TERRORISM IN THE UNITED STATES AND EUROPE, 1800–1959

GARLAND REFERENCE LIBRARY
OF SOCIAL SCIENCE
(VOL. 449)

TERRORISM IN THE UNITED STATES
AND EUROPE, 1800–1959
An Annotated Bibliography

Michael Newton
Judy Ann Newton

GARLAND PUBLISHING, INC. • NEW YORK & LONDON
1988

Library of Congress Cataloging-in-Publication Data

Newton, Michael, 1951–
    Terrorism in the United States and Europe, 1800–1959: an
annotated bibliography / Michael Newton, Judy Ann Newton.
        p.   cm. — (Garland reference library of social science ; vol.
449)
    Includes index.
    ISBN 0–8240–5747–3 (alk. paper)
    1. Terrorism—United States—History—Bibliography. 2. Terrorism—
Europe—History—Bibliography. I. Newton, Judy Ann, 1952–
II. Title. III. Series: Garland reference library of social science;
v. 449.
Z7164.T3N48   1988
[HV6432]
016.3036'25'094—dc19   88–21848
                                                                  CIP

Printed on acid-free, 250-year-life paper
Manufactured in the United States of America

To Kevin Wilson, for services above and beyond.
Hang in there, "Harry."

CONTENTS

PREFACE

Terrorism has become a crucial issue in our modern world.
Within the past ten years, the ruthless acts of dedicated
terrorists have toppled governments, ignited wars, and threatened national economies by altering patterns of trade and international tourism. At the same time, terrorist attacks have
been responsible for the creation of a new growth industry,
specifically designed to guarantee security for diplomats and
politicians, corporate executives, and military personnel.
Each day brings new reports of car bombs, sniping and abduction,
massacres and riots from around the world. No country is im-
mune from what appears to be a modern epidemic of concerted,
finely orchestrated savagery.

And yet, for all the recent headlines, terrorism should not
be mistaken for a new phenomenon. The term itself was coined
by Edmund Burke, in reference to French upheavals of the late
eighteenth century, but Burke was merely christening a concept
recognized by rulers—and their adversaries—from the dawn of
human history. A century before the Baader-Meinhof Gang and
Red Brigades began to ply their bloody trade, their spiritual
ancestors were planting bombs and stalking heads of state from
Pennsylvania's coal fields to St. Petersburg. Russian tsars
and American presidents were numbered among their victims, in
the company of countless governors and legislators, military
officers, civilians prominent and otherwise. Within a quarter-
century, from August 1914 to September 1939, concerted action
on the part of terrorists provoked two global conflicts and
imposed the world's first communist regime upon a captive population. Still, ironically, the venerable roots of terrorism
and its role in shaping history have been neglected, for the
most part, in the recent glut of theses dealing with contain-
ment, countermeasures, and security.

The present volume is designed to offer students of the
modern terrorist phenomenon the necessary background and
foundation for a survey of the history behind the headlines.
Only when the roots of terrorism are identified and understood,
can scholars hope to find a workable solution to the problem
that endangers all of us.

ix

For purposes of this examination, terrorism is defined as
any resort to violence or coercive action by a group in pursuit
of social, economic, or political objectives. Thus excluded are
the acts of mentally unbalanced individuals—psychotic subway
bombers, freeway snipers, and the like—together with the
strictly mercenary acts of covert criminal fraternities. By
definition, terrorism is conducted in a public forum, hence
excluding the activities of cults alleged to practice human
sacrifice and other groups that consciously attempt to cover
up their crimes. While terrorists, on rare occasions, have
employed professional assassins, those who kill primarily for
money, or in the pursuit of other mercenary crimes, are not
considered here as terrorists themselves, because their goals
are limited to personal enrichment.

Terroristic acts committed by established governments
against their citizens have likewise been excluded from con-
sideration here, because those acts, however brutal and re-
pugnant, constitute established policy. (The German Nazi
movement, for example, has been here considered terroristic
only prior to 1933, when it became the ruling force in Germany
with Hitler's elevation to the chancellery.) The violence of
open warfare, generally, is not considered terrorism, but
exceptions have been made: the Spanish civil war, incorporat-
ing terrorist activities by communist and fascist elements,
is here included, while America's own War Between the States
is not. In short, while terrorists are quick to light the
fuse of war, once conflicts are declared and openly engaged,
they properly become the province of diplomacy and military
history. To paraphrase Voltaire, while murder is forbidden,
it becomes acceptable when men are slaughtered "in large com-
panies, and to the sound of trumpets."

The work in hand is limited, in geographic scope, to the
United States and Europe; chronologically, it spans 160 years,
from 1800 to 1959. [Another volume, covering the terrorist
proliferation after 1960, is available from Garland.] Entries
have been organized both topically and geographically, for
the convenience of the reader. A preliminary section covers
general works, examining the terrorist phenomenon without
specific focus on a given ideology or nation. Europe's section is divided geographically, with subject countries listed
alphabetically. America's historical experience with terrorism is presented topically, with sections covering specific
acts (assassination, lynching), movements (anarchists, the
Ku Klux Klan), and driving motivations (social, racial, economic, and political). The sources listed here include both
books and periodicals, originally published in America and
Europe. In the interests of convenience, space, and practi-
cality, all sources listed have been published in the English

language. Annotations are provided in the case of books and articles whose titles are not self-explanatory.

The authors hope their contribution toward the scholarship on modern terrorism and its history may help, in some small way, to fill the gap in current research and present a more coherent view of the phenomenon, its roots in generations past, and possible solutions for the future. Understanding necessarily precedes the cure of any epidemic, and until we understand the terrorists among us, we are doomed to be the living targets of their rage.

Terrorism in the United States
and Europe, 1800–1959

PART 1
GENERAL WORKS

Books

1. Adams, Brooks. THE THEORY OF SOCIAL REVOLUTION. New
   York: Macmillan, 1914.

2. Alexander, Yonah (ed). INTERNATIONAL TERRORISM: NATIONAL,
   REGIONAL, AND GLOBAL PERSPECTIVES. New York: Praeger
   Publishers, 1976.

3. ————, and Kenneth A. Meyers (eds). TERRORISM IN EUROPE.
   New York: St. Martin's Press, 1982.

   Includes valuable historical background on the major
   terrorist movements of Europe, their roots and driving
   philosophies, with a discussion of official reactions and
   countermeasures.

4. Arendt, Hannah. ON REVOLUTION. New York: Viking Press,
   1963.

5. ————. ON VIOLENCE. New York: Harcourt, Brace and
   World, 1970.

6. Bell, J. Bowyer. ON REVOLT: STRATEGIES OF NATIONAL LIB-
   ERATION. Cambridge, Mass.: Harvard University Press,
   1976.

   Compares the strategies and tactics employed by various
   "armies of liberation," placing terrorism and political
   rebellion in sociological perspective on a global scale.

7. Bienen, Henry. VIOLENCE AND SOCIAL CHANGE: A REVIEW OF
   CURRENT LITERATURE. Chicago: University of Chicago
   Press, 1968.

   Examines the role of individual and mass violence in
   effecting social change in contemporary societies. Causal

factors of modern political and socio-economic violence
are examined in general terms.

8. Bishop, Charles M. "The Causes, Consequences and Cure of
    Mob Violence." DEMOCRACY IN EARNEST. Washington, D.C.:
    1918.

9. Brinton, Crane. THE ANATOMY OF REVOLUTION. New York:
    Random House, 1965.

    Compares historical "phases" of the American, French,
    and Russian revolutions, from the first stirrings of
    popular unrest through rebellion and paramilitary action,
    to the semi-inevitable "reign of terror" experienced in
    the wake of most (but not all) successful revolutions.

10. Bronowski, Jacob. THE FACE OF VIOLENCE. New York: G.
    Braziller, 1955.

11. Brown, Gene. TERRORISM. New York: The New York Times
    Co., 1979.

    A collection of news clippings from the NEW YORK TIMES
    about terrorist violence in various parts of the world,
    covering the period from 1900 to the late 1970s.

12. Canetti, Elias. CROWDS AND POWER. London: V. Gollancz,
    1962.

13. Chaplin, James P. RUMOR, FEAR AND THE MADNESS OF CROWDS.
    New York: Ballantine Books, 1959.

    Surveys the role of rumor and hysteria in mob violence,
    with an examination of causal factors and potential means
    of defusing explosive situations.

14. Chomsky, Noam. COUNTER-REVOLUTIONARY VIOLENCE: BLOODBATHS
    IN FACT AND PROPAGANDA. Andover, Mass.: Warner Modular
    Publications, Inc., 1973.

    Presents a leftist view of anti-revolutionary "propagan-
    da," deliberately downplaying the "reign of terror" phase
    of revolution examined in item 9 above.

15. Colton, Ethan Theodore. FOUR PATTERNS OF REVOLUTION:
    COMMUNIST U.S.S.R., FASCIST ITALY, NAZI GERMANY, NEW
    DEAL AMERICA. Freeport, N.Y.: Books for Libraries Press,
    1970.

16. Crotty, William J. ASSASSINATION AND POLITICAL ORDER.
    New York: Harper & Row, 1971.

17. Davies, James Chowning (ed). WHEN MEN REVOLT AND WHY:
    A READER IN POLITICAL VIOLENCE AND REVOLUTION. New
    York: Free Press, 1970.

18. Dollard, John Adrian. FRUSTRATION AND AGGRESSION. New
    Haven, Conn.: 1939.

19. Edelman, Jacob Murray. PUBLIC POLICY AND POLITICAL VIO-
    LENCE. Madison, Wis.: Wisconsin University Institute
    for Research on Poverty, 1968.

20. Edwards, Lyford Paterson. THE NATURAL HISTORY OF REVO-
    LUTION. Chicago: University of Chicago Press, 1927.

21. Ford, Franklin L. POLITICAL MURDER: FROM TYRANNICIDE
    TO TERRORISM. Cambridge, Mass.: Harvard University
    Press, 1985.

    Presents the best single history of assassination with
    case studies drawn from Biblical times to the present,
    including coverage of Europe and America, with surveys
    of the Third World. Coverage of the anarchist movement
    in Russia, under the Tsars, is especially informative.

22. Friederich, Car Joachin. THE PATHOLOGY OF POLITICS:
    VIOLENCE, BETRAYAL, CORRUPTION, SECRECY, AND PROPAGAN-
    DA. New York: Harper & Row, 1972.

23. Gaucher, Roland. THE TERRORISTS: FROM TSARIST RUSSIA TO
    THE O.A.S. London: Secker & Warburg, 1968.

24. Greenstein, Fred I., and Nelson Polsby. HANDBOOK OF
    POLITICAL SCIENCE. Reading, Mass.: Addison-Wesley,
    1975.

    Contains item 56 below.

25. Grundy, Kenneth W. THE IDEOLOGIES OF VIOLENCE. Colum-
    bus, Ohio: Merrill, 1974.

26. Gurr, Ted Robert. WHY MEN REBEL. Princeton, N.J.:
    Princeton University Press, 1970.

27. Havens, Murray Clark, Carl Leiden, and Karl M. Schmidt.
    THE POLITICS OF ASSASSINATION. Englewood Cliffs, N.J.:
    Prentice-Hall, 1970.

28. Hibbs, Douglas A. MASS POLITICAL VIOLENCE: A CROSS-
    NATIONAL CAUSAL ANALYSIS. New York: Wiley, 1973.

29. Hobsbawm, E.J. PRIMITIVE REBELS: STUDIES IN ARCHAIC
    FORMS OF SOCIAL MOVEMENTS IN THE 19th AND 20th
    CENTURIES. New York: Praeger, 1963.

    Examines "social bandits" and their role in fomenting
    revolution, their adoption by depressed or demoralized
    societies as hero-figures, and their ability to cloak
    mercenary criminal activity in the guise of social
    activisim.

30. Honderich, Ted. POLITICAL VIOLENCE. Ithaca, N.Y.: Cor-
    nell University Press, 1976.

31. Hyams, Edward S. TERRORISTS AND TERRORISM. New York:
    St. Martin's Press, 1974.

32. Jenkins, Brian Michael. TERRORISM AND KIDNAPPING. Santa
    Monica, Calif.: Rand Corp., 1974.

33. Kirkham, James F., Sheldon G. Levy, and William J. Crotty
    (eds). ASSASSINATION AND POLITICAL VIOLENCE. Vol. III
    of A REPORT TO THE NATIONAL COMMISSION ON THE CAUSES
    AND PREVENTION OF VIOLENCE. Washington, D.C.: U.S.
    Government Printing Office, 1969.

    Contains a detailed analysis of assassination and
    terrorism, replete with historical examples, quotations
    from the extremist literature of both political wings,
    and detailed statistical analysis of modern trends in
    political murder.

34. Laqueur, Walter. TERRORISM. Boston: Little, Brown, 1977.

35. ——— (ed). THE TERRORISM READER: A HISTORICAL ANTHOL-
    OGY. New York: New American Library, 1978.

36. Le Bon, Gustave. THE CROWD: A STUDY OF THE POPULAR MIND.
    London: Unwin, 1909.

37. Liston, Robert A. TERRORISM. Nashville, Tenn.: Nelson,
    1977.

38. McConnell, Brian. THE HISTORY OF ASSASSINATION. Nash-
    ville, Tenn.: Aurora Publishers, 1969.

39. McKnight, Gerald. THE TERRORIST MIND. Indianapolis,
    Ind.: Bobbs-Merrill, 1974.

40. Mickolus, Edward F. TRANSNATIONAL TERRORISM: A CHRON-
    OLOGY OF EVENTS, 1968-1979. Westport, Conn.: Green-
    wood Press, 1980, pp. 3-48.

    Despite the title, pages cited cover terrorist activi-
    ties from Biblical times through 1959, providing students
    in the subject area with a valuable launching pad for
    more specific detailed research in periodicals and the
    daily press.

41. Mommsen, Wolfgang J., and Gerhard Hirschfield. SOCIAL
    PROTEST, VIOLENCE AND TERROR IN NINETEENTH- AND
    TWENTIETH-CENTURY EUROPE. New York: St. Martin's
    Press, 1982.

    Contains items 707, 1403, 2300, and 2692 below.

42. Most, Johann. SCIENCE OF REVOLUTIONARY WAR: MANUAL FOR
    INSTRUCTION IN THE USE AND PREPARATION OF NITRO-
    GLYCERINE, DYNAMITE, GUN-COTTON, FULMINATING MERCURY,
    BOMBS, FUSES, AND POISONS, ETC., ETC. New York:
    International Zeitung Verein, 1884.

43. Nieburg, Harold L. POLITICAL VIOLENCE: THE BEHAVIORAL
    PROCESS. New York: St. Martin's Press, 1969.

44. O'Ballance, Edgar. LANGUAGE OF VIOLENCE: THE BLOOD
    POLITICS OF TERRORISM. San Rafael, Calif.: Presidio
    Press, 1979.

45. Parry, Albert. TERRORISM: FROM ROBESPIERRE TO ARAFAT.
    New York: Vanguard Press, 1976.

46. Payne, Pierre Stephen Robert. ZERO: THE STORY OF
    TERRORISM. London: Wingate, 1951.

47. Postgate, Raymond William. REVOLUTION FROM 1798-1906.
    London: Grant Richards, Ltd., 1920.

48. Rappaport, David C., and Yonah Alexander (eds). THE
    MORALITY OF TERRORISM: RELIGIOUS AND SECULAR JUSTIFI-
    CATIONS. New York: Pergamon Press, 1982.

    Examines the most common religious and political "ex-
    cuses" for condoning—or participating in—terrorist

activity. The authors are generally unsympathetic to
apologists of terrorism, revealing their "justifications" to be thread-bare, at best.

49. Richardson, Lewis F. STATISTICS OF DEADLY QUARRELS.
London: Stevens, 1960.

50. Rivera, Charles R. VIOLENCE. Rochelle Park, N.Y.: Hayden Book Co., 1976.

51. Sorel, Georges. REFLECTIONS ON VIOLENCE. New York:
Collier Books, 1950.

52. Sorokin, Pitirim A. THE SOCIOLOGY OF REVOLUTION. Philadelphia: J.B. Lippincott, 1925.

53. Sterling, Claire. THE TERROR NETWORK: THE SECRET WAR OF
INTERNATIONAL TERRORISM. New York: Holt, Rinehart
and Winston, 1981.

54. Swomley, John M. LIBERATION ETHICS. New York: Macmillan,
1972.

   Examines modern justifications for terroristic "wars of
   liberation," dissecting the motives and rhetoric of contemporary rebel spokesmen. Causal factors of political
   rebellion are examined in conjunction with perceived or
   expressed motivations.

55. Tilly, Charles. FROM MOBILIZATION TO REVOLUTION. Reading, Mass.: Addison-Wesley, 1978.

56. ———. "Revolution and Collective Violence." HANDBOOK
OF POLITICAL SCIENCE. Cited above as item 24.

57. ———, Louise Tilly, and Richard Tilly. THE REBELLIOUS
CENTURY, 1830-1930. Cambridge, Mass.: Harvard University Press, 1975.

58. Van den Haog, Ernest. POLITICAL VIOLENCE AND CIVIL DIS-
OBEDIENCE. New York: Harper & Row, 1972.

59. Van der Mehden, Fred P. COMPARATIVE POLITICAL VIOLENCE.
Englewood Cliffs, N.J.: Prentice-Hall, 1973.

60. Watson, Francis M. POLITICAL TERRORISM: THE THREAT AND
THE RESPONSE. Washington, D.C.: R.E. Luce Co., 1976.

61. Welch, Claude Emerson. ANATOMY OF REBELLION. Albany,
    N.Y.: State University Press of New York, 1980.

62. Wolf, E.R. PEASANT WARS OF THE TWENTIETH CENTURY. New
    York: Harper & Row, 1969.

63. Wolff, Robert Lee. THE BALKANS IN OUR TIME. Cambridge,
    Mass.: Harvard University Press, 1956.

    Includes lively, informative discussion of various
    terrorist movements and political upheavals in the Bal-
    kan region, concentrating on the post-World War II
    struggles against communist incursion from the East.

64. Wright, Gordon. INSIDERS AND OUTLIERS: THE INDIVIDUAL
    IN HISTORY, 1910-1926. Madison, Wis.: University of
    Wisconsin Press, 1978.

65. Zimmermann, Ekkart. POLITICAL VIOLENCE, CRISES, AND
    REVOLUTIONS. Cambridge, Mass.: Schenkman Publishing
    Co., 1983.

                            Articles

66. Abbott, L. "Our God is Marching On." LIVING AGE 298
    (July 6, 1918): 1-12.

    Reviews the course of contemporary revolutions.

67. Amann, Peter. "Revolution: A Redefinition." POLITICAL
    SCIENCE QUARTERLY 77 (1962): 36-53.

68. Bailey, Sydney D. "The United Nations and the Termination
    of Armed Conflict, 1946-64." INTERNATIONAL AFFAIRS
    58 (1982): 465-475.

69. Bernstein, E. "Revolutions in Theory and Practice."
    LIVING AGE 304 (February 21, 1920): 452-454.

70. Bettelheim, Bruno. "Individual and Mass Behavior in Ex-
    treme Situations." JOURNAL OF ABNORMAL AND SOCIAL
    PSYCHOLOGY 38 (1943): 417-452.

    Includes examination of mob violence.

71. Binkley, R.C. "An Anatomy of Revolution." VIRGINIA
    QUARTERLY REVIEW 10 (October 1934): 502-514.

72. Blind, K. "Modern Revolutions and Their Results." NORTH AMERICAN 154 (June 1892): 655-665.

73. Brandes, G. "War and Civil War." NATION 107 (December 21, 1918): 768-769.

    Reviews contemporaneous European unrest and civil wars in the wake of World War I. Includes discussion of the global conflict's destabilizing effect on colonial empires.

74. "Bread, Agents and Bullets." TIME 40 (December 21, 1942): 36.

    Describes wartime terror tactics in Europe.

75. Brown, P.M. "International Revolution." AMERICAN JOURNAL OF INTERNATIONAL LAW 29 (October 1935): 670-673.

76. ———, and L. Rogers. "Examination of Fascism." CURRENT HISTORY 34 (May 1931): 161-168.

77. Buckley, J.M. "Assassination of Kings and Presidents." CENTURY 63 (November 1901): 136-142.

78. Calvocoressi, M.D. "Music and Revolution." 19th CENTURY AND AFTER 115 (June 1934): 691-704.

    Examines the alleged relationship between performing art and socio-political upheaval in Europe.

79. Cantril, Hadley. "Causes and Control of Riot and Panic." PUBLIC OPINION QUARTERLY 7 (1943): 669-679.

80. Carver, T.N. "The Basis of Social Conflict." AMERICAN JOURNAL OF SOCIOLOGY 13 (1907): 628-648.

81. "Causes of Revolution." NATION 85 (December 12, 1907): 532-533.

82. Chesterton, G.K. "Fascist Method." CATHOLIC WORLD 132 (November 1930): 216-217.

83. Colvin, I.D. "Revolutions: Their Cause and Cure." LIVING AGE 295 (October 13, 1917): 73-79.

84. "Conflict Between Groups." CATHOLIC WORLD 139 (May 1934): 233-235.

85. Cowley, M. "Art of Insurrection." NEW REPUBLIC 74 (April
    13, 1933): 248-250.

    Reviews modern techniques of fomenting rebellion, in
    light of violent fascist ascendancy in several European
    nations.

86. Crozier, B. "Anatomy of Terrorism." NATION 188 (March
    21, 1959): 250-252.

87. Davies, James C. "Toward a Theory of Revolution." AMER-
    ICAN SOCIOLOGY REVIEW 27 (1962): 5-19.

88. Davis, Allison. "Caste, Economy, and Violence." AMERI-
    CAN JOURNAL OF SOCIOLOGY 51 (1945): 7-15.

    Reviews the socio-economic factors behind mass violence
    in Europe and America.

89. Davis, J. "Challenge of Dictatorship, Red or Black."
    CENTURY 120 (April 1930): 170-179.

    Compares the tactics of fascist and communist strong
    men in contemporary Europe.

90. "Delusion of the Crank." NEW REPUBLIC 3 (July 10, 1915):
    242-243.

    Laments the contemporary rash of European assassinations.

91. Dewey, John. "Force and Coercion." INTERNATIONAL JOUR-
    NAL OF ETHICS 26 (1916): 359-367.

    Examines the practicality and ethics of violent means
    in modern society.

92. Duchamel, Luc. "Lenin, Violence, and Eurocommunism."
    CANADIAN JOURNAL OF POLITICAL SCIENCE 13 (1980):
    97-120.

    Compares Lenin's views on revolutionary violence with
    the practices of communist parties in France, Italy,
    and Spain.

93. Durham, M.E. "Writing on the Wall." CONTEMPORARY
    OPINION 146 (December 1934): 650-657.

    Charts contemporary trends toward political violence

and terrorism in Depression-era Europe.

94. Elliott, W.Y. "Perils of Fascism." WORLD TOMORROW 12
    (November 1929): 452-455.

95. Ellwood, C.A. "Psychological Theory of Revolutions."
    AMERICAN JOURNAL OF SOCIOLOGY 11 (July 1905): 49-59.

96. Feierabend, Ivo K., and Rosalind L. Feierabend. "Aggres-
    sive Behaviors Within Politics, 1948-1962: A Cross-
    National Study." JOURNAL OF CONFLICT RESOLUTION 10
    (1966): 249-271.

97. Flanigan, William H., and Edwin Fogelman. "Patterns of
    Political Violence in Comparative Historical Perspec-
    tive." COMPARATIVE POLITICS 3 (1970): 1-20.

98. Godkin, E.L. "Mob Violence." NATION 63 (October 29,
    1896): 322.

99. Handman, M. "Bureaucratic Culture Pattern and Political
    Revolutions." AMERICAN JOURNAL OF SOCIOLOGY 39 (Novem-
    ber 1933): 301-313.

100. Hatto, Arthur. "Revolution: An Enquiry into the Useful-
     ness of an Historical Term." MIND 58 (1949): 495-517.

     Debates semantics on the applicability of labels such
     as "revolution" and "rebellion."

101. Hibben, P. "Why is a Revolution?" NORTH AMERICAN 198
     (July 1913): 60-74.

102. Huber, J.B. "Psychology of a Revolution." HARPER'S
     WEEKLY 58 (January 17, 1914): 11.

103. Hyndman, H.M. "Evolution of Revolution." LIVING AGE
     298 (July 6, 1918): 1-12.

104. "In July Nations Tread Carefully." LITERARY DIGEST 114
     (July 16, 1932): 34.

     Examines historical trends toward revolution in the
     summer months, citing examples from the late nineteenth
     century through World War I.

105. "International Contagion." SPECTATOR 65 (August 2, 1890):
     140-141.

Examines the contemporary rash of political upheaval in
Europe, decrying the tendency toward violent settlement
of public issues.

106. Kebbel, T.E. "Mobs." BLACKWELL'S MAGAZINE 153 (January
     1893): 109-125.

107. "Keeping Our Heads with Assassins About." NATION 101
     (July 8, 1915): 36-37.

108. Kort, Fred. "The Quantification of Aristotle's Theory of
     Revolution." AMERICAN POLITICAL SCIENCE REVIEW 46
     (1952): 486-493.

109. Kuttner, A.B. "Cycle of Revolution." NEW REPUBLIC 20
     (August 20, 1919): 86-88.

110. Landfield, J. "Convalescence from Utopia." REVIEW 3
     (October 13, 1920): 310-311.

     Examines the unexpected aftershocks of contemporary
     revolutions, including Russia's recent upheaval as a
     prime example.

111. Langtoft, G. "Assassination a Fruit of Socialism."
     FORTUNE 76 (October 1901): 571-580.

     Brands socialism as the root of contemporary terrorism
     in Europe and the United States.

112. Laufkotter, F. "Goethe and the Revolution." LIVING AGE
     307 (October 9, 1920): 85-89.

113. "Law of Riot." SPECTATOR 71 (September 30, 1893): 421-
     422; 71 (Ocobter 7, 1893): 465.

114. Lewisohn, L. "New Meaning of Revolution." NORTH AMERI-
     CAN 238 (September 1934): 210-218.

     Charts the contemporary trend toward totalitarian sei-
     zure of power in major European nations, utilizing terror-
     istic methods to pave the way for imposition of dictator-
     ships.

115. McKay, C. "Constitutional Changes; Force Should Not Be
     Necessary." CANADIAN FORUM 13 (October 1932): 35.

     Pleads for moderation in an era racked by violence.

116. "Making Martyrs of Assassins." CHRISTIAN CENTURY 50 (October 4, 1933): 1227.

    Condemns the tendency of certain groups to deify selected terrorists.

117. Masaryk, T.G. "Revolutionary Theory in Europe." LIVING AGE 310 (July 9, 1921): 73-77.

118. "Menace of Fascism." NATION 131 (November 12, 1930): 515-516.

119. "Mr. Wiseman on Revolutions." NATION 107 (December 14, 1918): 731.

120. "Murder in the Mails." LITERARY DIGEST 112 (January 16, 1932): 5-6.

    Examines early usage of parcel bombs by terrorist groups in Europe.

121. "New Order: The March of Death in High Places." NEWSWEEK 17 (April 14, 1941): 34.

    Examines contemporary trends in international assassination.

122. Nitti, F. "From War to Revolution." CURRENT HISTORY 37 (December 1932): 281-284.

123. Oswald, F.L. "The Assassination Mania." NORTH AMERICAN 171 (September 1900): 314-319.

    Examines recent terrorist attempts on heads of state.

124. Parker, R. "Scheduled Terror." 19th CENTURY AND AFTER 131 (January 1942): 21-26.

125. Phillips, J.B. "Use of Terror as a Weapon." NEWSWEEK 33 (February 21, 1949): 37.

126. "Political Assassination." LIVING AGE 262 (August 14, 1909): 434-436.

127. Post, A.T. "Modern Revolutions." PUBLIC OPINION 22 (August 30, 1919): 932-933.

128. Postgate, R. "Critique of Communist Tactics." AMERICAN
     MERCURY 32 (July 1934): 281-289.

     Condemns red participation in fomenting political vio-
     lence in various parts of Depression-era Europe.

129. ———. "How to Make a Revolution." AMERICAN MERCURY
     32 (May 1934): 12-20.

     Examines the role of terrorists and agitators in cre-
     ating modern revolutions.

130. Prince, J.F.T. "Necessity of Revolution." CATHOLIC
     WORLD 138 (October 1933): 106-108.

     Concedes the occasional inevitability of violent means
     in resolving political conflict.

131. Reed, T.B. "Historic Political Upheavals." NORTH AMER-
     ICAN 160 (January 1895): 109-116.

132. Renan, M. "On Revolutions." SPECTATOR 69 (October 15,
     1892): 521-522.

133. "Revolution by Due Course of Law." NATION 108 (February
     15, 1919): 243.

     Seeks alternatives to violent rebellion in solution of
     political conflicts.

134. "Revolution, New Style." REVIEW 1 (July 5, 1919): 159-
     160.

     Compares modern rebellions to the historical "norm,"
     with an examination of changing tactics and causal
     factors.

135. "Revolutions." LIVING AGE 293 (April 28, 1917): 246-248.

136. "Revolutions and Revolutions." NATION 110 (June 12, 1920):
     788.

137. "Right of Revolution." LITERARY DIGEST 52 (January 29,
     1916): 216-217.

     Debates the right of subject populations to revolt
     against their rulers.

138. "Right of Revolution." OUTLOOK 112 (January 19, 1916): 128-129.

139. Rosney, J.H. "Revolutionary Messianism." LIVING AGE 302 (September 27, 1919): 783-785.

    Surveys the character of recent revolutionary leaders, with a discussion of their charismatic qualities.

140. Roucek, Joseph S. "The Sociology of Violence." JOURNAL OF HUMAN RELATIONS 5 (1957): 8-21.

141. ————. "Sociological Elements of a Theory of Terror and Violence." AMERICAN JOURNAL OF ECONOMICS AND SOCIOL-OGY 21 (1962): 165-172.

142. ————. "What Can Start Student Riots in Europe." SCHOOL AND SOCIETY 41 (March 2, 1935): 293-294.

143. Rummel, Rudolph J. "Dimensions of Conflict Behavior Within Nations." JOURNAL OF CONFLICT RESOLUTION 10 (1966): 65-74.

144. Sears, J.H. "Cycle of Revolution." FORUM 65 (January 1921): 77-89.

145. Shaw, R. "In Re Assassination." COMMONWEAL 22 (September 27, 1935): 513-515.

146. ————. "Revolutions." REVIEW OF REVIEWS 89 (February 1934): 21-22+.

147. Shinn, C.H. "The Reason Behind Revolutions." PUBLIC OPINION 15 (December 13, 1912): 1180-1181.

148. Slater, G. "Politics and Assassination." WESTMINSTER'S 151 (February 1899): 211-217.

149. "Spread of Fascism." OUTLOOK 156 (November 5, 1930): 366-367.

150. Stack, R.E.H. "Some Aspects of Fascism." CATHOLIC WORLD 128 (January 1929): 482-484.

151. Stoddard, T.L. "Some Reflections on Revolution." UN-POPULAR REVIEW 9 (April 1918): 385-392.

152. Strachey, J. St. L. "Mechanism of Revolution." 19th
     CENTURY AND AFTER 88 (October 1920): 582-594.

153. Thompson, B. "Spread of the Fascist Movement in Europe
     and Mexico." SATURDAY EVENING POST 155 (March 10, 1923):
     11.

154. Vannus. "Assassination False Cure for Ills of State."
     CHRISTIAN SCIENCE MONITOR MAGAZINE (March 11, 1936):
     7.

     Condemns terrorism as a remedial tool for eliminating
     the problems of despotic societies.

155. Wada, George, and James C. Davies. "Riots and Rioters."
     WESTERN POLITICAL QUARTERLY 10 (1957): 864-874.

156. "War and Revolution." NEW REPUBLIC 10 (March 24, 1917):
     212-214.

157. "Westward Course of Revolution." LIVING AGE 304 (Febru-
     ary 21, 1920): 455-457.

     Postulates a rising trend toward rebellion in the West,
     with the recent Russian revolution cited as a harbinger
     of things to come.

158. White, A.D. "Assassins and Their Apologists." INDEPEN-
     DENT 54 (August 21, 1902): 1989-1990.

159. Zimmern, H. "Lombroso's New Theory of Political Crime."
     BLACKWELL'S MAGAZINE 149 (February 1891): 202-211.

PART 2: EUROPE

ALBANIA

Articles

160. Pollo, Stefanaq. "Luigi Gurakuqi: A Distinguished Revo-
     lutionary Democrat." STUDIME HISTORY 33 (1979): 17-32.

     Presents a communist party-line biography of a militant
     Albanian nationalist who led the Ottoman "liberation"
     movements of 1911-1912. Gurakuqi was assassinated in
     Italian exile, in 1924, following the collapse of the
     government he helped create.

AUSTRIA

Books

161. Bauer, O. THE AUSTRIAN REVOLUTION. London: Parsons, 1925.

     Presents a detailed examination of the 1848 revolution,
     including a discussion of causal factors, military action,
     and results.

162. Bell, Mary Margaret. POST-WAR GERMAN-AUSTRIAN RELATIONS:
     THE ANSCHLUSS MOVEMENT, 1918-1936. Stanford, Calif.:
     Stanford University Press, 1937.

     Examines Nazi terrorism in the early 1930s, culminating
     in seizure of the Austrian government by pro-German
     fascist elements.

163. Bulloch, Malcolm. AUSTRIA, 1918-1938: A STUDY IN FAILURE.
     London: Macmillan, 1939.

     Describes the rise of right-wing terrorism in Austria
     after World War I, culminating in the ascendancy of pro-
     fascist elements and annexation by Hitler's Germany.

164. Dedijer, Vladmir. THE ROAD TO SARAJEVO. New York:
     Simon & Schuster, 1966.

     Examines violent nationalist movements in the Austro-
     Hungarian empire, including terror tactics by the Black
     Hand and similar groups, ultimately leading to the out-
     break of global war.

165. Florence, Ronald. FRITZ: THE STORY OF A POLITICAL ASS-
     ASSINATION. New York: Dial, 1971.

     Examines the 1916 asssassination of Austro-Hungarian
     Prime Minister Karl von Sturgkh.

166. Fuchs, Martin. A PACT WITH HITLER: THE DEATH OF AUSTRIA.
     London: Victor Gollancs, Ltd., 1939.

     Includes a discussion of Nazi terrorism prior to German
     annexation of Austria.

167. Galantai, Jozsef. AUSTRIA-HUNGARY AND THE WAR: THE OC-
     TOBER 1913 CRISIS—PRELUDE TO JULY 1914. Budapest:
     Akademiai Kiado, 1980.

     Examines political upheavals and terrorist activities
     in the Austro-Hungarian empire prior to the assassination
     of the Archduke Ferdinand at Sarajevo.

168. Gehl, Jurgen. AUSTRIA, GERMANY AND THE ANSCHLUSS, 1931-
     1938. London: Oxford University Press, 1963.

     Includes detailed coverage of Nazi terrorism in the
     1930s.

169. Goldmark, Josephine Clara. PILGRIMS OF '48: ONE MAN'S
     PART IN THE AUSTRIAN REVOLUTION OF 1848, AND A FAMILY
     MIGRATION TO AMERICA. New Haven, Conn.: Yale Univer-
     sity Press, 1930.

170. Klein, Ernst. ROAD TO DISASTER. London: George Allen &
     Unwin, Ltd., 1940.

     Includes a discussion of Nazi terrorism in Austria,
     culminating in the rise of a pro-fascist government and
     ultimate annexation by Germany.

171. Mason, John W. THE DISSOLUTION OF THE AUSTRO-HUNGARIAN
     EMPIRE, 1867-1918. London: Longman, 1985.

172. Pribichevich, Stoyan. WORLD WITHOUT END: THE SAGA OF
     SOUTHEASTERN EUROPE. New York: Reynal & Hitchcock,
     1939.

     Examines the terrorist assassination of four Serbian
     rulers between 1804 and 1934, including information on
     the background and motivations of their assassins.

173. Rath, Reuben John. THE VIENNESE REVOLUTION OF 1848.
     Austin, Tex.: University of Texas Press, 1957.

174. Seton-Watson, R.W. SARAJEVO: A STUDY IN THE ORIGINS OF
     THE GREAT WAR. London: Hutchinson, 1925.

     Includes discussion of the nationalist violence leading
     to the outbreak of World War I, with discussion of the
     Black Hand and details of the plot to murder Archduke
     Ferdinand.

175. Stiles, William Henry. AUSTRIA IN 1848-49: BEING A HIS-
     TORY OF THE LATE POLITICAL MOVEMENTS IN VIENNA, MILAN,
     VENICE, AND PRAGUE; WITH DETAILS OF THE CAMPAIGNS OF
     LOMBARDY AND NOVARA; A FULL ACCOUNT OF THE REVOLUTION
     IN HUNGARY. London: S. Low, 1852.

176. Ward, David. 1848: THE FALL OF METTERNICH AND THE YEAR
     OF REVOLUTION. New York: Weybright & Talley, 1970.

177. Zeman, Zbynek A. TWILIGHT OF THE HAPSBURGS: THE COLLAPSE
     OF THE AUSTRO-HUNGARIAN EMPIRE. New York: American
     Heritage Press, 1971.

     Examines political upheaval in the late nineteenth and
     early twentieth centuries.

                              Articles

178. Alder, Douglas D. "Assassination as Political Efficacy:
     Two Case Studies from World War I." EASTERN EUROPEAN
     QUARTERLY 12 (1978): 209-231.

     Compares the assassinations of Archduke Ferdinand in
     1914 and Austrian President Karl Sturgkh in 1916, con-
     trasting the victims, killers, and consequences of the
     two politically-motivated murders.

179. ————. "Friedrich Adler: Evolution of a Revolutionary."
     GERMAN STUDIES REVIEW 1 (1978): 260-284.

     Traces the career of Karl Sturgkh's assassin.

180. Allen, D. "Peace is Dead! Long Live Peace!" WORLD TO-
     MORROW 17 (March 15, 1934): 127-129.

     Examines political upheaval and violence in the 1930s.

181. ————. "Why the Austrian Socialists Fought." WORLD TO-
     MORROW 17 (March 1, 1934): 103-105.

182. "American Aid to Dolfuss." WORLD TOMORROW 17 (March 29,
     1934): 149.

     Examines American intervention in Austrian political
     unrest, prior to the fascist takeover.

183. "Attempt on Life of Dolfuss." NEWSWEEK 2 (October 14,
     1933): 13.

     Reports a Nazi murder attempt against Austria's demo-
     cratic leader.

184. "Austria and After." NEW REPUBLIC 79 (August 8, 1934):
     331-332.

     Examines events in Austria after the Nazi assassination
     of Prime Minister Dolfuss.

185. "Austria Relinquishes Democratic Government." NEWSWEEK
     3 (March 31, 1934): 14.

186. "Austria Stands Firm." WORLD TOMORROW 16 (September 14,
     1933): 509.

187. "Austrian Counter-Revolution." CONTEMPORARY REVIEW 145
     (April 1934): 385-395.

188. "Austrian Fascism in the Open." CHRISTIAN CENTURY 50
     (September 27, 1933): 1196.

189. "Austrian Nazis Protest with Bombs." NEWSWEEK 3 (May 19,
     1934): 11.

190. "Austrian Strife and Europe's Future." LITERARY DIGEST
     117 (February 24, 1934): 5-6.

191. "Austria's Struggle Against Hitlerism." LITERARY DIGEST
      115 (June 3, 1933): 11-12.

192. "Austro-Italian Friendship Reenforced: Meeting of Schus-
      chnigg and Mussolini." LITERARY DIGEST 118 (September
      1, 1934): 15.

      Examines efforts of Dollfuss's successors to appease
      fascist neighbors, at the ultimate expense of their na-
      tion's sovereignty.

193. Bouissounouse, J. "Major Fey, the Goring of Austria."
      LIVING AGE 346 (May 1934): 230-232.

      Continues coverage of Nazi terrorism in Austria, with
      a profile of a ranking fascist leader.

194. Brailsford, N. "Austria Confronts Fascism." NEW REPUB-
      LIC 76 (October 4, 1933): 202-204.

195. ————. "Austria's Alternatives." WORLD TOMORROW 16
      (June 1933): 422-423.

      Discusses the prospect of a Nazi victory in Austria.

196. ————. "That Worker-Peasant Deadlock." WORLD TOMORROW
      16 (September 28, 1933): 545-546.

197. Calice, F. "Austria and the Nazis." COMMONWEAL 18 (Sep-
      tember 22, 1933): 480-482.

198. "Chancellor vs. Vice-Chancellor in Austria." LITERARY
      DIGEST 118 (November 10, 1934): 14.

      Examines divided government opinions on the proper tac-
      tics to be used in coping with fascist terrorism.

199. "Civil Law Once More Rules." NEW REPUBLIC 78 (March 7,
      1934): 85-86.

200. "Class-War Failure." WORLD TOMORROW 16 (May 1933): 390.

      Presents an overly-optimistic view of the terrorist
      "cease-fire" in Austria.

201. Creed, V. "Hapsburgs on the Horizon." NORTH AMERICAN
      238 (October 1934): 331-339.

Predicts a return to monarchy under pro-fascist rulers.

202. ———. "Unhappy Austria." NORTH AMERICAN 237 (April 1934): 331-338.

203. Danubian. "Austria's Struggle for Life." CONTEMPORARY REVIEW 144 (July 1933): 24-30.

204. "Death of Austrian Democracy." NATION 138 (February 28, 1934): 234-235.

205. "Dictator Dollfuss Calls Rule Authoritarian." NEWSWEEK 2 (September 30, 1933): 15.

206. "Disunion in Vienna." NEWSWEEK 3 (February 24, 1934): 5-7.

207. "Dollfuss as Dictator." WORLD TOMORROW 16 (November 9, 1933): 617.

208. "Dollfuss Killed by Nazis." NEWSWEEK 4 (August 4, 1934): 3-5.

209. "Dollfuss Now Fascist Dictator." NEWSWEEK 3 (May 12, 1934): 12.

210. "Dollfuss Outlaws Nazis." NEWSWEEK 1 (June 24, 1933): 13-14.

211. "Dollfuss's Slayers are Hanged, Country Gossips About a Royalist Restoration." NEWSWEEK 4 (August 11, 1934): 11.

212. Eibl, H. "Youth in Reaction." LIVING AGE 342 (August 1932): 507-514.

Examines political upheaval and violence among Austrian youth in the Depression era, including discussion of the factors which lured youth into participation in extremist movements of the radical left and fascist right.

213. "Europe and the Murder of Dollfuss." LITERARY DIGEST 118 (August 4, 1934): 3+.

214. "Europe Marches." NEW REPUBLIC 78 (February 21, 1934): 32-33.

Places Austrian violence in international perspective.

215. "Ex Cathedra." WORLD TOMORROW 17 (March 1, 1934): 98.

    Continues coverage of terrorism in Austria, as the Doll-
    fuss regime attempts to suppress violent Nazi activity.

216. "Fascism in Austria." CANADIAN FORUM 14 (November 1933):
    46.

217. Fay, S.B. "Dollfuss: Victim of Nazi Crime." CURRENT
    HISTORY 40 (September 1934): 729-741.

218. "Feeling the Way Toward a Fascist Austria." LITERARY
    DIGEST 116 (September 23, 1933): 11.

219. "Form of Fascism May Be Adopted by Dollfuss." NEWSWEEK
    2 (September 23, 1933): 12.

220. Fredenburgh, R.L. "Austrian Checkmate." QUEEN'S QUAR-
    TERLY 41 (August 1934): 383-396.

    Examines political upheaval and continuing violence in
    the wake of the Dollfuss assassination.

221. "Garrotting of Viennese Socialism." NEW REPUBLIC 75
    (July 5, 1933): 194-195.

    Examines suppression of leftist dissent in Austria.

222. Gedye, G.E.R. "Austria's Dark Outlook." FORTUNE 142
    (September 1934): 257-272.

    Anticipates a Nazi take-over in Austria.

223. ————. "Fascist Factor in Austrian Politics." CONTEMP-
    ORARY REVIEW 134 (December 1928): 723-728.

224. ————. "Some Aspects of the Vienna Disorders." CONTEMP-
    ORARY REVIEW 132 (September 1927): 305-311.

225. ————. "Tragedy of Dollfuss." CONTEMPORARY REVIEW 146
    (September 1934): 276-284.

    Examines the murder of Dollfuss by Nazi gunmen, predict-
    ing dire consequences for the nation at large.

226. ————. "Viennese Shambles." NATION 125 (August 10,
    1927): 128-129.

Describes political violence in Austria's capital, as communist and fascist groups battle in the streets for ultimate political control.

227. Germains, V.W. "Problem of Austrian Neutrality in a European War." CONTEMPORARY REVIEW 145 (January 1934): 47-55.

228. "German Nazi Warning to Austria: Habicht Threat." LITER-ARY DIGEST 117 (March 3, 1934): 15.

229. Goldberg, B.Z. "Austria Resists Nazi Imperialism." CUR-RENT HISTORY 38 (August 1933): 541-546.

230. Gould, K.M. "Agony of Austria." SCHOLASTIC 24 (March 3, 1934): 18.

231. Grant, D. "Austria in Crisis." WORLD TOMORROW 16 (April 5, 1933): 329.

232. ———. "Austria Quiet and Terrible." CHRISTIAN CENTURY 50 (November 29, 1933): 1516.

233. ———. "Austria Resists German Threats: Bavaria's Fate Rouses Deepened Concern." CHRISTIAN CENTURY 50 (July 26, 1933): 965-966.

234. ———. "Church Favors Austrian Fascism." CHRISTIAN CENTURY 50 (November 1, 1933): 1388.

235. ———. "Hold Dollfuss Nazi Forerunner." CHRISTIAN CENTURY 51 (January 3, 1934): 35.

236. ———. "Keeping Hitler Out of Austria." NATION 138 (February 14, 1934): 180-181.

237. ———. "Sees Vienna as Conquered City." CHRISTIAN CEN-TURY 51 (April 4, 1934): 471.

238. ———. "Will the Nazis Win Austria?" CHRISTIAN CENTURY 50 (September 27, 1933): 1220.

239. Grimm, W. "Three Ruritarians: Schuschnigg of Austria." LIVING AGE 347 (December 1934): 317-319.

Examines continuing political terrorism, along with government efforts to suppress escalating violence.

240. Gunther, J. "After the Dollfuss Murder." NATION 139
     (August 22, 1934): 204-205.

241. ————. "Dollfuss and the Future of Austria." FOREIGN
     AFFAIRS 12 (January 1934): 306-318.

242. ————. "Hapsburgs Again?" FOREIGN AFFAIRS 12 (July
     1934): 579-591.

     Anticipates a return to monarchy after the Dollfuss
     murder.

243. ————. "Policy by Murder: Story of the Dollfuss Killing."
     HARPER 169 (November 1934): 651-652.

244. ————. "Slaughter in Austria." NATION 133 (March 21,
     1934): 328-330.

245. ————. "Struggle for Power in Austria." NATION 138
     (May 16, 1934): 557-559.

246. ————. "Will Austria Go Fascist?" NATION 136 (April
     12, 1933): 393-395.

247. Gwynn, S. "Vienna Tragedy." FORTUNE 141 (April 1934):
     482-484.

248. Gyomai, I. "Fascism in Vienna." LIVING AGE 344 (July
     1933): 401-404.

249. "Hapsburg Restoration Rumored." NEWSWEEK 3 (April 14,
     1934): 16-17.

250. "Heimwehr Acts Up." NEWSWEEK 3 (March 24, 1934): 22.

     Examines continuing terrorism in Austria, perpetrated
     by German-sponsored fascist groups.

251. "Heimwehr Movements Disturb Austria." NEWSWEEK 3 (March
     3, 1934): 13.

252. "Hide-and-Seek Game of Austrian Monarchists." LITERARY
     DIGEST 118 (August 18, 1934): 13.

     Examines the monarchist role in continuing terrorism.

253. High, S. "Austria's Vest-Pocket Chancellor." LITERARY
     DIGEST 116 (October 28, 1933): 5+.

Examines the continuing war against terrorism.

254. "Hitlerism Conquers Austria." WORLD TOMORROW 16 (November 13, 1933): 628.

255. "Hitlerism in Middle Europe." NEW REPUBLIC 74 (May 3, 1933): 324-325.

256. Holden, O.W. "Austria is Not Germany." NATION 137 (July 5, 1933): 14-15.

Continues coverage of the war against on-going terror.

257. "July Revolt in Vienna." QUARTERLY 249 (October 1927): 363-378.

258. Lengyel, E. "Starhemberg's Power in Austria." CURRENT HISTORY 40 (Auguat 1934): 542-546.

Examines violence in the wake of the Dollfuss murder.

259. "Making Austria a Fascist State." LITERARY DIGEST 117 (April 7, 1934): 17.

260. Markham, R.H. "Austrian Church Backs Tyranny." CHRISTIAN CENTURY 52 (January 30, 1935): 150-151.

261. Melville, C.F. "Austrian Aftermath: Consequences for Europe." FORTUNE 141 (April 1934): 404-412.

Anticipates a Nazi victory in Austria.

262. ———. "Austrian Crisis." FORTUNE 140 (July 1933): 41-46.

263. ———. "Can Austria Survive?" FORTUNE 140 (November 1933): 542-549.

264. Menczer, B. "Should the Hapsburgs be Restored?" CONTEMPORARY REVIEW 146 (July 1934): 44-48.

Examines one alternative in the war on terrorism, namely a restoration of the traditional monarchy.

265. Minkus, F. von. "New Austria Once and Now." COMMONWEAL 21 (March 22, 1935): 592-594.

Describes political results of the Dollfuss murder.

266. "Mob Rule in Vienna." LIVING AGE 333 (September 1, 1927):
     394-397.

267. "Murder of the Empress of Austria." SPECTATOR 81 (April
     28, 1892): 317-318.

268. "Mussolini-Schuschnigg Conference." NEWSWEEK 4 (September 1, 1934): 10.

     Examines Austrian appeasement of fascist neighbors in
     the wake of the Dollfuss murder.

269. "Nazi Agitation and Propaganda Tempt Nation to Adopt
     Fascism." NEWSWEEK 1 (September 16, 1933): 13.

270. "Nazi Bomb Terror." NEWSWEEK 2 (June 16, 1934): 10-11.

271. "Nazism's Defeat in Austria." NATION 139 (August 8,
     1934): 144.

     Presents a unique perspective of the Dollfuss murder's
     aftermath.

272, "New Austria Comes Into Being: Republic is Succeeded by
     Fascist Regime." LITERARY DIGEST 117 (May 12, 1934):
     14.

273. "New Austrian Constitution." NATION 138 (April 4, 1934):
     371.

274. "New Austrian Constitution." NEW REPUBLIC 78 (April 4,
     1934): 199.

275. "New Triple Alliance." NATION 133 (March 28, 1934): 347-
     348,

     Continues coverage of political upheavals in Austria,
     as the Dollfuss regime takes steps to suppress fascist
     terrorism.

276. "Not Another Sarajevo: Assassination of the Austrian
     Chancellor." CHRISTIAN CENTURY 51 (August 8, 1934):
     1014-1015.

277. Orlow, Dietrich. "Neo-Nazis in Austria." PATTERNS OF
     PREJUDICE 16 (1982): 13-18.

     Describes the integration of ex-Nazis and neo-fascists

into post-war Austrian politics, from 1945 to the present.

278. Pastorelli, Pietro I. "Italo-Austrian Relations from the De Gasperi-Gruber ACcord to More Recent Agreements (1946-69)." STORIA E POLITICA 13 (1974): 283-307.

Examines political extremism and terrorism in the continuing Austro-Italian dispute over the Tyrol region.

279. "Revolution Flares in Austria." NEWSWEEK 15 (February 17, 1934): 15.

280. Roosevelt, N. "Austria and the Peace of Europe." CURRENT HISTORY 40 (April 1934): 20-24+.

281. "Schuschnigg Discusses the Times with Goemboes." NEWSWEEK 4 (August 18, 1934): 13.

Examines the aftermath of the Dollfuss murder, and Austria's slippage into neo-fascism, anticipating the subsequent annexation by Hitler's Germany.

282. Shaw, R. "Germany, France, Austria! Grave Internal Problems Beset Three Key Countries of Europe." REVIEW OF REVIEWS 89 (March 1934): 37.

283. ————. "Starhemberg." REVIEW OF REVIEWS 91 (February 1935): 49-51.

Examines the aftermath of the Dollfuss murder, with emphasis on the rise to power of German-backed Austrian fascists.

284. Shuster, G.N. "Death of Dollfuss." COMMONWEAL 20 (August 17, 1934): 381-382.

285. Simon, H. "Austria and the Nazi Movement." 19th CENTURY AND AFTER 114 (November 1933): 561-572.

286. Smyser, W.L. "Dollfuss, Chancellor of Austria." CONTEMPORARY REVIEW 144 (November 1933): 532-540.

287. "Socialist Revolt in Austria." CATHOLIC WORLD 138 (March 1934): 747-748.

288. "Starhemberg: Prince Who Commands Austria's Heimwehr." NEWSWEEK 3 (February 24, 1934): 16-17.

289. Steel, J. "Europe Moves Toward War." NATION 138 (March
     7, 1934): 269-270.

     Places Austrian terrorism in international perspective.

290. Stevens, E. "Austria After the Terror." NEW REPUBLIC
     78 (May 9, 1934): 359-360.

291. Thompson, D. "Wreath for Toni." HARPER'S 169 (July 1934):
     136-147.

     Describes the continuation of Nazi terror in Austria,
     with focus upon a particular victim of political murder.

292. "Trouble in Austria." COMMONWEAL 19 (February 23, 1934):
     450.

293. "Turbulent Regime of Austria's Dictator." LITERARY DI-
     GEST 118 (August 4, 1934): 15.

294. "Vienna Outbreak." LITERARY DIGEST 94 (July 30, 1927):
     230-241.

295. "Vienna Riots." NEW REPUBLIC 51 (July 27, 1927): 239-241.

296. "Vienna Today." CANADIAN FORUM 15 (October 1934): 9-10.

297. Walser, Harald. "Who Stood Behind the NSDAP? A Contri-
     bution to the History of Vorarlberg 1933 and 1934."
     ZEITGESCHICHTE 7 (1980): 288-297.

     Examines the birth and rise of Nazi terrorism in the
     early 1930s, sponsored by Hitler's German regime and
     supported by wealthy textile magnates.

298. "What Has Dollfuss Done?" CHRISTIAN CENTURY 51 (February
     28, 1934): 278-279.

299. Wirsing, G. "Germany Looks at Europe." LIVING AGE 346
     (May 1934): 249-256.

     Examines Hitler's role in continued Austrian terror.

300. Wiskemann, E. "Catholic Austria and the Hapsburgs."
     19th CENTURY AND AFTER 115 (June 1934): 643-654.

     Examines religious issues in Austria's political turmoil.

301. ————. "Problem of Austria." 19th CENTURY AND AFTER 114
     (September 1933): 290-302.

302. "World Over." LIVING AGE 347 (November 1934): 191-193.

     Examines the aftermath of the Dollfuss murder, placing
     Austrian terrorism in international perspective.

BULGARIA

Articles

303. Iliercu, Crisan. "1923—Bulgaria." AMALE DE ISTORIE
     25 (1979): 169-186.

     Presents a Romanian communist view of events in Bulgaria
     from the rightist coup of June 1923, to the successful
     "liberation" struggle by the Bulgarian Communist Party in
     September 1944.

CYPRUS

Books

304. Alastos, Doros. CYPRUS GUERILLA: GRIVAS, MAKARIOS AND
     THE BRITISH. London: Heinemann, 1960.

     Profiles guerilla leaders in the Cypriot war for inde-
     pendence from Britain.

305. ————. CYPRUS IN HISTORY: A SURVEY OF 5,000 YEARS.
     London: Zeno Publishers, 1955.

     Includes discussion of the war against British colon-
     ialism.

306. Bilge, Al Suat. "The Cyprus Conflict and Turkey." TUR-
     KEY"S FOREIGN POLICY IN TRANSITION, 1950-1974. Cited
     below as item 336, pp. 135-185.

     Examines Turkish participation in the Cypriot war for
     independence from Britain, with a discussion of on-going
     ethnic antagonism between Turks and Greeks, leading to
     commission of various atrocities.

307. Bitsios, D. CYPRUS: THE VULNERABLE REPUBLIC. Thessa-
     loniki: Institute for Balkan Studies, 1975.

308. Byford-Jones, W. GRIVAS AND THE STORY OF THE EOKA.
     London: Cassell, 1960.

     Examines the career of legendary nationalist hero George
     Grivas, who led the campaign against British colonialism.
     Includes historical coverage of the terrorist Ethniki
     Organosis Kyprion Agoniston (EOKA).

309. Campbell, Arthur. GUERILLAS. A HISTORY AND ANALYSIS.
     London: Arthur Barker, 1967.

310. Condit, D.M. (ed). CHALLENGE AND RESPONSE IN INTERNAL
     CONFLICT, Vol. II. Washington, D.C.: Center for Re-
     search in Social Systems, American University, 1967.

     Contains item 342 below.

311. Coyle, Dominick J. MINORITIES IN REVOLT. POLITICAL VIO-
     LENCE IN IRELAND, ITALY, AND CYPRUS. New Jersey: Fair-
     leigh Dickinson University Press, 1983, pp. 151-234.

     Presents a brief history of Cyprus and the movement for
     "Enosis"—union of Cyprus and Greece—with coverage of
     the EOKA terrorist campaigns of 1955-1959. Includes dis-
     cussion of the "holy alliance" between guerilla leader
     Grivas and Archbishop Makarios, a religious leader and
     political strategist.

312. Crawshaw, Nancy. THE CYPRUS REVOLT: AN ACCOUNT OF THE
     STRUGGLE FOR UNION WITH GREECE. London: G. Allen &
     Unwin, 1978.

313. Cross, Colin. THE FALL OF THE BRITISH EMPIRE, 1918-1968.
     London: Hodder & Stoughton, 1968.

     Includes discussion of the Cypriot crisis in a general
     review of the British empire's decline and dissolution
     after World War I.

314. THE CYPRIOT DILEMMA: OPTIONS FOR PEACE. New York: Insti-
     tute for Greek-American Historical Studies, 1965.

315. Denktash, Rauf R. THE CYPRUS TANGLE. London: Allen &
     Unwin, 1982.

     Examines the often-hostile foreign relations of Turkey,
     Cyprus, Greece, and Britain, culminating in acts of
     terrorism and ultimate revolution against colonial rule.

316. Durrell, Lawrence George. BITTER LEMONS. London: Faber
     & Faber, 1957.

     Presents an inside view of the continuing Cypriot strug-
     gle for independence from Britain.

317. Ehrlich, Thomas. CYPRUS, 1958-1967. New York: Oxford
     University Press, 1974.

318. European Commission of Human Rights. REPORT IN RESPONSE
     TO CHARGES BY THE GOVERNMENT OF CYPRUS CONCERNING ATRO-
     CITIES COMMITTED BY TURKISH TROOPS IN CYPRUS. Stras-
     bourg: 1971.

319. Foley, Charles. ISLAND IN REVOLT. London: Longman, 1962.

     Presents a history of the EOKA independence struggle.

320. ————. LEGACY OF STRIFE: CYPRUS FROM REBELLION TO CIVIL
     WAR. London: Penguin Books, 1964.

321. ————, and W.I. Scobie. THE STRUGGLE FOR CYPRUS. Stan-
     ford, Calif.: Hoover Institute on War, Revolution and
     Peace Press, 1975.

322. Foot, Hugh. A START TO FREEDOM. London: Hodder & Stough-
     ton, 1964.

     Examines the EOKA independence movement on Cyprus.

323. Foot, Michael, and Mervin Jones. QUIETLY MEN: SUEZ AND
     CYPRUS. New York: Rinehart, 1957.

     Presents a British soldier's "inside" view of conflict
     on Cyprus and in the Middle East. Includes discussion of
     EOKA terror tactics, with the war against Britain still
     in progress.

324. Foot, Sylvia. EMERGENCY EXIT. London: Chatto & Windus,
     1960.

     Examines the war for Cypriot independence and its after-
     math, in the withdrawal of British colonial forces.

325. Fraser, J. "The Conflict on Cyprus, 1952-1964." THE
     CONTROL OF LOCAL CONFLICT, Vol. 3. Cited below as
     item 831, pp. 777-880.

326. Gourlay, B.I.S. "Terror in Cyprus." THE GUERILLA—AND
     HOW TO FIGHT HIM. Cited below as item 842, pp. 232-248.

327. Great Britain, Central Office of Information. CYPRUS:
     EOKA'S CAMPAIGN OF TERROR. London: Her Majesty's
     Stationery Office, 1956.

328. Great Britain, Colonial Office. TERRORISM CYPRUS. Lon-
     don: H.M.S.O., 1956.

329. ————. CYPRUS 1956. London: H.M.S.O., 1957.

330. ————. TERRORISM IN CYPRUS; THE CAPTURED DOCUMENTS.
     London: H.M.S.O., 1956.

331. Greek Youth of Cyprus. A CYPRUS POCKET BOOK CONTAINING
     INDISPUTABLE ALL-BRITISH DOCUMENTARY EVIDENCE OF THE
     SEVENTY-EIGHT YEARS COLONIAL EXPLOITATION. Athens:
     Greek Youth of Cyprus, 1956.

     Presents the nationalist view of the Cypriot revolt,
     citing captured British documents to support EOKA claims
     od discrimination and oppression.

332. Grivas, George. GENERAL GRIVAS ON GUERILLA WARFARE. New
     York: Praeger, 1965.

     Presents the EOKA leader's views on guerilla tactics
     and the war against British colonialism.

333. ————. THE MEMOIRS OF GENERAL GRIVAS. Edited by Charles
     Foley. London: Longman, 1964.

334. Home, Gordon Cochrane. CYPRUS, THEN AND NOW. London:
     J.M. Dent, 1960.

335. Karouses, Girogos. PROPOSALS FOR A SOLUTION TO THE CY-
     PRUS PROBLEM. Nicosia: The Author, 1976.

336. Karpat, Kemal E., (ed). TURKEY'S FOREIGN POLICY IN
     TRANSITION 1950-1974. Leiden, Netherlands: E.J. Brill,
     1975.

     Contains items 306 and 337.

337. ————. "War on Cyprus: the Tragedy of Enosis." TUR-
     KEY's FOREIGN POLICY IN TRANSITION 1950-1974. Cited
     above as item 336, pp. 186-205.

338. Kinross, Lord. ATATURK. London: Weidenfeld & Nicholson, 1964.

     Includes background of the Cypriot independence move-
     ment in a biography of Mustafa Kemal Ataturk, father of
     the modern Turkish nation. Examines historic ethnic ri-
     valries between Greeks and Turks, together with resultant
     acts of terrorism.

339. Kosut, Hal. CYPRUS, 1946-68. New York: Facts on File, 1970.

340. Koumoulides, John T. CYPRUS AND THE WAR OF GREEK INDE-
     PENDENCE, 1821-1829. London: Zeno Books, 1974.

341. Kyle, Keith. CYPRUS. London: Minority Rights Group, 1984.

342. Lagoudakis, C.G. "Cyprus, 1954-1958." CHALLENGE AND RE-
     SPONSE IN INTERNAL CONFLICT, Vol. II. Cited above as
     item 310, pp. 335-380.

343. Lang, Robert Hamilton. CYPRUS: ITS HISTORY, ITS PRESENT
     RESOURCES, AND FUTURE PROSPECTS. London: Macmillan &
     Co., 1878.

     Includes discussion of 19th-century political upheavals
     and violence on Cyprus, laying groundwork for subsequent
     unrest in the 20th century.

344. Laqueur, Walter. THE STRUGGLE FOR THE MIDDLE EAST, THE
     SOVIET UNION IN THE MEDITERRANEAN 1958-1968. New York:
     Macmillan, 1968.

     Examines Soviet influence in Cypriot political violence,
     citing examples of communist support for guerilla move-
     ments on Cyprus and elsewhere.

345. Lee, Dwight Erwin. GREAT BRITAIN AND THE CYPRUS CONVEN-
     TION OF 1878. Cambridge, Mass.: Harvard University
     Press, 1934.

     Examines British 19th-century relations with Cyprus and
     Turkey, including efforts to forestall further violence
     between Greeks and Turks.

346. Luke, Harry Charles Joseph. CYPRUS UNDER THE TURKS, 1571-
     1878: A RECORD BASED ON THE ARCHIVES OF THE ENGLISH CON-
     SULATE IN CYPRUS UNDER THE LEVANT COMPANY AND AFTER.
     London: Oxford University Press, 1921.

347. McKinnon, Campbell. TURKEY AND GREECE: CLOSER UNITY——NOW!
     New York: Vantage Press, 1968.

348. Maier, Franz Georg. CYPRUS FROM EARLIEST TIMES TO THE
     PRESENT DAY. London: Elek, 1968.

349. Mariti, G. TRAVELS IN THE ISLAND OF CYPRUS. Cambridge:
     Cambridge University Press, 1909.

     Presents contemporaneous eyewitness accounts of the
     battles for Nicosia and Famagusta, with Greek forces
     waging guerilla war against the Turks.

350. Mayes, Stanley. CYPRUS AND MAKARIOS. London: Putnam,
     1960.

351. ————. MAKARIOS: A BIOGRAPHY. New York: St. Martin's
     Press, 1981.

     Includes discussion of the EOKA's anti-colonial campaign
     within a general biography of the Cypriot leader Makarios.

352. Modino, Peter. THE EVENTS IN CYPRUS. Paris: American
     Hellenic Institute, 1974.

353. Pantelli, Stavros. A NEW HISTORY OF CYPRUS: FROM THE
     EARLIEST TIMES TO THE PRESENT DAY. London: East-West
     Publications, 1984.

354. Papandreou, Andreas. DEMOCRACY AT GUNPOINT. London:
     Deutsch, 1971.

     Examines modern terrorism and political upheaval in
     Cyprus, together with a discussion of harsh anti-terrorist
     tactics imposed by the government in power.

355. Polyviou, P. CYPRUS: THE TRAGEDY AND THE CHALLENGE.
     London: John Swain, 1975.

356. Public Information Office. CYPRUS: THE PROBLEM IN PER-
     SPECTIVE. Nicosia: Public Information Office, 1969.

357. ————. THE CYPRUS QUESTION: A BRIEF ANALYSIS. Nicosia:
     Public Information Office, 1969.

358. Richter, Heinz A. GREECE AND CYPRUS SINCE 1920: BIBLIO-
     GRAPHY OF CONTEMPORARY HISTORY. Heidelberg, Germany:
     Wissenschaftlicher Verlag Nea Hellas, 1984.

359. Royal Institute of International Affairs, Information
     Department. CYPRUS, BACKGROUND TO ENOSIS. London:
     Oxford University Press, 1957.

360. ———. CYPRUS: THE DISPUTE AND THE SETTLEMENT. London:
     Oxford University Press, 1959.

361. Salih, Halil Ibrahim. CYPRUS: AN ANALYSIS OF CYPRIOT
     POLITICAL DISCORD. Brooklyn, N.Y.: T. Gaus's Sons, 1968.

362. ———. CYPRUS, THE IMPACT OF DIVERSE NATIONALISM ON A
     STATE. Tuscaloosa, Ala.: University of Alabama Press,
     1978.

363. Sonyel, Salahi Ramsdan. THE TURCO-GREEK CONFLICT. An-
     kara: Cyprus Turkish Culture Assn., 1985.

     Examines historical roots of "Enosis," with discussion
     of the long-standing animosity between Greeks and Turks
     on Cyprus.

364. Spyridakis, Konstantinos. A BRIEF HISTORY OF CYPRUS.
     Nicosia: Publication Department, Greek Communal Chamber,
     1964.

365. Stephens, Robert Henry. CYPRUS: A PLACE OF ARMS: POWER
     POLITICS AND ETHNIC CONFLICT IN THE EASTERN MEDITER-
     RANEAN. London: Pall Mall, 1966.

366. Union of Journalists of the Athens Daily Newspapers.
     CYPRUS, TOUCHSTONE FOR DEMOCRACY. Athens: 1958.

367. Vanezis, P.N. CYPRUS: THE UNFINISHED AGONY. London:
     Abelard Schuman, 1977.

368. ———. MAKARIOS: FAITH AND POWER. London: Abelard
     Schuman, 1971.

369. ———. MAKARIOS, LIFE AND LEADERSHIP. London: Abelard
     Schuman, 1979.

     Continues the biography begun in item 368, including
     discussion of the EOKA anti-colonial struggle.

370. ———. MAKARIOS, PRAGMATISM V. IDEALISM. London:
     Abelard Schuman, 1974.

371. Windsor, Philip. NATO AND THE CYPRUS CRISIS. London:
     Institute of Strategic Studies, Adelphi Papers, 1964.

372. Xydis, Stephen George. CYPRUS: RELUCTANT REPUBLIC. The
     Hague: Mouton, 1973.

                              Articles

373. "After the Cease-Fire?" NEWSWEEK 48 (September 3, 1956):
     38.

374. "Again, Violence." TIME 68 (September 19, 1956): 39.

375. Alan, R. "Cyprus: Nationalism Through a Looking Glass."
     REPORTER 10 (April 27, 1954): 36-39.

376. "Ally Adrift?" NEWSWEEK 46 (October 3, 1955): 40.

     Continues coverage of the Cypriot revolt against Britain.

377. "Along the Mason-Dixon Line." TIME 71 (June 23, 1958):
     19.

     Presents further coverage of violence in Cyprus.

378. "Another Country Heard From." TIME 68 (July 16, 1956):
     26.

     Examines foreign intervention in Cyprus.

379. "Answering Blast." TIME 71 (April 28, 1958): 26+.

380. Baker, E. "Cyprus: Island of Frustration." CHRISTIAN
     CENTURY 75 (October 15, 1958): 1180-1181.

381. Barco, J.W. "Problem of Cyprus: Statement, November 28,
     1958." U.S. DEPARTMENT OF STATE BULLETIN 40 (January
     5, 1959): 41-42.

382. "Beyond the Truce." NEWSWEEK 49 (March 25, 1957): 53.

383. "Bitter Breakdown." TIME 72 (November 10, 1958): 36+.

384. "Bridge Builder." TIME 72 (January 13, 1958): 19.

     Describes attempts at negotiated settlement on Cyprus.

385. "British Free Makarios." SENIOR SCHOLASTIC 70 (April 12,
       1957): 20.

386, Buckley, K.O. "Cyprus." AUSTRALIAN OUTLOOK 11 (1957):
       33-39.

387. "Church Spurs Drive for Cyprus Independence." CHRISTIAN
       CENTURY 71 (August 18, 1954): 965.

388. Comstock, A. "Uneasy Cyprus." CURRENT HISTORY 34 (June
       1958): 352-356.

389. "Counter-Terror." TIME 69 (March 11, 1957): 28+.

390. "Cyprus: New Issue, Old Land; Case of Greece; United
       Kingdom's Position." UNITED NATIONS REVIEW 1 (December
       1954): 44-51.

391. "Cyprus Solution?" U.S. NEWS AND WORLD REPORT 42 (April
       5, 1957): 12.

392. "Cyprus, Three-Way Tug of Diplomacy." SENIOR SCHOLASTIC
       73 (October 31, 1958): 10-12.

393. "Dead and Angry." NEWSWEEK 52 (November 24, 1958): 58.

       Continues coverage of the Cypriot revolt.

394. Durrell, L. "Cyprus: Personl Reflections." NATION 187
       (July 19, 1958): 23-24.

395. "Enosis and Its Background." ROUND TABLE 186 (1957):
       129-140.

396. "Eruption." NEWSWEEK 51 (June 23, 1958): 46+.

397. "Flight to the East." TIME 72 (August 18, 1958): 22.

       Continues coverage of the Cypriot revolt and the escape
       of certain rebel forces into Turkey.

398. Good, R.C. "Riddle of Cyprus." COMMONWEAL 65 (February
       15, 1957): 503-506.

399. Gould, K.M. "Isle of Venus." SCHOLASTIC 65 (October 13,
       1954): 14.

       Places the Cypriot revolt in historical perspective.

400. "Greece Brings Cyprus Issue Before the U.N." CHRISTIAN
     CENTURY 71 (September 15, 1954): 1093.

401. "Greeks for Greece." NEWSWEEK 44 (August 30, 1954): 34-35.

402. "Grief of Cyprus." LIFE 44 (June 30, 1958): 32-33.

403. Griffiths, E. "Hate is the Barrier." NEWSWEEK 52 (Aug-
     ust 11, 1958): 34+.

404. ————. "On the Scene." NEWSWEEK 51 (June 10, 1958): 38+.

     Continues coverage of the war on Cyprus.

405. "Haggling and Hopes." TIME 72 (November 3, 1958): 26.

     Follows the course of negotiations on Cyprus.

406. "Half Speed Ahead." TIME 72 (August 25, 1958): 25-26.

     Continues coverage of attempts to negotiate a settlement.

407. "Hard Way Out." NEWSWEEK 50 (July 22, 1957): 39.

408. Healey, D. "Cyprus Before the UN." NEW REPUBLIC 131
     (September 13, 1954): 6.

409. "Hostile Partners." TIME 72 (September 22, 1958): 26.

     Continues coverage of foreign involvement in Cyprus.

410. "In the Box." TIME 72 (July 7, 1958): 22+.

     Follows the course of continuing terrorism in the Cyp-
     riot revolt against Britain.

411. "In the Fateful Hours." NEWSWEEK 52 (October 6, 1958): 39.

     Examines the on-going Cypriot revolt.

412. "In the Front Line." TIME 72 (November 24, 1958): 31-32.

413. "Makarios Gets His Own Way." CHRISTIAN CENTURY 74 (April
     24, 1957): 508.

414. N., C. "Cyprus: Conflict and Reconciliation." THE WORLD
     TODAY 15 (1959): 13-47.

415. ————. "The Uneasy Truce in Cyprus." THE WORLD TODAY
     13 (1957): 422-432.

416. "New Rinkle: Passive Resistance." TIME 71 (March 17,
     1958): 31.

     Examines the shifting tactics of EOKA rebels.

417. "Next?" NEWSWEEK 51 (February 24, 1958): 48+.

     Attempts to project the future in troubled Cyprus.

418. "Ominous Hours for Cyprus." LIFE 44 (June 23, 1958): 43.

419. "Pale Hope in Cyprus." NEWSWEEK 52 (August 18, 1958): 43.

     Examines recent attempts to negotiate a cease-fire.

420. Panter-Downes, M. "Letter from London." NEW YORKER 34
     (July 12, 1958): 76+.

     Capsulized British opinion on the Cypriot revolt.

421. Patsavos, Christos C. "Archbishop Makarios III: A Bio-
     graphical Sketch." INTERNATIONAL REVIEW OF HISTORY AND
     POLITICAL SCIENCE 12 (1976): 89-92.

422. "Perpetual Prize." COMMONWEAL 61 (December 31, 1954): 350.

     Continues coverage of the Cypriot revolt against Britain.

423. Pipinelis, P. "Greco-Turkish Feud Revived." FOREIGN
     AFFAIRS 37 (January 1959): 306-316.

424. Radcliffe, Cyril John. "The Problem of Cyprus." UNITED
     EMPIRE 49 (January-February 1958): 15-19.

425. "Return of the Exiled Churchman to His Political Crusade."
     LIFE 42 (April 29, 1957): 40-41.

     Follows the activities of Archbishop Makarios in Cyprus.

426. "Return of Makarios?" NEWSWEEK 52 (September 22, 1958):
     53.

427. "Return of the Archbishop." TIME 69 (April 29, 1957):
     27.

428. "Riots and Resolution." TIME 70 (December 23, 1957): 18.

429. "Romans 5:3-4; Patience Worketh Hope." TIME 71 (June 30, 1958): 22.

Examines the sluggish progress of Cypriot negotiations.

430. "Sir Hugh Foot, Governor of Turbulent Cyprus." U.S. NEWS AND WORLD REPORT 43 (December 20, 1957): 18.

431. "Soldier's Mission." TIME 69 (April 1, 1957): 24.

432. "Solution for Cyprus?" NEWSWEEK 51 (January 13, 1958): 40.

433. "South from Cyprus." TIME 70 (July 22, 1957): 29.

Continues coverage of the Cypriot revolt and the flight of refugees from the on-going violence.

434. "Spring Thaw in Cyprus." CHRISTIAN CENTURY 74 (April 10, 1957): 443-444.

Follows the resumption of attempted negotiations.

435. Stevens, G.G. "Cyprus: Another Case for Nationalism." FOREIGN POLICY BULLETIN 34 (October 1, 1954): 9-10.

436. "Stifling Voices." TIME 64 (August 16, 1954): 25.

437. Sutton, H. "Paradise Lost." SATURDAY REVIEW 40 (November 2, 1957): 26-28.

438. "Time for a Change." TIME 70 (November 4, 1957): 28.

Proposes British settlement of nationalist claims.

439. "Trouble on Cyprus." NATION 179 (August 28, 1954): 161.

440. "Truce in Tatters." NEWSWEEK 50 (December 23, 1957): 33.

441. "Truce's End." TIME 71 (March 31, 1958): 17.

442. "Uproar." NEWSWEEK 44 (December 27, 1954): 29.

Examines the early days of the EOKA revolt on Cyprus.

443. "Warring Partners." TIME 72 (October 13, 1958): 33.

   Follows the course of political dissent among nationalist forces on Cyprus.

444. "Worst to Come?" NEWSWEEK 51 (May 5, 1958): 51.

   Examines escalating terrorism in Cyprus.

445. "Worst Yet." TIME 71 (February 10, 1958): 25.

CZECHOSLOVAKIA

Books

446. Bilek, Bohumil. FIFTH COLUMN AT WORK. London: Trinity
   Press, 1945.

   Examines the activities of underground communist forces
   in post-war Czechoslovakia, citing examples of terrorism
   and deliberate destabilization of the current regime.

447. Bolton, Glorney. CZECH TRAGEDY. London: Watts, 1955.

   Reviews the communist takeover after World War II, with
   examples of terrorism and subversion plotted and sponsored
   in the Soviet Union.

448. Brown, John. WHO'S NEXT? THE TERROR OF CZECHOSLOVAKIA.
   London: Hutchinson, 1951.

   Examines red terrorism and the fall of the Czech government, anticipating a "domino effect" in Eastern Europe.

449. Korbel, Josef. THE COMMUNIST SUBVERSION OF CZECHOSLOVAKIA,
   1938-1948: THE FAILURE OF COEXISTENCE. Princeton, N.J.:
   Princeton University Press, 1959.

450. Uhlir, Franticek. PRAGUE AND BERLIN, 1918-1938. London:
   Hutchinson and Co., 1944.

   Examines Czech relations with Germany prior to World
   War II, including a discussion of Nazi terrorism in
   Czechoslovakia prior to the German invasion.

ENGLAND

Books

451. Aldred, Guy Alfred. NO TRAITOR'S GAIT. Glasgow: Strick-
     land Press, 1955.

     Examines the 19th-century Fenian conspiracy and the
     bombing of Clerkenwell Gaol to free Irish prisoners.
     The Fenians stand as an historical precursor of the mod-
     ern Irish Republican Army, and their tactics were strik-
     ingly similar in terms of bombing and other terroristic
     acts.

452. Allen, H.C. GREAT BRITAIN AND THE UNITED STATES. London:
     1954.

     Includes an examination of the role which Irish-Americans
     have played in subsidizing and otherwise supporting acts
     of terrorism committed by Irish activists in England.

453. Anderson, Robert. THE FENIAN CONSPIRACY. London: The
     Author, 1905.

     Examines early Irish terrorism in London, from the view-
     point of a former assistant police commissioner who organ-
     ized covert activities against the Fenians.

454. ———. A GREAT CONSPIRACY. London: The Author, 1910.

     Presents further "inside" details on the Fenian move-
     ment and its terrorist activities.

455. ———. SIDELIGHTS ON THE HOME RULE MOVEMENT. London:
     The Author, 1906.

     Continues coverage of Fenian crimes and conspiracies
     in the late 19th century, with details of bomb plots,
     assassination attempts, and political maneuvers by overt
     spokesmen for the movement.

456. Bohstedt, John. RIOTS AND COMMUNITY POLITICS IN ENGLAND
     AND WALES, 1790-1810. Cambridge, Mass.: Harvard Uni-
     versity Press, 1983.

457. Clutterbuck, Richard L. BRITAIN IN AGONY: THE GROWTH OF
     POLITICAL VIOLENCE. London: Faber & Faber, 1978.

458. Cobb, G.B. CRITICAL YEARS AT THE YARD. London: B.T. Batsford, 1956.

Examines police efforts to suppress terrorism by the IRA and other groups in the years since World War II.

459. Critchley, Thomas Alan. A HISTORY OF THE POLICE IN ENGLAND AND WALES, 1900-1966. London: Constable, 1967.

460. ———. THE CONQUEST OF VIOLENCE: ORDER AND LIBERTY IN BRITAIN. London: Constable, 1970.

461. Cronin, Sean. THE REVOLUTIONARIES. Dublin: Republican Publications, 1971.

Examines the Fenian movement for Irish home rule, and the terrorist acts for which it was responsible in England.

462. Darvall, Frank Angley. POPULAR DISTURBANCES AND PUBLIC ORDER IN REGENCY ENGLAND; BEING AN ACCOUNT OF THE LUDDITE AND OTHER DISORDERS IN ENGLAND DURING THE YEARS 1811-1817. London: Oxford University Press, 1934.

463. Denvir, John. THE IRISH IN BRITAIN. London: The Author, 1892.

464. ———. LIFE STORY OF AN OLD REBEL. Dublin: Sealy, Bryers & Walker, 1910.

Presents the personal memoirs of a Fenian activist.

465. Dilnot, George. SCOTLAND YARD. London: Houghton Mifflin, 1929.

466. Fairfield, L. TRIAL OF PETER JONES AND OTHERS: THE I.R.A. COVENTRY EXPLOSION OF 1939. London: W. Hodge, 1953.

467. Glynn, A. HIGH UPON THE GALLOWS TREE. Tralee: Anvil Books, 1967.

Examines Irish republican violence in England, resulting in the trial and execution of captured terrorists.

468. Gregory, Isabella Augusta. GODS AND FIGHTING MEN. Gerrards Cross, England: C. Smythe, 1970.

469. Griffiths, A. CHRONICLES OF NEWGATE. London: Chapman & Hall, 1884.

Includes a discussion of Fenian terrorist cases with other criminal cases fromthe police logs of 19th-century London.

470. ———. MYSTERIES OF POLICE AND CRIME: A GENERAL SURVEY OF WRONGDOING AND ITS PURSUIT. London: Cassell & Co., 1898.

471. Gwynn, Denis Rolleston. GREAT BRITAIN: ENGLAND AND WALES. Dublin: Gill, 1968.

472. Hart, Herbert Lionel Adolphus. PUNISHMENT AND RESPONSI-BILITY. London: Oxford University Press, 1968.

Examines the continuing controversy over suppression and punishment of political "conscience crimes" in modern England.

473. Hayes, L.M. REMINISCENCES OF MANCHESTER FROM THE YEAR 1850. London: The Author, 1958.

Includes discussion of socio-economic rioting which rocked Manchester in the mid-19th century.

474. Le Caron, Henri. TWENTY-FIVE YEARS IN THE SECRET SERVICE. London: W. Heinemann, 1892.

Presents the memoirs of a leading British agent against the Fenian terrorists, with discussion of Fenian activities and profiles of ranking leaders.

475. Medlicott, W.N. CONTEMPORARY ENGLAND 1914-1964. London: Longmans, 1967.

476. Mowat, Charles Loch. BRITAIN BETWEEN THE WARS 1918-1940. London: Methuen, 1955.

477. Mudd, David. CORNWALL IN UPROAR. Cornwall: Bossiney Books, 1983.

Presents an historical view of British socio-economic turmoil, including violence on the part of Welsh coal miners seeking higher wages and improved working conditions.

478. Norman, Edward R. ANTI-CATHOLICISM IN VICTORIAN ENGLAND. New York: Barnes & Noble, 1968.

479. O'Donovan Rossa, Jeremiah. ROSSA'S RECOLLECTIONS, 1838
     TO 1898. New York: Arno, 1898.

     Presents the memoirs of a Fenian activist in Britain,
     including first-hand accounts of participation in certain
     terrorist activities against the British government.

480. Peacock, Alfred James. BREAD OR BLOOD: A STUDY OF THE
     AGRARIAN RIOTS IN EAST ANGLIA IN 1816. London: Victor
     Gollancz, 1965.

481. Prill, Felician. IRELAND, BRITAIN AND GERMANY, 1871-1914.
     PROBLEMS OF NATIONALISM AND RELIGION IN NINETEENTH-
     CENTURY EUROPE. Dublin: Gill & Macmillan, 1975.

482. Quinlivan, Patrick, and Paul Rose. THE FENIANS IN ENG-
     LAND, 1865-1872: A SENSE OF INSECURITY. London: John
     Calder Publishers, 1982.

     Presents a concise and compact history of the Fenian
     rebellion in England. Covers the Chester Castle raid,
     the Murphy riots, the Manchester rescue, the Clerkenwell
     explosion trials and executions, and the amnesty movement.

483. Quinault, R., and J. Stevenson (eds). POPULAR PROTEST
     AND PUBLIC ORDER: SIX STUDIES IN BRITISH HISTORY, 1790-
     1920. London: Allen & Unwin, 1974.

     Presents historical coverage of socio-economic turmoil
     in Britain. Contains item 2673 below.

484. Richter, Donald C. RIOTOUS VICTORIANS. Athens, Ohio:
     Ohio University Press, 1981.

     Includes British riots and public demonstrations in the
     period from 1837 to 1901.

485. Rude, George. THE CROWD IN HISTORY: A STUDY OF POPULAR
     DISTURBANCES IN FRANCE AND ENGLAND, 1730-1848. New
     York: Wiley, 1964.

486. Short, K.R.M. THE DYNAMITE WAR: IRISH-AMERICAN BOMBERS
     IN VICTORIAN BRITAIN. Atlantic Highlands, N.J.: Human-
     ities Press, 1979.

     Chronicles early British bombings by two Irish organi-
     zations based in the United States, Victorian precursors
     of the IRA.

487. Stevenson, John. POPULAR DISTURBANCES IN ENGLAND, 1700-
     1870. London: Longman, 1979.

Articles

488. "Aldersgate Explosion." SPECTATOR 78 (May 25, 1897): 762.

     Reports the latest incident of Fenian violence.

489. "Anarchist Propaganda in England." FORTUNE 95 (February
     1911): 333-343.

490. Bach, J.S. "Fascism, and the British Fuehrer." LITERARY
     DIGEST 124 (July 24, 1937): 13-15+.

     Examines Sir Oswald Mosley's British fascists.

491. Blakeney, R.B.D. "British Fascism." 19th CENTURY AND
     AFTER 97 (January 1925): 132-141.

492. Brailsford, H.N. "Fascism in England." NEW REPUBLIC 80
     (August 22, 1934): 42-43.

493. "Britain's Black Shirt Leader." NEWSWEEK 3 (May 5, 1934):
     22.

     Profiles Oswald Mosley and his fascist movement.

494. Brooks, S. "London's Startling Lesson; Houndstitch Mur-
     der." HARPER'S WEEKLY 55 (January 21, 1911): 8-9.

     Examines a recent political murder in Britain.

495. Calverton, V.F. "Swastika Over England?" CURRENT HISTORY
     46 (September 1937): 25-29.

     Follows the growth of Mosley's British fascist movement,
     with speculation on its particular significance to England.

496. Catlin, G.E.G. "Fascist Stirrings in Britain." CURRENT
     HISTORY 39 (February 1934): 542-547.

497. Clarke, J.W. "Assassins, British State, and the Plea of
     Insanity." ATLANTIC MONTHLY 48: 780.

498. Dutt, R.P. "B.U.F., Oswald Mosley and British Fascism."
     LIVING AGE 346 (July 1934): 441-445.

499. "Easton Bombs." NEW REPUBLIC 69 (January 13, 1932): 227; 69 (January 27, 1932): 297-298.

500. "English Fascists Hold Huge Rally." SCHOLASTIC 24 (May 12, 1934): 21.

501. "Fascists Come to England." LIVING AGE 346 (March 1934): 46-48.

502. "Hair-Pulling at Fascist Rally." NEWSWEEK 3 (June 16, 1934): 13.

503. Hodson, H.V. "London Letter." CANADIAN FORUM 14 (May 1934): 286.

     Continues coverage of the growing fascist movement in Britain.

504. Janeway, E. "England Moves Toward Fascism; the New Economic Pattern." HARPER'S WEEKLY 178 (January 1929): 113-125.

505. "John Bull's Fascists; Mosely Black Shirts Are Tamed but Provocative Ideas Spread." NEWSWEEK 13 (February 13, 1939): 22-23.

506. "Lessons of Southampton." SPECTATOR 65 (September 13, 1890): 328.

     Examines an outbreak of socio-economic rioting in Britain during the late 19th century.

507. "London Melodrama: Houndstitch Murders." OUTLOOK 97 (January 14, 1911): 41-42.

     Reports a contemporary political assassination.

508. Milner, L.B. "Fighting Fascism by Law: Public Order Act." NATION 146 (January 15, 1938): 65-67.

509. Mosley, Oswald. "Our Policy." LIVING AGE 346 (April 1934): 114-116.

     Presents the fascist case first-hand, from the pen of Britain's leading black-shirt.

510. "Mr. Asquith and the Coal-Riots; Relations of Home Office and Local Governments in Preserving Order." SPECTATOR 71 (September 23, 1893): 392.

511. "Near East Riots Spread, Vex Britain." LITERARY DIGEST
        121 (June 6, 1936): 12.

512. Oliphant, J.B. "Fighting Fascism by Law; Reply with
        Rejoinder." NATION 146 (April 30, 1938): 515-516.

        Refutes item 508 above.

513. Rawdon, J. "Mosley's British Fascists." CURRENT HISTORY
        40 (August 1934): 601-602.

514. "Relation of Great Britain to Anarchy." SPECTATOR 72
        (February 24, 1894): 257.

515. Rosten, L.C. "Rise of Oswald Mosley." HARPER 169 (Sep-
        tember 1934): 492-501.

516. Scarborough, H.E. "British Fascism: Force or Farce?"
        LITERARY DIGEST 117 (June 30, 1934): 14.

517. "Soldiers and the People; the Featherstone Riot." SPEC-
        TATOR 71 (September 16, 1893): 357.

518. Steel, J. "Is Britain Going Fascist?" NATION 138 (April
        4, 1934): 384-386; 138 (April 18, 1934): 446-447; 138
        (June 13, 1934): 675.

519. Strachey, E.G. St. L. "Fascism in Great Britain." NEW
        REPUBLIC 78 (May 2, 1934): 331-332.

520. Tait, S. "English Theatre Riots During the Eighteenth
        and Early Nineteenth Centuries." THEATRE ARTS 24 (Feb-
        ruary 1940): 97-105.

521. Williams, Dale Edward. "Were 'Hunger' Rioters Really
        Hungry? Some Demographic Evidence." PAST AND PRESENT
        71 (May 1976).

        Takes a new look at historic socio-economic violence in
        Britain.

522. Ybarra, T.R. "England's Hitler." COLLIER'S 94 (Septem-
        ber 1, 1934): 11+.

        Profiles Oswald Mosley and his fascist movement.

523. Zukerman, W. "Strange Story of Sir Oswald Mosley."
        HARPER'S WEEKLY 188 (February 1944): 257-263.

FINLAND

Articles

524. "Fascism in Finland." NATION 131 (Septembet 3, 1930): 255.

525. "Fascist Fiasco in Finland." LITERARY DIGEST 112 (March 12, 1932): 14-15.

526. Kirby, D.G. "Revolutionary Ferment in Finland and the Origins of the Civil War, 1917-1918." SCANDANAVIAN ECONOMIC HISTORY REVIEW 26 (1978): 15-35.

Examines the economic causal factors and activities of paramilitary groups leading to Finnish civil war.

527. Siltala, Juha. "The Lapua Movement and the Kidnappings of 1930." HISTORIA AIKAKANSKIRJA 80 (1982): 105-123.

Examines 213 incidents of violence in the period from May to December 1930, 110 of them directly traceable to the far-right Lapua movement.

528. Wright, H. "Finland Before and Since the Russian Revolution." CONTEMPORARY REVIEW 113 (April 1918): 447-452.

Includes political upheavals since 1917.

FRANCE

Books

529. Amann, Peter. REVOLUTION AND DEMOCRACY: THE PARIS CLUB MOVEMENT IN 1848. Princeton, N.J.: Princeton University Press, 1975.

530. Blanc, Louis. 1848—HISTORICAL REVELATIONS: INSCRIBED TO LORD NORMANBY. London: Chapman & Hall, 1858.

Examines causal factors in the upheavals which rocked France and other European nations during 1848.

531. Bezucha, Robert J. THE LYON UPRISING OF 1834: SOCIAL AND POLITICAL CONFLICT IN THE EARLY JULY MONARCHY. Cambridge, Mass.: Harvard University Press, 1974.

532. Bosher, J.F. (ed). FRENCH GOVERNMENT AND SOCIETY, 1500-
     1850: ESSAYS IN MEMORY OF ALFRED COBBAN. London: Ath-
     lone, 1973.

533. Clark, Michael K. ALGERIA IN TURMOIL. New York: Praeger,
     1959.

     Traces the Algerian revolt to terrorism by the OAS and
     other groups in France, culminating in attempts upon the
     life of Charles DeGaulle by right-wing fanatics who op-
     posed the liberation of Algeria from colonial rule.

534. Cobb, R.C. THE POLICE AND THE PEOPLE: FRENCH POPULAR
     PROTEST, 1784-1820. Oxford: Clarendon Press, 1970.

535. Colton, Charles Caleb. NARRATIVE OF THE FRENCH REVOLU-
     TION IN 1830: AN AUTHENTIC DETAIL OF EVENTS WHICH TOOK
     PLACE ON THE 26th, 27th, 28th, AND 29th OF JULY; WITH
     THE OCCURRENCES PRECEDING AND FOLLOWING THOSE MEMORABLE
     DAYS. Paris: A. & W. Galignani, 1830.

536. De Luna, Frederich A. THE FRENCH REPUBLIC UNDER CAVAIG-
     NAC, 1848. Princeton, N.J.: Princeton University Press,
     1969.

     Examines causal factors of the 1848 revolution, with a
     discussion of its aftermath.

537. Denholm, Anthony. FRANCE IN REVOLUTION, 1848. Sydney,
     Australia: John Wiley & Sons, 1972.

538. Duvean, Georges. 1848, THE MAKING OF A REVOLUTION. New
     York: Pantheon Books, 1967.

539. Elton, Godfrey Elton. THE REVOLUTIONARY IDEA IN FRANCE,
     1789-1871. New York: Longmans, Green & Co., 1923.

540. Fabian Society. FRANCE FACES FASCISM. London: V. Gol-
     lancz, 1940.

     Presents a contemporary leftist view of the fascist
     threat in France, including a discussion of right-wing
     terrorism prior to the German occupation.

541. Forshufvud, Sten. WHO KILLED NAPOLEON? London: Hutchin-
     son, 1962.

Theorizes that the former emperor was assassinated in
exile, citing medical evidence in favor of death by slow
arsenic poisoning, with speculation on the identity of
probable suspects.

542. ————, and Ben Weider. ASSASSINATION AT ST. HELENA.
Vancouver: Mitchell Press, 1978.

Elaborates on the theory propounded in item 541.

543. Hutchinson, Martha Crenshaw. REVOLUTIONARY TERRORISM:
THE FLN IN ALGERIA 1954-1962. Stanford, Calif.: Stanford University Press, 1978.

544. Joesten, Joachin. DE GAULLE AND HIS MURDERERS; A FACTUAL
ACCOUNT OF A DRAMATIC PIECE OF CONTEMPORARY HISTORY.
Douglas, Isle of Man: Times Press, 1964.

Examines the terrorist activities of the OAS in France,
as an outgrowth of the Algerian crisis, culminating in
attempts on the life of the French chief of state.

545. La Hodde, Lucien de. THE CRADLE OF REBELLION: A HISTORY
OF THE SECRET SOCIETIES OF FRANCE. New York: J. Brad-
burn, 1864.

546. Lamartine, A.M.C. de Prat d. HISTORY OF THE FRENCH REV-
OLUTION OF 1848. London: G. Bell & Son, 1888.

547. Lansdowne, Henry William, and Edmund Petty FitzMaurice.
THE SECRET OF THE COUP D'ETAT. London: Constable, 1924.

548. Lougee, Robert W. MIDCENTURY REVOLUTION, 1848: SOCIETY
AND REVOLUTION IN FRANCE AND GERMANY. Lexington, Mass.:
Heath, 1972.

549. Margadant, T.W. FRENCH PEASANTS IN REVOLT: THE INSURREC-
TION OF 1851. Princeton, N.J.: Princeton University
Press, 1979.

550. Maupas, C.E. de. THE STORY OF THE COUP D'ETAT. London:
J.S. Virtue, 1884.

551. Meisel, James Hans. THE FALL OF THE REPUBLIC: MILITARY
REVOLT IN FRANCE. Ann Arbor, Mich.: University of
Michigan Press, 1962.

552. Meltzer, Milton. THE TERRORISTS. New York: Harper &
Row, 1983.

553. Merriman, John M. (ed). 1830 IN FRANCE. New York: New
     Viewpoints, 1975.

554. Mithcell, Donald Grant. THE BATTLE OF SUMMER: BEING
     TRANSCRIPTS FROM PERSONAL OBSERVATION IN PARIS, DURING
     THE YEAR 1848. New York: Charles Scribner, 1852.

555. Moxon-Browne, Edward. TERRORISM IN FRANCE. London: In-
     stitute for the Study of Conflict, 1983.

556. Normanby, Constantine Henry Phipps. A YEAR OF REVOLU-
     TION FROM A JOURNAL KEPT IN PARIS IN 1848. London:
     Longman, Brown, Green, Longmans & Roberts, 1857.

557. Pinkney, David H. THE FRENCH REVOLUTION OF 1830. Prince-
     ton, N.J.: Princeton University Press, 1972.

   * Rude, George. THE CROWD IN HISTORY: A STUDY OF POPULAR
     DISTURBANCES IN FRANCE AND ENGLAND, 1730-1848. Cited
     above as item 485.

558. Sarrans, Bernard Alexis. MEMOIRS OF GENERAL LAFAYETTE
     AND OF THE FRENCH REVOLUTION OF 1830. London: R. Bent-
     ley, 1832.

559. Sobel, Lester (ed). POLITICAL TERRORISM. New York:
     Facts on File, 1978.

560. Soucy, Robert. FRENCH FASCISM: THE FIRST WAVE, 1924-1933.
     New Haven, Conn.: Yale University Press, 1986.

     Examines the rise of the fascist underground in France,
     citing acts of right-wing terrorism a decade before the
     eventual occupation by Nazi Germany.

561. Stewart-McDougall, Mary Lynn. THE ARTISAN REPUBLIC:
     REVOLUTION, REACTION, AND RESISTANCE IN LYON, 1848-
     1851. Gloucester: A. Sutton, 1984.

562. Sue, Eugene. THE GALLEY SLAVE'S RING: OR THE FAMILY OF
     LEBRENN; A TALE OF THE FRENCH REVOLUTION OF 1848. New
     York: New York Labor News Co., 1911.

563. Traugott, Mark. ARMIES OF THE POOR: DETERMINANTS OF
     WORKING-CLASS PARTICIPATION IN THE PARISIAN INSURREC-
     TION OF JUNE 1848. Princeton, N.J.: Princeton Univer-
     sity Press, 1985.

564. Weider, Ben, and David Hapgood. THE MURDER OF NAPOLEON.
     New York: Congdon & Lattes, 1982.

565. Williams, Roger L.   MANNERS AND MURDERS IN THE WORLD OF
     LOUIS-NAPOLEON.   Seattle: University of Washington
     Press, 1975.

566. ————.   THE MORTAL NAPOLEON III.   Princeton, N.J.:
     Princeton University Press, 1971.

Articles

567. "Anarchism in America and France." SPECTATOR 73 (August
     11, 1894): 167.

568. "Anarchist Scare." SPECTATOR 68 (April 2, 1892): 452.

569. "Anarchist Trial in Paris." SPECTATOR 68 (April 30,
     1892): 596.

570. "Anarchists in Paris." SPECTATOR 71 (December 16, 1893):
     860-861.

571. "Anti-German Riots in Alsace." LITERARY DIGEST 47 (De-
     cember 20, 1913): 1217-1218.

572. "Barricades Up Once More in Paris Streets." NEWSWEEK 3
     (May 12, 1934): 12.

573. Black, C.E. "Blood Over France." CURRENT HISTORY 1
     (December 1941): 340-343.

     Examines French terrorism under German occupation.

574. Blatt, Joel. "Relatives and Rivals: The Responses of
     the Action Francaise to Italian Fascism, 1919-26."
     EUROPEAN STUDIES REVIEW 11 (1981): 263-292.

     Charts the career of the Action Francaise, a pro-fascist
     group in France, during the years 1919-1926.

575. "Blum Glum; French Half-Day General Strike Follows Clichy
     Uprising." LITERARY DIGEST 123 (March 27, 1937): 11.

576. Brailsford, H.N. "Fascism and Finance in France." NEW
     REPUBLIC 84 (August 14, 1935): 8-10.

     Traces financial backers of the French fascist movement.

577. "Clichy Riot." NATION 144 (March 27, 1937): 341.

578. Cowley, M. "Two Sides of the Barricades." NEW REPUBLIC 85 (January 15, 1936): 287.

579. Dell, R. "Is France Going Fascist?" NATION 122 (February 3, 1926): 108-109.

580. "Fascism in France." LIVING AGE 328 (January 9, 1926): 87-91.

581. "France Echoes to Scandal." NEWSWEEK 3 (February 17, 1934): 8-10.

    Presents further coverage of Depression-era rioting, inspired by right- and left-wing extremist agitation.

582, Fraval, C. "Apostles of Fascism." LIVING AGE 328 (January 9, 1926): 85-87.

583. "French Anarchists." HARPER'S WEEKLY 36 (May 7, 1892): 437,

584. "French Anarchy Legislation." SPECTATOR 73 (July 14, 1894): 38-39.

585. Godkin, E.L. "Anarchists in Paris." NATION 54 (May 5, 1892): 335.

586. Laugel, A. "Government and Anarchists in France." NATION 59 (August 2, 1894): 77-78.

587. Lengyel, E. "Decline and Fall of French Fascism; Rise of the Front Populaire." NATION 141 (October 2, 1935): 380-381.

588. Malato, C. "Some Anarchist Portraits." FORTUNE 62 (September 1894): 315-333.

    Profiles leading French anarchists.

589. "Outrage of Paris." SPECTATOR 69 (November 12, 1892): 676.

    Examines outbreaks of political violence in the late 19th century.

590. "Paris and the Social Revolution." ARENA 39 (June 1908): 724-727.

591. "Patient Fascisti: French Leader Awaiting Chance for a
     Coup." LITERARY DIGEST 122 (July 11, 1936): 12.

592. Ravage, M.E. "Decline of French Fascism." NATION 142
     (March 18, 1936): 347-348.

593. ———. "Doriot, France's Would-Be Fuhrer." NATION 143
     (September 12, 1936): 299-300.

     Profiles the leader of the French fascist movement.

594. Rosny, J.H. "Anarchy in Paris." HARPER'S WEEKLY 39
     (October 12, 1895): 967-969.

595. Sanborn, A.F. "French Anarchists." INDEPENDENT 67 (August 5, 1909): 312-316.

596. Seldes, G. "Fascist Uprising in France?" NEW REPUBLIC
     91 (May 12, 1937): 11-12.

597. Shaw, R. "France and Spain Are Beset by the Fascist
     Threat to Republicanism." REVIEW OF REVIEWS 93 (April
     1936): 63.

598. "Stream of Blood; France Undergoes a Nightmare on Collaboration Anniversary." NEWSWEEK 18 (November 3, 1941):
     26.

     Reports terrorist attacks on pro-German elements, as
     resistance fighters settle old scores dating from the
     onset of German occupation.

599. "Students' Riots in Paris, in 1893." AMERICAN ARCHIVE
     $!: 132.

600. "Suburban Revolution, Paris." TIME 29 (March 29, 1937):
     21-22.

601. "Trial of the Thirty." SPECTATOR 73 (August 18, 1894):
     200-201.

     Follows the prosecution of French anarchists for various terroristic acts in the late 19th century.

602. Werner, M. "Frere Jacques." LIVING AGE 351 (October
     1936): 132-135.

     Examines the tactics of French fascist groups.

603. Werth, A. "French Fascism." FOREIGN AFFAIRS 15 (October 1936): 141-154.

GERMANY

Books

604. Abbotson, Martin (pseud). THE LIBERATION OF GERMANY. London: Watts, 1939.

Examines the Nazi rise to power from a sympathetic viewpoint, condemning enemies of the state and rationalizing Hitler's tactics in seizing control of the government.

605. Allen, William Sheridan. THE NAZI SEIZURE OF POWER: THE EXPERIENCE OF A SINGLE GERMAN TOWN, 1930-1935. Chicago: Quadrangle, 1965.

606. Angebert, Jean Michael. THE OCCULT AND THE THIRD REICH: THE MYSTICAL ORIGINS OF NAZISM AND THE SEARCH FOR THE HOLY GRAIL. New York: Macmillan, 1974.

607. Baynes, Helton Godwin. GERMANY POSSESSED. London: Jonathan Cape, 1941.

608. Beaumont, Maurice. THE FALL OF THE KAISER. New York: A.A. Knopf, 1931.

609. Bendersky, Joseph W. A HISTORY OF NAZI GERMANY. Chicago: Nelson-Hall, 1985.

610. Bessel, Richard. POLITICAL VIOLENCE AND THE RISE OF NAZISM: THE STORM TROOPERS IN EASTERN GERMANY, 1925-1934. New Haven, Conn.: Yale University Press, 1984.

611. Bondy, Louis W. RACKETEERS OF HATRED. London: N. Wolsey, 1946.

Presents a critical appraisal of the early Nazi movement, including discussion of terrorist activities by the brownshirts and other factions.

612. Braun, R. FASCISM—MAKE OR BREAK? GERMAN EXPERIENCE SINCE THE "JUNE DAYS." New York: International Publishers, 1935.

613. Brosart, Martin. GERMAN NATIONAL SOCIALISM, 1919-1945. Santa Barbara, Calif.: Clio Press, 1966.

614. Burdick, Charles, and Ralph H. Luts (eds). THE POLITICAL
     INSTITUTIONS OF THE GERMAN REVOLUTION, 1918-1919.
     Stanford, Calif.: Stanford University Press, 1966.

     Examines political violence in post-World War Germany,
     laying the groundwork for later charges of betrayal from
     spokesmen of the fledgling Nazi movement.

615. Clark, Robert Thompson. THE FALL OF THE GERMAN REPUBLIC;
     A POLITICAL STUDY. London: G. Allen & Unwin, 1935.

616. Dahlinger, Charles William. THE GERMAN REVOLUTION OF
     1849: BEING AN ACCOUNT OF THE FINAL STRUGGLE, IN BADEN,
     FOR THE MAINTENANCE OF GERMANY'S FIRST NATIONAL REPRE-
     SENTATIVE GOVERNMENT. New York: G. Putnam's Sons, 1903.

617. De Wilde, John Charles. BUILDING THE THIRD REICH. New
     York: Foreign Policy Assn., 1929.

618. Dornberg, John. THE PUTSCH THAT FAILED: MUNICH, 1923:
     HITLER'S REHEARSAL FOR POWER. London: Weidenfeld &
     Nicholson, 1982.

619. Engels, Friederich. THE GERMAN REVOLUTION: THE PEASANT
     WAR IN GERMANY: REVOLUTION AND COUNTER-REVOLUTION.
     Chicago: University of Chicago Press, 1967.

     Presents a communist view of the 1848 revolution, citing
     the inevitability of a popular uprising against oppressive
     capitalist regimes.

620. Epstein, Klaus. MATTHIAS ERZBERGER AND THE DILEMMA OF
     GERMAN DEMOCRACY. Princeton, N.J.: Princeton University
     Press, 1959.

     Examines contemporary political violence in post-war
     Germany, weighing the balance between Soviet-influenced
     red forces and latent pro-Nazi groups.

621. Feuchtwanger, Lion. DOUBLE, DOUBLE, TOIL AND TROUBLE.
     New York: Viking Press, 1943.

     Profiles leaders of the early Nazi movement, with a
     discussion of party terrorist acts in the 1920s and 1930s.

622. Fried, Hans Ernest. THE GUILT OF THE GERMAN ARMY. New
     York: Macmillan, 1942.

Discusses military involvement in Hitler's rise to power, including the gullible acceptance of Nazi scape-goating by senior officers who should have known better.

623. Goebbels, Joseph. MY PART IN GERMANY'S FIGHT. London: Hurst & Blackett, 1938.

Presents a personal memoir of the early Nazi movement, delivered with all the passion of a twisted mind.

624. Golding, Claud. FROM VERSAILLES TO DANZIG. London: G. Allen & Unwin, 1940.

625. Gordon, Harold. HITLER AND THE BEER HALL PUTSCH. Princeton, N.J.: Princeton University Press, 1972.

626. Greenberger, Richard. RED RISING IN BAVARIA. New York: St. Martin's Press, 1973.

Examines leftist violence in Germany after World War I, setting the stage for fascist reaction and eventual triumph.

627. Gross, Felix. HITLER'S GIRLS, GUNS, AND GANGSTERS. London: Hurst & Blackett, 1941.

Presents a critical, if sensationalized, view of the early Nazi movement, its leaders and activities. Incidents of terrorism on the road to power are included in a propaganda broadside.

628. Haffner, Sebastian. FAILURE OF A REVOLUTION: GERMANY 1918-1919. London: Deutsch, 1973.

629. Hanser, Richard. PUTSCH! HOW HITLER MADE REVOLUTION. New York: P.H. Wyden, 1970.

630. Heiden, Konrad. A HISTORY OF NATIONAL SOCIALISM. London: Methuen, 1934.

631. Herzstein, Robert Edwin. ADOLF HITLER AND THE GERMAN TRAUMA, 1913-1945. New York: Putnam, 1974.

632. Hitler, Adolf. THE HITLER TRIAL BEFORE THE PEOPLE'S COURT IN MUNICH. Arlington, Va.: University Publications of America, 1976.

Presents Hitler's views on the beer hall prosecution
and his own imprisonment, predictably skewed, but fascinating all the same.

633. Kater, Michael H. THE NAZI PARTY: A SOCIAL PROFILE OF
     MEMBERS AND LEADERS, 1919-1945. Cambridge, Mass.:
     Harvard University Press, 1975.

634. Kessler, Count Harry. WALTER RATHENAU: HIS LIFE AND
     WORK. New York: Harcourt, Brace, 1930.

     Profiles Foreign Minister Rathenau, with coverage of
     his assassination in 1922, by Nazi gunmen.

635. Knauerhase, Ramon. AN INTRODUCTION TO NAZI SOCIALISM,
     1920-1939. Columbus, Ohio: C.E. Merrill, 1972.

636. Koenigwald, Harald Von. REVOLUTION 1918. Breslan: W.G.
     Korn, 1933.

637. Lewis, Wyndham. THE HITLER CULT. London: J.M. Dent,
     1939.

   * Lougee, Robert W. MIDCENTURY REVOLUTION, 1848: SOCIETY
     AND REVOLUTION IN FRANCE AND GERMANY. Cited above as
     item 548.

638. Malraux, Andre. DAYS OF WRATH. New York: Random House,
     1936.

     Examines early terrorism by the Nazi party, culminating
     in Hitler's elevation to the chancellery and imposition
     of the first anti-Jewish laws in Germany.

639. Marx, Karl. THE REVOLUTION OF 1848-49. New York:
     International Publishers, 1972.

640. Maurice, C.E. THE REVOLUTIONARY MOVEMENT OF 1848-49 IN
     ITALY, AUSTRIA HUNGARY, AND GERMANY; WITH SOME EXAM-
     INATION OF THE PREVIOUS THIRTY-THREE YEARS. New York:
     G.P. Putnam's Sons, 1887.

641. Mehring, Franz. ABSOLUTISM AND REVOLUTION IN GERMANY,
     1525-1848. London: New Park Publications, 1975.

642. Meissner, Erich. GERMANY IN PERIL. London: Oxford
     University Press, 1942.

Presents a critical assessment of the Nazi party and
its violent rise to power, with documentation of terrorist incidents.

643. Merkl, Peter H. THE MAKING OF A STORMTROOPER. Princeton, N.J.: Princeton University Press, 1980.

644. Mitchell, Allan. REVOLUTION IN BAVARIA, 1918-1919.
Princeton, N.J.: Princeton University Press, 1965.

645. Mosse, Werner E. (ed). REVOLUTION AND EVOLUTION, 1848
IN GERMAN-JEWISH HISTORY. Tubingen, Germany: Mohr, 1981.

646. Mowrer, Edgar Ansel. GERMANY PUTS THE CLOCK BACK. Harmondsworth, England: Penguin Books, 1939.

647. Nathan, Peter Wilfred. THE PSYCHOLOGY OF FASCISM. London:
Faber & Faber, 1943.

648. Noakes, Jeremy. DOCUMENTS ON NAZISM, 1919-1945. New
York: Viking, 1974.

649. Noyes, P.H. ORGANIZATION AND REVOLUTION: WORKING-CLASS
ASSOCIATIONS IN THE GERMAN REVOLUTION OF 1848-1849.
Princeton, N.J.: Princeton University Press, 1966.

650. Pridham, Geoffrey. HITLER'S RISE TO POWER: THE NAZI
MOVEMENT IN BAVARIA, 1923-1933. New York: Harper &
Row, 1973.

* Prill, Felician. IRELAND, BRITAIN AND GERMANY, 1871-1914.
PROBLEMS OF NATIONALISM AND RELIGION IN NINETEENTH-
CENTURY EUROPE. Cited above as item 481.

Examines political and religious upheaval in disparate
cultures of the 19th and 20th centuries, with discussion
of terrorist activities in each area.

651. Rauschning, Herman. MEN OF CHAOS. New York: G.P. Putnam's Sons, 1942.

Profiles the early Nazi movement and its violent tactics, with discussion of assassinations and other terroristic acts which paved the way for Hitler's rise to
power.

652. Reed, Douglas. NEMESIS? THE STORY OF OTTO STRASSER AND
THE BLACK FRONT. London: Jonathan Cape, 1940.

653. Remak, Joachin. THE NAZI YEARS: A DOCUMENTARY HISTORY.
     Englewood Cliffs, N.J.: Prentice-Hall, 1969.

654. Rosenhaft, Eve. "The KPD in the Wiemar Republic and the
     Problem of Terror During the 'Third Period,' 1929-33."
     SOCIAL PROTEST, VIOLENCE AND TERROR IN NINETEENTH- AND
     TWENTIETH-CENTURY EUROPE. Cited above as item 41, pp.
     342-366.

655. Ryder, A.J. THE GERMAN REVOLUTION OF 1918: A STUDY OF
     GERMAN SOCIALISM IN WAR AND REVOLT. Cambridge: Cam-
     bridge University Press, 1967.

656. Stadelman, Rudolf. SOCIAL AND POLITICAL HISTORY OF THE
     GERMAN 1848 REVOLUTION. Athens, Ohio: Ohio University
     Press, 1975.

657. Stone, Norman. HITLER. Boston: Little, Brown, 1980.

658, Turner, Henry Ashby. GERMAN BIG BUSINESS AND THE RISE
     OF HITLER. New York: Oxford University Press, 1985.

659. ————. NAZISM AND THE THIRD REICH. New York: Quadrangle,
     1972.

660. Valentin, Veit. 1848. CHAPTERS OF GERMAN HISTORY. Lon-
     don: G. Allen & Unwin, 1940.

661, Von Maltitz, Horst. THE EVOLUTION OF HITLER'S GERMANY.
     New York: McGraw-Hill, 1973.

662. Watt, Richard M. THE KINGS DEPART: THE TRAGEDY OF
     GERMANY: VERSAILLES AND THE GERMAN REVOLUTION. New
     York: Simon & Schuster, 1968.

663. Young, George. THE NEW GERMANY. New York, Harcourt,
     Brace & Howe, 1920.

     Includes a discussion of political violence in the
     post-World War era, preceding the rise of the Nazi party.

664. Zucher, Adolf Eduard. THE FORTY-EIGHTERS, POLITICAL
     REFUGEES OF THE GERMAN REVOLUTION OF 1848. New York:
     Columbia University Press, 1950.

Articles

665. "Adolf Hitler States His Case." LITERARY DIGEST 111
     (November 21, 1931): 15.

666. "Among the German Fascisti." LIVING AGE 319 (December
     29, 1923): 593-596.

667. "Anarchist Plot Against the German Emperor." SPECTATOR
     81 (October 22, 1898): 549.

668. "Avenging Spirit of Germany." LITERARY DIGEST 103 (No-
     vember 2, 1929): 17-18.

     Examines the growth of the early Nazi movement.

669. Bargenhausen, J. "German Political Labyrinth." REVIEW
     OF REVIEWS 84 (November 1931): 80.

     Includes discussion of the early Nazi party.

670. Bartholdy, A. Mendelssonn. "Political Dilemma in Germany."
     FOREIGN AFFAIRS 8 (July 1930): 620-631.

671. "Bruening Stops the Hitler Drive." LITERARY DIGEST 111
     (October 31, 1931): 13-14.

     Presents a premature obituary of German Nazism.

672. "Bruening's Last Stand." NATION 133 (December 23, 1931):
     685-686.

673. Cambon, J. "Bulow and the War." FOREIGN AFFAIRS 10
     (April 1932): 402-416.

     Examines German political upheaval in the Depression
     era, charting the rise of communist and Nazi movements
     to greater influence with a disaffected population.

674. Carman, H.S., and S. McKee, Jr. "Parliamentary Crisis
     in Germany." CURRENT HISTORY 30 (April 1929): 156-159.

675. Carter, W.H. "Germany Struggling to Her Feet." FORTUNE
     137 (March 1932): 337-346.

676. Dawson, W.H. "Mending the German Constitution." CON-
     TEMPORARY REVIEW 135 (April 1929): 424-431.

677. "Dictator or Parliament." NATION 131 (October 8, 1930): 365.

678. "Driving Germany Bolshevik." LITERARY DIGEST 108 (February 14, 1931): 12.

679. Dumont-Wilden, L. "Germany's Aches and Pains." LIVING AGE 338 (March 1, 1930): 18-22.

680. Eberlein, H. "German Fascist Organizations." LIVING AGE 319 (October 27, 1923): 170-172.

681. Eddy, S. "Crisis in Europe." CHRISTIAN CENTURY 48 (October 14, 1931): 1278-1281.

     Places German turmoil in international perspective.

682. Elliott, J. "Germany Seeks a President." NATION 134 (March 2, 1932): 255-257.

     Examines continuing Nazi gains in German politics.

683. "Europe in Extremis; Dismissal of the Bruning Government." NATION 134 (June 3, 1932): 639.

     Sets the stage for a Nazi seizure of power in Germany.

684. Fairweather, N. "Hitler and Hitlerism." ATLANTIC 149 (March-April 1932): 509-516.

685. Farbman, M. "Deadlock in Berlin." NEW REPUBLIC 69 (December 16, 1931): 124-126.

686. ———. "Decline of Capitalism in Germany." CONTEMPORARY 141 (February 1932): 155-162.

687. Fay, S.B. "Fascist Victory." CURRENT HISTORY 33 (November 1930): 291-295.

688. ———. "German Constitutional Crisis." CURRENT HISTORY 32 (September 1930): 1213-1216.

689. Freeman, A.C. "Fascist Menace in Germany." FREEMAN 7 (May 9, 1923): 206-208.

690. "French Fears of Hitler." LITERARY DIGEST 113 (April 23, 1932): 15.

Places the growing Nazi movement in international perspective.

691. Friederich, C.J. "Dictatorship in Germany?" FOREIGN
AFFAIRS 9 (Ocobter 1930): 118-132.

692. Friters, G. "Who Are the German Fascists?" CURRENT
HISTORY 35 (January 1932): 532-536.

693. "From Hitler to Moscow; Symposium." LIVING AGE 340 (May
1931): 238-247.

Contrasts Nazi and communist philosophies, on a contin-
ent suddenly dominated by totalitarian states.

694. "From Left to Right of the German Parties: Posters in
the Presidential Campaign, 1925." SURVEY 61 (February
1, 1929): 546-547.

695. "From Six to Six Millions: National Socialist German
Workers' Party." LIVING AGE 339 (November 1930): 243-
245.

696. Gavit, J.P. "Much Ado About Hitler." SURVEY 68 (June 1,
1932): 239.

697. ————. "Through the Brandenburg Tor." SURVEY 61 (February 1, 1929): 540-545.

Continues coverage of political violence in Germany.

698. ————. "'Ware Germany and China!" SURVEY 64 (September
1, 1930): 475-476.

Compares political violence in two disparate cultures,
citing similar causes for widespread unrest and dissent.

699. "German Election." NATION 131 (September 24, 1930): 309.

Examines Nazi political gains.

700. "German Election." REVIEW OF REVIEWS 82 (October 1930):
60-61.

701. "German Elections." WORLD TOMORROW 15 (May 1932): 131.

702. "German Fascism." OUTLOOK 156 (October 8, 1930): 216.

703. "German Politics Sizzling." LITERARY DIGEST 106 (August 2, 1930): 12.

704. "German Thoughts on Revolution." LITERARY DIGEST 111 (December 26, 1931): 11.

705. "Germany and Democracy." WORLD TOMORROW 13 (September 1930): 355.

    Laments the approach of totalitarianism in Germany.

706. "Germany Decides." COMMONWEAL 13 (January 7, 1931): 255.

    Examines Nazi political gains.

707. "Germany Faces a Winter of Strife." CHRISTIAN CENTURY 47 (October 22, 1930): 1269-1270.

708. "Germany Fears Unsettlement Following Provincial Elections." BUSINESS WEEK (April 27, 1932): 34.

709. "Germany on the Brink. CHRISTIAN CENTURY 47 (October 29, 1930): 1303-1305.

    Examines the growth of red and fascist movements.

710. "Germany's Brown Terror." LITERARY DIGEST 115 (May 6, 1933): 10-11.

711. "Germany's Fascist Drive." LITERARY DIGEST 106 (September 6, 1930): 14.

712. "Germany's Inflamed Youth." LITERARY DIGEST 107 (November 1, 1930): 16.

    Examines the susceptibility of unemployed youth to recruitment by political extremists.

713. "Germany's Political Babel." LIVING AGE 336 (May 1929): 167.

714. "Germany's Political Murders." NATION 115 (Ocobter 4, 1922): 342-343.

    Examines three recent political assassinations.

715. "Germany's Political Pot Boils Over." LITERARY DIGEST 109 (April 11, 1931): 12.

716. "Germany's Radical Ballot Revolt." LITERAY DIGEST 106
       (September 27, 1930): 9-10.

717. "Germany's Red Dictatorship." LITERARY DIGEST 103 (No-
       vember 39, 1929): 18.

       Attempts to label the current government, with unfor-
       tunate results.

718. "Germany's Sack-Suit Chancellor." LITERARY DIGEST 105
       (May 3, 1930): 17.

       Follows the rise of the early Nazi party.

719. "Germany's Supreme Effort to End the Terror." LITERARY
       DIGEST 114 (August 20, 1931): 10-11.

720. Glasgow, G. "Conference Preliminaries; Germany." CON_
       TEMPORARY REVIEW 141 (January 1932): 112-116.

       Continues coverage of political turmoil.

721. ————. "German Crisis." CONTEMPORARY REVIEW 138 (No-
       vember 1930): 645-657.

722. Goebbels, Josef. "What Hitler Will Do: Doctrines of
       National Socialism." LIVING AGE 341 (January 1932):
       388-395.

723. Gooch, G.P. "New Germany." SURVEY 61 (February 1, 1929):
       605.

724. Gribble, F. "German Political Murders." FORTUNE 120
       (October 1923): 563-573.

725. "Handsome Adolf, the Man Without a Country." LITERARY
       DIGEST 107 (October 18, 1930): 34+.

726. Hellpach, W. "Hazards of the Democracy." SURVEY 61
       (February 1, 1929): 548-550.

727. "Hindenburg Making Germany Safe for Everybody." LITERARY
       DIGEST 112 (March 26, 1932): 15-16.

       Follows government efforts to suppress terrorism.

728. "Hindenburg Uses Dictatorial Powers to Avoid a Dictator-
       ship." CHRISTIAN CENTURY 47 (December 10, 1930): 1517-
       1518.

729. "Hindenburg Victory." NEW REPUBLIC 70 (March 23, 1923):
     140-141.

730. Hirschfield, G. "Brazen Dr. Bruening." OUTLOOK 159 (Sep-
     tember 16, 1931): 75+.

     Continues coverage of fascist violence in Germany.

731. Hitler, Adolph. "Germany, Awake!" LIVING AGE 340 (March
     1931): 12-14.

     Presents the Nazi party line for international perusal.

732. ————. "To Victory and Freedom: National Socialist Labor
     Party." LIVING AGE 342 (March 1932): 24-25.

     Offers Hitler's view of Nazi party history.

733. "Hitler Control in Prussia Depends on Concessions."
     BUSINESS WEEK (May 4, 1932): 29.

734. "Hitler, Germany's Would-Be Mussolini." LITERARY DIGEST
     107 (October 11, 1930): 15-16.

735. "Hitler Versus Prussia." NATION 134 (April 20, 1932):
     455.

736. "Hitlerism Shows Its Strength." CHRISTIAN CENTURY 49
     (May 4, 1932): 563.

737. "Hitler's Astounding Outburst." LITERARY DIGEST 111 (De-
     cember 19, 1931): 10.

738. "Hitler's Battle of the Marne." REVIEW OF REVIEWS 83
     (April 1931): 80-81.

739. "Hitler's Great Walkout." LITERARY DIGEST 108 (February
     28, 1931): 15.

740. "Hitler's Star Still in the Ascendent." LITERARY DIGEST
     113 (May 7, 1932): 12-13.

741. "Hitler's Victory." NATION 134 (May 4, 1932): 501.

742. "Hope of Peace." COMMONWEAL 12 (October 29, 1930): 652.

     Examines efforts to suppress political violence.

743. "Hugenberg Campaign to Tear Germany Assunder." LITERARY
     DIGEST 103 (November 23, 1929): 15-16.

     Reviews continuing political violence in Germany.

744. "Is Time Up for Hindenburg?" LITERARY DIGEST 111 (Octo-
     ber 3, 1931): 12-13.

745. Jackh, E. "Spirit of the New Germany." SURVEY 61 (Feb-
     ruary 1, 1929): 551-553.

746. Jordan, M. "Germany Elects a President." COMMONWEAL 15
     (April 20, 1932): 682-684.

     Examines Nazi political gains.

747. ————. "Reforming the Reich." COMMONWEAL 15 (January
     6, 1932): 261-262.

748. Kecskemeti, G. "Rudolf Breitscheid, Social Democratic
     Leader' Interview." LIVING AGE 342 (March 1932): 40-42.

     Interviews a major leftist leader in Germany during a
     time of continuing political turmoil and violence.

749. Koch-Weser, E. "Radical Forces in Germany." FOREIGN
     AFFAIRS 9 (April 1931): 435-440.

750. Lorab, H. de. "Republic Police of Berlin." REVIEW OF
     REVIEWS 84 (December 1931): 71.

751. Lafue, P. "Germany's Last Six Years; How Stresemann
     Out-Bismarcked Bismarck." LIVING AGE 337 (January 15,
     1930): 606-611.

752. Laidler, H.W. "German Socialism in the Balance." NATION
     133 (October 14, 1931): 384-385.

753. "Lease on Life." OUTLOOK 156 (Ocobter 29, 1930): 328.

     Examines continuing political turmoil in Germany.

754. Lore, L. "Hitler's Bid for German Power: With the Text
     of National Socialist Program." CURRENT HISTORY 36
     (May 1932): 166-172.

755. McClatchie, S. "Germany Awake." FORUM 85 (April 1931):
     217-224.

Examines Nazi political gains and violent activities.

756. Mackie, J.M. "German Revolution of 1848." BLACKWELL'S
     64: 373; 66: 206, 424.

757. Marcossin, I.F. "Germany Goes to Extremes." SATURDAY
     EVENING POST 203 (November 1, 1930): 8-9+.

758. ————. "New German Leadership." SATURDAY EVENING POST
     203 (May 16, 1931): 3-5+.

759. Mason, J.B. "How the Centre Party Votes." COMMONWEAL
     12 (October 8, 1930): 574-576.

Examines continuing political turmoil in Germany.

760. Mattern, J. "Gustav Stresemann." COMMONWEAL 11 (Decem-
     ber 4, 1929): 134-136.

Reviews continuing political unrest in Germany, with
emphasis on the career of one rightist spokesman.

761. ————. "National-Socialist Movement." COMMONWEAL 16
     (May 18, 1932): 63-65.

762. "New York in International Incidents; Bremen Riot." LIT-
     ERARY DIGEST 120 (August 10, 1935): 11.

Presents implications of recent Germany violence for
the United States.

763. Niebuhr, R. "German Crisis." NATION 131 (October 1,
     1930): 358.

764. ————. "Germany, a Prophecy of Western Civilization."
     CHRISTIAN CENTURY 49 (March 2, 1932): 287-289.

Places German political unrest in international perspective.

765. Norton, H.K. "Germany Shows Her Irritation." STATE OF
     THE NATION 58 (November 1930): 46-47.

766. ————. "Leaders of the New Germany." WORLD'S WORK 58
     (April 1929): 64-69.

767. Ogg, F.A. "Germany and Italy: A Contrast in Government."
     CURRENT HISTORY 33 (November 1930): 228-233.

Compares pre-Hitler Germany with Italy's fascist regime.

768. "Old Home Week of the German Social Democrats." LITERARY
     DIGEST 101 (June 22, 1929): 14-15.

     Profiles Germany's leftist faction as turmoil continues.

769. Ossietzky, C. von. "Trotski on Germany: Shall Fascism
     Really Conquer?" LIVING AGE 342 (March 1932): 29-31.

     Presents a red revolutionary's view of turmoil in Ger-
     many, erroneously anticipating a socialist victory in
     the near future.

770. Pavlov, E.A. "Inspired by October: the 90th Birthday of
     Max Holz." VOPROSY ISTORII KPSS 10 (1979): 128-131.

     Presents a Soviet profile of a German revolutionary
     activist who fled to Czechoslovakia in 1921.

771. Price, M.P. "Fascisti Movement in Germany." LIVING AGE
     316 (March 3, 1923): 514-520.

772. "Prussia's Good Sense Victorious." NATION 133 (August
     19, 1931): 172.

     Charts Nazi electoral gains and losses.

773. Radek, K. "Hitler." NATION 134 (April 20, 1932): 462-
     464.

774. "Reaction in Germany." LIVING AGE 339 (November 1930):
     237-245.

775. "Red Watch on the Rhine." LITERARY DIGEST 106 (August
     16, 1930): 13.

     Examines leftist political action in Germany.

776. "Religious War in Germany." COMMONWEAL 13 (April 8, 1934):
     617-618.

     Examines anti-semitic violence in Germany.

777, Remmele, H. "German Communism Speaks." LIVING AGE 342
     (March 1932): 26-29.

778. "Riots in Berlin." INDEPENDENT 69 (October 6, 1910):
     727-728.

779. "Scare That Prussia Gave Germany." LITERARY DIGEST 110
     (August 22, 1931): 10-11.

780. Scharfe, S. "Holds Hitler Small Danger." CHRISTIAN CEN-
     TURY 48 (December 16, 1931): 1603.

     Minimizes the Nazi threat in Germany.

781. Scheffer, P. "Hitler: Phenomenon and Portent." FOREIGN
     AFFAIRS 10 (April 1932): 382-390.

782. Schwarz, W. "Germany on the Road to Peace." CONTEMPOR-
     ARY REVIEW 139 (June 1931): 718-727.

783. "Scramble of Parties in Germany." LITERARY DIGEST 106
     (August 30, 1930): 14.

784. "Secret Orders and Murder in Germany." LITERARY DIGEST
     77 (May 5, 1923): 52-56.

785. Sencourt, R. "Germany's Centre Party." COMMONWEAL 9
     (May 1, 1929): 742-744.

786. Sforza, C. "Monarchy a Lost Cause in Germany." CURRENT
     HISTORY 33 (October 1930): 29-32.

787. Shaw, R. "Germany Votes for President." REVIEW OF RE-
     VIEWS 84 (March 1932): 44-45.

788. Shuster, G.N. "Sunrise in the West." COMMONWEAL 13 (No-
     vember 26, 1930): 98.

     Examines political extremism in Depression-era Germany.

789. Simonds, F.H. "German Mess." REVIEW OF REVIEWS 82 (Sep-
     tember 1930): 53-54.

790. ————. "If Hitler Comes to Power." REVIEW OF REVIEWS
     85 (June 1932): 35-37.

     Predicts the results of a Nazi ascendency.

791. ————. "New Germany Serves Notice." REVIEW OF REVIEWS
     82 (November 1930): 65-68.

792. ———. "Watch Germany!" REVIEW OF REVIEWS 85 (January 1932): 35-36+.

Places German Nazism in international perspective.

793. Smith, R. "National-Socialist Movement in Germany." CONTEMPORARY REVIEW 139 (March 1931): 297-302.

794. Soloveytchik, G. "Enigma of Germany." 19th CENTURY AND AFTER 111 (March 1932): 293-304.

Covers continuing political chaos in Germany.

795. ———. "Germany in the Melting Pot." 19th CENTURY AND AFTER 108 (September 1930): 364-375.

Examines German ethnic and religious turmoil.

796. Speed, H. "Terrorism in the Balkans." FORTUNE 142 (December 1934): 693-700.

797. "Stranger with a Package in Bonn." TIME 59 (April 7, 1952): 32.

Covers a post-World War II bombing incident in Germany.

798. "Stresemann." NATION 129 (October 16, 1929): 400.

Continues coverage of German political unrest, with focus on a contemporary rightist spokesman.

799. "Terror in Germany." LIVING AGE 344 (May 1933): 198-202.

800. "Terrorism Rules Germany." NATION 136 (March 29, 1933): 332.

801. Thalheimer, A. "Real Trend in Germany." LIVING AGE 342 (June 1932): 338-344.

Examines Nazi electoral gains.

802. Thompson, D. "Something Must Happen; German Youth Demands a Different World." SATURDAY EVENING POST 203 (May 23, 1931): 18-19+.

803. ———. "State Dictates; The Economic Evolution of Germany." SATURDAY EVENING POST 204 (February 6, 1932): 6-7+.

804. "Transformation of Adolf Hitler." LITERARY DIGEST 112
     (January 9, 1932): 13-14.

805. Troje, E. "Trend in Germany; Reply to L. Trotsky." FORUM
     87 (June 1932): 10.

     Refutes item 806 below.

806. Trotsky, Leon. "I See War with Germany if the Hitlerites
     Gain the Upper Hand." FORUM 87 (April 1932): 224-227.

807. Tschuppik, K. "Hindenburg." FOREIGN AFFAIRS 10 (October
     1931): 54-69.

     Examines continuing political unrest in Germany, as
     Nazi electoral gains undermine democracy.

808. Unruh, F.F. von. "Hitler in Action: Account of a Typical
     Hitler Meeting." LIVING AGE 340 (August 1931): 550-554.

809. Vermeil, E. "Danger from Germany." LIVING AGE 339 (Oc-
     tober 1930): 137-143.

810. Villard, O.G. "On the German Front." NATION 132 (Jan-
     uary 14, 1931): 37-39.

811. ———. "Soldiers Old, Soldiers New." NATION 131 (Octo-
     ber 29, 1930): 463-465.

812. Walter, F. "German Michael and the Doctors." CANADIAN
     FORUM 12 (October 1931): 11-13.

813. "War on the People." OUTLOOK 94 (March 5, 1910): 577-578.

     Examines contemporary political riots in Germany.

814. "Watching Germany's Communists." LITERARY DIGEST 101
     (June 8, 1929): 15.

815. Wertheimer, M.S. "Germany: Thunder on the Right." NEW
     REPUBLIC 66 (March 4, 1931): 66-68.

816. "Which Way Germany?" WORLD TOMORROW 13 (November 1930):
     437.

     Examines political alternatives in the Depression era,
     while communists and fascists brawl in the streets.

817. White, W.C. "Bolshevism a la Carte." SCRIBNER'S MAGA-
     ZINE 91 (May 1932): 395-398.

     Examines Germany's extreme left wing.

818. ————. "Hail Hitler!" SCRIBNER'S MAGAZINE 91 (April
     1932): 229-231.

819. "Wildfire Spread of German Fascism." LITERARY DIGEST 111
     (November 28, 1931): 13-14.

820. "World Over." LIVING AGE 339 (December 1930): 331-334.

     Examines the rise of German fascism, and its conse-
     quences for the world at large.

821. Ybarra, T.R. "Best Since Bismarck." COLLIER'S 89 (Feb-
     ruary 6, 1932): 12-13+.

     Examines continuing political unrest in Germany.

822. ————. "Germany's Brown Shirt." COLLIER'S 89 (March 5,
     1932): 11+.

823. ————. "Hindenburg Losing His Grip." OUTLOOK 156 (No-
     vember 26, 1930): 495.

824. ————. "Hugenberg, Hindenburg, Hitler." OUTLOOK 155
     (August 27, 1930): 665.

825. ————. "Stresemann's Successor." OUTLOOK 153 (November
     20, 1929): 460-461.

     Continues coverage of German political turmoil.

826. ————. "Watch Von Seeckt!" OUTLOOK 156 (December 24,
     1930): 657.

     Presents further coverage of German political unrest,
     with emphasis on the latest in a string of rightist
     leaders.

GREECE

Books

827. Albright, David E. (ed). COMMUNISM AND POLITICAL SYSTEMS
     IN WESTERN EUROPE. Denver: Westview Press, 1979.

Contains item 846 below.

828. Alivizatos, Nicos C. "The 'Emergency Regime' and Civil Liberties, 1946-1949." GREECE IN THE 1940's. A NATION IN CRISIS. Cited below as item 845, pp. 220-228.

829. Archer, Laird. BALKAN TRAGEDY. Kansas: Kansas State University, 1977.

     Examines communist efforts to subvert the Greek government after World War II, with discussion of the American military response and UN intervention.

830. Averof, Evangelos. BY FIRE AND AXE. THE COMMUNIST PARTY AND THE CIVIL WAR IN GREECE, 1944-49. New Rochelle, N.Y.: Caratzas, 1978.

831. Bloomfield, Lincoln Palmer. THE CONTROL OF LOCAL CONFLICT: A DESIGN STUDY ON ARMS CONTROL AND LIMITED WAR IN THE DEVELOPING AREAS. Washington, D.C.: U.S. Government Printing Office, 1967.

     Contains items 325 and 838.

832. Borkenau, Franz (ed). EUROPEAN COMMUNISM. New York: Harper, 1953, pp. 409-437.

     Includes a discussion of the communist effort to subvert and capture Greece after World War II.

833. Campbell, John. "The Greek Civil War." THE INTERNATIONAL REGULATION OF CIVIL WARS. Cited below as item 851, pp. 37-64.

834. Campbell, M.A., E.W. Downs, and L.V. Schuetta. THE EMPLOYMENT OF AIRPOWER IN THE GREEK GUERILLA WAR, 1947-1949. Houston: Aerospace Studies Institute, 1964.

835. Chandler, Geofrey. THE DIVIDED LAND, AN ANGLO-GREEK TRAGEDY. London: Macmillan, 1959.

836. Cloff, Richard. "Greece 1943-1949." COMMUNIST POWER IN EUROPE, 1944-1949. Cited below as item 853.

837. Eudes, Dominique. THE KAPETANIOS: PARTISANS AND CIVIL WAR IN GREECE, 1943-1949. New York: Monthly Review Press, 1972.

838. Fraser, J. "The Greek Insurgency. 1944-1949." THE CON-
     TROL OF LOCAL CONFLICT, Vol. 3. Cited above as item
     831, pp. 727-776.

839. Gage, Nicholas. ELENI. A SAVAGE WAR, A MOTHER'S LOVE,
     AND A SON'S REVENGE. A PERSONAL STORY. New York: Ran-
     dom House, 1983.

     Presents a personal memoir of the Greek civil war, as
     a best-selling author pursues—and finally confronts—
     the man responsible for his mother's execution.

840. Greene, A. (ed). THE GUERILLA—AND HOW TO FIGHT HIM.
     New York: 1962.

     Contains items 326 and 856.

841. Gunther, John (ed). BEHIND THE CURTAIN. New York:
     Harper, 1949.

     Examines the on-going Greek civil war between communist
     and nationalist forces.

844. Heilbrunn, Otto. PARTISAN WARFARE. London: George Allen
     & Unwin, 1962.

843. Iatrides, John O. "Civil War, 1945-1949: National and
     International Aspects." GREECE IN THE 1940's. A NATION
     IN CRISIS. Cited below as item 845, pp. 195-219.

844. ———. "Greece and the Origins of the Cold War."
     GREECE IN TRANSITION. Cited below as item 847, pp.
     236-251.

845. ——— (ed). GREECE IN THE 1940's. A NATION IN CRISIS.
     Hanover: University Press of New England, 1981.

     Contains items 828, 839, 860, and 861.

846. Kitsikis, Dimitri. "Greece: Communism in a Non-Western
     Setting." COMMUNISM AND POLITICAL SYSTEMS IN WESTERN
     EUROPE. Cited above as item 827, pp. 211-242.

847. Koumoulides, John T.A. (ed). GREECE IN TRANSITION.
     London: Zeno Publishers, 1977.

     Contains item 844.

848. Kousoulas, Dimitrios George. THE PRICE OF FREEDOM;
     GREECE IN WORLD AFFAIRS, 1939-1953. Syracuse, N.Y.:
     Syracuse University Press, 1953.

849. ————. REVOLUTION AND DEFEAT, THE STORY OF THE GREEK
     COMMUNIST PARTY. London: Oxford University Press, 1965.

850. Leeper, Sir Reginald. WHEN GREEK MEETS GREEK. London:
     Chatto & Windus, 1950.

     Examines the background and course of the civil war,
     with a discussion of the communist role in attempting to
     subvert and overthrow the Greek government after World
     War II.

851. Luard, Evan (ed). THE INTERNATIONAL REGULATION OF CIVIL
     WARS. London: Thames & Hudson, 1972.

     Contains item 833.

852. Matthews, Kenneth. MEMORIES OF A MOUNTAIN WAR: GREECE,
     1944-1949. London: Longman, 1972.

853. McCauley, M. (ed). COMMUNIST POWER IN EUROPE, 1944-1949.
     London: Macmillan, 1977.

     Contains item 836.

854. Murray, J.C. "Winning in the Mountains—Greece: The
     Anti-Bandit War (1945-1949)." THE GUERILLA—AND HOW
     TO FIGHT HIM. Cited above as item 840, pp. 63-112.

855. O'Ballance, Edgar. THE GREEK CIVIL WAR 1944-1949.
     London: Faber, 1966.

856. Osanka, Franklin Mark (ed). MODERN GUERILLA WARFARE.
     FIGHTING COMMUNIST GUERILLA MOVEMENTS, 1941-1961.
     New York: 1962.

     Contains items 857 and 866.

857. Papagos, A. "Guerilla Warfare." MODERN GUERILLA WAR-
     FARE. Cited above as item 856.

858. Richter, Heinz. GREECE 1945-1946: FROM BRITISH INTER-
     VENTION TO CIVIL WAR. London: Merlin Press, 1984.

* ———. GREECE AND CYPRUS SINCE 1920. Cited above as
    item 358.

859. Sissons, Michael (ed). AGE OF AUSTERITY. London: Hodder
     & Stoughton, 1963.

     Contains item 867.

860. Svoronos, Nikolas. "Greek History, 1940-1950: The Main
     Problems." GREECE IN THE 1940's. A NATION IN CRISIS.
     Cited above as item 845, pp. 1-16.

861. Tsoucalas, Constantine. "The Idealogical Impact of the
     Civil War." GREECE IN THE 1940's. A NATION IN CRISIS.
     Cited above as item 855, pp. 319-341.

862. United States Congress, House Committee on Foreign Affairs.
     THE STRATEGY AND TACTICS OF WORLD COMMUNISM. SUPPLEMENT
     IV: FIVE HUNDRED LEADING COMMUNISTS IN THE EASTERN
     HEMISPHERE. Washington, D.C.: U.S. Government Print-
     ing Office, 1948.

863. United States, Department of State. PROBLEMS OF GREECE,
     KOREA AND PALESTINE: SELECTED STATEMENTS, UNITED
     NATIONS RESOLUTIONS, SEPT. 21-DEC. 12, 1948. Washing-
     ton, D.C.: U.S. Government Printing Office, 1949.

864. ———. THE UNITED NATIONS AND THE PROBLEM OF GREECE.
     Washington, D.C.: U.S. Dept. of State, 1947.

865.United States, Office of the Chief of Military History.
     SUPPRESSION OF IRREGULAR (BANDITS) OPERATIONS, TR.
     BY THE WRITING OF DEPUTY CHIEF OF STAFF, GREEK ARMY.
     Washington, D.C.: n.d.

866, Wainhouse, Edward R. "Guerilla War in Greece, 1946-49:
     A Case Study." MODERN GUERILLA WARFARE, FIGHTING
     COMMUNIST GUERILLA MOVEMENTS, 1941-1961. Cited above
     as item 856.

867. Watt, D. "Withdrawal from Greece." AGE OF AUSTERITY,
     1945-51. Cited above as item 859, pp. 106-131.

     Examines British evacuation from Greece in 1947, at
     the height of the civil war between communist and nation-
     alist forces.

868. Wittner, Lawrence S. AMERICAN INTERVENTION IN GREECE
     1943-1949. A STUDY IN COUNTERREVOLUTION. New York:
     Columbia University Press, 1982.

869. Ypourgeion, Exoterikon. INCIDENTS ON THE GREEK FRONTIER,
     FROM JANUARY 1 TO DECEMBER 31, 1946. Athens: 1947.

     Examines communist attempts to subvert the Greek gov-
     ernment after World War II.

870. ————. OF CONCILIATION AND IRRECONCILABLES. Athens:
     1949.

                              Articles

871. "Albanian Frontier: Ignition Point; Escape of 9000 Greek
     Guerillas to Camps in Albania." U.N. WORLD 3 (October
     1949): 3.

872. Alvarez del Vayo, J. "Report from Athens." NATION 166
     (January 3, 1948): 5-6.

     Examines the continuing Greek civil war.

873. Anthem, Thomas. "Challenge in Greece." CONTEMPORARY
     REVIEW 173 (March 1948): 146-150.

874. ————. "Greek Cauldron." CONTEMPORARY REVIEW 172
     (September 1947): 148-153.

875. ————. "New Balkan Cockpit." CONTEMPORARY REVIEW 170
     (November 1946): 268-274.

     Presents early coverage of the Greek civil war.

876. ————. "The Prospect in Greece." CONTEMPORARY REVIEW
     176 (September 1949): 142-147.

     Anticipates the outcome of the civil war.

877. Balkos, Anastasios A. "Guerilla Warfare." MILITARY
     REVIEW (March 1958).

878. "Captain of the Crags." TIME 51 (April 5, 1948): 26-29.

     Profiles partisan fighters in the civil war against
     communism.

879. Chandler, Geoffrey. "The Unnecessary War: The Greek Civil War of 1946-1949." HISTORY TODAY 8 (October 1958): 715-724.

880. "Crucified; Naousa." TIME 53 (January 31, 1949): 27.

Continues coverage of the on-going civil war, with focus on the outcome of one particular engagement.

881. Curtin, E.P. "American Advisory Group Aids Greece in War on Guerillas." ARMOURED CAVALRY JOURNAL 58 (January-February 1949): 8-11, 34.

882. Daniell, R. "Great Challenge of the Greek Crisis." NEW YORK TIMES MAGAZINE (April 20, 1947): 8.

883. ———. "Where the Cold War is a Shooting War." NEW YORK TIMES MAGAZINE (February 15, 1948): 12-13.

884. "Days of Victory." TIME 54 (August 29, 1949): 22.

Covers the final days of the civil war, with communist forces in retreat.

885. "Despite Rumbles from the Greek Police." NATION 167 (September 25, 1948).

Continues coverage of the struggle against communist terrorism in Greece.

886. "Diary." TIME 50 (August 25, 1947): 27.

Presents a personal narrative of the civil war.

887. Dodds, Norman. "Europe's Hell Hole." CAVALCADE (May 1, 1948).

888. "Eleven Miles from Athens." TIME 50 (October 20, 1947): 32-33.

Continues coverage of the civil war, as communist forces advance on the Greek capital.

889. Falls, Cyril. "Communist Campaign Against Greece." MILITARY REVIEW (May 1949): 77-80.

890. ———. "Greek Army and the Guerillas." MILITARY REVIEW (March 1948): 73-76.

891. "Flickering Freedom." NEW REPUBLIC 16 (February 12, 1947): 10.

892. "Flushing the Hares." TIME 51 (May 3, 1948).

     Follows the hunt for communist guerillas in Greece.

893. "Free Greece." COMMONWEAL 47 (January 9, 1948): 316.

894. "From No Matter Where You Sit, the Greek Drama..." NATION 165 (July 19, 1947).

895. "Greece's Three-Year Ordeal." U.N. WORLD 3 (September 1949): 36-37.

896. "Greece in Agony." SCHOLASTIC 52 (February 9, 1948): 7-8.

897. "Greek Balance Sheet." NEW STATESMAN AND NATION 35 (June 12, 1948): 475.

     Examines relative wins and losses in the continuing civil war.

898. "Greek Executions." COMMONWEAL 48 (May 21, 1948): 128.

899. "Greek Executioner." NATION 166 (May 15, 1948): 518.

900. "Greek Situation Nears Showdown." LIFE 23 (August 25, 1947): 32-33.

901. "Greek Skirmishes Cause War Scare." LIFE 23 (July 28, 1947): 34-35.

902. "Guerillas on Parade." NEWSWEEK 31 (February 23, 1948): 34.

903. "Guinea Pig." NATION 166 (March 27, 1948).

     Places the civil war in international perspective, with an overview of communist and Western strategies.

904. Hasbrouck, J. "Greece: Halfway to Failure." NEW REPUB-LIC 118 (February 23, 1948): 11-14.

905. Hauser, E.O. "Something Rotten in Greece." SATURDAY EVENING POST 219 (April 5, 1947): 26-27.

906. Howard, Harry Nicholas. "Greece and Its Balkan Neighbors (1948-1949): The United Nations Attempts at Conciliation." BALKAN STUDIES 7 (1966): 1-26.

907. "International Brigade." NEWSWEEK 30 (July 28, 1947): 16.

     Examines the role of foreign volunteers in the civil war.

908. "In Greece the Guerillas Announced." NATION (June 18, 1949).

909. Katris, John. "Political Assassinations." JOURNAL OF THE HELLENIC DIASPORA 3 (1976): 17-23.

     Includes Greek political murders in the twenty-year period beginning in 1956.

910. Kendrick, A. "Greece's Ultimate Solution." NEW REPUBLIC 120 (March 7, 1949): 14-16.

911. Kippax, H.G. "Greek People in the Long War." LIFE 25 (September 23, 1948): 21-22.

912. Kirchwey, Freda. "Mr. Churchill's War." NATION 164 (April 19, 1947): 439-441.

     Examines British intervention in the Greek war against communism.

913. Kitroeff, Alexander. "A Divided Land: Greece in the Nineteen Forties." JOURNAL OF THE HELLENIC DIASPORA 9 (Summer 1982): 118-136.

914. Kousoulas, Dimitrios George. "Guerilla War the Communists Lost." NAVAL INSTITUTE PROCEEDINGS (May 1963): 66-73.

915. Laski, Harold J. "Power Politics Spells War." NATION (October 4, 1947): 355-358.

916. "Local Insurrection in Greece." COMMONWEAL 50 (August 26, 1949): 476.

917. "Long, Long Trail." TIME 52 (October 11, 1948): 33.

     Continues coverage of the Greek civil war.

918. Low, R. "Battle for Greece." TIME 50 (November 17, 1947)
     37.

919. ―――. "So Long, Fella." TIME 53 (January 3, 1949): 20.

     Continues coverage of the civil war.

920. Lyford, J.P. "Nazis Who Never Left Greece." NEW REPUB-
     LIC 117 (December 8, 1947): 13.

     Examines the far-right wing in the civil war.

921. McNeill, William Hardy. "Struggle for Greece, 1944-1947."
     CURRENT HISTORY 14 (February 1948): 71-75.

922. Murray, J.C. "The Anti-Bandit War. Part 1." MARINE CORPS
     GAZETTE 38 (January 1954): 14-23.

923. ―――. "The Anti-Bandit War. Part 2." MARINE CORPS
     GAZETTE 38 (February 1954): 50-59.

924. ―――. "The Anti-Bandit War. Part 3." MARINE CORPS
     GAZETTE 38 (March 1954): 51-59.

925. ―――. "The Anti-Bandit War. Part 4." MARINE CORPS
     GAZETTE 38 (April 1954): 52-60.

926. ―――. "The Anti-Bandit War. Part 5." MARINE CORPS
     GAZETTE 38 (May 1954): 52-58.

927. "Not So Stupid." TIME 49 (March 31, 1947): 26.

     Covers tactics on both sides in the civil war.

928. "No Compliments." TIME 50 (September 1, 1947): 19.

     Continues coverage of the Greek civil war.

929. "No Telltale Tongue." TIME 52 (November 1, 1948): 34.

     Follows covert action in the civil war.

930. Papagos, A. "Guerilla Warfare." FOREIGN AFFAIRS 30
     (1952): 215-230.

931. Pendle, G. "Storm Centre: Greece." FORTNIGHTLY 168
     (September 1947): 198-200.

932. "People's Shame." NEWSWEEK 29 (May 5, 1947): 40.

    Reports on alleged civil war atrocities.

933. "Plans and Fears." TIME 51 (March 29, 1948): 37.

934. "Plan of Operation." TIME 50 (July 28, 1947): 11.

935. Porter, A. "Wanted: A Miracle in Greece." COLLIET'S
     (September 20, 1947).

936. Poulos, Constantine. "Cold War: No One is Neutral in
     the Balkans." NEW REPUBLIC 117 (September 15, 1947):
     14.

937, ———. "Greek Frontier." NATION 164 (May 24, 1947):
     620-622.

938. ———. "Lesson of Greece." NATION 166 (March 27,
     1948): 343-345.

939. ———. "Meet Our Greek Allies." NATION 164 (June 28,
     1947): 761-763.

940. ———. "Who Killed George Polk?" NATION (May 28, 1949):
     605-608.

    Seeks solutions in the murder of an American journalist
    covering the civil war.

941. ———, and A.W. Sheppard. "Fiasco in Greece." NATION
     165 (December 6, 1947): 614-617.

942. "Protector." TIME 54 (August 8, 1949): 23.

    Profiles right-wing leadership in the civil war.

943. Pryor, Don. "The Greek Tragedy." NEW STATESMAN AND
     NATION 34 (July 5, 1947): 4.

944. "Red Sky at Morning." TIME 50 (July 21, 1947): 31.

945. Roubatis, Yiamin, and Elias Vlanton. "Who Killed
     George Polk?" MORE, THE MEDIA MAGAZINE 7 (May 1977):
     12-14.

    Seeks suspects in the murder of an American newsman
    covering the civil war.

946. Salisbury, Harrison E. "Reflection on an Unsolved Mystery." THE PROGRESSIVE 41 (May 1977): 24.

Examines the Polk murder in retrospect.

947. Schmidt, Dana Adams. "The Front in Greece and Everywhere." NEW YORK TIMES MAGAZINE (December 7, 1947): 12-13, 52-55.

Places the civil war in international perspective.

948. ———. "The Modern Tragedy in Ancient Greece." NEW YORK TIMES MAGAZINE (August 24, 1947): 9, 20-21.

949. Sedwick, A.C. "Plot Against Greece." FOREIGN AFFAIRS 26 (April 1948): 486-496.

950. Selton, Robert. "Communist Errors in the Anti-Bandit War 1946-1949 in Greece." MILITARY REVIEW 65 (September 1965): 66-77.

951. Sheppard, A.W. "Golden Opportunity for Peace in Greece." NATION 167 (August 7, 1948): 167.

952. "Showdown in Greek War: US Dollars for New Drive." U.S. NEWS & WORLD REPORT 24 (June 25, 1948): 30.

953. "Siege of Konitsa." TIME 51 (January 12, 1948): 22.

954. "Smashing Markos." NEWSWEEK 32 (August 23, 1948): 29.

955. Smogorzewski, K.M. "Greece: Three Years of Civil War." FORTNIGHTLY 172 (September 1949): 179-184.

956. ———. "The Greek Tragedy." WORLD AFFAIRS (January 1948): 1-18.

957. Sofianopoulos, Ioannis. "Greece: Prescription for Peace." NATION 169 (July 2, 1949): 5-7.

958. ———. "How to End the Greek Tragedy." NATION 167 (December 25, 1948): 715-718.

959. "Something Must Be Done in Greece." NEW STATESMAN AND NATION 34 (November 22, 1947): 406.

960. Spencer, Kenneth. "Report on Greece." NEW STATESMAN AND NATION 36 (August 7, 1948):

961. "Squeeze Play." TIME 52 (August 16, 1948): 28.

   Follows the lates civil war maneuvers.

962. "That the British, No Longer Able to ..." NATION 164
   (March 8, 1947).

   Examines British involvement in the civil war, and the
   eventual withdrawal of troops from Greece.

963. "Three-Headed Baby." TIME 53 (January 31, 1949): 26.

   Speculates on possible results of the civil war.

964. "Top of the Pot." TIME 51 (March 22, 1948): 32.

   Continues coverage of the Greek civil war.

965. "Truman or Stalin in Greece." NATION 166 (January 3,
   1948): 4-5.

966. United Nations. "Assembly Establishes Special Balkan
   Committee." U.N. BULLETIN 3 (October 28, 1947): 547-
   548.

967. ————. "Assembly Takes Up Greek Question." U.N. BUL-
   LETIN 3 (October 7, 1947): 453-458.

968. ————. "Balkan Commission Accepts Partisan Documents."
   U.NN BULLETIN 2 (April 19, 1947): 461-462.

969. ————. "Balkan Commission Adopts Report." U.N. BUL-
   LETIN 2 (June 10, 1947): 630-632.

970. ————. "Balkan Commission and Delay of Executions."
   U.N. BULLETIN 2 (February 18, 1947): 126-129.

971. ————. "Balkan Commission Concludes Hearings." U.N.
   BULLETIN 2 (April 8, 1947): 373-375.

972. ————. "Balkan Commission Drafting Report." U.N. BUL-
   LETIN 2 (April 22, 1947): 435.

973. ————. "Balkan Commission Ends Inquiry in Greece."
   U.N. BULLETIN 2 (April 1, 1947): 307.

974. ————. "Balkan Commission Forming Subsidiary Groups."
   U.N. BULLETIN 2 (May 6, 1947): 488.

975. ———. "Balkan Commission Moves Headquarters." U.N. BULLETIN 2 (March 4, 1947): 196-197.

976. ———. "Balkan Commission Opens Inquiry." U.N. BULLETIN 2 (February 11, 1947): 117.

977. ———. "Balkan Commission Proceeds to Athens." U.N. BULLETIN 2 (January 28, 1947): 63.

978. ———. "Balkan Commission Resolution Fails." U.N. BULLETIN 3 (August 5, 1947): 183-190.

979. ———. "Balkan Commission's Hearings." U.N. BULLETIN 2 (February 25, 1947): 152-156.

980. ———. "Balkan Commission's Investigations." U.N. BULLETIN 2 (March 11, 1947): 227-232.

981. ———. "The Balkan Commission's Report." U.N. BULLETIN 3 (July 1, 1947): 17-26.

982. ———. "Balkan Committee Faces New Problems." U.N. BULLETIN 4 (January 15, 1948): 53-54.

983. ———. "Balkan Committee Investigates New Charges." U.N. BULLETIN 4 (April 1, 1948): 277-278.

984. ———. "Balkan Committee Reports on Refugees." U.N. BULLETIN 4 (April 15, 1948): 344.

985. ———. "Balkan Group Investigates Fresh Allegations." U.N. BULLETIN 3 (July 29, 1947): 177.

986. ———. "Balkan Group Reports on Bulgarian Conduct." U.N. BULLETIN 3 (July 1, 1947): 36-37.

987. ———. "Balkan Group Reports on Work." U.N. BULLETIN 3 (August 5, 1947): 204-206.

988. ———. "Balkan Group to Cross Bulgarian Border." U.N. BULLETIN 2 (June 17, 1947): 658-659.

989. ———. "Balkan Inquiry Nearing Conclusion." U.N. BULLETIN 2 (March 25, 1947): 287-289.

990. ———. "Balkan Observation Groups to be Established." U.N. BULLETIN 3 (December 16, 1947): 809-810.

991. ———. "Commission Group to Remain in Balkans. Security
       Council Rejects Proposal to Supervise US Aid to Greece."
       U.N. BULLETIN 2 (April 29, 1947).

992. ———. "Committee Recommends New Balkan Body." U.N.
       BULLETIN 3, (October 21, 1947): 511-514.

993. ———. "Concluding Phases of Balkan Investigations."
       U.N. BULLETIN 2 (April 15, 1947): 406-407.

994. ———. "Council Rejects Restrictions on Balkan Groups."
       U.N. BULLETIN 2 (June 3, 1947): 583-591.

995. ———. "Council Rejects Soviet Balkan Resolution." U.N.
       BULLETIN 3 (August 12, 1947): 226-227.

996. ———. "Directives for Balkan Subsidiary Group." U.N.
       BULLETIN 2 (May 16, 1947): 523-524.

997. ———. "Economic Rehabilitation of Greece. FAO Mission
       Recommends Comprehensive Measures." U.N. BULLETIN 2
       (April 1, 1947): 336-339.

998. ———. "Effort to Establish Normal Relations in Balkans."
       U.N. BULLETIN 4 (March 15, 1948): 243-244.

999. ———. "Effort to Restore Balkan Diplomatic Relations."
       U.N. BULLETIN 4 (May 15, 1948): 419-420.

1000. ———. "Efforts for Balkan Settlement Continue." U.N.
       BULLETIN 5 (December 15, 1948): 1017-1019.

1001. ———. "For Peace and Security in the Balkans." U.N.
       BULLETIN 5 (September 1, 1948): 700-702.

1002. ———. "Fresh Efforts for Balkan Peace." U.N. BULLETIN
       5 (November 15, 1948): 938-945.

1003. ———. "Further Discussion of Balkan Report." U.N.
       BULLETIN 3 (July 22, 1947): 115-121.

1004. ———. "Further Discussion of Greek Question." U.N.
       BULLETIN 2 (April 22, 1947): 417-422.

1005. ———. "Furthermore Efforts At Balkan Settlement."
       U.N. BULLETIN 3 (October 14, 1947): 484-487.

1006. ————. "General Debate on Balkan Report Concluded." U.N. BULLETIN 3 (July 29, 1947): 169-175.

1007. ————. "General Debate: The Balkans Situation." U.N. BULLETIN 5, (October 15, 1948): 800-802.

1008. ————. "Greek Attitude on Diplomatic Relations with Bulgaria." U.N. BULLETIN 5 (September 15, 1948): 749.

1009. ————. "Greek Question Before General Assembly." U.N. BULLETIN 3 (September 30, 1947): 423.

1010. ————. "Greek Question Goes to Assembly." U.N. BULLETIN 3 (September 23, 1947): 385-386.

1011. ————. "Greek Question Goes to General Assembly." U.N. BULLETIN 3 (September 2, 1947): 301-302.

1012. ————. "More Frontier Incidents Before Balkan Group." U.N. BULLETIN 3 (July 15, 1947): 103-104.

1013. ————. "New Commission Proposed for Aid to Greece: Summary of Discussions of U.S. Program, by. A.A. Gromyko and Others." U.N. BULLETIN 2 (April 15, 1947): 383-388.

1014. ————. "Progress of Balkan Inquiry." U.N. BULLETIN 2 (March 28, 1947): 263.

1015. ————. "Security Council's Discussion of Balkan Report." U.N. BULLETIN 3 (July 15, 1947): 86-90.

1016. ————. "Serious Warning to Greece's Neighbors Suggested." U.N. BULLETIN 5 (October 1, 1948): 764-765.

1017. ————. "The Situation in Greece." U.N. BULLETIN 4 (January 1, 1948): 6-7.

1018. ————. "Special Balkan Committee Begins Work." U.N. BULLETIN 3 (December 9, 1947): 781-782.

1019. ————. "Stalemate Balks Action in Greek Question." U.N. BULLETIN 3 (August 26, 1947): 282-285.

1020. ————. "Subsidiary Group Continues Investigations." U.N. BULLETIN 3 (July 22, 1947): 132-133.

1021. ———. "Unanimous Approval for Balkan Peace Efforts."
U.N. BULLETIN 5 (December 1, 1948): 958-965.

1022. ———. "United States Aid to Greece and Turkey." U.N.
BULLETIN 2 (April 8, 1947): 362-365.

1023. ———. "United States Resolution on Balkan Report."
U.N. BULLETIN 3 (July 8, 1947): 67-74.

1024. ———. "UNSCOB Calls for Return of Greek Children."
U.N. BULLETIN 4 (June 15, 1948): 486.

1025. ———. "UNSCOB Group Crosses Bulgarian Frontier."
U.N. BULLETIN 4 (June 15, 1948): 456.

1026. ———. "USSR Criticizes Balkan Group's Directives."
U.N. BULLETIN 2 (May 20, 1947): 563-564.

1027. United Nations Department of Public Information. "Es-
tablishment of an Interim Committee of the General
Assembly." YEARBOOK OF THE UNITED NATIONS 2 (1947-
48): 75.

1028. ———. "The Greek Question." YEARBOOK OF THE UNITED
NATIONS 2 (1947-48): 337-352.

1029. ———. "The Greek Question (Greek Complaint)."
YEARBOOK OF THE UNITED NATIONS 1 (1946-47): 360-375.

1030. ———. "The Greek Question (Soviet Complaint)."
YEARBOOK OF THE UNITED NATIONS 1 (1946-47): 336-338.

1031. ———. "The Greek Question (Ukrainian Complaint)."
YEARBOOK OF THE UNITED NATIONS 1 (1946-47): 351-360.

1032. ———. "Threats to the Political Independence and
Territorial Integrity of Greece." YEARBOOK OF THE
UNITED NATIONS 2 (1947-48): 63-75.

1033. ———. "Trheats to the Political Independence and
Territorial Integrity of Greece." YEARBOOK OF THE
UNITED NATIONS 3 (1948-49): 238-256.

1034. ———. "United Nations Special Committee on the
Balkans (UNSCOB)." YEARBOOK OF THE UNITED NATIONS
2 (1947-48): 298-302.

1035. United States Department of State. "American Observers
      in Greek Elections." DEPARTMENT OF STATE BULLETIN
      14 (January 20, 1946).

1036. ————. "Case of Slain Correspondent to be Tried in
      Greece." DEPARTMENT OF STATE BULLETIN 20 (March 13,
      1949).

1037. ————. "CBS Correspondent Slain in Greece." DEPART-
      MENT OF STATE BULLETIN 18 (May 30, 1948): 713.

1038. ————. "Communists Attempt to Overthrow Recognized
      Greek Government." DEPARTMENT OF STATE BULLETIN 18
      (January 11, 1948): 59.

1039. ————. "Frontier Violations Basic Issue in Greek
      Situation." DEPARTMENT OF STATE BULLETIN 20 (May 29,
      1949): 696.

1040. ————. "Greek Guerillas Cease Activities." DEPART-
      MENT OF STATE BULLETIN 21 (October 31, 1949): 658.

1041. ————. "Greek Investigation into Death of CBS Corre-
      spondent." DEPARTMENT OF STATE BULLETIN 18 (June 6,
      1948): 748.

1042. ————. "The Refugee Problem in Greece." DEPARTMENT
      OF STATE BULLETIN 18 (March 7, 1948): 291-293.

1043. ————. "The Struggle for Freedom in Greece." DEPART-
      MENT OF STATE BULLETIN 19 (November 7, 1948): 584.

1044. Van Fleet, James. "How We Won in Greece." BALKAN
      STUDIES 8 (1967): 387-393.

1045. Voight, Frederick August. "Battle of Konitsa." 19th
      CENTURY AND AFTER 143 (February 1948): 68-70.

1046. ————. "Present State of Greece. Part 1." 19th
      CENTURY AND AFTER 139 (June 1946): 253-266.

1047. ————. "Present State of Greece. Part 2." 19th
      CENTURY AND AFTER 140 (July 1946): 1-19.

1048. ————. "Present State of Greece. Part 3." 19th
      CENTURY AND AFTER 141 (August 1949): 74-93.

1049. Wallace, Henry. "The Way to Help Greece." NEW REPUB-
      LIC 116 (March 17, 1947): 12-13.

      Suggests avenues of American assistance in the war.

1050. "War Risks in Greek-aid Plans." U.S. NEWS & WORLD REPORT
      24 (March 5, 1948): 30-31.

1051. "Wastebasket Amnesty." NEWSWEEK 30 (September 22, 1947):
      43.

1052. "What We Haven't Learned in Greece." NEW REPUBLIC 120
      (January 17, 1949): 10.

1053. "Who Runs Greece?" NATION (February 28, 1948): 228-229.

1054. Wilkes, Lyall. "Greek Ulcer." NEW STATESMAN AND NATION
      34 (September 27, 1947): 255.

1055. "Winged Victory." TIME (October 24, 1949).

1056. "With Will to Win." TIME 53 (May 23, 1949): 26-29.

1057. Xydis, Stephen George. "The Polk Murder Case Revisited."
      SOUTHEASTERN EUROPE 2 (1975): 194-198.

      Presents a retrospective view of an American journal-
      ist's murder during the civil war.

1058. "Year of Explosion in Greece?" NEWSWEEK 31 (January 5,
      1948): 27.

1059. Zacharakis, E.E. "Lessons Learned from the Anti-Guerilla
      War in Greece, 1946-1949." REVUE MILITAIRE GENERALE
      (July 1960).

HUNGARY

Books

1060. Andrassy, Gyula. DIPLOMACY AND THE WAR. London: J.
      Bale, Sons & Danielson, 1921.

      Includes a discussion of pro-nationalist terrorism
      in the Austro-Hungarian empire, culminating in the
      assassination of Archduke Ferdinand and the outbreak of
      World War I.

1061. Bandholtz, Harry Hill. AN UNDIPLOMATIC DIARY. New
      York: Columbia University Press, 1933.

      Includes discussion of Depression-era political vio-
      lence in the memoirs of an American diplomat assigned
      to Hungary after World War I.

1062. Deak, Istvan. THE LAWFUL REVOLUTION: LOUIS KOSSUTH
      AND THE HUNGARIANS, 1848-1849. New York: Columbia
      University Press, 1979.

1063. Deme, Laszlo. THE RADICAL LEFT IN THE HUNGARIAN REVO-
      LUTION OF 1848. New Y-rk: Columbia University Press,
      1976.

1064. De Puy, Henry Walter. THE HISTORY OF HUNGARY AND THE
      LATE HUNGARIAN WAR, KOSSUTH AND HIS GENERALS. Buf-
      falo, New York: Phinney, 1858.

1065. Ecknardt, Tibor. REGICIDE AT MARSEILLE. New York:
      American Hungarian Library and Historical Society,
      1964.

      Recounts the assassination of a Hungarian head of
      state in France, by nationalist gunmen.

1066. Gorgei, Arthur. MY LIFE AND ACTS IN HUNGARY IN THE
      YEARS 1848 AND 1849. London: David Bosue, 1852.

      Offers a personal narrative of the 1848 revolution,
      with first-hand descriptions of widespread political
      upheaval and acts of terrorism.

1067. Janos, Andrew C., and William B. Slottman. REVOLUTION
      IN PERSPECTIVE: ESSAYS ON THE HUNGARIAN SOVIET RE-
      PUBLIC OF 1919. Berkeley, Calif.: University of
      California Press, 1971.

1068. Kune, Julian. REMINISCENCES OF AN OCTEGENARIAN HUNGAR-
      IAN EXILE. Chicago: The Author, 1911.

      Includes a personal narrative of political dissent
      and violence in the late nineteenth and early twentieth
      century, by an activist forced to seek refuge in Amer-
      ica.

1069. Low, Alfred D. THE SOVIET HUNGARIAN REPUBLIC AND THE
      PARIS PEACE CONFERENCE. Philadelphia: American
      Philosophical Society, 1963.

1070. Pastor, Peter. HUNGARY BETWEEN WILSON AND LENIN: THE
      HUNGARIAN REVOLUTION OF 1918-1919 AND THE BIG THREE.
      New York: Columbia University Press, 1976.

1071. Peteri, Gyorgy. EFFECTS OF WORLD WAR I: WAR COMMUNISM
      IN HUNGARY. New York: Columbia University Press, 1983.

1072. Pulszky, Terezia. MEMOIRS OF A HUNGARIAN LADY. Phila-
      delphia: Lea & Blanchard, 1850.

      Includes a personal narrative of the 1848 revolution,
      as views through the eyes of a native aristocrat.

1073. Spira, Gyrogy. A HUNGARIAN COUNT IN THE REVOLUTION OF
      1848. Budapest: Akademiai Kiado, 1974.

1074. Sproxton, Charles. PALMERSTON AND THE HUNGARIAN REVO-
      LUTION. Cambridge: Cambridge University Press, 1919.

1075. Stroup, Edsel Walter. HUNGARY IN EARLY 1848: THE CON-
      STITUTIONAL STRUGGLE AGAINST ABSOLUTISM IN CONTEMP-
      ORARY EYES. Buffalo, N.Y.: Hungarian Cultural Foun-
      dation, 1977.

1076. Szilassy, Sandor. REVOLUTIONARY HUNGARY, 1918-1921.
      Astor Park, Fl.: Danubian Press, 1971.

      Examines the violent advent of communism in Hungary,
      with a discussion of political upheaval and terrorist
      acts of the period.

1077. Tefft, Benjamin Franklin. HUNGARY AND KOSSUTH: OR, AN
      AMERICAN EXPOSITION OF THE LATE HUNGARIAN REVOLUTION.
      Philadelphia: J. Ball, 1852.

1078. Tokes, Rudolf L. BELA KUN AND THE HUNGARIAN SOVIET
      REPUBLIC; THE ORIGINS AND ROLE OF THE COMMUNIST PARTY
      OF HUNGARY IN THE REVOLUTIONS OF 1918-1919. Stanford,
      Calif.: F.A. Praeger, 1967.

1079. Tormay, Cecile. AN OUTLAW'S DIARY: THE COMMUNE. New
      York: R.M. McBride, 1924.

1080. Volgyes, Ivan. HUNGARY IN REVOLUTION. Lincoln, Neb.:
      University of Nebraska Press, 1971.

1081. ———. THE HUNGARIAN SOVIET REPUBLIC, 1919: AN EVALU-
      ATION AND A BIBLIOGRAPHY. Stanford, Calif.: Hoover
      Institution Press, 1970.

Includes a valuable bibliography of foreign-language sources on the Hungarian revolution of 1918-1919.

Articles

1082. "When Fascism Stoops to Conquer." INDEPENDENT 116 (March 6, 1926): 258-259.

Examines the rising tide of fascist violence in Hungary, including deliberate exacerbation of Serbo-Croatian ethnic antagonism.

IRELAND

Books

1083. Abel, Jules. THE PARNELL TRAGEDY. London: Collier-Macmillan, 1964.

Examines the struggle of the 19th-century Land Leagues, in search of rent control and other forms of relief for destitute tenants.

1084. Addison, Christopher. POLITICS FROM WITHIN, 1911-1918, INCLUDING SOME RECORDS OF A GREAT NATIONAL EFFORT. London: H. Jenkins, 1924.

1085. Akenson, Donald Harman. THE UNITED STATES AND IRELAND. Cambridge, Mass.: Harvard University Press, 1973.

Presents an overview of United States foreign policy toward Ireland through the years. Includes a review of grass-roots Irish-American support for the terrorist activities of the IRA.

1086. Ardmore, Patrick. THE IRISH REPUBLIC, A HISTORICAL MEMOIR OF IRELAND AND HER OPPRESSORS. St. Paul, Minn.: The Author, 1871.

Presents a biased account, of little historical value byond its delivery of undiluted republican rhetoric for the reader's perusal and occasional amusement.

1087. Armour, W.S. FACING THE IRISH QUESTION. London: Duckworth, 1955.

1088. ———. ULSTER, IRELAND, BRITAIN: A FORGOTTEN TRUST. London: Duckworth, 1938.

1089. Bagenal, P.H.   THE AMERICAN-IRISH AND THEIR INFLUENCE
      ON IRISH POLITICS. London: K. Paul, Trench, & Co.,
      1882.

      Examines the influence of Irish-Americans on the con-
      tinuing violence in Northern Ireland, with a discussion
      of American support for terrorists abroad.

1090. Baker, Ernest.   IRELAND IN THE LAST FIFTY YEARS, 1866-
      1916. Oxford: Clarendon Press, 1919.

      Presents a general analysis of Irish problems in the
      areas of agriculture, labor, politics, and religion,
      suggesting that "the Irish Question" is basically a
      clash of two disparate cultures, oversimplified by re-
      duction to simple issues of politics or religion.

1091. Baker, Sybil E.   "Orange and Green. Belfast 1832-1912."
      THE VICTORIAN CITY. IMAGES AND REALITIES. Cited below
      as item 1259.

1092. Barnett, Correlli.   THE COLLAPSE OF BRITISH POWER. Lon-
      don: Eyre Methuen, 1972.

      Examines the Irish troubles as a symptom of British
      decline, reviewing major acts of terrorism and rebel-
      lion by Irish republican forces against continued Brit-
      ish rule.

1093. Barritt, Denis P., and Charles F. Carter.   THE NORTHERN
      IRELAND PROBLEM: A STUDY IN GROUP RELATIONS. London:
      Oxford University Press, 1962.

1094. Barry, Tom.   GUERILLA DAYS IN IRELAND. Cork: The Mer-
      cier Press, 1950.

      Presents the memoirs of an IRA flying squad commander,
      covering the violent period of Ireland's civil war,
      1919-1921.

1095. Beach, Thomas Miller.   TWENTY-FIVE YEARS IN THE SECRET
      SERVICE: THE RECOLLECTIONS OF A SPY. London: William
      Heinemann, 1892.

      Presents a personal narrative of official efforts to
      suppress the Fenian movement in the 19th century, re-
      called by one of the agents assigned to infiltrate and
      disrupt the republican group.

1096. Beasli, Piaras. MICHAEL COLLINS AND THE MAKING OF A NEW
      IRELAND. Vol. 1 and 2. Dublin: Phoenix Publishing
      Co., 1930.

      Examines the life of a Sinn Fein leader assassinated
      in 1922. The author was editor of the underground rebel
      paper AN T'OGLACH, and worked closely with Collins dur-
      ing the civil war.

1097. ————. MICHAEL COLLINS, SOLDIER AND STATESMAN. Dublin:
      Talbot Press, 1937.

      Presents a revised, updated version of item 1096.

1098. Beaverbrook, Lord Max Aitken. POLITICIANS AND THE WAR,
      1914-1916. 2 vols. Garden City, N.Y.: Doubleday,
      Doran & Co., 1928.

      Includes a discussion of the World War's impact on
      Ireland and Irish responses to continued British rule,
      culminating in the Easter rising and civil war.

1099. Beck, George Andrew (ed). THE ENGLISH CATHOLIC, 1850-
      1950. London: Burns, Oates, 1950.

      Contains item 1373 below.

1100. Beckett, J.C. A SHORT HISTORY OF IRELAND. London:
      Hutchinson, 1952.

1101. ————. THE ANGLO-IRISH TRADITION. Ithaca, N.Y.: Cor-
      nell University Press, 1976.

1102. ————. THE MAKING OF MODERN IRELAND, 1603-1923. Lon-
      don: Faber & Faber, 1966, pp. 277-461.

      Presents a masterful account of the political, social,
      and economic forces at work in Ireland over three cen-
      turies. Excellent groundwork for understanding modern
      Irish terrorism.

1103. Bell, Geoffrey. THE PROTESTANTS OF ULSTER. London:
      Pluto Press, 1976.

1104. Bell, J. Bowyer. THE SECRET ARMY: THE IRA, 1916-1970.
      New York: The John Day Co., 1971.

      Presents an excellent, fast-paced account of IRA

history from the group's origins to the early 1970s.

1105. ————. THE SECRET ARMY: THE IRA, 1916-1974. Cambridge,
      Mass.: Massachusetts Institute of Techonology Press,
      1974.

      Updates item 1104 above.

1106. ————. THE SECRET ARMY: THE IRA, 1916-1979. Cambridge,
      Mass.: Massachusetts Institute of Technology Press,
      1980.

      Updates items 1104 and 1105 above.

1107. Beloff, Max. IMPERIAL SUNSET: BRITAIN'S LIBERAL EMPIRE,
      1897-1921. New York: Alfred A. Knopf, 1970.

      Includes discussion of the Irish question in a general
      survey of declining British colonialism.

1108. Bennett, Richard. THE BLACK AND TANS. London: Edward
      Hulton & Co., 1959.

      Examines the history and activities of the despised
      Protestant militia in Northern Ireland, including dis-
      cussion of actual and alleged atrocities committed
      against Catholic prisoners.

1109. Bergin, J.J. HISTORY OF THE ANCIENT ORDER OF HIBERNIANS.
      Dublin: The Author, 1910.

      Presents the history of a nationalist society organ-
      ized as an answer to the loyalist Orange League. The
      Hibernians emerged as primary guardians of Catholic
      liberties in Ireland, and were active internationally.
      In America, a violent faction better known as the Molly
      Maguires saw action in the Pennsylvania coal fields,
      committing various assassinations and acts of industrial
      sabotage.

1110. Bew, Paul. C.S. PARNELL. Dublin: The Author, 1980.

      Examines the Land League struggles of the 19th century.

1111. ————. CONFLICT AND CONCILIATION IN IRELAND, 1890-1910,
      PARNELLITES AND RADICAL AGRARIANS. Oxford: Clarendon
      Press, 1987.

Covers the United Irish League and the development of agrarian rebellion in three decades following the Irish "Land War" of 1879-1882.

1112. ─────. LAND AND THE NATIONAL QUESTION IN IRELAND, 1858-82. Atlantic Highland, N.J.: Humanities Press, 1979.

1113. ─────, and Henry Patterson. THE BRITISH STATE AND THE ULSTER CRISIS FROM WILSON TO THATCHER. London: Verso, 1985.

1114. ─────, Peter Gibbon, and Henry Patterson. THE STATE OF NORTHERN IRELAND, 1921-72, POLITICAL FORCES AND SOCIAL CLASSES. New York: St. Martin's Press, 1979.

1115. ─────, and Frank Wright. "The Agrarian Opposition in Ulster Politics, 1848-87." IRISH PEASANTS, VIOLENCE AND POLITICAL UNREST, 1780-1914. Cited below as item 1180, pp. 192-229.

1116. Biggar, F.J. THE ULSTER LAND WAR. London: The Author, 1910.

1117. Biggs-Davidson, John. GEORGE WYNDHAM, A STUDY IN TORY-ISM. 1951.

Presents a biography of the statesman who attempted to "kill Home Rule with kindness."

1118. ─────. THE HAND IS RED. London: Johnson Publications, 1973.

1119. Birrell, Augustine. THINGS PAST REDRESS. London: Faber & Faber, 1937.

1120. Bixley, W. THE GUILTY AND THE INNOCENT. MY FIFTY YEARS AT THE OLD BAILEY. London: Souvenir Press, 1957.

Includes reports of various IRA prosecutions through the years in a chronicle of British criminal cases.

1121. Black, R.D Collison. ECONOMIC THOUGHT AND THE IRISH QUESTION, 1817-70. Cambridge: Cambridge University Press, 1960.

1122. Blake, John W. NORTHERN IRELAND IN THE SECOND WORLD WAR. Belfast: Her Majesty's Stationery Office, 1966.

1123. Bleakley, David. PEACE IN ULSTER. London: Mowbrays,
      1972.

1124. Blunt, Wilfred Scawen. THE LAND WAR IN IRELAND. BEING
      A PERSONAL NARRATIVE OF EVENTS, IN CONTINUATION OF "A
      SECRET HISTORY OF THE ENGLISH OCCUPATION OF EGYPT."
      London: S. Swift, 1912.

      Examines the course of Irish agrarian rebellion, led
      by members of the Land League during the years 1879-1903.
      Includes discussion of the roles played by Parnell, John
      Dillon, Michael Davitt, and others, along with coverage
      of the Land Acts which effected transfer of ownership
      from landlords to tenants in the early 20th century.

1125. Bolton, G.C. THE PASSING OF THE IRISH ACT OF UNION.
      London: Oxford University Press, 1966, pp. 185-222.

1126. Boulton, David. THE UVF: 1966-73: AN ANATOMY OF A LOYAL-
      IST REBELLION. Dublin: Torch Books, 1973.

      Examines the violent activities of militant Protestants
      in Northern Ireland, frequently overlooked in reports
      that concentrate upon the terrorism of the IRA. The
      Ulster Volunteer Force has been linked to numerous mur-
      ders and other acts of violence aimed at Catholics in
      Ulster. Boulton's volume places the UVF's modern activ-
      ities in historical perspective, with background on other
      militant loyalist societies.

1127. Bourke, Marcus. JOHN O'LEARY. A STUDY IN IRISH SEPAR-
      ATISM. Albany, Ga.: University of Georgia Press, 1967.

      Examines the life and career of an Irish separatist
      leader, active between 1848 and his death in 1907.
      Imprisoned by the British for publishing inflammatory
      editorials, O'Leary spent nine years in jail and emerged
      to become president of the Irish Republican Brotherhood,
      a post which he retained until his death.

1128. Bowden, Tom. THE BREAKDOWN OF PUBLIC SECURITY: THE
      CASE OF IRELAND, 1916-1921, AND PALESTINE, 1936-1939.
      Beverly Hills, Calif.: Sage, 1977.

1129. Bowen, Desmond. THE PROTESTANT CRUSADE IN IRELAND,
      1800-70: A STUDY OF PROTESTANT-CATHOLIC RELATIONS
      BETWEEN THE ACT OF UNION AND DISESTABLISHMENT. Dub-
      lin: Gill & Macmillan, 1978.

1130. Bowman, John. DE VALERA AND THE ULSTER QUESTION, 1917-
       1973. Oxford: Clarendon Press, 1982.

       Examines the career of Eamon De Valera, senior surviv-
       ing leader of the 1916 rising, later a prime mover in
       the Sinn Fein political movement and founder, in 1926,
       of a new republican party, the Soldiers of Destiny. Bow-
       man's work reviews Valera's influence on the modern re-
       publican movement and the continuing "troubles" in Ulster.

1131. Boyce, D.G. ENGLISHMEN AND IRISH TROUBLES: BRITISH PUB-
       LIC OPINION AND THE MAKING OF IRISH POLICY, 1918-22.
       London: Jonathan Cape, 1972.

1132. Boyd, Andrew. HOLY WAR IN BELFAST. Tralee: Anvil Books,
       1969.

1133. ———. THE UVF. Dublin: Torch Books, 1973.

       Examines the history of the Protestant Ulster Volun-
       teer Force and its on-going war against Catholic repub-
       licans.

1134. Boyle, John F. "Connolly, the Citizen Army and the
       Rising." THE MAKING OF 1916. Cited below as item
       1546, pp. 51-68.

1135. ———. THE IRISH REBELLION OF 1916: A BRIEF HISTORY OF
       THE REVOLT AND ITS SUPPRESSION. London: Constable,
       1916.

1136. Boyle, John W. (ed). LEADERS AND WORKERS. Cork: The
       Author, 1966.

       Contains item 1522 below.

1137. Brady, C. POLICE AND GOVERNMENT IN THE IRISH FREE STATE,
       1922-1933. Dublin: University College, 1977.

1138. Brady, L.W. T.P. O'CONNOR AND THE LIVERPOOL IRISH.
       London: Royal Historical Society, 1983.

       Examines attitudes and activities of Irish living in
       Britain, including campaigns of disruption conducted by
       Fenian militants.

1139. Breen, Dan. MY FIGHT FOR IRISH FREEDOM. Dublin: Anvil
       Books, 1924.

Presents the memoirs of an IRA leader in the Easter
rising and subsequent civil war. Breen was the commander of a republican flying squad, sought by British authorities for involvement in political assassinations
and other acts of terrorism.

1140. Brennan, Michael. THE WAR IN CLARE 1911-21: PERSONAL
      MEMOIRS OF THE IRISH WAR OF INDEPENDENCE. Dublin:
      Four Courts Press, 1980.

      Covers activities of the IRA, Irish Republican Brother-
      hood, and the Irish Volunteers in the period including
      the Easter rising and civil war.

1141. Brennan, Robert. ALLEGIANCE. Dublin: Browne & Nolan,
      1950.

      Presents the memoirs of a Sinn Fein political director
      in the elections of 1918. Strongly republican in view-
      point, Brennan's account scores some telling points
      against the conduct of British colonial rule in Northern
      Ireland.

1142. British Broadcasting Company. ULSTER SINCE 1800. London:
      B.B.C., 1954.

1143. British and Irish Communist Organization. THE CULT OF
      THE INDIVIDUAL: THE CONTROVERSY WITHIN BRITISH COMMU-
      NISM, 1956-58. Belfast: British and Irish Communist
      Org., 1975.

1144. ————. ULSTER AS IT IS. A REVIEW OF THE DEVELOPMENT
      OF CATHOLIC-PROTESTANT POLITICAL CONFLICT IN BELFAST
      BETWEEN CATHOLIC EMANCIPATION AND THE HOME RULE BILL.
      Belfast: British and Irish Communist Org., 1973.

      Examines upheavals of the period from 1828-1880, from
      a communist perspective.

1145. Broad, Richard. THE TROUBLES. London: Macdonald-Futura,
      1980.

1146. Broderick, John F. THE HOLY SEE AND THE IRISH MOVEMENT
      FOR THE REPEAL OF THE UNION WITH ENGLAND, 1829-1847.
      Rome: Universitatis Gregorianne Press, 1951.

1147. Broeker, Galen. RURAL DISORDER AND POLICE REFORM IN
      IRELAND, 1912-1836. London: Routledge & Kegan Paul,
      1970.

106 TERRORISM IN THE UNITED STATES AND EUROPE

1148. Bromage, Mary C. DE VALERA AND THE MARCH OF A NATION. New York: Noonday Press, 1956.

1149. ————. CHURCHILL AND IRELAND. South Bend, Ind.: Notre Dame University Press, 1965.

Examines tensions between Britain and Ireland in the years surrounding World War II.

1150. Brooks, Sydney. ASPECTS OF THE IRISH QUESTION. Dublin: Maunsel & Co., 1912.

1151. Brown, Malcolm. THE POLITICS OF IRISH LITERATURE: FROM THOMAS DAVIS TO W.B. YEATS. Seattle: University of Washington Press, 1972.

1152. Brown, Thomas N. IRISH-AMERICAN NATIONALISM, 1870-90. Philadelphia: Lippincott, 1966.

Presents useful background on Irish-American support for militant action by 19th-century Irish separatists.

1153. Bryant, Sophie. LIBERTY, ORDER AND LAW UNDER NATIVE IRISH RULE. London: Hardung & More, 1923.

1154. Brynn, Edward. CROWN AND CASTLE, BRITISH RULE IN IRELAND 1800-1830. Dublin: The O'Brien Press, 1978.

1155. ————. IRISH UNIONISM: Vol. 1. THE ANGLO-IRISH AND THE NEW IRELAND 1885-1922. Dublin: Gill & Macmillan, 1972.

1156. ————. IRISH UNIONISM: Vol. 2. ULSTER UNIONISM AND THE ORIGINS OF NORTHERN IRELAND 1886-1922. Dublin: Gill & Macmillan, 1973.

1157. ————. IRISH UNIONISM: 1885-1922. London: The Historical Assn., 1973.

Condenses items 1155 and 1156 to present a light overview of the Irish union movement and its failure to defeat the cause of Home Rule.

1158. Budge, Ian, and Cornelius O'Leary. BELFAST: APPROACH TO CRISIS. New York: Macmillan, 1973, pp. 14-198.

Examines the relevant period of Belfast history, within a general coverage of the area from 1613 to 1970.

1159. Burns, Elinor. BRITISH IMPERIALISM IN IRELAND. Dublin:
      City and County Dublin Press, 1931.

1160. Bussy, Frederick Moir (ed). IRISH CONSPIRACIES: RECOL-
      LECTIONS OF JOHN MALLON (THE GREAT IRISH DETECTIVE)
      AND OTHER REMINISCENCES. London: Everett & Co., 1910.

      Presents the memoirs of a detective assigned to suppress
      Irish terrorist societies in the late 19th century.

1161. Butler, Ewan. BARRY'S FLYING COLUMN. London: Leo Cooper,
      1971.

      Follows the action of an IRA fighting unit in the
      Easter rising and subsequent civil war.

1162. Byrne, Mrs. Miles (ed). MEMOIR OF MILES BYRNE. Shannon:
      Irish University Press, 1972.

      Presents a personal account of political turmoil in
      Ireland, authored by a farmer who joined the United
      Irishmen and commanded pikemen at the battle of Anklow
      in 1798. Five years later, Byrne was involved in the
      rising led by Robert Emmet, and was sent to France by
      Emmet in an effort to organize French support. Byrne
      there joined the Irish Legion, believing it would return
      to Ireland, but wound up fighting on the continent in-
      stead. He was awarded the Legion of Honour by Louis
      Phillipe in 1830.

1163. Callaghan, James. A HOUSE DIVIDED: THE DILEMMA OF
      NORTHERN IRELAND. London: Collins, 1973.

1164. Calwell, C.E. SIR HENRY WILSON. 2 Vols. London: 1927.

      Presents a general biography of a British military
      leader, assassinated by the IRA in 1921. Though not
      primarily of Irish interest, material of critical im-
      portance for understanding the Irish situation is in-
      cluded.

1165. Campbell, T.J. FIFTY YEARS OF ULSTER 1890-1940. Dublin:
      Irish News, 1941.

1166. Carlyle, Thomas. THE REPEAL OF THE UNION CONSPIRACY.
      London: Field & Tuer, 1889.

1167. Carroll, F.M.   AMERICAN OPINION AND THE IRISH QUESTION:
      1910-1923.   Dublin: Gill & Macmillan, 1978.

      Examines American involvement from the influx of Irish
      immigrants in the 1940s through foundation of the Irish
      Free State in 1921-1923.

1168. Carroll, Joseph T.   IRELAND IN THE WAR YEARS, 1939-1945.
      London: David & Charles, Newton Abbot, 1975.

1169. Carson, William.   ULSTER AND THE IRISH REPUBLIC.   Belfast
      William Cleland, 1956.

1170. Carty, Xavier.   IN BLOODY PROTEST——THE TRAGEDY OF PATRICK
      PEARSE.   Dublin: Able Press, 1978.

      Follows the career of Patrick Pearse, a founder of the
      Irish Volunteers in 1913, later inducted into the Irish
      Republican Brotherhood.   Pearse subsequently became a
      member of the Military Council which planned the Easter
      rising of 1916.   Named chairman of the Provisional Gov-
      ernment of the Irish Republic, he was imprisoned by
      British authorities and was executed in May 1916.

1171. Cashman, D.B.   THE LIFE OF MICHAEL DAVITT, FOUNDER OF
      THE NATIONAL LAND LEAGUE TO WHICH IS ADDED, THE SECRET
      HISTORY OF THE LAND LEAGUE BY MICHAEL DAVITT.   Glasgow:
      The Author, n.d.

1172. Caulfield, Malachy Francis.   THE EASTER REBELLION.   New
      York: Holt, Rinehart & Winston, 1963.

      Presents detailed accounts of the Easter rising in
      Dublin, but scarcely addresses the general political
      situation.   Useful and informative, despite occasional
      lapses into obvious fiction.

1173. Chamberlain, Joseph.   HOME RULE AND THE IRISH QUESTION.
      London: C. Routledge, 1887.

1174. Chart, David A.   IRELAND FROM THE UNION TO CATHOLIC
      EMANCIPATION.   THE HISTORY OF THE PARTITION IN IRE-
      LAND.   London: Victor Gollancz, 1957.

1175. Chenevix Trench, Charles.   THE GREAT DANIEL. A BIOGRA-
      PHY OF DANIEL O'CONNELL.   London: Jonathan Cape, 1984.

Follows the career of a leader in the movement to repeal the Irish Act of Union. O'Connell's activities
made Irish nationalism a force to be reckoned with, but
his militant Catholicism also succeeded in deepening
Irish religious divisions, exacerbating an already tense
situation.

1176. Childers, Erskine. MILITARY RULE IN IRELAND: A SERIES
      OF EIGHT ARTICLES CONTRIBUTED TO THE DAILY NEWS, MARCH
      -MAY 1920. Dublin: The Talbot Press, 1920.

1177. Chubb, Basil. THE GOVERNMENT AND POLITICS OF IRELAND.
      London: Oxford University Press, 1974.

1178. Clark, Dennis J. IRISH BLOOD: NORTHERN IRELAND AND THE
      AMERICAN CONSCIENCE. Port Washington, N.Y.: Kennikat
      Press, 1977.

1179. Clark, Samuel. SOCIAL ORIGINS OF THE IRISH LAND WAR.
      Princeton, N.J.: Princeton University Press, 1979.

1180. ————, and James S. Donnelly, Jr. (eds). IRISH PEAS-
      ANTS: VIOLENCE AND POLITICAL UNREST, 1780-1914. Madi-
      son, Wis.: University of Wisconsin Press, 1983.

      Contains items 1115, 1279, 1643, and 1717.

1181. Clarkson, J. Dunsmore. LABOUR AND NATIONALISM IN IRE-
      LAND. New York: Columbia University Press, 1925.

1182. Coffey, Tom. AGONY AT EASTER. THE 1916 IRISH UPRISING.
      Toronto: The Macmillan Co., 1969.

1183. Cohane, John Philip. THE INDESTRUCTIBLE IRISH. New
      York: Meredith Press, 1969.

1184. Cole, J.A. PRINCE OF SPIES, HENRI LE CARON. London:
      Faber & Faber, 1984.

      Examines foreign involvement in Irish terrorism.

1185. Colles, Ramsay. THE HISTORY OF ULSTER FROM THE EARLIEST
      TIMES TO THE PRESENT DAY, Vol. 4. London: Gresham
      Publishing Co., pp. 158-274.

1186. Collins, Michael. ARGUMENTS FOR THE TREATY. Dublin:
      Lester, 1922.

Presents the reluctant arguments of an IRA leader and
Sinn Fein political activist in favor of a treaty ending
the Irish civil war with Britain. Collins's background
in militant IRA activity made him an unlikely proponent
of peace, but he made sincere efforts to curtail violence
in Northern Ireland. When British pressure forced the
Irish government to move against republican forces in
the summer of 1922, Collins rejoined the struggle as
commander-in-chief of the National Army. He was killed
in an ambush on August 22, 1922.

1187. ———. THE PATH TO FREEDOM. Dublin: The Mercier Press,
1922.

1188. Colum, Padraic. ARTHUR GRIFFITH. Dublin: Browne & Nolan
1959.

Presents the most thorough biography of a leading Sinn
Fein spokesman who died (of natural causes) during the
late days of the civil war.

1189. ———. THE IRISH REBELLION OF 1916 AND ITS MARTYRS:
ERIN'S TRAGIC EASTER. New York: Macmillan, 1916.

1190. ———. ON JAMES STEPHENS. New York: Macmillan, 1928.

Examines the career of a 19th-century Fenian activist,
also associated with revolutionary groups in France.

1191. ———. OURSELVES ALONE! THE STORY OF ARTHUR GRIFFITH
AND THE ORIGIN OF THE IRISH FREE STATE. New York:
Crown Publishers, 1959.

1192. Comerford, R.V. THE FENIANS IN CONTEXT: IRISH POLITICS
AND SOCIETY 1848-82. Dublin: Wolfhound Press, 1985.

Follows the turbulent history of the Fenian movement,
a forerunner of the modern IRA.

1193. Conlon, Lil. CUMANN na mBAN AND THE WOMEN OF IRELAND,
1913-25. Kilkenny: Kilkenny People, Ltd., 1969.

Presents a history of the Irish Women's Council, with
profiles of original members, group protests and militant actions, arrests, trials, and imprisonments.

1194. Connolly, James. AXE TO THE ROOT. Dublin: The Author,
1921.

Presents a posthumous view of the Irish republican
struggle, collected from writings of a prominent socialist and trade union organizer. A committed Marxist,
Connolly organized a Citizen's Army in 1916 and joined
forces with Patrick Pearse's Irish Volunteers in the
Easter rising against British rule. Sentenced to death
by military tribunal for his role in the rising, Connolly
was executed in May 1916.

1195. ————. ERIN'S HOPE: THE END AND THE MEANS. New York:
National Executive Committee, Socialist Labor Party,
1897.

1196. ————. LABOUR AND EASTER WEEK 1916. Dublin: The Author,
1916.

1197. ————. LABOUR IN IRELAND: LABOUR IN IRISH HISTORY:
THE RECONQUEST OF IRELAND. Dublin: At the Sign of
Three Candles, 1917.

1198. Coogan, O. THE WAR IN MEATH 1913-23. Dublin: The Author,
1983.

Presents a retrospective view of events surrounding
the Easter rising and civil war.

1199. Coogan, Timothy Patrick. THE I.R.A. London: Pall Mall
Press, 1970.

Provides an excellent history of the IRA, from its
formation and the Easter rising through the 1960s.
Sympathetic but fair.

1200. ————. THE I.R.A. London: Fontana Books, 1980.

Updates item 1199.

1201. ————. IRELAND SINCE THE RISING. London: Pall Mall
Press, 1966.

1202. Corfe, Thomas. THE PHOENIX PARK MURDERS. CONFLICT,
COMPROMISE AND TRAGEDY IN IRELAND, 1879-1882. London:
Hodder & Stoughton, 1968.

Examines the assassination of Lord Frederick Caven-
dish and Thomas Burke by a Fenian splinter group, the
Invincibles, in 1882.

1203. Corish, Patrick J. "Political Problems, 1860–1878."
      A HISTORY OF IRISH CATHOLICISM. Cited below as item
      1204.

1204. ———— (ed). A HISTORY OF IRISH CATHOLICISM, Vol. V.
      Dublin: H.M. Gill & Sons, 1967.

      Contains items 1203 and 1731.

1205. Cosgrove, Art, and Donal McCartney (eds). STUDIES IN
      IRISH HISTORY. Dublin: University College, 1979.

      Contains items 1226, 1276, 1470, and 1687.

1206. Coxhead, E. DAUGHTERS OF ERIN. FIVE WOMEN OF THE IRISH
      RENASCENCE. London: Secker & Warburg, 1965.

      Profiles outspoken republican women, including the
      flamboyant Countess Markievicz.

   * Coyle, Dominick J. MINORITIES IN REVOLT. POLITICAL
      VIOLENCE IN IRELAND, ITALY, AND CYPRUS. Cited above
      as item 311, pp. 33–86.

      Covers Irish republican activities from 1920.

1207. Crawford, Frederick Hugh. GUNS FOR ULSTER. Belfast:
      Graham & Heslip, 1947.

      Describes military efforts to arm the pro-British
      Ulster Volunteer Force for action against the republi-
      can forces in 1914, authored by a leader of the campaign.

1208. Crilly, F.L. THE FENIAN MOVEMENT: THE STORY OF THE
      MANCHESTER MARTYRS. London: John Ouseley, 1908.

1209. Cronin, Sean. IRELAND SINCE THE TREATY. FIFTY YEARS
      AFTER. Dublin: Irish Freedom Press, 1971.

1210. ————. IRISH NATIONALISM: A HISTORY OF ITS ROOTS AND
      IDEOLOGY. Dublin: Academy Press, 1980.

1211. ————. OUR OWN RED BLOOD. Dublin: Academy Press, 1966.

1212. ————. THE REVOLUTIONARIES: THE STORY OF TWELVE GREAT
      IRISHMEN. Dublin: Republican Publications, 1971.

1213. Crosland, Thomas William Hodgson. THE WILD IRISHMAN.
      London: Stanley Paul & Co., 1905.

      Examines life and politics in Ireland around the turn
      of the century, including discussion of the continuing
      "land wars" between tenants and landlords.

1214. Crozier, Brigadier Frank P. IMPRESSIONS AND RECOLLEC-
      TIONS. London: T. Werner Laurie, 1930.

      Includes discussion of the Easter rising and civil
      war, from the viewpoint of a British military officer
      assigned to suppress the rebellion.

1215. Curran, Joseph M. THE BIRTH OF THE IRISH FREE STATE,
      1921-1923. Tuscaloosa, Ala.: University of Alabama
      Press, 1980.

      Examines the movement for Irish home rule, from 1890
      through days of terrorism and counter-terrorism, the
      Easter rising and the civil war.

1216. Curtis, L.P., Jr. COERCION AND CONCILIATION IN IRELAND,
      1800-1892: A STUDY IN CONSERVATIVE UNIONISM. Prince-
      ton, N.J.: Princeton University Press, 1963.

1217. Cusack, Sister M.F. THE LIFE OF DANIEL O'CONNELL THE
      LIBERATOR. HIS TIMES—POLITICAL, SOCIAL AND RELIGIOUS.
      New York: Kenmare Publications, 1872.

1218. Dalton, Charles. WITH THE DUBLIN BRIGADE 1917-1921.
      London: Peter Davies, 1929.

      Presents a personal narrative of the civil war period
      in Ireland, describing action by the early IRA in its
      campaign against British colonialism.

1219. Daly, Cathal B. VIOLENCE IN IRELAND. Dublin: Clonmore,
      1973.

1220. ———, and R.D.E. Gallagher. VIOLENCE IN IRELAND: A
      REPORT TO THE CHURCHES. Dublin: Veritas Publications,
      1977.

      Revises and updates item 1219.

1221. Daly, Martin (pseud.). MEMORIES OF THE DEAD ... SOME
      IMPRESSIONS OF ROGER CASEMENT, EAMUNN CEANNT [AND
      OTHERS]. Dublin: Powell Press, 1917.

      Profiles republican martyrs executed by the British
      military for their involvement in the Easter rising.

1222. Dane, Mervyn. THE FERMANAGH 'B' SPECIALS. Enniskillen:
      William Trimble, 1970.

      Examines the history of the Protestant security police
      in Northern Ireland, including accounts of documented
      atrocities against Catholics.

1223. D'Angelo, Giovanni. ITALY AND IRELAND IN THE 19th
      CENTURY. CONTACTS AND MISUNDERSTANDINGS BETWEEN TWO
      NATIONAL MOVEMENTS. Athlone: St. Paul Publications,
      1975.

      Examines political violence and terrorism in two dis-
      parate cultures of the 19th century, including discus-
      sion of the Irish "land wars."

1224, Dangerfield, George. THE DAMNABLE QUESTION: A STUDY IN
      ANGLO-IRISH RELATIONS. Boston: Little, Brown, 1976.

1225. Darby, John. CONFLICT IN NORTHERN IRELAND: THE DEVEL-
      OPMENT OF A POLARIZED COMMUNITY. Dublin: Gill &
      Macmillan, 1976.

1226. D'Arcy, Fergus. "Charles Bradlaugh and the Irish Ques-
      tion: A Study in the Nature and Limits of British
      Radicalism, 1853-91." STUDIES IN IRISH HISTORY.
      Cited above as item 1205, pp. 228-256.

1227. Daunt, William Joseph O'Neill. PERSONAL RECOLLECTIONS
      OF THE LATE DANIEL O'CONNELL M.P. London: T.F. Unwin,
      1848.

      Presents a sympathetic profile of a leading national-
      ist hero and martyr. In 1823, O'Connell organized the
      Catholic Association, campaigning for Catholic emanci-
      pation. Elected to parliament in 1828, although as a
      Catholic he was not legally qualified to serve, O'Connell
      fought for—and won—passage of the Catholic Emancipa-
      tion Bill, emerging as the major voice of Irish minority
      dissent in the 1830s and 1840s.

1228. ―――――. IRELAND AND HER AGITATORS. Dublin: John Browne, 1845.

1229. Davies, Noelle. CONNOLLY OF IRELAND, PATRIOT AND SOCIAL-IST. Caernarfon, Ireland: Swyddfa'r Blaid, 1946.

1230. Davis, Richard. ARTHUR GRIFFITH AND NON-VIOLENT SINN FEIN. Tralee: Anvil Books, 1974.

Covers organization of Sinn Fein and ideological controversies over use of violence in the period from 1890 to 1921. Concludes that the nonviolent wing of the movement was ultimately self-defeating through its own timidity.

1231. Davitt, Michael. THE FALL OF FEUDALISM IN IRELAND OR THE STORY OF THE LAND LEAGUE REVOLUTION. London: Harper & Brothers, 1904.

1232. ―――――. LEAVES FROM A PRISON DIARY: OR, LECTURES TO A "SOLITARY" AUDIENCE. London: Chapman & Hall, 1885.

Presents the memoirs of an incarcerated Land League activist.

1233. Dawson, Richard. RED TERROR AND GREEN. London: John Murray, 1920.

Examines political terrorism committed by both loyalist and nationalist factions during the Easter rising and civil war.

1234. de Blacam, A. WHAT SINN FEIN STANDS FOR. Dublin: Mellifont Press, 1921.

1235. De Burca, Padraig, and John F. Boyle. FREE STATE OR REPUBLIC? Dublin: Talbot Press, 1922.

1236. Denieffe, Joseph. A PERSONAL NARRATIVE OF THE IRISH REVOLUTIONARY BROTHERHOOD GIVING A FAITHFUL REPORT OF THE PRINCIPAL EVENTS FROM 1855 TO 1867, WRITTEN AT THE REQUEST OF FRIENDS. New York: The Gael Publishing Co.. 1906.

1237. Denvir, John. THE IRISH IN BRITAIN FROM THE EARLIEST TIME TO THE FALL AND DEATH OF PARNELL. London: Kegan, Paul, Trench, Trubner & Co., 1892.

1238. ———. LIFE STORY OF AN OLD REBEL. Dublin: Sealy,
      Bryers & Waler, 1910.

      Presents a personal narrative of the nationalist strug-
      gle prior to the Easter rising and civil war.

1239. De Paor, Liam. DIVIDED ULSTER. London: Pelican Press,
      1970, pp. 15–168.

      Presents one of the best published histories of Nor-
      thern Ireland, authored by a professor at the University
      of Dublin.

1240. Deutsch, Richard, and Vivien Magowan. NORTHERN IRELAND:
      A CHRONOLOGY OF EVENTS. 3 Vols. Belfast: Blackstaff
      Press, 1968–1974.

      Includes near-comprehensive coverage of terrorist ac-
      tivities in a lengthy chronology. Valuable for reference
      purposes, as a launching pad for more specific research
      in periodicals and newspapers.

1241. Devoy, John. RECOLLECTIONS OF AN IRISH REBEL. London:
      The Author, 1929.

      Presents an admittedly-biased memoir of a Fenian acti-
      vist, more entertaining than historically reliable.

1242. ———. THE LAND OF EIRE. THE IRISH LAND LEAGUE. ITS
      ORIGIN, PROGRESS AND CONSEQUENCES. PRECEDED BY A CON-
      CISE HISTORY OF THE VARIOUS MOVEMENTS WHICH HAVE CUL-
      MINATED IN THE LAST GREAT AGITATION. New York: Pat-
      terson & Neilson, 1882.

1243. Dewar, Michael. THE BRITISH ARMY IN NORTHERN IRELAND.
      London: Arms & Armour Press, 1985, pp. 11–26.

      Presents a comprehensive military history of British
      movements in Northern Ireland, prepared by a retired
      army officer.

1244. ———, John Brown, and S.E. Long. ORANGEISM. A NEW
      HISTORICAL APPRECIATION. Belfast: Grand Orange Lodge
      of Ireland, 1967, pp. 83–198.

      Presents a sympathetic survey of the Orange loyalist
      movement which has historically opposed unification of
      Ireland under home rule. Succeeds in glossing over most

of the crimes committed against innocent Catholics by
Orange bullies, a campaign of terrorism which is today
recognized as a major factor in the birth of the IRA as
a pro-Catholic counter-force.

1245. Dillon, Martin, and Denis Lehane. POLITICAL MURDER IN
      NORTHERN IRELAND. Baltimore: Penguin Books, 1974.

1246. Dillon, William. LIFE OF JOHN MITCHEL. 2 Vols. London:
      Kegan, Paul, Trench & Co., 1888.

      Profiles a 19th-century journalist and spokesman for
      the United Irishmen, who advocated violent tactics on
      the eve of the Irish "land wars."

1247. Doheny, Michael. THE FELON'S TRACK. Dublin: M.H. Gill
      & Son, 1914.

      Presents the personal account of a Young Ireland mem-
      ber, driven into European exile by the fear of prosecu-
      tion for pro-nationalist activities.

1248. Dooley, Pat. UNDER THE BANNER OF CONNOLLY. London:
      Irish Freedom, 1945.

1249. Doumitt, Donald P. CONFLICT IN NORTHERN IRELAND. New
      York: Peter Lang, 1985.

1250. DUBLIN'S FIGHTING STORY. Tralee: Kerryman Press, 1949.

      Offers an anonymous, pro-republican view of the con-
      tinuing violence in Ireland.

1251. Duff, Charles. SIX DAYS TO SHAKE AN EMPIRE: EVENTS AND
      FACTORS BEHIND THE IRISH REBELLION OF 1916—AN ACCOUNT
      OF THAT REBELLION AND ITS SUPPRESSION AND OF THE FINAL
      STRUGGLE FOR SELF GOVERNMENT, WITH AN EPILOGUE ON THE
      DISSOLUTION OF THE BRITISH EMPIRE INTO THE BRITISH
      COMMONWEALTH OF NATIONS. London: J.M. Dent & Sons,
      1966.

1252. Duffy, Sir Charles Gavan. DANIEL O'CONNELL. London:
      G. Routledge, 1844.

1253. ————. FOUR YEARS OF IRISH HISTORY, 1845-49. London:
      1883.

Examines the Young Ireland movement in a continuing
history which includes items 1254 and 1256 below. Written thirty years after the fact, these volumes are based
on historical documents, standing as indispensable
sourcebooks for an understanding of socio-economic turmoil in the 1840s.

1254. ————. THE LEAGUE OF THE NORTH AND THE SOUTH: AN EPI-
SODE IN IRISH HISTORY, 1850-54. London: Chapman &
Hall, 1886.

Completes Duffy's examination of the Young Ireland
movement, occasionally exaggerating Duffy's personal
role.

1255. ————. THOMAS DAVIS: THE MEMOIRS OF AN IRISH PATRIOT
1840-46. London: Kegan Paul, Trench, Trubner & Co.,
1890.

Examines the career of a Young Ireland activist in the
years of famine and political upheaval. A co-founder
of THE NATION, a nationalist periodical, Davis contributed patriotic poetry which gave the paper its distinc-
tive character.

1256. ————. YOUNG IRELAND: A FRAGMENT OF IRISH HISTORY
1840-1850. 2 Vols. London: Cassell, Petter & Co.,
1880-1883.

Launches Duffy's epic historical examination of the
Young Ireland movement and its aftermath.

1257. Dunlop, Robert. DANIEL O'CONNELL AND THE REVIVAL OF
NATIONAL LIFE IN IRELAND. New York: G.P. Putnam's
Sons, 1908.

1258. Dwyer, T. Ryle. IRISH NEUTRALITY AND THE USA, 1937-1947.
Dublin: Gill & Macmillan, 1977.

Examines the impact of Irish neutrality in World War
II on Irish-Americans and U.S. foreign policy. Includes
discussion of occasional IRA cooperation with Axis agents

1259. Dyos, H.J., and Michael Wolff (eds). THE VICTORIAN
CITY. IMAGES AND REALITIES. London: Routledge & Kegan
Paul, 1973.

Contains item 1091 above.

1260. EASTER COMMEMORATION DIGEST. Dublin: Graphic Publications, 1966.

Contains nostalgic retrospective material dealing with
the Easter rising and martyrdom of republican heroes
executed on the order of British military tribunals.

1261. Edmonds, Sean. THE GUN, THE LAW AND THE IRISH PEOPLE.
Tralee: Anvil Books, 1971.

Presents a critical study of the violence and contempt
for law and order by both sides in the "Irish question,"
covering terrorist activities from 1912 onward.

1262. Edwards, Owen Dudley. THE MIND OF AN ACTIVIST—JAMES
CONNOLLY. Dublin: Gill & Macmillan, 1971.

1263. ———. THE SINS OF OUR FATHERS: ROOTS OF CONFLICT IN
NORTHERN IRELAND. Dublin: Gill & Macmillan, 1970.

1264. ———, and Fergus Pyle (eds). 1916: THE EASTER RISING.
London: MacGibbon & Kee, 1968.

Contains items 1538 and 1550 below.

1265. Edwards, Ruth Dudley. DANIEL O'CONNELL AND HIS WORLD.
London: Thames & Hudon, 1975.

1266. ———. JAMES CONNOLLY. Dublin: Gill & Macmillan, 1981.

1267. ———. PATRICK PEARSE, THE TRIUMPH OF FAILURE. London:
Victor Gollancz, 1977.

1268. Edwards, Robert Dudley, and T. Desmond Williams (eds).
THE GREAT FAMINE. STUDIES IN IRISH HISTORY 1845-52.
New York: New York University Press, 1957.

1269. Elliott, Marianne. PARTNERS IN REVOLUTION. THE UNITED
IRISHMEN AND FRANCE. London: Yale University Press,
1982.

Examines the activities of the United Irishmen, an
early nationalist group composed primarily of Belfast
Presbyterians opposed to the dominant Anglican church.
Organized in the 1790s, when England was at war with
revolutionary France, the United Irishmen sought to
"subvert the tyranny of our execrable government,"
without significant result. Ex-members of the group,

including Robert Emmet, led their own revolts against
British rule in the early 19th century.

1270. Ellis, P. Berresford. A HISTORY OF THE IRISH WORKING
      CLASS. London: Victor Gollancz, 1972.

1271. Emmer, Thomas Addis. IRELAND UNDER ENGLISH RULE OR A
      PLEA FOR THE PLAINTIFF. New York: The Knickerbocker
      Press, 1903.

      Delineates the economic, political, and social failures
      of Ireland under (and because of) British rule. Appen-
      dices list the various Coercion Acts passed in the in-
      terest of the landlords, with a list of rejected Land
      Bills from 1829.

1272. Ervine, St. John. CRAIGAVON: ULSTERMAN. London: Allen
      & Unwin, 1949.

      Presents the official, uncritical biography of John
      Craig, an Ulster Unionist Party leader and first prime
      minister of Northern Ireland during the civil war period
      of the 1920s. Until his retirement in 1940, Craig's
      battle cry of "No surrender" rallied Orange forces
      against all efforts to unify Ireland under home rule,
      further exacerbating tensions in a divided society.

1273. ———. PARNELL. Boston: Little, Brown, 1925.

1274. Eversley, Baron. PEEL AND O'CONNELL. London: Kegan
      Paul, Trench & Co., 1887.

1275. Falls, C. "Northern Ireland and the Defence of the
      British Isles." ULSTER UNDER HOME RULE: A STUDY OF
      THE POLITICAL AND ECONOMIC PROBLEMS IN NORTHERN IRE-
      LAND. Cited below as item 1736.

      Examines IRA collaboration with Axis agents in World
      War II, along with other problems of military defense
      in a divided land.

1276. Fanning, Ronan. "The Irish Policy of Asquith's Govern-
      ment and the Cabinet Crisis of 1910." STUDIES IN
      IRISH HISTORY. Cited above as item 1205, pp. 279-303.

1277. Farrell, Michael. NORTHERN IRELAND: THE ORANGE STATE.
      London: Pluto Press, 1976, pp. 21-226.

1278. Feehan, John M. THE SHOOTING OF MICHAEL COLLINS. Cork:
      The Mercier Press, 1981.

      Refutes the offical theory that Collins was killed by
      a stray shot or ricochet bullet, citing evidence of de-
      liberate murder in the death of an Irish nationalist
      hero.

1279. Feingold, William L. "Land League Power: The Tralee
      Poor-Law Election of 1881." IRISH PEASANTS, VIOLENCE
      AND POLITICAL UNREST, 1780-1914. Cited above as item
      1180, pp. 285-310.

1280. Fergusson, Sir James. THE CURRAGH INCIDENT. London:
      Faber & Faber, 1964.

      Presents an excellent authoritative account of the Cur-
      ragh mutiny, in which various military officers refused
      to take up arms against loyalists in Ulster. Prepared
      by a descendant of a principal participant, the account
      is detailed and admirably objective.

1281, Figgis, Darrell. A CHRONICLE OF JAILS. Dublin: Talbot
      Press, 1917.

      Examines the Sinn Fein movement and its various im-
      prisoned martyrs from the viewpoint of a leading party
      spokesman.

1282. ————. RECOLLECTIONS OF THE IRISH WAR. London: Ernest
      Nemm, 1927.

1283. ————. A SECOND CHRONICLE OF JAILS. Dublin: Talbot
      Press, 1919.

      Updates item 1281 above.

1284. Finegan, John J. (ed). THE ANNE DEVLIN JAIL JOURNAL.
      Cork: The Mercier Press, 1968.

      Examines the life of Anne Devlin, female compatriot
      of Robert Emmet in the uprising of 1803, who was jailed
      for her involvement. Written by Devlin's contemporary,
      Brother Luke Cullen, who befriended Devlin during and
      after her detention in Kilmainham Jail.

1285. FitzGerald, Desmond. MEMOIRS OF DESMOND FITZGERALD,
      1913-16. London: Routledge & Kegan Paul, 1968.

Examines activities of the Irish Volunteers and the
Irish Republican Brotherhood through the Easter rising,
presented from the viewpoint of an active participant.

1286. Fitzgerald, Redmond. CRY BLOOD, CRY ERIN. London:
Barrie & Rockliff, 1966.

1287. FitzGibbon, Constantine. THE IRISH IN IRELAND. London:
David & Charles, 1983.

Includes a discussion of "the troubles" in a general,
often romantic survey of Irish history from pre-Celtic
times to the present day.

1288. ————. OUT OF THE LION'S PAW. IRELAND WINS HER FREE-
DOM. London: Macdonald & Co., 1969.

1289. ————. RED HAND: THE ULSTER COLONY. Garden City, N.Y.:
Doubleday, 1972.

1290. Fitzpatrick, David. POLITICS AND IRISH LIFE, 1913-1921:
PROVINCIAL EXPERIENCE OF WAR AND REVOLUTION. Dublin:
Gill & Macmillan, 1977.

1291. ————. QUEEN'S REBELS: ULSTER LOYALISM IN HISTORICAL
PERSPECTIVE. Dublin: Gill & Macmillan, 1978.

1292. Flood, Sean. "God Damn You, England! Has History Taught
You Nothing?" IRELAND UNFREE. Cited below as item
1530, pp. 13-18.

Examines treatment of republican prisoners in British
jails.

1293. ————. "A Protestant Parliament, A Protestant State."
IRELAND UNFREE. Cited below as item 1530, pp. 47-53.

Examines the history of Irish partition and attendant
violence.

1294. Fogarty, L. (ed). JAMES FINIAN LAWLOR: THE PATRIOT AND
POLITICAL ESSAYIST, 1807-1899. Dublin: The Talbot
Press, 1918.

Profiles a Fenian spokesman and activist of the 19th
century.

1295. Forester, Margery. MICHAEL COLLINS—THE LOST LEADER.
      London: Sidgwick & Jackson, 1971.

1296. Foster, R.F. CHARLES STEWART PARNELL. Sussex: The Har-
      vester Press, 1976.

1297. Fox, Michael. GREEN BANNERS: THE STORY OF THE IRISH
      STRUGGLE. London: Secker & Warburg, 1938.

1298. ———. HISTORY OF THE IRISH CITIZEN ARMY. Dublin:
      J. Duffy & Co., 1943.

      Studies the history of the Citizen Army during the
      Easter rising and civil war, including lists of active
      personnel with their length of service and post.

1299. ———. JAMES CONNOLLY: THE FORERUNNER. Tralee: The
      Kerryman Ltd., 1946.

1300. ———. REBEL IRISHWOMEN. Dublin: The Talbot Press,
      1935.

      Profiles twelve heroines of Ireland's rebellion, in-
      cluding their contributions and participation in para-
      military action.

1301. ———. SMOKY CRUSADE. London: The Hogarth Press, 1938.

1302. Gallagher, Frank. THE INDIVISIBLE LAND: THE HISTORY OF
      THE PARTITION OF IRELAND. London: Victor Gollancz,
      1957.

1303. Gallagher, Thomas. PADDY'S LAMENT: IRELAND 1846-1847.
      PRELUDE TO HATRED. New York: Harcourt, Brace, Jovan-
      ovich, 1982.

1304. Galliher, John F., and Jerry L. Degregory. VIOLENCE IN
      NORTHERN IRELAND: UNDERSTANDING PROTESTANT PERSPEC-
      TIVES. Dublin: Gill & Macmillan, 1965.

1305. Garvin, Tom. DEFENDERS, RIBBONMEN AND OTHERS. Dublin:
      University College, 1980.

      Examines militant secret societies organized to de-
      fend poor tenants and oppose financial obligations im-
      posed by the church. Organized in 1826, the Ribbonmen
      attempted to intimidate landlords with threats of vio-
      lence. When simple coercion proved ineffective, they

sometimes resorted to maiming of cattle, destruction of
crops, and murder of selected targets.

1306. ———. THE EVOLUTION OF IRISH NATIONAL POLITICS. New
York: Holmes & Meier, 1981.

Concludes that Ireland, "far from being an oddity, [is]
in many ways a classic example of the development of
popular anti-colonial nationalism in a conquered country."

1307. Gibbons, Peter. THE ORIGINS OF ULSTER UNIONISM: THE
FORMATION OF POPULAR PROTESTANT POLITICS AND IDEOLOGY
NINETEENTH-CENTURY IRELAND. Manchester: Manchester
University Press, 1975.

1308. Gleeson, James. BLOODY SUNDAY. London: Four Square
Books, 1962.

Presents an account of the IRA's liquidation of British intelligence agents on November 21, 1920. The assassination of eleven spies by members of Michael Collins's
IRA Special Intelligence Unit provoked a violent reaction
by Black and Tans later in the day. Firing on a crowd
of spectators at an athletic event, the soldiers killed
12 persons and wounded 60. Rounding off the grisly
afternoon, three republican prisoners were executed at
Dublin Castle, in reprisal for the original murders.

1309. Glynn, Anthony. HIGH UPON THE GALLOWS TREE. Tralee:
Anvil Books, 1967.

Examines the case of the Manchester Martyrs, three
Fenians executed for slaying a police sergeant during
the rescue of Fenian leaders from Manchester gaol in
September 1867. Five men were originally sentenced to
die in the case, but two were subsequently freed when
further doubt was cast upon their guilt. The three
martyrs went to their deaths with cries of "God save
Ireland," providing a motto for the later Irish Republican Brotherhood.

1310. Gnathai Gan Iarraidh. THE SACRED EGOISM OF SINN FEIN.
Dublin: Maunsel & Co., 1918.

1311. Gogarty, Oliver St. John. AS I WAS GOING DOWN SACKVILLE
STREET. New York: Reynal & Hitchcock, 1937.

Describes the author's abduction by IRA soldiers during the Irish civil war.

1312. Good, James Winder. IRISH UNIONISM. London: Kennikat Press, 1920.

1313. ————. ULSTER AND IRELAND. Dublin: Maunsel & Co., 1919.

1314. Gray, John. CITY IN REVOLT: JAMES LARKING AND THE BELFAST DOCK STRIKE OF 1907. Belfast: Blackstaff Press, 1985.

1315. Greaves, Charles Desmond. DE VALERA. London: Connolly Books, 1969.

Profiles a major Irish republican leader and his career, in relation to political turmoil of the times. A survivor of the Easter rising, Eamon De Valera emerged as a driving force behind the Sinn Fein political movement. Elected to Parliament on his release from prison, De Valera became a leading spokesman in favor of Irish unification under home rule. Initially involved in IRA guerilla activities, in later years De Valera sought to divorce himself from the violent side of the republican struggle, opting for constitutional means.

1316. ————. THE IRISH CRISIS. New York: International Publishers, 1972.

Provides historical background to the "clash of interest between English monopoly capitalism on the one hand and the Irish people on the other."

1317. ————. LIAM MELLOWS AND THE IRISH REVOLUTION. London: Lawrence & Wishart, 1971.

Profiles another principal of the Irish civil war. Held by the British as an IRA activist, Mellows was executed at Mountjoy Prison, in Dublin, in December 1922.

1318. ————. THE LIFE AND TIMES OF JAMES CONNOLLY. London: Lawrence & Wishart, 1961.

1319. Green, Alice Stopford. OURSELVES ALONE IN ULSTER. Dublin: Maunsel & Co., 1918.

Examines Northern Ireland from the inside, in the wake of the Easter rising.

1320. Green, E.R.R. "The Beginnings of Fenianism." THE FEN-
IAN MOVEMENT. Edited by T.W. Moody. Cork: The
Mercier Press, 1968.

1321. Griffith, Arthur. THE SINN FEIN POLICY. Dublin: James
Duffy & Co., 1907.

1322. ——— (ed). THOMAS DAVIS: THE THINKER AND TEACHER.
Dublin: Gill & Macmillan, 1914.

1323. Griffith, Kenneth, and Timothy E. O'Grady. CURIOUS
JOURNEY. AN ORAL HISTORY OF IRELAND'S UNFINISHED REV-
OLUTION. London: Hutchinson & Co., 1982.

1324. Griffiths, A.R.G. "Finland, Norway and the Easter Rising." IRISH CULTURE AND NATIONALISM, 1750-1950. Cited
below as item 1442, pp. 149-160.

Examines foreign contributions to the Irish rebellion
of 1916.

1325. Gwynn, Denis Rolleston. DANIEL O'CONNELL. THE IRISH
LIBERATOR. Oxford: B.H. Blackwell, 1947.

1326. ———. DE VALERA. New York: E.P. Dutton, 1933.

1327. ———. EAMON DE VALERA. London: Jarrolds, 1933.

Presents a slightly revised version of item 1326.

1328. ———. THE HISTORY OF PARTITION, 1912-1925. Dublin:
Browne & Nolen, 1950.

Begins with Home Rule and ends with failure of the
Boundary Commission in 1925.

1329. ———. THE IRISH FREE STATE, 1922-27. London: Macmillan & Co., 1928.

1330. ———. LIFE AND DEATH OF ROGER CASEMENT. London:
Newnes, 1931.

Profiles a Protestant spokesman converted to the home
rule cause and support for Irish independence. With
World War I in progress, Casement visited Germany to

obtain arms and ammunition for Irish rebels. Arrested
prior to the Easter rising, he was convicted of treason.
Circulation of his private diaries, indicating Casement
may have been a homosexual, scuttled popular support
for a reprieve, and he was hanged in August 1916.

1331. ————. THE LIFE OF JOHN REDMOND. London: Harrap, 1932.

Profiles a leader of the Irish Parliamentary Party,
once a member of the Irish Republican Brotherhood, who
split with the IRB on the issue of violent means in
September 1914, organizing his own moderate National
Volunteers. Redmond described the Easter rising of 1916
as a "German intrigue," proving himself out of touch
with the new nationalist trend in Ireland. He died of
natural causes in 1918, nine months before Sinn Fein
annihilated his party at the polls.

1332. ————. THE STRUGGLE FOR CATHOLIC EMANCIPATION, 1750-
1829. London: Longmans & Co., 1928.

1333. ————. TRAITOR OR PATRIOT: THE LIFE AND DEATH OF ROGER
CASEMENT. New York: J. Cape & H. Smith, 1931.

Presents a slightly revised version of item 1330.

1334. ————. YOUNG IRELAND AND 1848. Cork: Cork University
Press, 1949.

Presents a survey of the Young Ireland movement and
19th-century unrest, drawing heavily on information
contained in items 1253, 1254, and 1256 above.

1335. Gwynn, Stephen. JOHN REDMOND'S LAST YEARS. New York:
Longmans, Green & Co., 1919.

1336. Hachey, Thomas E. BRITISH AND IRISH SEPARATISM: FROM
THE FENIANS TO THE FREE STATE, 1867-1922. Chicago:
McNally & Co., 1977.

1337. Hackett, Francis. IRELAND. A STUDY IN NATIONALISM. New
York: B.W. Huebsch, 1918.

1338. Hamilton, Iaian. THE IRISH TANGLE. London: Institute
for the Study of Conflict, 1970.

1339. Hancock, W.K. SMUTS, Vol. II. THE FIELDS OF FORCE
1919-1950. London: Cambridge University Press, 1968.

Includes memoirs of military activity against the IRA.

1340. HANDBOOK OF THE ULSTER QUESTION. Dublin: Dublin Stationery Office, 1923.

1341. Harbison, J.F. THE ULSTER UNIONIST PARTY, 1832-1973: ITS DEVELOPMENT AND ORGANISATION. Belfast: Blackstaff Press, 1973.

1342. Harkness, David W. NORTHERN IRELAND SINCE 1920. Dublin: Helicon, 1983.

1343. ————. THE RESTLESS DOMINION: THE IRISH FREE STATE AND THE BRITISH COMMONWEALTH OF NATIONS, 1921-1931. London: Macmillan, 1969.

1344. Harmon, Maurice (ed). FENIANS AND FENIANISM: CENTENARY ESSAYS. Dublin: Scepter Books, 1968.

1345. Harris, Rosemary. PREJUDICE AND TOLERANCE IN ULSTER: A STUDY OF NEIGHBORS AND STRANGERS IN A BORDER COMMUNITY. Manchester: Manchester University Press, 1972.

Contains items 1374, 1469, 1475, 1617, and 1673 below.

1346. Harrison, Henry. IRELAND AND THE BRITISH EMPIRE, 1937: CONFLICT OR COLLABORATION? A STUDY OF ANGLO-IRISH DIFFERENCES FROM THE INTERNATIONAL STANDPOINT. London: R. Hale & Co., 1937.

1347. ————. THE NEUTRALITY OF IRELAND: WHY IT WAS INEVITABLE. London: R. Hale, 1942.

Examines Irish neutrality in World Warr II, and IRA cooperation with Axis agents.

1348. ————. PARNELL VINDICATED, THE LIFTING OF THE VEIL. London: Constable & Co., Ltd.

Provides a useful account of Parnell's last years and the activities of his unionist movement. Despite his Protestant religion, Parnell emerged, with IRB veteran Michael Davitt, of the Land League, demanding the "three F's": fair rents, fixity of tenure, and free sale of tenancy.

1349. ————. THE PARTITION OF IRELAND: HOW BRITAIN IS RESPONSIBLE. London: R. Hale, 1939.

1350. ————. ULSTER AND THE BRITISH EMPIRE. London: Hale, 1939.

1351. Haslip, Joan. PARNELL: A BIOGRAPHY. London: Cobden & Sanderson, 1936.

1352. Hawkins, John. THE IRISH QUESTION TODAY: THE PROBLEMS AND DANGERS OF PARTITION. London: Victor Gollancz, 1941.

1353. Hawkins, R. "Dublin Castle and the Royal Irish Constabulary, 1916-1922." THE IRISH STRUGGLE, 1916-1926. Cited below as item 1734.

Examines the role of the R.I.C. in the Easter rising and subsequent suppression of terrorism.

1354. Hayes, Michael. "Thomas MacDonagh and the Rising." THE EASTER RISING AND UNIVERSITY COLLEGE, DUBLIN. Cited below as item 1504, pp. 35-49.

Profiles a leading figure in the early struggle for Irish independence. MacDonagh was a founding member of the Irish Volunteers in 1913, serving as the group's training director and as organizer of the Howth gunrunning expedition in July 1914. Joining the Irish Republican Brotherhood in 1915, he was a key planner of the Easter rising a year later. Arrested by the British for his role in the rebellion, he was executed in May 1916.

1355. Hayes-McCoy, Gerard Anthony. THE IRISH AT WAR. Cork: Mercier Press, 1964.

1356. ————. "A Military History of the 1916 Rising." THE MAKING OF 1916: STUDIES IN THE HISTORY OF THE RISING. Cited below as item 1544.

1357. ———— (ed). HISTORICAL STUDIES IV. Cambridge: Cambridge University Press, 1963.

Contains item 1546 below.

1358. Hazlett, Arthur. THE "B" SPECIALS, A HISTORY OF THE ULSTER SPECIAL CONSTABULARY. Shannon: Irish University Press, 1969.

Examines the history and tactics of Protestant special police in Northern Ireland. Organized by Lord Brookeborough in 1919, to combat the IRA, members of the B-Specials were frequently accused of cruelty and atrocities against Catholics. In addition to their duties as auxilliary police in Belfast, it is documented that various members took part in "unofficial"—and illegal—raids against the homes of Catholic families suspected of IRA connections. In 1969, following exposure of lawless activities by B-Special members, the group was abolished and replaced by the Ulster Defense Regiment.

1359. ———. THE FERMANAGH 'B' SPECIALS. London: Tom Stacey, 1972.

Updates item 1358 above.

1360. Henry, Robert Mitchell. THE EVOLUTION OF SINN FEIN. Dublin: T. Fisher Union, 1920.

1361. Hepburn, A.C. THE CONFLICT OF NATIONALITY IN MODERN IRELAND. New York: St. Martin's Press, 1980.

1362. Hewitt, James (ed). EYE-WITNESS TO IRELAND IN REVOLT. England: Osprey Publishers, Ltd.

Includes two chapters on 19th-century uprisings and the 1916 Easter revolt.

1363. Heyck, Thomas William. THE DIMENSIONS OF BRITISH RADICALISM: THE CASE OF IRELAND, 1874-1895. Urbana, Ill.: University of Illinois Press, 1974.

1364. Hickey, D.J., and J.E. Doherty. A DICTIONARY OF IRISH HISTORY SINCE 1800. Dublin: Gill & Macmillan, 1980.

Provides an invaluable sourcebook for major characters, organizations, incidents, and themes in Irish history.

1365. Hogan, David (pseud.). THE FOUR GLORIOUS YEARS. Dublin: Irish Press, 1921.

1366. Holt, Edgar. PROTEST IN ARMS: THE IRISH TROUBLES, 1916-1923. London: McClelland, 1960.

Presents one of the most balanced accounts of the early "troubles" in Ireland.

1367. Hone, Joseph M. IRELAND SINCE 1922. London: Faber & Faber, 1932.

1368. Horgan, J.J. (ed). THE COMPLETE GRAMMAR OF ANARCHY—BY MEMBERS OF THE WAR CABINET AND THEIR FRIENDS. London: Nisbet & Co., 1919.

1369. ————. PARNELL TO PEARSE, SOME RECOLLECTIONS AND RE-FLECTIONS. Dublin: Browne & Nolan, 1948.

1370. House of Commons. MINUTES OF EVIDENCE OF THE ROYAL COM-MISSION ON THE REBELLION IN IRELAND. London: Her Majesty's Stationery Office, 1916.

1371. Hughes, Katherine. ENGLISH ATROCITIES IN IRELAND. New York: 1920.

1372. Hull, Roger H. THE IRISH TRIANGLE: CONFLICT IN NORTHERN IRELAND. Princeton, N.J.: Princeton University Press, 1976.

1373. Hurst, Michael. "Fenianism in the Context of World History." FENIANS AND FENIANISM. Cited above as item 1099, pp. 82-89.

1374. ————. PARNELL AND IRISH NATIONALISM. London: Rout-ledge and Kegan Paul, 1968.

1375. Inglis, Brian. ROGER CASEMENT. London: Hodder & Stough-ton, 1973.

1376. ————. THE STORY OF IRELAND. London: Faber & Faber, 1956.

1377. I.O. (pseud.) THE ADMINISTRATION OF IRELAND IN 1920. London: Philip Allan & Co., 1921.

1378. ————. THE ADMINISTRATION OF IRELAND IN 1921. London: Philip Allan & Co., 1922.

1379. Ireland, Denis. FROM THE JUNGLE OF BELFAST: FOOTNOTES TO HISTORY, 1904-1972. Belfast: Blackstaff Press, 1973.

1380. Ireland, Tom. IRELAND PAST AND PRESENT. New York: G.P. Putnam's Sons, 1942, pp. 225-965.

Presents a detailed national history, delivered from
an admittedly republican viewpoint. IRA terrorism is
covered under a heading on "disorders."

1381. Irish Times. SINN FEIN REBELLION HANDBOOK: EASTER 1916.
      Dublin: Irish Times, 1917.

1382. THE IRISH UPRISING 1916-1922. New York: CBS Legacy
      Collection Books, 1966.

1383. Independent Television. THE TROUBLES. London: I.T.V.,
      1980.

1384. Jackson, Spencer. THE LAND MONOPOLISTS OF IRELAND AND A
      PLAN FOR THEIR GENERAL EXTINCTION. London: E. Stan-
      ford, 1880.

1385. Jackson, Thomas A. IRELAND HER OWN. London: Cobbett
      Press, 1947.

      Presents a Marxist view of Irish history, authored by
      a founder of the British Communist Party.

1386. JAMES STEPHENS CHIEF ORGANIZER OF THE FENIAN BROTHER-
      HOOD. New York: Private printing, 1866.

      Presents a "semi-biographical" sketch of the Irish
      Revolutionary Brotherhood's founding father. Influenced
      by contact with French secret societies, Stephens organ-
      ized the IRB—better known as the Fenians—in 1858.
      Imprisoned by the British in 1865, he escaped two months
      later with aid from two Fenian jailers. Within a year,
      he was replaced by more radical members of the IRB, who
      launched a dynamite campaign against the British govern-
      ment in London. An American branch of the Fenians also
      planned—and executed—an invasion of Canada in 1866.

1387. Jervis, H.J.W. IRELAND UNDER BRITISH RULE. London:
      Chapman & Hall, 1868.

1388. Jones, Francis P. HISTORY OF THE SINN FEIN MOVEMENT
      AND THE IRISH REBELLION OF 1916. New York: P.J.
      Kenedy & Sons, 1917.

      Offers a solidly pro-republican view of the Easter
      rising, complete with rosters of republican activists
      jailed or executed by the British.

1389. Joy, Maurice (ed). THE IRISH REBELLION OF 1916 AND ITS
       MARTYRS: ERIN'S TRAGIC EASTER. New York: The Devin-
       Adair Co., 1916.

       Includes chapters written by some of the best-known
       adherents of Sinn Fein. Fairly restrained, providing a
       great deal of information on Gaelic nationalism as well
       as the rebellion.

1390. Kee, Robert. THE GREEN FLAG: A HISTORY OF IRISH NATION-
       ALISM. London: Weidenfeld & Nicolson, 1972.

1391. Kelly, Kevin. THE LONGEST WAR: NORTHERN IRELAND AND THE
       IRA. Dingle, County Kerry: Brandon Books, 1973.

1392. Kenna, G.B. FACTS AND FIGURES OF THE BELFAST POGROM
       1920-1922. Dublin: O'Connell Publishing Co., 1922.

       Presents a Catholic view of Ulster violence in the
       civil war, authored by a Belfast priest.

1393. Kennedy, D. "Ulster During the War and After." IRELAND
       IN THE WAR YEARS AND AFTER, 1939-1951. Cited below
       as item 1548.

1394. Kerr, Donal A. PEEL, PRIESTS AND POLITICS. Oxford:
       Clarendon Press, 1982.

       Examines Sir Robert Peel's treatment of Irish Catholics
       in the 1840s.

1395. Kiely, Benedict. COUNTIES IN CONTENTION. Cork: Mercier
       Press, 1945.

1396. Killfeather, T.P. THE CONNAUGHT RANGERS. Tralee: Anvil
       Books, 1969.

       Examines the June 1920 mutiny of British soldiers who
       protested atrocities against the Irish in the civil war.
       Ironically, the mutiny took place in India, far removed
       from the scene of Irish violence. Two mutineers died in
       an attempt to seize the military arsenal at Solon; a
       third died from harsh treatment in custody, and 75 were
       convicted in various courts martial, including one
       soldier—a member of the Irish Republican Brotherhood—
       who was shot by a firing squad in November.

1397. King, Clifford. THE ORANGE AND THE GREEN. London:
      Macdonald & Co., 1965.

      Examines the tumultuous period of 1912-1920, with em-
      phasis on the Easter rising and Belfast barricade revolts
      of 1920.

1398. Kirkpatrick, R.W. "Origins and Development of the Land
      War in Mid-Ulster, 1879-85." IRELAND UNDER THE UNION.
      Cited below as item 1433.

1399. ————. THE PARTITION OF IRELAND, 1911-1925. Dundalk:
      Dundalgan Press, 1983.

1400. Laffan, Peter. "Violence and Terror in Twentieth-century
      Ireland: IRB and IRA." SOCIAL PROTEST, VIOLENCE AND
      TERROR IN NINETEENTH- AND TWENTIETH-CENTURY EUROPE.
      Cited above as item 41, pp. 155-174.

1401. Landon, Michael de L. ERIN AND BRITANNIA: THE HISTORICAL
      BACKGROUND TO A MODERN TRAGEDY. Chicago: Nelson-Hall,
      1981.

1402. Landreth, Helen. THE PURSUIT OF ROBERT EMMET. New York:
      McGraw-Hill, 1948.

1403. Larkin, Emmett. THE ROMAN CATHOLIC CHURCH AND THE CRE-
      ATION OF THE MODERN IRISH STATE, 1876-1886. Philadel-
      phia: American Philosophical Society, 1975.

1404. ————. THE ROMAN CATHOLIC CHURCH IN IRELAND AND THE
      FAILURE OF PARNELL, 1888-1891. Chapel Hill, N.C.:
      University of North Carolina Press, 1979.

      Presents the story of the second and final phase of
      consolidation of the modern Irish state, from the
      Clerical-Nationalist Alliance of 1889 to the fall of
      Parnell and the rise of Catholic power in 1891.

1405. Lawlor, Sheila. BRITAIN AND IRELAND, 1914-23. Dublin:
      Gill & Macmillan, 1983.

1406. Leamy, Margaret. PARNELL'S FAITHFUL FEW. New York:
      Macmillan, 1936.

1407. Lecky, William Edward Hartpole. THE LEADERS OF PUBLIC
      OPINION IN IRELAND: SWIFT, FLOOD, GARTTAN, O'CONNELL.
      New York: D. Appleton, 1883, pp. 223-320.

Includes laudatory chapters on Jonathan Swift, Henry
Flood, Henry Grattan, and Daniel O'Connell.

1408. Lee, Alfred McClung. TERRORISM IN MODERN IRELAND. New
York: General Hall, Inc., Publishers, 1983, pp. 19-74.

1409. Lee, Joseph. "The Ribbonmen." SECRET SOCIETIES IN
IRELAND. Cited below as item 1735, pp. 26-35.

1410. Leech, H. Brougham. 1848 AND 1912: THE CONTINUITY OF
THE IRISH REVOLUTIONARY MOVEMENT. London: Simpkin,
Marshall & Co., 1912.

1411. Le Roux, L.N. TOM CLARKE AND THE IRISH FREEDOM MOVEMENT.
Dublin: Talbot Press, 1936.

1412. Leslie, Sir Shane. THE IRISH TANGLE FOR ENGLISH READERS.
London: MacDonald & Co., 1946.

1413. ———. THE IRISH ISSUE IN ITS AMERICAN ASPECT. New
York: Charles Scribner's Sons, 1917.

1414. Levenson, Samuel. JAMES CONNOLLY: A BIOGRAPHY. London:
Martin Brian & O'Keefe, 1973.

1415. ———. MAUD GONNE. London: Cassell, 1976.

Profiles a prominent Irish suffragette and republican
spokeswoman. Dissatisfied with the Fenian movement's
lack of aggressive behavior, Gonne led agitation in
Donegal and Mayo during the famine of the 1890s, later
rising to prominence in the Amnesty Association, fighting for the release of political prisoners. Gonne's
estranged husband, John MacBride, was executed for his
role in the Easter Rising of 1916, and a year later she
was jailed for involvement in alleged "German plots"
against England. Escaping from Holloway prison, Gonne
was active with republican forces during the civil war,
and was again imprisoned by the British, winning release
after a hunger strike lasting 23 days.

1416. Lieberson, Goddard. THE IRISH UPRISING, 1916-1922.
New York: Macmillan, 1960.

1417. Livingstone, P. THE FERMANAGH STORY. Enniskillen:
Cumann Seanchais Chlochair, 1969.

1418. Lloyd George, David. IS IT PEACE? London: Hodder &
      Stoughton, 1923.

1419. ————. WAR MEMOIRS. 2 Vols. London: Oldhams Press,
      1938.

1420. Longford, Frank Lakenham, and Thomas P. O'Neill. EAMONN
      DE VALERA. London: Hutchinson, 1926.

      Presents the best single biography of De Valera, pre-
      pared with the subject's complete cooperation.

1421. Longford, Lord, and Anne McHardy. ULSTER. London: Weid-
      enfield & Nicolson, 1981, pp. 26-103.

1422. Lynch, Arthur. IRELAND: VITAL HOUR. London: Stanley
      Paul & Co., 1915.

1423. ————. MY LIFE STORY. London: John Long, 1924.

      Presents the memoirs of an Australian-born Irish re-
      publican spokesman. While covering the Boer war as a
      journalist, Lynch joined Major John MacBride in forming
      a pro-Boer "Irish Brigade" for action against British
      troops. Elected to parliament from Galway in 1900,
      Lynch was arrested for treason upon his return to England
      and was sentenced to death in 1903. Pardoned in 1907,
      he was subsequently reelected to parliament, but his
      republican zeal had faded. By 1914, Lynch was serving
      in the British army, recruiting troops in Ireland.
      Defeated by Sinn Fein opponents in a parliamentary cam-
      paign four years later, he retired to the quiet practice
      of medicine in London.

1424. Lynch, Diarmuid. THE I.R.B. AND THE 1916 INSURRECTION.
      Edited by Florence O'Donoghue. Cork: The Mercier
      Press, 1957.

      Presents an insider's view of rebellion in Ireland,
      from an author who joined the Irish Republican Brother-
      hood in 1908, serving on the IRB's supreme council from
      1911 to 1916. Active in gun-running prior to the Easter
      rising, Lynch was imprisoned for his role in the rebel-
      lion, winning release a year later. Traveling to the
      United States, he organized the Friends of Irish Freedom,
      and subsequently spent three years in the government
      led by Eamon De Valera.

1425. Lyons, Francis Steward Leland. THE BURDEN OF OUR HISTORY. Belfast: Queen's University, 1978.

1426. ———. CHARLES STEWART PARNELL. London: William Collins Sons & Co., 1977.

1427. ———. CULTURE AND ANARCHY IN IRELAND 1890-1939. Oxford: Oxford University Press, 1979.

1428. ———. THE FALL OF PARNELL, 1890-1901. London: Routledge & Kegan Paul, 1960.

1429. ———. IRELAND SINCE THE FAMINE. New York: Charles Scribner's Sons, 1971.

1430. ———. THE IRISH PARLIAMENTARY PARTY, 1890-1910. London: Faber & Faber, 1951.

1431. ———. JOHN DILLON. A BIOGRAPHY. London: Routledge & Kegan Paul, 1968.

1432. ———. PARNELL. Dundalk, Ireland: Dundalgan Press, 1965.

1433. ———, and R.AJ. Hawkins (eds). IRELAND UNDER THE UNION. Oxford: Clarendon Press, 1980.

Contains item 1398 above.

1434. MacBride, Maud Gonne. A SERVANT OF THE QUEEN, HER OWN STORY. Dublin: Golden Eagle Books, 1950.

1435. MacCarthy, J.M. (ed). LIMERICK'S FIGHTING STORY. Tralee.

Contains item 1597.

1436. MacDonagh, Donagh. "Plunkett and MacDonagh." LEADERS AND MEN OF THE EASTER RISING: DUBLIN 1916. Cited below as item 1504, pp. 165-176.

1437. MacDonagh, Michael. DANIEL O'CONNELL AND THE STORY OF CATHOLIC EMANCIPATION. Dublin: Talbot Press, 1929.

1438. ———. THE HOME RULE MOVEMENT. Dublin: Talbot Press, 1920.

1439. ———. THE LIFE OF WILLIAM O'BRIEN, THE IRISH NATIONALIST. London: Ernest Benn, 1928.

Profiles an Irish journalist and land agitator who
supported the Land League and authored its "No Rent
Manifesto" in 1881. Jailed with Parnell through April
1882, O'Brien later participated in the Fenian Plan of
Campaign, ans was imprisoned in November 1887, following
the deaths of three persons at a rally he was scheduled
to address. Escaping from an Irish courtroom in January
1889, he was subsequently recaptured and served four
months in jail. In 1890, O'Brien skipped bail with activist John Dillon and fled into exile, remaining active
in the republican cause from a distance, as an author
and lecturer.

1440. MacDonagh, Oliver. STATES OF MIND. A STUDY OF ANGLO-
      IRISH CONFLICT 1780-1980. London: George Allen &
      Unwin, 1983.

1441. ————. IRELAND: THE UNION AND ITS AFTERMATH. London:
      George Allen & Unwin, 1977.

1442. ————, W.F. Mandle, and Pauric Travers (eds). IRISH
      CULTURE AND NATIONALISM, 1750-1950. New York: St.
      Martin's Press, 1983.

      Contains item 1435.

1443. MacEntee, Sean. EPISODE AT EASTER. Dublin: Gill & Son,
      1966.

1444. MacEoin, Gary. NORTHERN IRELAND: CAPTIVE OF HISTORY.
      New York: Holt, Rinehart & Winston, 1974.

1445. MacEoin, Uinseann (ed). SURVIVORS. Dublin: Argenta
      Publications, 1980.

1446. MacGiolla, Breandan Choille (ed). INTELLIGENCE NOTES:
      1913-1916. Dublin: Government Publications Office,
      1966.

      Presents formerly-classified police reports from a
      period preceding and including the Easter rising. The
      information to be gathered from these reports should
      be used with caution indicated by the editor in his
      admirable introduction. It must be remembered especial-
      ly that the INTELLIGENCE NOTES are only a precis of
      general reports, which themselves were compiled from a
      multitude of legal documents, and also that the police
      —though knowledgeable—did not know everything, but
      were, in fact frequently isolated from the community.

1447. MacInerney, Michael. THE RIDDLE OF ERSKINE CHILDERS.
      Dublin: The O'Brien Press, 1971.

      Examines the career of a politician who succeeded
      Eamon De Valera as president of Ireland and died in
      office two years later.

1448. MacIntyre, Angus. THE LIBERATOR: DANIEL O'CONNELL AND
      THE IRISH PARTY 1830-1847. London: Hamish Hamilton,
      1965.

1449. MacKnight, Thomas. ULSTER AS IT IS. 2 Vols. London:
      Macmillan & Co., 1896.

1450. MacLochlainn, Piaras Finnbarr (ed). LAST WORDS: LETTERS
      AND STATEMENTS OF THE LEADERS EXECUTED AFTER THE RISING
      AT EASTER 1916. Dublin: Kilmainham Jail Restoration
      Society, 1971.

1451. MacLysaght, Edward. CHANGING TIMES: IRELAND SINCE 1898.
      Bucks, England: Colin Smyth, 1978.

1452. ———. "Larkin, Connolly, and the Labour Movement."
      LEADERS AND MEN OF THE EASTER RISING: DUBLIN 1916.
      Cited below as item 1504, pp. 121-133.

1453. MacManus, Francis (ed). THE YEARS OF THE GREAT TEST
      1926-39. Cork: The Mercier Press, 1967.

      Contains item 1478 below.

1454. MacManus, M.J. EAMON DE VALERA. Dublin: The Talbot
      Press, 1944.

1455. ——— (ed). THOMAS DAVIS AND YOUNG IRELAND. Dublin:
      The Talbot Press, 1945.

1456. MacManus, Seumas (ed). THE YEARS OF THE GREAT TEST,
      1926-1939. Cork: Mercier Press, 1967.

1457. MacNeill, Eoin. PHASES OF IRISH HISTORY. Dublin: M.H.
      Gill & Son, 1920.

      Examines Irish history through the eyes of a Sinn Fein
      activist and spokesman. Appointed chief of staff for
      the Irish Volunteers in 1913, MacNeill participated in
      the Howth gun-running incident, but he opposed the Easter
      rising in the planning stages. Using his position as IV

chief of staff to countermand orders from Patrick Pearse,
MacNeill created chaos among rebel forces. He was generally blamed for the failure of the rising, but Pearse
and Thomas MacDonagh exonerated him of all blame prior
to their execution. Reconciled with De Valera in prison,
where they served time together in 1916-17, MacNeill
later held various high-ranking posts in the Irish government.

1458. MacNeill, John Gordon Swift. THE IRISH ACT OF UNION AND
HOW IT WAS CARRIED. Dublin: Talbot, 1912.

1459. MacNeill, R.J. ULSTER'S STAND FOR UNION. Belfast: J.
Cleeland, 1906.

1460. MacVeagh, Jeremiah. HOME RULE IN A NUTSHELL. A POCKET
BOOK FOR SPEAKERS AND ELECTORS. London: Daily Chronicle, 1911.

1461. ———. "HOME RULE OR ROME RULE." THE TRUTH ABOUT RE-
LIGIOUS INTOLERANCE IN IRELAND. Sheffield: 1912.

1462. McAnally, Sir Henry William Watson. THE IRISH MILITIA,
1793-1816: A SOCIAL AND MILITARY STUDY. Dublin: Clonmore & Reynolds, 1949.

1463. McCaffrey, Lawrence J. DANIEL O'CONNELL AND THE REPEAL
YEAR. Lexington, Ky.: University of Kentucky Press,
1966.

1464. ———. THE IRISH QUESTION 1800-1922. Lexington, Ky.:
University of Kentucky Press, 1968.

1465. ——— (ed). IRISH NATIONALISM AND THE AMERICAN CONTRI-
BUTION. New York: Arno Press, 1976.

1466. McCann, Eamon. WAR IN AN IRISH TOWN. Middlesex: Penguin,
1974.

1467, McCartan, Patrick. WITH DE VALERA IN AMERICA. Dublin:
Fitzpatrick, 1932.

1468. McCarthy, Michael John Fitzgerald. THE IRISH REVOLUTION
VOL. 1: THE MURDERING TIME, FROM THE LAND LEAGUE TO
THE FIRST HOME RULE BILL. Edinburgh: William Black-
wood & Sons, 1912.

1469. McCartney, Donal. "The Church and Fenians." FENIANS
      AND FENIANISM. Cited above as item 1325, pp. 11-23.

1470, ———. "De Valera's Mission to the United States."
      STUDIES IN IRISH HISTORY. Cited above as item 1205,
      pp. 304-423.

1471. ———. "The Sinn Fein Movemenr." THE MAKING OF 1916.
      Cited below as item 1546, pp. 31-47.

1472. McCay, Hedley. PADRAIC PEARSE. Cork: Mercier Press,
      1966.

1473. McClelland, Aiken. "The Later Orange Order." SECRET
      SOCIETIES IN IRELAND. Cited below as item 1735, pp.
      126-137.

1474. McColl, Rene. ROGER CASEMENT: A NEW JUDGEMENT. London:
      1956.

1475. McCord, Norman. "The Fenians and Public Opinion in
      Great Britain." FENIANS AND FENIANISM. Cited above
      as item 1345, pp. 35-48.

1476. McCracken, John Leslie. "The Consequences of the Land
      War." ULSTER SINCE 1800: A POLITICAL AND ECONOMIC
      SURVEY. Cited below as item 1526, pp. 60-69.

1477. ———. "Northern Ireland, 1921-66." THE COURSE OF
      IRISH HISTORY. Cited below as item 1527.

1478. ———. "The Political Scene in Northern Ireland,
      1926-57." THE YEARS OF THE GREAT TEST, 1926-39.
      Cited above as item 1453.

1479. McDowell, Robert Brendan. PUBLIC OPINION AND GOVERNMENT
      IN IRELAND, 1801-1846. London: Faber & Faber, 1952.

      Presents a comprehensive study of the political atmos-
      phere in the pre-famine period, including a digest of
      the many strands of opinion in Ireland which helped
      form (1) the Volunteer movement and the first active
      display of Protestant Irish patriotism, (2) the radical
      movement which developed from that, and (3) the state
      of mind which accepted Union.

142   TERRORISM IN THE UNITED STATES AND EUROPE

1480. McGuffin, John. INTERNMENT. Tralee: Anvil Books, 1973.

1481. McGruire, James K. WHAT COULD GERMANY DO FOR IRELAND?
New York: Wolf Tone Co., 1916.

1482. McHugh, Roger. "Casement and German Help." LEADERS
AND MEN OF THE EASTER RISING: DUBLIN 1916. Cited
below as item 1507.

1483. ———— (ed). DUBLIN 1916. London: Arlington Books, 1966

1484. McNeill, Ronald. ULSTER'S STAND FOR UNION. London:
John Murray, 1922.

1485, Macardle, Dorothy. THE IRISH REPUBLIC: A DOCUMENTED
CHRONICLE OF THE ANGLO-IRISH CONFLICT AND THE PAR-
TITIONING OF IRELAND WITH A DETAILED ACCOUNT OF THE
PERIOD 1916-1923. London: Victor Gollancz, 1937.

Presents the most detailed available study of Ireland's
rebellious era, firmly biased toward the republican side
of the struggle. Contains an encyclopedic wealth of information on the Easter rising and civil war, including
republican perspectives on the eventual treaty and
boundary disputes between Ulster and the Irish state.

1486. ————. "James Connolly and Patrick Pearse." THE SHAP-
ING OF MODERN IRELAND. Cited below as item 1552, pp.
185-195.

1487. Macken, Ultan. THE STORY OF DANIEL O'CONNELL. Cork:
Mercier Press, 1976.

1488. Mackey, Herbert O. THE LIFE AND TIMES OF ROGER CASE-
MENT. Dublin: Apollo Press, 1954.

1489. Madden, Richard R. THE UNITED IRISHMEN, THEIR LIVES
AND TIMES. 7 Vols. London: J. Madden, 1842-1846.

1490. ————. THE LIFE AND TIMES OF ROBERT EMMET, ESQ. Dublin: James Duffy, 1847.

1491. Magee, John. NORTHERN IRELAND: CRISIS AND CONFLICT.
London: Routledge & Kegan Paul, 1974.

1492. Malins, Edward. YEATS AND THE EASTER RISING. Dublin:
Domen Press, 1965.

Presents transcripts of lectures delivered at Yeats International Summer School in Sligo, in August 1962.

1493. Manhattan, Auro. RELIGIOUS TERROR IN IRELAND. London: Paravision Books, 1973.

Describes "subversion" by the Catholic church in Ulster, promoting the Protestant (UVF) view that Catholics in general, and the IRA in particular, are responsible for all terrorist violence in Northern Ireland. An interesting look at the militant Protestant mind.

1494. Manning, Maurice. THE BLUESHIRTS. Dublin: Gill & Macmillan, 1970.

Examines the history of the Army Comrades Association, dubbed Blueshirts after the uniforms adopted by the group in April 1933. Drawing inspiration from Mussolini's fascist regime in Italy, Blueshirts vigorously opposed the Sinn Fein government of Eamon De Valera and clashed with members of the IRA. The organization merged with the National Center Party in September 1933, creating the new United Ireland Party. Steady decline through the mid-1930s ended with dissolution of the Blueshirts after a brigade was sent to aid Franco's fascist rebels in the Spanish civil war.

1495. Mansbach, Richard W. (ed). NORTHERN IRELAND: HALF A CENTURY OF PARTITION. New York: Facts on File, 1973, pp. 9-20.

1496. Mansergh, Nicholas. BRITAIN AND IRELAND. London: Longmans, Green, and Co., 1942, pp. 22-96.

Offers liberal, conservative, and Sinn Fein "solutions" to continuing Irish turmoil, contained within an official British Commonwealth publication.

1497. ————. THE GOVERNMENT OF NORTHERN IRELAND: A STUDY IN DEVOLUTION. London: G. Allen & Unwin, 1936.

1498. ————. IRELAND IN THE AGE OF REFORM AND REVOLUTION. London: Allen & Unwin, 1940.

1499. ————. THE IRISH QUESTION 1840-1921. Toronto: University of Toronto Press, 1967.

Completely revises and updates item 1498.

1500. ————. "Ireland and the British Commonwealth of Nations the Dominion Settlement." THE IRISH STRUGGLE 1916-1926 Cited below as item 1734.

1501. ————. "Ireland: External Relations 1926-1939." THE YEARS OF THE GREAT TEST. Cited above as item 1453.

1502. Marrecco, Anne. THE REBEL COUNTESS: THE LIFE AND TIMES OF CONSTANCE MARKIEVICZ. Philadelphia: Chilton Books, 1967.

Profiles the rebellious career of a Sinn Fein spokesperson who quarreled with leader Arthur Griffith over his adherence to nonviolent tactics. In 1918, Countess Markievicz became the first woman elected to the House of Commons, but she spent much of the next three years in prison for her militant republican activities. Jailed again in 1923-24 for her support of guerilla forces in the Irish civil war, she ran for office once more in 1927, but died in the midst of her campaign.

1503. Marrinan, Patrick. PAISLEY. MAN OF WRATH. Tralee: 1973.

1504. Martin, Francis X. (ed). THE EASTER RISING 1916, AND UNIVERSITY COLLEGE, DUBLIN. Dublin: Browne & Nolan, 1966.

Contains items 1354, 1436, and 1593.

1505. ———— (ed). THE HOWTH GUN-RUNNING AND THE KILCOOLE GUN-RUNNING, 1914. Dublin: Browne & Nolan, 1964.

1506. ————. THE IRISH VOLUNTEERS, 1913-1915. Dublin: James Duffy & Co., 1963.

1507. ———— (ed). LEADERS AND MEN OF THE EASTER RISING: DUBLIN, 1916. London: Methuen & Co., 1967.

Contains items 1483, 1508, 1545, 1578, 1608, 1693, 1708, and 1733.

1508. ————. "McCullough, Hobson and Republican Ulster." LEADERS AND MEN OF THE EASTER RISING: DUBLIN, 1916. Cited above as item 1507.

1509. ————. "The Origins of the Irish Rising of 1916." THE IRISH STRUGGLE, 1916-1926. Cited below as item 1734.

1510. ————, and Francis J. Byrne (eds). THE SCHOLAR REVO-
       LUTIONARY: EOIN MACNEILL, 1867-1945, AND THE MAKING
       OF THE NEW IRELAND. Shannon: Irish University Press,
       1973.

1511. Martin, Hugh. INSURRECTION IN IRELAND OR IRELAND IN
       INSURRECTION. AN ENGLISHMAN'S RECORD. London: The
       Author, 1921.

1512. Marx, Karl, and Friederich Engels. IRELAND AND THE
       IRISH PROBLEM: A COLLECTION OF WRITINGS. New York:
       International Publishers, 1945.

1513. Maxwell, W.H. HISTORY OF THE IRISH REBELLION IN 1798;
       WITH MEMOIRS OF THE UNION AND ROBERT EMMET'S INSURREC-
       TION OF 1803. New York: Charles Scribner & Co., 1845,
       pp. 399-433.

1514. Miller, David W. CHURCH, STATE AND NATION IN IRELAND:
       1898-1921. Pittsburgh: University of Pittsburgh Press,
       1973.

1515. ————. QUEEN'S REBELS: ULSTER LOYALISM IN HISTORICAL
       PERSPECTIVE. Dublin: Gill & Macmillan, 1978, pp. 51-
       139.

1516. Mitchel, John. JAIL JOURNAL. PRISONER IN THE HANDS OF
       THE ENGLISH. Dublin: Gill & Macmillan, 1913.

1517. ————. THE LAST CONQUEST OF IRELAND (PERHAPS). Glas-
       gow: The Author, 1876.

1518. Moley, Richard. DANIEL O'CONNELL, NATIONALISM WITHOUT
       VIOLENCE. New York: Fordham University Press, 1974.

1519. Molony, John Chartres. IRELAND'S TRAGIC COMEDIANS.
       Freeport, N.Y.: Books for Library Press, 1934, pp.
       233-312.

       Pages cited cover the career of agrarian rebel Robert
       Emmet.

1520. Monteith, Robert. CASEMENT'S LAST ADVENTURE. Dublin:
       F. Moynihan, 1953.

1521. Moody, T.W. DAVITT AND IRISH REVOLUTION, 1846-82.
       Oxford: Clarendon House, 1981.

Profiles a member of the Irish Revolutionary Brotherhood, active in the February 1867 raid on Chester Castle.
Davitt was chief arms purchaser for the Fenians until
1870, when he was jailed for fifteen years on a dubious
charge of incitement to murder. Released after seven
years of harsh treatment, he spent two years in the
United States before returning to Ireland and active
participation in the land wars of the 1880s. More
prison time followed, but in 1892 he was elected to parliament, where he supported the cause of Irish home rule.

1522. ————. "Michael Davitt." LEADERS AND WORKERS. Cited
      above as item 1136.

1523. ————. THOMAS DAVIS 1814-1845. Dublin: Hodges, Figgis,
      1945.

1524. ————. THE ULSTER QUESTION, 1603-1973. Cork: Mercier
      Press, 1967.

1525. ———— (ed). THE FENIAN MOVEMENT. Cork: Mercier Press,
      1968.

1526. ————, and F.X. Martin (eds). THE COURSE OF IRISH
      HISTORY. Cork: Mercier Press, 1967.

      Contains item 1476.

1527. ————, and J.C. Beckett (eds). ULSTER SINCE 1800: A
      POLITICAL AND ECONOMIC SURVEY. London: British Broad-
      casting Co., 1955.

      Contains item 1477.

1528. Mowat, Charles Loch. BRITAIN BETWEEN THE WARS, 1918-
      1940. Chicago: University of Chicago Press, 1955.

1529. ————. "The Irish Question in British Politics (1916-
      1922)." THE IRISH STRUGGLE 1916-1926. Cited below
      as item 1734.

1530. Mulligan, Martin (ed). IRELAND UNFREE. Sydney:
      Pathfinder Press, 1981, pp. 135-144.

      Contains items 1292 and 1293. Includes a chronology
      of violent events spanning 800 years, with various essays
      generally sympathetic to the IRA.

1531. Munck, Ronnie. IRELAND: NATION, STATE AND CLASS STRUG-
      GLE. Colorado: Westview Books, 1985.

1532. Murphy, John A. IRELAND IN THE TWENTIETH CENTURY. Dub-
      lin: Gill & Macmillan, 1975.

1533. ———. "The New IRA, 1925-1962." SECRET SOCIETIES IN
      IRELAND. Cited below as item 1735, pp. 150-165.

1534. Neeson, Eoin. THE CIVIL WAR IN IRELAND, 1921-1923.
      Cork: The Mercier Press, 1966.

1535. ———. THE LIFE AND DEATH OF MICHAEL COLLINS. Cork:
      The Mercier Press, 1968.

1536. Neligan, David. THE SPY IN THE CASTLE. London: MacGib-
      bon & Kee, 1968.

      Presents the author's memoirs of service with Michael
      Collins as republican intelligence agents during the
      civil war era.

1537. Nelson, Sarah. ULSTER'S UNCERTAIN DEFENDERS: PROTESTANT,
      POLITICAL, PARAMILITARY AND COMMUNIST GROUPS AND THE
      NORTHERN IRELAND CONFLICT. Syracuse, N.Y.: Appletree
      Press, 1984.

1538. Nevin, D. "The Irish Citizen Army." 1916: THE EASTER
      RISING. Cited above as item 1264.

1539. Norman, Edward R. ANTI-CATHOLICISM IN VICTORIAN ENGLAND.
      New York: Barnes & Noble, 1968.

1540. ———. THE CATHOLIC CHURCH AND IRELAND IN THE AGE OF
      REBELLION, 1859-1873. Ithaca, N.Y.: Cornell University
      Press, 1965.

1541. Northern Friends Peace Board. ORANGE AND GREEN: A
      QUAKER STUDY OF COMMUNITY RELATIONS IN NORTHERN IRE-
      LAND. Sedbergh, Yorkshire: N.F.P.B., 1969.

1542. Norway, Mrs. Hamilton. THE SINN FEIN REBELLION AS I
      SAW IT. London: Smith, Elder & Co., 1916.

1543. Nowlan, Kevin B. "Dail Eireann and the Army: Unity and
      Division, 1916-1922." THE IRISH STRUGGLE. Cited
      below as item 1734.

1544. ———. "The Meaning of Repeal in Irish History."
       HISTORICAL STUDIES IV. Cited above as item 1356.

1545. ———. "Tom Clarke, McDermott and the IRB." LEADERS
       AND MEN OF THE EASTER REBELLION: DUBLIN 1916. Cited
       above as item 1507.

1546. ——— (ed). THE MAKING OF 1916; STUDIES IN THE HISTORY
       OF THE RISING. Dublin: Healy Thom, 1969.

       Contains items 1134, 1357, 1471, 1573, 1720, and 1721.

1547. ———, and Maurice R. O'Connell (eds). DANIEL O'CONNELL
       PORTRAIT OF A RADICAL. New York: Fordham University
       Press, 1985.

1548. ———, and T. Desmond Williams (eds). IRELAND IN THE
       WAR YEARS AND AFTER 1939-51. Dublin: Gill & Macmillan,
       1969.

       Contains item 1393.

1549. O'Ballance, Edgar. TERROR IN IRELAND: THE HERITAGE OF
       HATE. Novato, Calif.: Presidio Press, 1981.

1550. O'Brien, Conor Cruise. "The Embers of Easter." 1916:
       THE EASTER RISING. Cited above as item 1264.

1551. ———. PARNELL AND HIS PARTY, 1880-90. Oxford: The
       Clarendon Press, 1957.

       Offers a detailed examination of the membership and
       organization of the home rule party under Parnell's
       leadership. An authoritative and specialized work,
       including an impressive analysis of the composition
       of the parliamentarians.

1552. ——— (ed). THE SHAPING OF MODERN IRELAND. London:
       Routledge & Kegan Paul, 1960.

       Contains items 1486 and 1727.

1553. O'Brien, Francis W. DIVIDED IRELAND: THE ROOTS OF THE
       CONFLICT. Rockford, Ill.: Rockford College Press,
       1971.

1554. O'Brien, Nora Connolly. WE SHALL RISE AGAIN. London:
       Mosquito Press, 1981.

Presents a less than objective view of Irish turmoil,
authored by the daughter of James Connolly. Personal
recollections and insight are interesting, but contri-
bute little new historical information.

1555. O'Brien, Richard Barry. THE LIFE OF CHARLES STEWART
PARNELL, 1846-1891. 2 Vols. London: Smith, Elder and
Co., 1898.

1556. ———. THOMAS DRUMMOND: UNDER-SECRETARY IN IRELAND,
1835-40. London: K. Paul, Trench & Co., 1889.

Examines the career of a tolerant and constructive
Irish politician, who encouraged Catholics to join the
Royal Irish Constabulary in the 1830s. Drummond's handling of unrest over tithes—converting land tithes to
fixed rents and eliminating the use of troops in rent
collection—led to a sharp decline in violent protest
during 1840. Drummond's stance made him very unpopular
with landlords, but he remained a champion of the Irish
people until his death in office, following a chronic
illness.

1557. O'Brien, William. THE IRISH REVOLUTION AND HOW IT CAME
ABOUT. London: George Allen & Unwin, 1923.

1558. O'Broin, Leon. CHARLES GAVAN DUFFY: PATRIOT AND STATES-
MAN...1816-1903. Dublin: J. Duffy, 1967.

1559. ———. DUBLIN CASTLE AND THE 1916 RISING. Dublin:
Helicon, 1966.

1560. ———. FENIAN FEVER: AN ANGLO-IRISH DILEMMA. London:
Chatto & Windus, 1971.

1561. ———. THE PRIME INFORMER, A SUPPRESSED SCANDAL.
London: Sidgwick & Jackson, 1971.

Profiles a noted Nazi sympathizer and propagandist,
William Joyce, who was educated in Ireland and subsequently moved to England, there joining Oswald Mosley's
British Union of Fascists in 1933. Expelled four years
later, Joyce formed his own National Socialist League,
departing England for Germany in 1939. Dubbed "Lord
Haw-Haw," after his mock British accent, adopted for
propaganda broadcasts on the radio, Joyce became a
naturalized German citizen in 1940. Captured near the
Danish border in 1945, he was returned to London, tried
for treason, and hanged.

1562. ———. PROTESTANT NATIONALISTS IN REVOLUTIONARY IRE-
      LAND. Dublin: 1985.

1563. ———. REVOLUTIONARY UNDERGROUND: THE STORY OF THE
      IRISH REPUBLICAN BROTHERHOOD, 1858-1924. Dublin:
      Gill & Macmillan, 1976.

1564. ———. THE UNFORTUNATE MR. ROBERT EMMET. Dublin:
      Clonmore & Reynolds, 1958.

1565. O'Callaghan, Sean. THE EASTER LILLY. THE STORY OF THE
      I.R.A. London: Allen Wingate, 1956.

      Presents an excellent inside account of the IRA, from
      a member who joined in 1934. The text covers activities
      of the Blueshirts, raids for arms, the Broy Harriers,
      and IRA bombing campaigns in England.

1566. O'Casey, Sean. DRUMS UNDER THE WINDOW. London: Mac-
      millan & Co., 1945.

1567. ———. THE STORY OF THE IRISH CITIZEN ARMY. Dublin:
      Maunsel & Co., 1919.

1568. O'Connor, Batt. WITH MICHAEL COLLINS IN THE FIGHT FOR
      IRISH INDEPENDENCE. London: Peter Davies, 1929.

1569. O'Connor, Frank. THE BIG FELLOW: A LIFE OF MICHAEL
      COLLINS. London: T. Nelson & Sons, 1937.

1570. ———. THE BIG FELLOW: MICHAEL COLLINS AND THE IRISH
      REVOLUTION. Dublin: Clonmore & Reynolds, 1965.

1571. ———. DEATH IN DUBLIN: MICHAEL COLLINS AND THE IRISH
      REVOLUTION. New York: Doubleday, 1937.

1572. O'Connor, Ulick. A TERRIBLE BEAUTY IS BORN. THE IRISH
      TROUBLES, 1912-1922. London: Hamish Hamilton, 1975.

1573. O'Cuiv, Brian. "The Gaelic Cultural Movements and the
      New Nationalism" THE MAKING OF 1916. Cited above
      as item 1546.

1574. O'Day, Alan. PARNELL AND THE FIRST HOME RULE EPISODE,
      1884-87. Dublin: Gill & Macmillan, 1986.

1575. O'Doherty, Eamonn. THE I.R.A. AT WAR 1916 TO THE PRES-
      ENT. Cork: Mercier Press, 1985.

Billed by the author as "not a history of the IRA, but an attempt by the use of available photos to trace the career of an organisation whose roots go back to at least the 18th century." Heavily illustrated with photos, also including a list of IRA war dead and executed "martyrs."

1576. O'Donnell, Charles James. OUTRAGED ULSTER: WHY IRELAND IS REBELLIOUS. London: Cecil Palmer, 1932.

1577. O'Donnell, Patrick. THE IRISH FACTION FIGHTERS OF THE 19th CENTURY. Dublin: 1975.

1578. O'Donoghue, F. "Ceannt, Devoy, O'Rahlly and the Military Plan." LEADERS AND MEN OF THE EASTER RISING: DUBLIN 1916. Cited above as item 1507.

1579. O'Donoghue, Florence. NO OTHER LAW (THE STORY OF LIAM LYNCH AND THE IRISH REPUBLICAN ARMY 1916-1923). Dublin: Irish Press, 1954.

1580. ————. THE IRB AND THE RISING. London: 1956.

1581. ————. THOMAS MacCURTAIN. Tralee: Anvil Books, 1971.

Profiles a Sinn Fein politician who became the first republican Lord Mayor of Cork in 1920. Active in Irish guerilla organizations from 1907 through the Easter rising, MacCurtain was assassinated at his home in March 1920. A coroner's report blamed the assassination on specific policemen assigned to the Royal Irish Constabulary, one of whom was later killed in reprisal by "persons unknown."

1582. O'Dubhghaill, M. (ed). INSURRECTION FIRES AT EASTERTIDE. Cork: The Mercier Press, 1966.

1583. O'Duffy, Eimar. THE WASTED LAND. Dublin: M. Lester, 1919.

1584. O'Faolain, Sean. CONSTANCE MARKIEVIECZ: OR THE AVERAGE REVOLUTIONARY: A BIOGRAPHY. London: Jonathan Cape, 1934.

1585. ————. KING OF THE BEGGARS: A LIFE OF DANIEL O'CONNELL. London: Nelson, 1938.

1586. ————. DE VALERA. Harmondsworth, England: Penguin Books, 1939.

1587. O'Farrell. Fergus. CATHOLIC EMANCIPATION, DANIEL O'CON-
      NELL AND THE BIRTH OF IRISH DEMOCRACY, 1820-30. Dub-
      lin: Gill & Macmillan, 1985.

1588. ————. DANIEL O'CONNELL. Dublin: Gill & Macmillan,
      1981.

1589. O'Farrell, Patrick. ENGLAND AND IRELAND SINCE 1800.
      New York: Oxford University Press, 1975.

      Presents a New Zealander's view that, while violence
      and prejudice are abhorrent, they have been effective
      forces in Anglo-Irish affairs.

1590. ————. IRELAND'S ENGLISH QUESTION: ANGLO-IRISH RELA-
      TIONS, 1534-1970. London: Batsford, 1971.

1591. ————. WHO'S WHO IN THE IRISH WAR OF INDEPENDENCE,
      1916-1921. Dublin: Mercier Press, 1980.

1592. O'Flaherty, Liam. CIVIL WAR. London: E. Archer, 1925.

1593. ————. FAMINE. London: Victor Gollancz, 1937.

1594. ————. INSURRECTION. London: Gollancz, 1950.

1595. ————. THE LIFE OF TIM HEALY. London: Jonathan Cape,
      1927.

1596. ————. THE TERRORIST. London: E. Archer, 1926.

1597. O'Hannigan, D. "Origins and Activities of the First
      Flying Column." LIMERICK'S FIGHTING STORY. Cited
      above as item 1435, pp. 85-87.

1598. O'Hegarty, Patrick Sarsfield. A HISTORY OF IRELAND UNDER
      THE UNION, 1801-1922. London: Methuen & Co., 1952.

      Easily the most readable survey of Irish nationalism,
      enlivened at points by the author's distinctive republi-
      can bias. O'Hegarty, a former member of the Irish Re-
      publican Brotherhood, includes a nationalist interpre-
      tation of the Great Famine.

1599. ————. SINN FEIN: AN ILLUMINATION. Dublin: Maunsel &
      Co., 1919.

1600. ————. ULSTER. A BRIEF STATEMENT OF FACT. Dublin:
      Maunsel & Co., 1919.

1601. ————. THE VICTORY OF SINN FEIN. HOW IT WON IT, AND
      HOW IT USED IT. Dublin: The Talbot Press, 1924.

1602. O'Higgins, Brian. THE SOLDIER'S STORY OF EASTER WEEK.
      Dublin: Brian O hUigginn, 1925.

1603. O'Higgins, Kevin. CIVIL WAR AND THE EVENTS WHICH LED TO
      IT. Dublin: The Talbot Press, 1922.

1604. O'Kelly, Seamus. THE GLORIOUS SEVEN, 1916-1966. [BRIEF
      BIOGRAPHIES OF SEVEN IRISH REVOLUTIONARIES. WITH IL-
      LUSTRATIONS.] Dublin: Irish News Service, 1965.

1605. O'Leary, John. RECOLLECTIONS OF FENIANS AND FENIANISM.
      2 Vols. London: Downey & Co., 1896.

1606. Oliver, Frederick Scott. THE ANVIL OF WAR. London:
      Macmillan & Co., 1936.

1607. ————. THE IRISH QUESTION: FEDERATION OR SECESSION.
      New York: Civil Service Print Co., n.d.

1608. O'Luing, Sean. "Arthur Griffith and Sinn Fein." LEAD-
      ERS AND MEN OF THE EASTER RISING: DUBLIN 1916. Cited
      above as item 1507, pp. 55-65.

1609. ————. I DIE IN A GOOD CAUSE: A STUDY OF THOMAS ASHE,
      IDEALIST AND REVOLUTIONARY. Dublin: Anvil Books, 1970.

Profiles a republican martyr who led the local force
of Irish Volunteers at Ashbourne, County Meath, in the
Easter rising of 1916. Sentenced to life imprisonment
by court martial, Ashe was released in the general amnesty of 1917 and became an active Sinn Fein organizer.
Arrested in August of that year, on charges of inciting
the civil population, he was sentenced to another two
years in prison, there organizing a hunger strike among
political prisoners. Ashe died in September 1917,
while being forcibly fed by his jailers. A two-month
inquest censured those responsible for his death.

1610. O'Malley, Earnan. ARMY WITHOUT BANNERS. London: Four
      Square Books, 1936.

Examines the Easter rising from an IRA perspective,

prepared by a captain of the Third Tipperary Brigade.
Wounded and imprisoned in 1922, his sentence of death
was eventually commuted and he was elected to the Irish
parliament, refusing to take his seat when he learned
an oath of allegiance to Britain was required. O'Malley
spent two years with Basque separatists in Spain before
returning home to Ireland and the life of an author.

1611. ———. ON ANOTHER MAN'S WOUND. London: Four Square
      Books, 1936.

1612. ———. THE SINGING FLAME. Dublin: Anvil Books, 1978.

1613. O'Neil, Daniel J. THREE PERENNIAL THEMES OF ANTI-
      COLONIALISM: THE IRISH CASE. Denver: University of
      Denver, 1976.

      Examines themes of self-reliance, self-sacrifice, and
      exploitation, as personified by major players in the
      Irish melodrama. In the author's opinion, Arthur Grif-
      fith represented self-reliance, Patrick Pearse embodied
      self-sacrifice, and James Connolly displayed the charac-
      teristics of exploitation.

1614. O'Neill, Brian. THE WAR FOR THE LAND IN IRELAND. Lon-
      don: Martin Lawrence, 1933.

1615. ———. EASTER WEEK. London: Martin Lawrence, 1936.

1616. O'Suilleabhain, Michael. WHERE MOUNTAINY MEN HAVE SOWN.
      Tralee: Anvil Books, 1965.

      Presents an account of war and peace in rebel Cork,
      between the years 1916 and 1921.

1617. O'Suilleabhain, Sean. "The Iveragh Fenians in Oral
      Tradition." FENIANS AND FENIANISM. Cited above as
      item 1345, pp. 24-34.

1618. Pakenham, Francis. PEACE BY ORDEAL. London: Jonathan
      Cape, 1935.

1619. Palmer, N. Dunbar. THE IRISH LAND LEAGUE CRISIS. New
      Haven, Conn.: Yale Historical Publications, 1940.

1620. Palmer, S.H. POLICE AND PROTEST IN ENGLAND AND IRELAND,
      1780-1850: THE ORIGINS OF MODERN POLICE FORCES. Cam-
      bridge, Mass.: Harvard University Press, 1973.

1621. Parmiter, Geoffrey de Clinton. ROGER CASEMENT. London:
      Arthur Barker, 1936.

1622. Parnell, John Howard. CHARLES STEWART PARNELL, A MEMOIR.
      New York: Henry Holt & Co., 1914.

1623. Paul, W. THE IRISH CRISIS, 1921. London: Communist
      Party of Great Britain, 1921.

1624. Paul-Dubois, Louis Francois Alphonse. THE IRISH STRUG-
      GLE AND ITS RESULTS. London: Longmans, Green & Co.,
      1934.

1625. Pearse, Padraic H. COLLECTED WORKS OF PADRAIC H. PEARSE.
      5 Vols. Dublin: The Phoenix Publishing Co., 1924.

1626. Phillips, W. Alison. THE REVOLUTION IN IRELAND, 1906-
      1923. London: Longmans, Green & Co., 1923.

1627. Pigott, Richard. PERSONAL RECOLLECTIONS OF AN IRISH
      NATIONAL JOURNALIST. Dublin: Hodges, Figgis & Co.,
      1883.

1628. Pollard, Hugh Bertie Campbell. THE SECRET SOCIETIES OF
      IRELAND, THEIR RISE AND PROGRESS. London: P. Allan
      & Co., 1922.

1629. Pomfret, John E. THE STRUGGLE FOR LAND IN IRELAND 1800-
      1923. Princeton, N.J.: Princeton University Press, 1930.

1630. Postgate, Raymond W. ROBERT EMMET. London: Martin
      Secker, 1931.

1631. Prill, Felician. IRELAND, BRITAIN AND GERMANY, 1871-
      1914. PROBLEMS OF NATIONALISM AND RELIGION IN NINE-
      TEENTH CENTURY EUROPE. Dublin: Gill & Macmillan, 1975.

1632. Provisional IRA. FREEDOM STRUGGLE. London: Red Books,
      1933.

1633. Purdie, Bob. IRELAND UNFREE. London: 1972.

1634. ————, and Austen Morgan (eds). IRELAND, DIVIDED NATION,
      DIVIDED CLASS. London: Ink Links, 1980.

1635. REBEL CORK'S FIGHTING STORY. Tralee: Anchor Books.

1636. Redmond-Howard, L.G.   SIX DAYS OF THE IRISH REPUBLIC.
       Dublin: The Author, 1916.

1637. Reed, David.   IRELAND: THE KEY TO THE BRITISH REVOLUTION.
       London: Larkin Publishers, 1984.

1638. Reeve, Carl.   JAMES CONNOLLY AND THE UNITED STATES: THE
       ROAD TO THE 1916 IRISH REBELLION.   Atlantic Highland,
       N.J.: Humanities Press, 1978.

1639. Reynolds, J.A.   THE CATHOLIC EMANCIPATION CRISIS IN IRE-
       LAND, 1823-29.   New Haven, Conn.: Yale University Press
       1954.

1640. Riddell, Lord.   INTIMATE DIARY OF THE PEACE CONFERENCE
       AND AFTER, 1918-1923.   London: Ivor Nicholson & Watson,
       1933.

1641. Riddell, Patrick.   FIRE OVER ULSTER.   London: Hamilton,
       1970.

1642. Roberts, Paul E.W.   "Caravats and Shanavests: Whiteboyism
       and Faction Fighting in East Munster, 1802-11."   IRISH
       PEASANTS, VIOLENCE & POLITICAL UNREST, 1780-1914.
       Cited above as 1180, pp. 64-101.

1643. Roebuck, Peter (ed).   PLANTATION TO PARTITION: ESSAYS IN
       ULSTER HISTORY IN HONOUR OF J.L. McCRACKEN.   Belfast:
       Blackstaff Press, 1981.

       Contains item 1718 below.

1644. Rose, Paul.   THE MANCHESTER MARTYRS. THE STORY OF A
       FENIAN TRAGEDY.   London: Lawrence & Wishart, 1970.

1645. Rose, Richard.   GOVERNING WITHOUT CONSENSUS.   London:
       Faber & Faber, 1971.

1646. Rumpf, E., and A.C. Hepburn.   NATIONALISM AND SOCIALISM
       IN TWENTIETH CENTURY IRELAND.   New York: Barnes & Noble,
       1977.

1647. Russell, George.   CO-OPERATION AND NATIONALITY: A GUIDE
       FOR RURAL REFORMERS FROM THIS TO THE NEXT GENERATION.
       Dublin: Maunsel & Co., 1912.

1648. ————.   THE DUBLIN STRIKE.   Dublin: Irish Worker Press,
       1913.

1649. ————. A PLEA FOR JUSTICE. Dublin: The Irish Homestead. 1920.

1650. Russell, T.O. IS IRELAND A DYING NATION? Dublin: M.H. Gill & Son, 1906.

1651. Rutherford, J. THE SECRET HISTORY OF THE FENIAN CONSPIRACY, ITS ORIGINS, OBJECTS AND RAMIFICATIONS. 2 vols. London: C. Kegan Paul & Co., 1877.

Draws on official police records to present a fascinating account of the Fenian movement. Flawed by numerous small inaccuracies, Rutherford's work examines Fenian activities from the perspective of a Unionist reporter with government connections. Heavily criticized (and, to some extent, unfairly so) by Fenian apologists.

1652. Ryan, A.P. MUTINY AT THE CURRAGH. London: Macmillan & Co., 1956.

1653. Ryan, Desmond. THE FENIAN CHIEF: A BIOGRAPHY OF JAMES STEPHEN. Dublin: H.M. Gill & Son, 1967.

1654. ————. JAMES CONNOLLY: HIS LIFE AND WORK. Dublin: Talbot Press, 1924.

1655. ————. THE MAN CALLED PEARSE. Dublin: Maunsel & Co., 1919.

1656. ————. MICHAEL COLLINS AND THE INVISIBLE ARMY. London: Arthur Barker, 1932.

1657. ————. THE PHOENIX FLAME: A STUDY OF FENIAN JOHN DEVOY. London: Arthur Barker, 1937.

1658. ————. REMEMBERING SION. London: Arthur Barker, 1934.

1659. ————. THE RISING: THE COMPLETE STORY OF EASTER WEEK. Dublin: Standard House, 1949.

1660. ————. "Sinn Fein Policy and Practice." THE IRISH STRUGGLE, 1916-26. Cited below as item 1734.

1661. ————. UNIQUE DICTATOR: A STUDY OF EAMON DE VALERA. London: Arthur Barker, 1936.

1662. Ryan, Mark. FENIAN MEMORIES. Dublin: M.H. Gill & Son, 1645.

1663. Ryan, Meda. THE TOM BARRY STORY. Cork: Mercier Press, 1962.

1664. Ryan, William P. LABOUR REVOLT AND LARKINISM. London: The Daily Herald, 1913.

1665. Savage, John. FENIAN HEROES AND MARTYRS. Boston; The Author, 1868.

    Examines the history of the Irish Revolutionary Brother-hood from the prospective of a one-time "center," or section leader, of the secret society. Predictably biased as it is, Savage's account remains readable and informa-tive.

1666. Sawyer, Roger. CASEMENT, THE FLAWED HERO. London: Routledge & Kegan Paul, 1984.

1667. Schaeffer, Werner. ENGLAND'S OPPRESSION OF IRELAND. Berlin: M. Muller & Fils, 1940.

    Discourses on the Irish question from a Nazi viewpoint, originally published as a piece of anti-British propa-ganda in wartime.

1668. Schutz, Barry M. NATIVES AND SETTLERS: A COMPARATIVE ANALYSIS OF THE POLITICS OF OPPOSITION AND MOBILIZA-TION IN NORTHERN IRELAND AND RHODESIA. Denver: Uni-versity of Denver Press, 1974.

1669. Senior, Herewood. ORANGEISM IN IRELAND AND BRITAIN, 1795-1836. London: Routledge & Kegan Paul, 1966.

1670. ———. "The Place of Fenianism in the Irish Republican Tradition." FENIANS AND FENIANISM. Cited above as item 1345, pp. 58-67.

1671. Shaw, George Bernard. THE MATTER WITH IRELAND. David H. Greene and Dan H. Lawrence editors. London: Rupert Hart-Davis, 1962.

1672. Shea, Patrick. VOICES AND THE SOUND OF DRUMS. Belfast: 1981.

1673. Shearman, Hugh. NORTHERN IRELAND 1921-1971. Belfast: Her Majesty's Stationery Office, 1971.

1674. ————. NOT AN INCH: A STUDY OF NORTHERN IRELAND AND
        LORD CRAIGAVON. London: Faber & Faber, 1942.

1675. Sheehan, D.D. IRELAND SINCE PARNELL. London: Daniel
        O'Connor, 1921.

1676. Sheehy, Michael. DIVIDED WE STAND. London: Faber &
        Faber, 1955.

1677. ————. IS IRELAND DYING? London: Hollis & Carter, 1968.

1678, Sheehy-Skeffington, Francis. MICHAEL DAVITT: REVOLUTION-
        ARY, AGITATOR AND LABOUR LEADER. London: T. Fisher
        Unwin, 1908.

1679. Short, Kenneth R.M. THE DYNAMITE WAR: IRISH AMERICAN
        BOMBERS IN VICTORIAN BRITAIN. Atlantic Highlands,
        N.J.: Humanities Press, 1979.

        Examines the British dynamite campaign conducted by
        a Fenian triumvirate, dubbed the Triangle, in the mid-
        19th century. Bombings were financed by the Fenian
        "skirmishing fund," and many of the bombers were trained
        by Dr. Thomas Gallagher. Moderate Fenian leaders opposed
        the radical campaign, which included attacks on Chester
        Castle, Liverpool Town Hall, and numerous other targets.
        Random violence further alienated British voters and
        legislators from the Irish cause, and numerous Fenians
        were tried for treason as a result of their participa-
        tion in the campaign.

1680. Sibbett, R.M. ORANGEISM IN IRELAND AND THROUGHOUT THE
        EMPIRE. 2 Vols. Belfast: Henderson & Co., 1914.

1681. Sigerson, George. "CUSTODIA HONESTA": TREATMENT OF
        POLITICAL PRISONERS IN GREAT BRITAIN. London: The
        Woman's Press, 1913.

1682. Skinnider, Margaret. DOING MY BIT FOR IRELAND. New
        York: 1917.

1683. Smith A.D. (ed). NATIONALIST MOVEMENTS. London: 1976.

1684. Snoddy, Patrick. IRISH REVOLUTIONARY MOVEMENTS 1913-1916.
        Dublin: University College, 1963.

1685. Spindler, Captain Karl. GUN RUNNING FOR CASEMENT IN THE
        EASTER REBELLION, 1916. London: W. Collins, 1921.

1686. ————. THE MYSTERY OF THE CASEMENT SHIP. Berlin: Kribe-Verlag, 1931.

1687. Steele, E.D. "Gladstone, Irish Violence and Concilia- tion." STUDIES IN IRISH HISTORY. Cited above as item 1205, pp. 257-278/

1688. ————. IRISH LAND AND BRITISH POLITICS: TENANT-RIGHT AND NATIONALITY, 1865-1870. Cambridge: Cambridge University Press, 1974.

1689. Stephens, James. THE INSURRECTION IN DUBLIN. Dublin: Maunsel & Co., 1916.

1690. Stevens, Patricia Bunning. GOD SAVE IRELAND! THE IRISH CONFLICT IN THE TWENTIETH CENTURY. London: Collier Macmillan Publishers, 1974.

1691. Stewart, Anthony Terence Quincey. THE NARROW GROUND: ASPECTS OF ULSTER, 1609-1969. London: Faber & Faber, 1977.

1692. ————. THE ULSTER CRISIS. London: Faber & Faber, 1967.

1693. ————. "Craig and the Ulster Volunteer Force." LEADERS AND MEN OF THE EASTER RISING: DUBLIN 1916. Cited above as item 1507, pp. 701-715.

1694. Strauss, Eric. IRISH NATIONALISM AND BRITISH DEMOCRACY. London: Methuen & Co., 1951, pp. 67-291.

1695. Sullivan, M.F. IRELAND OF TODAY: THE CAUSES AND AIMS OF IRISH AGITATION. Philadelphia: J.C. McCurdy, 1881.

1696. Sullivan, T.D. RECOLLECTIONS OF TROUBLED TIMES. Dublin: 1905.

1697. ————, A.M. Sullivan, and D.B. Sullivan (eds). SPEECHES FROM THE DOCK: OR, PROTESTS OF IRISH PATRIOTISM: THE MANCHESTER TRAGEDY AND THE CRUISE OF THE JACKMELL PACKET: THE WEARING OF THE GREEN: OR, THE PROSECUTED FUNERAL PROCESSION AND ETC. Providence, R.I.: H. McElroy, Murphy and McCarthy, 1879.

1698. Sweetman, Rosita. ON OUR KNEES. London: Pan Books, 1972.

1699. SWORN TO BE FREE: THE COMPLETE BOOK OF IRA JAILBREAKS 1918-1921. Tralee: Anvil Books, 1971.

1700. Talbot, Hayden. MICHAEL COLLINS' OWN STORY. London:
      Hutchinson & Co., 1923.

1701. Tansill, Charles Callan. AMERICA AND THE FIGHT FOR IRISH
      FREEDOM, 1886-1922, AN OLD STORY BASED UPON NEW DATA.
      New York: The Devin-Adair Co., 1957.

1702. Taylor, George. A HISTORY OF THE REBELLION IN THE
      COUNTY OF WEXFORD. Dublin: The Author, 1800.

1703. Taylor, Rex. ASSASSINATION. THE DEATH OF SIR HENRY WIL-
      SON AND THE TRAGEDY OF IRELAND. London: Hutchinson,
      1961.

1704. ————. MICHAEL COLLINS. London: Hutchinson, 1958.

1705. Thayer, George. THE BRITISH POLITICAL FRINGE. London:
      Anthony Blond, 1955.

1706. Thompson, William Irwin. THE IMAGINATION OF AN INSUR-
      RECTION: DUBLIN, EASTER 1916. New York: Harper &
      Row, 1967.

1707. Thornley, David. ISAAC BUTT AND HOME RULE. London:
      Ambassador Press, 1964.

      Profiles an Irish Unionist politician and barrister,
      who opposed Daniel O'Connell in a fight to repeal the
      Irish Act of Union. Undergoing a change of heart during
      the famine, Butt emerged as defense counsel for jailed
      members of Young Ireland, and later for accused terror-
      ists of the Irish Republican Brotherhood. Despite his
      spirited defense of republican guerillas, Butt remained
      a constitutionalist, committed for the most part to
      change through the electoral process.

1708. ————. "Patrick Pearse—the Evolution of a Republican."
      LEADERS AND MEN OF THE EASTER RISING: DUBLIN 1916.
      Cited above as item 1507, pp. 151-163.

1709. Tierney, Mark (ed). DANIEL O'CONNELL. Dublin: Browne
      & Nolan, 1949.

1710. Touhill, Blanche. WILLIAM SMITH O'BRIEN AND HIS IRISH
      REVOLUTIONARY COMPANIONS IN PENAL EXILE. Columbia,
      Mo.: University of Missouri Press, 1981.

1711. Townshend, Charles. THE BRITISH CAMPAIGN IN IRELAND,
      1919-1921: THE DEVELOPMENT OF POLITICAL AND MILITARY
      POLICIES. London: Oxford University Press, 1975.

1712. ————. POLITICAL VIOLENCE IN IRELAND: GOVERNMENT AND
      RESISTANCE SINCE 1848. Oxford: Clarendon Press, 1983.

1713. Trevelyan, Charles E. THE IRISH CRISIS. London: Longman,
      Brown, Green & Longmans, 1848.

1714. Tynan, P.J.P. THE HISTORY OF THE IRISH NATIONAL INVIN-
      CIBLES AND THEIR TIMES. New York: Irish National In-
      vincible Publishing Co., 1874.

      Examines the career of the Irish National Invincibles,
      a splinter faction of the IRB founded during the Land
      League agitation of 1881. A terrorist organization led
      by prominent Fenians and Land League members, the group
      plotted to murder various police officials and politi-
      cians. Five members of the order were convicted and
      executed for their role in the infamous Phoenix Park
      murders, after which the Invincibles largely disappeared.

1715. Valiulis, Maryann Gialanella. ALMOST A REBELLION: THE
      IRISH ARMY MUTINY OF 1924. Cork: Tower Books, 1985.

1716. Van Voris, Jacqueline. CONSTANCE DE MARKIEVICZ IN THE
      CAUSE OF IRELAND. Amherst, Mass.: University of
      Massachusetts Press, 1967.

1717. Walker, Brian M. "The Land Question and Elections in
      Ulster, 1868-86." IRISH PEASANTS, VIOLENCE AND
      POLITICAL UNREST, 1780-1914. Cited above as item
      1180, pp. 230-270.

1718. ————. "Party Oranisation in Ulster, 1805-92: Regis-
      tration Agents and Their Activities." PLANTATION TO
      PARTITION: ESSAYS IN ULSTER HISTORY IN HONOUR OF J.L.
      McCRACKEN. Cited above as item 1643, pp. 191-209.

1719. Walker, Mabel Gregory. THE FENIAN MOVEMENT. Colorado
      Springs, Colo.: Ralph Myles Publisher, 1969.

      Sheds light on a neglected phase of American history
      by examining conditions under which it was possible for
      Irish immigrants to organize the Fenian Brotherhood on
      American soil in the 1850s, subsequently launching an
      invasion of Canada in 1866.

1720. Wall, Maureen. "The Background to the Rising from 1914 Until the Issue of the Countermanding Order on Easter Sunday, 1916." THE MAKING OF 1916: STUDIES IN THE HISTORY OF THE RISING. Cited above as item 1546.

1721. ————. "The Plans and the Countermand: The Country and Dublin." THE MAKING OF 1916: STUDIES IN THE HISTORY OF THE RISING. Cited above as item 1546.

1722. ————. "The Whiteboys." SECRET SOCIETIES IN IRELAND. Cited below as item 1735, pp. 13-25.

1723. Ward, Alan J. IRELAND AND ANGLO-AMERICAN RELATIONS 1899-1921. London: Weidenfeld & Nicolson, 1969.

1724. Weekly Irish Times. SINN FEIN REBELLION HANDBOOK. Dublin: Irish Times, 1917.

1725. Wells, Warren, and N. Marlowe. A HISTORY OF THE IRISH REBELLION OF 1916. Dublin: Maunsel & Co., 1916.

1726. Wheeler, H.F.B., and A.M. Bradley. THE WAR IN WEXFORD. London: 1910.

1727. White, Terence de Vere. "Arthur Griffith." THE SHAPING OF MODERN IRELAND. Cited above as item 1552, pp. 63-73.

1728. ————. KEVIN O'HIGGINS. Tralee: Anvil Books, 1966.

1729. ————. THE ROAD TO EXCESS: A BIOGRAPHY OF ISAAC BUTT. Dublin: Browne & Nolan, 1946.

1730. Whyte, John H. THE INDEPENDENT IRISH PARTY, 1850-59. London: Oxford University Press, 1958.

1731. ————. "Political Problems, 1850-1860." A HISTORY OF IRISH CATHOLICISM. Cited above as item 1204.

1732. ————. THE TENANT LEAGUE AND IRISH POLITICS IN THE EIGHTEEN-FIFTIES. Dundalk: Dundalgon Press, 1966.

1733. Williams, T. Desmond. "Eoin MacNeill and the Irish Volunteers." LEADERS AND MEN OF THE EASTER RISING: DUBLIN 1916. Cited above as item 1507, pp. 135-149.

1734, ——— (ed). THE IRISH STRUGGLE, 1919-26. London:
        Routledge & Kegan Paul, 1966.

        Contains items 1353, 1500, 1509, 1529, 1543, and 1660.

1735. ——— (ed). SECRET SOCIETIES IN IRELAND. New York:
        Barnes & Noble, 1973.

        Contains items 1409, 1473, 1533, and 1722.

1736. Wilson, Thomas (ed). ULSTER UNDER HOME RULE: A STUDY
        OF THE POLITICAL AND ECONOMIC PROBLEMS OF NORTHERN
        IRELAND. London: Oxford University Press, 1955.

        Contains item 1275.

1737. Woodham-Smith, Cecil. THE GREAT HUNGER: IRELAND 1845-9.
        London: Hamish Hamilton, 1962.

1738. Younger, Carlton. IRELAND'S CIVIL WAR. London: Fred-
        erick Muller, 1968.

1739. ———. A STATE OF DISUNION. London: Frederick Muller,
        1972.

                              Articles

1740. Ackerman, W. "Ireland From a Scotland Yard Notebook."
        ATLANTIC 129 (April-June 1922): 433-444, 603-614,
        800-812.

        Presents a policeman's perspective of the Sinn Fein/
        IRA insurrection.

1741. "Action of the English Government with Regard to the
        Settlement of the Irish Question." CATHOLIC WORLD
        103 (September 1916): 850-863.

1742. Akenson, D.H., and J.F. Fallin. "The Irish Civil War
        and the Drafting of the Free State Constitution."
        EIRE-IRELAND 5 (Spring 1970): 10-26; 5 (Summer 1970):
        42-93; 5 (Winter 1970): 28-70.

1743. "America as the Decisive Factor in the Irish Truce."
        CURRENT OPINION 71 (August 1921): 155-158.

1744. "America. Ireland's Western Front." LITERARY DIGEST 64
        (January 17, 1920): 25-26.

1745. "American Meddling with Ireland." LITERARY DIGEST 65
      (May 22, 1920): 32.

1746. "America's Alleged Dictation of the Irish Settlement to
      England." CURRENT OPINION 68 (January 1920): 28-32.

1747. "An American Statesman on Atrocities in Ireland." BLACK-
      WELL'S MAGAZINE 127: 271.

1748. Andrews, C.M. "Irish and American Independence: Reply to
      L. Colcord, with Rejoinder." NATION 112 (April 13,
      1921): 538-539.

1749. "Arthur Griffith, the Father of Sinn Fein." CURRENT
      OPINION 70 (March 1921): 325-328.

1750. Atherley-Jones, L.A. "English Home Ruler's View." 19th
      CENTURY AND AFTER 81 (April 1917): 932-944.

1751. "Background to Home Rule." CURRENT HISTORY 6 (June 1917):
      447-453.

1752. Bagenal, H. "Royal Irish Constabulary and Sinn Fein."
      19th CENTURY AND AFTER 92 (July 1922): 118-120.

1753. "Bandying Phrases Over the Irish Crisis." OUTLOOK 129
      (September 28, 1921): 123-124.

1754. Barrett, W.F. "Irish Problem." CONTEMPORARY REVIEW 110
      (August 1916): 165-173.

1755. Battine, C. "Safety for Ireland." FORTUNE 109 (March
      1918): 462-469.

1756. Beames, M.R. "Rural Conflict in Pre-famine Ireland:
      Peasant Assassinations in Tipperary, 1837-1847."
      PAST & PRESENT 81 (November 1978): 75-91.

1757. Bethell, Nicholas. "How Britain Nearly Invaded Ireland
      in 1939." THE TIMES (January 1, 1970).

      Explores the issue of IRA complicity with Axis agents
      during World War II, the London bombing campaigns, and
      the near-miss of another civil war.

1758. "Bitterness of Life on the Road to Ulster." LITERARY
      DIGEST 69 (June 18, 1921): 40-41.

1759. Blaghd, E. De. "Cold War in the Dublin GAA, 1887."
      DUBLIN HISTORICAL RECORD 12 (1968): 252-262.

      Examines the creation and early days of the Gaelic
      Athletic Association, ostensibly a sporting club, which
      used the background of Irish sports as a platform for
      anti-British agitation. Most members of the GAA belonged
      simultaneously to the Irish Volunteers, participating in
      the paramilitary activities of that organization.

1760. Blake, H.A. "Irish Settlement? A Southern Unionist's
      View." 19th CENTURY AND AFTER 82 (July 1917): 26-30.

1761. ————. "Is There a Way Out of the Chaos in Ireland?"
      19th CENTURY AND AFTER (October 1916): 734-739.

1762. Bohn, W.E. "Justice for Ireland." INTERNATIONAL SOCIAL-
      IST REVIEW 18 (August 1917): 110-111.

1763. Boulger, D.C. "Irish Clan Regiments." FORTUNE 110
      (September 1918): 443-451.

1764. Bourke, M. "The Early GAA in South Ulster." CLOGHER
      RECORD 7 (1967): 5-26.

1765. Bowden, Tom. "The Irish Underground and the War of
      Independence, 1919-21." JOURNAL OF CONTEMPORARY HIS-
      TORY 8 (1973): 3-23.

      Examines the covert war between British intelligence
      agents and the Irish Volunteers of Michael Collins,
      played out against the backdrop of general insurrection
      in Ireland.

1766. Boyce, D.G. "British Conservative Opinion, the Ulster
      Question, and the Partition of Ireland, 1912-21."
      IRISH HISTORICAL STUDIES 17 (March 1970).

1767. Boyle, John. "Irish Labour and the Rising." EIRE-
      IRELAND II 3 (Autumn 1967): 122-131.

1768. ————. "The Belfast Protestant Association and the
      Independent Orange Order." IRISH HISTORICAL STUDIES
      13 (September 1962): 117-152.

1769. "British Correspondence and Sinn Fein." NATION 111
      (October 20, 1920): 459-460.

1770. "British Press Split on Ireland." LITERARY DIGEST 69
      (April 2, 1921): 20-21.

1771. "British Labor and the Irish Settlement." NATION 110
      (April 10, 1920): 467-470.

1772. "British Sketches on the Sinn-Fein Front." LITERARY
      DIGEST 67 (November 27, 1920): 46-54.

1773. "British View of Irish Nationalism." LIVING AGE 301
      (May 17, 1919): 387-389.

1774. "British View of Irish Reluctance." LITERARY DIGEST 71
      (October 8, 1921): 21.

1775. Brooks, S. "Irish Insurrection." NORTH AMERICAN 204
      (July 1916): 57-69.

1776. ————. "Let the Irish Work it Out." INDEPENDENT 87
      (August 21, 1916): 265-266.

1777. Brown, Thomas N. "The Origin and Character of Irish
      American Nationalism." REVIEW OF POLITICS 18 (July
      1956): 327-358.

1778. ————. "Nationalism and the Irish Peasant, 1800-1848."
      REVIEW OF POLITICS 15 (October 1953): 403-445.

1779. Buckland, P.J. "The Southern Irish Unionists, the Irish
      Question, and British Politics, 1906-14." IRISH HIS-
      TORICAL STUDIES 15 (March 1967): 228-250.

1780. "Bullying of Ireland." NEW REPUBLIC 27 (June 15, 1921):
      63.

1781. Byrne, J.F. "Irish Grievance; the Case for the Anti-
      English Party." CENTURY 93 (January 1917): 465-473.

1782. Cahill, Gilbert. "Irish Catholicism and English Tory-
      ism." THE REVIEW OF POLITICS 19 (January 1957): 62-76.

1783. ————. "Irish Popery and British Nativism: 1800-1848."
      CITHARA 13 (May 1974): 3-18.

1784. ————. "The Protestant Association and the Anti-Maynooth
      Agitation of 1845." THE CATHOLIC HISTORICAL REVIEW
      43 (October 1957): 273-308.

1785. ———. "Some Nineteenth-century Roots of the Ulster
       Problem, 1829-1848." IRISH UNIVERSITY REVIEW 1 (1970).

1786. Carroll, P.J. "Irish Men of Easter Week; A Reapprais-
       ment." CATHOLIC WORLD 123 (April 1926): 28-37.

1787. "Case for Irish Freedom." NATION 108 (April 5, 1919):
       489-490.

1788. Chesterton, G.K. "Fenians and a Fallacy." LIVING AGE
       299 (December 14, 1918): 683-685.

1789. Christianson, G.E. "Secret Societies and Agrarian Vio-
       lence in Ireland, 1790-1840." AGRICULTURAL HISTORY
       46 (October 1972): 369-384.

1790. Clarke, R. "The Relations Between O'Connell and the
       Young Irelanders." IRISH HISTORICAL STUDIES 3 (March
       1942): 18-30.

1791. "Clashing Ultimatums in Ireland." LITERARY DIGEST 70
       (September 1921): 9.

1792. Cluseret, General Gustave P. "My Connection with Fenian-
       ism." FRASER'S MAGAZINE 6 (July 1872).

       Presents the memoirs of a soldier of fortune, briefly
       Fenian commander-in-chief. Born in France, Cluseret won
       his own country's Legion of Honour before moving on to
       fight for Garibaldi in Sicily, later joining the Union
       army in the American Civil War. In 1866, he became the
       Fenian commander-in-chief, on a recruiter's promise
       that his army would number 10,000 men. A tour of Ireland
       was interrupted by the premature Kerry rising in March
       1867. Cluseret had advised against military rebellion
       in the face of overwhelming odds, and returned to France
       in disgust when his advice was ignored.

1793. Colcord, L. "Irish and American Independence." NATION
       112 (March 9, 1921): 373-374.

1794. ———. "Why Lloyd George Negotiates with De Valera."
       NATION 113 (October 5, 1921): 369-370.

1795. Colum, P. "Sinn Fein Victory in the Irish Elections."
       NATION 108 (January 11, 1919): 42-43.

1796. "Condition of an Irish Settlement." NEW REPUBLIC 24
      (October 27, 1920): 205-207.

1797. "Condition of Ireland Under the British Bayonet." CUR-
      RENT OPINION 62 (June 1917): 380.

1798. "Conflict in Ireland." CURRENT HISTORY 13 (February
      1921): 307-309.

1799. Connolly, James. "Ireland—Disaffected or Revolutionary?"
      WORKERS REPUBLIC (November 13, 1915).

1800. ———. "The Irish Flag." LABOUR AND EASTER WEEK (1966):
      175.

1801. ———. "The Man and His Cause." WORKERS REPUBLIC
      (July 31, 1915).

1802. Cooke, A.B., and J.R. Vincent. "Lord Spencer and the
      Phoenix Park Murders." IRISH HISTORICAL STUDIES 18
      (1973): 583-591.

      Reprints an 1889 retrospective of the 1882 assassina-
      tion of Lord Frederick Charles Cavendish and the under
      secretary of Ireland by Irish terrorists.

1803. Coote, W. "Sinn Fein Demands Examined and Statements
      Exposed." CURRENT OPINION 68 (February 1920): 171-173.

1804. Costigan, Giovanni. "The Anglo-Irish Conflict, 1919-
      1922: A War of Independence or Systematized Murder."
      UNIVERSITY REVIEW 5 (Spring 1968): 64-86.

1805. ———. "The Treason of Sir Roger Casement." AMERICAN
      HISTORICAL REVIEW 60 (January 1955).

1806. "Court-Martial Justice in Ireland." NATION 111 (October
      20, 1920): 461.

1807. Crammond, E. "Ireland's Part in the War." 19th CENTURY
      AND AFTER 81 (May 1917): 974-990.

1808. Cronin, S. "The Fenian Tradition." IRISH TIMES (April
      9, 1969).

1809. Curran, Joseph M. "The Decline and Fall of the IRB."
      EIRE-IRELAND 10 (Spring 1975): 14-23.

1810. ———. "Ireland Since 1916." EIRE-IRELAND 1 (1966):
       14-28.

1811. ———. "The Irish Free State." UNIVERSITY REVIEW 5
       (Spring 1968).

1812. ———. "Ulster Repartition: A Possible Answer?" AMERICA
       134 (January 31, 1976): 66-68.

1813. Curtis, L.P., Jr. "Government Policy and the Irish
       Party Crisis, 1890-92." IRISH HISTORICAL STUDIES 13
       (September 1962): 293-315.

1814. Desmond, S. "Ireland: Now It Can Be Told." CURRENT
       HISTORY 16 (April 1923): 9-11d.

1815. De Valera, Eamon. "American Liberty and the Spirit of
       the Irish Republic." CURRENT OPINION 67 (August 1919):
       83-85.

1816. ———. "Ireland Can Stand Alone." INDEPENDENT 99
       (July 19, 1919): 89+.

1817. ———. "Ireland's Right to Independence." NATION 108
       (June 7, 1919): 906.

1818. "De Valera's Order Outlaws Blue-Shirt Fascists." NEWS-
       WEEK 2 (September 2, 1933): 16.

       De Valera's government moves to disband the right-wing
       Army Comrades Organization, dubbed Blueshirts after their
       chosen uniforms. Adopting their philosophy from Italy's
       Benito Mussolini, the Blueshirts were led by Eoin McDuffy
       whom De Valera had earlier dismissed from his post as
       leader of the Irish national police force. At the time
       of this article, proposed public demonstrations by the
       Blueshirts had just been officially banned, in hopes of
       preventing violent clashes with the IRA. The movement
       withered by 1935, with a brief "last fling" in 1936-
       1937, when selected members joined the fascist ranks in
       Spain's civil war.

1819. Dicey, A.V. "Ireland as a Dominion." 19th CENTURY AND
       AFTER 82 (October 1917): 700-726.

1820. ———. "Irish Settlement: Is It Wise to Establish Home
       Rule Before the End of the War?" 19th CENTURY AND
       AFTER 82 (July 1917): 1-25.

1821. Dilnot, F. "Can the Irish Settle the Irish Question?"
      WORLD'S WORK 34 (August 1917): 413-424.

1822. ———. "Ireland Under Sinn Fein." OUTLOOK 121 (Janu-
      ary 15, 1919): 106-108.

1823. ———. "What Ireland Would Be Like as a Sinn Fein Re-
      public." CURRENT OPINION 69 (October 1920): 467-471.

1824. "Does Ireland Matter?" NEW REPUBLIC 26 (March 2, 1921):
      6-8.

1825. "Drawn Into the Vortex: The Remaking of an Irish Mind."
      LIVING AGE 311 (October 22, 1921): 197-201.

1826. Dresser, H.W. "Struggle for Home Rule." HOME PROGRESS
      6 (February 1917): 245-246.

1827. Dublin, J. "Ireland in 1916." LIVING AGE 291 (November
      11, 1916): 331-338.

1828. Edwards, J.H. "Lloyd George Appeals to Rome." CURRENT
      OPINION 70 (March 1921): 323-324.

1829. "Election to Settle the Irish Question." CURRENT OPINION
      71 (October 1921): 415-418.

1830. Elliott, Marianne. "The Origins and Transformation of
      Early Irish Republicanism." INTERNATIONAL REVIEW OF
      SOCIAL HISTORY 23, (1978): 405-428.

1831. "England's Efforts to Secure the Pope as an Ally in
      Ireland." CURRENT OPINION 58 (February 1915): 82-83.

1832. "England's Iron Hand on Ireland." LITERARY DIGEST 62
      (September 27, 1919): 15-16.

1833. "England's Iron Heel on Ireland." LITERARY DIGEST 66
      (August 14, 1920): 20-21.

1834. E.R.R. "The Fenians." HISTORY TODAY 8 (1958): 698-705.

1835. Fanning, J. Ronan. "The Unionist Party and Ireland,
      1906-1910." IRISH HISTORICAL STUDIES 15 (September
      1966): 147-171.

1836. "Fascists Organize." NEWSWEEK 1 (July 29, 1933): 14.

1837. "Feeling the Way Toward Irish Peace." CURRENT HISTORY
      15 (October 1921): 147-151.

1838. Feingold, William. "The Tenant's Movement to Capture
      the Irish Poor Law Board, 1879-1885." ALBION 7 (Decem-
      ber 1975): 216-231.

1839. Fisher, J.R. "Federal Panacea for Ireland." 19th CEN-
      TURY AND AFTER 84 (July 1918): 59-67.

1840. ———, and J.V. Bates. "Ulster and the Irish Tangle."
      19th CENTURY AND AFTER 83 (May 1918): 1088-1100.

1841. ———, J.C. Sheridan, and R.H. Murray. "Irish Enigma
      Again." 19th CENTURY AND AFTER 79 (June 1916): 1184-
      1220.

1842. "For and Against the Irish Republic." REVIEW OF REVIEWS
      62 (July 1920): 97-98.

1843. "Free Ireland." NEW REPUBLIC 18 (March 1, 1919): 132-
      134.

1844. "Ghost of Home Rule Rises." INDEPENDENT 90 (April 7,
      1917): 61.

1845. Gibbs, P. "Anarchy in Ireland." HARPER 142 (March 1921)
      409-418.

1846. Glandon, Virginia E. "The Irish Press and Revolutionary
      Irish Nationalism." EIRE-IRELAND 16 (1981): 21-33.

      Samples newspaper reactions and treatment of Irish
      nationalist and revolutionary violence in the period
      between 1896 and 1927.

1847. Glaser, John A. "Parnell's Fall and the Nonconformist
      Conscience." IRISH HISTORICAL STUDIES 12 (September
      1960): 119-138.

1848. Good, J.W. "Ulster Nationalist." CONTEMPORARY REVIEW
      112 (November 1917): 542-549.

1849. "Good Name of Britain." NEW REPUBLIC 25 (December 29,
      1920): 124-125.

1850. Gorman, H.S. "America and Ireland." NEW REPUBLIC 11
      (June 23, 1917): 219.

1851. Grasty, C.H.   "Irish Realities."   ATLANTIC 126 (September 1920): 383-394.

1852. Graves, A.P.   "Ulster Home Rule."   CONTEMPORARY REVIEW 111 (May 1917): 588-597.

1853. Grigg, John.   "The Irish Question."   WORLD SURVEY 40 (1972): 1-15.

       Presents an overview of "the troubles," with special emphasis on ethnic and religious causal factors.

1854. Gwynn, S.   "Chances for Ireland."   REVIEW 5 (July 2, 1921): 9-10.

1855. ———.   "Dark Possibilities in Ireland."   REVIEW 4 (May 7, 1921): 436-437.

1856. ———.   "Dawn of Sanity in Ireland."   INDEPENDENT 107 (October 1, 1921): 3-4.

1857. ———.   "Decade of Ireland."   LIVING AGE 329 (May 15, 1926): 349-353.

1858. ———.   "End of a Year in Ireland."   REVIEW 4 (January 26, 1921): 76-77.

1859. ———.   "From Bad to Worse in Ireland."   REVIEW 4 (January 5, 1921): 10-11.

1860. ———.   "Ireland To-Day."   REVIEW 3 (October 6, 1920): 286-287.

1861. ———.   "Sidelights on Revolutionary Ireland."   FORTUNE 125 (January 1926): 57-67.

1862. ———.   "St. Patrick's Day."   REVIEW 4 (April 6, 1921): 314-315.

1863. Hackett, F.   "Hands Off Ireland?"   NEW REPUBLIC 22 (April 28, 1920): 283-284.

1864. ———.   "Impasse in Ireland."   NEW REPUBLIC 24 (October 13, 1920): 161-163.

1865. ———.   "In Contempt of Ireland."   NEW REPUBLIC 8 (August 19, 1916): 61-62.

1866. ———. "Irish Conscription." NEW REPUBLIC 14 (April 20, 1918): 354-355.

1867. ———. "On Her Majesty's Service." NEW REPUBLIC 29 (January 18, 1922): 203-204.

1868. ———. "Policy for Ireland." NEW REPUBLIC 6 (March 25, 1916): 209-211.

1869. ———. "Silver Lining in Ireland." HARPER 143 (June 1921): 1-8.

1870. ———. "Where the Irish Radical Stands." NEW REPUBLIC 1 (December 26, 1914): 16-18.

1871. Hannay, J.O. "Recruiting in Ireland To-Day." 19th CENTURY AND AFTER 79 (January 1916): 173-180

1872. Harding, J.W. "Ireland's Reign of Terror—and Why." CURRENT HISTORY 12 (September 1920): 1039-1046.

1873. Hawkins, Richard. "Gladstone, Forster and the Release of Parnell 1882-8." IRISH HISTORICAL STUDIES 16 (March 1968).

1874. Hepburn, A.C. "The Ancient Order of Hibernians in Irish Politics 1905-14." CITHARA 10 (1971).

1875. Herbert, S.A. "Convention or Esle?" 19th CENTURY AND AFTER 82 (December 1917): 1216-1233.

    Examines stormy efforts to create a national constitu-
    tion in the wake of the 1916 Easter rising. With civil
    war already looming, Irish statesmen try to save their
    homeland with a resolution short of violence.

1876. Herdman, J.O. "Sinn Fein Trials and Parliamentary Dis-qualification." CONTEMPORARY REVIEW 115 (February 1919): 177-182.

1877. "Heroic Effort to Settle the Irish Question." CURRENT OPINION 63 (July 1917): 14-16.

1878. Hoare, S. "Irish War and English Peace." FORUM 66 (August 1921): 91-102.

1879. "Home Rule and Conscription." OUTLOOK 118 (April 24, 1918): 661-662.

1880. "Home Rule at Last." OUTLOOK 113 (July 19, 1916): 636-
      637.

1881. "Home Rule for Ireland; Events Attending the British
      Government's New Proposal of an Irish Council." CUR-
      RENT HISTORY 6 (June 1917): 444-446.

1882. Hone, J.M. "Ireland During the War." CONTEMPORARY RE-
      VIEW 109 (March 1916): 360-368.

1883. "Hopes for Peace in Ireland." OUTLOOK 128 (July 20,
      1921): 469-470.

1884. "Hostilities Increase in Ireland." CURRENT HISTORY 14
      (April 1921): 130-134.

1885. "Hour Has Come! I.R.A. Terrorist Activities." TIME 33
      (January 20, 1939): 16.

      Examines the IRA bombing campaign of 1939, carried out
      in conjunction with Axis moves abroad, thereby seeking
      to weaken the British military establishment and bring
      the government to its knees.

1886. "How Military Experts Consider the War in Ireland."
      CURRENT HISTORY 68 (June 1920): 739-742.

1887. "How to Save Ireland." LITERARY DIGEST 55 (August 25,
      1917): 17-18.

1888. Howard, C.H.D. "Joseph Chamberlain, W.H. O'Shea and
      Parnell, 1884, 1891-2." IRISH HISTORICAL STUDIES 13
      (September 1962): 33-37.

1889. "Ideals of Sinn Fein." LIVING AGE 300 (March 22, 1919):
      762-764.

1890. "In Tara's Halls." LIVING AGE 293 (June 2, 1917): 565-
      567.

1891. "Increasing Turbulence in Ireland." CURRENT HISTORY 12
      (June 1920): 418-422.

1892. "I.R.A. Again; London Greets New Bombings with Raid on
      Irish Suspects." NEWSWEEK 14 (August 7, 1939): 22.

1893. "Ireland." LIVING AGE 311 (October 1, 1921): 7-12.

1894. "Ireland." NEW REPUBLIC 19 (May 17, 1919): 74.

1895. "Ireland." OUTLOOK 129 (September 7, 1921): 10.

1896. "Ireland a Volcano Near Eruption." LITERARY DIGEST 55
      (November 24, 1917): 22-23.

1897. "Ireland a War-Factor." LITERARY DIGEST 54 (May 12,
      1917): 1400.

      Examines the repercussions of Ireland's Easter rising
      on the British military effort in World War I.

1898. "Ireland an American Question." LITERARY DIGEST 67 (No-
      vember 6, 1920): 20-21.

1899. "Ireland: An Appeal." LIVING AGE 293 (June 9, 1917):
      631-633.

1900. "Ireland Asks Our Aid and Money." LITERARY DIGEST 62
      (July 12, 1919): 14-15.

1901. "Ireland Between the Vatican and the Wilhelmstrasse."
      CURRENT OPINION 65 (July 1918): 14-16.

      Politics and religion clash in Ireland as the World
      War nears its end and Irish terrorism escalates toward
      open civil war against Britain.

1902. "Ireland Drifting into Anarchy." LITERARY DIGEST 57
      (April 6, 1918): 29.

1903. "Ireland Forever—Ireland." OUTLOOK 116 (June 21, 1917):
      321-322.

1904. "Ireland in Revolt." CURRENT HISTORY 11 (March 1920):
      421-422.

1905. "Ireland in the Grip of an Army of Occupation." CURRENT
      OPINION 68 (May 1920): 608-611.

1906. "Ireland on the Eve of Another Sanguinary Insurrection."
      CURRENT OPINION 61 (December 1916): 377-379.

1907. "Ireland on the Verge of Peace?" NATION 113 (July 20,
      1921): 59.

1908. "Ireland, Propserous but Not Content." NATION 105 (November 15, 1977): 529.

1909. "Ireland Under Sinn Fein." LIVING AGE 306 (July 17, 1920): 130-133.

1910. "Ireland's Better Day." LITERARY DIGEST 70 (July 23, 1921): 8-9.

1911. "Ireland's Chance to Govern Herself." LITERARY DIGEST 54 (June 2, 1917): 1688.

1912. "Ireland's Cry to Us for Help." LITERARY DIGEST 54 (March 24, 1917): 805-806.

1913. "Ireland's Evil Genius." LITERARY DIGEST 54 (April 21, 1917): 1159.

1914. "Ireland's Great Opportunity." LITERARY DIGEST 53 (December 9, 1916): 1530-1531.

1915. "Irish and English Views of the Sinn-Fein Republic." LITERARY DIGEST 60 (February 8, 1919): 19-20.

1916. "Irish-British Peace." NATION 113 (September 21, 1921): 326-332.

1917. "Irish Civil War." SURVEY 45 (January 8, 1921): 528-529.

1918. "Irish Impediment." NORTH AMERICA 205 (May 1917): 652-655.

1919. "Irish Military Rule Especially Hard on Women, Children, and Constables." LITERARY DIGEST 66 (June 24, 1920): 52-55.

1920. "Irish Muddle." INDEPENDENT 87 (September 25, 1916): 441.

1921. "Irish Muddle." LITERARY DIGEST 65 (May 15, 1920): 34-35.

1922. "Irish Negotiations." NEW REPUBLIC 27 (July 13, 1921): 179-181.

1923. "Irish Peace Conference." CURRENT HISTORY 15 (November 1921): 334-337.

1924. "Irish Peace in Sight." LITERARY DIGEST 70 (September 17, 1921): 7-9.

1925. "Irish Peace Negotiations." CURRENT HISTORY 14 (September 1921): 952-954.

1926. "Irish Preliminaries." NEW REPUBLIC 28 (September 21, 1921): 83-85.

1927. "Irish Prolem." OUTLOOK 114 (November 1, 1916): 478-480.

1928. "Irish Problem: the Dawn of a Better Day." OUTLOOK 116 (May 30, 1917): 182-183.

1929. "Irish Question." OUTLOOK 117 (November 14, 1917): 407-408.

1930. "Irish Question, Referred to Irishmen." INDEPENDENT 90 (May 26, 1917): 362.

1931. "Irish Realities." EDINBURGH REVIEW 228 (July 1918): 125-146.

1932. "Irish Republic." LITERARY DIGEST 64 (January 3, 1920): 40.

1933. "Irish Republican Army Ire." TIME 33 (April 10, 1939): 24.

       Takes another look at IRA terrorism in the days just prior to the outbreak of World War II in Europe.

1934. "Irish Responsibility." NEW REPUBLIC 11 (May 12, 1917): 38-40.

1935. "Irish Situation." OUTLOOK 113 (August 2, 1916): 760-76

1936. "Irish Soldier." LIVING AGE 288 (January 1, 1916): 52-5

1937. "Irish Tangle." OUTLOOK 128 (August 24, 1921): 637-638.

1938. "Irish Terrorism; Drive Seeks to Worry Britons and Stress Division at Home." NEWSWEEK 13 (February 13, 1939): 2

1939. "Irish the Arbiters." NATION 113 (August 24, 1921): 190.

1940. "Irish Triangle." LITERARY DIGEST 70 (July 30, 1931): 10-11.

1941. "Irish War." TIME 34 (August 7, 1939): 18.

1942. "Irish Women and the Republican Army." NATION 112 (March 2, 1921): 353-354.

1943. "Issues in Ireland: Official Report of the Irish Convention." CURRENT HISTORY 8 (June 1918): 496-504.

1944. "John Redmond: the Man Who Dominates the New Situation in Ireland." CURRENT OPINION 60 (June 1916): 400-402.

1945. Johnston, C. "Can the Irish Barrier Be Removed?" OUTLOOK 119 (August 21, 1918): 632-633.

1946. Judson, H.P. "Will Ireland Seize the Golden Moment?" REVIEW OF REVIEWS 57 (June 1918): 616-617.

1947. "Labor's Indictment of Britain's Irish Policy." LITERARY DIGEST 68 (February 5, 1921): 18-19.

1948. Laffan, M. "The Sinn Fein Party, 1916-1921." CAPUCHIN ANNUAL (1970): 227-237.

1949. ————. "The Unification of Sinn Fein in 1917." IRISH HISTORICAL STUDIES 17 (1970): 353-379.

1950. Larkin, Emmet. "The Devotional Revolution in Ireland, 1870-75." AMERICAN HISTORICAL REVIEW 77 (June 1972): 625-652.

1951. ————. "Church and State in Ireland in the Nineteenth Century." CHURCH HISTORY 21 (September 1962): 294-306.

1952. ————. "The Roman Catholic Hierarchy and the Fall of Parnell." VICTORIAN STUDIES 4 (June 1961): 315-336.

1953. ————. "Mounting the Counter Attack: The Roman Catholic Church and the Destruction of Parnellism." THE REVIEW OF POLITICS 15 (April 1963): 157-182.

1954. Lathbury, D.C. "Cabinet and Convention." 19th CENTURY AND AFTER 82 (August 1917): 283-300.

1955. ————. "Latest Irish Problem." 19th CENTURY AND AFTER 80 (November 1916): 952-965.

1956. ————. "Ways Out of the Irish Labyrinth." 19th CENTURY AND AFTER 80 (July 1916): 209-220.

1957. Law, H.A. "Humpty-Dumpty Up Again." CONTEMPORARY REVIEW 110 (September 1916): 290-296.

1958. ————. "Ireland, 1918." CONTEMPORARY REVIEW 113 (June 1918): 601-609.

1959. ————., "Pacata Hibernia." CONTEMPORARY REVIEW 109 (June 1916): 690-700.

        Examines the restoration of "peace" in Ireland, one month after the Easter rising.

1960. ————. "Plea for Irish History." CONTEMPORARY REVIEW 113 (March 1918): 272-279.

1961. ————. "Plus Fait Douceur." CONTEMPORARY REVIEW 112 (July 1917): 6-13.

1962. Lawlor, S.M. "Ireland from Truce to Treaty: War or Peace? July to October 1921." IRISH HISTORICAL STUDIES 22 (1980): 49-64.

1963. Lea, John. "W.S. Caine and Irish Home Rule—a Study of the Radical Opposition of 1886." HISTORICAL STUDIES 1 (1968).

1964. "Liberty by Bayonetting." NEW REPUBLIC 25 (January 19, 1921): 216-217.

1965. Lucy, H. "Most Distressful Country." NATION 103 (August 24, 1916): 172.

1966. ————. "Mr. Redmond's Dictatorship." NATION 101 (July 1, 1915): 92.

1967. ————. "Recruiting in Ireland." NATION 103 (November 9, 1916): 439.

1968. ————. "Unmuzzled!" NATION 103 (August 31, 1916): 194.

1969. Lynn, R.J. "Ulster and Sinn Fein." EDINBURGH REVIEW 230 (October 1919): 279-296.

1970. MacDonald, J.A.M. "Devolution or Destruction." CONTEMPORARY REVIEW 114 (August 1918): 134-140.

1971. MacDonald, W. "Direct Action in Ireland." NATION 110 (June 19, 1920): 822-823.

1972. ———. "Underground Ireland." NATION 110 (June 12, 1920): 800-801.

1973. ———. "Will Sinn Fein Succeed?" NATION 110 (June 26, 1920): 846-847.

1974. MacGiolla Choille, Breandan. "Fenian Documents in the State Paper Office." IRISH HISTORICAL STUDIES 16 (March 1969).

1975. ———. "Mourning the Martyrs." NORTH MUNSTER ANTI-QUARIAN JOURNAL 10 (1966): 173-205.

Describes Fenianism in 1863 as a localized town movement just tapping into the well-established traditions of the Ribbonmen in the midlands and south Ulster.

1976. MacHugh, F. "Who Killed the 'Bad Earl' of Leitrim?" IRISH TIMES (May 27, 1978).

Examines the continuing mystery of William Sydney Clements's assassination during 1878. As Earl of Leitrim, Sydney was notorious for harsh treatment of his peasant tenants. Nearly 200 were hauled into court for failure to pay rent on time, and there were accusations that Clements used his social position to seduce farm girls in the vicinity of his home. Murdered by three men in 1878, the case was never solved. The assassination is considered a prelude to the land war, which erupted one year later.

1977. MacLochlainn, Ailfrie. "The Racism of Thomas Davis: Root and Branch." THE HOURNAL OF IRISH LITERATURE 5 (May 1976): 112-122.

1978. MacManus, S. "In the Matter of Ireland." INDEPENDENT 91 (July 14, 1917): 61-62.

1979. MacNeill, J.G.S. "Breakdown of the Dublin Castle Regime." CONTEMPORARY REVIEW 110 (July 1916): 22-31.

1980. ———. "Irish Rights and British Honour." CONTEMPORARY REVIEW 11 (May 1918): 499-508.

1981. McCaffrey, Lawrence J. "Home Rule and the General Election of 1874 in Ireland." IRISH HISTORICAL STUDIES 9 (September 1954): 190-212.

1982. ———. "The Roots of the Irish Troubles." AMERICA 134 (January 31, 1976): 69-70.

1983. McCartney, Donal. "The Church and Fenianism." UNIVERSITY REVIEW 4 (Winter 1967): 203-215.

1984. McCord, Norman. "The Fenians and Public Opinion in Great Britain." UNIVERSITY REVIEW 4 (Winter 1967).

1985. McGrath, J. "Irish National Leaders and a Federal Solution." FORTUNE 109 (June 1918): 924-933.

1986. ———. "Mr. Redmond as Irish Leader; and His Legacy." FORTUNE 109 (May 1918): 744-754.

1987. ———. "Sinn Fein Tragedy." FORTUNE 111 (May 1919): 771-784.

1988. ———. "Sir Horace Plunkett, Sinn Fein and the Irish Situation." FORTUNE 108 (December 1917): 865-874.

1989. McInerney, M. "From Sinn Fein to Fianna Fail." IRISH TIMES (July 23, 1976).

1990. McNeill, R. "Ulster Standpoint." 19th CENTURY AND AFTER 81 (April 1917): 922-931.

1991. Magee, John. "The Monaghan Election of 1883 and the 'Invasion of Ulster.'" CLOGHER RECORD 8 (1974): 147-166.

1992. Mandle, W.F. "The IRB and the Beginnings of the Gaelic Athletic Association." IRISH HISTORICAL STUDIES 20 (September 1977): 418-438.

1993. Markell, E. "Can the People of Ireland Unite?" OUTLOOK 128 (June 8, 1921): 257-259.

1994. Marlowe, N. "Irish Bishops, the War, and Home Rule." CONTEMPORARY REVIEW 114 (October 1918): 402-406.

1995. ———. "Week in Clare." CONTEMPORARY REVIEW 113 (April 1918): 434-439.

1996. Marlowe, Terry. "Easter Rising." HANDS OFF IRELAND! 10
      (April 1980): 16-18.

1997. Marriott, J.A.R. "Heel of Achilles." 19th CENTURY AND
      AFTER 87 (June 1920): 1100-1110.

1998. ————. "Prussia, Poland, and Ireland." EDINBURGH RE-
      VIEW 225 (January 1917): 158-177.

1999. "Martial Law in Ireland." CURRENT HISTORY 13 (January
      1921): 86-89.

2000. Martin, Francis X. "Eoin MacNeill on the 1916 Rising."
      IRISH HISTORICAL STUDIES 12 (March 1961): 234-240.

2001. ————. "The 1916 Rising—a Coup d'Etat or a 'Bloody
      Protest'?" STUDIA BIBERNICA 8 (1968): 106-137.

2002. ———— (ed). "1916—Myth, Fact and Mystery." STUDIA
      HIBERNICA 7 (1967): 1-124.

      Presents a penetrating analysis of recent literature
      on the Easter rising and its historical antecedents.

2003. Massingham, H.W. "Ireland 1916—and Beyond." ATLANTIC
      188 (December 1916): 839-845.

2004. "May Visit to Dublin." LIVING AGE 310 (July 2, 1921):
      36-39.

2005. "Michael Collins, Most Terrifying of All Sinn Feiners."
      CURRENT OPINION 71 (December 1921): 721-724.

2006. "Mr. Redmond's Position as Head of Government in Dublin."
      CURRENT OPINION 61 (August 1916): 87-88.

2007. Murphy, J.J. "Ireland Her Own." PUBLIC 22 (March 2,
      1919): 291-292.

2008. Murray, R.H., and J.O. Hannay. "Ireland in Two Wars."
      19th CENTURY AND AFTER 79 (January 1916): 153-180.

2009. "Neutral View of Ireland." LIVING AGE 306 (August 7-14,
      1920): 320-324.

2010. Nevinson, H.W. "Anglo-Irish War." CONTEMPORARY REVIEW
      120 (July 1921): 20-26.

2011. "New Developments in Ireland." CURRENT HISTORY 13 (November 1920): 278-280.

2012. "New Scheme for Ireland." LITERARY DIGEST 54 (January 27, 1917): 183-184.

2013. Newman, E.M. "Ireland Roday." MENTOR 9 (April 1921): 2-12.

2014, Newsinger, John. "Revolution and Catholicism in Ireland, 1848-1923." EUROPEAN STUDIES REVIEW 9 (1979): 457-480.

Examines the gradual identification of the Irish church with revolutionary nationalist activities. Spanning a period between the famine and civil war, this article surveys religious polarization in Ireland, including examples of Protestant intransigence which made Catholic radicalization inevitable.

2015. ————. "'I Bring Not Peace but a Sword': the Religious Motif in the Irish War of Independence." JOURNAL OF CONTEMPORARY HISTORY 13 (July 1978): 609-628.

2016. O'Beirne-Ravelagh, John. "The I.R.B. From the Treaty to 1924." IRISH HISTORICAL STUDIES 20 (1976): 26-39.

Reviews the history of the Irish Republican Brotherhood in the wake of the civil war against Britain.

2017. O'Brien, W. "Is There a Way Out of the Chaos in Ireland? 19th CENTURY AND AFTER 80 (September 1916): 489-506.

2018. ————. "Parnell and His Liberal Allies." 19th CENTURY AND AFTER 83 (January 1918): 170-183.

2019. O'Connell, J.R. "What Ireland Wants." FORTUNE 108 (July 1917): 101-110.

2020. O'Connor, R.F. "Irish Volunteers." CATHOLIC WORLD 101 (July 1915): 513-521.

2021. O'Donnell, Frank Hugh. "Fenianism Past and Present." CONTEMPORARY REVIEW 43 (May 1883).

2022. O'Donnell, P. "Why Bombs Are Being Thrown." NEW REPUBLIC 99 (May 10, 1939): 14.

2023. O'Donoghue, F. "Plans for the 1916 Rising." UNIVERSITY
       REVIEW 3 (1962).

2024. O'Donoghue, Patrick. "Causes of the Opposition to Tithes,
       1830-38." STUDIA HIBERNICA 5 (1965): 13-19.

2025. O'Faolain, Sean. "The Admirer and the Disillusioned."
       IRISH TIMES (April 21, 1976): 335-336.

       Presents a fond memory of James Connolly.

2026. O'Fiach, T. "The Clergy and Fenianism, 1860-70." IRISH
       ECCLESIASTICAL RECORD 109 (February 1968): 81-103.

2027. O'Mahoney, John. "Fenianism." IRISH PEOPLE (January-
       July 1868).

2028. "Order and Anarchy in Ireland." LIVING AGE 305 (June 5,
       1920): 580-583.

2029. O'Regan, T. "Prussianization of Ireland." NATION 109
       (November 29, 1919): 678-679.

2030. O'Riley, M. "Ireland's Independence; the Rights of Ire-
       land as Seen from the Sinn Fein Viewpoint." CURRENT
       HISTORY MAGAZINE, NEW YORK TIMES 12 (September 1920):
       1046-1049.

2031. O'Riordan, M., and B. Sinclair. "Irish Communists and
       Terrorism." WORLD MARXIST REVIEW 19 (1976): 87-96.

       Communist authors dispute claims of red participation
       in Irish terrorism through the years. Biased at best,
       but fundamentally accurate in its contention that "the
       troubles" were not initially inspired by outside agita-
       tors. Conversely, Soviet military support for the vio-
       lent IRA is exhaustively documented and no longer open
       to serious debate.

2032. "Outside Help Needed for Irish Settlement." LIVING AGE
       293 (April 21, 1917): 183-184.

2033. Payne, P. "The Third Sinn Fein Party, 1923-1926."
       ECONOMIC AND SOCIAL REVIEW 1 (1969): 29-50.

2034. ———. "The Politics of Parliamentary Abstentionism:
       Ireland's Four Sinn Fein Parties, 1905-26." JOURNAL
       OF COMMONWEALTH AND COMPARATIVE POLITICS 12 (July 1974):
       206-227.

2035. "Peace or War in Ireland." REVIEW 5 (August 20, 1921): 156-157.

2036. Pim, H.M. "Sinn Fein: Past, Present, and Future." 19th CENTURY AND AFTER 85 (June 1919): 1165-1174.

2037. "Plight of Ireland." CURRENT OPINION 69 (November 1920): 595-597.

2038. Plunkett, Geraldine. "The Insurrection of 1916." UNIVERSITY REVIEW 2 (1959).

2039. Plunkett, H. "Message from Ireland to America." LIVING AGE 304 (January 17, 1920): 125-127.

2040. "Pope Urges Irish Peace." INDEPENDENT 105 (June 4, 1921): 588.

2041. "Present State of Ireland: Statement of the Cardinal Primate and the Archbishops of Ireland." NATION 111 (December 1, 1920): 624-625.

2042. "Protestant Ireland's Opinion." LITERARY DIGEST 53 (November 4, 1916): 1165.

2043. "Real Sinn Feiners." LIVING AGE 297 (April 6, 1918): 54-56.

2044. Redmond, W. "From the Trenches; a Plea and a Claim." LIVING AGE 293 (May 26, 1917): 501-504.

2045. "Report of the British Labor Commission to Ireland." NATION 112 (January 26, 1921): 131-160.

2046. "Republican Movement in Ireland." LIVING AGE 305 (May 22, 1920): 440-442.

2047. "Road to Irish Peace." NEW REPUBLIC 27 (August 24, 1921): 337-338.

2048. Roberts, R. "Irish Nights." NATION 110 (January 31, 1920): 138-140.

2049. Savage, D.C. "The Irish Unionists: 1867-1886." EIRE-IRELAND 2 (Autumn 1967).

2050. ———. "The Origins of the Ulster Unionist Party, 1885-6." IRISH HISTORICAL STUDIES 12 (March 1961): 185-208.

2051. ———. "The Attempted Home Rule Settlement of 1916."
      EIRE-IRELAND 2 (Autumn 1967).

2052. Scarborough, H.E. "Most Distressful Country." OUTLOOK
      127 (March 30, 1921): 505-508.

2053. ———. "Turbulent Isle." OUTLOOK 127 (April 6, 1921):
      544-547.

2054. "Sedition in Ireland." LIVING AGE 284 (January 9, 1915):
      111-114.

2055. "Shadow of Gunman Over Erin; Admiral Slain in New Irish
      Republican Drive to Keep Ireland's Sons Out of British
      Army." LITERARY DIGEST 121 (April 4, 1936): 15.

      Examines the IRA assassination of Admiral H.B. Somer-
      ville on March 25, 1936.

2056. "Sinn Fein." INDEPENDENT 90 (May 19, 1917): 317-318.

2057. "Sinn Fein and the Civil War in Ireland." CURRENT OPIN-
      ION 68 (February 1920): 154-158.

2058. "Sinn Fein and the Irish Convention." LITERARY DIGEST
      55 (September 29, 1917): 20.

2059. "Sinn Fein Fixes the World's Gaze on Ireland Again."
      CURRENT OPINION 69 (October 1920): 440-443.

2060. "Sinn Fein Gets on the International Stage." CURRENT
      OPINION 66 (April 1919): 215-218.

2061. "Sinn Fein Growing." LITERARY DIGEST 53 (October 14,
      1916): 944.

2062. "Sinn Fein is Determined Upon Self-Determination." CUR-
      RENT OPINION 66 (February 1919): 84-85.

2063. "Sinn Fein Justice." NATION 110 (June 26, 1920): 864.

2064. "Sinn Fein Prepares a New Dilemma for Anglo-American
      Diplomacy." CURRENT OPINION 69 (August 1920): 164-167.

2065. "Sinn Fein Psychology." LIVING AGE 308 (March 19-26,
      1921): 688-694, 760-766.

2066. "Sinn Feiners Win." INDEPENDENT 101 (January 31, 1920): 180-181.

2067. Skeffington, H.S. "Conscription in Ireland?" INDEPEN-DENT 89 (January 29, 1917): 181-182.

2068. Spender, H. "Ireland: A Plea for Conciliation." CON-TEMPORARY REVIEW 119 (March 1921): 299-309.

2069. ————. "Ireland and the War." CONTEMPORARY REVIEW 110 (November 1916): 565-573.

2070. ————. "Ireland Under the Truce." CONTEMPORARY REVIEW 120 (November 1921): 585-592.

2071. "Split in Sinn Fein." CURRENT OPINION 70 (March 1921): 308-310.

2072. Spring, Roy. "Connolly and Irish Freedom." HANDS OFF IRELAND! 5 (September 1978): 18-20.

2073. "State of Ireland." SURVEY 45 (December 25, 1920): 447-448.

2074. Stewart, H.L. "Ireland's Attitude to the War." NATION 102 (March 30, 1916): 352-353.

2075. ————. "Last Fifty Years of Irish Agitation." INDE-PENDENT 108 (January 28, 1923): 87-89.

2076. "Straightening the Irish Line." LITERARY DIGEST 58 (July 6, 1918): 22-23.

2077. "Suppression of Sinn Fein." INDEPENDENT 99 (September 27, 1919): 439-440.

2078. "Suppression of Sinn Fein." INDEPENDENT 101 (February 1920): 254-256.

2079. Sweeney, Joseph. "Why 'Sinn Fein'?" EIRE-IRELAND 6 (Summer 1971).

2080. "Talking Ireland into Peace." LITERARY DIGEST 70 (Octo-ber 1, 1921): 10-12.

2081. "Taming of Sinn Fein." CURRENT OPINION 70 (May 1921): 583-586.

2082. "Temper of Ireland." LIVING AGE 295 (December 15, 1917):
      682-685.

2083. Terchek, Ronald H. "Conflict and Cleavage in Northern
      Ireland." ANNALS OF THE AMERICAN ACADEMY OF POLITICAL
      AND SOCIAL SCIENCE 433 (1977): 47-59.

      Contends that modern ethnic conflict in Ireland is
      more than a mere continuance of ancient antagonisms be-
      tween Catholics and Protestants. Modern trends in Irish
      violence are charted from 1921, at the end of the civil
      war.

2084. "Terence MacSwiney, an Irish Spearhead." LITERARY DIGEST
      66 (September 25, 1920): 44-48.

2085. Thompson, R. "Riots in Ireland." CURRENT HISTORY 42
      (September 1935): 644-645.

2086. "Threats of a Fresh Insurrection in Ireland." CURRENT
      OPINION 61 (November 1916): 304-305.

2087. "Three Crises in the British Empire—India, Egypt, Ire-
      land." CURRENT OPINION 66 (June 1919): 350-352.

2088. Townsend, Charles. "The Irish Railway Strike of 1920:
      Industrial Action and Civil Resistance in the Struggle
      for Independence." IRISH HISTORICAL STUDIES 21 (1979):
      265-282.

      Examines the Irish railroad workers' 1920 embargo on
      transport of British troops and military supplies, con-
      ducted in an effort to hamper suppression of republican
      activists by military force.

2089. ———. "The Irish Republican Army and the Development
      of Guerilla Warfare, 1916-1921." ENGLISH HISTORY RE-
      VIEW 94 (1979): 318-345.

2090. Travers, C.J. "Sean MacDiarmada, 1883-1916." BREIFNE
      (1966).

      Examines the life and career of an Irish republican
      whose activities progressed from membership in the
      Ancient Order of Hibernians to an active role in the
      IRB in 1906. An organizer of Sinn Fein political cam-
      paigns in 1908, MacDiarmada became a full-time organ-
      izer for the IRB that same year. Despite a crippling

attack of polio in 1912, he continued his activities in
the republican cause, aiding both the IRB and Irish Volunteers. Briefly imprisoned by the British in 1915, he
emerged from jail to become a member of the Provisional
Government organized by Irish rebels during the 1916
Easter rising. Captured by British troops during the
revolt, he was executed in May 1916.

2091. Tristram, J.W. "Sources and Lessons of the Recent Irish
      Revolt." FORTUNE 106 (September 1916): 436-446.

2092. "Truce in the Irish Warfare." CURRENT HISTORY 14 (Aug-
      ust 1921): 851-854.

2093. "Turbulent Days in Ireland." CURRENT HISTORY 12 (May
      1920): 187-191.

2094. Turner, E.R. "Nationalist Ireland—the Case for Home
      Rule." NATION 104 (March 15, 1917): 307-310.

2095. ———. "Sinn Fein and Ireland." WORLD'S WORK 41 (No-
      vember 1920): 69-72.

2096. ———. "Sinn Fein and the United States." WORLD'S
      WORK 40 (October 1920): 544-549.

2097. ———. "Ulster—An Exposition Based on the Writings
      of Both Sides." NATION 104 (January 25, 1917): 97-101.

2098. "Two Weeks of Terror in Ireland." NATION 113 (July 6,
      1921): 23-27.

2099. "Ulster's Case Against Home Rule." LITERARY DIGEST 59
      (October 12, 1918): 18-19.

2100. "Unsettling Settlement of Ireland." LITERARY DIGEST 53
      (August 19, 1916): 399-400.

2101. "Village Discusses Sinn Fein Raid." LIVING AGE 301
      (June 28, 1919): 783-784.

2102. "Viscount Grey as an Irish Peacemaker." LITERARY DIGEST
      67 (October 16, 1920): 22-24.

2103. Walsh, F.P. "Ireland at Truce." NATION 113 (October
      12, 1921): 393-394.

2104. Walsh, J.C. "John Dillon's Task." NATION 106 (March 21, 1918): 316-318.

2105. "War Robbed Redmond of a Realization of His Life's Dream." LITERARY DIGEST 56 (March 23, 1918): 55-58.

2106. Ward, A.J. "America and the Irish Problem, 1899-1921." IRISH HISTORICAL STUDIES 16 (March 1968).

2107. ———. "Army and Ireland." 19th CENTURY AND AFTER 89 (January 1921): 1-7.

2108. ———. "Issue in Ireland." 19th CENTURY AND AFTER 90 (October 1921): 557-562.

2109. "Warfare in Ireland." CURRENT HISTORY 13 (March 1921): 495-497.

2110. Warren, G.A. "Irish Home Rule Versus Separation." PUBLIC 21 (Jnue 22, 1918): 799-800.

2111. Warren, M.R. "Soul of Ireland." DELIN 93 (December 1918): 9+.

2112. ———. "What They Are Saying in Ireland." COLLIER'S 67 (January 29, 1921): 8-9.

2113. "Way Out for Ireland." LIVING AGE 293 (April 7, 1917): 59-61.

2114. "What Ireland Wants." LIVING AGE 197 (May 4, 1918): 301-302.

2115. "What is Happening in Ireland; the Ulster View." PUBLIC 21 (March 30, 1918): 396-398.

2116. "What the Irish Wish." OUTLOOK 120 (September 4, 1918): 11-12.

2117. "When the Irish Government Was Run on the Run." LITERARY DIGEST 71 (December 24, 1921): 34.

2118. Whyte, J.H. "Daniel O'Connell and the Repeal Party." IRISH HISTORICAL STUDIES 11 (September 1959): 297-316.

2119. Wilkinson, Burke. "Erskine Childers: the Boston Connection." MASSACHUSETTS HISTORICAL SOCIETY PROCEEDINGS 86 (1974): 53-63.

Examines the life of an Irish-American novelist, born in Boston, who died fighting for the IRA in 1922.

2120. Withington, P.R. "Against Sinn Fein." NEW REPUBLIC 19 (July 2, 1919): 285.

2121. "Word for Ireland." LIVING AGE 291 (November 25, 1916).

2122. "Words and Facts in the Irish Controversy." REVIEW 5 (September 24, 1921): 267.

2123. "Work of the Sinn Fein in Ireland." REVIEW OF REVIEWS 62 (September 1920): 307-308.

ITALY

Books

2124. Absalom, Roger Neil Lewis. MUSSOLINI AND THE RISE OF ITALIAN FASCISM. London: Methuen, 1969.

2125. Alexander, Yonah. TERRORISM IN ITALY. New York: Crane, Russack, 1979.

2126. Allum, P.A. THE ITALIAN COMMUNIST PARTY SINCE 1945. Reading, England: University of Reading Press, 1970.

2127. Aya, Roderick. THE MISSED REVOLUTION: THE FATE OF RURAL REBELS IN SICILY AND SOUTHERN SPAIN, 1840-1950. Amsterdam: Anthropologisch-Sociologisch Centrum, 1975.

2128. Borgese, Giuseppe Antonio. GOLIATH: THE MARCH OF FASCISM. New York: Viking Press, 1938.

2129. Borghi, Armando. MUSSOLINI, RED AND BLACK. New York: Freie Arbeiter Stimme, 1938.

Includes an ironic epilogue referring to Adolf Hitler as "Mussolini's disciple."

2130. Carocci, Giampiero. ITALIAN FASCISM. Baltimore: Penguin, 1975.

2131. Cassels, Alan. FASCIST ITALY. New York: Crowell, 1968.

2132. Chabod, Federico. A HISTORY OF ITALIAN FASCISM. London: Weidenfeld & Nicolson, 1963.

2133. Clark, Martin. THE FAILURE OF REVOLUTION IN ITALY, 1919-
      1920. Reading, Pa.: University of Reading, 1973.

  * Coyle, Dominick J. MINORITIES IN REVOLT. POLITICAL VIO-
      LENCE IN IRELAND, ITALY, AND CYPRUS. Cited above as
      item 311, pp. 89-147.

      Charts Italian violence through the rise of fascism
      and the Italian communist party, on to the growth of
      the Red Brigades in more modern times.

2134. Darrah, David. HAIL CAESAR! New York: Hale, Cushman &
      Flint, 1936.

      Examines the rise of Benito Mussolini to power in Italy,
      including a discussion of terroristic methods used by his
      fascist Blackshirts.

2135. DeGrand, Alexander J. THE ITALIAN NATIONALIST ASSOCIA-
      TION AND THE RISE OF FASCISM IN ITALY. Lincoln, Neb.:
      University of Nebraska Press, 1978.

2136. Ebenstein, William. FASCIST ITALY. New York: American
      Book Co., 1939.

2137. Finer, Herman. MUSSOLINI'S ITALY. London: V. Gollancz,
      1935.

2138. Halperin, Samuel William. MUSSOLINI AND ITALIAN FASCISM.
      Princeton, N.Y.: Van Nostrand, 1964.

2139. Hambloch, Ernest. ITALY MILITANT. London: Duckworth,
      1941.

2140. Hibbert, Christopher. GARIBALDI AND HIS ENEMIES: THE
      CLASH OF ARMS AND PERSONALITIES IN THE MAKING OF
      ITALY. Boston: Little, Brown, 1966.

2141. Keene, Frances (ed). NEITHER LIBERTY NOR BREAD: THE
      MEANING AND TRAGEDY OF FASCISM. New York: Harper &
      Brothers, 1940.

2142. Kirkpatrick, Sir Ivone. MUSSOLINI: STUDY OF A DEMA-
      GOGUE. London: Oldhams Books, 1964.

2143. Lyttleton, Adrian. THE SEIZURE OF POWER: FASCISM IN
      ITALY, 1919-1929. New York: Charles Scribner's Sons,
      1973.

2144. Macgregor-Hastie, Roy. THE DAY OF THE LION: THE LIFE
      AND DEATH OF FASCIST ITALY. 1922-1945. New York:
      Coward-McCann, 1963.

2145. Mach Smith, Denis. MUSSOLINI. New York: Knopf, 1982.

2146. Matteotti, Giacomo. THE FASCISTI EXPOSED: A YEAR OF
      FASCIST DOMINATION. New York: H. Fertig, 1969.

2147. Monelli, Paolo. MUSSOLINI: THE INTIMATE LIFE OF A DEM-
      AGOGUE. New York: Vanguard Press, 1954.

2148. Morgan, Thomas Brynmor. SPURS ON THE BOOT: ITALY UNDER
      HER MASTERS. New York: Longmans, Green & Co., 1941.

2149. Munro, Ion Smeaton. THROUGH FASCISM TO WORLD POWER: A
      HISTORY OF THE REVOLUTION IN ITALY. London: A. Mac-
      lehose & Co., 1933.

2150. Orsini, Felice. THE AUSTRIAN DUNGEONS OF ITALY. London:
      G. Routledge, 1856.

      Presents the prison memoirs of an Italian anarchist
      noted for his resort to violence and terrorism.

2151. ————. MEMOIRS AND ADVENTURES OF FELICE ORSINI, WRITTEN
      BY HIMSELF. Edinburgh: Thomas Constable, 1857.

2152. Packe, Michael St. John. THE BOMBS OF ORSINI. London:
      Secker & Warburg, 1957.

2153. Por, Odom. FASCISM. London: Labor Publishing Co., 1923.

2154. Roberts David D. THE SYNDICALIST TRADITION AND ITALIAN
      FASCISM. Chapel Hill, N.C.: University of North Caro-
      lina Press, 1979.

2155. Salvemini, Gaetano. UNDER THE AXE OF FASCISM. New York:
      Viking Press, 1936.

2156. Sarti, Roland (ed). THE AX WITHIN: ITALIAN FASCISM IN
      ACTION. New York: New Viewpoints, 1974.

2157. ————. FASCISM AND THE INDUSTRIAL LEADERSHIP OF ITALY,
      1919-1940. Berkeley, Calif.: University of California
      Press, 1971.

2158. Schneider, Herbert Wallace. MAKING FASCISTS. Chicago: University of Chicago Press, 1929.

2159. Selder, George. SAWDUST CAESAR: THE UNTOLD HISTORY OF MUSSOLINI AND FASCISM. New York: Harper & Brothers, 1935.

2160. Sked, Alan. THE SURVIVAL OF THE HABSBURG EMPIRE: RE-DETZKY, THE IMPERIAL ARMY AND THE CLASS WAR, 1848. London: Longman, 1979.

2161. Snowden, Frank Martin. VIOLENCE AND GREAT ESTATES IN THE SOUTH OF ITALY: APULIA, 1900-1922. New York: Cambridge University Press, 1986.

2162. Sturzo, Luigi. ITALY AND FASCISM. New York: H. Fertig, 1967.

2163. Tannenbaum, Edward R. THE FASCIST EXPERIENCE: ITALIAN SOCIETY AND CULTURE, 1922-1945. New York: Basic Books, 1972.

2164. Tasca, Angelo. THE RISE OF ITALIAN FASCISM, 1918-1922. New York: H. Fertig, 1966.

   * Williams, Roger L. MANNERS AND MURDERS IN THE WORLD OF LOUIS-NAPOLEON. Cited above as item 565, pp. 68-101.

      Presents a chapter on Orsini and the Italian anarchist movement in the late 19th century.

2165. Wiskeman, Elizabeth. FASCISM IN ITALY: ITS DEVELOPMENT AND INFLUENCE. New York: St. Martin's Press, 1970.

2166. Woolf, S.J. (ed). THE REBIRTH OF ITALY, 1943-50. London: Longman, 1972.

Articles

2167. "After the Matteotti Murder." OUTLOOK 137 (August 6, 1294): 538-539.

      Examines the assassination of Giacomo Matteotti by fascist gunmen, and the political aftermath of his death.

2168. "Anarchy and Italy." OUTLOOK 65 (August 11, 1900): 853-855.

2169. Austin, F.B. "Black Shirt and Black Cassock, Italy's Two Masters." FORTUNE 119 (February 1923): 210-213.

2170. Baldwin, E.F. "Fascism in Italy." OUTLOOK 132 (December 13, 1922): 654-655.

2171. Barnes, J.S. "Basis of Fascism." EDINBURGH REVIEW 240 (July 1924): 1-15.

2172. Beals, C. "Black-Shirt Revolution." NATION 115 (December 13, 1923): 655-656.

2173. ————. "Dictatorship of Benito Mussolini." CURRENT HISTORY 18 (May 1923): 207-217.

2174. ————. "Dictatorship of the Middle Class." NATION 116 (January 17, 1923): 64-65.

2175. ————. "Fascismo: The Reaction in Italy." NATION 112 (May 4, 1921): 656-657.

2176. ————. "Fascist Labor Movement in Italy." NATION 115 (October 4, 1922): 329-330.

2177. ————. "Rise of the Fascisti in Italy." CURRENT HISTORY 15 (March 1922): 941-946.

2178. Berkes, T. "Fiume and the Fascisti." LIVING AGE 351 (December 9, 1922): 572-574.

2179. "Black-Shirted Princes of Italy; Disciplinary Regulation for the Fascist Militia." NATION 115 (November 15, 1922): 532-534.

2180. "Blood in the Palace." TIME 43 (October 21, 1946): 35.

    Examines the attempted assassination of Sir Noel Charles.

2181. Blythe, S.G. "Latin Cromwell." SATURDAY EVENING POST 195 (February 24, 1923): 25.

2182. Bugeja, V. "Fascism and Its Political Influences in Italy." QUARTERLY 237 (January 1922): 134-154.

2183. Child, R.W. "Making of Mussolini." SATURDAY EVENING POST 196 (June 28, 1924): 3-4.

2184. ————. "Open the Gates!" SATURDAY EVENING POST 197 (July 12, 1924): 5.

2185. ————. "What Does Mussolini Mean?" SATURDAY EVENING POST 197 (July 26, 1924): 23.

2186. Coote, C. "Fascist Victory and After." 19th CENTURY AND AFTER 94 (October 1923): 604-613.

2187. ————. "Modern Samurai." 19th CENTURY AND AFTER 95 (May 1924): 755-762.

2188. ————. "Prologue to Fascismo." 19th CENTURY AND AFTER 93 (February 1923): 189-198.

2189. Cortesi, A. "Tide That Swept Italy's Fascisti to Power." CURRENT HISTORY 17 (January 1923): 567-574.

2190. ————. "Year of Fascism in Italy." CURRENT HISTORY 19 (January 1924): 628-635.

2191. "Crisis in Italy." CONTEMPORARY REVIEW 122 (September 1922): 384-387.

2192. Dell, R. "Fascist Rule in South Tyrol." NATION 118 (May 21, 1924): 581-582; 118 (May 28, 1924): 609-610.

2193. Denny, L. "Mystery of Fascismo." FREEMAN 6 (February 21, 1923): 563-565.

2194. "Fascism Defended and Denounced." LITERARY DIGEST 77 (May 5, 1923): 25.

2195. "Fascismo on the Wane." LIVING AGE 310 (July 9, 1921): 63-64.

2196. "Fascism's First Anniversary." LITERARY DIGEST 79 (December 1, 1923): 22-23.

2197. "Fascism's Iron Hand." LITERARY DIGEST 81 (June 21, 1924): 22.

2198. "Fascism's Triumph Explained by Italian Writers." LITERARY DIGEST 75 (December 23, 1922): 17-18.

2199. "Fascist Coyness on Political Cooperation." LITERARY DIGEST 83 (October 4, 1924): 20-21.

2200. "Fascist Rule." CONTEMPORARY REVIEW 125 (April 1924): 432-437.

2201. "Fascisti." CURRENT OPINION 71 (October 1921): 431.

2202. "Fascisti." LIVING AGE 309 (May 14, 1921): 403-406.

2203. "Fascisti and Italy's Future." LIVING AGE 315 (November 11, 1922): 312-315.

2204. "Fascisti At Work." CURRENT OPINION 74 (February 1923): 205-207.

2205. "Fascisti Episode." LIVING AGE 315 (December 2, 1922): 498-500.

2206. "Fascisti in Italy." CONTEMPORARY REVIEW 120 (September 1921): 400-402.

2207. "Fascisti Triumphant." OUTLOOK 132 (November 15, 1922): 469-470.

2208. "Fascisti vs. Bolsheviki in Italy." LITERARY DIGEST 69 (June 11, 1921): 17-18.

2209. "Fascisti; Whither Bound?" LIVING AGE 315 (November 18, 1922): 379-384.

2210. Fuchs, J. "Why Matteotti Had to Die." NATION 119 (July 30, 1924): 114-115.

2211. Galtier, J. "Some Fascist Doctrines; Interview with Mussolini." LIVING AGE 317 (May 26, 1923): 439-442.

2212. Giglio, G. "Situation in Italy." NATION 113 (April 10, 1921): 148-149.

2213. Godkin, E.L. "Italian Trouble: Riots." NATION 166 (May 19, 1898): 378.

2214. Hackett, F. "Under the Black Shirt." SURVEY 51 (October 1, 1923): 13-17.

2215. "How Fascism Came to Be." LITERARY DIGEST 76 (January 6, 1923): 22.

2216. "Italian Fascistis, Political Crusaders." REVIEW OF REVIEWS 64 (October 1921): 438-439.

2217. "Italy: The Fury of Fear." NEWSWEEK 28 (October 31, 1946): 56.

2218 "Italy's New Political Crisis." LITERARY DIGEST 74 (August 12, 1922): 16-17.

2219. "Italy's Social Unrest." CURRENT HISTORY 17 (October 1922): 160-161.

2220. "Italy's Stormy Waters." LIVING AGE 322 (August 9, 1924): 244-246.

2221. "Italy's War Between the Red Unions and Fighting Fascisti." LITERARY DIGEST 75 (October 28, 1922): 45-47.

2222. "Italy's White Terror." NATION 116 (March 28, 1923): 374-375.

     Examines fascist violence against left-wing elements during the 1920s.

2223. Livingston, A. "Italy and the Fascisti." CENTURY 106 (June 1923): 265-272.

2224. Lyttleton, Adrian. "Fascism and Violence: Social Conflict and Political Action in Italy After World War I." STORIA CONTEMPORANEA 13 (1982): 965-983.

2225. McCracken, W.D. "Riot in Rome, February 1889." ARENA 5 (May 1892): 743-747.

2226. Mancini, V.F. di G. "Memoirs of a Fascist Organizer." NATION 115 (December 20, 1922): 698-700.

2227. "March on Rome." LIVING AGE 319 (December 22, 1923): 552-555.

2228. "Matteotti Mystery." OUTLOOK 137 (July 2, 1924): 340-341.

     Continues a search for clues and responsibility in the political murder of Giacomo Matteotti.

2229. Mondolfo, R. "Some Causes of Fascism." LIVING AGE 312 (January 7, 1922): 53-56.

2230. Morgan, E.S. "Fascisti." EDINBURGH REVIEW 236 (July 1922): 152-165.

2231. "Mussolini and the Klan." NATION 119 (July 2, 1924): 5.

   Examines the abortive flirtation between Mussolini's
   blackshirts and America's own white-robed fascists.

2232. "Mussolini, Garibaldi or Caesar?" LITERARY DIGEST 75
   (November 18, 1922): 17-18.

2233. "Mussolini Reactionary?" LIVING AGE 316 (March 31, 1923):
   742-743.

2234. "Mussolini Reaps a Whirlwind." CURRENT OPINION 77 (August 1924): 147-149.

2235. "Mussolini's Aim at Conciliation." LITERARY DIGEST 82
   (September 13, 1924): 21.

2236. Nitti, F.S. "Italian Anarchists." NORTH AMERICAN REVIEW
   167 (November 1898): 598-608.

2237. "Nobility of Violence." NATION 112 (June 29, 1921): 928-
   929.

2238. "Oath of the Fascisti." NATION 115 (November 22, 1922):
   541-542.

2239. Perillo, Gaetano I. "Communists and Class Struggle in
   Liguria, November 1922—November 1926." MOVIMENTO
   OPERAIO E SOCIALISTA 17 (1971): 57-104.

   Describes the four-year battle between communists and
   fascists for political control in one section of Italy.

2240. Peterson, Jens. "The Problem of Violence in Italian
   Fascism." STORIA CONTEMPORANEA 13 (1982): 985-1008.

2241. "Political Murder in Italy." LITERARY DIGEST 82 (July 5,
   1924): 18.

   Reviews the fascist slaying of Giacomo Matteotti.

2242. Pollakoff, V. "Mussolini and His Methods." FORTUNE 119
   (May 1923): 742-747.

2243. Poole, E. "Is Fascism Dead?" OUTLOOK 134 (July 4, 1923):
   316-318.

2244. Prezzolini, G. "Fascism on Trial." NEW REPUBLIC 39
      (August 6, 1924): 295-297.

2245. ─────. "Fascista Movement in Italy." CONTEMPORARY
      REVIEW 119 (June 1921): 796-800.

2246. ─────. "Fascisti and the Class Struggle." NEW REPUB-
      LIC 32 (November 1, 1922): 242-244.

2247. ─────. "Italian Fascisti." CENTURY 102 (September
      1921): 683-691.

2248. Quagliariello, Ernesto. "The Witness of Giovanni Amen-
      dola." STUDIUM 78 (1982): 545-554.

      Profiles another victim of fascist assassins, slain in
      July 1925.

2249. Roberts, K.L. "Ambush of Italy." SATURDAY EVENING POST
      196 (August 25, 1923): 6-7.

2250. ─────. "Fight of the Black Shirts." SATURDAY EVENING
      POST 196 (September 8, 1923): 19.

2251. ─────. "Salvage of a Nation." SATURDAY EVENING POST
      196 (September 22, 1923): 20-21.

2252. Roselli, B. "Fascisti." OUTLOOK 132 (November 8, 1922):
      428-429.

2253. Showerman, G. "Dead and Quick in Eternal Rome." INDE-
      PENDENT 108 (January 28, 1922): 69-70.

2254. Smith, Denis Mack. "The Matteotti Affair." HISTOIRE
      52 (1983): 10-18.

2255. ─────. "The Murder of Matteotti." ITALIAN QUARTERLY
      24 (1983): 11-20.

2256. "Socialist-Fascisti Truce in Italy." NATION 113 (Novem-
      ber 2, 1921): 514-516.

2257. "Some Fascist Tactics." NATION 115 (December 20, 1922):
      698.

2258. Speranza, G. "Fascismo." INDEPENDENT 109 (November 11,
      1922): 258-259.

2259. Turati, F. "Sanity Out of Italy." NATION 116 (January 24, 1923): 104-106.

2260. "Vigilantes of Italy." INDEPENDENT 109 (September 2, 1923): 90.

2261. Villari, L., and G. Bruccoleri. "Advent of Fascismo." CONTEMPORARY REVIEW 123 (February 1923): 145-155.

2262. Waterfield, L. "Decline of the Fascisti." LIVING AGE 311 (October 29, 1921): 300-303.

2263. "What Keeps Mussolini in Power." LITERARY DIGEST 82 (August 9, 1924): 16-17.

2264. "What Mussolini and the Fascisti Mean to Italy." CURRENT OPINION 73 (October 1922): 469-471.

2265. "Who the Italian Fascisti Are." LITERARY DIGEST 59 (April 16, 1921): 18.

2266. Wood, L.J.S. "Ho, Lictors, Clear the Way! Fascismo and the Fascisti." ATLANTIC 131 (February 1923): 250-258.

2267. Woolf, L. "Fascista Revolution." CONTEMPORARY REVIEW 122 (December 1922): 789-792.

Netherlands

Articles

2268. Herman, Valentine, and Rob van der Laars Bouma. "Nationalists Without a Nation: South Moluccan Terrorism in the Netherlands." TERRORISM 4 (1980): 223-257.

Examines the status of South Moluccan separatists and their resort to violence spanning two decades, from the 1950s to the 1970s.

2269. "Holland and Its Fascism." REVIEW OF REVIEWS 71 (March 1926): 321-322.

2270. Wenner, T.J.B. "Dutch Cure for Fascism." CURRENT HISTORY 48 (May 1938): 39-42.

POLAND

Books

2271. Coleman, Arthur Prudden, and Marin More Coleman. THE
POLISH INSURRECTION OF 1863 IN THE LIGHT OF NEW YORK
EDITORIAL OPINION. Williamsport, Pa.: Bayard Press,
1934.

2272. Day, William Ansell. THE RUSSIAN GOVERNMENT IN POLAND;
WITH A NARRATIVE OF THE POLISH INSURRECTION OF 1863.
London: Longmans, Green, Reader & Dyer, 1867.

2273. Lutsiv, Vasyl'. UKRAINIANS AND THE POLITICAL REVOLT OF
1863; A CONTRIBUTION TO THE HISTORY OF UKRAINIAN-POLISH
RELATIONS. New Haven, Conn.: Slavia Library, 1961.

Articles

2274. Cardwell, A. "Poland: A Nazi Blueprint of France?"
CHRISTIAN SCIENCE MONITOR MAGAZINE (June 29, 1940): 2.

2275. Korzec, Pawel. "The Steiger Affair." SOVIET JEWISH
AFFAIRS 3 (1973): 38-57.

Chronicles the upsruge in Polish antisemitism following an alleged attempt by Jews to kill the Polish president in 1925.

PORTUGAL

Books

2276. Wheeler, Douglas L. REPUBLIC PORTUGAL: A POLITICAL HIS-
TORY, 1910-1926. Madison, Wis.: University of Wisconsin Press, 1978.

Includes discussion of political assassinations which
rocked Portugal's government in December 1918 and October 1921.

ROMANIA

Books

2277. Eidelberg, Philip Gabriel. THE GREAT RUMANIAN PEASANT
REVOLT IN 1907. Leiden: Brill, 1974.

2278. Georgescu-Buzau, Gh. THE 1848 REVOLUTION IN THE RUMAN-
       IAN LANDS. Bucharest" Meridiane Publishing House, 1965

2279. Hitchins, Keith Arnold. THE RUMANIAN NATIONAL MOVEMENT
       IN TRANSYLVANIA, 1780-1849. Cambridge, Mass.: Har-
       vard University Press, 1969.

2280. Pascu, Stefan (ed). THE INDEPENDENCE OF ROMANIA. Bu-
       charest: Editura, Academici Republici Socialiste Ro-
       mania, 1977.

       Presents a carefully-edited communist view of revolu-
       tionary trends in Romanian history, climaxing with the
       nation's "independence" under Soviet leadership.

2281. Roberts, Henry L. RUMANIA: POLITICAL PROBLEMS OF AN
       AGRARIAN STATE. New Haven, Conn.: Yale University
       Press, 1951.

       Includes an examination of unrest and occasional vio-
       lence among Romanian peasants after the Soviet occupa-
       tion.

                              Articles

2282. "Assassination an Anti-Semitic Weapon in Roumania."
       LITERARY DIGEST 117 (January 13, 1934): 13.

       Examines the political murder of Ion Duca in December
       1933.

2283. Chirot, Daniel, and Charles Ragin. "The Market, Tra-
       dition, and Peasant Rebellion: The Case of Romania
       in 1907." AMERICAN SOCIOLOGICAL REVIEW 40 (August
       1975): 429.

2284. Spalatelu, Ion. "The Militant Position of the Democratic
       Progressive Forces with the Romanian Communist Party
       at Their Head Against the Social-Political Concepts of
       Legionarism." ROMANIA 6 (1981): 64-85.

       Presents a communist view of history, charting Romanian
       communist party resistance against the Iron Guard, a
       group of extreme nationalists sponsored by German Nazis.

2285. Wolfe, H.C. "Fascism in Rumania." NEW REPUBLIC 93
       (November 24, 1937): 67-68.

RUSSIA

Books

2286. Abramovitch, Raphael R. THE SOVIET REVOLUTION, 1917-1939. New York: International Studies Press, 1962.

2287. Alioshin, Dmitri. ASIAN ODYSSEY. New York: H. Holt & Co., 1940.

An officer of the Tsar's imperial army describes his flight from Russia after the Bolshevik revolution.

2288. Ascher, Abraham (ed). THE MENSHIVIKS AND THE RUSSIAN REVOLUTION. New York: Cornell University Press, 1976.

2289. Astrov, Vladimir. AN ILLUSTRATED HISTORY OF THE RUSSIAN REVOLUTION. 2 Vols. New York: International Publishers, 1928-1929.

2290. Avrich, Paul. THE RUSSIAN ANARCHISTS. Princeton, N.J.: Princeton University Press, 1967.

2291. Beatty, Bessie. THE RED HEART OF RUSSIA. New York: The Century Co., 1919.

2292. Berkman, Alexander. THE RUSSIAN REVOLUTION AND THE COMMUNIST PARTY. Berlin: Der Syndikalist, 1922.

Presents an anarchist's view of the Bolshevik revolt in Russia.

2293. ———. THE RUSSIAN TRAGEDY. Sanday: Cienfuegos Press, 1976.

Examines the "betrayal of the people's revolution" by elitist elements of the communist party in Russia. An old anarchist clings to his chaotic principles to the bitter end.

2294. Bettelheim, Charles. CLASS STRUGGLES IN THE USSR. New York: Monthly Review Press, 1976.

2285. Bochkareva, Maria Leontievna. YASHKA, MY LIFE AS PEAS- ANT, OFFICER AND EXILE. New York: Frederick A. Stokes, 1919.

Presents a revolutionary memoir from the commander of the Russian "women's battalion of death."

2296. Boleslavski, Richard. LANCES DOWN: BETWEEN THE FIRES IN MOSCOW. Indianapolis, Ind.: Bobbs-Merrill, 1932.

2297. ————, and Helen Woodward. WAY OF THE LANCES. New York: The Literary Guild, 1932.

2298. Borcke, Astrid von. "Violence and Terror in Russian Revolutionary Populism: The Narodnaya Volya, 1879-83." SOCIAL PROTEST, VIOLENCE AND TERROR IN NINETEENTH- AND TWENTIETH-CENTURY EUROPE. Cited above as item 41, pp. 48-62.

2299. Botcharsky, Sophie. THE KINSMEN KNOW HOW TO DIE. New York: W. Morrow & Co., 1931.

2300. Bradley, John Francis Nejez. CIVIL WAR IN RUSSIA, 1917-1920. London: B.T. Batsford, 1975.

2301. Breshko-Breshkovskaia, Ekaterina Konstantinova. HIDDEN SPRINGS OF THE RUSSIAN REVOLUTION: PERSONAL MEMOIRS OF KATERINA BRESHKOVSKAIA. London: H. Milford, 1931.

2302. Brower, Daniel R. THE RUSSIAN REVOLUTION: DISORDER OR NEW ORDER? St. Louis: Forum Press, 1979.

2303. Brown, Arthur Jackson. RUSSIA IN TRANSFORMATION. New York: Fleming H. Revell, 1917.

2304. Brown, Douglas. DOOMSDAY 1917: THE DESTRUCTION OF RUSSIA'S RULING CLASS. New York: G.P. Putnam, 1975.

2305. Bryant, Louis. SIX RED MONTHS IN RUSSIA. New York: George H. Doran Co., 1918.

2306. Buchanan, Meriel. THE DISSOLUTION OF AN EMPIRE. London: J. Murray, 1932.

2307. ————. PETRODGRAD, THE CITY IN TROUBLE, 1914-1918. London: W. Collins Sons, 1918.

2308. Bullard, Arthur. THE RUSSIAN PENDULUM: AUTOCRACY—DEMOCRACY—BOLSHEVISM. New York: Macmillan, 1919.

2309. Carmichael, Joel. A SHORT HISTORY OF THE RUSSIAN REVOLUTION. New York: Basic Books, 1964.

2310. Carr, Edward Hallett. MICHAEL BAKUNIN. London: Macmillan, 1937.

Examines the anarchist movement in Russia and its persistent efforts to topple the Tsarist regime through acts of terror and assassination.

2311. ————. THE OCTOBER REVOLUTION: BEFORE AND AFTER. New York: Knopf, 1969.

2312. Cash, Anthony. THE RUSSIAN REVOLUTION. London: Benn, 1967.

2313. Chamberlin, William Henry. THE RUSSIAN REVOLUTION, 1917-1923. New York: Macmillan, 1935.

2314. Chernov, Viktor Mikhailovich. THE GREAT RUSSIAN REVOLUTION. New Haven, Conn.: Yale University Press, 1936.

2315. Chernova-Kolbasima, Olga E. NEW HORIZONS: REMINISCENCES OF THE RUSSIAN REVOLUTION. London: Hutchinson, 1936.

2316. Curtiss, John Shelton. THE RUSSIAN REVOLUTIONS OF 1917. Princeton, N.Y.: Van Nostrand, 1957.

2317. Daily, Kenneth Irving. THE RUSSIAN PROVISIONAL GOVERNMENT OF 1917. Ann Arbor, Mich.: University Microfilms, 1957.

2318. Daniels, Robert Vincent. RED OCTOBER: THE BOLSHEVIK REVOLUTION OF 1917. New York: Scribner, 1967.

2319. Davitt, Michael. WITHIN THE PALE: THE TRUE STORY OF ANTI-SEMITIC PERSECUTIONS IN RUSSIA. London: Hurst & Blackett, 1903.

Presents the unique perspective of an Irish rebel active in the Russian cause.

2320. Deniken, Anton Ivanovich. THE RUSSIAN TURMOIL: MEMOIRS, MILITARY, SOCIAL, AND POLITICAL. London: Hutchinson, 1922.

2321. ————. THE WHITE ARMY. London: J. Cape, 1930.

2322. Dolgoff, Sam (ed). BAKUNIN ON ANARCHY: SELECTED WORKS BY THE ANARCHIST-FOUNDER OF WORLD ANARCHISM. New York: Knopf, 1972.

2323. Dorr, R.C. INSIDE THE RUSSIAN REVOLUTION. New York: Macmillan, 1917.

2324. Dziewanowski, M.K. (ed). THE RUSSIAN REVOLUTION: AN ANTHOLOGY. New York: Crowell, 1977.

2325. Eichenbaum, Vsevolod Mikhailovich. NINETEEN-SEVENTEEN: THE RUSSIAN REVOLUTION BETRAYED. London: Freedom Press, 1954.

2326. ————. THE UNKNOWN REVOLUTION, 1917-1921. New York: Free Life Editions, 1974.

2327. Engel, Barbara Alpern, and Clifford N. Rosenthal (eds). FIVE SISTERS: WOMEN AGAINST THE TSAR. New York: Knopf, 1975.

2328. Farbman, Michael. BOLSHEVISM IN RETREAT. London: W. Collins Sons, 1923.

2329. Ferro, Marc. OCTOBER 1917: A SOCIAL HISTORY OF THE RUSSIAN REVOLUTION. London: Routledge & Kegan Paul, 1980.

2330. Figner, Vera. MEMOIRS OF A REVOLUTIONIST. New York: International Publishers, 1927.

2331. Fleming, Peter. THE FATE OF ADMIRAL KOLCHAK. New York: Harcourt, Brace & World, 1963.

2332. Floyd, David. RUSSIA IN REVOLT: 1905: THE FIRST CRACK IN TSARIST POWER. London: Macdonald & Co., 1969.

2333. Footman, David. THE ALEXANDER CONSPIRACY: A LIFE OF A.I. ZHELYABOV. LaSalle, Ill.: Open Court Publishing Co., 1974.

2334. ————. CIVIL WAR IN RUSSIA. London: Faber & Faber, 1961.

2335. ————. THE RUSSIAN REVOLUTIONS. London: Faber & Faber, 1962.

2336. Foster, William Z. THE RUSSIAN REVOLUTION. Chicago: Trade Union Educational League, 1921.

    The leader of America's communist party offers bound-
    less praise for Russia's Bolshevik revolutionaries.

2337. Francis, David Rowland. RUSSIA FROM THE AMERICAN EMBAS-
      SY, APRIL 1916—NOVEMBER 1918. New York: C. Scribner's
      Sons, 1921.

2338. Gill, Graeme J. PEASANTS AND GOVERNMENT IN THE RUSSIAN
      REVOLUTION. New York: Barnes & Noble, 1975.

2339. Goldman, E. THE CRUSHING OF THE RUSSIAN REVOLUTION.
      London: Freedom Press, 1922.

2340. Goldston, Robert C. THE RUSSIAN REVOLUTION. Indianap-
      olis, Ind.: Bobbs-Merrill, 1966.

2341. Gordon, Alban Godwin. RUSSIAN YEAR: A CALENDAR OF REV-
      OLUTION. London: Cassell & Co., 1935.

2342. Gross, Feliks. VIOLENCE IN POLITICAL TERROR AND POLITI-
      CAL ASSASSINATION IN EASTERN EUROPE AND RUSSIA. The
      Hague: Mouton, 1972.

2343. Halliday, Ernest Milton. RUSSIA IN REVOLUTION. New
      York: American Heritage Publishing Co., 1967.

2344. Harcave, Sidney Samuel. FIRST BLOOD: THE RUSSIAN REV-
      OLUTION OF 1905. New York: Macmillan, 1964.

2345. Harper, Florence MacLeod. RUNAWAY RUSSIA. New York:
      The Century Co., 1918.

2346. Hill, John Edward Christopher. LENIN AND THE RUSSIAN
      REVOLUTION. London: English Universities Press, 1961.

2347. Hillquit, Morris. FROM MARX TO LENIN. New York: The
      Hanford Press, 1921.

2348. Hindus, Maurice Gerschon. THE RUSSIAN PEASANT AND THE
      REVOLUTION. New York: H. Holt & Co., 1920.

2349. Hingley, Ronald. NIHILISTS: RUSSIAN RADICALS AND REV-
      OLUTIONARIES IN THE REIGN OF ALEXANDER II, 1855-81.
      London: Weidenfeld & Nicolson, 1967.

2350. Hodgson, John Ernest. WITH DENIKIN'S ARMIES: BEING A
      DESCRIPTION OF THE COSSACK COUNTER-REVOLUTION IN
      SOUTH RUSSIA, 1918-1920. London: L. Williams, 1932.

2351. Hough, Richard Alexander. THE POTEMKIN MUTINY. London:
      H. Hamilton, 1960.

2352. Houghteling, James Lawrence. A DIARY OF THE RUSSIAN
      REVOLUTION. New York: Dodd, Mead, 1918.

2353. Hyndman, Henry Mayers. THE EVOLUTION OF REVOLUTION.
      London: G. Richards, 1920.

2354. Katkov, George. RUSSIA, 1917: THE FEBRUARY REVOLUTION.
      New York: Harper & Row, 1967.

2355. Keep, John Leslie Howard. THE RUSSIAN REVOLUTION: A
      STUDY IN MASS MOBILIZATION. London: Weidenfeld &
      Nicolson, 1976.

2356. Kempz, Peter. CIVIL WAR IN SOUTH RUSSIA: THE FIRST YEAR
      OF THE VOLUNTEER ARMY. Berkeley, Calif.: University
      of California Press, 1971.

2357. ————. CIVIL WAR IN SOUTH RUSSIA, 1919-1920: THE DE-
      FEAT OF THE WHITES. Berkeley, Calif.: University of
      California Press, 1977.

2358. Kerensky, Alexander Feodorovich. THE CATASTROPHE: KER-
      ENSKY'S OWN STORY OF THE RUSSIAN REVOLUTION. New
      York: D. Appleton & Co., 1927.

      The deposed Menshevik leader, responsible for the
      actual overthrow of the Tsarist regime, describes the
      betrayal of his popular revolution by Bolshevik agents.

2359. ————. THE CRUCIFIXION OF LIBERTY. New York: The
      John Day Co., 1934.

2360. ————. RUSSIA AND HISTORY'S TURNING POINT. New York:
      Duell, Sloan & Pearce, 1965.

2361. Kettle, Michael. THE ALLIES AND THE RUSSIAN COLLAPSE,
      MARCH 1917-MARCH 1919. St. Paul, Minn.: University
      of Minnesota Press, 1981.

2362. Kirby, Louis Paul. THE RUSSIAN REVOLUTION. Boston:
      Meador Publishing Co., 1940.

2363, Kochan, Lionel. RUSSIAN IN REVOLUTION 1890-1918. Lon-
      don: Weidenfeld & Nicolson, 1966.

2364. Koenker, Diane. MOSCOW WORKERS AND THE 1917 REVOLUTION.
      Princeton, N.J.: Princeton University Press, 1981.

2365. Korff, Sergiei Aleksandrovich. AUTOCRACY AND REVOLUTION
      IN RUSSIA. New York: Macmillan, 1923.

2366. Kravchinsky, Sergei. UNDERGROUND RUSSIA: REVOLUTIONARY
      PROFILES AND SKETCHES FROM LIFE. New York: Scribner,
      1883.

      An interesting revolutionary memoir from the killer
      who assassinated General Mesentov in 1878.

2367. Lange, Christian Louis. RUSSIA, THE REVOLUTION AND THE
      WAR. Washington, D.C.: The Endowment, 1917.

2368. Lansbury, George. WHAT I SAW IN RUSSIA. New York: Boni
      & Liveright, 1920.

2369. Larsson, Reidar. THEORIES OF REVOLUTION: FROM MARX TO
      THE FIRST RUSSIAN REVOLUTION. Stockholm: Almqvist &
      Wiksell, 1970.

2370. Lawton, Lancelot. THE RUSSIAN REVOLUTION. London: Mac-
      millan, 1927.

2371. Lehovich, Dimitri V. WHITE AGAINST RED: THE LIFE OF
      GENERAL ANTON DENIKIN. New York: Norton, 1974.

2372. Lenin, Vladimir Ilich. COLLECTED WORKS. Moscow: Pro-
      gress, 1962.

2373. ———, and Leon Trotsky. THE PROLETARIAN REVOLUTION IN
      RUSSIA. New York: The Communist Press, 1918.

2374. Levine, Isaac Don. THE MAN LENIN. New York: T. Seltzer,
      1924.

2375. ———. THE RUSSIAN REVOLUTION. New York: Harper, 1917.

2376. Levy, Roger. TROTSKY. Paris: Librairie de Parti
      Socialiste et de l'Humanite, 1920.

2377. Liebman, Marcel. THE RUSSIAN REVOLUTION. New York;
      Random House, 1970.

2378. Litvinov, Maksim Maksimovich. THE BOLSHEVIK REVOLUTION:
      ITS RISE AND MEANING. Chicago: Socialist Party of
      the U.S., 1920.

2379. Lobanov-Rostovsky, Prince Andrei. THE GRINDING MILL:
      REMINISCENCES OF WAR AND REVOLUTION IN RUSSIA, 1913–
      1920. New York: Macmillan, 1935.

2380. Lomonosov, George V. MEMOIRS OF THE RUSSIAN REVOLUTION.
      New York: The Rand School of Social Science, 1919.

2381. McDonald, Lawrence Patton. TROTSKYISM AND TERROR: THE
      STRATEGY OF THE REVOLUTION. Washington, D.C.: ACU
      Educational and Research Institute, 1977.

2382. McNeal, Robert Hatch. THE RUSSIAN REVOLUTION: WHY DID
      THE BOLSHEVIKS WIN? New York: Rinehart, 1959.

2383. Mailloux, Kenneth Frank. LENIN: THE EXILE RETURNS.
      Princeton, N.J.: Aurebach Publishers, 1971.

2384. Maksimov, Grigorii Petrovich. THE GUILLOTINE AT WORK:
      TWENTY YEARS OF TERROR IN RUSSIA. Chicago: The Chi-
      cago Section of the Alexander Berkman Fund, 1940.

2385. Malia, Martin. ALEXANDER HERZEN AND THE BIRTH OF RUS-
      SIAN SOCIALISM. Cambridge, Mass.: Harvard University
      Press, 1961.

2386. Marcasson, Isaac Frederick. THE REBIRTH OF RUSSIA.
      London: John Lane, 1917.

2387. Marcu, Valerin. LENIN. New York: Macmillan, 1928.

2388. Maxton, J. LENIN. London: P. Davies, 1932.

2389. Matzel, Matitiahu. GENERALS AND REVOLUTIONARIES: THE
      RUSSIAN GENERAL STAFF DURING THE REVOLUTION. Osna-
      bruck: Biblio-Verlag, 1979.

2390. Mehlinger, Howard D. COUNT WITTE AND THE TSARIST GOV-
      ERNMENT IN THE 1905 REVOLUTION. Bloomington, Ind.:
      Indiana University Press, 1972.

2391. Meiendorf, Baron Aleksandr Feliksovich. THE BEGINNING
      OF THE RUSSIAN REVOLUTION. New York: H. Holt & Co.,
      1929.

2392. Milinkov, Pavel Nikolaevich. BOLSHEVISM: AN INTERNATION-
      AL DANGER, ITS DOCTRINE AND ITS PRACTICE THROUGH WAR
      AND REVOLUTION. London: G. Allen & Unwin, 1920.

2393. Mirsky, D.S. LENIN. Boston: Little, Brown, 1931.

2394. Moorehead, Alan. THE RUSSIAN REVOLUTION. New York:
      Harper, 1958.

2395. Naimark, Norman M. TERRORISTS AND SOCIALISTS: THE RUS-
      SIAN REVOLUTIONARY MOVEMENT UNDER ALEXANDER III. Cam-
      bridge, Mass.: Harvard University Press, 1983.

2396. Nevison, Henry Wood. THE DAWN IN RUSSIA. New York:
      Arno Press, 1971.

2397. Nikitin, B.V. THE FATAL YEARS: FRESH REVELATIONS ON A
      CHAPTER OF UNDERGROUND HISTORY. Westport, Conn.:
      Alfred Knox, 1977.

2398. Ossendowski, Ferdynand Antoni. FROM PRESIDENT TO PRISON.
      New York: E.P. Dutton, 1925.

2399. Pares, Sir Bernard. THE FALL OF THE RUSSIAN MONARCHY.
      London: Jonathan Cape, 1938.

2400. ————. MY RUSSIAN MEMOIRS. London: Jonathan Cape, 1931.

2401. Payne, Pierre Stephen Robert. THE LIFE AND DEATH OF
      LENIN. New York: Simon & Schuster, 1964.

2402. ————. THE TERRORISTS: THE STORY OF THE FORERUNNERS
      OF STALIN. New York: Funk & Wagnalls, 1957.

2403. Pearson, Michael. THE SEALED TRAIN. New York: Putnam,
      1975.

      Examines German involvement in fomenting Russian rev-
      olution during World War I, as a strategic ploy. The
      exiled Lenin was transported across Europe in a sealed
      train for insertion into Russia, a tactic later compared
      by Winston Churchill to deliberate infection of a healthy
      body with "a plague bacillus."

2404. Pethybridge, Roger William. THE SPREAD OF THE RUSSIAN
      REVOLUTION. London: Macmillan, 1972.

2405. Petrunkevitch, Alexander Ivanovitch. THE RUSSIAN REV-
      OLUTION. Cambridge, Mass.: Harvard University Press,
      1968.

2406. Pettit, Walter William. THE RUSSIAN REVOLUTION. New
      York: Institute for International Education, 1920.

2407. Polloch, John. THE BOLSHEVIK ADVENTURE. New York:
      Dutton, 1919.

2408. Rabinowitch, Alexander. THE BOLSHEVIKS COME TO POWER.
      New York: W.W. Norton, 1976.

2409. ———. PRELUDE TO REVOLUTION. Bloomington, Ind.:
      Indiana University Press, 1968.

2410. Radkey, Oliver Henry. THE UNKNOWN REVOLUTION: A STUDY
      OF THE GREEN MOVEMENT IN THE TAMBOV REGION, 1920-1921.
      Stanford, Calif.: Hoover Institution Press, 1976.

2411, Radziwill, E.R. RASPUTIN AND THE RUSSIAN REVOLUTION.
      New York: John Lane Co., 1918.

2412. Rappoport, Angelo Solomon. PIONEERS OF THE RUSSIAN
      REVOLUTION. London: S. Paul & Co., 1918.

2413. Reed, John. TEN DAYS THAT SHOOK THE WORLD. New York:
      Boni & Liveright, 1919.

      An American communist gadfly offers his observations
      on contemporary upheaval in Russia. Reed's memoirs were
      subsequently transformed into a long, boring motion pic-
      ture with Warren Beatty in the leading role.

2414. Robinson, Geroid Tanquary. RURAL RUSSIA UNDER THE OLD
      REGIME: A HISTORY OF THE LANDLORD-PEASANT WORLD AND A
      PROLOGUE TO THE PEASANT REVOLUTION OF 1917. Berkeley,
      Calif.: University of California Press, 1960.

2415. Rosenberg, Arthur. A HISTORY OF BOLSHEVISM, FROM MARX
      TO THE FIRST FIVE YEAR PLAN. London: Oxford Univer-
      sity Press, 1934.

2416. Rosenbery, William G. A.I. DENIKIN AND THE ANTI-BOLSHE-
      VIK MOVEMENT IN SOUTH RUSSIA. Amherst, Mass.: Amherst
      College Press, 1961.

2417. Ross, Edward Alsworth. RUSSIA IN UPHEAVAL. New York:
      The Century Co., 1918.

2418. ———. THE RUSSIAN BOLSHEVIK REVOLUTION. New York:
      The Century Co., 1921.

2419. Russell, Charles Edward. BOLSHEVISM AND THE UNITED
      STATES. Indianapolis, Ind.: Bobbs-Merrill, 1919.

2420. ————. UNCHAINED RUSSIA. New York: D. Appleton & Co.,
      1918.

2421. Sablinsky, Walter. THE ROAD TO BLOODY SUNDAY: FATHER
      GAPON AND THE ST. PETERSBURG MASSACRE OF 1905. Prince-
      ton, N.J.: Princeton University Press, 1976.

2422. Salisbury, Harrison Evans. BLACK NIGHT, WHITE SNOW:
      RUSSIA'S REVOLUTION (1905-1917). New York: Doubleday,
      1978.

2423. Sayler, Oliver M. RUSSIA, WHITE OR RED. Boston: Little,
      Brown, 1919.

2424. Schwarz, Solomon M. THE RUSSIAN REVOLUTION OF 1905: THE
      WORKERS' MOVEMENT AND THE FORMATION OF BOLSHEVISM AND
      MENSHEVISM. Chicago: University of Chicago Press, 1967.

2425. Shukman, Harold. LENIN AND THE RUSSIAN REVOLUTION. New
      York: Putnam, 1967.

2426. Sisson, Edgar Grant. ONE HUNDRED RED DAYS: A PERSONAL
      CHRONICLE OF THE BOLSHEVIK REVOLUTION. New Haven,
      Conn.: Yale University Press, 1931.

2427. Smith, Clarence Jay. FINLAND AND THE RUSSIAN REVOLUTION,
      1917-1922. Athens, Ga.: University of Georgia Press,
      1958.

2428. Spargo, John. BOLSHEVISM, THE ENEMY OF POLITICAL AND
      INDUSTRIAL DEMOCRACY. New York: Harper & Brothers,
      1919.

2429. Spector, Ivar. THE FIRST RUSSIAN REVOLUTION: ITS IMPACT
      ON ASIA. Englewood Cliffs, N.J.: Prentice-Hall, 1962.

2430. Spinka, Matthew. THE CHURCH AND THE RUSSIAN REVOLUTION.
      New York: Macmillan, 1927.

2431. Stalin, Joseph. THE ROAD TO POWER. New York: Inter-
      national Publishers, 1937.

2432. Stebbing, Edward Percy. FROM CZAR TO BOLSHEVIK. London:
      John Lane, 1918.

2433. Steinberg, Isaac Nachman. IN THE WORKSHOP OF THE REVO-
      LUTION. New York: Rinehart, 1953.

2434. ———. SPIRIDONOVA: THE REVOLUTIONARY TERRORIST. Lon-
      don: Methuen, 1935.

      Presents the biography of revolutionary Maria Aleksan-
      drovna Spiridonova.

2435. Stewart, George. THE WHITE ARMIES OF RUSSIA: A CHRONI-
      CLE OF COUNTER-REVOLUTION AND ALLIED INTERVENTION.
      New York: Macmillan, 1933.

2436. Sukhamov, Nikolai Nikolaevich. THE RUSSIAN REVOLUTION,
      1917, A PERSONAL RECORD. London: Oxford University
      Press, 1955.

2437. Summers, Anthony. THE FILE ON THE TSAR. New York:
      Harper & Row, 1976.

2438. Thompson, Arthur William. THE UNCERTAIN CRUSADE: AMER-
      ICA AND THE RUSSIAN REVOLUTION OF 1905. Amherst, Mass.
      University of Massachusetts Press, 1970.

2439. Treviranus, Gottfried Reinhold. REVOLUTIONS IN RUSSIA:
      THEIR LESSONS FOR THE WESTERN WORLD. New York: Harper
      & Brothers, 1944.

2440. Trotsky, Leon. BETWEEN RED AND WHITE. London: Commu-
      nist Party of Great Britain, 1922.

      A leading architect of the Bolshevik revolution pre-
      sents his memoirs of the Russian civil war.

2441. ———. THE DEFENCE OF TERRORISM. London: Labour
      Publishing Co., 1920.

2442. ———. FROM OCTOBER TO BREST-LITOVSK. New York:
      The Socialist Publishing Society, 1919.

2443. ———. THE HISTORY OF THE RUSSIAN REVOLUTION. New
      York: Simon & Schuster, 1932.

2444. ———. LENIN. New York: Minton, Balch & Co., 1925.

2445. ———. LESSONS OF OCTOBER. New York: Pioneer Publish-
      ers, 1937.

2446. ————. OUR REVOLUTION: ESSAYS ON WORKING-CLASS AND
      INTERNATIONAL REVOLUTION, 1904-1917. New York: H.
      Holt & Co., 1918.

2447. ————. THE REVOLUTION BETRAYED. New York: Doubleday,
      Doran & Co., 1937.

      Bitter in exile, Trotsky laments the betrayal of rev-
      olutionary ideals by Soviet leaders, counting down the
      days to his own pick-ax assassination in Mexico.

2448. ————. THE RUSSIAN REVOLUTION: THE OVERTHROW OF TZARISM
      AND THE TRIUMPH OF THE SOVIETS. New York: Doubleday,
      1959.

2449. Tucker, Robert C. PATHS OF COMMUNIST REVOLUTION. Prince-
      ton, N.J.: Woodrow Wilson School of Public and Interna-
      tional Affairs, 1968.

2450. Ulam, Adam. THE BOLSHEVIKS. New York: Macmillan, 1965.

2451. Ullman, Richard Henry, INTERVENTION AND THE WAR: ANGLO-
      SOVIET RELATIONS, 1917-1921. Princeton, N.J.: Prince-
      ton University Press, 1961.

2452. Vandervelde, Emile. THREE ASPECTS OF THE RUSSIAN REVO-
      LUTION. London: G. Allen & Unwin, 1918.

2453. Varsavsky, Vladimir. THE REVOLUTION OF 1905 AS REPORTED
      IN THE RUSSIAN PRESS FIFTY YEARS AGO. New York: Amer-
      ican Committee for Liberation from Bolshevism, 1955.

2454. Vasiliev, Alekiei Tikhonovich. THE OCHRANA—THE RUSSIAN
      SECRET POLICE. London: G.G. Harrap & Co., 1930.

      Presents an interesting examination of the police state
      in action, written by the last active chief under Tsar
      Nicholas.

2455. Venturi, Franco. ROOTS OF REVOLUTION. London: Weiden-
      feld & Nicolson, 1960.

2456. Vernadsky, George. LENIN, RED DICTATOR. London: Oxford
      University Press, 1931.

2457. ————. THE RUSSIAN REVOLUTION, 1917-1931. New York:
      H. Holt & Co., 1932.

2458. Vining, L. HELD BY THE BOLSHEVIKS: THE DIARY OF A BRIT-
      ISH OFFICER IN RUSSIA, 1919-1920. London: The St.
      Catherine Press, 1924.

2459. Von York, Tania. RUSSIA'S ROAD TO REVOLUTION: A SOCIAL,
      CULTURAL AND INTELLECTUAL HISTORY OF THE RUSSIAN REVO-
      LUTION. Boston: Christopher Publishing House, 1963.

2460. Wallace, Sir Donald Mackenzie. RUSSIA ON THE EVE OF WAR
      AND REVOLUTION. New York: Vintage, 1961.

2461. Wheatley, Dennis. RED EAGLE, THE STORY OF THE RUSSIAN
      REVOLUTION AND OF KLEMENTY EFREMOVITCH VOROSHILOV,
      MARSHAL AND COMMISSAR FOR DEFENCE OF THE UNION OF
      SOCIALIST SOVIET REPUBLICS. London: Hutchinson, 1938.

2462. Wheeler-Bennett, John. BREST-LITOVSK, THE FORGOTTEN
      PEACE, MARCH 1918. London: Macmillan, 1956.

2463. White, Dimitri Fedotoff. SURVIVAL THROUGH WAR AND REVO-
      LUTION IN RUSSIA. London: H. Milford, 1939.

2464. Wildman, Allan K. THE END OF THE RUSSIAN IMPERIAL ARMY:
      THE OLD ARMY AND THE SOLDIERS' REVOLT (MARCH-APRIL
      1917). Princeton, N.J.: Princeton University Press,
      1980.

2465. Williams, Albert Rhys. THROUGH THE RUSSIAN REVOLUTION.
      New York: Boni & Liveright, 1921.

2466. Williams, Ariadna. FROM LIBERTY TO BREST-LITOVSK, THE
      FIRST YEAR OF THE RUSSIAN REVOLUTION. London: Mac-
      millan, 1919.

2467. Wilson, Colin. RASPUTIN AND THE FALL OF THE ROMANOVS.
      London: Arthur Barker, 1964.

2468. Wilton, Robert. RUSSIA'S AGONY. London: E. Arnold, 1918

2469. Wolfe, Bertram D. THREE WHO MADE A REVOLUTION. New
      York: Dial Press, 1981.

2470. Wood, Anthony. THE RUSSIAN REVOLUTION. London: Long-
      man, 1979.

2471. Yarmolinsky, Avrahm. ROAD TO REVOLUTION, A CENTURY OF
      RUSSIAN RADICALISM. New York: Macmillan, 1959.

Articles

2472. Alder, H.M. "World's Great Object-Lesson." HARPER'S
      WEEKLY 136 (April 1918): 758-760.

2473, "Among Hunted Terrorists." LITERARY DIGEST 45 (July 13,
      1912): 77.

      Examines the life-style of anti-Tsarist revolutionaries
      five years prior to Russia's ultimate revolution.

2474. "Assassination Regulated by the Police in Russia." OUT-
      LOOK 91 (March 6, 1909): 515.

2475. Atkinson, R.O. "Red Flag in Siberia." FORTUNE 110 (No-
      vember 1918): 673-690.

2476. ————. "Traveling Through Siberian Chaos." HARPER'S
      WEEKLY 137 (November 1918): 813-827.

2477. ————. "Watching the Russian Army Die." HARPER'S
      WEEKLY 137 (October 1918): 618-631.

2478. Barrows, I.C. "After the Verdict." OUTLOOK 94 (April
      16, 1910): 844-846.

      Examines the trial and sentencing of anarchist revo-
      lutionaries in Tsarist Russia.

2479. ————. "Madame Breshkovsky in Prison." OUTLOOK 94
      (March 5, 1910): 538-542.

2480. Beatty, B. "Fall of the Winter Palace." CENTURY 96
      (August 1918): 523-532.

2481. ————. "Grave of Hope; Fortress of St. Peter and St.
      Paul Under the Bolshevik Revolution." CENTURY 96
      (October 1918): 805-812.

2482. ————. "Rise of the Proletariat; Overturning a Nation
      in Two Days of Civil War in Petrograd." ASIA 18 (July
      1918): 542-548.

2483. "Bolshevik Freedom." LITERARY DIGEST 56 (January 19,
      1918): 21.

2484. "Bolsheviki at Home." LIVING AGE 296 (March 2, 1918):
      566-567.

2485. Bradford, J.A. "Madness of Russia." BELLMAN 24 (December 2, 1918): 241-253; 24 (December 9, 1918): 263-369.

2486. Brailsford, H.N. "Bolsheviki and Jacobins." NEW REPUBLIC 14 (March 9, 1918): 167-170.

2487. ────. "Clue to Russia." NEW REPUBLIC 12 (October 20, 1917): 321-324.

2488. Brown, A.J. "Struggle to Save Russia." ASIA 17 (June 1917): 246-256.

2489. Buchanan, M. "Rule of the Red Guard." SCRIBNER'S MAGAZINE 64 (October 1918): 443-449.

2490. Bullard, A. "Russian Revolution in a Police Station." HARPER'S WEEKLY 136 (February 1918): 335-340.

2491. Camus, A. "The Combat Organisation of the Revolutionary Socialist Party; the Sensitive Murderers." WORLD REVIEW 9 (November 1940): 30-33.

      Examines terrorist assassinations in the Soviet Union during the early days of World War II.

2492. "Clearing Skies in Russia." NATION 104 (June 21, 1917): 726-727.

2493. Coghlan, J.O. "Fall of Kerensky." OVERLAND 71 (March 1918): 265-270.

      Examines the Bolshevik revolution which overthrew the Kerensky government in Russia, leading directly to annihilation of the Tsar's family and imposition of a Soviet state.

2494. "Critical Situation in Russia." CURRENT HISTORY 6 (June 1917): 478-487.

2495. Dillon, E.J. "Russia's Eclipse." FORTUNE 108 (December 1917): 812-825.

2496. Dosch, Fleurot, A. "In Petrograd During the Seven Days." WORLD'S WORK 34 (July 1917): 255-263.

2497. ────. "Russia Pulls Itself Together." WORLD'S WORK 34 (August 1917): 424-430.

2498. Doty, M.Z. "Revolutionary Justice." ATLANTIC 122 (July
       1918): 129-139.

2499. "Dreamers." INTERNATIONAL SOCIALIST REVIEW 18 (August
       1917): 112.

2500. Eastman, M. "Syndicalist-Socialist Russia." INTERNATION-
       AL SOCIALIST REVIEW 18 (August 1917)L 77-79.

2501. "Entente and the German Press on the Russian Revolt."
       LITERARY DIGEST 54 (March 31, 1917): 889-890.

2502. "Execution That Failed—a Tale of Russia Under the Bol-
       sheviki." CURRENT OPINION 64 (February 1918): 135.

2503. "Fall of Kerensky." CURRENT HISTORY 7 (February 1918):
       302-307.

2504. Farbman, M.S. "Maxim Gorky and the Revolution." NATION
       107 (November 30, 1918): 641-643.

2505. ————. "Year of Bolshevism." NEW REPUBLIC 17 (Novem-
       ber 2, 1918): 13-15.

2506. Felter, W. "Revolution and Religion in Russia." MISCEL-
       LANEOUS REVIEW 40 (May 1917): 339-349.

2507. "For and Against the Bolsheviki." NEW REPUBLIC 15 (April
       6, 1918): 280-282.

2508. "General Gurko on the Revolution." CURRENT HISTORY 7
       (January 1918): 18-19.

2509. "German Alarm at the Collapse of Russia's Counter-
       Revolution." CURRENT OPINION 63 (September 1917): 155-
       156.

2510. Goldenwieser, N. "Bolshevism as a World Problem." RE-
       VIEW OF REVIEWS 57 (February 1918): 188-190.

2511. "Good Effect of the Korniloff Rebellion." LITERARY DI-
       GEST 55 (September 22, 1917): 11-13.

2512. Gorski, W.O. "Russia and Her Terrorists." HARPER'S
       WEEKLY 52 (August 22, 1908): 33.

       Examines recent anarchist efforts to topple the Tsarist
       government through acts of terrorism.

2513. Graham, S. "Inside Russia." CENTURY 94 (July 1917):
      461-468.

2514. ———. "Thoughts on the Russian Revolution." LIVING
      AGE 294 (August 25, 1917): 451-459.

2515. Grey, S. "Sidelights on the Russian Revolution." LIVING
      AGE 294 (July 14, 1917): 71-79.

2516. Harper, S.N. "Is Russia Playing Germany's Game?" INDE-
      PENDENT 92 (December 15, 1917): 507.

2517. ———. "What Russia Wants." INDEPENDENT 92 (December
      22, 1917): 552.

2518. Hegan, E.T. "Russian Revolution from a Hospital Window."
      HARPER'S WEEKLY 135 (September 1917): 555-561.

2519. Heyking, A. "Aftermath of Revolution and the Future of
      Russia." CONTEMPORARY REVIEW 113 (May 1918): 509-518.

2520. "His Last Day as Czar." LITERARY DIGEST 54 (April 7,
      1917): 996.

2521. "Historic Turning Point; the Russian Revolution." REVIEW
      OF REVIEWS 55 (April 1917): 339-346.

2522. Holme, J.G. "Break Up of Russia." ASIA 18 (March 1918):
      182-187.

2523. ———. "Russian Upheaval." ASIA 17 (November 1917):
      689-697.

2524. Hourwich, I.A. "Marxism in Russia." SURVEY 40 (May 11,
      1918): 159-160.

2525. ———. "Russian Police and Political Assassination."
      INDEPENDENT 53 (October 3, 1901): 2343-2345.

      Examines the role of Russia's secret police in arrang-
      ing selective political murders, utilizing provocateurs,
      and otherwise waging war against suspected revolution-
      aries.

2526. Johnston, C. "Russia and the Revolution." NORTH AMER-
      ICAN 205 (May 1917): 715-723.

2527. ————. "Russia and the War After the War." NORTH
       AMERICAN 207 (March 1918): 378-387.

2528. ————. "Russia's Danger; Its Cause and Cure." NORTH
       AMERICAN 206 (September 1917): 384-393.

2529. ————. "Russia's Two Revolutions." REVIEW OF REVIEWS
       57 (January 1918): 59-62.

2530. ————. "What Happened in Russia." NORTH AMERICAN 205
       (June 1917): 865-873.

2531. Kennan, G. "Early Days of the Russian Revolution." OUT-
       LOOK 116 (June 6, 1917): 217-219.

2532, ————. "Escape of Prince Kapotkin." CENTURY 84 (June
       1917): 246-253.

2533. ————. "Russian Revolution." OUTLOOK 119 (July 3,
       1918): 379-381.

2534. ————. "Victory of the Russian People." OUTLOOK 115
       (March 28, 1917): 546-547.

2535. ————. "Will the Russian Political I.W.W.'s Succeed?"
       OUTLOOK 117 (November 21, 1917): 455-456.

2536. "Key to the Mysteries of the Latest Russian Upheaval."
       CURRENT OPINION 6 (December 1917): 371-375.

2537. Lane, W.D. "Making of a Russian Revolutionist; an Inter-
       view with Marie Sukloff." SURVEY 32 (June 1914): 257-
       263.

2538. Lange, C.L. "Story of the Russian Upheaval." CURRENT
       HISTORY 6 (July 1917): 105-114.

2539. Lauzanne, S. "A Comparison of French and Russian Revo-
       lutions." NATIONAL REVIEW 80 (September 1922): 41-45.

2540. Lawton, N. "Mother of Revolutionists." HARPER'S WEEKLY
       57 (August 9, 1913): 7+.

2541. "Leader; Scenes of Revolutionary Life in Russia." FOR-
       TUNE 96 (December 1911): 1145-1156; 97 (January 1912):
       191-203.

2542. Levine, I.D. "Russia in the Throes of Re-Birth." REVIEW
      OF REVIEWS 55 (June 1917): 619-622.

2543. ———. "Russian Crisis." NEW REPUBLIC 13 (December 15,
      1917): 181-183.

2544. ———. "Russian Revolution." REVIEW OF REVIEWS 55
      (April 1917): 385-390.

2545. "Liberty Through the Guillotine." LITERARY DIGEST 57
      (May 11, 1918): 18.

2546. Long, R.C. "Black Hundred of Russia." COSMOPOLITAN 44
      (January 1908): 229-238.

      Focuses on activities of anti-semitic terrorists in
      Tsarist Russia.

2547. "Lucid Intervals in the Russian Delirium." LITERARY DI-
      GEST 56 (March 9, 1913): 19.

2548. "Man with the Gun." BELLMAN 24 (February 16, 1918): 174-
      175.

2549. Marcosson, I.F. "March 1917." EVERYBODY'S MAGAZINE 36
      (May 1917): 527-528,

2550. ———. "Seven Days; the Story of the Rebirth of Russia."
      EVERYBODY'S MAGAZINE 37 (July 1917): 25-40.

2551. Mason, G. "Eyes Left! In Russia." OUTLOOK 116 (July
      11, 1917): 399-401.

2552. ———. "Russia Upside Down." OUTLOOK 116 (August 15,
      1917): 584+.

2553. Masson, F. "Causes of the Russian Revolution." CURRENT
      HISTORY 7 (February 1918): 307-308.

2554. Melamed, S.M. "Anthropological Causes of the Revolution."
      RUSSIAN REVIEW 3 (July 1917): 45-49.

2555. Michalovsky, A. "Kerensky and Kornilov." RUSSIAN RE-
      VIEW 4 (April 1918): 88-100.

2556. "Month's Developments in Russia." CURRENT HISTORY 7
      (November 1917): 259-262.

2557. Morgan, G. "New Russia." NORTH AMERICAN 205 (April
      1917): 502-510.

2558. "Moscow's Misery." CURRENT HISTORY 8 (September 1918):
      484-486.

2559. Naudeau, L. "Life in Revolutionary Russia." CURRENT
      HISTORY 7 (February 1918): 293-299.

2560. Nevinson, H.W. "Dayspring in Russia." CONTEMPORARY RE-
      VIEW 111 (April 1917): 409-418.

2561. "New Aspect of Revolutionary Russia." CURRENT OPINION
      63 (November 1917): 303-305.

2562. "New Crisis in Russia." OUTLOOK 117 (September 19, 1917):
      77.

2563. "New Era in Russia." LIVING AGE 293 (April 21, 1917):
      184-186.

2564. "Nine Days; Diary of an American During the Russian Rev-
      olution." NEW REPUBLIC 11 (June 23, 1917): 212-217.

2565. Palmieri, F.A. "Church and the Russian Revolution."
      CATHOLIC WORLD 105 (May 1917): 153-161; 105 (August
      1917): 577-586.

2566. ————. "Russian Church and the Revolution." CATHOLIC
      WORLD 106 (June 1918): 661-670.

2567. ————. "Theorist of the Russian Revolution; Mikhail
      Alexandrovitch Bakunin." CATHOLIC WORLD 110 (Decem-
      ber 1919): 331-343.

2568. Paquet, A. "Russia's Reign of Terror." LIVING AGE 299
      (November 30, 1918): 521-525.

2569. "Passing of Old Russia." INDEPENDENT 89 (March 26, 1917):
      523-525.

2570. Pasvolsky, L. "Russia's Tragedy." RUSSIAN REVIEW 4
      (April 1918): 7-38.

2571. Pollock, J. "Russian Revolution." 19th CENTURY AND
      AFTER 81 (May 1917): 1068-1082.

2572. Prelooker, J. "Why Count Vassili Danilovitch Stroganoff Became a Revolutionist." FORTUNE 95 (April 1911): 743-758.

2573. "Premature Pessimism Over Russia's Stormy Month Under the New Freedom." CURRENT OPINION 63 (July 1917): 9-11.

2574. Prins, J.W. "Siberian Chaos." SCRIBNER'S MAGAZINE 64 (November 1918): 625-633.

2575. "Progress of the Latest Upheaval in Petrograd." CURRENT OPINION 63 (October 1917): 232-233.

2576. Ransome, A. "Desperate Conditions Under Bolshevist Rule." CURRENT HISTORY 8 (April 1918): 72-74.

2577. Rappoport, A.S. "Philosophic Basis of the Russian Revolution." EDINBURGH REVIEW 226 (July 1917): 113-133.

2578. Recouly, R. "Contrasts Between the French and Russian Revolutions." WORLD'S WORK 42 (September 1923): 329-342.

2579. ———. "Russia in Revolution." SCRIBNER'S MAGAZINE 62 (July 1917): 29-38.

2580. ———. "Russian Army and the Revolution." SCRIBNER'S MAGAZINE (November 1917): 554-563.

2581. Reed, John. "Bolsheviki." PUBLIC 21 (October 19, 1918): 1312-1313.

    An American communist presents his biased view of the Bolshevik revolution in Russia.

2582. ———. "Case for the Bolsheviki." INDEPENDENT 95 (July 13, 1918): 55.

    Reed attempts to persuade Americans that the Bolshevik revolution will be beneficial for Russian peasants and the world at large.

2583. Reinach, J. "Causes of Russia's Downfall." CURRENT HISTORY 8 (April 1918): 84-88.

2584. "Revolution and Dogma." NEW REPUBLIC 16 (August 24, 1918): 91-93.

2585. Reynolds, R. "Russian Church and the Revolution." CON-
      TEMPORARY REVIEW 113 (April 1918): 397-405.

2586. Ross, E.A. "Roots of the Russian Revolution." CENTURY
      95 (December 1917): 192-198.

2587. "Russia and Retribution." LIVING AGE 295 (December 22,
      1917): 756-759.

2588. "Russia and Revolutionary Experiment." PUBLIC 21 (Sep-
      tember 21, 1918): 1199-1201.

2589. "Russia Finding Herself." LITERARY DIGEST 55 (September
      8, 1917): 16-18.

2590. "Russia From Within." LITERARY DIGEST 57 (June 29, 1918):
      21-22.

2591. "Russia in Revolution." CURRENT HISTORY (April 1917):
      1-13.

2592. "Russia Passes Through Deep Waters." CURRENT HISTORY 6
      (September 1917): 433-438.

2593. "Russia Under the Terror." LITERARY DIGEST 55 (December
      29, 1917): 24-25.

2594. "Russian and French Revolutions." CURRENT HISTORY 6
      (July 1917): 118-123.

2595. "Russian Chaos." INDEPENDENT 91 (July 7, 1917): 11.

2596. "Russian Crisis." INDEPENDENT 90 (May 26, 1917): 365.

2597. "Russian Cross Currents." NATION 105 (November 1, 1917):
      476-477.

2598. "Russian Muddle." LITERARY DIGEST 54 (June 23, 1917):
      1917-1918.

2599. "Russian Napoleon Due." LITERARY DIGEST 54 (May 19,
      1917): 1491-1492.

      Anticipates the rise of a military strong man to bring
      order out of chaos in revolutionary Russia.

2600. "Russian Outlook." NATION 104 (April 26, 1917): 482-483.

228   TERRORISM IN THE UNITED STATES AND EUROPE

2601. "Russian Peasant." BELLMAN 22 (June 9, 1917): 622.

2602. "Russian Phenomena." WORLD'S WORK 34 (June 1917): 126-128.

2603. "Russian Problem." NATION 104 (May 17, 1917): 592-593.

2604. "Russian Revolution." BELLMAN 22 (May 5, 1917): 495-496.

2605. "Russian Revolution." INDEPENDENT 89 (March 26, 1917): 528.

2606. "Russian Revolution." INTERNATIONAL SOCIALIST REVIEW 17 (April 1917): 619-620.

2607. "Russian Revolution." INTERNATIONAL SOCIALIST REVIEW 17 (June 1917): 709-714.

2608. "Russian Revolution." LITERARY DIGEST 54 (March 24, 1917): 799-800.

2609. "Russian Revolution and Democracy." REVIEW OF REVIEWS 56 (July 1917): 91-92.

2610. "Russian Revolution; the History of Four Days." OUTLOOK 115 (March 28, 1917): 544-545.

2611. "Russian Situation." OUTLOOK 116 (May 16, 1917): 94.

2612. "Russia's Escape from Civil War." CURRENT HISTORY 7 (October 1917): 63-72.

2613. "Russia's Greatest Danger." LITERARY DIGEST 54 (May 12, 1917): 1403-1404.

2614. "Russia's Perilous Transition Stage." CURRENT HISTORY 6 (July 1917): 53-57.

2615. "Russia's Radicals in Revolt." CURRENT HISTORY 7 (December 1917): 419-423.

2616. "Russia's Reign of Terror." CURRENT HISTORY 9 (October 1918): 74-81.

2617. "Russia's Revolution Gets a Fresh Start." CURRENT OPINION 64 (January 1918): 11-15.

2618. Sack, A.J. "Factors in the Russian Revolution." CURRENT
        HISTORY 6 (June 1917): 473-478.

2619. ———. "Problems of the New Russia." NATION 104 (March
        19, 1917): 361-362.

2620. Sakhnovshy, A.N. "Certain Phases of the Revolution."
        RUSSIAN REVOLUTION 3 (July 1917): 24-25.

2621. "Salvation of Russia." NEW REPUBLIC 12 (September 22,
        1917): 202-204.

2622. Scott, E.F. "Comparison of the French and Russian Rev-
        olutions." QUEEN'S QUARTERLY 25 (April-June 1918):
        403-414.

2623. "Secret of the Revolution." LITERARY DIGEST 54 (April
        7, 1917): 1001.

2624. Shatsky, B.E. "New Russia." OUTLOOK 116 (May 2, 1917):
        16-18.

2625. Shaviro, N. "Russian Thought and the Revolution." NATION
        104 (May 24, 1917): 627-628.

2626. Simkhovitch, V.G. "Terrorism in Russia." INTERNATIONAL
        QUARTERLY 11 (July 1905): 266-287.

2627. Simonds, F.H. "Russian Revolution." REVIEW OF REVIEWS
        55 (April 1917): 384.

2628. Simpson, J.Y. "After the Great Days of the Revolution."
        19th CENTURY AND AFTER 82 (July 1917): 136-149.

2629. ———. "Russian Revolution in Retrospect and Forecast."
        19th CENTURY AND AFTER 83 (April 1918): 715-733.

2630. Slobodin, H.L. "Russian Revolution." INTERNATIONAL
        SOCIALIST REVIEW 17 (May 1917): 645-647.

2631. Soskice, D. "Story of Eugene Azeff; Unmasking of Russia's
        Secret Police System." McCLURE 34 (January 1910):
        282-299.

        Examines the Ochrana's secret war against anarchists
        and revolutionaries in Tsarist Russia.

2632. Sosnowsky, G.J. "Freeing Russia." INDEPENDENT 80 (March 26, 1917): 536.

2633. Steffens, Lincoln. "Rasputin—the Real Story." EVERY-BODY'S MAGAZINE 37 (September 1917): 276-285.

2634. Stone, M.E. "Remember Russia." NORTH AMERICAN 206 (August 1917): 324-328.

2635. ———. "Russian Revolution." RUSSIAN REVIEW 3 (July 1917): 37-44.

2636. "Struggle for Supreme Power in Petrograd." CURRENT OPINION 62 (June 1917): 390-391.

2637. Strunsky, R. "Little Darling." FORUM 45 (January 1911): 31-43.

Reviews the recent activities of Russian terrorists against the Tsarist government.

2638. ———. "Russian Revolution—an Interpretation." CENTURY 96 (June 1918): 215-221.

2639. ———. "Siberia and the Russian Woman." FORUM 44 (August 1910): 129-141.

Examines the treatment of imprisoned Russian revolutionaries and their continuing war against the Tsar.

2640. Sukloff, Marie. "Making of a Russian Terrorist." CENTURY 89 (November 1914): 93-105.

Reviews recent anarchist attacks on the Tsarist government, with an examination of some motivating factors, presented from the viewpoint of a militant female activist.

2641. ———. "Story of My Escape." CENTURY 88 (August 1914): 499-506.

Marie Sukloff recreates her escape from a Tsarist jail, where she was serving time for acts of terrorism against the state.

2642. "Swift Success of the Russian Revolution." CURRENT OPINION 62 (April 1917): 235-236.

2643. "Trotzky and Lenin in Another Agony of Bolshevism."
      CURRENT OPINION 64 (March 1918): 167-169.

2644. Vinogradoff, P. "Some Elements of the Russian Revolution."
      QUARTERLY 228 (July 1917): 184-200.

2645. ————. "Some Impressions of the Russian Revolution."
      CONTEMPORARY REVIEW 111 (May 1917): 553-561.

2646. "War and Revolution." NEW REPUBLIC 10 (March 24, 1917):
      212-214.

2647. Wharton, P. "Russian Ides of March." ATLANTIC 120
      (July 1917): 21-30.

2648. "Why Korniloff Rebelled." LITERARY DIGEST 55 (November
      3, 1917): 18.

2649. "Why the Russian Revolution Failed." LITERARY DIGEST 58
      (August 3, 1918): 27-28.

2650. Wilcox, E.H. "Kerenski and Korniloff." FORTUNE 110
      (September 1918): 330-343; 110 (October 1918): 502-
      517.

2651. ————. "Kerensky and the Revolution." ATLANTIC 120
      (November 1917):693-703.

2652, ————. "Lenin and Bolshevism." FORTUNE 109 (March
      1918): 371-383.

2653. ————. "Protopopoff and the Revolution." FORTUNE 108
      (July 1917): 69-81.

2654. ————. "Revolution and the War." FORTUNE 107 (May
      1917): 744-756.

2655. ————. "Sidelights on the Revolution." FORTUNE 107
      (June 1917): 963-971.

2656. "Worse Anarchy Due in Russia." LITERARY DIGEST 59
      (October 5, 1918): 21.

2657. Wright, C.H. "Rebirth of Russia." CONTEMPORARY REVIEW
      113 (April 1918): 361-368.

2658. ————. "Trials of Russia." CONTEMPORARY REVIEW 112
      (August 1917): 121-129.

2659. "Zionism and the Russian Revolution." NATION 104 (May
      17, 1917): 594-595.

SCOTLAND

Books

2660. Ellis, Peter Beresford, and Seamus Mac A'Ghobhainn. THE
      SCOTTISH INSURRECTION OF 1820. London: Victor Gollancz,
      1970.

2661. Grimble, I. THE TRIAL OF PATRICK SELLAR: THE TRAGEDY OF
      HIGHLAND EVICTIONS. London: Routledge & Kegan Paul,
      1962.

2662. Logue, Kenneth J. POPULAR DISTURBANCES IN SCOTLAND,
      1780-1815. Edinburgh: John Donald Publishers, 1979.

      Includes discussion of violent activities by assorted
      meal mobs, militia riots, anti-recruitment riots, indus-
      trial disturbances, and patronage riots.

2663. MacKenzie, Alexander. THE HIGHLAND CLEARANCES. Glasgow:
      A. MacLaren, 1946.

2664. MacLeod, D. GLOOMY MEMORIES. Glasgow: A. MacLaren, 1892.

2665. MacLeod, John. THE NORTH COUNTRY SEPARATISTS. Inverness:
      1920.

2666. Prebble, J. THE HIGHLAND CLEARANCES. London: Penguin,
      1969.

2667. ———. MUTINY: HIGHLAND REGIMENTS IN REVOLT, 1743-1804.
      London: Secker & Warburg, 1975.

2668. Richards, Eric. THE LAST SCOTTISH FOOD RIOT. Oxford:
      The Past and Present Society, 1982.

2669. ———. "Patterns of Highland Discontent, 1790-1860."
      POPULAR PROTEST AND PUBLIC ORDER: SIX STUDIES IN
      BRITISH HISTORY, 1790-1920. Cited above as item 531.

2670. Saunders, L.J. SCOTTISH DEMOCRACY, 1815-1840. Edinburgh:
      Oliver & Boyd, 1950.

2671. Sherry, Frank Andrew. THE RISING OF 1820. Glasgow:
      William MacLellan, 1968.

Examines the Glasgow rising of 1820, the events that
led to it, the trials and execution of John Baird and
Andrew Hardie which resulted from the abortive movement.

2672. Somers, Robert. LETTERS FROM THE HIGHLANDS: OR, THE
      FAMINE OF 1847. London: The Author, 1848.

2673. Taylor, A.J.P. THE TROUBLE-MAKERS: DISSENT OVER FOREIGN
      POLICY, 1792-1939. London: Hamosh Hamilton, 1967.

2674. Vaughan, W.E. SIN, SHEEP, AND SCOTSMEN: JOHN GEORGE
      ADAIR AND THE DERRYVEAGH EVICTIONS, 1861. Belfast:
      1983.

2675. Young, Robert. THE PARISH OF SPYNIE IN THE COUNTY OF
      ELGIN. Elgin: The Author, 1871.

      Covers the food riots and dock disturbances of the
      Invergordon riots, circa 1847.

                              Articles

2676. Richards, Eric. "The Prospect of Economic Growth in
      Sutherland at the Time of the Clearances, 1809-1813."
      SCOTTISH HISTORICAL REVIEW 49 (1970).

      A Scottish historian examines socio-economic violence
      during the 19th-century land clearances which displaced
      peasants in the countryside.

2677. ———. "How Tame Were the Highlanders During the Clear-
      ances?" SCOTTISH STUDIES 17 (1973).

2678. ———. "Structural Change in a Regional Economy:
      Sutherland and the Industrial Revolution, 1780-1830."
      ECONOMIC HISTORY REVIEW 26 (1973).

2679. Western, J.R. "The Volunteer Movement as an Anti-Revolu-
      tionary Force: 1793-1801." ENGLISH HISTORICAL REVIEW
      71 (1956).

                               SPAIN

                               Books

2680. Agirre, Julen. OPERATION OGRO: THE EXECUTION OF ADMIRAL
      LUIS CARRERO BLANCO. New York: Quadrangle/New York
      Times Books, 1974.

2681. Alvarez del Vayo, Julio. FREEDOM'S BATTLE. New York:
      Hill & Wang, 1971.

   * Aya, Roderick. THE MISSED REVOLUTION: THE FATE OF RURAL
      REBELS IN SICILY AND SOUTHERN SPAIN, 1840-1950. Cited
      above as item 2127.

2682. Beevor, Anthony. THE SPANISH CIVIL WAR. New York:
      P. Bedrick Books, 1982.

2683. Bessie, Alvah Cecil. MEN IN BATTLE: A STORY OF AMERICANS
      IN SPAIN. San Francisco: Chandler & Sharp, 1975.

2684. Bolloten, Burnett. THE GRAND CAMOUFLAGE: THE COMMUNIST
      CONSPIRACY IN THE SPANISH CIVIL WAR. New York:
      Praeger, 1961.

2685. ————. THE SPANISH REVOLUTION: THE LEFT AND THE STRUG-
      GLE FOR POWER DURING THE CIVIL WAR. Chapel Hill, N.C.
      University of North Carolina Press, 1979.

2686. Borkenau, Franz. THE SPANISH COCKPIT, AN EYE-WITNESS
      ACCOUNT OF THE POLITICAL AND SOCIAL CONFLICTS OF THE
      SPANISH CIVIL WAR. Ann Arbor, Mich.: University of
      Michigan Press, 1963.

2687. Broue, Pierre, and Emile Temime. THE REVOLUTION AND THE
      CIVIL WAR IN SPAIN. Cambridge, Mass.: M.I.T. Press,
      1972.

2688. Brunn, Gerhard. "Nationalist Violence and Terror in the
      Spanish Border Provinces: ETA." SOCIAL PROTEST, VIO-
      LENCE, AND TERROR IN NINETEENTH- AND TWENTIETH-CENTURY
      EUROPE. Cited above as item 41, pp. 112-136.

2689. Carr, Raymond. THE REPUBLIC AND THE CIVIL WAR IN SPAIN.
      New York: St. Martin's Press, 1971.

2690. ————. THE SPANISH TRAGEDY: THE CIVIL WAR IN PERSPEC-
      TIVE. London: Weidenfeld & Nicolson, 1977.

2691. Casado, Segismundo. THE LAST DAYS OF MADRID: THE END OF
      THE SECOND SPANISH REPUBLIC. London: P. Davies, 1939.

2692. Cattell, David Tredwell. COMMUNISM AND THE SPANISH
      CIVIL WAR. Berkeley, Calif.: University of California
      Press, 1955.

2693. ————. SOVIET DIPLOMACY AND THE SPANISH CIVIL WAR.
      Berkeley, Calif.: University of California Press, 1957.

2694. Cleugh, James. SPANISH FURY: THE STORY OF A CIVIL WAR.
      London: G.G. Harrap, 1962.

2695. Colodny, Robert Garland. SPAIN: THE GLORY AND THE TRAG-
      EDY. New York: Humanities Press, 1970.

2696. Cortada, James W. (ed). HISTORICAL DICTIONARY OF THE
      SPANISH CIVIL WAR. Westport, Conn.: Greenwood Press,
      1982.

2697. Coverdale, John F. ITALIAN INTERVENTION IN THE SPANISH
      CIVIL WAR. Princeton, N.J.: Princeton University Press,
      1975.

2698. Cox, Geoffrey. DEFENCE OF MADRID. London: V. Gollancz,
      1937.

2699. Dundas, Lawrence. BEHIND THE SPANISH MASK. London: R.
      Hale, Ltd., 1943.

2700. Eby, Cecil D. BETWEEN THE BULLET AND THE LIE; AMERICAN
      VOLUNTEERS IN THE SPANISH CIVIL WAR. New York: Holt,
      Rinehart & Winston, 1969.

2701. Edwards, Jill. THE BRITISH GOVERNMENT AND THE SPANISH
      CIVIL WAR. London: Macmillan, 1979.

2702. Fischer, Louis. THE WAR IN SPAIN. New York: The Nation,
      1937.

2703. Foss, William. THE SPANISH ARENA. London: Catholic
      Book Club, 1938.

2704. Francis, Hywel. MINERS AGAINST FASCISM: WALES AND THE
      SPANISH CIVIL WAR. London: Lawrence & Wishart, 1984.

2705. Fraser, Ronald. BLOOD OF SPAIN: AN ORAL HISTORY OF THE
      SPANISH CIVIL WAR. New York: Pantheon Books, 1979.

2706. Gannes, Harry, and Theodore Repard. SPAIN IN REVOLT.
      New York: A.A. Knopf, 1936.

2707. Geiser, Carl. PRISONERS OF THE GOOD FIGHT: THE SPANISH
      CIVIL WAR. Westport, Conn.: L. Hill, 1986.

2708. Gibbs, Jack. THE SPANISH CIVIL WAR. London: E. Benn,
      1973.

2709. Greenwall, Harry James. MEDITERRANEAN CRISIS. London:
      Nicholson & Watson, 1939.

2710. Gurney, Jason. CRUSADE IN SPAIN. London: Faber & Faber,
      1974.

2711. Guttman, Allen (ed). AMERICAN NEUTRALITY AND THE SPANISH
      CIVIL WAR. Boston: Heath, 1963.

2712. ———. THE WOUND IN THE HEART: AMERICA AND THE SPANISH
      CIVIL WAR. New York: Free Press of Glencoe, 1962.

2713. Ibarruri, Dolores. THEY SHALL NOT PASS: THE AUTOBIOGRAPHY
      OF LA PASSIONARIA. London: Lawrence & Wishart, 1967.

      Presents the memoirs of a female activist in the Span-
      ish civil war.

2714. Jackson, Gabriel. A CONCISE HISTORY OF THE SPANISH CIVIL
      WAR. London: Thames & Hudson, 1974.

2715. ———. THE SPANISH CIVIL WAR. Chicago: Quadrangle
      Books, 1972.

2716. ———. THE SPANISH CIVIL WAR: DOMESTIC CRISIS OR INTER-
      NATIONAL CONSPIRACY? Boston: Heath, 1967.

2717. Jellinek, Frank. THE CIVIL WAR IN SPAIN. New York: H.
      Fertig, 1969.

2718. Johnston, Verle B. LEGIONS OF BABEL; THE INTERNATIONAL
      BRIGADES IN THE SPANISH CIVIL WAR. University Park,
      Pa.: University of Pennsylvania Press, 1967.

2719. Kurzman, Dan. MIRACLE OF NOVEMBER: MADRID'S EPIC STAND,
      1936. New York: Putnam, 1980.

2720. Landis, Arthur H. THE ABRAHAM LINCOLN BRIGADE. New
      York: Citadel Press, 1967.

      Reviews the activities of American volunteers who fought
      for the Loyalist side in Spain's civil war. Members of
      the brigade were later reviled as communists in America,
      during the "red scare" of the 1940s and 1950s.

2721. ————. SPAIN; THE UNFINISHED REVOLUTION. Baldwin Park,
      Calif.: Camelot Publishing Co., 1972.

2722. Legaretta, Dorothy. THE GUERNICA GENERATION: BASQUE
      REFUGEE CHILDREN OF THE SPANISH CIVIL WAR. Reno, Nev.:
      University of Nevada Press, 1984.

2723. Lewis, Wyndham. COURT YOUR DEAD: THEY ARE ALIVE! OR, A
      NEW WAR IN THE MAKING. London: L. Dickson, 1937.

2724. Little, Douglas. MALEVOLENT NEUTRALITY: THE UNITED
      STATES, GREAT BRITAIN AND THE ORIGINS OF THE SPANISH
      CIVIL WAR. Ithaca, N.Y.: Cornell University Press,
      1985.

2725. Loveday, Arthur Frederic. WORLD WAR IN SPAIN. London:
      J. Murray, 1939.

2726. Lunn, Arnold Henry Moore. SPANISH REHEARSAL. New York:
      Sheed & Ward, 1937.

      Examines the Spanish civil war as a proving ground for
      fascist and communist military tactics later used to good
      effect in World War II.

2727. Matthews, Herbert Lionel. HALF OF SPAIN DIED: OR REAP-
      PRAISAL OF THE SPANISH CIVIL WAR. New York: Scribner,
      1973.

2728. ————. TWO WARS AND MORE TO COME. New York: Carrick &
      Evans, 1938.

2729. ————. THE YOKE AND THE ARROWS: A REPORT ON SPAIN.
      New York: G. Braziller, 1961.

2730. Mendizabal Villalba, Alfredo. THE MARTYRDOM OF SPAIN,
      ORIGINS OF A CIVIL WAR. London: G. Bles, the Centen-
      ary Press, 1938.

2731. Mitchell, David C. THE SPANISH CIVIL WAR. New York:
      Franklin Watts, 1983.

2732. Morrow, Felix. REVOLUTION AND COUNTER-REVOLUTION IN
      SPAIN. New York: Pioneer Publications, 1938.

2733. North, Joseph. MEN IN THE RANKS, THE STORY OF TWELVE
      AMERICANS IN SPAIN. New York: Friends of the Abraham
      Lincoln Brigade, 1939.

2734. O'Riordan, Michael. CONNOLLY COLUMN: THE STORY OF THE
      IRISHMEN WHO FOUGHT IN THE RANKS OF THE INTERNATIONAL
      BRIGADES IN THE NATIONAL-REVOLUTIONARY WAR OF THE
      SPANISH PEOPLE, 1936-1939. Dublin: New Books, 1979.

2735. Paul, Elliot Harold. THE LIFE AND DEATH OF A SPANISH
      TOWN. London: P. Davies, 1937.

2736. Payne, Stanley G. FALANGE: A HISTORY OF SPANISH FASCISM.
      Stanford, Calif.: Stanford University Press, 1961.

2737. ————. THE SPANISH REVOLUTION. New York: Norton, 1970.

2738. Paz, Abel. DURRUTI, THE PEOPLE ARMED. New York: Free
      Life Editions, 1977.

2739. Peers, Edgar Allison. THE SPANISH TRAGEDY, 1930-1936;
      DICTATORSHIP, REPUBLIC, CHAOS. London: Methuen & Co.,
      1936.

2740. Pitcairn, Frank. REPORTER IN SPAIN. London: Lawrence
      & Wishart, 1936.

2741. Powell, Thomas G. MEXICO AND THE SPANISH CIVIL WAR.
      Albuquerque, N.M.: University of New Mexico Press, 1981

2742. Preston, Paul (ed). REVOLUTION AND WAR IN SPAIN, 1931-
      1939. New York: Methuen, 1984.

2743. Purcell, Hugh. THE SPANISH CIVIL WAR. London: Wayland,
      1973.

2744. Puzzo, Dante Anthony. THE SPANISH CIVIL WAR. New York:
      Van Nostrand Reinhold Co., 1969.

2745. Richardson, R. Dan. COMINTERN ARMY: THE INTERNATIONAL
      BRIGADES AND THE SPANISH CIVIL WAR. Lexington, Ky.:
      University Press of Kentucky, 1982.

2746. Rogers, F.T. SPAIN: A TRAGIC JOURNEY. New York: The
      Macaulay Co., 1937.

2747. Rosenstone, Robert A. CRUSADE ON THE LEFT: THE LINCOLN
      BRIGADE IN THE SPANISH CIVIL WAR. New York: Pegasus,
      1969.

2748. Sanchez, Jose Mariano. REFORM AND REACTION: THE POLITICO-
      RELIGIOUS BEGINNINGS OF THE SPANISH CIVIL WAR. Chapel
      Hill, N.C.: University of North Carolina Press, 1964.

2749. Sheean, Vincent. THE ELEVENTH HOUR. London: H. Hamilton, 1939.

2750. ————. NOT PEACE, BUT A SWORD. New York: Doubleday, Doran & Co., 1939.

2751. Sommerfield, John. VOLUNTEER IN SPAIN. New York: Alfred A. Knopf, 1937.

2752. Steer, George Lowther. THE TREE OF GERNIKA: A FIELD STUDY OF MODERN WAR. London: Hodder & Stoughton, 1938.

2753. Taylor, Foster Jay. THE UNITED STATES IN THE SPANISH CIVIL WAR. New York: Bookman Associates, 1956.

2754. Terrant, Eleonora. SPANISH JOURNEY; PERSONAL EXPERIENCES OF THE CIVIL WAR. London: Eyre & Spottisworde, 1936.

2755. Thomas, Gordon. THE DAY GUERNICA DIED. London: Hodder & Stoughton, 1975.

2756. Thomas, Hugh. THE SPANISH CIVIL WAR. New York: Harper & Row, 1977.

2757. Watson, Keith Scott. SINGLE TO SPAIN. London: A. Barker, 1937.

   Presents the memoirs of a foreign volunteer in the Spanish civil war.

2758. Whaley, Barton. GUERILLAS IN THE SPANISH CIVIL WAR. Detroit: Management Information Services, 1969.

2759. Wilson, Hugh Robert. DESCENT INTO VIOLENCE—SPAIN, JANUARY-JULY 1936. Ilfracombe: Stockwell, 1969.

2760. Wyden, Peter. THE PASSIONATE WAR: THE NARRATIVE HISTORY OF THE SPANISH CIVIL WAR, 1936-1939. New York: Simon & Schuster, 1983.

Articles

2761. "Abies and Georgies." TIME 31 (April 18, 1938): 21.

   Covers American volunteers in the civil war.

2762. "After Barcelona?" NATION 148 (February 4, 1939): 135-136.

Follows events in Spain's civil war.

2763. "After Barcelona; Press Comments." COMMONWEAL 29 (February 10, 1939): 439-440.

2764. Allen, J. "City of Horrors: Badajoz." SCHOLASTIC 29 (November 7, 1936): 10-11+.

Presents scenarios from the civil war.

2765. "American War Birds in Spain." CURRENT HISTORY 45 (January 1937): 107-108.

Examines the role of American volunteers in the civil war.

2766. "Anarchist Blood-Feud." SPECTATOR 79 (August 14, 1897): 201-202.

Describes internecine warfare between terrorist groups.

2767. "Appalling Catastrophe." TIME 28 (December 7, 1936): 21.

Covers the on-going civil war.

2768. Araquistain, L. "Defending the Spanish Republic." NATION 143 (August 8, 1936): 146.

Presents a Loyalist view of civil war activity.

2769. Arrupe, P. "Spanish War Psychology." COMMONWEAL 25 (January 29, 1937): 377-379.

2770. Atkinson, W.C. "Civil War and After." FORTUNE 146 (October 1936): 412-421.

2771. "Attack Orders; Andre Malraux Seeks Aid for Loyal Air Corps." LITERARY DIGEST 123 (April 3, 1937): 15-16.

2772. Attwater, D. "Passing the Buck." COMMONWEAL 24 (October 2, 1936): 517-518.

Condemns Allied failure to defend the Spanish republic.

2723. "Back from Spain: Return of Nazis and Italians Clarifies
      Submarine Policy." NEWSWEEK 13 (June 19, 1939): 26-27.

2724. "Background to War." FORTUNE 15 (March 1937): 154.

2775. "Bad-Guesser Franco." LITERARY DIGEST 123 (March 27,
      1937): 14.

      Chronicles recent setbacks for fascist forces.

2776. "Barcelona Falls to Franco; Italy, Germany Hail Victory."
      SCHOLASTIC 34 (February 11, 1939): 7.

2777. "Barcelona Pinch." NEWSWEEK 13 (January 23, 1939): 16-17.

      Follows the fascist advance on Barcelona.

2778. "Barcelona's Peril; Franco's Push Carries War to the Be-
      leaguered Capital." NEWSWEEK 13 (January 30, 1939):
      20.

2779. Barry, D. "Soldier of Misfortune." SATURDAY EVENING
      POST 209 (May 1, 1937): 20-21+.

      Presents the personal narrative of a civil war volun-
      teer.

2780. "Basque Children." COMMONWEAL 26 (June 18, 1937): 197-
      198.

      Examines the plight of civil war refugees.

2781. "Basque Shambles." LITERARY DIGEST 123 (May 8, 1937):
      14.

      Reports Basque resistance to fascist forces.

2782. "Basques Make Final Stand Against Rebels." SCHOLASTIC
      30 (May 15, 1937): 12.

2783. Bates, R. "Castilian Drama." NEW REPUBLIC 92 (October
      20, 1937): 286-290; 92 (October 27, 1937): 333-337.

2784. ————. "Companero Sagasta Burns a Church." NEW REPUB-
      LIC 88 (October 14, 1936): 274-276.

2785. ————. "Of Legendary Time." VIRGINIA QUARTERLY REVIEW
      15 (January 1939): 21-36.

2786. "Battleground in Spain." REVIEW OF REVIEWS 95 (February 1937): 22.

2787. "Battleships Steam Into Civil War Spotlight." NEWSWEEK 8 (August 15, 1936): 10-12.

2788. "Behind the Franco Lines." NATION 148 (December 31, 1938): 3-4.

2789. "Besieged Madrid." LITERARY DIGEST 122 (December 19, 1936): 7.

2790. "Beyond the Ebro." NATION 147 (August 20, 1938): 168-169.

     Follows the action in Spain's civil war.

2791. "Bilbao and the World's Conscience." NATION 144 (May 8, 1937): 523-524.

     Discusses reports of Spanish atrocities.

2792. "Bitter Spanish Pill: Mussolini Annoyed by Gibes at Defeat of His Iberian Legions." LITERARY DIGEST 123 (April 3, 1937): 15.

2793. "Blackshirt in Spain." LIVING AGE 352 (June 1937): 299-304.

     Presents the personal narrative of a fascist volunteer in the civil war.

2794. "Blondes Fight for Both Fascists and Communists." NEWS-WEEK 8 (December 19, 1936): 13.

2795. "Bomb from Barcelona." NATION 147 (July 2, 1938): 5.

     Discusses foreign intervention in the civil war.

2796. "Bombs Slaughter Spanish Civilians." LITERARY DIGEST 123 (March 20, 1937): 10.

2797. "Bombs vs. Civilians, Gold vs. Ore, Oranges vs. Olives." NEWSWEEK 11 (January 31, 1938): 9-11.

2798. "Bombshells: Spanish War Thunders On, Reporter Hints at Diplomatic Revelations." LITERARY DIGEST 123 (May 22, 1937): 12.

2799. Borkenau, F. "Situation in Spain." 19th CENTURY AND
      AFTER 125 (March 1939): 295-302.

      Examines the current status of Spain's civil war.

2800. ———. "Spain Calls Its Own Tune." CHRISTIAN SCIENCE
      MONITOR MAGAZINE (November 24, 1937): 1-2+.

      Follows the course of the on-going civil war.

2801. "Boys from Brunete." TIME 33 (January 2, 1939): 7.

      Examines volunteer activities in the civil war.

2802. Brenner, A. "Calling for Protest; Persecution of Left
      Labor Elements." NATION 145 (August 21, 1937): 206.

      Examines anti-union violence during the civil war.

2803. ———. "Who's Who in Spain." NATION 143 (August 15,
      1936): 174-177.

      Examines opposing sides in the civil war.

2804. Brereton, G. "Can Franco Win the Spanish War?" CONTEM-
      PORARY REVIEW 152 (December 1937): 656-663.

2805. ———. "Spanish Peasants at War." CURRENT HISTORY 48
      (April 1938): 38-40.

2806. Brierly, J.L. "Bombs and the Law; Sinking of British
      Ships in Spanish Ports." VITAL SPEECHES 4 (July 15,
      1938): 605-606.

2807. "British Call Bluff; Piracy Conference Shows Nations
      Still Playing Cards." BUSINESS WEEK (September 18,
      1937): 18.

      Covers submarine operations in the civil war.

2808. "British Oppose Mystery Pirates with a Conference, a
      Plan, and Sixty Destroyers." NEWSWEEK 10 (September
      20, 1937): 7-8.

2809. Brower, J. "Spain's Little World War." SCHOLASTIC 32
      (May 7, 1938): 31S.

2810. Buckley, H. "Inside Spain." FORTUNE 149 (March 1938):
      299-307.

2811. Buell, R.L. "Revolt in Spain, and in Europe and the
      United States." VITAL SPEECHES 2 (August 15, 1936):
      698-701.

2812. "Bumping Off Parties." TIME 29 (January 11, 1937): 22-
      23.

      Reports current political murders in Spain.

2813. Burkett, P.H. "Murder in Madrid; Reply." COMMONWEAL 24
      (September 24, 1936): 488.

      Refutes item 3046 below.

2814. "Business and Blood." TIME 29 (April 19, 1937): 22-23.

      Continues coverage of the civil war.

2815. Calverton, V.F. "Benavente and the Spanish Revolution."
      CURRENT HISTORY 49 (November 1938): 48.

2816. Campbell, G.W., and O.D. Bell. "I've Stopped Killing
      for Money." AMERICAN MERCURY 125 (June 1938): 35+.

      Presents a personal narrative of the civil war.

2817. "Capture of Barcelona Points to End of the Spanish War."
      NEWSWEEK 13 (February 6, 1939): 18-20.

2818. "Carmens in Spanish Death Dance." LITERARY DIGEST 122
      (August 22, 1936): 10-11.

      Covers the on-going civil war.

2819. Carter, W.H. "Avalanche." FORTUNE 149 (April 1938):
      385-390.

      Examines the progress of foreign intervention in Spain

2820. ————. "Calvary in Spain." FORTUNE 151 (March 1939):
      285-294.

      Examines the declining days of the civil war.

2821. ————. "Spain from the Inside." FORTUNE 146 (November
       1936): 553-561.

2822. ————. "Spanish Imbroglio." CONTEMPORARY REVIEW 150
       (December 1936): 656-664.

       Continues coverage of the civil war.

2823. ————. "Spanish Tragedy." CONTEMPORARY REVIEW 150
       (September 1936): 265-279.

2824. Castle, T.M. "General Franco's War." LIVING AGE 144
       (May 15, 1937): 555-557.

2825. "Catholics and Fascists; Reply." COMMONWEAL 29 (Novem-
       ber 18, 1938): 99.

2826. "Cats and Seagulls." TIME 29 (April 26, 1937): 20.

       Continues coverage of the civil war.

2827. Cazalet, V.A. "Civil War; Conditions in General Franco's
       Area." 19th CENTURY AND AFTER 121 (April 1937): 493-
       499.

2828. Chamberlain, Neville. "War Odds, July 1937; Spain a
       Second Sarajevo?" VITAL SPEECHES 3 (July 15, 1937):
       589-590.

2829. "Charges Against Negrin." NEW REPUBLIC 99 (June 7, 1939):
       114.

       Covers alleged war crimes in the Spanish conflict.

2830. Chaves-Nogales, M. "Franco's Spain." FORTUNE 150
       (October 1938): 412-423.

2831. ————. "General Franco." 19th CENTURY AND AFTER 125
       (January 1939): 18-25.

2832. "Chewed Up." TIME 29 (April 5, 1937): 21-22+.

       Reports new casualties in the civil war.

2833. Chiaromonte, N. "Spain: The War." ATLANTIC MONTHLY 159
       (March 1937): 359-364.

2834. "Civil War and Intervention." NATION 143 (August 29, 1936): 228-229.

2835. "Civil War Climax of Spain's Long Suffering History." SCHOLASTIC 29 (September 19, 1936): 12-13.

2836. "Civil War in Spain." CATHOLIC WORLD 143 (September 1936): 747-748.

2837. "Civil War in Spain and the United States." COMMONWEAL 28 (June 24, 1938): 229-230, 241; 28 (July 15, 1938): 324-327.

2838. "Civil War in Spain May Cost World Its Masterpieces." NEWSWEEK 8 (September 5, 1936): 20-21.

2839. "Civil War Within Civil War Hastens Collapse of Loyalists." SCHOLASTIC 34 (March 25, 1939): 9.

2840. "Closing Phase of Spanish War Marked by Loyalist Upheavals." NEWSWEEK 13 (March 13, 1939): 20.

2841. Colvin, I. "Case for Franco." ATLANTIC MONTHLY 161 (March 1938): 397-402.

    Presents a sympathetic view of Spain's leading fascist.

2842. ―――. "Six and Half-a-Dozen: or, One as Bad as the Other." 19th CENTURY AND AFTER 120 (November 1936): 556-558.

    Compares opposing sides in Spain's civil war.

2843. "Compromise on Spain Fails to Bring Peace Closer." NEWSWEEK 12 (July 4, 1938): 14.

2844. Cornford, J. "On the Catalonian Front." NEW REPUBLIC 89 (December 2, 1936): 136-138.

    Presents a front-line view of the civil war.

2845. "Counter-Revolution in Spain." NEW REPUBLIC 87 (July 29, 1936): 337-338.

2846. Courtney, W.B. "Rehearsal in Spain; Show Window of the Next War." COLLIER'S 99 (January 23, 1937): 12-13+.

2847. Cowley, M. "To Madrid." NEW REPUBLIC 92 (August 25, 1937): 63-65; 92 (September 1, 1937): 93-96; 92 (September 15, 1937): 152-155; 92 (September 22, 1937): 179-182; 92 (October 6, 1937): 233-238.

2848. Cox, G. "Eyewitness in Madrid." HARPER'S 175 (June 1937): 27-37.

2849. "Crisis: The Unconquered are Conquered." NEWSWEEK 9 (June 26, 1937): 5-6.

       Covers the on-going civil war.

2850. "Crumbling Republic." TIME 28 (October 5, 1936): 20-21.

2851. Daura, L. de. "Soldier Returns; Spanish Letters." ATLANTIC MONTHLY 161 (January 1938): 28-34.

2852. Davis, R. "Spanish Scene." CANADIAN FORUM 16 (November 1936): 18-19.

2853. "Death of Mola." TIME 29 (June 14, 1937): 21.

       Examines the continuing civil war.

2854. "Democracy in Retreat." NATION 143 (September 19, 1936): 320-321.

       Reports fascist victories in Spain's civil war.

2855. Dennis, L. "Russia's Private War in Spain." AMERICAN MERCURY 40 (February 1937): 158-166.

2856. "Deutschland and Almeria." NEW REPUBLIC 91 (June 9, 1937): 116.

       Examines German intervention in the civil war.

2857. Dewey, S. "Anarchist Movement in Spain." CONTEMPORARY REVIEW 81 (May 1902): 741-749.

2858. DeWilde, J.C. "Struggle Over Spain." FOREIGN POLICY REPORT 14 (April 1, 1938): 140-144.

2859. "Dictators Meet." NATION 145 (October 2, 1937): 336.

       Reviews foreign intervention in the civil war.

2860. "Diplomacy: Fuhrer Settles Crisis." NEWSWEEK 9 (January 23, 1937): 14.

Reports German involvement in the civil war.

2861. "Diplomacy: November 18 Day of Ignominy." NEWSWEEK 8 (November 28, 1936): 5-6.

Examines foreign intervention in the civil war.

2862. "Diplomacy: Powers Confine the War to Spain." NEWSWEEK 9 (February 27, 1937): 13.

2863. "Diplomatic Dogfight." TIME 28 (October 19, 1936): 22-23.

Examines foreign intervention in the civil war.

2863. "Diplomats Bury Quarrels, Brave Continue to Bury the Dead." NEWSWEEK 9 (June 19, 1937): 18-20.

2865. "Discouraged Celts." TIME 29 (May 10, 1937): 21-23.

Reports on Spain's continuing war of attrition.

2866. "Disease Area." TIME 29 (March 8, 1937): 25-26.

2867. "Disorders in Spain." CATHOLIC WORLD 143 (April 1936): 109.

2868. "Drift to War; Shelling of Almeria." NATION 144 (June 12, 1937): 655.

Examines Nazi activity in the civil war.

2869. "Duce Continues Spanish War on the Front and in London." NEWSWEEK 10 (October 25, 1937): 16-17.

2870. "Duce Speaks." CURRENT HISTORY 47 (December 1937): 106-107.

Examines Italian intervention in the civil war.

2871. "Duce's Forces Overshadow Hitler's in Spain." NEWSWEEK 9 (February 20, 1937): 7-9.

2872. Duff, C. "Malaga and After." FORTUNE 147 (April 1937): 405-412.

2873. Durant, W. "Spanish Crazy Quilt." COLLIER'S 98 (December 12, 1936): 10-11+.

Examines opposing sides in the civil war.

2874. "Dying Spaniards." LITERARY DIGEST 122 (September 12, 1936): 12-13.

2875. Earle, G.H. "Spain in Flames." NATION 144 (April 25, 1937): 396.

2876. "Easter and an Anniversary Brings Insurgents Luck." NEWSWEEK 11 (April 25, 1938): 18.

Charts the changing fortunes of war in Spain.

2877. "Easter Brings Victories, Resurrection of Hope to Madrid." NEWSWEEK 9 (April 3, 1937): 15.

2878. Eddy, S. "Tragedy of Spain." CHRISTIAN CENTURY 54 (September 22, 1937): 1163-1165.

2879. Ehrenbourg, I. "Volunteers for Murder." LIVING AGE 354 (August 1938): 491-495.

Examines aerial operations in the civil war.

2880. Elliott, J. "With the Rebels." ATLANTIC MONTHLY 158 (November 1936): 534-542.

Follows the progress of Franco's fascist troops.

2881. Emanuel, W.V. "Naval Side of the Spanish War." FORTUNE 150 (July 1938): 83-91.

2882. Enters, A. "Ramon, Miguel, and Dolores; Air Raid Toll." NEW REPUBLIC 95 (May 18, 1938): 47.

2883. "Exit." TIME 32 (October 3, 1938): 19.

Covers volunteer activities in the civil war.

2884. "Failure at Teruel Dooms Insurgents' Plan." NEWSWEEK 11 (January 17, 1938): 17-20.

2885. "Farmers and Workers Rise Against Military Coup." NEWSWEEK 8 (August 1, 1936): 5-8.

2886. "Fascist Aid to the Rebels." NEW REPUBLIC 88 (October 14, 1936): 267.

2887. "Fascist and Red March in Spain." LITERARY DIGEST 122 (August 1, 1936): 11-12.

2888. "Fascist Bombs Distress Madrid, Encourage Barcelona." NEWSWEEK 8 (December 26, 1936): 11-12.

2889. "Fascist Front Holds On." NATION 144 (January 23, 1937): 88.

    Examines victories by Franco's rebel troops.

2890. "Fascist Internationale." CHRISTIAN CENTURY 53 (December 2, 1936): 1600-1602.

    Reviews right-wing intervention in the civil war.

2891. "Fascist Terror in Majorca." NATION 143 (December 5, 1936): 655-656.

    Criticizes Franco's military conduct.

2892. "Fascists Are Fed Up but Reds Sing for First Time." NEWSWEEK 9 (April 10, 1937): 16-17.

2893. Feistman, R. "Franco's Nazi Advisor." LIVING AGE 352 (June 1937): 327-330.

2894. Fernsworth, L.A. "Back of the Spanish Rebellion." FOREIGN AFFAIRS 15 (October 1936): 87-101.

    Examines causal factors in the fascist uprising.

2895. ———. "Civil War in Spain." FORTUNE 146 (September 1936): 268-278.

2896. ———. "Next Round in Spain." NATION 147 (October 29, 1938): 448-450.

2897. ———. "Revolutionary Forces in Catalonia." FOREIGN AFFAIRS 15 (July 1937): 674-684.

2898. ———. "Spain Balks the Fascists." CURRENT HISTORY 46 (June 1937): 27-32.

2899. ———. "Spain's Schedule of War." NATION 147 (November 26, 1938): 560-561.

2900. ———. "Twentieth-Century Piracy." CURRENT HISTORY 47 (November 1937): 59-64.

Examines submarine activity in the civil war.

2901. ———. "Whose Fault in Spain?" CURRENT HISTORY 49 (December 1938): 31-33.

2902. ———. "With the Spanish Anarchists." CURRENT HISTORY 46 (July 1937): 71-75.

2903. ———, and J. Stevens. "Driven People." NEW REPUBLIC 98 (March 15, 1939): 158-160.

Continues coverage of the civil war.

2904. Finick, E. "I Fly for Spain." HARPER'S 176 (January 1938): 138-148.

2905. Fischer, L. "Barcelona Holds Out." NATION 146 (April 2, 1938): 374-375.

Describes a fascist siege in progress.

2906. ———. "Cable from the Front." NATION 146 (April 23, 1938): 458.

2907. ———. "Can Madrid Hold On?" NATION 144 (January 16, 1937): 62.

Examines the declining strength of republican forces in the civil war.

2908. ———. "Drive Along the Ebro." NATION 147 (September 3, 1938): 219-221.

2909. ———. "Franco Cannot Win." NATION 145 (August 7, 1937): 148-150.

Oops.

2910. ———. "Loyalist Spain Gathers Its Strength." NATION 145 (July 3, 1937): 7-8.

2911. ———. "Loyalist Spain Takes the Offensive." NATION 145 (July 17, 1937): 62.

2912. ———. "Loyalists Push Ahead." NATION 146 (January 1, 1938): 736-737.

2913. ———. "Madrid Fights Off Franco." NATION 143 (November 21, 1936): 595-596.

2914. ———. "Madrid Keeps Its Nerve." NATION 143 (November 7, 1936): 539.

2915. ———. "Madrid's Foreign Defenders." NATION 145 (September 4, 1937): 235-237.

Examines volunteers on the loyalist side.

2916. ———. "On Madrid's Front Line." NATION 143 (October 24, 1936): 469-470.

2917. ———. "Peace on Earth." NATION 147 (December 24, 1938): 686-688.

Covers aerial operations in the civil war.

2918. ———. "Pirates and British Policy." NATION 145 (September 18, 1937): 282.

Covers submarine operations in the civil war.

2919. ———. "Spain Won't Surrender." NATION 146 (April 30, 1938): 495-497.

2920. ———. "Spain's Final Tragedy." NATION 148 (March 18, 1939): 312-313.

Assess the fascist victory and its aftermath.

2921. ———. "Spain's Red Foreign Legion." NATION 144 (January 9, 1937): 36-38.

Examines Russian intervention in the civil war.

2922. ———. "Spain's Tragic Anniversary." NATION 147 (July 30, 1938): 103-105.

Continues coverage of the civil war.

2923. ———. "Thirty Months of War in Spain." NATION 148
      (January 7, 1939): 28-30.

2924. ———. "Under Fire in Madrid." NATION 143 (December
      12, 1936): 693-694.

2925. ———. "What Can Save Spain?" NATION 146 (March 26,
      1938): 348-349.

      Discusses foreign intervention in Spain.

2926. ———. "Will Moscow Save Madrid?" NATION 143 (October
      31, 1936): 508-509.

2927. "Flight from Madrid." TIME 28 (November 16, 1936): 35-36.

      Describes the evacuation of republican forces.

2928. "Fog in Spain." NEWSWEEK 12 (November 21, 1938): 20.

      Follows the progress of the civil war.

2929. "Foreign Airmen Steal the Show from Native Troops."
      NEWSWEEK 9 (May 8, 1937): 9-10.

2930. "Foreigners Bring Gas and Flame-Throwers to Madrid."
      NEWSWEEK 8 (December 12, 1936): 14.

2931. "Franco Besieges Most Excellent City of Madrid." NEWS-
      WEEK 8 (November 14, 1936): 9-10.

2932. "Franco Blockades Loyal Ports, Japan Recognizes Rebels."
      SCHOLASTIC 31 (December 18, 1937): 14S.

2933. "Franco Drives for Bilbao Touchdown, and Catalonia Takes
      Time Out for Private Scrimmage." NEWSWEEK 9 (May 15,
      1937): 18.

2934. "Franco in Striking Distance of Madrid, Becomes Dictator."
      NEWSWEEK 8 (October 10, 1936): 15-17.

2935. "Franco Launches Drive to End Spanish Civil War." SCHO-
      LASTIC 33 (January 7, 1939): 10.

2936. "Franco Prepares to Use Roman Design for Victory."
      NEWSWEEK 10 (November 8, 1937): 16-18.

2937. "Franco Setback." NEWSWEEK 12 (August 8, 1938): 14-15.

Examines changing fortunes in the civil war.

2938. "Franco Wins North Coast, Duce Plots New Victories."
NEWSWEEK 10 (November 1, 1937): 16-18.

2939. "Franco's Conquest of the Atlantic." NATION 146 (February 26, 1938): 233-234.

2940. "Franco's Final Drive." NATION 148 (January 7, 1939): 24.

2941. "Franco's Onrush Scares Paris with Back-Door Fascist Threat." NEWSWEEK 11 (April 11, 1938): 14.

2942. "Franco's Parade; Long-Delayed Entry of Madrid." NEWSWEEK 13 (May 29, 1939): 20-21.

2943. "Franco's Push." NEWSWEEK 13 (January 9, 1939): 18-19.

2944. "Franco's Smashing Drives Prove Speed Best Weapon."
NEWSWEEK 11 (April 4, 1938): 15-16.

2945. "Franco's Timetable; Valencia and Madrid, Then Catalonia in Spring." NEWSWEEK 12 (July 18, 1938): 14.

2946. Frank, W. "Spain in War." NEW REPUBLIC 95 (July 13, 1938): 269-272, 298-301; 95 (July 27, 1938): 325-327.

2947. "Frantic Franco." LITERARY DIGEST 123 (April 17, 1937): 15-16.

2948. Frewen, O. "Watch on the Spanish Shores." FORTUNE 151 (April 1939): 429-436.

Describes civil war naval blockades.

2949. Fulano, F. "Fifth Column: Franco's Secret Army." LIVING AGE 353 (November 1937): 219-222.

Examines political subersion in Spain.

2950. "Gallant Spaniards Still Die in Vain." LITERARY DIGEST 122 (October 10, 1936): 12-13.

Updates front-line reports from the civil war.

2951. Gellhorn, M. "City at War." COLLIER'S 101 (April 2, 1938): 18-19+.

   Presents a personal narrative of the civil war.

2952. ———. "Men Without Medals: Abraham Lincoln Battalion." COLLIER'S 101 (January 15, 1938): 9-10+.

2953. ———. "Only Shells Whine." COLLIER'S 100 (July 17, 1937): 12-13+.

2954. ———. "Visit to the Wounded." SCHOLASTIC 31 (November 6, 1937): 19E-20E.

   Presents a personal narrative of the civil war.

2955. "General Franco's Next Move." CURRENT HISTORY 48 (January 1939): 73.

2956. Gittler, L.F. "Spain's Rebel Chiefs." CURRENT HISTORY 46 (May 1937): 55-60.

2957. "Glad Reds; International Column in Spain." TIME 29 (April 5, 1937): 18-19.

   Examines the communist faction in the civil war.

2958. Glasgow, G. "Spanish Cockpit." CONTEMPORARY REVIEW 151 (June 1937): 742-745.

   Examines aerial combat in the civil war.

2959. Goodman, E., and A. Jacob. "Construction and Destruction in Spain." CONTEMPORARY REVIEW 150 (October 1936): 416-426.

2960. "Gory Year." LITERARY DIGEST 123 (June 19, 1937): 11.

2961. Greene, M.T. "North Africa's Turmoil; Franco Brings the Moor Back to Europe, Fanning Islam's Smoldering Nationalism." CURRENT HISTORY 47 (December 1937): 86-89.

2962. Grenfell, R. "Navy and the Spanish War." 19th CENTURY AND AFTER 125 (May 1939): 567-574.

2963. Gruyth, R. de. "Soviet Agents; Leftist Cause in Spain Directed by a Sort of Moscow Triumvirate." LIVING AGE 352 (April 1937): 143-146.

2964. Gwynn, S. "Freebooting and Swashbuckling." FORTUNE 149 (March 1938): 359-360.

    Examines foreign intervention in the civil war.

2965. ———. "Volunteers for Spain." FORTUNE 147 (February 1937): 230-233.

2966. Haldane, J.B.S., and G.H. Keeling. "Below the Pyrenees." LIVING AGE 352 (March 1937): 35-37.

    Presents a personal narrative of the civil war.

2967. Hanighen, F. "Axis Over Spain; Economic Interests." NEW REPUBLIC 97 (November 30, 1938): 89-91.

2968. ———. "Spanis Volcano." REVIEW OF REVIEWS 94 (October 1936): 40-43.

2969. ———. "War for Raw Materials in Spain." NATION 144 (April 24, 1937): 456-458.

2970. ———. "Women at War; Four Types of the Spanish Amazon." REVIEW OF REVIEWS 94 (November 1936): 75-76.

2971. Hart, B.H. Liddell. "Military Lessons from Spain." NEW REPUBLIC 91 (August 4, 1937): 357-359.

2972. Hart, M.K. "America, Look at Spain! The Agony Will Be Repeated Here." VITAL SPEECHES 5 (November 1, 1938): 57-58.

2973. ———. "Our Position Respecting Spain; Red Propaganda in America." VITAL SPEECHES 5 (January 1, 1939): 187-191.

2974. Hellman, L. "Day in Spain." NEW REPUBLIC 94 (April 13, 1938): 297-298.

    Presents a personal narrative of the civil war.

2975. Hemingway, Ernest. "Reports from the Madrid Battlefront." NEW REPUBLIC 90 (May 5, 1937): 376-379.

2976. "Hemingway Finds That Americans Know Their Trade." NEWS-
        WEEK 10 (October 4, 1937): 23.

        Reviews the activities of civil war volunteers in Spain.

2977. "Hemingway; LIFE Documents FOR WHOM THE BELL TOLLS with
        War Shots." LIFE 10 (January 6, 1941): 52-57.

        Photo layouts on the civil war complement excerpts from
        Hemingway's best-selling novel about Spain.

2978. "Hemingway Reports Spain; Selections from Dispatches."
        NEW REPUBLIC 90 (January 12, 1937): 273-276; 93 (April
        27, 1937): 273-276; 94 (May 5, 1937): 350-351; 95 (June
        8, 1938): 124-126.

2979. "Hero of Madrid; Kleber Checks Rightists." LITERARY
        DIGEST 122 (December 5, 1936): 11-12.

2980. "Hitler Over Bilbao." CURRENT HISTORY 46 (August 1937):
        90-91.

        Covers aerial operations in the civil war.

2981. House, R.T. "Spain's Holy War." CHRISTIAN CENTURY 54
        (October 6, 1937): 1228-1229.

2982. ———. "Spain's Useful Reminder; Offensive Warfare
        Doesn't Pay." CHRISTIAN CENTURY 54 (July 7, 1937):
        867-868.

2983. Hughes, L. "Laughter in Madrid." NATION 146 (January
        29, 1938): 123-124.

        Follows the course of Spain's civil war.

2984. "Iberian Blockade." LITERARY DIGEST 123 (March 6, 1937):
        13.

2985. "If Barcelona Falls." CHRISTIAN CENTURY 56 (February 1,
        1939): 143-145.

2986. "International Naval Line-Up." TIME 30 (July 5, 1937):
        15.

        Covers naval operations in the civil war.

2987. "Irish and Italians Find Spain is a Distressful Country."
      NEWSWEEK 9 (March 27, 1937): 18-19.

      Presents foreign views on the civil war.

2988. "Irun's Fall." TIME 28 (September 14, 1936): 22.

      Reports from the front lines in the civil war.

2989. "Italian Aid." NEWSWEEK 11 (June 6, 1938): 16.

2990. "Italy Admits Having 40,000 Men in Franco's Army." CHRIS-
      TIAN CENTURY 54 (October 27, 1937): 1317.

2991. "Itsly Charges French Aid as Loyalists Gain." SCHOLASTIC
      30 (April 24, 1937): 14.

      The pot calls the kettle black in Spain's civil war.

2992. "Italy Defies Britain, France on Spain." SCHOLASTIC 31
      (October 23, 1937): 14S.

2993. "Italy Partially Accepts Withdrawal Plan." SCHOLASTIC
      31 (November 6, 1937): 13S.

2994. "Italy Willing to Withdraw Troops from Spain." SCHOLAS-
      TIC 30 (May 1, 1937): 30.

2995. Jerrold, D. "Issues in Spain." AMERICAN REVIEW 9 (April
      1937): 1-34.

2996. ————. "Red Propaganda in Spain." AMERICAN REVIEW 9
      (May 1937): 129-151.

2997. Jones, S. "Eyewitness in Spain." CHRISTIAN CENTURY 54
      (April 7, 1937): 452-454.

2998. Kaminsky. "Piracy Eyewitness." LITERARY DIGEST 124
      (October 9, 1937): 26.

      Covers submarine operations in the civil war.

2999. Kemp, P. "People's Army." 19th CENTURY AND AFTER 123
      (March 1938): 365-377.

3000. Kennedy, Joseph P., Jr. "Here They Come! Air Raid,
      Valencia." ATLANTIC MONTHLY 164 (October 1939): 545-54

3001. Koltsov, M. "Besieged in a Tank." LITERARY DIGEST 124
      (November 27, 1937): 26-27.

      Presents a personal narrative of the civil war.

3002. ————. "Don Quixote's Villages: El Toboso and Don Fab-
      rique." LIVING AGE 352 (May 1937): 201-206.

      Presents an on-site examination of the continuing war.

3003. Krivitsky, W.G. "Stalin's Hand in Spain." SATURDAY
      EVENING POST 211 (April 15, 1939): 5-7+.

3004. "Lack of Troops Stalls Franco in Battle of Men and Mer-
      cury." NEWSWEEK 12 (August 22, 1938): 16-17.

3005. Laird, M. "Diary of a Revolution." ATLANTIC MONTHLY 158
      (November 1936): 513-533.

3006. Langdon-Davies, J. "Bombs Over Barcelona; Analysis of
      the Official Minute-to-Minute Log Kept by the Air
      Defense." LIVING AGE 355 (September 1938): 58-61.

3007. "Last Chance; Bilbao." TIME 29 (June 21, 1937): 24-25.

      Follows continuing violence in the civil war.

3008. "Last Ditch: Loyalists Prepare for Counterattack After
      Bilbao Falls to Franco." LITERARY DIGEST 123 (June
      26, 1937): 12-13.

3009. Leider, B. "Last Letters from Spain." CURRENT HISTORY
      46 (April 1937): 46.

3010. "Letters from Spain." CANADIAN FORUM 17 (December 1937):
      310-311.

3011. Lingelbach, W.E. "Clash of Spanish Parties." CURRENT
      HISTORY 43 (March 1936): 653-655.

      Covers political violence on the eve of civil war.

3012. "Little World War." TIME 29 (January 18, 1937): 20-21.

      Examines foreign intervention in the civil war.

3013. "Little World War Begins to Grow." NATION 143 (November
      28, 1936): 620.

3014. "Little World War's Worst Crisis." NEWSWEEK 9 (June 12, 1937): 5-9.

3015. "Long Live Dynamite!" TIME 28 (August 31, 1936): 18-20.

Examines escalating violence in Spain.

3016. "Loyalist Dilemma." NATION 145 (August 21, 1937): 185-186.

Examines continuing action in the civil war.

3017. "Loyalist Hopes Rise as Rebels Falter." SCHOLASTIC 30 (April 17, 1937): 16.

3018. "Loyalist Surrender Near, Negrin Ousted at Madrid." SCHOLASTIC 34 (March 18, 1939): 7.

3019. "Loyalists Elated at Holding Rebel Drive at a Stalemate." NEWSWEEK 11 (May 16, 1938): 18-19.

3020. "Loyalists Strike in South to Divert Franco Offensive." SCHOLASTIC 33 (January 21, 1939): 10.

3021. "Loyalists Take the Offensive but Unseen Enemies Cut Off Supplies." NEWSWEEK 10 (Septemebr 13, 1937): 14.

3022. "Lucky Among Moors." TIME 30 (August 2, 1937): 19.

Covers aerial operations in the civil war.

3023. M., Mary. "A Catholic Speaks Her Mind." NATION 145 (December 18, 1937): 683-685.

Examines religious issues in the civil war.

3024. McGuire, O.B. "New Spain." COMMONWEAL 27 (October 29, 1937): 5-8.

Covers action in the on-going civil war.

3025. ————. "Peace in Spain." COMMONWEAL 26 (August 27, 1937): 413-415.

3026. Macauley, T. "Spain: When Peace Explodes." SURVEY GEOGRAPHIC 28 (March 1939): 212-213+.

Continues coverage of the civil war.

3027. "Macgowan, G. "Red Vultures in the Pyrenees." COMMON-
      WEAL 27 (February 18, 1938): 458-460.

      Examines communist conduct in the civil war.

3028. ———. "Scarlet Pimpernels of Spain." COMMONWEAL 27
      (January 21, 1938): 341-342.

      Follows action in the continuing civil war.

3029. "Madrid Impasse." LITERARY DIGEST 122 (December 12,
      1936): 10-11.

3030. "Madrid: Shambles of Warring Spain." LITERARY DIGEST
      122 (November 14, 1936): 13.

3031. Malraux, Andre. "Forging Man's Fate in Spain." NATION
      144 (March 20, 1937): 315-316.

      Speculates on the consequences of the civil war.

3032. ———. "This is War." COLLIER'S 99 (May 29, 1937):
      9-10+.

      Presents a personal narrative of the civil war.

3033. Mangold, W.P. "Why Franco Has Hesitated." NEW REPUBLIC
      93 (December 22, 1937): 192-193.

3034. Mann, T. "I Stand with the Spanish People." NATION 144
      (April 17, 1937): 429-430.

      Reports on progress of the civil war.

3035. Manuel, F.E. "Background of the Spanish Revolt." NATION
      143 (July 25, 1936): 94-97.

3036. "Mass Torture?" TIME 33 (March 20, 1939): 19-20.

      Examines the plight of civil war refugees.

3037. "Massacre in Spain." NEW REPUBLIC 98 (April 5, 1939):
      238.

      Reports alleged civil war atrocities.

3038. "Mediterranean Crisis." NEW REPUBLIC 92 (September 15,
      1937): 145.

Covers submarine operations in the civil war.

3039. "Mediterranean Piracy." CURRENT HISTORY 47 (October 1937): 17-18.

Continues coverage of submarine operations.

3040. Mitchell, J. "Death Rides the Wind; Destruction of Guernica." NEW REPUBLIC 91 (May 26, 1937): 63-64.

3041. "Modern Saracens Capture Key Citadel, Reds Obtain Chief Posts in New Madrid Government." NEWSWEEK 8 (September 12, 1936): 9-10.

3042. "Moors to Lusitania." TIME 28 (August 17, 1936): 19.

Continues civil war coverage.

3043. "Morocco Front." NATION 144 (January 16, 1937): 60.

Describes new action in the civil war.

3044. Morrow, F. "Spain: A Battle Behind the Lines." NEW REPUBLIC 93 (November 10, 1937): 18-20.

3045. "Moscow Uses Civil War as Lever to Raise Prestige; Madrid Evacuates Children." NEWSWEEK 8 (October 17, 1936): 5-7.

3046. "Murder in Madrid." COMMONWEAL 24 (August 28, 1936): 413-414.

Covers fascist bombing attacks on republican forces.

3047. "Murder in Spain." LITERARY DIGEST 122 (July 25, 1936): 12-13.

Covers the assassination of Calvo Sotelo.

3048. "Mussolini Weighs His Chances." NATION 144 (April 3, 1937): 369.

Reports Italian intervention in the civil war.

3049. "Mussolini Wins a Round." NATION 145 (October 30, 1937): 463-464.

3050. "New Crisis in Spain." NATION 144 (June 5, 1937): 635.

   Continues coverage of the civil war.

3051. "Next Phase in Spain." NEW REPUBLIC 91 (June 23, 1937): 173-174.

3052. "Nine to Nyon." TIME 30 (September 20, 1937): 15.

   Covers submarine operations in the civil war.

3053. "No Duds; Blast of Spanish Loyalist Bombs on German War-Ship Heard Round the World." LITERARY DIGEST 123 (June 5, 1937): 12-13.

3054. "No Military Objective Explains the Bombs." NEWSWEEK 11 (February 7, 1938): 20-21.

   Covers aerial operations in the civil war.

3055. "No Restraint in Spain; Nation Torn by Civil War Has Long Been Divided." LITERARY DIGEST 123 (February 27, 1937): 12-13.

3056. "Now It Can Be Told; Full Extent of German and Italian Intervention." NATION 148 (June 17, 1939): 688-689.

3057. O'Donnell, P. "Irishman in Spain." 19th CENTURY AND AFTER 120 (December 1936): 698-706.

   Presents a personal narrative of the civil war.

3058. Oman, C. "British Blockade-Runners, 1861-65 and 1936-38." 19th CENTURY AND AFTER 124 (September 1938): 279-284.

   Includes naval operations in the Spanish civil war.

3059. "125 Days." TIME 28 (November 30, 1936): 20-21.

   Follows the early course of the civil war.

3060. "One Year of Fighting and Both Sides Only Beginning." NEWSWEEK 10 (July 17, 1937): 17.

3061. "One Year of the Spanish War." CURRENT HISTORY 46 (September 1937): 16-17.

3062. "Others Play at War as Spain Fights; Line-Up of Embattled
      Spaniards." LITERARY DIGEST 122 (August 29, 1936): 12-
      13.

3063. "Outcome Again in the Balance on Teruel Front." NEWS-
      WEEK 11 (January 10, 1938): 20.

3064. "Panic in Spain." NEWSWEEK 11 (March 28, 1938): 15-16.

      Continues coverage of the civil war.

3065. "Passion Flowers." TIME 28 (August 10, 1936): 24-26.

      Follows the action in Spain's civil war.

3066. "Patience Exhausted; Threat of War Unless Piracy Stops."
      NEWSWEEK 11 (February 14, 1938): 20-21.

      Covers submarine operations in the civil war.

3067. Paul, E. "Life and Death of a Spanish Town." READER'S
      DIGEST 31 (October 1937): 111-128.

3068. "Peace and Pirates." TIME 30 (September 27, 1937): 15-
      16.

      Covers submarine operations in the civil war.

3069. "Peace-Loving Powers Put the War in a Steel Cage; Musso-
      lini's Moors Arrive." NEWSWEEK 9 (March 20, 1937):
      7-9.

3070. Pearsall, R., and S. Huddleston. "Strategy in the Bale-
      arics." CHRISTIAN SCIENCE MONITOR MAGAZINE (December
      29, 1937): 5+.

3071. Peers, E.A. "Catalonia in Arms." CONTEMPORARY REVIEW
      151 (May 1937): 530-537.

3072. ———. "Pendulum Over Spain." 19th CENTURY AND AFTER
      120 (September 1936): 275-286.

      Assesses progress in the civil war.

3073. ———. "Spain That Had No Easter." COMMONWEAL 26 (May
      7, 1937): 39-40.

      Continues coverage of the civil war.

3074. Pflaum, L. "Russia's Role in Spain." AMERICAN MERCURY 47 (May 1939): 9-17.

3075. Phillips, T.R. "Preview of Armageddon." SATURDAY EVENING POST 210 (March 12, 1938): 12-13+.

3076. Pineda, E.R. "Chaos in Spain." COMMONWEAL 24 (October 9, 1936): 551-554.

3077. Pitcairn, F. "On the Firing Line in Defense of Madrid." TRAVEL 68 (February 1937): 18-22+.

   Presents a personal narrative of the civil war.

3078. "Portugal Speaks Up; What Has Moscow Been Doing?" REVIEW OF REVIEWS 95 (January 1937): 46.

3079. "Preparing for Mussolini's Next Move." CHRISTIAN CENTURY 56 (February 22, 1939): 238-239.

   Examines Italian intervention in the civil war.

3080. Prince, A.E. "Spain, a Ship of Fools." QUEEN'S QUARTERLY 43 (August 1936): 280-287.

3081. Pritchett, V.S. "Spain, the Ancient Struggle." CHRISTIAN SCIENCE MONITOR MAGAZINE (December 20, 1936): 1-2.

3082. "Progress of the Revolt." CURRENT HISTORY 44 (September 1936): 20-24.

3083. "Proposed Spanish Truce." NEW REPUBLIC 91 (June 2, 1937): 90.

3084. Putnam, Mrs. G.H. "Street Scene." ATLANTIC MONTHLY 158 (November 1936): 636-639.

   Relates more violent incidents from the civil war.

3085. Ravage, M.E. "Hopeful Catalonia." NEW REPUBLIC 89 (December 9, 1936): 171-173.

   Reports developments in the civil war.

3086. "Real Problem in Spain." CATHOLIC WORLD 145 (June 1937): 257-265.

3087. "Rebel Gains in Spain." CURRENT HISTORY 47 (October
       1937): 16-17.

3088. "Rebels Promise Dictatorship; Rabbles Promise Confisca-
       tion." NEWSWEEK 8 (September 5, 1936): 13.

3089. "Reconnaissance in Spain." LIVING AGE 353 (December
       1937): 333-336.

3090. Recouly, R. "Hour Has Struck." CATHOLIC WORLD 143 (Sep-
       tember 1936): 742-743.

       Updates dispatches from the civil war front.

3091. ————. "Technique of Revolt; Siam and Spain." REVIEW
       OF REVIEWS 87 (January 1933): 51-52.

3092. "Red Snow in Spain." NEWSWEEK 10 (December 27, 1937):
       23.

       Follows continuing action in the civil war.

3093. "Reds Blow Up Alcazar." NEWSWEEK 8 (September 26, 1936):
       15.

3094. "Relics of the Whirlwind." COMMONWEAL 24 (October 16,
       1936): 569-570.

       Examines continuing violence in the civil war.

3095. "Republic vs. Republic." TIME 28 (August 24, 1936):
       25-28.

3096. "Revolution and Conversation." CURRENT HISTORY 46 (April
       1937): 103.

3097. "Riots in Spain, Palestine, Yugoslavia and Poland."
       NEWSWEEK 7 (April 25, 1936): 14-15.

3098. "Rival Spains." REVIEW OF REVIEWS 95 (March 1937): 68-
       69.

       Assesses opposing factions in the civil war.

3099. Roberts, W. "Outlook in Spain." CONTEMPORARY REVIEW
       155 (March 1939): 274-279.

       Projects the aftermath of civil war.

3100. ————. "Reflections on Spain." CONTEMPORARY REVIEW
      151 (February 1937): 137-144.

      Covers the continuing civil war.

3101. ————. "War in Spain." CONTEMPORARY REVIEW 152 (Sep-
      tember 1937): 277-284.

3102. Robson, K.S. "Third Winter of the Spanish Civil War;
      Falange Program." 19th CENTURY AND AFTER 124 (Decem-
      ber 1938): 666-676.

3103. Romer, S. "I Was Franco's Prisoner." NATION 147 (Novem-
      ber 19, 1938): 529-533.

      Presents a personal narrative of the civil war.

3104. ————. "Pacifism and Revolution." NATION 145 (October
      9, 1937): 387-388.

3105. "Royalist Rabbit Out of Franco Hat; How Ex-King Financed
      20 Days of Revolt." LITERARY DIGEST 123 (April 24,
      1937): 10-11.

3106. "Russia Calls a Bluff." NEW REPUBLIC 88 (October 21,
      1936): 295-296.

      Follows the action with red troops in Spain.

3107. Ryan, W.G. "Escape from Loyalist Spain; Final Episode
      of an American Communist's Adventure in Spain." AMER-
      ICAN MERCURY 46 (April 1939): 456-462.

3108. ————. "Men Against Machines." CATHOLIC WORLD 153
      (June 1941): 294-299.

3109. Ryerson, B. "Foreign Volunteer in Spain." NEW REPUBLIC
      90 (April 21, 1937): 317-319.

3110. "Safety First; Anarchism; White Aims." TIME 28 (Septem-
      ber 7, 1936): 15-17.

      Examines political goals in the civil war.

3111. Sauerwine, J. "Powers and the Peninsula." REVIEW OF
      REVIEWS 94 (November 1936): 74.

      Examines foreign intervention in the civil war.

3112. Schwinn, G. "We Escape from Madrid." NATIONAL GEOGRAPH-
      IC 71 (February 1937): 251-268.

      Presents a personal narrative of the civil war.

3113. Scott, W.L. "Spanish Situation." COMMONWEAL 25 (March
      26, 1937): 613-614.

      Continues coverage of the civil war.

3114. Sedgwick, E. "On Franco's Side in Spain." READER'S
      DIGEST 32 (December 1937): 27-29.

3115. ————. "Patron Saint of Andalusia." ATLANTIC MONTHLY
      161 (June 1938): 777-784.

      Continues coverage of the on-going civil war.

3116. "Seesaw in Spain." NEW REPUBLIC 88 (September 2, 1936):
      91-92.

      Examines shifting fortunes in the civil war.

3117. "Seesaw in the Spanish War; Franco Pauses, Foes Reorgan-
      ize." NEWSWEEK 11 (April 13, 1938): 18-19.

3118. Sencourt, R. "Turn in Spain." 19th CENTURY AND AFTER
      123 (June 1938): 733-744.

3119. Sender, R. "Peasant's War." NATION 145 (October 30,
      1937): 475-477.

3120. Shaw, R. "Franco's Big Push; Turning Point of Spain's
      Civil War." CURRENT HISTORY 50 (March 1939): 15-16+.

3121. ————. "Hell Over Spain." REVIEW OF REVIEWS 94 (Sep-
      tember 1936): 56-58.

      Describes aerial combat in the civil war.

3122. ————. "Meet General Kleber." REVIEW OF REVIEWS 95
      (February 1937): 30-31.

      Profiles a military leader in Spain's civil war.

3123. ————. "Twilight in Spain." REVIEW OF REVIEWS 94
      (November 1936): 47.

3124. "Shipping Arms to Spain." NEW REPUBLIC 89 (January 13, 1937): 315-316.

3125. "Sidewalks of Madrid." TIME 28 (November 2, 1936): 18-19.

   Presents a front-line view of the civil war.

3126. "Situation in Spain." 19th CENTURY AND AFTER (September 1936): 287-297.

   Charts the early course of Spain's civil war.

3127. "Slow Help; Catalonians Tussel Enemy Within and Bilbao Dodges Bombs and Bullets." LITERARY DIGEST 123 (May 29, 1937): 12-13.

3128. "Smashing of War Within a War Unifies Madrid to Talk Peace." NEWSWEEK 13 (March 20, 1939): 19-20.

   Covers the final days of the civil war.

3129. Sommerfield, J. "Volunteer in Spain." NEW REPUBLIC 91 (July 7, 1937): 239-241.

   Presents a personal narrative of the civil war.

3130. "Soviets Force a Showdown." NATION 143 (October 17, 1936): 435.

   Reports Russian involvement in the civil war.

3131. Spaight, J.M. "Bombing of Harbours and Shipping Therein." 19th CENTURY AND AFTER 124 (September 1938): 270-278.

3132. "Spain: A Chapter of Horrors." CURRENT HISTORY 46 (June 1937): 19-20.

3133. "Spain Blockaded." REVIEW OF REVIEWS 95 (June 1937): 18.

   Describes foreign involvement in the civil war.

3134. "Spain: British Action Helps Fascists Fight Against Reds Who Threaten to Sovietize Peninsula." NEWSWEEK 8 (August 22, 1936): 5-6.

3135. "Spain Fights On While Europe Trembles." SCHOLASTIC 31 (September 18, 1937): 19.

3136. "Spain is Not Lost." NATION 146 (April 16, 1938): 429–430.

3137. "Spain is Not Russia." NEW REPUBLIC 93 (November 10, 1937): 5.

Examines Soviet intervention in the civil war.

3138. "Spain: Pawn in Little World War." LITERARY DIGEST 122 (November 28, 1936): 11.

3139. "Spain's Pains; Fight to the Death." LITERARY DIGEST 123 (July 10, 1937): 13.

3140. "Spain's Volunteers; Number of Aliens Fighting Alarms Both Sides." LITERARY DIGEST 123 (January 30, 1937): 15–16.

3141. "Spaniards Scorn Talk of Armistice." LITERARY DIGEST 122 (September 19, 1936): 13.

3142. "Spanish Anarchists." SPECTATOR 68 (April 9, 1982): 484–486.

3143. "Spanish Casualties; Two Illusions." CURRENT HISTORY 46 (May 1937): 19–20.

Examines the human cost of civil war.

3144. "Spanish Cauldron." CANADIAN FORUM 16 (October 1936): 4–5.

3145. "Spanish Crises." CURRENT HISTORY 46 (July 1937): 17–18.

3146. "Spanish Helpers; Extent of the German, Italian, and Red Intervention Revealed." NEWSWEEK 13 (June 12, 1939): 20–21.

3147. "Spanish Left and Right." CHRISTIAN SCIENCE MONITOR MAGAZINE (February 10, 1937): 5.

Examines opposing sides in the civil war.

3148. "Spanish Mosaic." LIVING AGE 252 (June 1937): 290–305.

Assesses the issues in Spain's civil war.

3149. "Spanish Mud." NEWSWEEK 11 (May 9, 1938): 19.

Continues coverage of the civil war.

3150. "Spanish Pawn." NEW REPUBLIC 92 (October 27, 1937): 329.

Reports continuing action in the civil war.

3151. "Spanish Rebels Copying Wellington." LITERARY DIGEST
122 (September 26, 1936): 12.

3152. "Spanish Shake-Ups." LITERARY DIGEST 122 (May 1, 1937):
15.

Examines changing fortunes in the civil war.

3153. "Spanish Strategy; Franco's Brilliant Lunges Ascribed
to Reich Experts." NEWSWEEK 11 (May 2, 1938): 20.

3154. "Spanish Threat: Morocco Situation Tries Patience of
Britain and France." LITERARY DIGEST 123 (January 16,
1937): 13.

3155. "Spanish Volcano: Victory Eruptions Threaten to Destroy
Peace of Europe." LITERARY DIGEST 122 (October 17,
1936): 13.

3156. "Spanish Volunteers; Dictators Indicate Intention to
Evacuate Spain." NEWSWEEK 12 (October 17, 1938): 18.

3157. "Spanish War." REVIEW OF REVIEWS 95 (April 1937): 18;
95 (May 1937): 18.

3158. "Spanish War Turns to Tussle of Powers for Franco's
Favor." NEWSWEEK 12 (February 27, 1939): 17-18.

3159. "Spirit of Spain; Letter from Madrid." NATION 144 (April
3, 1937): 391.

Charts the course of continuing civil war.

3160. "Spotlight on Spain; Civil War Facts in a Nutshell."
SCHOLASTIC 30 (February 6, 1937): 18; 30 (April 17,
1937): 25.

3161. "Stalin and Spain; How Reds Aided Loyalists." NEWSWEEK
13 (May 29, 1939): 21-22.

3162. Starkle, W. "Spanish Kaleidoscope; A Background." FOR-
      TUNE 146 (December 1936): 682-688.

      Places the civil war in historical perspective.

3163. Stewart, M.S. "Catalonia in Revolution." NATION 143
      (August 15, 1936): 173.

      Examines the fascist rebellion in Spain.

3164. ————. "Inside Spain." NATION 143 (August 29, 1936):
      233-236.

3165. "Still Bilbao." TIME 29 (May 31, 1937): 25-26.

      Reports from the civil war's front lines.

3166. "Story of the War." NEWSWEEK 13 (March 6, 1939): 18-23.

3167. Stowe, L. "Evelyn the Truck-Driver; an American Girl
      with the Spanish Armies." HARPER'S 178 (February
      1939): 278-286.

3168. ————. "Franco Lies to Win." NEW REPUBLIC 91 (May 19,
      1937): 40-41.

3169. ————. "Loyalists Can Still Win." NEW REPUBLIC 96
      (August 31, 1938): 93-95.

3170. ————. "Spain's Shirt-Sleeve Heroes; Generals of the
      Loyalist Army." NATION 146 (April 23, 1938): 467-469.

3171. "Stranded Volunteers." NATION 147 (October 8, 1938):
      341-342.

3172. "Submerged Pirates." TIME 30 (September 13, 1937): 14-15

      Covers submarine operations in the civil war.

3173. "Tantrums Into Triumphs?" TIME 30 (July 5, 1937): 14-15.

      Continues coverage of the civil war.

3174. "Terrific Toledo." TIME 28 (September 28, 1936): 20-21.

      Examines one city's survival during civil war.

3175. "Terror in Barcelona." LITERARY DIGEST 125 (February 12, 1938): 7-8.

3176. "Terrorist in Spain." LIVING AGE 351 (October 1936): 123-127.

3177. "Teruel Destroyed; Value of Franco's Victory Discounted by Experts." NEWSWEEK 11 (March 7, 1938): 19.

3178. "Thanks, General Franco." NATION 144 (October 1936): 174.

   Examines fascist gains in the civil war.

3179. Thomas, Norman. "Pacifist's Dilemma." NATION 144 (January 16, 1937): 66-68.

3180. ———. "Spain: A Socialist View." NATION 144 (June 19, 1937): 698-700.

3181. Thomson, C.A. "Spain: Civil War." FOREIGN POLICY REPORT 12 (January 15, 1937): 258-268.

3182. ———. "Spain: Issues Behind the Conflict." FOREIGN POLICY REPORT 12 (January 1, 1937): 246-256.

3183. ———. "War in Spain." FOREIGN POLICY REPORT 14 (May 1, 1938): 38-48.

3184. "Tide Turns for Spanish Loyalists." LITERARY DIGEST 123 (April 10, 1937): 13.

3185. Tinker, F.G. "Some Still Live." SATURDAY EVENING POST 210 (April 9, 1938): 5-7+; 210 (April 16, 1938): 10-11+; 210 (April 23, 1938): 16-17+; 210 (April 30, 1938): 18-19+.

   Presents a personal narrative of the civil war.

3186. "Tokens for Spain." NEWSWEEK 12 (October 24, 1938): 16-17.

   Examines continuing action in the civil war.

3187. "Tomato Juice and Blood." TIME 28 (August 17, 1936): 16-17.

   Continues coverage of the civil war.

3188. "Torture in Spain; Designer Condemned for Aiding Loyal-
       ists on Cruelty Devices." NEWSWEEK 13 (June 28, 1939):
       21.

3189. "Trumpets in Spain." NEWSWEEK 11 (February 28, 1938):
       26.

       Continues coverage of the civil war.

3190. "Turmoil in Spain." MISCELLANEOUS REVIEW 59 (November
       1936): 515-516.

3191. "Turn in Spanish Fortunes." NEW REPUBLIC 89 (November
       11, 1936): 34.

3192. "Uneasy Christmas." TIME 29 (January 4, 1937): 17-18.

       Continues coverage of the civil war.

3193. "Unfortunate Manure: Italians of the Foreign Legion."
       TIME 29 (March 22, 1937): 21-22.

3194. "Unity in Rebel Spain?" NEW REPUBLIC 96 (September 21,
       1938): 173.

       Examines fascist political upheaval in the civil war.

3195. "U.S. Warship Under Fire Off Spain." LITERARY DIGEST
       122 (September 5, 1936): 14.

3196. "Unpleasant Surprises for Both the Whites and Reds."
       NEWSWEEK 8 (November 7, 1936): 19.

3197. Val, Marquis Merry de. "In the Wake of the Reds."
       CATHOLIC WORLD 147 (June 1938): 359-361.

3198. Van Slyke, B., and C. Ofaire. "Letters from a Spanish
       Outpost." YALE REVIEW 26 (March 1937): 449-474.

       Presents a personal narrative of the civil war.

3199. "Victory at Teruel." NATION 146 (January 15, 1938): 60.

3200. "Victory for Loyalists." LITERARY DIGEST 125 (January
       8, 1938): 9.

       Reviews the leftist victory at Teruel.

3201. Villard, O.G. "Stage Set for Massacre." NATION 148
      (April 1, 1939): 378.

      Predicts dire consequences of Franco's victory.

3202. "War Cloud from Moroccan Hills Overshadows Battle of the
      Volunteers in Spain." NEWSWEEK 9 (January 16, 1937):
      13-14.

3203. "War, East and West." NATION 145 (September 18, 1937):
      279-281.

3204. "War Goes On." NATION 148 (February 18, 1939): 191-192.

3205. "War in Spain." TIME 30 (July 5, 1937): 15-17; 30 (July
      12, 1937): 24-25; 30 (July 19, 1937): 19; 30 (July 26,
      1937): 17; 30 (August 2, 1937): 19; 30 (August 9,
      1937): 17; 30 (August 16, 1937): 15; 30 (August 23,
      1937): 18; 30 (August 30, 1937): 22; 30 (September 6,
      1937): 20-22+; 30 (September 13, 1937): 14-16; 30 (Sep-
      tember 20, 1937): 15; 30 (September 27, 1937): 15-16;
      30 (October 4, 1937): 19; 30 (October 11, 1937): 21-22;
      30 (October 18, 1937): 22-23; 30 (October 25, 1937): 19;
      30 (November 1, 1937): 23-25; 30 (November 8, 1937):
      20; 30 (November 15, 1937): 20-22; 30 (November 22,
      1937): 21; 30 (November 30, 1937): 17-18; 30 (December
      6, 1937): 17-18; 30 (December 6, 1937): 20; 30 (Decem-
      ber 13, 1937): 19; 30 (December 27, 1937): 14; 31 (Jan-
      uary 3, 1938): 16; 31 (January 10, 1938): 17-18; 31
      (January 17, 1938): 23; 31 (January 24, 1938): 14; 31
      (January 31, 1938): 13; 31 (February 7, 1938): 15; 31
      (February 14, 1938): 15-17; 31 (February 21, 1938):
      23; 31 (February 28, 1938): 21; 31 (March 7, 1938):
      17-18; 31 (March 14, 1938): 17; 31 (March 21, 1938):
      23; 31 (March 28, 1938): 15-16; 31 (April 4, 1938):
      16-17; 31 (April 11, 1938): 17; 31 (April 18, 1938):
      21; 31 (April 25, 1938): 14-15; 31 (May 2, 1938): 14;
      31 (May 9, 1938): 15-16; 31 (May 16, 1938): 19; 31
      (May 23, 1938): 15; 31 (May 30, 1938): 16; 31 (June 6,
      1938): 18; 31 (June 13, 1938): 17; 31 (June 20, 1938):
      16-17; 31 (June 27, 1938): 16; 32 (July 4, 1938): 14;
      32 (July 11, 1938): 15; 32 (July 25, 1938): 13-15; 32
      (August 1, 1938): 16; 32 (August 8, 1938): 14; 32 (Aug-
      ust 15, 1938): 14; 32 (August 22, 1938): 27; 32 (August
      29, 1938): 15; 32 (September 5, 1938): 14; 32 (Septem-
      ber 12, 1938): 30; 32 (September 19, 1938): 21; 32
      (September 26, 1938): 18-19; 32 (October 3, 1938):19;

32 (October 24, 1938): 17; 32 (October 31, 1938): 15-
16; 32 (November 7, 1938): 12; 32 (November 14, 1938):
23; 32 (November 21, 1938): 18; 32 (November 28, 1938):
16; 32 (December 19, 1938): 20; 33 (January 2, 1939):
16; 33 (January 9, 1939): 19; 33 (January 16, 1939):
22-23; 33 (January 23, 1939): 14; 33 (January 30, 1939)
15; 33 (February 6, 1939): 14; 33 (February 13, 1939):
17-19; 33 (February 20, 1939): 16-18; 33 (February 27,
1939): 21; 33 (March 6, 1939): 16; 33 (March 13, 1939):
19-20; 33 (March 20, 1939): 18-19; 33 (March 27, 1939):
21-22; 33 (April 3, 1939): 22.

Presents weekly coverage of the Spanish civil war.

3206. "War of the Air." LITERARY DIGEST 122 (November 21,
1936): 13.

Recounts aerial campaigns of the civil war.

3207. "War Produces Two Outstanding Martyrs; Madrid Rescues
Art Masterpieces but Loses Warship." NEWSWEEK 8 (November 28, 1936): 7-8.

3208. "War-ridden Madrid." LITERARY DIGEST 122 (November 7,
1936): 12-13.

3209. "War Tide Turns in Spain." CHRISTIAN CENTURY 54 (April
14, 1937): 475-476.

3210. Watts, R., Jr. "Madrid's Victory Complex." CURRENT HIS-
TORY 47 (October 1937): 45-48.

3211. "We Need Rifles; Other Side of Neutrality Pacts." REVIEW
OF REVIEWS 95 (January 1937): 70.

Examines the impact of foreign neutrality in the civil
war.

3212. Weisbord, A. "Running the International Blockade."
NATION 145 (July 17, 1937): 64-66.

Examines foreign intervention in the civil war.

3213. "Welsh Basques; Bilbao Blockade." TIME 29 (May 3, 1937):
19.

3214. Wertheim, B. "We Saw Democracy Fail." NEW REPUBLIC 99
(May 17, 1939): 38-40.

3215. "Western Front." LITERARY DIGEST 124 (October 30, 1937):
       9; 124 (November 6, 1937): 9.

3216. "Where Moors and Christians Feared to Tread Carlists
       Hope to Rush In." NEWSWEEK 9 (May 29, 1937): 11-12.

       Continues coverage of the civil war.

3217. Whitaker, J.T. "Incident in Spain; Dispatch on the Re-
       lief of the Alcazar." REVIEW OF REVIEWS 94 (November
       1936): 75.

3218. White, L. "Rebellion in Rebel Spain." NATION 145 (De-
       cember 11, 1937): 635-638.

3219. "White Noose Tightens Around Red Capital." NEWSWEEK 8
       (October 24, 1936): 9-10.

3220. "White Victors and Epic Alcazar Siege, Franco Drives
       Relentlessly on Fear-Stricken Madrid." NEWSWEEK 8
       (October 3, 1936): 10.

3221. "Who Won the Spanish Civil War?" CHRISTIAN CENTURY 56
       (June 14, 1939): 756.

3222. "Who's Winning in Spain?" NATION 143 (September 5, 1936):
       262.

3223. "Will the Spanish Blaze Spread?" CHRISTIAN CENTURY 54
       (September 15, 1937): 1126-1127.

       Covers submarine operations in the civil war.

3224. Williams, M. "How Many Slain? Summary of Reported Anti-
       Clerical Atrocities in Spain." CURRENT HISTORY 45
       (December 1936): 46-50.

3225. ————. "Truth About Spain; Open Letter to the Press."
       COMMONWEAL 26 (May 7, 1937): 33-37; 26 (May 21, 1937):
       85-87; 26 (June 4, 1937): 113-115, 151-153.

3226. Willis, J. "Barcelona Silhouette." 19th CENTURY AND
       AFTER 125 (January 1939): 26-33.

3227. "Winter Gale Fans War Sparks on Coast." NEWSWEEK 8 (De-
       cember 5, 1936): 9-10.

3228. "With Guns and Words Fascists Meet Red Challenge." NEWS-
      WEEK 8 (November 21, 1936): 17.

3229. "With the International Brigade in Spain." NATION 144
      (May 8, 1937): 531-432.

3230. "Women Rout Red Army from New Siege of the Alcazar."
      NEWSWEEK 9 (March 13, 1937): 18-19.

3231. Woodlock, T.F. "War Upon God; Conflict in Spain."
      COMMONWEAL 25 (November 13, 1936): 77-78.

      Examines religious aspects of the civil war.

3232. Woodside, W. "Tragedy in Spain." CANADIAN MAGAZINE
      87 (March 1937): 6-7+.

3233. "World Over; German Bombing of Guernica." LIVING AGE
      352 (June 1937): 63-64.

3234. "World Revolution." COMMONWEAL 24 (August 14, 1936):
      373-374.

      Places the civil war in international perspective.

3235. Young, G. "Spain the Insuppressible." FORTUNE 147
      (June 1937): 661-669.

3236. Ziffren, L. "I Lived in Madrid; Horrors of the Weeks of
      the Siege." CURRENT HISTORY 46 (April 1937): 35-41.

                        SWITZERLAND

                         Articles

3237. "Again An Assassin's Pistol Makes Europe Shiver." NEWS-
      WEEK 7 (February 15, 1936): 7.

      Examines the assassination of Sigmund Gustluss, execu-
      ted by fascist agents on February 4, 1936.

3238. Brown, P. "Swiss Democracy in Retreat." NATION 145
      (September 18, 1937): 290-291.

3239. Fehr, J.C. "Fascism in Switzerland." COMMONWEAL 27
      (January 28, 1938): 369-370.

3240. "Geneva's Massacre: More Light." WORLD TOMORROW 15 (December 14, 1932): 555-559.

    Examines the violent government response to rioting in Switzerland.

3241. Hooft, W.A.V. "Geneva Rules By Machine Guns; Killing of Rioters." CHRISTIAN CENTURY 49 (December 14, 1932): 1551.

WALES

Books

3242. Bohstedt, John. RIOTS AND COMMUNITY POLITICS IN ENGLAND AND WALES, 1790-1810. Cambridge, Mass.: Harvard University Press, 1983.

3243. Jones, David J. BEFORE REBECCA: POPULAR PROTESTS IN WALES, 1793-1835. London: Allen Lane, 1973.

    Examines the "Rebecca riots" of 1839 and 1842, in which the toll gates of western Wales became targets of popular socio-economic violence.

3244. Williams, D. THE REBECCA RIOTS. Cardiff: The Author, 1955.

YUGOSLAVIA

Books

3245. Graham, Stephen. ALEXANDER OF YUGOSLAVIA. New Haven, Conn.: Yale University Press, 1939.

    Presents a biography of Alexander I of Serbia, climaxed by his assassination.

3246. West, Rebecca. BLACK LAMB AND GREY FALCON. New York: Viking, 1941.

    Examines the assassination of Alexander, and his replacement by Peter I.

Articles

3247. Wilamowski, Jacek, and Krzysztof Szczepanik. "The Ustase
      and Croatian Separatism: A Contribution to the Study of
      the Croatian Nationalist Movement." PRZEGLAD HISTORY
      74 (1983): 75-94.

      Presents a communist perspective of the conflict be-
      tween Croatian separatists and King Alexander I during
      1921-1934. The violence climaxed with Alexander's ass-
      assination, in France, on October 9, 1934. An "indepen-
      dent" Croatian state was established in 1941, but it
      collapsed with the end of World War II and leading sep-
      aratists were driven into exile abroad.

3248. Zaharescu, Vladimir. "1929 - Yugoslavia." ANALE DE
      ISTORIE 25 (1979): 150-162.

      Chronicles events between the foundation of Yugoslavia,
      in 1918, to King Alexander's assumption of dictatorial
      power in 1929, examined from a post-war communist per-
      spective.

PART 3: UNITED STATES

1. General Sources

a. Books

3249. Allen, Rodney F. VIOLENCE AND RIOTS IN URBAN AMERICA.
      Worthington, Ohio: Jones Publishing Co., 1969.

3250. Archer, James. RIOT!: A HISTORY OF MOB ACTION IN THE
      UNITED STATES. New York: Hawthorn Books, 1974.

3251. Berthoff, Rowland. AN UNSETTLED PEOPLE. SOCIAL ORDER
      AND DISORDER IN AMERICAN HISTORY. New York: Harper &
      Row, 1971.

3252. Bingham, Jonathan B. VIOLENCE AND DEMOCRACY. New York:
      World Publishing Co., 1970.

3253. Brown, Richard Maxwell (ed). AMERICAN VIOLENCE. Engle-
      wood Cliffs, N.J.: Prentice-Hall, 1970.

3254. ————. "Historical Patterns of Violence in America."
      VIOLENCE IN AMERICA: HISTORICAL AND COMPARATIVE PER-
      SPECTIVES. Edited by Hugh Davis Graham and Ted Robert
      Gurr. Cited below as item 3265, pp. 45-84.

3255. ————. STRAIN OF VIOLENCE: HISTORICAL STUDIES OF AMER-
      ICAN VIOLENCE AND VIGILANTISM. New York: Oxford Uni-
      versity Press, 1977.

3256. Bruce, Dickson D. VIOLENCE AND CULTURE IN THE ANTEBELLUM
      SOUTH. Austin, Tex.: University of Texas Press, 1979.

3257 Connery, Robert H. URBAN RIOTS: VIOLENCE AND SOCIAL
      CHANGE. New York: Academy of Political Science, 1968.

3258. Crawford, Fred Roberts. VIOLENCE AND DISSENT IN URBAN
      AMERICA. Atlanta, Ga.: Southern Newspaper Publishers
      Association, 1969.

281

3259. Curtis, Lynn A. VIOLENCE, RACE AND CULTURE. Lexington, Mass.: Lexington Books, 1975.

3260. DeWitt, Howard A. IMAGES OF ETHNIC AND RADICAL VIOLENCE IN CALIFORNIA POLITICS, 1917-1930. San Francisco: R. & E. Research Associates, 1975.

3261. Dick, James C. VIOLENCE AND OPPRESSION. Athens, Ga.: University of Georgia Press, 1979.

3262. Eisinger, Peter K. THE CONDITIONS OF PROTEST BEHAVIOR IN AMERICAN CITIES. Madison, Wis.: University of Wisconsin, 1972.

3263. Feldburg, Michael. THE TURBULENT ERA: RIOT AND DISORDER IN JACKSONIAN AMERICA. New York: Oxford University Press, 1980.

3264. Friederich, Carl J. THE PATHOLOGY OF POLITICS, VIOLENCE, CORRUPTION, SECRECY, AND PROPAGANDA. New York: Harper & Row, 1972.

3265. Graham, Hugh Davis, and Ted Robert Gurr (eds). VIOLENCE IN AMERICA: HISTORICAL AND COMPARATIVE PERSPECTIVES. New York: Bantam Books, 1970.

      Contains items 3254, 3267, 3592, 5358, 5378, and 5851.

3266. Green, Gilbert. TERRORISM: IS IT REVOLUTIONARY? New York: New Outlook Publishers, 1920.

3267. Hackney, Sheldon. "Southern Violence." VIOLENCE IN AMERICA: HISTORICAL AND COMPARATIVE PERSPECTIVES. Edited by Hugh Davis Graham and Ted Robert Gurr. Cited above as item 3265, pp. 505-527.

3268. HATE GROUPS IN AMERICA: A RECORD OF BIGOTRY AND VIOLENCE. New York: Anti-Defamation League of B'nai B'rith, 1982.

3269. Heaps, Willard A. RIOTS, U.S.A., 1765-1965. New York: Seabury Press, 1966.

3270. Hofstadter, Richard, and Michael Wallace (eds). AMERICAN VIOLENCE. A DOCUMENTARY HISTORY. New York: Vintage Books, 1970.

3271. Hollon, William Eugene. FRONTIER VIOLENCE: ANOTHER LOOK. New York: Oxford University Press, 1974.

3272. Iglitzin, Lynne B. VIOLENT CONFLICT IN AMERICAN SOCIETY.
       San Francisco: Chandler Publishing Co., 1972.

3273. Jeffreys-Jones, R. VIOLENCE AND REFORM IN AMERICAN HIS-
       TORY. New York: New Viewpoints, 1978.

3274. Jenkins, Brian Michael. TERRORISM IN THE UNITED STATES.
       Santa Monica, Calif.: Rand Corp., 1980.

3275. Madison, Arnold. VIGILANTISM IN AMERICA. New York:
       Seabury Press, 1973.

3276. Manheim, Jarol B. DEJA VU: AMERICAN POLITICAL PROBLEMS
       IN HISTORICAL PERSPECTIVE. New York: St. Martin's
       Press, 1976.

3277. Parker, Thomas F. VIOLENCE IN THE UNITED STATES. New
       York: Facts on File. 1974.

3278. Pinkney, Alfonso. THE AMERICAN WAY OF VIOLENCE. New
       York: Random House, 1972.

3279. Porges, Irvin. THE VIOLENT AMERICANS. Derby, Conn.:
       Monarch Books, 1963.

3280. Rable, George C. BUT THERE WAS NO PEACE: THE ROLE OF
       VIOLENCE IN THE POLITICS OF RECONSTRUCTION. Athens,
       Ga.: University of Georgia Press, 1984.

3281. Rose, Thomas (ed). VIOLENCE IN AMERICA. A HISTORICAL
       AND CONTEMPORARY READER. New York: Vintage Books,
       1970.

       Contains item 3871 below.

3282. Rubenstein, Richard E. REBELS IN EDEN: MASS POLITICAL
       VIOLENCE IN THE UNITED STATES. Boston: Little, Brown,
       1970.

3283. Short, James F. (ed). COLLECTIVE VIOLENCE. Chicago:
       Aldine-Atherton, 1972.

3284. Skolnick, Jerome. THE POLITICS OF PROTEST: VIOLENT AS-
       PECTS OF PROTEST AND CONFRONTATION. New York: Simon &
       Schuster, 1969.

3285. Sloan, Irving J. OUR VIOLENT PAST: AN AMERICAN CHRONI-
       CLE. New York: Random House, 1970.

3286. Stohl, Michael. WAR AND DOMESTIC POLITICAL VIOLENCE: THE
      AMERICAN CAPACITY FOR REPRESSION AND REACTION. Beverly
      Hills, Calif.: Sage, 1976.

3287. Upton, James N. A SOCIAL HISTORY OF 20th CENTURY URBAN
      RIOTS. Bristol, Ind.: Wyndham Hall Press, 1984.

3288. Victor, Orville J. HISTORY OF AMERICAN CONSPIRACIES: A
      RECORD OF TREASON, INSURRECTION, REBELLION, ETC., IN
      THE UNITED STATES OF AMERICA, FROM 1760 TO 1860. New
      York: J.D. Torrey, 1864.

3289. Wasko, Arthur L. RUNNING RIOT: OFFICIAL DISASTERS AND
      CREATIVE DISORDER IN AMERICAN SOCIETY. New York: Her-
      der & Herder, 1970.

3290. Wolfe, Alan. THE SEAMY SIDE OF DEMOCRACY: REPRESSION IN
      AMERICA. New York: Longman, 1978.

                          b. Articles

3291. Adams, James T. "Our Lawless Heritage." ATLANTIC MONTH-
      LY 142 (1928): 732-740.

3292. "Applied Violence." NEW REPUBLIC 28 (August 31, 1921):
      5-6.

      Examines recent examples of mob violence in America.

3293. Bellows, H.A. "Crowd in Action." BELLMAN'S MAGAZINE
      26 (June 28, 1919): 721-723.

      Considers mob violence as a factor in contemporary
      American life.

3294. Clark, Malcolm, Jr. "The Bigot Disclosed: 90 Years of
      Nationalism." OREGON HISTORICAL QUARTERLY 75 (1974):
      108-190.

      Presents a history of violent bigotry in the Pacific
      Northwest, including the 1920s Ku Klux Klan, the Know-
      Nothing movement, violence against Catholics, Chinese,
      and organizers of the Industrial Workers of the World.

3295. Eisinger, Peter K. "The Conditions of Protest Behavior
      in American Cities." AMERICAN POLITICAL SCIENCE RE-
      VIEW 67 (1973): 11-28.

3296. Feinstein, I. "How to Make a Riot." NEW REPUBLIC 79
      (June 27, 1934): 178-180.

3297. Feldburg, Michael J. "The Crowd in Philadelphia History:
      A Comparative Perspective." LABOR HISTORY 15 (1974):
      323-336.

3298. Geffen, Elizabeth M. "Violence in Philadelphia in the
      1840s and 1850s." PENNSYLVANIA HISTORY 36 (1969):
      381-410.

3299. Grimsted, David. "Rioting in Its Jacksonian Setting."
      AMERICAN HISTORY REVIEW 77 (1972): 361-397.

3300. Ivanian, E.A. "Political Terror is an Inseparable Fact
      of the American Way of Life." VOPROSY ISTORII 3 (1982):
      91-104.

      Presents the Soviet view of American presidential ass-
      assinations and failures to enact gun-control laws.

3301. "Law and Order Anarchy." NATION 113 (August 1, 1921):
      113.

      Examines recent outbreaks of mob violence in America.

3302. "Lawlessness and Human Nature." REVIEW 1 (November 22,
      1919): 595-596.

      Seeks the sociological roots of American mob violence.

3303. "Mob Violence." PUBLIC OPINION 22 (May 10, 1919): 481-
      482.

3304. Siegel, Bernard J. "The Paradox of American Violence."
      ANNALS OF THE AMERICAN ACADEMY OF POLITICAL SCIENCE
      391 (September 1970): 74-82.

3305. Wallace, Michael. "The Uses of Violence in American
      History." AMERICAN SCHOLAR 40 (1971): 81-102.

                          2. Anarchism

                          a. Books

3306. Adamic, Louis. DYNAMITE, THE STORY OF CLASS VIOLENCE IN
      AMERICA. New York: Viking Press, 1931.

3307. Adams, Grace K., and Edward Hutter. THE MAD FORTIES.
      New York: Harper & Brothers, 1942.

      Includes discussion of activities by anarchists in the
      United States.

3308. Berkman, Alexander. NOW AND AFTER: THE ABC OF COMMUNIST
      ANARCHISM. New York: Vanguard Press, 1929.

      America's most infamous anarchist spells out his phil-
      osophy for the masses.

3309. ─────. PRISON MEMOIRS OF AN ANARCHIST. New York:
      Schocken Books, 1970.

3310. Bool, Henry. HENRY BOOL'S APOLOGY FOR HIS JEFFERSONIAN
      ANARCHISM. Ithaca, N.Y.: The Author, 1901.

3311. Destler, Chester MacArthur. AMERICAN RADICALISM, 1865-
      1901. New London, Conn.: Connecticut College, 1946.

3312. Drinnon, Richard. REBEL IN PARADISE: A BIOGRAPHY OF
      EMMA GOLDMAN. Chicago: University of Chicago Press,
      1961.

3313. Eltzbacher, Paul. ANARCHISM. New York: B.R. Tucker,
      1908.

3314. Fleming, Marie. THE ANARCHIST WAY TO SOCIALISM. Totowa,
      N.J.: Rowman & Littlefield, 1979.

3315. Goldman, Emma. LIVING MY LIFE. 2 Vols. New York: Alfred
      A. Knopf, 1931.

      Another leading anarchist spokesperson offers her auto-
      biography as an example for future revolutionary genera-
      tions.

3316. Greene, William Batchelder. THE BLAZING STAR. Boston:
      A. Williams & Co., 1872.

      A leftist author argues the "good points" of anarchism
      in the era before radical violence became a potent pol-
      itical issue.

3317. ─────. EQUALITY. West Brookfield, Mass.: O.S. Cooke
      & Co., 1849.

Presents utopian anarchy as an alternative to the
built-in inequalities of American society in the last
century.

3318. ———. FREE SPEECH: REPORT OF EZRA H. HEYWOOD'S DEFENSE
BEFORE THE UNITED STATES COURT IN BOSTON, APRIL 10, 11
AND 12, 1883; TOGETHER WITH JUDGE NELSON'S CHARGE TO
THE JURY. Princeton, N.J.: Co-operative Publishing
Co., 1883.

Examines the highly politicized prosecution of an
American anarchist in the 19th century.

3319. ———. UNITED STATES VS. HEYWOOD: WHY THE DEFENDANTS
SHOULD BE RELEASED. New York: National Defense Assn.,
1891.

3320. Horowitz, Irving Louis (ed). THE ANARCHISTS. New York:
Dell Publishers, 1964.

3321. Jacker, Corinne. THE BLACK FLAG OF ANARCHY. ANTISTATISM
IN THE UNITED STATES. New York: Charles Scribner's
Sons, 1968.

3322. Joll, James. THE ANARCHISTS. London: Eyre & Spottis-
woode, 1964.

3323. Labadie, Joseph A. ANARCHISM. Detroit: The Author,
1932.

3324. ———. ANARCHISM: GENUINE AND ASININE. Wixom, Mich.:
The Author, 1925.

3325. ———. ANARCHISM: WHAT IT IS AND WHAT IT IS NOT.
Detroit: The Author, 1896.

3326. Leech, Margaret. IN THE DAYS OF McKINLEY. New York:
Harper & Brothers, 1959, pp. 592-603.

Pages cited include a review of anarchist activities
in America, culminating in the murder of a president.

3327. Lum, Dyer Daniel. A CONCISE HISTORY OF THE GREAT TRIAL
OF THE CHICAGO ANARCHISTS. Chicago: Socialistic Publishing Co., 1887.

Presents a leftist view of the Chicago Haymarket trial
and subsequent conviction of anarchist defendants.

3328. ———. THE ECONOMICS OF ANARCHY, A STUDY OF THE INDUS-
      TRIAL TYPE. Chicago: Socialistic Publishing Co., 1890.

3329. Martin, James J. MEN AGAINST THE STATE. DeKalb, Ill.:
      Adrian Allen, 1953.

3330. Russell, Bertrand. PROPOSED ROADS TO FREEDOM: SOCIALISM,
      ANARCHISM AND SYNDICALISM. New York: Henry Holt, 1919.

3331. Spooner, Lysander. ILLEGALITY OF THE TRIAL OF JOHN W.
      WEBSTER. Boston: B. Marsh, 1850.

      Examines the prosecution of another anarchist.

3332. Wenley, R.M. ANARCHIST IDEAL. Boston: R.G. Badger,
      1913.

3333. Westrup, Alfred B. OUR REVOLUTION: ESSAYS IN INTERPRE-
      TATION. Boston: R.G. Badger, 1920.

3334. Woodcock, George. ANARCHISM. New York: World Publish-
      ing Co., 1971.

3335. ———. ANARCHISM; A HISTORY OF LIBERTARIAN IDEAS AND
      MOVEMENTS. Cleveland: Meridian Books, 1962.

3336. Yarros, Victor S. ANARCHISM: ITS AIMS AND METHODS.
      Boston: B.R. Tucker, 1887.

3337. Zenker, Ernst Victor. ANARCHISM, A CRITICISM AND HISTORY
      OF ANARCHIST THEORY. New York: G.P. Putnam's Sons,
      1897.

b. Articles

3338. Abbott, L. "Anarchism; Its Cause and Cure." OUTLOOK 70
      (February 1922): 465-471.

3339. "After the Crime." EDUCATION REVIEW 22 (October 1901):
      320-323.

3340. Aldrich, E. "Power of the Federal Government to Protect
      Its Agents." NORTH AMERICAN 173 (December 1901): 746-
      757.

3341. "Amiable Anarchists." CURRENT LITERATURE 29 (July 1900):
      30.

3342. "Anarchism and the Law." INDEPENDENT 53 (September 12, 1901): 2187-2189.

3343. "Anarchism as an Advertisement." SATURDAY REVIEW 90: 166.

   *   "Anarchism in America and France." SPECTATOR. Cited above as item 567.

3344. "Anarchism Versus Anarchists." INDEPENDENT 99 (August 2, 1919): 145.

3345. "Anarchist Bombs and Socialist Theories and the Union Square Demonstration." CURRENT LITERATURE 44 (May 1908): 461-468.

3346. "Anarchist Campaign." SPECTATOR 71 (December 30, 1893): 934-935; 72 (January 13, 1894): 48.

3347. "Anarchist Deportations." NEW REPUBLIC 21 (December 24, 1919): 96-98.

3348. "Anarchist Exclusion Law." OUTLOOK 75 (November 21, 1903): 678-679.

3349. "Anarchist Experiment Station." INDEPENDENT 53 (November 7, 1901): 2661-2663.

3350. "Anarchist Interior; Views of M. Henry." SPECTATOR 72 (May 5, 1894): 610-611.

3351. "Anarchist Literature." SPECTATOR 73 (July 14, 1894): 41-42.

3352. "Anarchist or Paranoiac? Union Square Demonstration." OUTLOOK 88 (April 11, 1908): 808-809.

3353. "Anarchist Spirit." INDEPENDENT 53 (September 26, 1901): 2307-2308.

3354. "Anarchist Wave." SPECTATOR 71 (September 30, 1893): 424-425.

3355. "Anarchists." INDEPENDENT 64 (March 5, 1908): 538; 64 (April 2, 1908): 760-761.

3356. "Anarchists and Their Whims." HARPER'S WEEKLY 49 (June 24, 1905): 896.

3357. "Anarchy and Its Suppression." HARPER'S WEEKLY 45 (October 5, 1901): 997.

3358. "Anarchy: From Below and From Above." SURVEY 28 (June 1, 1912): 351-352/

3359. Anderson, R. "Problem of the Criminal Alien." 19th CENTURY AND AFTER 69 (February 1911): 217-224.

3360. "Anti-Anarchy Measures in Congress." CHATAUQUA 34 (February 1902): 461-462.

3361. "At Close Quarters." REVIEW OF REVIEWS 26 (November 1902): 604-605.

    Examines recent examples of anarchist violence in America, including the assassination of President McKinley.

3362. "Baptism of Blood." INDEPENDENT 60 (June 7, 1906): 1387-1388.

3363. Baty, T. "Can Anarchy Be a State?" AMERICAN JOURNAL OF INTERNATIONAL LAW 28 (July 1934): 444-445.

3364. Bennigaeu, G. "Anarchism - Communism - Christianity." DUBLIN REVIEW 204 (January 1889): 71-84.

3365. "Bill Against Anarchists." NATION 74 (February 20, 1902): 145.

3366. Blind, K. "Rise and Development of Anarchism." CONTEMPORARY REVIEW 65 (January 1894): 140-152.

3367. ———. "Rise and Progress of Anarchism." CONTEMPORARY REVIEW 65 (1894): 140.

3368. Boglietti, G. "Anarchist Utopia; Excerpt." REVIEW OF REVIEWS 10 (October 1894): 421.

3369. "Bomb-Thrower." NATION 86 (April 2, 1908): 300.

3370. Brandenburg, J.R. "Chicago Anarchists, 1887." OUTLOOK 76 (January 9, 1904): 117-125.

    Examines the role of anarchist agitators in fomenting the Haymarket violence in Chicago.

3372. Burrows, J.C.   "Need of National Legislation Against
      Anarchism."   NORTH AMERICAN 173 (December 1901): 727-
      745.

3373. "Can We Stamp Out Anarchy?"   GUNTON 21 (October 1901):
      349-353.

3374. Chafee, Z. "Legislation Against Anarchy."   NEW REPUBLIC
      19 (July 23, 1919): 379-385.

3375. "Character of the Anarchist in Politics and Literature."
      BLACKWELL'S 167 (May 1900): 688-694.

3376. Cleyre, V. De.   "Making of an Anarchist."   INDEPENDENT
      55 (September 24, 1903): 2276-2280.

3377. Conant, R.W.   "Anarchism at Close Quarters."   ARENA 28
      (October 1902): 337-345.

3378. "Control of Anarchists."   NATION 83 (June 7, 1906): 463-
      464.

3379. Cooley, S.   "Making Anarchists."   PUBLIC OPINION 18
      (January 1, 1915): 5-6.

3380. Cortesi, S.   "Anarchy in Its Birthplace."   INDEPENDENT
      53 (October 3, 1901): 2346-2348.

3381. "Criminality of Anarchism."   INDEPENDENT 53 (September
      19, 1901): 2250.

3382. Crosby, E.   "Freedom of Thought."   NORTH AMERICAN 178
      (April 1904): 605-616.

3383. "Czolgosz, Product of a Materialistic, Greed-Crazed
      World."   ARENA 27 (January 1902): 100-101.

3384. "Destructive Vanity."   SPECTATOR 73 (July 28, 1894): 106.

      Examines the philosophy and activities of contemporary
      American anarchists.

3385. "Disadvantages of Anarchism."   INDEPENDENT 54 (December
      25, 1902): 3103-3104.

3386. Doane, W.C.   "Anarchism and Atheism; A Sermon."   OUTLOOK
      69 (September 28, 1901): 218-221.

3387. Dodd, S.C. "Congress and Anarchy." NORTH AMERICAN 173 (October 1901): 433-436.

3388. Donisthorpe, W. "In Defense of Anarchy; Excerpt." REVIEW OF REVIEWS 10 (October 1894): 421.

3389. Duke of Acros. "International Control of Anarchists." NORTH AMERICAN 173 (December 1901): 758-767.

3390. Dunne, F.P. "Doings of Anarchists." HARPER'S WEEKLY 44 (August 11, 1900): 757.

3391. "Effects of Anarchy on Politics." SPECTATOR 73 (September 8, 1894): 295-296.

3392. Ely, R.T. "Anarchy." HARPER'S WEEKLY 37 (December 23, 1893): 1226.

3393. "Emma Goldman's Faith." CURRENT LITERATURE 50 (February 1911): 176-178.

3394. "Extradition of Anarchists." BLACKWELL'S 168 (September 1900): 402-404.

3395. Farnara, G. "Latest Anarchist Confession." SPECTATOR 73 (April 28, 1894): 579-581.

3396. Gary, J.E. "Chicago Anarchists of 1886." CENTURY 45 (April 1893): 803-837.

3397. Gaskine, J.W. "Anarchists at Home, Washington." INDE-PENDENT 68 (April 28, 1910): 914-922.

3398. Gladden, W. "Philosophy of Anarchism." OUTLOOK 69 (October 19, 1901): 449-454.

3399. Goldstein, Robert J. "The Anarchist Scare of 1908: A Sign of Tensions in the Progressive Era." AMERICAN STUDIES 15 (1974): 55-78.

3400. Goodwin, G.S. "What Anarchism Is." ERA 10 (December 1902): 599-607.

3401. Hill, F.T. "Chicago Anarchists' Case." HARPER'S WEEKLY 114 (May 1907): 889-900.

3402. ————. "Decisive Battles of Law." HARPER'S WEEKLY 114 (May 1907): 240-268.

3403. Holt, H. "Punishment of Anarchists and Others." FORUM 17 (August 1894): 644-658.

3404. ————. "Treatment of Anarchism." REVIEW OF REVIEWS 25 (February 1902): 192-200.

3405. Holyoake, G.J. "Causes of Anarchy." 19th CENTURY AND AFTER 50 (October 1901): 683-686.

3406. "How to Treat Anarchists." BLACKWELL'S 170 (October 1901): 560-565.

3407. "How to Treat Anarchists." LIVING AGE 231 (October 12, 1901): 128-131.

3408. "Immigration and Anarchists." INDEPENDENT 64 (March 12, 1908): 554-555.

3409. Johnson, C. "Anarchists and the President." NORTH AMERICAN 173 (October 1901): 437-444.

3410. Johnston, C. "Nihilism and Anarchy." NORTH AMERICAN 171 (September 1900): 302-313.

3411. Jouffray, T.L. "Warnings and Teachings of the Church on Anarchism." CATHOLIC WORLD 74 (November 1901): 202-209.

3412. Kidder, M.G. "Anarchy." OVERLAND 52 (August 1908): 129-133.

3413. Lamont, H. "Legislating Against Anarchists." NATION 74 (1901): 243.

3414. Langtoft, G. "Socialism and Anarchism." FORTUNE 74 (October 1900): 544-558.

3415. "Latest Attempt at Assassination." SPECTATOR 79 (November 13, 1897): 674.

3416. "Legislating Against Anarchists." NATION 74 (March 27, 1902): 243.

3417. Lombroso, C. "Paradoxical Anarchist." POPULAR SCIENCE 56 (January 1900): 312-315.

3418. McDermet, G. "Senor Ferrer and the Anarchists Again." AMERICAN CATHOLIC QUARTERLY 35 (October 1910): 569-589.

3419. Malagodi, O. "Psychology of Anarchist Conspiracies." WESTMINSTER'S 147 (January 1897): 87-91.

3420. Neill, C.P. "Anarchism." AMERICAN CATHOLIC QUARTERLY 27 (January 1902): 160-179.

3421. "New Paganism." SPECTATOR 72 (February 10, 1894): 191-192.

Presents a condemnatory view of modern anarchism.

3422. Newton, R.H. "Philosophical and Revolutionary Anarchism." ARENA 27 (January 1902): 1-12.

3423. ———. "Political, Economic, and Religious Causes of Anarchism." ARENA 27 (February 1902): 113-125.

3424. Nichols, F.H. "Anarchists in America." OUTLOOK 68 (August 10, 1901): 859-863.

3425. Ogden, R. "The Bill Against Anarchists." NATION 74: 145.

3526. ———. "The Bill for Control of Anarchists." NATION 82: 463.

3527. Osgood, Herbert L. "Scientific Anarchism." POLITICAL SCIENCE QUARTERLY 4 (March 1889): 1-36.

3528. Oswald, F.L. "Evolutionary Aspects." ARENA 26 (November 1901): 449-458.

3529. Pepper, G.W. "What is an Anarchist?" NORTH AMERICAN 210 (October 1919): 470-474.

3530. Pierson, A.T. "Spirit of Anarchy and the Weapon of Assassination." MISCELLANEOUS REVIEW 24 (November 1901): 801-807.

3431. Pinkerton, R.A. "Defective Surveillance of Anarchists." NORTH AMERICAN 173 (November 1901): 609-617.

3432. "Prison Memoirs of an Anarchist, by A. Berkman." SURVEY 29 (January 25, 1913): 550-551.

3433. "Problem of Anarchy." GUNTON 21 (October 1901): 301-310.

3434. "Qualities of the Anarchist." BLACKWELL'S 180 (July 1906): 128-130.

3435. "Red Flag and the Torch." WORLD'S WORK 16 (May 1908):
      10171-10172.

3436. "Reverence for Law." NATION 108 (March 8, 1919): 343.

3437. Roberts, E.H. "Cure for Anarchy." ARENA 26 (November
      1901): 453-458.

3438. Rodolf, C.C. "Unrighteousness of Government, as Viewed
      by a Philosophical Anarchist." ARENA 14 (November
      1895): 476-486.

3439. Salter, W.M. "Second Thoughts on the Treatment of Anar-
      chy." ATLANTIC MONTHLY 89 (May 1902): 581-588.

3440. Scholasticus, W.F.C. "Anarchy and Government." CATHOLIC
      WORLD 76 (October 1902): 44-49.

3441. Schuster, Eunice M. "Native American Anarchism." STUDIES
      IN HISTORY 17 (October 1931-July 1932): 5-197.

3442. Schurz, C. "Murder as a Political Agency." HARPER'S
      WEEKLY 41 (August 28, 1897): 847.

3443. Slosson, E.E. "Experiment in Anarchy." INDEPENDENT 55
      (April 2, 1903): 779-785.

3444. Slosson, P. "If We Had Anarchy Tomorrow." INDEPENDENT
      103 (August 14, 1920): 169.

3445. "Soul of the Assassin." LIVING AGE 226 (September 15,
      1900): 718-719.

3446. Speed, J.G. "Anarchists in Hard Times." OUTLOOK 48
      (November 11, 1893): 840-841.

3447. ————. "Anarchists in New York." HARPER'S WEEKLY 36
      (August 20, 1892): 798-799.

3448. Stone, M.E. "Chicago Anarchists." COLLIER'S 67 (Febru-
      ary 5, 1921): 16-17.

3449. Tobenkin, E. "Anarchists and Immigrants in America."
      WORLD TODAY 14 (May 1908): 482-485.

3450. Tosti, G. "Anarchistic Crimes." POLITICAL SCIENCE
      QUARTERLY 14 (September 1899): 404-417.

3451. Trumbull, M.M. "Judge Gary and the Anarchists." ARENA
      8 (October 1893): 544-561.

3452. Turner, J. "Protest of an Anarchist." INDEPENDENT 55
      (December 24, 1903): 3052-3054.

3453. "Vaillant On His Defence." SPECTATOR 72 (January 13,
      1894): 36-37.

3454. Wallace, L. "Prevention of Presidential Assassinations."
      NORTH AMERICAN 173 (December 1901): 721-726.

3455. "Wave of Anarchism, 1893." SPECTATOR 71 (1894): 424.

3456. Westrup, Alfred B. "The I.W.W. Trial." NATION 107
      (August 31, 1918): 220-223.

      Reviews the trial of radical labor organizers on
      charges of fomenting anarchist violence.

3457. Winslow, E. "Coddling Anarchy." NORTH AMERICAN 209
      (February 1919): 234-236.

3458. Woods, G.H. "Anarchism. Outline and Criticism." WEST-
      MINSTER'S 157 (February 1902): 181-186.

3459. Yarros, V. "Anarchism: What It Is, and What It Is Not."
      ARENA 7 (April 1893): 595-601.

                        3. Assassination

                          a. Books

3460. AMERICAN ASSASSINS: THE DARKER SIDE OF POLITICS. Prince-
      ton, N.J.: Princeton University Press, 1982.

3461. Balsiger, David, and Charles E. Sellier, Jr. THE LINCOLN
      CONSPIRACY. Los Angeles, Calif.: Schick Sun Classic
      Books, 1977.

      Theorizes that John Wilkes Booth actually escaped cap-
      ture in 1865, dying years later in India. Lincoln's
      Secretary of War is named as the prime mover in a subver-
      sive plot to kill the president and thus bring about
      harsh congressional treatment of the defeated Confederate
      states.

3462. Bishop, Jim. THE DAY LINCOLN WAS SHOT. New York: Ban-
      tam Books, 1955.

3463. Clarke, James W. AMERICAN ASSASSINS. Princeton, N.J.:
      Princeton University Press, 1987.

      Presents biographies of noted American assassins.

3464. Crotty, William J. (ed). ASSASSINATIONS AND THE POLITI-
      CAL ORDER. New York: Harper & Row, 1971.

3465. Cuthbert, Norma B. LINCOLN AND THE BALTIMORE PLOT, 1861:
      FROM PINKERTON RECORDS AND RELATED PAPERS. San Marino,
      Calif.: Huntington Library, 1949.

3466. Donaghue, Mary Agnes. ASSASSINATION: MURDER IN POLITICS.
      Chatsworth, Calif.: Major Books, 1975.

3467. Donovan, Robert J. THE ASSASSINS. New York: Harper &
      Brothers, 1955.

3468. Hanchett, William. THE LINCOLN MURDER CONSPIRACIES.
      Urbana, Ill.: University of Illinois Press, 1983.

3469. Havens, Murray Clark, Carl Leiden, and Karl M. Schmitt.
      THE POLITICS OF ASSASSINATION. Englewood Cliffs, N.J.:
      Prentice-Hall, 1970.

3470. Hurwood, Bernhardt J. SOCIETY AND THE ASSASSIN: A BACK-
      GROUND BOOK ON POLITICAL MURDER. New York: Parents'
      Magazine Press, 1970.

3471. Hyams, Edward S. KILLING NOT MURDER: A STUDY OF ASSASS-
      INATION AS A POLITICAL MEANS. London: Nelson, 1969.

3472. Johnson, Francis. FAMOUS ASSASSINATIONS OF HISTORY,
      FROM PHILIP OF MACEDONIA, 336 B.C., TO ALEXANDER OF
      SERVIA, A.D. 1903. Chicago: A.C. McClurg & Co., 1903.

3473. McConnell, Brian. ASSASSINATION. London: Frewin, 1969.

3474. McKinley, James. ASSASSINATION IN AMERICA. New York:
      Harper & Row, 1977.

3475. Nelson, Anne. MURDER UNDER TWO FLAGS: THE U.S., PUERTO
      RICO, AND THE CERRO MARAVILLA COVER-UP. New York:
      Ticknor & Fields, 1986.

3476. O'Sullivan, Dennis. FAMOUS ASSASSINATIONS OF HISTORY, FROM THE TIME OF JULIUS CAESAR TO THE PRESENT DAY. New York: F. Tousey, 1882.

3477. Paine, Lauran. THE ASSASSIN'S WORLD. New York: Taplinge Publishing Co., 1975.

3478. Rapoport, David C. ASSASSINATION AND TERRORISM. Toronto Canadian Broadcasting Corp., 1971.

3479. Roscoe, Theodore. THE WEB OF CONSPIRACY: THE COMPLETE STORY OF THE MEN WHO MURDERED ABRAHAM LINCOLN. New York: Prentice-Hall, 1959.

3480. Starkey, Larry. WILKES BOOTH CAME TO WASHINGTON. New York: Random House, 1976.

3481. Stern, Philip Van Doren. THE MAN WHO KILLED LINCOLN. New York: Random House, 1955.

3482. Weichmann, Louis J. A TRUE HISTORY OF THE ASSASSINATION OF ABRAHAM LINCOLN AND OF THE CONSPIRACY OF 1865. New York: Vintage Books, 1975.

3483. Zellner, Harold (ed). ASSASSINATION. Cambridge, Mass.: Schenkman Publishing Co., 1974.

b. Articles

3484. "Assassins." NEW YORKER 34 (August 2, 1958): 17.

3485. "Attempt to Kill the President-Elect." LITERARY DIGEST 115 (February 25, 1933): 5-6.

Reports the abortive attempt on Franklin Roosevelt's life which killed Chicago Mayor Anton Cermak.

3486. "Behind the Alabama Assassination." CHRISTIAN CENTURY 71 (July 7, 1954): 813.

Reviews the recent murder of an elected official in Dixie.

3487. Channing, Walter. "The Mental Status of Czolgosz, the Assassin of President McKinley." AMERICAN JOURNAL OF INSANITY 49 (1902): 233-278.

3488. Donovan, R.J. "Annals of Crime; Assassination of Pres-
      ident McKinley." NEW YORKER 29 (November 28, 1953):
      105-112+.

3489. Fine, Sidney. "Anarchism and the Assassination of Mc-
      Kinley." AMERICAN HISTORICAL REVIEW 60 (1955): 777-
      799.

3490. "Five Shots Startled the Nation; Roosevelt Escapes Ass-
      assination Miraculously." NEWSWEEK 1 (February 25,
      1933): 7-8.

3491. Flory, Claude R. "Garman, Black, and the 'Baltimore
      Plot'." PENNSYLVANIA MAGAZINE OF HISTORY AND BIOGRA-
      PHY 94 (1970): 101-103.

3492. Gehman. "Washington's Most Spectacular Crimes." COSMO-
      POLITAN 144 (May 1958): 52-55.

3493. Hastings, Donald W. "The Psychiatry of Presidential
      Assassination." LANCET 55 (1965): 93-100, 157-162,
      189-192, 294-301.

3494. "Insanity of Assassins." INDEPENDENT 53 (November 7,
      1901): 2663-2665.

      Postulates that presidential assassins may be deranged,
      thus minimizing public concern in the wake of McKinley's
      murder.

3495. Jaszi, Oscar. "The Stream of Political Murder." AMERICAN
      JOURNAL OF ECONOMICS AND SOCIOLOGY 3 (1944): 335-355.

3496. McLaws, Monte B. "The Attempted Assassination of Missouri's
      Ex-governor Lilburn W. Boggs." MISSOURI HISTORICAL
      REVIEW 60 (1965): 50-62.

      Reviews the evidence from an attempted political
      murder in 1842.

3497. Phillips, D.G. "Assassination of a Governor: William
      Goebel." COSMOPOLITAN 38 (April 1905): 611-624.

      Presents a five-year retrospective on the January
      1900 murder of Kentucky's governor by political rivals.

3498. "President Doumer and This Year's Growing List of Political Assassinations." LITERARY DIGEST 113 (May 21, 1932): 38-39.

3499. Ring, Nancy. "The Religious Affiliations of Our Presidential Assassins." MID-AMERICA 16 (October 1933): 89-104.

3500. ———. "Religious Affiliations of Our Presidential Assassins." MID-AMERICA 16 (January 1934): 147-156.

3501. Walker, Kenneth R. "The Third Assassination." NEW YORK HISTORICAL SOCIETY QUARTERLY 41 (October 1957): 407-422.

Deals with the assassination of President McKinley.

3502. Wallace, L. "Prevention of Presidential Assassinations." NORTH AMERICAN 173 (December 1901): 721-726.

3503. Winden, Kathe van. "The Assassination of Abraham Lincoln Its Effect in California." JOURNAL WEST 4 (1965): 211-230.

4. Economic Violence

a. Books

3504. Adams, Graham, Jr. AGE OF INDUSTRIAL VIOLENCE, 1910-1915 THE ACTIVITIES AND FINDINGS OF THE UNITED STATES COMMISSION ON INDUSTRIAL RELATIONS. New York: Columbia University Press, 1966.

3505. American Civil Liberties Union. THE KENTUCKY MINERS' STRIKE. New York: A.C.L.U., 1930.

3506. ———. THE TRUTH ABOUT THE I.W.W. New York: A.C.L.U., 1922.

3507. Aurand, Harold W. FROM THE MOLLY MAGUIRES TO THE UNITED MINE WORKERS: THE SOCIAL ECOLOGY OF AN INDUSTRIAL UNION. Philadelphia: Temple University Press, 1971.

3508. Bimba, Anthony. THE MOLLY MAGUIRES. New York: International Publishers, 1932.

Examines the terrorist activities of Irish miners in the Pennsylvania coalfields of the latter 19th century.

3509. Blaisdell, Lowell L. THE DESERT REVOLUTION, BAJA CALI-
      FORNIA, 1911. Madison, Wis.: University of Wisconsin
      Press, 1962.

      Examines the involvement of California labor organizers
      in a five-month revolutionary war fought by the Liberal
      Party of Mexico, in Baja California. Members of the IWW
      were employed as mercenary soldiers by the Liberals.

3510. Brissenden, Paul F. THE I.W.W.: A STUDY OF AMERICAN
      SYNDICALISM. New York: Columbia University Press, 1919.

      Reviews the violent history of the Industrial Workers
      of the World, from 1905 to 1917.

3511. ———. THE LAUNCHING OF THE INDUSTRIAL WORKERS OF THE
      WORLD. Berkeley, Calif.: University of California
      Press, 1913.

3512. Broehl, W.G. THE MOLLY MAGUIRES. Cambridge, Mass.:
      Harvard University Press, 1964.

3513. Brooks, John Graham. AMERICAN SYNDICALISM: THE IWW.
      New York: Macmillan, 1913.

3514. Bruce, Robert V. 1877: YEAR OF VIOLENCE. New York:
      Bobbs-Merrill, 1959.

3515. Burbank, David T. REIGN OF THE RABBLE: THE ST. LOUIS
      GENERAL STRIKE OF 1877. New York: A.M. Kelley, 1966.

3516. California Commissioner to Investigate Disturbances in
      San Diego. REPORT OF HARRIS WEINSTOCK, COMMISSIONER
      TO HIS EXCELLENCY HIRAM W. JOHNSON, GOVERNOR OF CALI-
      FORNIA. Sacramento, Calif.: 1912.

      Officially concludes that San Diego county and munici-
      pal officials conspired with right-wing vigilantes to
      deny IWW organizers and other radicals their First Amend-
      ment rights through acts of violence and extreme cruelty.

3517. California State Assembly. MAJORITY AND MINORITY REPORTS
      ON THE MODESTO DEFENDANTS, PURSUANT TO ASSEMBLY RESOLU-
      TION ADOPTED JANUARY 21, 1935. Sacramento, Calif.:
      California State Assembly, 1937.

      Reviews the trial of radical unionists held on charges
      of stealing dynamite for use in acts of industrial

terrorism. The report concludes that goons employed by
Standard Oil were guilty of a frame-up in the case.

3518. Cantor, Louis. A PROLOGUE TO THE PROTEST MOVEMENT. THE
      MISSOURI SHARECROPPER ROADSIDE DEMONSTRATION OF 1939.
      Durham, N.C.: Duke University Press, 1969.

3519. Caughy, John W. THEIR MAJESTIES THE MOB. Chicago: Uni-
      versity of Chicago Press, 1960, pp. 127-129.

      Pages cited survey vigilante action against organizers
      of the IWW in California.

3520. Chaplin, Ralph. WOBBLY: THE ROUGH-AND-TUMBLE STORY OF
      AN AMERICAN RADICAL. Chicago: University of Chicago
      Press, 1948.

3521. Cheyney, Edward P. ANTI-RENT AGITATION IN THE STATE OF
      NEW YORK, 1839-1846. Philadelphia: Porter & Gates,
      1887.

3522. Cleland, Robert Glass. CALIFORNIA IN OUR TIME. New
      York: Knopf, 1941, pp. 88-104.

      Pages cited examine the case of Thomas Mooney and War-
      ren Billings, radical labor organizers framed for the
      lethal Preparedness Day bombing of 1916. Both were sen-
      tenced to death on murder charges, subsequently winning
      pardons when the frame-up by police officials was exposed

3523. Coleman, J. Walter. THE MOLLY MAGUIRE RIOTS: INDUSTRIAL
      CONFLICT IN THE PENNSYLVANIA COAL REGION. Richmond,
      Va.: Garrett, 1936.

3524. Conlin, Joseph R. BIG BILL HAYWOOD AND THE RADICAL UNION
      MOVEMENT. Syracuse, N.Y.: Syracuse University Press,
      1969.

3525. ————. BREAD AND ROSES, TOO: STUDIES OF THE WOBBLIES.
      Westport, Conn.: Greenwood Publishing Corp., 1969.

3526. Conrad, David E. THE FORGOTTEN FARMERS: THE STORY OF
      SHARECROPPERS IN THE NEW DEAL. Urbana, Ill.: Univer-
      sity of Illinois Press, 1965.

      Examines violence aimed at organizers of the Southern
      Tenant Farmer's Union in the Great Depression.

3527. Crook, Wilfrid H.   COMMUNISM AND THE GENERAL STRIKE.
      Hamden, Conn.: Shoestring Press, 1960, pp. 107-148.

      Examines the role of communist agitators in the mari-
      time coal strike of 1934.

3528. Dacus, Joseph A.   ANNALS OF THE GREAT STRIKES IN THE
      UNITED STATES, 1877.   St. Louis: Scamel & Co., 1877.

3529. David, Henry.   THE HISTORY OF THE HAYMARKET AFFAIR: A
      STUDY IN THE AMERICAN SOCIAL-REVOLUTIONARY AND LABOR
      MOVEMENTS.   New York: Farrar & Rinehart, 1936.

      Goes beyond the Haymarket bombing to include a history
      of American anarchists and the post-riot campaign of red-
      baiting which lent a vigilante atmosphere to subsequent
      legal proceedings.

3530. Destler, Chester McArthur.   AMERICAN RADICALISM, 1865-
      1901.   New London, Conn.: Connecticut College, 1946.

3531. Dillon, Richard H.   EMBARCADERO.   New York: Coward-McCann,
      1959, pp. 291-313.

      Pages cited detail evidence of seamen being "Shang-
      haied" and forced to work against their will on ocean-
      going vessels.   The practice of kidnapping seamen con-
      tinued into the first decade of the 20th century.

3532. ————.   SHANGHAIING DAYS.   New York: Coward-McCann, 1961.

      Updates item 3531 above, with further case histories
      of maritime abductions and slave labor.

3533. Dowell, Eldridge F.   A HISTORY OF CRIMINAL SYNDICALISM
      LEGISLATION IN THE UNITED STATES.   Baltimore, Md.: The
      Johns Hopkins Press, 1939.

3534. Dubofsky, Melvyn.   WE SHALL BE ALL: A HISTORY OF THE
      INDUSTRIAL WORKERS OF THE WORLD.   Chicago: Quadrangle,
      1969.

3535. Duff, Harvey.   THE SILENT DEFENDERS: COURTS AND CAPITAL-
      ISM IN CALIFORNIA.   Chicago: Industrial Workers of the
      World, 1919.

      Examines the arrest and prosecution of 50 IWW members
      in December 1917, following a minor bomb explosion at the

California governor's mansion. "Wobbly" defendants conducted a "silent" defense in face of the charges, and were eventually cleared.

3536. Dyche, John A. BOLSHEVISM IN AMERICAN LABOR UNIONS. A PLEA FOR CONSTRUCTIVE UNIONISM. New York: Boni & Liveright, 1926.

3537. Ebert, Julius. THE TRIAL OF A NEW SOCIETY. Cleveland: I.W.W. Publishing Bureau, 1913.

Covers the Ettor, Giovanitti and Caruso case, of IWW members on trial for alleged acts of terrorism.

3538. Farris, J.K. THE HARRISON RIOT OR THE REIGN OF THE MOB. Wynne, Ark.: The Author, 1924.

3539. Foner, Philip S. (ed). THE AUTOBIOGRAPHIES OF THE HAYMARKET MARTYRS. New York: Humanities Press, 1969.

3540. Forrest, Earle R. ARIZONA'S DARK AND BLOODY GROUND. Caldwell, Idaho: The Caxton Printers, 1936.

Surveys the range wars fought between cattle ranchers and sheep herders who sought to "invade" the open range.

3541. Fulton, Maurice G. HISTORY OF THE LINCOLN COUNTY WAR. Tucson, Ariz.: University of Arizona Press, 1968.

Examines further conflict between sheepmen and cattle ranchers.

3542. Gambs, John S. THE DECLINE OF THE I.W.W. New York: Columbia University Press, 1932.

3543. Grover, David Hubert. DEBATERS AND DYNAMITERS: THE STORY OF THE HAYWOOD TRIAL. Corvallis, Ore.: Oregon State University Press, 1964.

3544. Harriman, Job. THE CLASS STRUGGLE IN IDAHO. New York: Labor Publishing Assn., 1904.

3545. Harrison, George. THE I.W.W. TRIAL. STORY OF THE GREATEST TRIAL IN LABOR HISTORY. New York: Arno Press, 1969

3546. Haywood, William D. BILL HAYWOOD'S BOOK. New York: International Publishers, 1929.

3547. Huberman, Leo. FREE THESE THREE. San Francisco: King-
      Ramsay-Conner Defense Committee, 1941.

      Reviews manufactured evidence in the murder of a marine
      engineer, falsely blamed on union organizers, which re-
      sulted in the trial and near-conviction of three innocent
      defendants.

3548. Hunter, Robert. VIOLENCE AND THE LABOR MOVEMENT. New
      York: Macmillan, 1914.

3549. Joint Marine Modesto Defense Committee. THE MODESTO
      FRAME-UP. San Francisco: J.M.M.D.C., 1935.

      Cites further proof that manufactured evidence was used
      by California authorities to frame union organizers for
      theft of explosives.

3550. Kester, Howard. REVOLT AMONG THE SHARECROPPERS. New
      York: Covici-Friede, 1936.

3551. King-Ramsay-Conner Defense Committee. NOT GUILTY! San
      Francisco: K-R-C D.C., 1937.

      Examines the official effort to frame three defendants
      for the murder of a marine engineer in California. In
      retrospect, it seems clear the defendants were charged
      on the basis of their union activities, rather than be-
      cause of any solid evidence against them in the case.

3552. ———. PUNISHMENT WITHOUT CRIME. San Francisco: K-R-C
      D.C., 1940.

3553. ———. THE SHIP MURDER: THE STORY OF A FRAME-UP. San
      Francisco: K-R-C D.C., 1937.

3554. Kluger, James R. THE CLIFTON-MORENCI STRIKE: LABOR
      DIFFICULTY IN ARIZONA, 1915-16. Tucson: University of
      Arizona Press, 1970.

      Examines violence aimed at union organizers after
      Mexican and Yaqui Indian miners went on strike.

3555. Kogan, Bernard R. (ed). THE CHICAGO HAYMARKET RIOT:
      ANARCHY ON TRIAL. Boston: Heath, 1959.

3556. Kornbluh, Joyce L. REBEL VOICES. AN I.W.W. ANTHOLOGY.
      Ann Arbor, Mich.: University of Michigan Press, 1964.

3557. Kroll, Harry H. RIDERS IN THE NIGHT. Philadelphia: University of Pennsylvania Press, 1965.

3558. Lane, Winthrop D. CIVIL WAR IN WEST VIRGINIA. New York: Arno Press, 1921.

3559. Latham, Frank B. THE PANIC OF 1893: A TIME OF STRIKES, RIOTS, HOBOS, CAMPS, COXEY'S "ARMY," STARVATION, WITHERING DROUGHTS AND FEARS OF REVOLUTION. New York: Cowles, 1971.

3560. Lee, H.B. BLOODLETTING IN APPALACHIA: THE STORY OF WEST VIRGINIA'S FOUR MAJOR MINE WARS AND OTHER THRILLING INCIDENTS OF THE COAL FIELDS. Morgantown, W. Va.: West Virginia University, 1969.

3561. Lens, Sidney. THE LABOR WARS: FROM THE MOLLY MAGUIRES TO THE SITDOWNS. Garden City, N.Y.: Doubleday, 1974.

3562. Lum, Dyer D. A CONCISE HISTORY OF THE GREAT TRIAL OF THE CHICAGO ANARCHISTS IN 1886. Chicago: Arno Press, 1886.

3563. McCabe, James D. HISTORY OF THE GREAT RIOTS. Philadelphia: National Publishing, 1877.

3564. McGowan, George S., and Leonard F. Guttridge. THE GREAT COALFIELD WAR. New York: Houghton Mifflin, 1972.

3565. McGowan, Joseph A. HISTORY OF THE SACRAMENTO VALLEY. New York: Lewis Historical Publishing Co., 1961, pp. 106-117.

      Reviews IWW involvement in the Wheatland riot, with treatment of "Kelly's Army" of the unemployed, responsible for economic violence during 1914.

3566. McMurray, Donald L. COXEY'S ARMY: A STUDY OF THE INDUSTRIAL ARMY MOVEMENT OF 1894. Boston: Little, Brown, 1929.

      Follows a native "industrial army" on its violent cross-country trek, including clashes with railroad detectives, local police, and state militias.

3567. McWilliams, Carey. FACTORIES IN THE FIELD: THE STORY OF MIGRATORY FARM LABOR IN CALIFORNIA. Boston: Little, Brown, 1939.

3568. Nall, James O. THE TOBACCO NIGHT RIDERS OF KENTUCKY AND
       TENNESSEE, 1905-1909. Louisville, Ky.: The Standard
       Press, 1939.

3569. National Advisory Committee on Farm Labor. FARM LABOR
       ORGANIZING, 1905-1967: A BRIEF HISTORY. New York:
       National Advisory Committee on Farm Labor, 1967, pp.
       18-28.

3570. National Civil Liberties Bureau. THE "KNIGHTS OF LIBERTY"
       MOB AND THE I.W.W. PRISONERS AT TULSA, OKLA. New York:
       N.C.L.B., 1918.

3571. National Committee for the Defense of Political Prisoners.
       HARLAN MINERS SPEAK: REPORT ON TERRORISM IN THE KENTUCKY
       COAL FIELDS. New York: Harcourt, Brace, 1932.

3572. Parker, Carleton H. THE CASUAL LABORER AND OTHER ESSAYS.
       New York: Harcourt, Brace & Howe, 1920.

       The author was deputized in 1914, by the federal gov-
       ernment, to investigate the California Wheatland riot.
       His conclusions place responsibility on both sides of
       the conflict.

3573. Parker, Cornelia Stratton. AN AMERICAN IDYLL: THE LIFE
       OF CARLETON H. PARKER. Boston: Atlantic Monthly Press,
       1919.

       Written by Parker's widow, this volume examines his
       fascination and interaction with the IWW and California's
       migrant laborers.

3574. Parsons, Lucy (ed). THE FAMOUS SPEECHES OF THE EIGHT
       CHICAGO ANARCHISTS IN COURT. Chicago: L.E. Parsons,
       1886.

3575. Petro, Sylvester. THE KOHLER STRIKE: UNION VIOLENCE AND
       ADMINISTRATIVE LAW. Chicago: H. Regnery, 1961.

3576. Pinkerton, Allan. THE MOLLY MAGUIRES AND THE DETECTIVES.
       New York: G.W. Carleton, 1878.

3577. Quin, Mike. THE BIG STRIKE. Olema, Calif.: Olema Pub-
       lishing Co. 1949.

       Presents a panoramic view of local labor violence,
       through its climax on "Bloody Thursday," in 1934.

3578. Raper, Arthur F. TENANTS OF THE ALMIGHTY. Chapel Hill,
      N.C.: University of North Carolina Press, 1943.

      Reviews the violence faced by organizers of the South-
      ern Tenant Farmer's Union during the Depression.

3579. ————, and Ira De A. Reid. SHARECROPPERS ALL. Chapel
      Hill, N.C.: University of North Carolina Press, 1941.

      Continues coverage of the Southern Tenant Farmer's
      Union and the violent response to same by Southern plan-
      ters, vigilantes, and the Ku Klux Klan.

3580. Riesenberg, Felix, Jr. GOLDEN GATE: THE STORY OF SAN
      FRANCISCO HARBOR. New York: Knopf, 1940, pp. 308-327.

      Pages cited cover the "Bloody Thursday" clash of 1934.

3581. Roney, Frank. FRANK RONEY, IRISH REBEL AND CALIFORNIA
      LABOUR LEADER. Berkeley, Calif.: University of Calif-
      ornia Press, 1931.

3582. Saint John, Vincent. THE I.W.W.: ITS HISTORY, STRUCTURE,
      AND METHODS. Newcastle, Pa.: I.W.W. Publishing Bureau
      1911.

3583. Saposs, David J. COMMUNISM IN AMERICAN UNIONS. New York
      McGraw-Hill, 1959.

3584. Selekman, Sylvia Kapald. REBELLION IN LABOR UNIONS.
      New York: McGraw-Hill, 1924.

3585. Schroeder, Theodore A. FREE SPEECH FOR RADICALS. New
      York: Free Speech League, 1916, pp. 116-190.

      Pages cited review the San Diego "free speech" strug-
      gle, during which police and vigilantes did their best
      to terrorize and silence labor organizers.

3586. Smith, Helena Huntington. THE WAR ON POWDER RIVER. New
      York: McGraw-Hill, 1966.

      Wealthy ranchers declare open season on "squatters" in
      Jackson County, Wyo., during 1892. The bloody range war
      subsequently made Hollywood history with production of
      Michael Cimino's "Heaven's Gate," an all-time box office
      loser.

3587. Smith, Robert W. THE COEUR D' ALENE MINING WAR OF 1892.
      A CASE STUDY OF AN INDUSTRIAL DISPUTE. Corvallis, Ore.:
      Oregon State University Press, 1961.

3588. Smith, Walker C. THE EVERETT MASSACRE: A HISTORY OF
      CLASS STRUGGLE IN THE LUMBER INDUSTRY. Chicago: I.W.W.
      Publicity Bureau, 1917.

3589. ————. WAS IT MURDER? Centralia, Wash.: Centralia
      Publicity Committee, 1919.

3590. ————. CENTRALIA. Chicago: I.W.W. Publicity Bureau,
      1925.

3591. Symes, Lillian, and Travers Clement. REBEL AMERICA. New
      York: Harper, 1934.

3592. Taft, Philip, and Robert Ross. "American Labor Violence:
      Its Causes, Character, and Outcome." VIOLENCE IN AMER-
      ICA: HISTORICAL AND COMPARATIVE PERSPECTIVES. Cited
      above as item 3265, p. 281+.

3593. Thompson, Fred. THE I.W.W., ITS FIRST FIFTY YEARS, 1905-
      1955: THE HISTORY OF AN EFFORT TO ORGANIZE THE WORKING
      CLASS. Chicago: Industrial Workers of the World, 1955.

3594. Tilley, Nannie M. THE BRIGHT-TOBACCO INDUSTRY, 1860-
      1929. Chapel Hill, N.C.: University of North Carolina
      Press, 1948.

      Includes violence by nightriders, directed at manage-
      ment of major tobacco companies in North Carolina, during
      a period of chaotic labor unrest.

3595. Towne, Charles W., and Edward N. Wendworth. SHEPHERDS'
      EMPIRE. Norman, Okla.: University of Oklahoma Press,
      1943.

      Examines violence on the range between cattle ranchers
      and sheepmen.

3596. Vanderwood, Paul J. NIGHTRIDERS OF REELFOOT LAKE.
      Memphis, Tenn.: Memphis State University Press, 1969.

      Local fishermen declare war on a land company for con-
      trol of property in Tennessee.

3597. Wedge, Frederick R.   INSIDE THE I.W.W.   Berkeley, Calif.:
      The Author, 1924.

3598. Wolff, Leon.   LOCKOUT. THE STORY OF THE HOMESTEAD STRIKE
      OF 1892: A STUDY OF VIOLENCE, UNIONISM, AND THE CARNE-
      GIE STEEL EMPIRE.   New York: Harper & Row, 1965.

3599. Wood, Robert.   TO LIVE AND DIE IN DIXIE.   New York:
      Southern Workers Defense Committee, 1936.

3600. Wright, Carroll D.   THE BATTLES OF LABOR.   Philadelphia:
      Jacobs, 1906.

3601. Yearley, Clifton K., Jr.   ENTERPRISE AND ANTHRACITE: ECON-
      OMICS AND DEMOCRACY IN SCHUYLKILL COUNTY, 1820-1875.
      Baltimore, Md.: Johns Hopkins Press, 1961.

      Includes discussion of Molly Maguire violence in the
      Pennsylvania coal fields of the 19th century.

3602. Yellen, Samuel.   AMERICAN LABOR STRUGGLES.   New York:
      Harcourt, Brace, 1936.

      Examines major strikes, including many marred by vio-
      lence, from the 1870s through the early years of the
      Great Depression.

                          b. Articles

3603. Abbott, M.   "Chicago Interlude."   NEW REPUBLIC 15 (July
      27, 1918): 367-368.

      Examines activities of the IWW in Illinois.

3604. "Activities of the I.W.W. Enjoined in California; Member-
      ship Forbidden."   LAW AND LABOR 5 (October 1923): 272-
      274.

3605. Alexander, Arthur J.   "Prelude to the Antirent War of
      1845 in Delaware County, New York."   AGRICULTURAL HIS-
      TORY 20 (April 1946): 104-107.

3606. "An Interesting Revelation of I.W.W. Methods."   LAW AND
      LABOR 4 (December 1922): 340-342.

3607. Anderson, Arlow W.   "American Labor Unrest in Norway's
      Press: The Haymarket Affair and the Pullman Strike."
      SWEDISH PIONEER HISTORICAL QUARTERLY 25 (1974): 208-219.

3608. Archie, David E. "Times of Trouble: the Cow War." IOWAN
       7 (April-May 1959): 28-35, 52-53.

3609. Ashleigh, Charles. "Defense Fires Opening Guns; Everett
       Brutality Revealed in Court." INTERNATIONAL SOCIALIST
       REVIEW 17 (May 1917): 673-674.

       Follows the prosecution of IWW members accused of vio-
       lent crimes in Everett, Wash. The case arose from vigi-
       lante acts against the union, prompting "Wobblies" to
       use violence in self-defense.

3610. ————. "From an I.W.W. in Jail." NEW REPUBLIC 14 (March
       23, 1918): 234.

3611. ————. "The Job War in Chicago." INTERNATIONAL SOCIAL-
       IST REVIEW 15 (1914): 262-266.

3612. ————. "Lumber Trust and Its Victims." INTERNATIONAL
       SOCIALIST REVIEW 17 (March 1917): 536-538.

       Examines the activities of IWW organizers in the Paci-
       fic Northwest, clashing with management and "patriotic"
       loggers as they tried to organize a local union.

3613. Athearn, Robert G. "Origins of the Royal Gorge Railroad
       War." COLORADO MAGAZINE 36 (January 1959): 37-57.

3614. Auerbach, Jerold S. "Southern Tenant Farmers: Socialist
       Critics of the New Deal." LABOR HISTORY 7 (1966): 3-18.

3615. Barnard, Daniel D. "The 'Anti-Rent' Movement and Out-
       break in New York." AMERICAN WHIG REVIEW 2 (1845):
       587-598.

3616. Beck, William. "Law and Order During the 1913 Copper
       Strike." MICHIGAN HISTORY 54 (1970): 275-292.

3617. Beecher, John. "The Share Croppers' Union in Alabama."
       SOCIAL FORCES 13 (1934): 124-132.

3618. "Behind the Iowa Farm Riots." LITERARY DIGEST 115 (May
       13, 1933): 8.

3619. Bell, George L. "Wheatland Hop-Field Riot." OUTLOOK
       107 (May 16, 1914): 118-123.

3620. Bemis, Edward W. "The Homestead Strike." JOURNAL OF
      POLITICAL ECONOMY 2 (1983): 369-396.

3621. Berthoff, Rowland. "The Social Order in the Anthracite
      Coal Region, 1825-1902." PENNSYLVANIA MAGAZINE OF
      HISTORY AND BIOGRAPHY 89 (1965): 261-291.

3622. "Bills Drafted to Curb the I.W.W." SURVEY 38 (August 25,
      1917): 457-458.

3623. "Bisbee Deportations." SURVEY 38 (July 21, 1917): 353.

      Arizona authorities forcibly eject IWW organizers from
      their community following local labor unrest. The action
      sparked further violence and a major constitutional battle
      in the courts.

3624. "Bisbee Deportations Illegal." SURVEY 39 (December 8,
      1917): 291-292.

      Federal courts intervene to discourage mass deportations
      of radical labor organizers.

3625. Blackwell, Gordon W. "The Displaced Tenant Farm Family
      in North Carolina." SOCIAL FORCES 13 (1934): 65-73.

3626. "Bloodshed at Everett." LITERARY DIGEST 53 (November 25,
      1916): 1395.

3627. Bogue, Allen G. "The Iowa Claim Clubs: Symbol and Sub-
      stance." MISSISSIPPI VALLEY HISTORICAL REVIEW 45
      (1958): 231-253.

3628. Booth, Edward Townsend. "Wild West." ATLANTIC MONTHLY
      126 (December 1920): 785-788.

      Violence continues as IWW organizers clash with self-
      styled guardians of Americanism on the West Coast.

3629. "Branding the I.W.W." LITERARY DIGEST 58 (August 31,
      1918): 14-16.

3630. Brissenden, P.F. "Lively Corpse." NEW REPUBLIC 8 (Aug-
      ust 26, 1916): 95.

      Reports of the IWW's demise are greatly exaggerated,
      as violence continues in the Pacific Northwest.

3631. Browne, L.A. "Bolshevism in America." FORUM 59 (June
      1918): 703-717.

      Presents a critical review of recent IWW activities,
      drawing comparison with the recent Russian revolution.

3632. Bruere, R. "Copper Camp Patriotism; An Interpretation."
      NATION 106 (February 21, 1918): 202-203; 106 (February
      28, 1918): 235-236.

      Examines IWW activities in the Western mining regions,
      with discussion of violent opposition to the union.

3633. ———. "Industrial Workers of the World; An Interpre-
      tation." HARPER'S 137 (July 1918): 250-257.

3634. Bubka, T. "The Harlan County Coal Strike of 1931."
      LABOR HISTORY 11 (Winter 1970): 41-57.

3635. Busch, Francis X. "The Haymarket Riot and the Trial of
      the Anarchists." JOURNAL OF THE ILLINOIS STATE HIS-
      TORICAL SOCIETY 48 (1955): 247-270.

3636. Byrkit, James W. "The IWW in Wartime Arizona." JOURNAL
      OF ARIZONA HISTORY 18 (1977): 149-170.

3637. "California Injunction Against the I.W.W. Sustained by
      the Supreme Court of California." LAW AND LABOR 6
      (September 1934): 240-243.

3638. Callahan, Daniel F. "Criminal Syndicalism and Sabotage."
      MONTHLY LABOR REVIEW 14 (April 1922): 803-812.

3639. Canlin, Joseph R. "The I.W.W. and the Question of Vio-
      lence." WISCONSIN MAGAZINE OF HISTORY 51 (1968): 316-
      326.

3640. Carr, Ralph. "Private Land Claims in Colorado." COLO-
      RADO MAGAZINE 25 (1948): 10-29.

3641. Carter, Everett. "The Haymarket Affair in Literature."
      AMERICAN QUARTERLY 2 (1950): 270-278.

3642. "Centralia." NEW REPUBLIC 22 (April 14, 1920): 217-220.

      Examines the case of right-wing vigilantes, including
      members of the American Legion, who assaulted leftist
      union organizers in 1920. Several members of the mob

were killed when their intended victims fired in self-
defense, and subsequent murder trials turned a spotlight
on suppression of labor in the Pacific Northwest.

3643. "Centralia Before the Court." SURVEY 44 (April 3, 1920):
13-15.

Follows the trial of Centralia defendants, including
members of the IWW, accused of killing "patriotic" vigilantes.

3644. "Centralia Murder Trial." REVIEW 2 (April 3, 1920):
321-322.

3645. Chaplin, Ralph. "The Background of Centralia." ONE BIG
UNION MONTHLY 1 (May 1920): 17-19.

3646. ————. "A Hunger 'Riot' in Chicago." INTERNATIONAL
SOCIALIST REVIEW 15 (1914): 517-519.

3647. ————. "Violence in West Virginia." INTERNATIONAL
SOCIALIST REVIEW 13 (1912): 729-735.

3648. Clark, Norman H. "Everett, 1916, and After." PACIFIC
NORTHWEST QUARTERLY 57 (1966): 57-64.

3649. Cleland, Hugh G. "The Effect of Radical Groups on the
Labor Movement." PENNSYLVANIA HISTORY 26 (1959): 119-
132.

3650. Clinch, Thomas A. "Coxey's Army in Montana." MONTANA
MAGAZINE OF HISTORY 15 (1965): 2-11.

3651. Colby, E. "Industrial Workers of the World." BELLMAN
22 (March 3, 1917): 233-235.

3652. Coleman, B.S. "I.W.W. and the Law; the Result of Everett's Bloody Sunday." SUNSET 39 (July 1917): 35.

3653. "Colonel Disque and the I.W.W." NEW REPUBLIC 14 (April
6, 1918): 284-285.

3654. "Common Sense and the I.W.W.: Programme for the Social
and Economic Rehabilitation of Our National and Agricultural Lands." NEW REPUBLIC 14 (April 27, 1918):
375-376.

3655. "Convention, 1916, Chicago." INTERNATIONAL SOCIALIST
      REVIEW 17 (January 1917): 406-409.

      Covers the IWW annual convention, including discussion
      of radical tactics by those present.

3656. "Conviction of 27 Starts General Strike in San Pedro."
      INDUSTRIAL PIONEER 1 (August 1923): 3-4.

      IWW members are jailed in California, launching a major
      strike in protest of their sentencing.

3657. Corbin, David A. "The Socialist and Labor Star: Strike
      and Suppression in West Virginia, 1912-13." WEST VIR-
      GINIA HISTORY 34 (1973): 168-186.

3658. "The Cossack Regime in San Diego." MOTHER EARTH 7 (June
      1912): 97-107.

      Covers official efforts to suppress the IWW in South-
      ern California.

3659. "County-Wide Free Speech Fights." MOTHER EARTH 7 (April
      1912): 46-49.

      Further treatment of the IWW in San Diego, standing in
      the face of violent opposition from police and vigilantes.

3660. Crombie, John N. (ed). "Account of the Pennsylvania
      Railroad Riots from a Young Girl's Diary, Helen Crombie."
      WESTERN PENNSYLVANIA HISTORY MAGAZINE 54 (1971): 385-
      389.

3661. "The Curse of California." INDUSTRIAL PIONEER 4 (May
      1926): 33-38.

      Examines the role of IWW organizers and their opponents
      in contemporary labor violence.

3662. Darcy, Sam. "The Great West Coast Maritime Strike."
      COMMUNIST 13 (July 1934): 664-686.

      Prepared by the communist party's district director
      for California, presenting a far-left view of recent
      labor unrest.

3663. ———. "The San Francisco Bay Area General Strike."
      COMMUNIST 13 (October 1934): 985-1004.

3664. Davis, Mike. "The Stop Watch and the Wooden Shoe: Scientific Management and the Industrial Workers of the World." RADICAL AMERICA 9 (January-February 1975).

3665. Delaney, Edward. "Wheatland: the Bloody Hop Field." INDUSTRIAL PIONEER 2 (February 1925): 34-36.

3666. "Deportations." SURVEY 41 (February 22, 1919): 722-724.

      Examines the forced evacuation of IWW members from Arizona.

3667. Doherty, William T., Jr. "Berkeley's Non-revolution: Law and Order in the Great Railway Strike of 1877." WEST VIRGINIA HISTORY 35 (1974): 271-289.

3668. Downing, Mortimer. "The Case of the Hop Pickers." INTERNATIONAL SOCIALIST REVIEW 14 (October 1913): 210-213.

3669. Dyson, Lowell K. "The Southern Tenant Farmers Union and Depression Politics." POLITICAL SCIENCE QUARTERLY 88 (1973): 230-252.

3670. Ebner, Michael H. "The Passaic Strike of 1912 and the Two I.W.W.s." LABOR HISTORY 11 (1970): 452-466.

3671. Edwards, George. "Free Speech in San Diego." MOTHER EARTH 10 (July 1915): 182-185.

3672. Eklund, Monica. "Massacre at Ludlow." SOUTHWESTERN ECONOMICS AND SOCIOLOGY 4 (1978): 21-30.

      Thirteen women and children died in this incident, climaxing a long, bitter strike in 1913-1914.

3673. Eldridge, P.W. "The Wheatland Hop Riot and the Ford and Suhr Case." INDUSTRIAL AND LABOR RELATIONS FORUM 10 (May 1974): 165-195.

3674. Elliott, Russell R. "Labor Troubles in the Mining Camp at Goldfield, Nevada, 1906-1908." PACIFIC HISTORICAL REVIEW 19 (November 1950): 369-384.

3675. Faires, C.C. "I.W.W. Patriotism in Globe." NATION 106 (March 21, 1918): 319-320.

3676. Falconer, George N. "Machine Guns and Coal Miners."
      INTERNATIONAL SOCIALIST REVIEW 14 (1914): 480-482.

3677. ————. "The Miners' War in Colorado." INTERNATIONAL
      SOCIALIST REVIEW 14 (1913): 327-329.

3678. "Farm Riots: Martial Law in Iowa." NEWSWEEK 1 (May 6,
      1933): 9.

3679. "A First-Hand Account of the Railroad Riots of July 1877."
      WESTERN PENNSYLVANIA HISTORY MAGAZINE 57 (July 1974).

3680. Fisker, Harry. "Over Eight Hundred Hear George Speed
      Expose the Truth About the San Pedro Raid." INDUSTRIAL
      PIONEER 2 (August 1924): 3-6, 43-44.

3681. Fitch, J.A. "Baiting the I.W.W." SURVEY 33 (March 16,
      1915): 634-635.

3682. ————. "Sabotage and Disloyalty." SURVEY 39 (October
      13, 1917): 35-36.

3683. Foner, Philip S. "The I.W.W. and the Black Worker."
      JOURNAL OF NEGRO HISTORY 55 (1970): 45-64.

3684. Ford, L. "Growing Menace of the I.W.W." FORUM 61 (Jan-
      uary 1919): 62-70.

3685. Fraina, L.C. "The I.W.W. Trial." CLASS STRUGGLE 1 (No-
      vember-December 1917): 1-5.

3686. French, George E. "The Coeur d'Alene Riots, 1892."
      OVERLAND MONTHLY 2 (July 1895): 32-49.

3687. Fry, Joseph A. "Rayon, Riot, and Repression: the Coving-
      ton Sit-Down Strike of 1937." VIRGINIA MAGAZINE OF
      HISTORY AND BIOGRAPHY 84 (1976): 3-18.

3688. "Future and the I.W.W." PUBLIC FORUM 22 (February 8,
      1919): 134-136.

3689. Gaboury, William J. "From State House to Bull Pen: Idaho
      Populism and the Coeur d'Alene Troubles of the 1890s."
      PACIFIC NORTHWEST QUARTERLY 58 (1967): 14-22.

3690. Gannett, L.S. "I.W.W." NATION 111 (October 20, 1920):
      448-449.

3691. Gartin, Edwin V. "The West Virginia Mine War of 1912-
      1913: the Progressive Response." NORTH DAKOTA QUAR-
      TERLY 41 (Fall 1973).

3692. Gatell, Frank O. "Roger B. Taney, the Bank of Maryland
      Rioters, and a Whiff of Grapeshot." MARYLAND HISTOR-
      ICAL MAGAZINE 59 (1964): 262-267.

3693. Gates, Paul W. "California's Embattled Settlers." CALI-
      FORNIA HISTORICAL SOCIETY QUARTERLY 41 (1962): 99-130.

3694. "The General Defense Committee of the I.W.W." INTERNA-
      TIONAL SOCIALIST REVIEW 18 (1917): 408-409.

3695. Gerhard, Peter. "The Socialist Invasion of Baja Califor-
      nia, 1911." PACIFIC HISTORICAL REVIEW 15 (September
      1946): 295-304.

3696. Gilmore, Inez Haynes. "Marysville Strike." HARPER'S
      WEEKLY 58 (April 4, 1914): 18-20.

      Examines the IWW's role in yet another violent labor
      dispute.

3697. Gill, R.S. "Four L's in Lumber." SURVEY 44 (May 1,
      1920): 165-170.

      Follows the activities of IWW organizers in the Pacific
      Northwest.

3698. Goldman, Emma. "The Outrage of San Diego." MOTHER
      EARTH 7 (June 1912): 115-122.

3699. Grab, Gerald. "The Railroad Strikes of 1877." MIDWES-
      TERN JOURNAL 6 (1954): 16-34.

3700. Grantham, Dewey W., Jr. "Black Patch War: The Story of
      the Kentucky and Tennessee Night Riders, 1905-1909."
      SOUTH ATLANTIC QUARTERLY 59 (1960): 215-225.

3701. Gressley, Gene M. "The American Cattle Trust: A Study
      in Protest." PACIFIC HISTORICAL REVIEW 30 (1961):
      61-77.

3702. Grinde, Donald A. "Erie's Railroad War: A Case Study of
      Purposive Violence for a Community's Economic Advance-
      ment." WESTERN PENNSYLVANIA HISTORY MAGAZINE 57 (Jan-
      uary 1974).

3703. "The Gruesome Story of American Terrorism." ONE BIG
       UNION MONTHLY 1 (March 1920): 5-21.

       Reports incidents of anti-union violence, catalogued
    by journalists sympathetic to the cause of labor.

3704. Gutman, Herbert G. "The Tompkins Square 'Riot' in New
       York City on January 13, 1874: A Re-examination of its
       Causes and Aftermath." LABOR HISTORY 6 (1965): 45-70.

3705. ————. "Trouble on the Railroads in 1873-1874: Prelude
       to the 1877 Crisis." LABOR HISTORY 2 (1961): 215-235.

3706. Gunns, Albert F. "Ray Becker, the Last Centralia Prison-
       er." PACIFIC NORTHWEST QUARTERLY 59 (1968): 88-99.

3707. Haywood, William D. "On the Paterson Picket Line." IN-
       TERNATIONAL SOCIALIST REVIEW 13 (1913): 847-851.

       The IWW's leader examines his union's role in New Jer-
    sey labor disputes.

3708. Hedrick, P.C. "I.W.W. and Mayor Hanson." UNPARTISAN
       REVIEW 12 (July 1919): 35-45.

3709. Henderson, James A. "The Railroad Riots in Pittsburgh,
       Saturday and Sunday, April 21st and 22nd, 1877."
       WESTERN PENNSYLVANIA HISTORICAL MAGAZINE 11 (July 1928):
       194-197.

3710. Henderson, William W. "The Night Riders Raid on Hopkins-
       ville." FILSON CLUB HISTORICAL QUARTERLY 24 (1950):
       346-358.

3711. Hill, Mary Anderson. "The Free Speech Fight at San
       Diego." SURVEY 28 (May 4, 1912): 192-194.

3712. Hofteling, C. "Sunkist Prisoners." NATION 113 (Septem-
       ber 21, 1921): 316.

       Examines IWW organizational activities in the citrus
    industry.

3713. Holmes, William F. "Whitecapping: Agrarian Violence in
       Mississippi, 1902-1906." JOURNAL OF SOUTHERN HISTORY
       35 (May 1969): 165-185.

3714. Hoxie, Robert. "The Truth About the I.W.W." JOURNAL OF
      POLITICS AND ECONOMICS 21 (November 1913): 785-797.

3715. Hudson, James Jackson. "The McCloud River Affair of
      1909: A Study in the Use of State Troops." CALIFORNIA
      HISTORICAL QUARTERLY 35 (March 1956): 29-35.

      The California National Guard suppressed a riot by
      Italian lumbermen during a violent strike in Siskiyou
      County.

3716. "Ill Weeds Grow Apace." LIVING AGE 295 (November 24,
      1917): 492-493.

      Charts the continuing growth of the IWW from a critical
      viewpoint.

3717. "Industrial Action News." INTERNATIONAL SOCIALIST REVIEW
      17 (June 1917): 727-728.

3718. "Industrial Workers Who Won't Work." LITERARY DIGEST 55
      (July 28, 1917): 20-21.

      Covers the IWW on strike.

3719. "I.W.W. As an Agent of Pan-Germanism." WORLD'S WORK 36
      (October 1918): 581-582.

3720. "I.W.W. Develops Into a National Menace." CURRENT REVIEW
      63 (September 1917): 153-154.

3721. "I.W.W. On Trial." OUTLOOK 119 (July 17, 1918): 448-450.

3722. "I.W.W. Raids and Others." NEW REPUBLIC 12 (September
      15, 1917): 175-177.

3723. Jackson, W.T. "The Wyoming Stock Growers' Association:
      Political Power in Wyoming Territory, 1873-1890."
      MISSISSIPPI VALLEY HISTORICAL REVIEW 33 (1946): 571-
      594.

3724. Jeffreys-Jones, Rhodri. "Theories of American Labour
      Violence." JOURNAL OF AMERICAN STUDIES 13 (1979):
      245-264.

      A British author examines the theoretical causes of
      American labor violence, including environment, ideology,
      race, and culture.

3725. ————. "Violence in American History: Plug Uglies in
       the Progressive Era." PERSPECTIVES IN AMERICAN HISTORY
       8 (1974): 465-583.

       Examines how isolated incidents were translated into
       widespread paranoia through the illusion of potential
       revolution, leading to the rise of labor spies, armed
       guards, and violence aimed at unions.

3726. Johnson, Dorothy M. "Flour Famine in Alder Gulch, 1864."
       MONTANA MAGAZINE OF HISTORY 7 (1957): 18-27.

3727. Johnson, Michael R. "The I.W.W. and Wilsonian Democracy."
       SCIENCE AND SOCIETY 28 (1964): 257-274.

3728. Johnson, O. "After the Dearborn Massacre." NEW REPUB-
       LIC 70 (March 30, 1932): 172-174.

3729. "Keep Your Eyes on Everett!" INTERNATIONAL SOCIALIST RE-
       VIEW 17 (April 1917): 608-609.

3730. Kent, Donald H. "The Erie War of the Gauges." PENNSYL-
       VANIA HISTORY 15 (1948): 253-275.

3731. Kimball, William J. "The Bread Riot in Richmond, 1863."
       CIVIL WAR HISTORY 7 (June 1961): 149-154.

3732. Kintzer, Edward H. "The Battling Miners of West Virgin-
       ia." NEW REVIEW 1 (1913): 374-375.

3733. ————. "The Battling Miners of West Virginia." INTER-
       NATIONAL SOCIALIST REVIEW 13 (1912): 295-303, 391-393.

3734. Kirk, Clara, and Rudolf Kirk. "William Dean Howells,
       Geroge William Curtis, and the 'Haymarket Affair.'"
       AMERICAN LITERATURE 40 (1969): 487-498.

3735. Knight, Robert M. "Fighting to Win in Colorado." INTER-
       NATIONAL SOCIALIST REVIEW 14 (1913): 330-334.

3736. "Labor Fight at Everett." OUTLOOK 114 (November 15,
       1916): 583-584.

3737. Lane, Ann J. "Recent Literature on the Molly Maguires."
       SCIENCE AND SOCIETY (1966).

3738. Lanier, A.S. "To the President: Open Letter in Regard to
       Case of United States vs. W.D. Haywood, et al." NEW
       REPUBLIC 18 (April 19, 1919): 383-384.

Criticizes federal efforts to prosecute IWW leader
Bill Haywood for alleged acts of terrorism. In the
final event, Haywood fled to the Soviet Union, where he
was briefly hailed as a revolutionary hero before being
shuffled aside and forgotten.

3739. La Piere, Richard T. "The General Strike in San Francisco. A Study of the Revolutionary Pattern." SOCIOL-
OGY AND SOCIAL RESEARCH 19 (April 1935): 335-363.

3740. Levinson, Lew. "California Casualty List." NATION
139 (August 29, 1934): 243-245.

Examines violence in the San Francisco maritime strike.

3741. Linaberger, James. "The Rolling Mills Riots of 1850."
WESTERN PENNSYLVANIA HISTORY MAGAZINE 47 (1964):
1-18.

3742. Lindquist, John H., and James Fraser. "A Sociological
Interpretation of the Bisbee Deportation." PACIFIC
HISTORICAL REVIEW 37 (1968): 401-422.

3743. ———. "The Jerome Deportation of 1917." ARIZONA
AND THE WEST 11 (1969): 233-246.

3744. Lore, Wudwig. "The I.W.W. Trial." CLASS STRUGGLE 2
(1918): 377-383.

3745. Lovin, Hugh T. "Moses Alexander and the Idaho Lumber
Strike of 1917: the Wartime Ordeal of a Progressive."
PACIFIC NORTHWEST QUARTERLY 66 (July 1975).

3746. Lynch, Lawrence B. "The West Virginia Coal Strike."
POLITICAL SCIENCE QUARTERLY 29 (1914): 626-663.

3747. "Lynch Law and Treason; Lynching of Frank Little in
Butte." LITERARY DIGEST 55 (August 18, 1917): 12-13.

3748. McMahon, T.S. "Centralia and the I.W.W." SURVEY 43
(November 29, 1919): 173-174.

3749. MacDonald, John. "From Butte to Bisbee." INTERNATIONAL
SOCIALIST REVIEW 18 (1917): 69-71.

3750. McClelland, John M. "Terror on Tower Avenue." PACIFIC
NORTHWEST QUARTERLY 57 (1966): 65-72.

3751. McCormick, Kyle. "The National Guard of West Virginia During the Strike Period, 1912-1913." WEST VIRGINIA HISTORY 22 (October 1960): 34-35.

3752. MacDonald, W. "Where Labor Points the Way." NATION 108 (April 5, 1919): 499-501.

Continues coverage of the IWW in action.

3753. Mackey, Philip E. "Law and Order, 1877: Philadelphia's Response to the Railroad Riots." PENNSYLVANIA MAGAZINE OF HISTORY AND BIOGRAPHY 96 (1972): 183-202.

3754. Macphee, Donald A. "The Centralia Incident and the Pamphleteers." PACIFIC NORTHWEST QUARTERLY 62 (1971).

3755. Mandel, Bernard. "The Great Uprising of 1877." CIGAR MAKERS OFFICIAL JOURNAL (December 1953).

3756. Marcy, Leslie. "Calumet." INTERNATIONAL SOCIALIST REVIEW 14 (1913): 453-461.

Seventy-two children of striking miners were killed in hostile actions by management-sponsored goons.

3757. ———. "The Class War in Colorado." INTERNATIONAL SOCIALIST REVIEW 14 (1914): 708-727.

3758. ———. "The Eleven Hundred Exiled Copper Miners." INTERNATIONAL SOCIALIST REVIEW 18 (1917): 160-162.

3759. ———. "Food Riots in America." INTERNATIONAL SOCIALIST REVIEW 17 (1916): 582-587.

3760. Marcy, Mary. "A Month of Lawlessness." INTERNATIONAL SOCIALIST REVIEW 18 (1917): 154-159.

3761. Martin, John. "News from the Lumber Workers' Strike." INTERNATIONAL SOCIALIST REVIEW 18 (1917): 144-148.

3762. Mattick, Hans W. "Between Riots in 1844." AMERICAN CATHOLIC HISTORICAL SOCIETY RECORD 62 (1951): 64-65.

3763. Merz, Charles. "Issue in Butte." NEW REPUBLIC 12 (September 22, 1917): 215-217.

Examines IWW activities in Montana.

324   TERRORISM IN THE UNITED STATES AND EUROPE

3764. ———. "Tying Up Western Lumber." NEW REPUBLIC 12
(September 29, 1917): 242-244.

3765. Meyerhuber, Carl I., Jr. "The Alle-Kiski Coal Wars,
1913-1919." WESTERN PENNSYLVANIA MAGAZINE 63 (1980):
197-213.

3766. Miller, Grace L. "The I.W.W. Free Speech Fight: San
Diego, 1912." SOUTHERN CALIFORNIA QUARTERLY 54 (1972):
211-238.

3767. Milne, Robert D. "Hoodlums on a Hop Ranch." CALIFORN-
IAN 1 (February 1980): 171-176.

3768. "Minneapolis Unemployed Riot." NEWSWEEK 3 (April 14,
1934): 11-12.

3769. "Mr. Kent and the I.W.W." PUBLIC OPINION 21 (July 13,
1918): 878-879.

3770. "Montesano—Is the I.W.W. On Trial?" SURVEY 43 (March
13, 1920): 734-735.

3771. Montgomery, David. "The Shuttle and the Cross: Weavers
and Artisans in the Kensington Riots of 1844." JOURNAL
OF SOCIAL HISTORY 5 (1972): 411-446.

3772. Morefield, Richard Henry. "Mexicans in the California
Mines, 1848-1953." CALIFORNIA HISTORICAL QUARTERLY
35 (March 1956): 37-46.

Vigilante violence deprives Hispanics of their right-
ful claim to mining digs.

3773. Morris, Wayne. "The Great Strike." WESTERN PENNSYLVAN-
IA HISTORY MAGAZINE 58 (January 1975).

3774. Morton, James. "The Cabin Creek Victory." INTERNATIONAL
SOCIALIST REVIEW 13 (1912): 541-543.

3775. Murray, David. "The Antirent Episode in the State of
New York." AMERICAN HISTORICAL ASSOCIATION ANNUAL
REPORT 1 (1896): 137-173.

3776. Newton, E.E. "Ant and the Grasshopper." SURVEY 38 (September 15, 1917): 522-523.

Examines the continuing struggles of the IWW.

3777. Niven, A.C. "A Chapter of Anti-Rent History." ALBANY
      LAW JOURNAL 24 (1881): 125-127.

3778. "Ol' Rags and Bottles." NATION 108 (January 25, 1919):
      114-116.

      IWW battles continue in the post-war era.

3779. "Organization and Anarchy." NEW REPUBLIC 11 (July 21,
      1917): 320-323.

      Presents a critical view of IWW organizational activi-
      ties.

3780. Overmyer, Grace. "The Baltimore Mobs and John Howard
      Payne." MARYLAND HISTORICAL MAGAZINE 58 (1963): 54-61.

3781. Parker, Carleton H. "The California Casual and His Re-
      volt." QUARTERLY JOURNAL OF ECONOMICS 30 (November
      1915): 110-126.

3782. ———. "I.W.W." ATLANTIC MONTHLY 120 (November 1917):
      651-662.

3783. ———. "The Wheatland Riot and What Lay in Back of It."
      SURVEY 31 (March 21, 1914): 768-770.

      Deputized by federal authorities, the author made a
      personal investigation of the 1913 riot by migratory
      workers that left four persons dead.

3784. Paul, Rodman W. "The Great California Grain War: the
      Grangers Challenge the Wheat King." PACIFIC HISTORICAL
      REVIEW 27 (1958): 331-349.

3785. Paxon, Frederic L. "The Cow County." AMERICAN HISTORY
      REVIEW 22 (1916): 65-82.

3786. "Pennsylvania's Constabulary." NATION 90 (March 24,
      1910): 281-282.

      Examines labor violence in the coalfields.

3787. Pound, Arthur. "Down-Rent War in Olde Ulster (1845)."
      NEW YORK HISTORY 23 (October 1942): 410-418.

3788. "President's Commission at Bisbee." NEW REPUBLIC 13
      (December 8, 1917): 140-141.

3789. Preston, William. "Shall This Be All? U.S. Historians Versus William D. Haywood et al." LABOR HISTORY 12 (1971): 435-453.

3790. Priddy, A. "Controlling the Passions of Men—in Lawrence. OUTLOOK 102 (October 19, 1912): 343-345.

Reviews violence in the Pennsylvania coalfields.

3791. "Raiding the I.W.W." LITERARY DIGEST 55 (September 22, 1917): 17.

3792. Rasch, Philip J. "The Tularosa Ditch War." NEX MEXICO HISTORICAL REVIEW 43 (1968): 229-235.

3793. Reed, Merl E. "The I.W.W. and Individual Freedom in Western Louisiana, 1913." LOUISIANA HISTORY 10 (1969): 61-69.

3794. ———. "Lumberjacks and Longshoremen: The I.W.W. in Louisiana." LABOR HISTORY 13 (1972): 41-59.

3795. Reitman, Ben L. "The Respectable Mob." MOTHER EARTH 7 (June 1912): 109-114.

3796. Renshaw, Patrick. "The I.W.W. and the Red Scare, 1917-1924." JOURNAL OF CONTEMPORARY HISTORY 3 (October 1968): 63-72.

3797. Reynolds, Albin L. "War in the Black Patch." KENTUCKY HISTORICAL SOCIETY REGISTER 56 (1958): 1-10.

3798. Reynolds, Arthur R. "Land Frauds and Illegal Fencing in Western Nebraska." AGRICULTURAL HISTORY 23 (1949): 173-179.

3799. Rhodes, James Ford. "The Molly Maguires in the Anthracite Region of Pennsylvania." AMERICAN HISTORICAL REVIEW 15 (April 1910): 547-561.

3800. ———. "Railroad Riots of 1877." SCRIBNER'S MAGAZINE 50 (July 1911): 86-96.

3801. Rice, Charles Owen. "Verdict at Kohler." COMMONWEAL (November 11, 1896).

3802. "Right to Murder Labor; Lynching of a Railroad Striker at Harrison, Arkansas." LITERARY DIGEST 78 (February 3, 1923): 13.

UNITED STATES   327

3803. "Riots in Pennsylvania; Bituminous Coal Region." SPEC-
      TATOR 79 (September 18, 1897): 361-362.

3804. "Rising Danger of Violence." CHRISTIAN CENTURY 49 (March
      30, 1932): 405.

3805. Rocha, Guy Lewis. "The I.W.W. and the Boulder Canyon
      Project: the Final Death Throes of American Syndical-
      ism." NEVADA HISTORICAL SOCIETY QUARTERLY 21 (1978):
      2-24.

3806. Rosen, Dale, and Theodore Rosengarten. "Shoot-Out at
      Reeltown: the Narrative of Jess Hull, Alabama Tenant
      Farmer." RADICAL AMERICA 6 (1972): 65-84.

3807. Rowan, J. "Imprisoned I.W.W. at Leavenworth." NATION
      113 (August 13, 1921): 123.

3808. Rowley, William D. "The Loup City Riot of 1934: Main
      Street vs. the 'Far-out' Left." NEBRASKA HISTORY 47
      (1966): 295-328.

3809. Royce, Josiah. "The Squatter Riot of 1850 in Sacramento."
      OVERLAND MONTHLY 2 (1885): 225-246.

3810. Rudolph, Frederick. "Chinamen in Yankeedom: Anti-Union-
      ism in Massachusetts in 1870." AMERICAN HISTORICAL
      REVIEW 53 (October 1947): 1-29.

3811. Russell, Phillips. "The Arrest of Haywood and Lessig."
      INTERNATIONAL SOCIALIST REVIEW 13 (1912): 789-792.

      Examines IWW activities in New Jersey, and the prose-
      cution of union leaders there.

3812. Russell, Sigurd. "West Virginia Senatorial Investigation."
      INTERNATIONAL SOCIALIST REVIEW 14 (1913): 85-87.

3813. Ryder, David Warren. "California: Ashamed and Repentant."
      NEW REPUBLIC 51 (June 1, 1927): 111-144.

3814. Sandgren, John. "Under the Spell of Terrorism." ONE
      BIG UNION MONTHLY 1 (March 1920): 23-28.

3815. Schwantes, Carlos A. "Making the World Unsafe for
      Democracy: Vigilantes, Grangers and the Walla Walla
      'Outrage' of June 1918." MONTANA 31 (1981): 18-29.

Examines the case of Grangers drive out of town by a vigilante mob.

3816. Scott, Alexander. "What the Reds Are Doing in Paterson." SOCIALIST REVIEW 13 (1912): 852-856.

Presents a critical review of IWW activities in New Jersey.

3817. Seeley, Evelyn. "San Francisco's Labor War." NATION 138 (June 13, 1934): 672-674.

3818. Shippy, Hartwell. "The Shame of San Diego." INTERNATIONAL SOCIALIST REVIEW 12 (May 1912): 718-723.

3819. Short, W.M. "How One Town Learned a Lesson in Free Speech." SURVEY 35 (October 30, 1915): 106-108.

Follows the continuing trials of IWW organizers.

3820. Sims, Robert C. "Idaho's Criminal Syndicalism Act: One State's Response to Radical Labor." LABOR HISTORY 15 (1974): 511-527.

3821. Sinclair, Upton. "Civil Liberties in Los Angeles." INDUSTRIAL PIONEER 1 (August 1923): 27-29.

3822. Slaner, Philip A. "The Railroad Strikes of 1877." MARXIST QUARTERLY (1937): 214-236.

3823. Smith, E. "Fireman's Riot at New Haven, 1858." BACHELOR OF ARTS 1: 167.

3824. Smith, W.C. "Remember the Fifth of November." INTERNATIONAL SOCIALIST REVIEW 17 (January 1917): 396-399.

Examines continuing violence against the IWW.

3825. "Solidarity Wins in Fresno." INTERNATIONAL SOCIALIST REVIEW 11 (April 1911): 634-636.

3826. Spargo, J. "Why the I.W.W. Flourishes." WORLD'S WORK 39 (January 1920): 243-247.

3827. Splitter, Henry Winfred. "Concerning Vinette's Los Angeles Regiment of Coxey's Army." PACIFIC HISTORICAL REVIEW 17 (1948): 29-36.

3828. "Spruce and the I.W.W." NEW REPUBLIC 14 (February 23, 1918): 99-100.

3829. Sterling, Jean. "Silent Defense in Sacramento." LIBER-ATOR 1 (February 1919): 15-17.

3830. "Strike Failures a Joy to the I.W.W. Leaders." CURRENT REVIEW 68 (June 1920): 835-836.

3831. Strong, A.L. "Centralia: An Unfinished Story." NATION 110 (April 17, 1920): 508-510.

3832. ———. "Everett's Bloody Sunday; a Free Speech Fight That Led to a Murder Trial." SURVEY 37 (January 27, 1917): 475-476.

3833. ———. "Verdict at Everett." SURVEY 38 (May 19, 1917): 160-162.

3834. Sugar, M. "Bullets, Not Food, for Ford Workers." NATION 134 (March 28, 1932): 333-335.

3835. Sullivan, William A. "The 1913 Revolt of the Michigan Copper Miners." MICHIGAN HISTORY 43 (September 1959): 3-23.

3836. Taft, Philip. "The Bisbee Deportation." LABOR HISTORY 13 (1972): 3-40.

3837. ———. "The Federal Trials of the I.W.W." LABOR HIS-TORY 3 (Winter 1962): 57-91.

3838. ———. "The I.W.W. in the Gain Belt." LABOR HISTORY 1 (Winter 1960): 53-67.

3839. Taylor, Marie. "Night Riders in the Black Patch." KENTUCKY HISTORICAL SOCIETY REGISTER 61 (1963): 279-299; 62 (1964): 24-40.

3840. Thomas, Emory M. "The Richmond Bread Riot of 1863: 'A Manifest Uneasiness in the Public Mind.'" VIRGINIA CAVALCADE 18 (1968): 41-47.

3841. Thompson, W.H. "How a Victory was Turned into a 'Settle-ment' in West Virginia." INTERNATIONAL SOCIALIST RE-VIEW 14 (1913): 12-17.

3842. Thrasher, Sue, and Leah Wise. "The Southern Tenant Far-
      mers' Union." SOUTHERN EXPOSURE 1 (Winter 1974): 1-34.

3843. Tice, Douglas O. "'Bread or Blood!' The Richmond Bread
      Riot." CIVIL WAR TIMES ILLUSTRATED 12 (February 1974).

3844. Tilley, Nannie M. "Agitation Against the American Tobac-
      co Company in North Carolina, 1890-1911." NORTH CARO-
      LINA HISTORICAL REVIEW 24 (1947): 207-223.

3845. "Treason Must Be Made Odious." NORTH AMERICAN 206 (Octo-
      ber 1917): 513-517.

      Calls for harsh action against the growing IWW.

3846. Tyler, Robert L. "The Everett Free Speech Fight." PACI-
      FIC HISTORICAL REVIEW 23 (1954): 19-30.

3847. ————. "The I.W.W. and the West." AMERICAN QUARTERLY
      12 (Summer 1960): 175-187.

3848. ————. "Violence at Centralia, 1919." PACIFIC NORTH-
      WEST QUARTERLY 45 (1954): 116-124.

3849. Van Valen, Nelson. "The Bolsheviki and the Orange Grow-
      ers." PACIFIC HISTORICAL REVIEW 22 (February 1953):
      39-50.

      Reviews the clash between Southern California citrus
      farmers and the IWW.

3850. Venkataramani, M.S. "Norman Thomas, Arkansas Sharecrop-
      pers, and the Roosevelt Agricultural Politics, 1933-
      1937." MISSISSIPPI VALLEY HISTORICAL REVIEW 47 (1960):
      225-246.

3851. "Violence Against the Hungry." WORLD TOMORROW 15 (April
      1932): 102-104.

3852. West, George P. "California Sees Red." CURRENT HISTORY
      40 (September 1934): 658-662.

      Examines the red scare that accompanied California's
      maritime strike.

3853. "What Haywood Says to the I.W.W." SURVEY 38 (August 11,
      1917): 429-430.

3854. "What the I.W.W Black Cat and Wooden Shoe Emblems Mean."
       LITERARY DIGEST 61 (April 19, 1919): 70-75.

3855. Whitaker, Robert. "What Ails California?" INDUSTRIAL
       PIONEER 2 (January 1925): 8-44; 2 (February 1925):
       45-46.

3856. Whitten, Woodrow C. "The Wheatland Episode." PACIFIC
       HISTORICAL REVIEW 17 (February 1948): 37-42.

3857. "Why We Hate the Bolsheviki." PUBLIC FORUM 23 (February
       8, 1919): 126-127.

       Castigates the IWW for alleges subversive activitites.

3858. Williams, William J. "Bloody Sunday Revisited." PACIFIC
       NORTHWEST QUARTERLY 71 (1980): 50-62.

       Reviews the Everett massacre which left seven dead and
       47 wounded in November 1916, following a vigilante mob's
       assault on an IWW meeting hall.

3859. Winstead, R. "Enter a Logger; An I.W.W. Reply to the
       Four L's." SURVEY 44 (July 3, 1920): 474-477.

3860. Witt, Robert W. "Robert Penn Warren and the Black Patch
       War." KENTUCKY HISTORICAL SOCIETY REGISTER 67 (October
       1969).

3861. Woehlke, Walter V. "Bolsheviks of the West." SUNSET
       40 (January 1918): 14-16, 70-72.

3862. ————. "The I.W.W." OUTLOOK 101 (July 6, 1912): 531-
       536.

3863. ————. "Red Rebels Declare War." SUNSET 39 (September
       1917): 20-21.

       Follows radical activities of the IWW.

3864. Wortman, Roy T. "An I.W.W. Document of the 1919 Rossford
       Strike." NORTHWEST OHIO QUARTERLY 43 (1971): 37-42.

3865. ————. The Resurgence of the IWW in Cleveland: A Neglec-
       ted Aspect of Labor History." NORTHWEST OHIO QUARTERLY
       47 (1974): 20-29.

3866. Yarros, V.S. "I.W.W. Judgment." SURVEY 45 (October 16, 1920): 87.

3867. ————. "I.W.W. Trial." NATION 107 (August 31, 1918): 220-223.

3868. ————. "Story of the I.W.W. Trial." SURVEY 40 (August 31, 1918): 603-604; 40 (September 7, 1918): 630-632; 40 (September 14, 1918): 660-663.

3869. Yoder, Dale. "Economic Changes and Industrial Unrest in the United States." JOURNAL OF POLITICS AND ECONOMICS 32 (1942): 261-306.

3870. Zieger, Robert H. "Robin Hood in the Silk City: The I.W.W. and the Paterson Silk Strike of 1913." PROCEEDINGS OF THE NEW JERSEY HISTORICAL SOCIETY 84 (1968): 182-195.

5. Ku Klux Klan

a. Books

3871. Abrams, Charles. "Invasion and Counterattack." VIOLENCE IN AMERICA. Cited above as item 3281, pp. 185-190.

Examines incidents of racial bombings aimed at nonwhite families that have "invaded" previously all-white neighborhoods. Independent evidence established that the members of assorted Klan factions were responsible for most, if not all, of the explosions.

3872. Alabama General Assembly. REPORT OF JOINT COMMITTEE ON OUTRAGES. Montgomery, Ala.: J.G. Stokes & Co., 1868.

A Southern legislature reviews the terrorist activities of Klansmen during Reconstruction.

3873. Alexander, Charles C. CRUSADE FOR CONFORMITY: THE KU KLUX KLAN IN TEXAS, 1920-1930. Houston: University of Texas Press, 1962.

3874. ————. THE KU KLUX KLAN IN THE SOUTHWEST. Lexington, Ky.: University of Kentucky Press, 1965.

Expands on item 3873, including coverage of KKK activity in Arkansas, Louisiana, Oklahoma, and Texas.

3875. Angle, Paul M. BLOODY WILLIAMSON; A CHAPTER IN AMERICAN
      LAWLESSNESS. New York: Alfred A. Knopf, 1952.

      Examines the local "war" between bootleggers and the
      KKK, which sought to enforce Prohibition laws without
      resort to established courts and procedures. The result
      was protracted, bloody conflict with numerous deaths on
      both sides.

3876. Bain, Donald. THE WAR IN ILLINOIS. Englewood Cliffs,
      N.J.: Prentice-Hall, 1978.

      Presents another version of the story told in item
      3875 above.

3877. Beard, James Melville. K.K.K. SKETCHES, HUMOROUS AND
      DIDACTIC, TREATING THE MORE IMPORTANT EVENTS OF THE
      KU KLUX KLAN MOVEMENT IN THE SOUTH. Philadelphia:
      Claxton, Remsen & Haffelfinger, 1877.

3878, Booth, Edgar Allen. THE MAD MULLAH OF AMERICA. Columbus,
      Ohio: Boyd Ellison, 1927.

      Offers a critical view of the 1920s Indiana Klan, pre-
      pared with benefit of "inside" information. The author
      spotlights KKK corruption, with coverage of violence on
      the side.

3879. Brewster, James. SKETCHES OF SOUTHERN MYSTERY, TREASON
      AND MURDER. THE SECRET POLITICAL SOCIETIES OF THE
      SOUTH, THEIR METHODS AND MANNERS. THE PHAGEDENIC CAN-
      CER ON OUR NATIONAL LIFE. Milwaukee: Evening Wisconsin
      Co., 1903.

3880. Brown, George Alfred. HAROLD THE KLANSMAN. Kansas City,
      Mo.: Western Baptist Publishing Co., 1923.

      Presents a pro-Klan view of 1920s America, with the
      fictional "Harold" standing firm against various perils
      of the modern age.

3881. Bryant, Benjamin. EXPERIENCE OF A NORTHERN MAN AMONG THE
      KU KLUX; OR, THE CONDITION OF THE SOUTH. Hartford,
      Conn.: The Author, 1872.

      A "carpetbagger" lives to write about his torture at
      the hands of Klan nightriders during Reconstruction.

3882. Burton, Annie Cooper. THE KU KLUX KLAN. Los Angeles:
      W.T. Potter, 1916.

      Examines the Reconstruction Klan from a traditional
      Southern viewpoint, painting violent Klansmen as the
      saviors of a prostrate South.

3883. Busch, Francis X. GUILTY OR NOT GUILTY? Indianapolis:
      Bobbs-Merrill, 1952.

      Reviews the case of Indiana's KKK Grand Dragon, D.C.
      Stephenson, accused—and ultimately convicted—in the
      rape and murder of a woman he abducted for immoral pur-
      poses. The highly publicized incident destroyed the
      KKK in Indiana and cost the order thousands of members
      nationwide.

3884. Butler, Benjamin Franklin. KU KLUX OUTRAGES IN THE
      SOUTH. Washington, D.C.: M'Gill & Witherow, 1871.

3885. Butler, Robert A. SO THEY FRAMED STEPHENSON. Huntington
      Ind.: The Author, 1940.

      Strives to picture D.C. Stephenson as the victim of a
      frame-up by rival Klansmen and their un-American cronies.
      The argument did not hold water in the 1920s, and it
      seems ridiculous today.

3886. Campbell, Sam H. THE JEWISH PROBLEM IN THE UNITED STATES
      Atlanta, Ga.: Ku Klux Klan, 1923.

      A Klan author views the "Jewish problem" from a KKK
      perspective, offering "solutions" in line with the
      groups traditional methods of handling "aliens."

3887. Carlton, Luther M. ASSASSINATION OF J.W. STEPHENS.
      Durham, N.C. The Author, 1989.

      Reviews the case of a state senator murdered by Klans-
      men in North Carolina, May 21, 1868. The KKK tried to
      blame his death on black Republicans, without success.

3888. Chalmers, David M. HOODED AMERICANISM: THE FIRST CEN-
      TURY OF THE KU KLUX KLAN, 1865-1965. Garden City, N.Y.
      Doubleday, 1965.

      Presents the best single volume of Klan history ever
      published, bar none. If there is any weakness in the

work, it must be Chalmers' relatively hasty disposition
of the Reconstruction period. The 1920s KKK is covered
in microscopic detail, and later chapters follow frag-
mentation of the movement and its terrorist activities
through summer, 1964.

3889. ———. HOODED AMERICANISM: THE HISTORY OF THE KU KLUX
      KLAN. New York: New Viewpoints, 1981.

      Updates item 3888 with new chapters covering the Klan
      from 1965 through 1980. Fortunately, editors resisted
      the temptation to delete any of Chalmers' original
      material.

3890. Clason, George S. CATHOLIC, JEW, KU KLUX KLAN. Chicago:
      Nutshell, 1924.

3891. Clayton, Powell. THE AFTERMATH OF THE CIVIL WAR IN AR-
      KANSAS. New York: Neale Publishing Co., 1915.

      Includes discussion of the violent razorback Klan
      during the post-war era.

3892. Committee for the Defense of Civil Rights in Tampa.
      TERROR IN TAMPA: KU KLUX KLAN IN FLORIDA. New York:
      Workers Defense League, 1937.

      Examines a Depression-era reign of terror led by Klans-
      men in central Florida. Major targets of violence were
      labor organizers, one of whom was tortured to death in
      1935, but blacks were not neglected, either.

3893. Cook, Ezra A. KU KLUX SECRETS EXPOSED. Chicago: Cook,
      1922.

3894. Cook, Fred J. THE KU KLUX KLAN: AMERICA'S RECURRING
      NIGHTMARE. New York: Julian Messner, 1980.

      A historical overview, intended primarily for younger
      readers.

3895. Cook, James G. THE SEGREGATIONISTS. New York: Apple-
      ton-Century-Crofts, 1962, pp. 118-131.

      Pages cited cover operations of the KKK between 1954
      and 1960, following the Supreme Court's call for deseg-
      regation of public schools. Other violent racist groups
      are also treated.

3896. Coughlan, Robert. "Klonklave in Kokomo." THE ASPIRIN
      AGE. Edited by Isabel Leighton. New York: Simon &
      Schuster, 1949.

      Describes a rally of the Indiana KKK in the 1920s.

3897. Curry, LeRoy Amos. THE KU KLUX KLAN UNDER THE SEARCH-
      LIGHT; AN AUTHORITATIVE, DIGNIFIED AND ENLIGHTENED
      DISCUSSION OF THE AMERICAN KLAN; REVISED AND CONDENSED
      BY LEROY A. CURRY, WITH A BIOGRAPHICAL INTRODUCTION BY
      BEULAH L. CURRY; HIS WIFE; A FAIR, CANDID AND JUDICIAL
      EXPLANATION OF AMERICANISM AS ADVOCATED BY THE KU KLUX
      KLAN AND VIEWED BY AN AMERICAN CITIZEN. Kansas City,
      Mo.: Western Baptist Publishing Co., 1924.

      More title than substance in this effort to portray
      Klansmen as guardians of "100% Americanism."

3898. Damer, Eyre. WHEN THE KU KLUX RODE. New York: The Neale
      Publishing Co., 1912.

3899. Davis, Lenwood G., and Janet L. Sims-Wood. THE KU KLUX
      KLAN: A BIBLIOGRAPHY. Westport, Conn.: Greenwood
      Press, 1984.

      Lists thousands of newspaper articles dealing with the
      KKK, subdivided topically and geographically. A valuable
      resource.

3900. Davis, Susan Lawrence. AUTHENTIC HISTORY: KU KLUX KLAN,
      1865-1877. New York: American Library Service, 1924.

3901. Dent, Sanders. THE ORIGIN AND DEVELOPMENT OF THE KU
      KLUX KLAN. Durham, N.C.: Duke University, 1897.

      Treats the Reconstruction KKK with lily-white kid
      gloves, two decades prior to its revival in Georgia.

3902. Dever, Lem A. CONFESSIONS OF AN IMPERIAL KLANSMAN. Port
      land, Ore.: The Author, 1924.

      One of many "inside" looks at modern KKK chicanery.
      At the "imperial" (i.e., national) level, Klan scandals
      revolved primarily around money, its acquisition and
      unscrupulous deployment. Dever does his best to rip the
      mask off of the Klan's "law-and-order Americanism."

3903. Dixon, Edward H. THE TERRIBLE MYSTERIES OF THE KU KLUX
      KLAN. New York: The Author, 1868.

      Despite the title, Dixon finds nothing "terrible" about
      the Reconstruction KKK in this account, published three
      years before the Klan's suppression by federal troops.

3904. THE ENGLEWOOD RAIDERS; A STORY OF THE CELEBRATED KU KLUX
      CASE AT LOS ANGELES, AND SPEECHES TO THE JURY. Los
      Angeles: L.L. Bryson, 1923.

      Examines the activities of Southern California Klansmen
      brought to trial for vigilante action against aliens and
      suspected bootleggers.

3905. Evans, Hiram Wesley. THE ATTITUDE OF THE KU KLUX KLAN
      TOWARD THE JEW. Atlanta, Ga.: Ku Klux Klan, 1923.

      The Klan's Imperial Wizard airs various hackneyed
      complaints against Jews, predictably denying Klan invol-
      vement in illegal harassment of Jewish citizens.

3906. ————. THE RISING STORM; AN ANALYSIS OF THE GROWING
      CONFLICT OVER THE POLITICAL DILEMMA OF ROMAN CATHOLICS
      IN AMERICA. Atlanta, Ga.: Buckhead Publishing Co.,
      1930.

      Having dealt with Jews in item 3905 above, Evans re-
      bounds with a broadside aimed at Catholics. The alleged
      "political dilemma" is a question of "divided loyalty,"
      with Catholics theoretically torn between natural alle-
      giance to the United States and their religious duty to
      obey the Pope.

3907. Fisher, William Harvey. THE INVISIBLE EMPIRE. Metuchen,
      N.J.: Scarecrow Press, 1980.

3908. Forster, Arnold. A MEASURE OF FREEDOM. Garden City,
      N.Y.: Doubleday, 1950, pp. 15-34, 222-226.

      Pages cited cover violent KKK activity from 1945 to
      1949, prepared under the auspices of the Anti-Defamation
      League of B'nai B'rith.

3909. ————, and Benjamin Epstein. THE TROUBLEMAKERS. Garden
      City, N.Y.: Doubleday, 1952, pp. 91. 248-249, 294-296.

      Updates item 3908, through the early 1950s.

3910. Frost, Stanley. THE CHALLENGE OF THE KLAN. Indianapolis
      Bobbs-Merrill, 1924.

3911. Fry, Gladys-Marie. NIGHT RIDERS IN BLACK FOLK HISTORY.
      Knoxville, Tenn.: University of Tennessee Press, 1975.

3912. Fry, Henry Peck. THE MODERN KU KLUX KLAN. Boston: Small
      Maynard & Co., 1922.

3913. Fuller, Edgar I. MAELSTROM; THE VISIBLE OF THE INVISIBLE
      EMPIRE: A TRUE HISTORY OF THE KU KLUX KLAN. Denver:
      Maelstrom Publishing Co., 1925.

      Published at the peak of KKK power in American, Fuller's
      work highlights dissension in the upper ranks, including
      coverage of the messy litigation which exposed the inner
      workings of the group to public scrutiny.

3914. Furness, Jim. TENNESSEE'S KLAN KLEAGLE ONLY 22, BUT HAS
      HE MASS MURDER PLAN? Atlanta, Ga.: Southern Regional
      Council, 1946.

      Examines the early career of lifelong Klansman J.B.
      Stoner, then founder of the Christian Anti-Jewish Party.
      Stoner's "platform" advocated passage of legislation
      that would make "being Jewish" a capital offense.

3915. Gannon, William Henry. THE G.A.R. VS. THE KU KLUX.
      Boston: W.F. Brown & Co., 1872.

      Examines the Grand Army of the Republic's campaign
      against the Reconstruction Klan.

3916. Garner, James W. RECONSTRUCTION IN MISSISSIPPI. New
      York: Macmillan, 1901, pp. 338-353.

      Pages cited cover Klan activities in the Magnolia
      State, presented from a viewpoint favorable to the KKK.

3917. Gerlach, Larry R. BLAZING CROSSES IN ZION: THE KU KLUX
      KLAN IN UTAH. Logan, Utah: Utah State University, 1982

3918. Gillette, Paul J., and Eugene Tillinger. INSIDE KU KLUX
      KLAN. New York: Pyramid Books, 1965.

      Presents a lurid paperback account of KKK activities,
      with emphasis on violent acts described in loving detail.

3919. Goldberg, Robert Alan. HOODED EMPIRE: THE KU KLUX KLAN
      IN COLORADO. Urbana, Ill.: University of Chicago
      Press, 1981.

3920. GREAT KU KLUX TRIALS, OFFICIAL REPORT OF THE PROCEEDINGS
      BEFORE THE U.S. CIRCUIT COURT ... NOVEMBER TERM, 1871.
      Columbia, S.C.: The Columbia Union, 1872.

3921. Green, John Patterson. RECOLLECTIONS OF THE INHABITANTS,
      LOCALITIES, SUPERSTITIONS AND KU KLUX OUTRAGES OF THE
      CAROLINAS, BY A "CARPET-BAGGER" WHO WAS BORN AND LIVED
      THERE. Cleveland: The Author, 1880.

3922. Gruening, Martha. RECONSTRUCTION AND THE KU KLUX KLAN
      IN NORTH CAROLINA. New York: National Association for
      the Advancement of Colored People.

3923. Haas, Ben. K.K.K. San Diego: Regency Books, 1963.

      A short paperback overview of Klan history, published
      at the height of civil rights violence in Dixie. Better
      than some.

3924. Herbert, Hilary Abner (ed). WHY THE SOLID SOUTH? OR,
      RECONSTRUCTION AND ITS RESULTS. Baltimore: R.H. Wood-
      ward & Co., 1890, pp. 192-210.

      Pages cited view the KKK as a necessary Southern re-
      action to the "horrors" of Radical Reconstruction.

3925. Hodsden, Harry E. STEPHENSON WAS FRAMED IN A POLITICAL
      CONSPIRACY. La Porte, Ind.: La Porte Press, 1936.

      Another lame attempt to retroactively acquit Indiana
      Klansman D.C. Stephenson of rape and murder charges.

3926. Horn, Stanley F. INVISIBLE EMPIRE: THE STORY OF THE KU
      KLUX KLAN, 1866-1871. Boston: Houghton Mifflin, 1939.

      For years, considered the outstanding history of Re-
      construction Klandom, Horn's volume adheres to the tra-
      ditional Southern view of Klansmen as knights in shining
      linen, riding to the defense of a helpless Confederacy.
      Contains valuable information on the inner workings of
      the Klan, if readers can abide the slanted, racist view
      of history.

3927. HORRIBLE DISCLOSURES. A FULL AND AUTHENTIC EXPOSE OF THE
      KU-KLUX KLAN, FROM ORIGINAL DOCUMENTS OF THE ORDER, AND
      OTHER OFFICIAL SOURCES. Cincinnati: Padrick & CO., 186

3928. Hughes, Llewellyn. IN DEFENSE OF THE KLAN. New York:
      The Author, 1924.

      An enthusiastic attempt to defend the indefensible.

3929. Huie, William Bradford. THREE LIVES FOR MISSISSIPPI.
      New York: WCC Books, 1965, pp. 18-34.

      Pages cited cover the sadistic mutilation of an Alabama
      black man, circa 1957, who was randomly selected as the
      sacrificial victim in a KKK initiation ceremony.

3930. Illinois Legislative Investigating Commission. KU KLUX
      KLAN. Chicago: State of Illinois, 1976, pp. 3-26,
      39-42.

      Pages cited cover historical background on KKK activi-
      ties in Illinois, contained in a survey of latter-day
      Klan organizational efforts.

3931. Ingalls, Robert P. HOODS. New York: Putnam, 1979.

      A young reader's look at the Klan, including some in-
      formation not contained in other sources.

3932. Jackson, Kenneth T. THE KU KLUX KLAN IN THE CITY, 1915-
      1930. New York: Oxford University Press, 1967.

3933. Jarvis, Mary Woodson. THE CONDITIONS THAT LED TO THE
      KU KLUX KLANS. Raleigh, N.C.: Capital Print Co., 1902.

3934. ———. THE KU KLUX KLANS. Raleigh, N.C.: Capital
      Print Co., 1902.

3935. Johnsen, Julia E. KU KLUX KLAN. New York: H.W. Wilson,
      1923.

3936. Jones, Winfield. KNIGHTS OF THE KU KLUX KLAN. New York:
      Tocsin Publishers, 1941.

3937. ———. STORY OF THE KU KLUX KLAN. Washington, D.C.:
      American Newspaper Syndicate, 1921.

3938. Kennedy, Stetson. I RODE WITH THE KU KLUX KLAN. London:
      Arco Publishers, 1954.

      Kennedy infiltrated the KKK on behalf of civil rights
      groups, relaying information to police and journalists.
      His accounts of modern violence by the Klan are classics
      of their kind.

3939. ———. SOUTHERN EXPOSURE. Garden City, N.Y.: Doubleday,
      1946.

      Preceded item 3938, including coverage of the author's
      career as a Klansman.

3940. Kent, Grady. FLOGGED BY THE KU KLUX KLAN. Cleveland,
      Tenn.: White Wing, 1942.

3941. King, Martin Luther, Jr. STRIDE TOWARD FREEDOM. New
      York: Ballantine Books, 1958, pp. 132, 140-141, 144-148.

      Pages cited examine KKK complicity in bombings and
      other acts of violence surrounding the Montgomery, Ala.,
      bus boycott of 1955-1957.

3942. THE KU KLUX KLANS. Raleigh, N.C. Capital Publishing Co.,
      1902.

3943. Leland, John A. A VOICE FROM SOUTH CAROLINA. TWELVE
      CHAPTERS BEFORE HAMPTON. TWO CHAPTERS AFTER HAMPTON.
      WITH A JOURNAL OF A REPUTED KU KLUX, AND AN APPENDIX.
      Charleston, S.C.: Walker, Evans & Cogswell, 1879.

3944. Lester, John C., and D.L. Wilson. KU KLUX KLAN. ITS
      ORIGINS, GROWTH AND DISBANDMENT. Nashville, Tenn.:
      Wheeler, Osborn & Duckworth, 1884.

3945. Lewis, Anthony. PORTRAIT OF A DECADE. New York: Bantam,
      1965, pp. 33-37.

      Pages cited cover KKK reactions to the Supreme Court's
      school desegregation order.

3946. Likens, William M. PATRIOTISM CAPITALIZED OR RELIGION
      TURNED INTO GOLD. Uniontown, Pa.: Watchamn, 1925.

      Presents a critical view of the 1920s KKK and its
      efforts to promulgate anti-Catholicism in America.

3947. Loucks, Emerson H.   THE KU KLUX KLAN IN PENNSYLVANIA:
      A STUDY IN NATIVISM.   New York: Telegraph Press, 1936.

3948. Lowe, David.   KU KLUX KLAN: THE INVISIBLE EMPIRE.   New
      York: W.W. Norton, 1967.

3949. Lumpkin, Benjamin, and Thomas Malone.   FULL REPORT OF THE
      GREAT KU KLUX TRIAL IN THE UNITED STATES CIRCUIT COURT
      AT OXFORD, MISS.   Memphis, Tenn.: W.J. Mansford, 1871.

3950. Lytle, Andrew.   BEDFORD FORREST AND HIS CRITTER COMPANY.
      New York: McDowell, Obolensky, 1960.

      Examines the Reconstruction Klan in a less than sympa-
      thetic light.

3951. McBee, William D.   THE OKLAHOMA REVOLUTION.   Oklahoma
      City: Modern Publishers, 1956.

      Examines the "war" between Klansmen and Oklahoma's
      headstrong governor in the 1920s, leading to declaration
      of martial law and eventual impeachment of the state's
      chief executive.

3952. McCorvey, Thomas C.   "The Invisible Empire."   ALABAMA
      HISTORICAL SKETCHES.   Edited by George B. Johnson.
      Charlottesville, Va.: University of Virginia Press,
      1960.

3953. McGill, Ralph.   THE SOUTH AND THE SOUTHERNER.   Boston:
      Little, Brown, 1964, pp. 129-144.

      Pages cited cover KKK activities through the Great
      Depression, to the point of national disbandment in 1944.

3954. McLennan, Paul, and Trisha McLennan.   SOLIDARITY OR
      DIVISION: THE TRUE STORY OF THE KU KLUX KLAN VS ORGAN-
      IZED LABOR.   Atlanta, Ga.: Center for Democratic Re-
      newal, 1985.

3955. McMillen, Neil R.   THE CITIZENS' COUNCIL.   Chicago:
      University of Illinois Press, 1971, pp. 23, 47-55, 71,
      283-284.

      Pages cited cover the overlap in membership between
      "respectable" White Citizens Councils and the modern KKK.
      In spite of Council disclaimers, its members have often
      cooperated with "lower class" racists in acts of violence

3956. Mahoney, William J. SOME IDEALS OF THE KU KLUX KLAN.
       Atlanta, Ga.: Ku Klux Klan, n.d.

3957. Martin, John Bartlow. THE DEEP SOUTH SAYS "NEVER."
       New York: Ballantine Books, 1959, pp. 32, 34, 101-109,
       116-123.

       Pages cited cover violent Klan activity in defiance
       of the Supreme Court's school desegregation ruling.

3958. Marshall, Roy. THE NEGRO AND ORGANIZED LABOR. New
       York: John Wiley & Sons, 1960, pp. 190-193.

       Pages cited describe historic Klan opposition to labor
       unions in general and racially-integrated unions in par-
       ticular.

3959. Mast, Blaine. K.K.K., FRIEND OR FOE: WHICH? Pittsburgh:
       Herbick & Held Printing Co., 1924.

3960. Mecklin, John Moffat. THE KU KLUX KLAN: A STUDY OF THE
       AMERICAN MIND. New York: Harcourt, Brace & Co., 1924.

3961. ————. THE KU KLUX KLAN IN PENNSYLVANIA. New York:
       Telegraph Press, 1936.

3962. Mendelsohn, Jack. THE MARTYRS: 16 WHO GAVE THEIR LIVES
       FOR CIVIL RIGHTS. New York: Harper & Row, 1966.

       Includes frequent references to KKK activity in the
       1950s and 1960s, reviewing cases of various civil rights
       murders in Dixie. Particular attention is given to the
       odious overlap of the KKK and Southern law enforcement.

3963. Meriwether, Elizabeth. THE KU KLUX KLAN; OR, THE CARPET-
       BAGGER IN NEW ORLEANS. Memphis, Tenn.: Southern Bap-
       tist Publishing Co., 1877.

3964. Mitchell, Robert Hayes. THE NATION'S PERIL. TWELVE
       YEARS' EXPERIENCE IN THE SOUTH. THEN AND NOW. THE
       KU KLUX KLAN, A COMPLETE EXPOSITION OF THE ORDER; ITS
       PURPOSE, PLANS, OPERATIONS, SOCIAL AND POLITICAL
       SIGNIFICANCE; THE NATION'S SALVATION. New York:
       Friends of the Compiler, 1872.

3965. Minh, Ho Chi. SELECTED WORKS. Hanoi, Vietnam: Foreign
       Languages Publishing House, 1960, Vol. I, pp. 99-105.

Pages cited offer a unique perspective from a foreign
student, later revolutionary warrior and president of
North Vietnam. While studying in the United States, Ho
Chi Minh observed the 1920s KKK in action, recording his
impressions for posterity.

3966. Moffat, John. THE KU KLUX KLAN. New York: Russell &
      Russell, 1963.

3967. Montveal, Marion (pseud.). THE KLAN INSIDE OUT. Chicago:
      The Author, 1924.

3968. Moore, Powell A. THE CALUMET REGION: INDIANA'S LAST
      FRONTIER. Indianapolis: Indiana Historical Bureau,
      1959, pp. 457-470, 553-558.

      Pages cited offer a localized view of KKK activity
      in 1920s Indiana.

3969. Muse, Benjamin. TEN YEARS OF PRELUDE. New York: The
      Viking Press, 1964, pp. 41, 46, 89, 93-103, 115, 118-
      119, 196-198.

      Pages cited cover KKK activity in response to the Su-
      preme Court's ruling on school desegregation.

3970. Myers, Gustavus. HISTORY OF BIGOTRY IN THE UNITED STATES.
      New York: Capricorn Books, 1960, pp. 211-276.

      Myers's epic history of American prejudice includes
      detailed coverage of the 1920s Ku Klux Klan. The author
      emphasizes politics and propaganda over violence, but the
      Klan's terrorist activities are not neglected.

3971. National Association for the Advancement of Colored
      People. "M" IS FOR MISSISSIPPI AND MURDER. New York:
      N.A.A.C.P., 1956.

3972. Olsen, Otto H. CARPETBAGGER'S CRUSADE: THE LIFE OF
      ALBION WINEGAR TOURGEE. Baltimore: Johns Hopkins
      Press, 1965, pp. 121, 137, 147-148, 153, 159-169,
      184-187.

      Pages cited cover a Northern carpetbagger's impressions
      of the Reconstruction KKK.

3973. Randel, William Pierce. THE KU KLUX KLAN: A CENTURY OF
      INFAMY. Philadelphia: Chilton Books, 1965.

3974. Reynolds, John S. RECONSTRUCTION IN SOUTH CAROLINA, 1865-
      1877. Columbia, S.C.: State Co., 1905, pp. 179-217.

      Pages cited deal sympathetically with activities of the
      original KKK in South Carolina, circa 1868-1872.

3975. Rice, Arnold. THE KU KLUX KLAN IN AMERICAN POLITICS.
      Washington, D.C.: Public Affairs Press, 1962.

3976. Richardson, William Thomas. HISTORIC PULASKI, BIRTHPLACE
      OF THE KU KLUX KLAN, SCENE OF THE EXECUTION OF SAM
      DAVIS. Nashville, Tenn.: Methodist Publishing Co.,
      1913.

3977. Rogers, John. THE MURDERS OF MER ROUGE. St. Louis:
      Security Publishing Co., 1923.

      Examines KKK complicity in the brutal murders of two
      young men in Louisiana. Federal investigation finally
      identified the killers, but they were never tried.

3978. Romine, William Bethel. A STORY OF THE ORIGINAL KU KLUX
      KLAN, BY MR. AND MRS. W.B. ROMINE. Pulaski, Tenn.:
      The Pulaski Citizen, 1924.

3979. Rose, Laura. THE KU KLUX KLAN OR INVISIBLE EMPIRE. New
      Orleans, La.: Graham, 1914.

3980. Rose, S.E.F. THE KU KLUX KLAN. New Orleans: L. Graham,
      1914.

3981. Rubin, J. THE KU KLUX KLAN IN BINGHAMTON, NEW YORK,
      1923-1928. Binghamton, N.Y.: Broome County Historical
      Society, 1973.

3982. Sawyer, Reuben H. THE TRUTH ABOUT THE INVISIBLE EMPIRE,
      KNIGHTS OF THE KU KLUX KLAN. Portland, Ore.: 1922.

      Examines the Klan's diverse activities in Oregon,
      including a briefly-successful effort to outlaw parochial
      schools in the state.

3983. Senter, D.W.C. SPECIAL MESSAGE OF THE GOVERNOR, D.W.C.
      SENTER, IN RELATION TO MOB VIOLENCE. Nashville, Tenn.:
      Jones, Purvis & Co., 1870.

3984. Sherill, Robert. GOTHIC POLITICS IN THE DEEP SOUTH.
      New York: Grossman Publishers, 1968, pp. 42, 48, 267.

      Pages cited offer evidence linking the modern KKK with
      segregationist politicians in several Southern states.

3985. Simmons, William Joseph. THE KLAN UNMASKED. Atlanta,
      Ga.: W.F. Thompson Publishing Co., 1923.

      Sour grapes from the founding father of the modern
      KKK. Muscled out of power by Hiram Evans in 1922, the
      "original" Imperial Wizard went on to found other racist
      groups, none of which were ultimately profitable. Here,
      the outcast vents his spleen by trying to destroy his
      brainchild through exposure of the Klan's "corruption"
      under Evans.

3986. ————. AMERICA'S MENACE OR THE ENEMY WITHIN. Atlanta,
      Ga.: Patriotic Books, 1926.

      Further lamentations from the exiled Wizard. By the
      time this volume went to press, internal scandals and
      excessive violence had already doomed the 1920s KKK.

3987. Sims, Patsy. THE KLAN. New York: Stein & Day, 1978.

3988. Skaggs, William H. THE SOUTHERN OLIGARCHY. AN APPEAL IN
      BEHALF OF THE SILENT MASSES OF OUR COUNTRY AGAINST THE
      DESPOTIC RULE OF THE FEW. New York: Devin-Adair Co.,
      1924.

3989. Sletterdahl, Peter J. THE NIGHTSHIRT IN POLITICS. Min-
      neapolis: Ajax Publishing Co., 1926.

3990. Stanton, E.F. CHRIST AND OTHER KLANSMEN OR LIVES OF
      LOVE. Kansas City: Stanton & Harper, 1924.

      A twisted, if amusing presentation of KKK "Christian-
      ity." The title says it all in this preposterous attem-
      pt to whitewash KKK violence and corruption.

3991. Tannenbaum, Frank. DARKER PHASES OF THE SOUTH. New
      York: G.P. Putnam's Sons, 1924.

3992. Tennessee General Assembly. COMMITTEE ON MILITARY AF-
      FAIRS. REPORT OF EVIDENCE TAKEN BEFORE THE MILITARY
      COMMITTEE IN RELATION TO OUTRAGES COMMITTED BY THE KU
      KLUX KLAN IN MIDDLE AND WEST TENNESSEE. Nashville:
      S.C. Mercer, 1868.

3993. TESTIMONY FOR THE PROSECUTION IN THE CASE OF THE UNITED
      STATES VERSUS ROBERT HAYES MITCHELL. Cincinnati:
      Phonographic Institute, 1913.

      Reproduces transcripts from the prosecution of a Re-
      construction Klansman.

3994. Tourgee, Albion Winegar. A FOOL'S ERRAND BY ONE OF THE
      FOOLS: THE FAMOUS ROMANCE OF AMERICAN HISTORY. THE
      INVISIBLE EMPIRE; A CONCISE REVIEW OF THE EPOCH ON
      WHICH THE TALE IS BASED. New York: Fords, Howard &
      Hulbert, 1879.

      The "fool" in question was a Northern carpetbagger.
      This account relays his personal impressions of the South
      in Reconstruction, including observations on the KKK.

3995. Trelease, Allen W. WHITE TERROR: THE KU KLUX KLAN CON-
      SPIRACY AND SOUTHERN RECONSTRUCTION. Westport, Conn.:
      Greenwood Press, 1971.

      The best existing history of Reconstruction KKK acti-
      vity. Trelease breaks new ground by rejecting the tra-
      ditional view of Klansmen as "saviors" of the South,
      objectively reporting their activities as what they
      really were: a native American terrorist rampage.

3996. Tyler, Charles Walter. THE K.K.K. New York: Abbey
      Press, 1902.

3997. United States Congress. JOINT SELECT COMMITTEE TO IN-
      QUIRE INTO THE CONDITION OF AFFAIRS IN THE LATE IN-
      SURRECTIONARY STATES. 13 Vols. Washington, D.C.:
      Government Printing Office, 1872.

      Collects testimony from numerous witnesses, describing
      KKK activities in Reconstruction. Ironically, the epic
      investigation followed enactment of federal anti-Klan
      legislation, rather than preceding same. In any case,
      the hearing transcripts stand as a definitive record
      of KKK terrorism in the period.

3998. United States Congress. House of Representatives.
      THE KU KLUX KLAN. HEARINGS BEFORE THE COMMITTEE ON
      RULES, HOUSE OF REPRESENTATIVES, 67th CONGRESS, 1st
      SESSION. Washington, D.C.: Government Printing
      Office, 1921.

A rather different Congressional probe, launched in 1921, as a response to media reports of rampant Klan violence. Wizard William Simmons won investigators over with his plea of good intentions, and the modern KKK received a clean bill of health from legislators more concerned with Eastern European immigration.

3999. United States Congress. Senate. HEARINGS BEFORE SUBCOMMITTEE ON PRIVILEGES AND ELECTIONS, UNITED STATES SENATE, 68th CONGRESS, 1st SESSION, PURSUANT TO S. RES. 97 AUTHORIZING THE INVESTIGATION OF ALLEGED UNLAWFUL PRACTICES IN THE ELECTION OF A SENATOR FROM TEXAS. MAY 8, 9, 12, 13, 14, AND 16, 1924. Washington, D.C.: Government Printing Office, 1924.

4000. ────. REPORT ON THE ALLEGED OUTRAGES IN THE SOUTHERN STATES, BY THE SELECT COMMITTEE OF THE SENATE, MARCH 10, 1871. Washington, D.C.: Government Printing Office, 1871.

4001. Wade, Wyn Craig. THE FIERY CROSS: THE KU KLUX KLAN IN AMERICA. New York: Simon & Schuster, 1987.

The best Klan history since item 3889 above. Incorporates recent evidence linking Klansmen with unsolved crimes dating from 1951, while bringing the organization's history immediately up to date.

4002. Weaver, Charles C. A KU KLUX KLAN RAID, AND WHAT BECAME OF IT. Durham, N.C.: The Author, 1897.

4003. Wells, James M. THE CHISOLM MASSACRE: A PICTURE OF HOME-RULE IN MISSISSIPPI. Washington, D.C.: Chisolm Monument Assn., 1878.

Examines the Klan assassination of Sheriff W.W. Chisolm, who attempted to suppress white terrorism in Kemper County, Mississippi, during Reconstruction.

4004. Whalen, William J. HANDBOOK OF SECRET ORGANIZATIONS. Milwaukee: Bruce Publishing Co., 1966, pp. 90-99.

Pages cited offer a capsule history of the KKK, in a volume also treating such diverse groups as the Masonic lodge and the Indian Thugee.

4005. White, Alma. HEROES OF THE FIERY CROSS. Zerephath, N.J.:
      Good Citizen, 1928.

      Another effort to paint Klansmen as heroic figures in
      the 1920s. By the date of publication, it was a futile
      effort, with membership already fading in the face of
      publicized corruption, violence, and scandals linking
      leaders of the KKK with immoral activities.

4006. ————. KLANSMEN: GUARDIANS OF LIBERTY. Zerephath, N.J.:
      Good Citizen, 1926.

4007. ————. THE KU KLUX KLAN IN PROPHECY. Zerephath, N.J.:
      Good Citizen, 1925.

      Attempts to dredge up Biblical sanctions for modern-
      day nightriders, demonstrating once again that scripture,
      properly interpreted, offers something for everyone.

4008. White, William Allen. "Criticism of the Ku Klux Klan."
      SELECTED LETTERS OF WILLIAM ALLEN WHITE, 1899-1943.
      Edited by Walter Johnson. New York: Henry Holt & Co.,
      1947, pp. 220-221.

      Pages cited reproduce anti-Klan correspondence from the
      KKK's leading political opponent in Kansas.

4009. Williams, Randall (ed). THE KU KLUX KLAN; A HISTORY OF
      RACISM AND VIOLENCE. Montgomery, Ala.: Klanwatch,
      1986.

4010. Winter, Paul. WHAT PRICE TOLERANCE. New York: All
      American Book, Lecture & Research Bureau, 1928.

4011. Witcher, Walter C. THE REIGN OF TERROR IN OKLAHOMA, A
      DETAILED ACCOUNT OF THE KLAN'S BARBAROUS PRACTICES
      AND BRUTAL OUTRAGES AGAINST INDIVIDUALS; ITS CONTROL
      OVER JUDGES AND JURIES AND GOVERNOR WALTON'S HEROIC
      FIGHT, INCLUDING A GENERAL EXPOSURE OF KLAN SECRETS,
      SHAM AND HYPOCRISY. Ft. Worth, Tex.: W.C. Witcher,
      1923.

4012. Wright, Walter C. RELIGIOUS AND PATRIOTIC ORDER OF THE
      KU KLUX KLAN. Waco, Tex.: The Author, 1926.

      A lame, self-published bid to justify the Klan's ex-
      istence in terms of scripture and national necessity.

b. Articles

4013. Abbey, Sue W. "The Ku Klux Klan in Arizona, 1921-1925." JOURNAL OF ARIZONA HISTORY 14 (Spring 1973): 10-30.

4014. "Again, the Klan." TIME 47 (May 20, 1946): 20.

Examines the post-World War II rebirth of the KKK.

4015. Aikman, Duncan. "Prairie Fire." AMERICAN MERCURY 6 (October 1925): 209-214.

Examines KKK activities in the American Midwest.

4016. ————. "Savonarola in Los Angeles." AMERICAN MERCURY 21 (December 1930): 423-430.

Reports KKK activities in Southern California.

4017. "Alabama Aroused." OUTLOOK 147 (November 2, 1927): 261.

4018. "Alabama's Floggers." LITERARY DIGEST 95 (October 29, 1927): 11-12.

4019. Alexander, Charles C. "Defeat, Decline, Disintegration: The Ku Klux Klan in Arkansas, 1924 and After." ARKANSAS HISTORICAL QUARTERLY 22 (Winter 1963): 310-331.

4020. ————. "Kleagles and Cash: The Ku Klux Klan as a Business Organization, 1915-1930." BUSINESS HISTORY REVIEW 39 (Autumn 1965): 348-367.

4021. ————. "Secrecy Bids for Power: The Ku Klux Klan in Texas Politics in the 1920s." MID-AMERICA 46 (January 1964): 3-28.

4022. ————. "White Robed Reformers: The Ku Klux Klan in Arkansas, 1921-1922." ARKANSAS HISTORICAL QUARTERLY 22 (Spring 1963): 8-23.

4023. ————. "White Robes in Politics: The Ku Klux Klan in Arkansas, 1922-1924." ARKANSAS HISTORICAL QUARTERLY 22 (Fall 1963): 195-214.

4024. Alexander, T.B. "Ku Kluxism in Tennessee, 1865-1869: A Technique for the Overthrow of Radical Reconstruction." TENNESSEE HISTORICAL QUARTERLY 8 (September 1949): 195-219.

4025. Allen, Devere. "Substitutes for Brotherhood." THE WORLD
      TOMORROW 7 (March 1924): 74-76.

      Discusses the growth of the 1920s KKK.

4026. Allen Frederick L. "KKK." LITERARY DIGEST 124 (October
      9, 1937): 15-17.

4027. Allen, Lee N. "The Democratic Presidential Primary Elec-
      tion of 1924 in Texas." SOUTHWESTERN HISTORICAL QUAR-
      TERLY 61 (April 1958): 474-493.

4028. ————. "The McAdoo Campaign for the Presidential Nom-
      ination in 1924." JOURNAL OF SOUTHERN HISTORY 29 (May
      1963): 211-228.

      Includes discussion of KKK support for McAdoo.

4029. Allen, Ward. "A Note on the Origin of the Ku Klux Klan."
      TENNESSEE HISTORICAL QUARTERLY 23 (June 1964): 182.

4030. "Alma Mater, K.K.K." NEW REPUBLIC 36 (September 5, 1923):
      35-36.

      Examines the Klan's effort to establish its own univer-
      sity in Indiana.

4031. "And These Are the Children of God." COLLIER'S 124 (Aug-
      ust 6, 1949): 74.

      Examines a new outbreak of KKK violence in the South.

4032. Arnall, Ellis. "My Battle Against the Klan." CORONET
      20 (October 1946): 3-8.

      Georgia's governor describes his efforts to dismantle
      the KKK after World War II.

4033. "Arnall Moves to Dissolve Klan." CHRISTIAN CENTURY 63
      (July 3, 1946): 829.

4034. Arnold, S.G. "Conspiracy of the Ku-Klux." METHODIST
      QUARTERLY 33: 89.

      Reviews activities of the Reconstruction KKK.

4035. "Attorney General Daugherty and the Ku Klux Klan." THE
      MESSENGER 4 (October 1922): 498.

4036. "Backfire; South Carolina's Myrtle Beach." TIME 56 (September 11, 1950): 26-27.

Examines the aftermath of a KKK shooting incident.

4037. "Bad Medicine for the Klan; Robeson County, N.C." LIFE 44 (January 27, 1958): 26-28.

Lumbee Indians take the warpath against Klansmen seeking to further segregate their tribe from local whites.

4038. Bagnall, Robert W. "The Spirit of the Ku Klux Klan." OPPORTUNITY 1 (September 1923): 265-267.

4039. Barrett, G. "Montgomery Testing Ground." NEW YORK TIMES MAGAZINE (December 16, 1956): 8-9+.

Examines KKK violence in response to the Montgomery bus desegregation campaign.

4040. Beckett, R.C. "Some Effects of Military Reconstruction in Monroe County, Mississippi." PUBLICATIONS OF THE MISSISSIPPI HISTORICAL SOCIETY 8 (1904): 177-186.

4041. Bell, Edward P. "Israel Zangwill on the Ku Klux Klan." LANDMARK 6 (June 1924): 414-418.

4042. Belman, I. "Alabama Rips Off the Hood." CHRISTIAN SCIENCE MONITOR MAGAZINE (July 2, 1949): 3.

Reports passage of an anti-mask law in Alabama.

4043. Benet, William R. "Fan Mail." SATURDAY REVIEW OF LITERATURE 32 (January 1, 1949): 32-33.

Examined post-war KKK activities in Georgia.

4044. ———. "Phoenix Nest." SATURDAY REVIEW OF LITERATURE 32 (January 1, 1949): 32.

4045. Bennett, Carl D. "Methodists Not Alone in Georgia." CHRISTIAN CENTURY 66 (January 26, 1949): 114-115.

Describes KKK interaction with established churches in Georgia after World War II.

4046. ———. "Ministers Denounce Georgia Klan; Reply." CHRISTIAN CENTURY 66 (January 26, 1949): 114.

4047. Bentley, Max. "The Ku Klux Klan in Indiana." McCLURE'S MAGAZINE 56 (May 1925): 23-25.

4048. ————. "Let's Brush Them Aside; How One Man Preached the Gospel of Fairness to All." COLLIER'S 74 (November 22, 1924): 21.

4049. ————. "Texan Challenges the Klan." COLLIER'S 72 (November 3, 1923): 12.

4050. Berman, Daniel M. "Hugo L. Black: The Early Years." CATHOLIC UNIVERSITY OF AMERICAN LAW REVIEW 8 (May 1959): 103-116.

    Examines the background of an Alabama Klansman nominated to sit on the United States Supreme Court.

4051. Betten, Neil. "Nativism and the Klan in Town and City: Valparaiso and Gary, Indiana." STUDIES IN HISTORY AND SOCIETY 4 (Spring 1973): 3-16.

4052. "Black: A Klan Member on the Supreme Court? New Evidence Comes to Light." NEWSWEEK 10 (September 20, 1937): 9-12.

4053. Blake, Aldrich. "Oklahoma's Klan-Fighting Governor." NATION 117 (October 3, 1923): 353.

4054. Blankenship, Gary R. "The Commercial Appeal's Attack on the Ku Klux Klan, 1921-1925." WEST TENNESSEE HISTORICAL SOCIETY PAPERS 31 (1977): 44-58.

4055. Bliven, B. "From the Oklahoma Front." NEW REPUBLIC 36 (October 17, 1923): 202-205.

4056. Bohn, Frank. "The Ku Klux Klan Interpreted." AMERICAN JOURNAL OF SOCIOLOGY 30 (January 1925): 385-407.

4057. Boyd, T. "Defying the Klan; Julian Harris and the Enquirer-Sun." FORUM 76 (July 1926): 48-56.

    A Southern newspaper editor stands against KKK threats and intimidation to report local violence by the Klan.

4058. Braden, George. "The Ku Klux Klan: An Apology." SOUTHERN BIVOUAC 4 (September 1885): 103-109.

4059. Bradley, P. "Psycho-Analyzing the Ku Klux Klan." AMER-
      ICAN REVIEW 2 (November-December 1924): 683-686.

4060. Braxton, Lee. "They Spoke Out for Democracy." ROTARIAN
      83 (September 1953): 29, 55-56.

      Reviews KKK attempts to silence hostile newspapers in
      North Carolina.

4061. Brier, Royce. "Nightshirt Knights." FORUM 106 (July
      1946): 54-55.

4062. "Broken Monopoly." TIME 55 (March 20, 1950): 20.

      Examines rifts within the post-war KKK.

4063. Broun, Heywood. "Up Pops the Wizard." NEW REPUBLIC 99
      (June 21, 1939): 186-187.

4064. Brown, William Garrott. "The Ku Klux Movement." ATLAN-
      TIC MONTHLY 87 (May 1901): 634-644.

4065. Brownell, Blaine. "Birmingham, Alabama: New South City
      in the 1920s." JOURNAL OF SOUTHERN HISTORY 38 (Febru-
      ary 1972): 21-48.

4066. Buckner, George W., Jr. "Probe a Rebirth of Hoosier
      Klan." CHRISTIAN CENTURY 63 (November 27, 1946): 1446.

4067. Budenz, Louis Francis. "There's Mud on Indiana's White
      Robes." NATION 125 (July 27, 1927): 81-82.

4068. Burbank, Garin. "Agrarian Rebels and Their Opponents:
      Political Conflict in Southern Oklahoma, 1910-1924."
      JOURNAL OF AMERICAN HISTORY 58 (June 1971): 5-23.

4069. Callaway, E.E. "Notes on a Kleagle." AMERICAN MERCURY
      43 (February 1938): 248-249.

4070. "Can the Ku Klux Klan Survive in Oklahoma?" HARLOW'S
      WEEKLY 23 (September 6, 1924): 6-7.

4071. "Canada's Keep-Out to Klanism." LITERARY DIGEST 76
      (February 3, 1923): 20-21.

4072. "Carter and the KKK." NEW REPUBLIC 136 (February 4,
      1957): 6.

Examines violent activities by Klansmen in and around Birmingham, Ala.

4073. Carter, Elmer A. "The Ku Klux Klan Marches Again." OPPORTUNITY 17 (June 1939): 163.

Covers depression-era KKK activities in Florida.

4074. Carter, L. Edward. "Rise and Fall of the Invisible Empre: Knights of the Ku Klux Klan." GREAT PLAINS JOURNAL 16 (1977): 82-106.

4075. "Casting Out the Klan." INDEPENDENT 113 (September 13, 1924): 141.

4076. Catt, C.C. "Three Super States." WOMAN CITIZEN 9 (October 18, 1924): 10-11.

Covers KKK political activities in the 1920s.

4077. "Caucasian Crusade." OUTLOOK 155 (August 6, 1930): 539.

4078. Chalmers, David M. "The Ku Klux Klan in Politics in the 1920s." MISSISSIPPI QUARTERLY 18 (1964): 234-247.

4079. ————. "The Ku Klux Klan in the Sunshine State." FLORIDA HISTORICAL QUARTERLY 43 (1964): 209-215.

4080. Chomel, M. "The Klan Issue in Indiana." AMERICA 32 (October 25, 1924): 31-32.

4081. "Clash in the Klan." LITERARY DIGEST 77 (April 21, 1923): 13.

Reviews the successful efforts of Hiram Evans to replace William Simmons as Imperial Wizard of the KKK.

4082. Cline, Leonard L. "In Darkest Louisiana." NATION 116 (March 14, 1293): 292-293.

4083. Coleman, Louis. "The Klan Revives." NATION 139 (July 4, 1934): 20.

Examines the depression-era KKK in Alabama.

4084. Collins, Frederick L. "Way Down East with the Ku Klux Klan." COLLIER'S 72 (December 15, 1293): 12, 29.

Examines KKK activity in Maine.

4085. "Colonel Simmons and $146,000, from K.K.K. to K.F.S."
LITERARY DIGEST 80 (March 8, 1924): 36-40.

Following his ouster by Hiram Evans, Simmons organizes
a competing organization to vie for Klan members and
dollars.

4086. Commager, Henry Steele. "Does the Klan Ride to Its
Death?" SCHOLASTIC 49 (October 7, 1946): 7.

4087. "Confirmation from a Strange Source." AMERICAN FEDERA-
TIONIST 29 (December 1922): 905-906.

Examines KKK activities in Kansas during the 1920s.

4088. Conroy, Thomas M. "The Ku Klux Klan and the American
Clergy." ECCLESIASTICAL REVIEW 70 (1924): 49.

4089. "Constitution Week in Oklahoma." LITERARY DIGEST 79
(October 13, 1923): 12-13.

4090. "Crackdown on the Klan." TIME 59 (February 25, 1952):
28.

Examines federal prosecution of Klansmen in the Carolinas.

4091. Craven, Charles. "The Robeson County Indian Uprising
Against the KKK." SOUTH ATLANTIC QUARTERLY 57 (Autumn
1958): 433-442.

4092. Cripps, Thomas R. "The Reaction of the Negro to the
Motion Picture 'Birth of a Nation.'" THE HISTORIAN
25 (May 1963): 347,

4093. "Crosses of Fire." NEWSWEEK 27 (April 8, 1946): 21-22.

4094. Crosson, David. "What's the Risk? Controversial Exhibits
Challenge the Romantic Past." HISTORY NEWS 36 (April
1981): 17-19.

Examines the 1920s KKK in Indiana.

4095. Crowell, C.T. "Collapse of Constitutional Government."
INDEPENDENT 109 (December 9, 1922): 333-334; 110 (January 6, 1923): 8-9.

4096. Crowther, Bosley. "The Birth of 'The Birth of a Nation.'"
       NEW YORK TIMES MAGAZINE 116 (February 7, 1965): 85.

4097. Daniel, Mike. "The Arrest and Trial of Ryland Randolph:
       April-May, 1868." ALABAMA HISTORICAL QUARTERLY 40
       (1978): 127-143.

       Reviews the prosecution of Reconstruction's ranking
       Alabama Klansman.

4098. Davis, James H. "Colorado Under the Klan." COLORADO
       MAGAZINE 42 (Spring 1965): 93-108.

4099. "A Defense of the Ku Klux Klan." LITERARY DIGEST 76
       (January 20, 1923): 18-19.

4100. Degler, Carl N. "A Century of the Klan:A Review Article."
       JOURNAL OF SOUTHERN HISTORY 31 (November 1965): 435-
       443.

4101. "Democracy or Invisible Empire?" CURRENT OPINION 75
       (November 1923): 521-523.

4102. De Silver, Albert. "The Ku Klux Klan: 'Soul of Chival-
       ry'." NATION 113 (September 14, 1921): 285-286.

4103. Desmond, Shaw. "K.K.K.: The Strongest Secret Society
       on Earth." WIDE WORLD MAGAZINE 47 (September 1921):
       355-365.

4104. Devine, E.T. "Klan in Texas." SURVEY 48 (April 1, 1922):
       10-11; 48 (April 8, 1922): 42-43; 48 (May 13, 1922):
       251-253.

4105. "Disrobing the Klan." NEW REPUBLIC 126 (May 26, 1952):
       6.

       Examines the anti-mask laws aimed at the KKK.

4106. "Divisible Invisible Empire." NEWSWEEK 32 (July 19,
       1948): 20.

4107. Doherty, Herbert J., Jr. "Florida and the Presidential
       Election of 1928." FLORIDA HISTORICAL QUARTERLY 26
       (October 1947): 174-186.

4108. Douglas, Lloyd C. "The Patriotism of Hatred." CHRIS-
       TIAN CENTURY 40 (October 25, 1923): 1371-1374.

4109. Douglas, W.A.S. "Ku Klux." AMERICAN MERCURY 13 (March
      1928): 272-279.

4110. Du Bois, W.E.B. "Fighting Race Calumny." THE CRISIS 10
      (May 1915): 40.

      Presents a scathing review of the motion picture "Birth
      of a Nation," which contributed directly to the KKK re-
      vival in 1915.

4111. ———. "Savings of Black Georgia." OUTLOOK 69 (Septem-
      ber 14, 1901): 128-130.

      Reviews black history in Georgia, including coverage
      of the Reconstruction KKK.

4112. ———. "The Shape of Fear." NORTH AMERICAN 223 (June
      1926): 291-304.

      Chronicles KKK violence in Louisiana during the 1920s.

4113. ———. "The Slanderous Film." THE CRISIS 10 (December
      1915): 76-77.

      Continues the attack on "Birth of a Nation."

4114. Duffus, Robert L. "Ancestry and End of the Ku Klux Klan."
      WORLD'S WORK 46 (September 1923): 527-536.

4115. ———. "Counter-mining the Ku Klux Klan." WORLD'S
      WORK 46 (July 1923): 275-284.

4116. ———. "The Ku Klux Klan in the Middle West." WORLD'S
      WORK 46 (August 1923): 367-373.

4117. ———. "Salesmen of Hate." WORLD'S WORK 46 (October
      1923): 461-469.

4118. Dunning, Frederick A. "Ku Klux Fulfills the Scripture."
      CHRISTIAN CENTURY 41 (September 18, 1924): 1205-1207.

4119. "1871: Visitor from Hell; Excerpts from Congressional
      Hearings on the KKK." SOUTHERN EXPOSURE 8 (Summer
      1980): 62-63.

4120. "Election Eve in Georgia." NEW REPUBLIC 32 (September
      6, 1948): 10.

Examines KKK intimidation of blacks in the gubernatorial race of 1948.

4121. "Episcopalians Assail Ku Klux." THE MESSENGER 4 (October 1922): 497-498.

4122. Evans, Hiram Wesley. "Ballots Behind the Ku Klux Klan." WORLD'S WORK 55 (January 1928): 243-252.

4123. ———. "The Catholic Question as Viewed by the Ku Klux Klan." CURRENT HISTORY 26 (July 1927): 563-568.

4124. ———. "The Klan: Defender of Americanism." FORUM 74 (December 1925): 801-814.

4125. ———. "The Klan's Fight for Americanism." NORTH AMERICAN 223 (March 1926): 33-63.

4126. Evans, Margaret. "Like a Thief." NEW REPUBLIC 28 (August 31, 1921): 16-17.

4127. "Even the Klan Has Rights." NATION 115 (December 13, 1922): 654.

4128. Feidelson, Charles N. "Alabama's Super Government." NATION 125 (September 28, 1927): 311-312.

4129. "Fight for Freedom of the Press." LITERARY DIGEST 90 (August 14, 1926): 9-10.

Examines KKK efforts to censor local newspapers in Indiana.

4130. Fleming, Walter Lynwood. "A Ku Klux Document." MISSISSIPPI VALLEY HISTORICAL REVIEW 1 (March 1915): 575-578.

Examines historical documents of the Reconstruction KKK in Louisiana.

4131. ———. "The Ku Klux Testimony Relating to Alabama." GULF STATES HISTORICAL MAGAZINE (November 1903).

4132. ———. "Prescript of the Ku Klux Klan." PUBLICATIONS OF THE SOUTHERN HISTORY ASSOCIATION 7 (September 1903): 327-348.

4133. "A Flogging for the Klan." TIME 60 (August 11, 1952):
       21.

       Reports KKK violence in North Carolina in the 1950s.

4134. Foley, Albert S. "KKK in Mobile, Ala." AMERICA 96
       (December 8, 1956): 298-299.

4135. "For and Against the Ku Klux Klan." LITERARY DIGEST 70
       (September 28, 1921): 34, 36, 38, 40.

4136. Frank, Glenn. "Christianity and Racialism." CENTURY 109
       (December 1924): 279.

4137. Franklin, John Hope. "'The Birth of a Nation'—Propagan-
       da as History." MASSACHUSETTS REVIEW 30 (1979): 433.

4138. "From the Kredd of Klanishness." THE WORLD TOMORROW 7
       (March 1924): 76-77.

4139. Frost, Stanley G. "Behind the White Hoods: The Regen-
       eration of Oklahoma." OUTLOOK 135 (November 21, 1923):
       492-494.

4140. ————. "The Klan, the King, and a Revolution: The Re-
       generation of Oklahoma." OUTLOOK 135 (November 28,
       1923): 530-531.

4141. ————. "The Klan Restates Its Case." OUTLOOK 138 (Oc-
       tober 15, 1924): 244-245.

4142. ————. "The Klan Shows Its Hand in Indiana." OUTLOOK
       137 (June 4, 1924): 187-190.

4143. ————. "Klan's ½ of 1 Percent Victory." OUTLOOK 137
       (July 9, 1924): 384-387.

       Describes KKK participation in the chaotic Democratic
       presidential nominating convention of 1924.

4144. ————. "Masked Politics of the Klan." WORLD'S WORK
       55 (February 1928): 399, 407.

4145. ————. "Night-Riding Reformers: The Regeneration of
       Oklahoma." OUTLOOK 135 (November 14, 1923): 438-440.

4146. ————. "The Oklahoma Regicides Act." OUTLOOK 135
       (November 7, 1923): 395-396.

4147. ———. "When the Klan Rules." OUTLOOK 135 (December
      19, 1923): 674-676, 716-718; 136 (February 27, 1924):
      20-24, 64-66, 100-103, 144-147. 183-186, 217-219, 261-
      264, 308-311, 350-353.

4148. Gardner, Virginia. "Klansmen Crusade for Dewey." NEW
      MASSES 53 (October 31, 1944).

4149. Godkin, E.L. "Bill to Repress the Ku Klux." NATION 12:
      284.

      Examines federal efforts to control the Reconstruction
KKK.

4150. ———. "Reign of the Ku Klux at the South." NATION
      12: 192, 212.

4151. Gohdges, Clarence. "The Ku Klux Klan and the Classics."
      GEORGIA REVIEW 7 (Spring 1953): 18-24.

4152. Goldberg, Robert A. "Beneath the Hood and Robe: A So-
      cioeconomic Analysis of Ku Klux Klan Membership in
      Denver, Colorado, 1921-1925." WESTERN HISTORICAL
      QUARTERLY 11 (April 1980): 181-198.

4153. ———. "The Ku Klux Klan in Madison, 1922-1927."
      WISCONSIN MAGAZINE OF HISTORY 58 (Autumn 1974): 31, 44.

4154. Goldenweiser, Alexander. "Prehistoric K.K.K." THE WORLD
      TOMORROW 7 (March 1924): 81-82.

4155. Grant, George S. "Garveyism and the Ku Klux Klan."
      THE MESSENGER 5 (October 1923): 835-836, 842.

      Examines KKK support for Marcus Garvey's "Back to
Africa" movement among black nationalists.

4156. Greene, Ward. "Notes for a History of the Klan." AMER-
      ICAN MERCURY 5 (June 1925): 240-243.

4157. Griffith, Charles B., and Donald W. Stewart. "Has a
      Court of Equity Power to Enjoin Parading by the Ku
      Klux Klan in Mask?" CENTRAL LAW JOURNAL 96 (November
      20, 1923): 384-393.

4158. Hall, Grover C. "We Southerners." SCRIBNER'S MAGAZINE
      83 (January 1928): 82-88.

4159. Harlow, Victor E. "The Achievement of the Klan." HAR-
      LOW'S WEEKLY 23 (June 19, 1924): 1.

4160. ————. "A New Place for the Klan." HARLOW'S WEEKLY 23
      (December 6, 1924): 1.

      Continues coverage of the Klan wars in Oklahoma.

4161. Harris, A.I. "Klan on Trial." NEW REPUBLIC 35 (June 13,
      1923): 67-69.

4162. Harrison, Morton. "Gentlemen from Indiana." ATLANTIC
      141 (May 1928): 676-686.

4163. Hartt, Rollin L. "The New Negro." INDEPENDENT 105 (Jan-
      uary 15, 1921): 59-60.

4164. Haskell, H.J. "Martial Law in Oklahoma." OUTLOOK 135
      (September 26, 1923): 133.

4165. Haynes, George E., and Horace J. Wolf. "How Shall We
      Meet the Klan?" THE WORLD TOMORROW 7 (March 1924):
      85-86.

4166. Herring, Hubert C. "Ku Klux to the Rescue." NEW REPUB-
      LIC 34 (May 23, 1293): 341-342.

4167. Herring, Mary W. "The Why of the Ku Klux." NEW REPUBLIC
      33 (February 7, 1923): 289.

4168. "The History of the Ku Klux Klan: Rule by Terror."
      AMERICAN HISTORY ILLUSTRATED 14 (January 1980): 8-15.

4169. Hoffman, Edwin D. "The Genesis of the Modern Movement
      for Equal Rights in South Carolina, 1930-1939." JOUR-
      NAL OF NEGRO HISTORY 44 (October 1959): 346-369.

4170. "Hold Everything." TIME 54 (July 25, 1949): 12.

      Examines post-war KKK activity in Alabama.

4171. Holsinger, M. Paul. "The Oregon School Controversy,
      1922-25." PACIFIC HISTORICAL REVIEW 37 (August 1968):
      341.

      Reviews the KKK's drive to outlaw parochial schools
      in Oregon during the 1920s. The Klan-sponsored law
      was ultimately declared unconstitutional.

4172. "The Hooded Knights Revive Rule by Terror in the 'Twen-
      ties'." AMERICAN HISTORY ILLUSTRATED 14 (February
      1980): 28-36.

4173. "Hoods Down in Claxton." NEWSWEEK 35 (April 17, 1950):
      67.

      Reports legal efforts to unmask the Georgia Klan.

4174. Howe, Elizabeth M. "Ku Klux Uniform." BUFFALO HISTOR-
      ICAL SOCIETY PUBLICATIONS 25 (1921): 9-41.

4175. Hull, Robert. "The Klan Aftermath in Indiana." AMERICA
      38 (October 15, 1927): 8.

4176. "The Imperial Emperor of the KKK Meets the Press." AMER-
      ICAN MERCURY 69 (November 1949): 529-538.

      Self-proclaimed KKK "Emperor" Lycurgus Spinks makes an
      ass of himself on national radio, severely damaging
      Klan prestige.

4177. "Imperial Lawlessness." OUTLOOK 129 (September 14, 1921):
      46.

      Examines the prosecution of ranking Klan organizers on
      morals charges.

4178. "Imperial Wizard and His Klan." LITERARY DIGEST 68 (Feb-
      ruary 5, 1921): 40-46.

4179. "Indians Back at Peace and the Klan at Bay." LIFE 44
      (February 3, 1958): 36-36A.

4180. "Indians Rout the Klan." COMMONWEAL 67 (January 31,
      1958): 446.

4181. Ingalls, Robert. "1935: The Murder of Joseph Shoemaker."
      SOUTHERN EXPOSURE 8 (Summer 1980): 64-68.

      Recaps the KKK torture-slaying of a CIO organizer in
      Florida.

4182. "Initiating a Negro into the Ku Klux Klan." MESSENGER
      5 (January 1923): 562-563.

      Recounts a curious incident with the Louisiana KKK of
      the early 1920s.

4183. "Interesting Facts About the Ku Klux Klan." THE MESSEN-
      GER 3 (March 1921): 194-195.

4184. "Intolerance in Oregon." SURVEY 49 (October 15, 1922):
      76-77.

4185. "Invisible Empire in the Spotlight." CURRENT OPINION 71
      (November 1921): 561-564.

4186. "Invisible Government." OUTLOOK 132 (December 13, 1922):
      643.

4187. Irwin, Theodore. "The Klan Kicks Up Again." AMERICAN
      MERCURY 50 (August 1940): 470-476.

4188. "Is the Ku Klux Klan Returning?" THE MESSENGER 4 (Feb-
      ruary 1922): 356-357.

4189. "Is the Ku Klux Klan Un-American; Pro and Con, Mostly
      Con!" FORUM 75 (February 1926): 305-308.

4190. "It Sure Was Pretty." TIME 54 (November 7, 1949): 24.

      Examines post-war KKK activity in Alabama. The title
      refers to a cross-burning at the home of a woman charged
      with "immoral" activities in Birmingham.

4191. "Jack, the Klan-Fighter in Oklahoma." LITERARY DIGEST
      79 (October 20, 1923): 38, 40, 42.

4192. Jackson, Charles O. "William J. Simmons: A Career in Ku
      Kluxism." GEORGIA HISTORICAL QUARTERLY 50 (December
      1966): 351-365.

4193. Jenkins, William D. "The Ku Klux Klan in Youngstown,
      Ohio: Moral Reform in the Twenties." HISTORIAN 41
      (1978): 80-87.

4194. Johnsen, J.E. "Ku Klux Klan." REFERENCE SHELF 1 (May
      1923): 1-105.

4195. Johnson, Gerald W. "The Battling South." SCRIBNER'S
      MAGAZINE (March 1926): 302-307.

4196. ———. "The Ku-Kluxer." AMERICAN MERCURY 1 (February
      1924): 207-211.

4197. Johnson, Guy B. "The Race Philosophy of the Ku Klux
        Klan." OPPORTUNITY 1 (September 9123): 268-270.

4198. ————. "A Sociological Interpretation of the New Ku
        Klux Movement." SOCIAL FORCES 1 (March 1923): 440-444.

4199. Johnson, Tom. "Dixie Jew." NEW MASSES 12 (July 24,
        1934): 21-22.

4200. Johnston, Frank, Jr. "Religious and Racial Prejudice
        in the United States." CURRENT HISTORY 20 (July 1924):
        573-578.

4201. "Joke That Became a Terror." ILLUSTRATED WORLD 33 (March
        1920): 110.

        Traces KKK history from 1865 to 1920.

4202. Jones, J.R. "Memories of Danbury." KATALLAGATE 3-4
        (Winter/Spring 1972): 26-27.

        Reviews activities of the 1920s KKK in Connecticut.

4203. Jones, Lila L. "The Ku Klux Klan in Eastern Kansas
        During the 1290s." EMPORIA STATE RESEARCH STUDIES 23
        (Winter 1975): 5-41.

4204. Jones, Paul. "The Ku Klux Goes Calling." NEW REPUBLIC
        85 (January 8, 1936): 251.

4205. ————. "What Brotherhood Demands." THE WORLD TOMORROW
        7 (March 1924): 82-83.

4206. "Judicial Spanking for the Klan." LITERARY DIGEST 97
        (April 28, 1928): 8-9.

4207. "'Justice' by Violence." THE WORLD TOMORROW 7 (March
        1924): 78-79.

4208. Keith, Adam. "K.K.K. ... Klose Kall in Kolorado."
        DENVER 1 (August 1965): 24-27.

4209. Kennedy, Stetson. "KKK vs. Labor: A Sampler." SOUTHERN
        EXPOSURE 8 (Summer 1980): 61.

4210. ————. "Klan Invades Southern Unions, Gets a Strangle-
        hold on Some." DAILY COMPASS (February 1950): 1.

4211. ————. "The Ku Klux Klan in America." NEW REPUBLIC 114 (July 1, 1946): 928-930.

4212. ————. "Murder Without Indictment." NATION 173 (November 24, 1951): 444-446.

Examines KKK violence in Florida.

4213. ————. "Who Cares Who Killed Harry T. Moore?" THE CRISIS 89 (May 1982): 18-21.

Reports KKK complicity in the 1951 assassination of a Florida civil rights leader.

4214. Kent, Frank R. "Ku Klux Klan in America." SPECTATOR 130 (February 17, 1923): 279-280.

4215. Keressy, John McPike. "How Shall We Meet the Klan?" THE WORLD TOMORROW 7 (March 1924): 86.

4216. "Kidnapped by the Klan." NEWSWEEK 29 (May 26, 1952): 30.

Covers KKK violence in the Carolinas.

4217. "Killed by Kluxers." NEWSWEEK 35 (March 13, 1950): 16.

Reports a Klan murder in Alabama.

4218. "KKK." INDIANA SENATE JOURNAL. 74th Session (1925): 132, 792.

4219. "K.K.K." THE MESSENGER 5 (February 1923): 594.

4220. "The K.K.K." NEW REPUBLIC 28 (September 21, 1921): 88-89.

4221. "K.K.K." OPPORTUNITY 2 (June 1924): 191.

4222. "K.K.K. in Florida." NEWSWEEK 10 (November 29, 1937): 18.

4223. "KKK in Oregon." NATION 113 (1921): 233-234.

4224. "KKK in Oregon." NATION 116 (1922): 6, 325.

4225, "KKK in Oregon." SURVEY 49 (1922): 76-77.

4226. "KKK in Pennsylvania." LITERARY DIGEST 68 (February 5, 1921): 42, 45-46.

4227. "KKK in Pennsylvania." NATION 113 (1921): 285-286.

4228. "K.K.K. Philosophy." OPPORTUNITY 2 (January 1924): 30.

4229. "Klan and the Bottle." NATION 117 (November 21, 1923):
       570-572.

       Examines KKK efforts to enforce Prohibition.

4230. "The Klan and the Candidates." LITERARY DIGEST 82 (Sep-
       tember 6, 1924): 10-11.

4231. "The Klan and the Democrats." LITERARY DIGEST 81 (June
       14, 1924): 12-13.

4232. "The Klan as a National Problem." LITERARY DIGEST 75
       (December 2, 1922): 12-13.

4233. "Klan as an Issue." OUTLOOK 138 (September 3, 1924):
       5-6.

4234. "Klan as the Victim of Mob Violence." LITERARY DIGEST
       78 (September 8, 1923): 12-13.

4235. "Klan at Bay." CURRENT OPINION 77 (October 1924): 419-
       422.

       Reviews KKK participation in the 1924 presidential
       campaign.

4236. "Klan Backs a College." LITERARY DIGEST 78 (September
       15, 1923): 42-46.

4237. "The Klan Defies a State." LITERARY DIGEST 77 (June 9,
       1923): 12-13.

       Examines legal efforts to disband the KKK in New York.

4238. "Klan Dissolves but Subject to Revival." PULSE 2 (July
       1944): 14.

4239. "The Klan Enters the Campaign." LITERARY DIGEST 82
       (July 12, 1924): 9-10.

4240. "Klan Fight Causes Statewide Martial Law." HARLOW'S
       WEEKLY 22 (September 22, 1923): 8-9.

       Covers efforts to suppress the KKK in Oklahoma.

4241. "Klan for Negroes?" NEWSWEEK 42 (October 26, 1953): 7.

    Spotlights a zany scheme to recruit "right-minded" blacks for a nonwhite Klan auxilliary in Florida.

4242. "Klan Goes in for Face-Lifting." LITERARY DIGEST 96 (March 10, 1928): 15-16.

4243. "Klan in Florida." NEW REPUBLIC 91 (June 9, 1937): 118.

4244. "The Klan in Oklahoma Attempts to Come Back." HARLOW'S WEEKLY 30 (September 24, 1931): 4-7.

4245. "The Klan in Retreat and Defeat." INDEPENDENT 113 (August 30, 1924): 114-115.

    Follows the continuing Oklahoma Klan wars.

4246. "The Klan in Texas and Maine." THE MESSENGER 6 (October 1924): 312.

4247. "Klan is Dead, Long Live the ——?" CHRISTIAN CENTURY 45 (March 8, 1928): 306-307.

4248. "Klan is Guilty." NEWSWEEK 39 (May 26, 1952): 31.

    Covers the conviction of Klan floggers in the Carolinas.

4249. "Klan is in Trouble." LIFE 32 (March 31, 1952): 44-46+.

    Reports KKK indictments in the Carolinas.

4250. "Klan is Outlawed in Kentucky." CHRISTIAN CENTURY 63 (September 25, 1946): 114-116.

4251. "Klan Issue." WORLD'S WORK 48 (October 1924): 580.

4252. "Klan Knights Put Out of Church." LITERARY DIGEST 77 (May 5, 1923): 37-38.

    Reports the KKK's rejection by a Pennsylvania pastor and his congregation.

4253. "Klan Kurbed in South Carolina." NEWSWEEK 35 (January 29, 1940): 15.

4254. "Klan Member on the Supreme Court?" NEWSWEEK 10 (September 20, 1937): 9-12.

4255. "The Klan Rears Its Head Again." LITERARY DIGEST 118
       (July 21, 1934): 19.

4256. "Klan Reborn on Stone Mountain." CHRISTIAN CENTURY 63
       (June 5, 1946): 726.

4257. "Klan Revives." COMMONWEAL 65 (October 12, 1956): 38.

4258. "A Klan Senator from Indiana." LITERARY DIGEST 87 (No-
       vember 14, 1925): 16-17.

4259. "The Klan Sheds Its Hood." NEW REPUBLIC 45 (February 10,
       1926): 310-311.

4260. "A Klan Shock in Indiana." LITERARY DIGEST 81 (May 24,
       1924): 14.

4261. "Klan Victories and Defeats." LITERARY DIGEST 83 (Novem-
       ber 22, 1924): 16.

4262. "Klan Victories in Oregon and Texas." LITERARY DIGEST
       75 (November 25, 1922): 12-13.

4263. "Klan Walks in Washington." LITERARY DIGEST 86 (August
       22, 1925): 7-8.

4264. "The Klan - Ye Shall Have Always." PULSE 5 (November
       1947): 8.

4265. "Klans and Councils." NEW REPUBLIC 137 (September 23,
       1957): 6.

       Compares the modern KKK to its "nonviolent" counter-
       part, the White Citizens Council.

4266. "Klan's Challenge and the Reply." LITERARY DIGEST 79
       (November 17, 1923): 32-33.

4267. "The Klan's Political Role." LITERARY DIGEST 79 (Novem-
       ber 24, 1923): 13-14.

4268. "Klansman Admits Theft." THE MESSENGER 6 (December 1924):
       373.

       Describes the prosecution of a Vermont Klansman.

4269. "Klansman Black?" COMMONWEAL 26 (September 24, 1937):
       483-484.

4270. "Klansmen Kluxed by the Klux: Just Kluxin' Around."
       THE MESSENGER 5 (December 1923): 920.

       Examines KKK violence in Georgia during the 1920s.

4271. "Klansmen Must Surrender Jobs." THE MESSENGER 4 (April
       1922): 387-388.

       Describes a legal move against the 1920s Texas Klan.

4272. Kleber, Louis C. "The Ku Klux Klan." HISTORY TODAY 21
       (1971): 567-574.

4273. "Klobbered in Karolina." NEWSWEEK 40 (August 11, 1952):
       24.

       Reports the federal prosecution of Klan floggers.

4274. "Kluxers on the Prowl." NEWSWEEK 34 (July 11, 1949):
       21-22.

4275. Knebel, Fletcher, and Clark Mollenhoff. "Eight Klans
       Bring New Terror to the South." LOOK 21 (April 30,
       1957): 59-60+.

4276. "The Koo Koo Klan Again." THE MESSENGER 4 (September
       1922): 489-490.

4277. "Ku Klux and Crime." NEW REPUBLIC 33 (January 17, 1923):
       189-190.

       Examines reports of KKK violence in Louisiana.

4278. "The Ku Klux Are Riding Again." THE CRISIS 17 (March
       1919): 229-231.

4279. "Ku Klux Condemned by the Religious Press." LITERARY
       DIGEST 71 (October 1, 1921): 30-31.

4280. "The Ku Klux in Politics." LITERARY DIGEST 73 (June 10,
       1922): 15.

4281. "Ku Klux Klan." AMERICAN FEDERATIONIST 30 (November
       1923): 919.

4282. "Ku Klux Klan." CATHOLIC WORLD 116 (January 1923): 433-
       443.

4283. "The Ku Klux Klan." CENTURY 28 (August 1884): 948-950.

4284. "The Ku Klux Klan." THE MESSENGER 5 (January 1923): 564.

4285. "The Ku Klux Klan." THE MESSENGER 8 (November 1926): 345.

4286. "Ku Klux Klan." NATION 162 (June 8, 1946): 678.

4287. "Ku Klux Klan Activities in Saskatchewan." QUEEN'S QUAR-
      TERLY 35 (Autumn 1928): 592-602.

4288. "Ku Klux Klan Again." NEW REPUBLIC 114 (June 10, 1946):
      822.

4289. "Ku Klux Klan Again." OUTLOOK 129 (September 21, 1921):
      79.

4290. "Ku Klux Klan and the Election." CHRISTIAN CENTURY 41
      (November 30, 1924): 1496-1497.

4291. "Ku Klux Klan and the Next Election." WORLD'S WORK 46
      (October 1923): 573-575.

4292. "Ku Klux Klan: Attempts to Establish the Ku Klux Klan in
      Canada." CANADIAN FORUM 10 (April 1930): 233.

4293. "Ku Klux Klan: Bigotry in the Guise of Politics." NATION
      173 (August 4, 1951): 82.

4294. "The Ku Klux Klan - How to Fight It." THE MESSENGER 3
      (November 1921): 276-277.

4295. "Ku Klux Klan in Germany." LIVING AGE 327 (October 17,
      1925): 128.

      The KKK makes a brief attempt to export its doctrine,
      but finds itself unable to compete with the home-grown
      Nazi movement.

4296. "Ku Klux Klan in Oklahoma." CURRENT OPINION 75 (Novem-
      ber 1923): 523-524.

4297. "Ku Klux Klan in Politics." LITERARY DIGEST 73 (June 10,
      1922): 15.

      Examines KKK activity in Oregon.

4298. "Ku Klux Klan Leaders Well Fitted to Correct Morals of Communities." THE MESSENGER 3 (October 1921): 261-262.

   Takes a scathing look at Georgia Klansmen in their self-appointed roles as arbiters of community morals.

4299. "The Ku Klux Klan Movement." AMERICAN MERCURY (May 1901) 634-644.

4300. "Ku Klux Klan on the Downgrade." CHRISTIAN CENTURY 40 (September 13, 1923): 1158-1160.

4301. "Ku Klux Klan Seizing the Government." THE MESSENGER 4 (December 1922): 537-538.

4302. "Ku Klux Klan; Symposium." NORTH AMERICAN 223 (March 1926): 33-63; 223 (June 1926): 268-309.

4303. "Ku Klux Klan Tokens." ANTIQUES JOURNAL 36 (October 1981): 48.

4304. "The Ku Klux Klan Tries a Comeback." LIFE 20 (May 27, 1946): 42-44.

4305. "Ku Klux Klan - Unmasked." TIME 11 (March 5, 1928): 10-1

4306. "Ku Klux Klans of the Reconstruction Period in Missouri." MISSOURI HISTORICAL REVIEW 37 (July 1943): 441-450.

4307. "Ku Klux Kourts." THE MESSENGER 6 (December 1929): 373.

4308. "The Ku Klux Trial." AMERICAN MISSIONARY MAGAZINE 16 (February 1872): 39-40.

4309. "The Ku Klux Victory in Texas." LITERARY DIGEST 74 (August 5, 1922): 14-15.

4310. "Ku Klux Violence in Haywood County, Tennessee." AMERICAN MISSIONARY MAGAZINE 13 (February 1869): 40-42.

4311. "Ku Klux Violence to Teachers in the South." AMERICAN MISSIONARY MAGAZINE 18 (September 1874): 208-209.

4312. "Law for Others, Not for the Ku Klux Klan!" OUTLOOK 134 (June 9, 1923): 109.

4313. Lay, Wilfrid. "Psychoanalyzing the Klan." THE WORLD TOMORROW 7 (March 1924): 79-80.

4314. Lee, Kendrick. "Ku Klux Klan." EDITORIAL RESEARCH RE-
PORT 2 (July 10, 1946): 449-464.

4315. Leuchtenberg, William E. "A Klansman Joins the Court:
The Appointment of Hugo L. Black." UNIVERSITY OF CHI-
CAGO LAW REVIEW 41 (1973): 1-31.

4316. Lindsey, Ben B. "The Beast in a New Form." NEW REPUBLIC
41 (December 24, 1924): 121.

Reviews KKK activity in Colorado during the 1920s.

4317. ————. "My Fight with the Ku Klux Klan." SURVEY GEO-
GRAPHIC 54 (June 1, 1925): 271-274.

4318. Lipset, Seymour M. "An Anatomy of the Klan." COMMENTARY
40 (October 1965): 78.

4319. "London's View of the Klan Row." LITERARY DIGEST 77
(May 19, 1923): 20.

4320. Lovejoy, G.W. "In Brotherhood Week: A Look at the South."
NEW YORK TIMES MAGAZINE (February 17, 1957): 13.

4321. MacKaye, Milton. "'The Birth of a Nation.'" SCRIBNER'S
MAGAZINE 102 (November 1937): 44.

4322. McClean, Phillip J. "Klan Reborn on Stone Mountain."
CHRISTIAN CENTURY 63 (June 5, 1946): 726.

4323. ————. "Southern Liberals Oppose the Klan." CHRISTIAN
CENTURY 63 (June 5, 1946): 726.

4324. McIver, Stuart. "The Murder of a Scalawag." AMERICAN
HISTORY ILLUSTRATED 8 (April 1973): 12-18.

Reviews a Klan assassination in North Carolina during
Reconstruction.

4325. McNeilly, J.S. "Enforcement Act of 1871 and Ku Klux Klan
in Mississippi." MISSISSIPPI HISTORICAL SOCIETY PUB-
LICATIONS (1906): 107-171.

4326. ————. "Reconstruction and the Ku Klux." CONFEDERATE
VETERAN 30 (March 1922): 96-97.

4327. McWhiney, H. Grady, and Francis F. Simpkins. "Ghostly
Legend of the Ku Klux Klan." THE NEGRO HISTORY BUL-
LETIN 14 (February 1951): 109-112.

4328. McWilliams, Carey. "The Klan: Post War Model." NATION 163 (December 14, 1946): 691-692.

4329. "Ma Ferguson and the K.K.K." NEW STATESMAN 23 (October 4, 1924): 728-729.

       Examines efforts of a female governor in Texas to disband the KKK.

4330. Markey, Morris. "Why Did Indiana Free the Klan Killer?" CORONET (October 1950): 94-100.

       Questions the wisdom of paroling D.C. Stephenson, KKK grand dradon convicted of rape and murder in 1924.

4331. Marriner, Gerald L. "Klan Politics in Colorado." JOURNAL OF THE WEST 15 (January 1976): 76-101.

4332. "Martial Law in Oklahoma." OUTLOOK 135 (September 26, 1923): 133-134.

4333. Martin, Harold H. "The Truth About the Klan Today." SATURDAY EVENING POST 222 (October 22, 1949): 17-18, 122-126.

4334. Martin, John Bartlow. "Beauty and the Beast: The Downfall of D.C. Stephenson, Grand Dragon of the Indiana K.K.K." HARPER'S 189 (September 1944): 319-329.

4335. "Masked Floggers of Tulsa." LITERARY DIGEST 78 (Setpember 22, 1923): 17-18.

4336. Mazzulla, Fred, and Joe Mazzulla. "A Klan Album." COLORADO MAGAZINE 42 (September 1965): 109-113.

4337. Mecklin, John M. "Ku Klux Klan and the Democratic Tradition." AMERICAN REVIEW 2 (May 1924): 241-251.

4338. Melching, Richard. "The Activities of the Ku Klux Klan in Anaheim, California, 1923-1925." SOUTHERN CALIFORNIA QUARTERLY 56 (Summer 1974).

4339. Mellett, Lowell. "Klan and Church in Indiana." ATLANTIC MONTHLY 132 (November 1923): 586-592.

4340. "Membership in the American Fascisti: Disclaimed." THE MESSENGER 4 (November 1, 1922): 518-519.

4341. Merritt, Dixon. "Klan and Anti-Klan in Indiana." OUTLOOK 144 (December 8, 1926): 465-469.

4342. ———. "Klan on Parade." OUTLOOK 140 (August 19, 1925): 553-554.

4343. "Mer Rouge Murders Unpunished." LITERARY DIGEST 76 (March 31, 1923): 10-11.

Reviews Klan violence in Louisiana.

4344. Merz, Charles. "The New Ku Klux Klan." INDEPENDENT 118 (February 12, 1927): 179-180, 196.

4345. "The Messenger Editors." THE MESSENGER 3 (March 1921): 194.

Levels an editorial broadside at recent KKK activities.

4346. Middlebrooks, A.E. "Alabama Votes to Unmask the Klan." CHRISTIAN CENTURY 66 (July 20, 1949): 871.

4347. Miller, Robert M. "Note on the Relationship Between the Protestant Churches and the Revived Ku Klux Klan." JOURNAL OF SOUTHERN HISTORY 22 (August 1956): 355-368.

4348. ———. "The Social Attitudes of the American Methodists, 1919-1920." RELIGION IN LIFE 28 (Spring 1958): 185-198.

Includes a discussion of overlapping membership between the church and the KKK.

4349. "Ministers Denounce Georgia Klan." CHRISTIAN CENTURY 66 (January 5, 1949): 6.

4350. "Miss KKK." NEWSWEEK 32 (December 20, 1948): 22.

The post-war Georgia Klan sponsors a beauty contest.

4351. "Mr. White Challenges the Klan." OUTLOOK 138 (October 1, 1924): 154.

Reviews William A. White's one-man war against the KKK in Kansas.

4352. Mitchell, Enoch L. "The Role of George Washington Gordon in the Ku Klux Klan." WEST TENNESSEE HISTORICAL SOCIETY PAPERS (1947): 73-80.

4353. "Mob Violence and the Ku Klux Klan." THE MESSENGER 3 (September 1921): 244-246.

4354. Mockler, William E. "Source of Ku Klux." NAMES 3 (March 1955): 14-18.

   Traces the origin of the Klan's name to ancient Greece.

4355. Mollenhoff, Clark. "Eight Klans Bring New Terror to the South." LOOK 21 (April 30, 1957): 59-69.

4356. Monk, A.D. "Knights of the Knightshirt Organized in Canada." CANADIAN MAGAZINE 66 (October 1926): 31.

4357. Moore, John H. "Communists and Fascists in a Southern City: Atlanta, 1930." SOUTH ATLANTIC QUARTERLY 67 (Summer 1968): 437-454.

   The Klan clashes with reds in Depression-era Georgia.

4358. Moore, Samuel T. "Consequences of the Klan." INDEPENDENT 113 (December 20, 1924): 534-536.

4359. ———. "How the Kleagles Collected the Cash." INDEPENDENT 113 (December 13, 1924): 517-519.

   Reviews KKK recruiting methods in Indiana.

4360. ———. "A Klan Kingdom Collapses." INDEPENDENT 113 (December 6, 1924): 473-475.

   Examines the Indiana KKK's decline after the conviction of its leader on felony charges.

4361. "Moral Lashes for Alabama Floggers." LITERARY DIGEST 95 (December 17, 1927): 32.

4362. Moseley, Clement Charlton. "Latent Klanism in Georgia, 1890-1915." GEORGIA HISTORICAL QUARTERLY 56 (1972): 115-135.

4363. ———. "The Political Influence of the Ku Klux Klan in Georgia, 1915-1925." GEORGIA HISTORICAL QUARTERLY 57 (Summer 1973): 235-255.

4364. Mugleston, William F. "Julian Harris, the Georgia Press, and the Ku Klux Klan." GEORGIA HISTORICAL QUARTERLY 59 (1975): 284-295.

4365. "Murders of Mer Rouge." LITERARY DIGEST 76 (January 13, 1923): 10-12.

4366. Murphy, Paul L. "Sources and Nature of Intolerance in the 1920s." JOURNAL OF AMERICAN HISTORY 51 (June 1964): 60-76.

4367. Murphy, Robert J. "The South Fights Bombing." LOOK 23 (January 6, 1959): 13-17.

4368. "Mutiny in the Invisible Empire." INDEPENDENT 116 (January 16, 1929): 58-59.

   Examines a rift in the Connecticut realm of the KKK.

4369. Myers, William Starr. "Know Nothing and Ku Klux Klan." NORTH AMERICAN 219 (January 1924): 1, 7.

4370. ————. "The Ku Klux Klan of Today." NORTH AMERICAN 223 (June-August 1926): 304-309.

4371. "The Nation and the Klan." THE MESSENGER 6 (March 1924): 69-70.

4372. "National Affairs - Ku Klux Klan." TIME 4 (August 18, 1924): 3-4.

4373. "Natives Are Restless." TIME 71 (January 27, 1958): 20.

   Examines violent reactions among Lumbee Indians to KKK rallies in Robeson County, North Carolina.

4374. "Negroes - Darrow vs. Klan." TIME 9 (March 21, 1927): 12.

   Attorney Clarence Darrow is threatened by the KKK while defending blacks accused of rape in Alabama.

4375. Nelson, Llewellyn. "The K.K.K. for Boredom." NEW RE-PUBLIC 41 (January 14, 1925): 196-198.

   Examines Klan activities in Oklahoma.

4376. Neruinger, Sheldon. "Governor Walton's War on the Ku Klux Klan: An Episode in Oklahoma History." CHRONICLES OF OKLAHOMA 45 (Summer 1967): 153-179.

4377. "The New Crusaders." OPPORTUNITY 2 (August 1924): 227-228.

4378. "New Ku Klux Klan Activity." SCHOLASTIC MAGAZINE 36 (May 13, 1940): 2.

4379. "New York's Anti-Klan Outburst." LITERARY DIGEST 75 (December 23, 1922): 31-32.

Klansmen find themselves on the receiving end of mob violence in New York.

4380. Nicholson, Meredith. "Hoosier Letters and the Ku Klux." BOOKMAN 67 (March 1928): 7.

4381. "Nightmare on Pine Mountain." TIME 51 (March 22, 1948): 24-25.

Reports Klan violence in post-war Georgia.

4382. "Night-riding in Alabama." COMMONWEAL 50 (July 8, 1949): 309.

4383. "1940: 'The Police Just Laughed.'" SOUTHERN EXPOSURE 8 (Summer 1950): 69.

Examines police complicity in crimes of the Georgia KKK.

4384. "No Place for Fanatics." COLLIER'S 100 (October 23, 1937): 74-75.

Opposes Hugo Black's nomination to the Supreme Court.

4385. "North Carolina: Indian Raid." NEWSWEEK 51 (January 27, 1958): 27.

4386. Oates, Stephen B. "Boom Oil! Oklahoma Strikes it Rich!" AMERICAN WEST 5 (January 1968): 64-66.

4387. "Oklahoma Kingless, Not Klanless." LITERARY DIGEST 79 (December 8, 1923): 9-11.

4388. "Oklahoma's Klan War from Over the Border." HARLOW'S WEEKLY 22 (September 22, 1924): 4-5.

4389. "Oklahoma's Uncivil Civil War." LITERARY DIGEST 78 (September 29, 1923): 10-11.

4390. Olsen, Otto H. "The Ku Klux Klan: A Study of Reconstruction Politics and Propaganda." NORTH CAROLINA HISTORICAL REVIEW 39 (July 1962): 340-362.

4391. O'Mahony, Joseph P. "The Ku Klux Klan in Indiana." AM-
      ERICA 30 (December 15, 1923): 202.

4392. "Oscar Underwood's Great Service." WORLD'S WORK 48 (July
      1924): 242-243.

      Reviews KKK participation in the 1924 elections.

4393. Ottley, Roy. "I Met the Grand Dragon." NATION 169 (July
      2, 1949): 10-11.

      A black journalist interviews the leader of the Georgia
      Klan.

4394. "Our Own Secret Fascisti." NATION 115 (November 15,
      1922): 514-515.

4395. "Out of the Cave." TIME 47 (June 3, 1946): 25.

      Examines the post-war rebirth of the KKK in Georgia.

4396. Owens, John W. "Does the Senate Fear the Ku Klux Klan?"
      NEW REPUBLIC 37 (December 26, 1923): 113-114.

4397. Papikolas, Helen Zeese. "The Greeks of Carbon County."
      UTAH HISTORICAL QUARTERLY 22 (April 1954): 163.

      Reviews KKK efforts to agitate against European immi-
      grants in Utah.

4398. ————. "Tragedy and Hate." UTAH HISTORICAL QUARTERLY
      38 (Spring 1970): 176-181.

      Examines Klan violence in Utah during the 1920s.

4399. Pattangall, William R. "Is the Ku Klux Klan Un-American?"
      FORUM 74 (September 1925): 321-332.

4400. Patterson, Barbara. "Defiance and Dynamite." NEW SOUTH
      18 (May 1963): 8-11.

      Presents a chronology of racist bombings between 1956
      and 1963, most of which were traced to members of the
      KKK and affiliated groups.

4401. Patton, R.A. "A Ku Klux Klan Reign of Terror." CURRENT
      HISTORY 28 (April 1928): 51-55.

4402. Paul, Justus F. "The Ku Klux Klan in the 1936 Nebraska Election." NORTH DAKOTA QUARTERLY 39 (Autumn 1971): 64-70.

4403. Payne, George H. "Does the Ku Klux Klan Need the Jew?" FORUM 74 (December 1925): 915-917.

4404. Peck, Ralph L. "Lawlessness in Florida: 1868-1871." FLORIDA HISTORICAL QUARTERLY 40 (October 1961): 164-185.

      Includes a discussion of the Reconstruction KKK.

4405. Percy, Leroy. "The Modern Ku Klux Klan." ATLANTIC MONTHLY 130 (July 1922): 122-128.

4406. Perlmutter, Nathan. "Bombing in Miami; Anti-Semitism and the Segregationists." COMMENTARY 25 (June 1958): 498-503.

      Klansmen and neo-Nazis take the blame for recent acts of anti-semitic violence in South Flordia, including the bombing of a synagogue and Jewish community center.

4407. Phillips, Paul D. "White Reaction to the Freedmen's Bureau in Tennessee." TENNESSEE HISTORICAL QUARTERLY 25 (Spring 1966): 50-62.

4408. "Pink Ballots for the Ku Klux Klan." OUTLOOK 137 (June 25, 1924): 306-309.

4409. "Platforms of the People and the Mind of the Ku Klux Klan." OUTLOOK 137 (June 25, 1924): 307-309.

4410. "Playing with Fire." TIME 53 (January 3, 1949): 42.

      Examines KKK violence and intimidation in Georgia.

4411. Pomeroy, J.N. "Bill to Repress the Ku-Klux." NATION 12: 268.

      Examines federal efforts to crush the Reconstruction Klan.

4412. Post, Louis F. "A 'Carpetbagger' in South Carolina." JOURNAL OF NEGRO HISTORY 10 (January 1925): 10-79.

4413. "Powerful Aid for the Klan." THE CRISIS 46 (August 1939): 241-242.

4414. Powell, John. "The Klan Un-Klandestine." NATION 173
      (September 29, 1951): 255.

4415. Preece, Harold. "The Klan Declares War." NEW MASSES 57
      (October 16, 1945): 3-7.

4416. ———. "Klan 'Murder, Inc.' in Dixie." THE CRISIS 53
      (October 1946): 299-301.

4417. ———. "The Klan's 'Revolution of the Right'." THE
      CRISIS 53 (July 1946): 202-203, 219-220.

4418. "Protectors of Womanhood." TIME 51 (February 16, 1948):
      26.

      Reviews Klan violence, including some against women,
      in Georgia.

4419. "Protestants Disowning the Ku Klux." LITERARY DIGEST 75
      (November 25, 1922): 33-34.

4420. "Quaint Customs and Methods of the Ku Klux Klan." LITER-
      ARY DIGEST 74 (August 5, 1922): 44-52.

4421. Racine, Phillip N. "The Ku Klux Klan, Anti-Catholicism,
      and Atlanta's Board of Education, 1916-1927." GEORGIA
      HISTORICAL QUARTERLY 57 (Spring 1973): 63-75.

4422. Rambow, Charles. "The Ku Klux Klan in the 1920s: A Con-
      centration on the Black Hills." SOUTH DAKOTA HISTORY
      4 (Winter 1973): 63-81.

4423. Reed, John C. "What I Know of the Ku Klux Klan." UNCLE
      REMUS'S MAGAZINE (January 1908).

4424. "The Reformation of Herrin." LITERARY DIGEST 86 (August
      1, 1925): 28-29.

4425. Reich, Frances. "The Klan Rides Hitler." JEWISH SURVEY
      2 (June 1942): 4-6.

      Examines KKK flirtation with the German American Bund.

4426. "The Reign of the Tar Bucket." LITERARY DIGEST 70 (Aug-
      ust 27, 1921): 12-13.

4427. "Revised and Amended Prescript of the Order of the ..."
      AMERICAN HISTORICAL SOCIETY QUARTERLY 5 (January 1900):
      3-26.

Reprints the constitution of the Reconstruction KKK, which represented its title with periods or asterisks, in the interest of secrecy.

4428. "The Riot at Niles." OUTLOOK 138 (November 12, 1924): 396.

Examines Klan-related violence in Ohio.

4429. "The Rise and Fall of the K.K.K." NEW REPUBLIC 53 (November 30, 1927): 33-34.

4430. "Rise and Fall of the Ku Klux Klan." OUTLOOK 138 (October 15, 1924): 237-238.

4431. Roberts, W. "The Ku-Kluxing of Oregon." OUTLOOK 133 (March 14, 1923): 490-491.

4432. Rogers, Joel A. "The Ku Klux Klan: A Menace of a Promise?" THE MESSENGER 5 (March 1923): 626-629; 5 (April 1923): 662-663, 675-678; 5 (June 1923): 738-740; 5 (August 1923): 785, 795; 5 (October 1923): 833-835.

4433. Rogers, William W. "Boyd Incident: Black Belt Violence During Reconstruction." CIVIL WAR HISTORY 21 (December 1975): 302-329.

Reviews activities of the early Alabama KKK.

4434. Rork, C.M. "A Defense of the Klan." NEW REPUBLIC 37 (December 5, 1923): 44-45.

4435. Rovere, Richard. "The Klan Rides Again." NATION 150 (April 6, 1940): 445-446.

4436. Ruark, H.G. "Fear Klan Revival in the Carolinas." CHRISTIAN CENTURY 75 (February 26, 1958): 257.

4437. Schaefer, Richard T. "The Ku Klux Klan: Continuity and Change." PHYLON 32 (1971): 143-157.

4438. Schieffelin, William J. "Most Unforgettable Character I've Met: R.R. Moton." READER'S DIGEST 57 (November 1950): 25-28.

Examines the life of a Klan opponent in Alabama.

4439. ———. "The Most Unforgettable Character I've Ever Met."
       THE NEGRO DIGEST 9 (February 1951): 66-68.

       Reprints item 4438 above.

4440. Shankman, Arnold. "Julian Harris and the Ku Klux Klan."
       MISSISSIPPI QUARTERLY 28 (Spring 1975): 147-169.

4441. ———. "Julian Harris and the Negro." PHYLON 35 (1974):
       442-456.

4442. Shapiro, Herman. "The Ku Klux Klan During Reconstruction:
       The South Carolina Episode." JOURNAL OF NEGRO HISTORY
       49 (January 1964): 35-55.

4443. "Shed a Tear for the Klan." NATION 119 (October 9, 1924):
       351-352.

4444. "Sheet, Sugar Sack and Cross." TIME 51 (March 15, 1948):
       29.

       Examines KKK violence in Georgia.

4445. "The 'Sheeted Jerks' of the Ku Klux Klan." NATION 169
       (July 2, 1949): 2-4.

4446. Shepherd, William G. "How I Put Over the Klan." COL-
       LIER'S 82 (July 14, 1928): 5-7. 32, 34-35.

       A retired Kleagle describes his career as a hate sales-
       man for the KKK in Pennsylvania.

4447. ———. "Indiana's Mystery Man." COLLIER'S 79 (January
       8, 1927): 8-9, 47-49.

4448. ———. "Ku Klux Koin." COLLIER'S 82 (July 21, 1928):
       8-9, 38-39.

4449. ———. "The Whip Hand in Alabama." COLLIER'S 81 (Jan-
       uary 7, 1928): 8-9, 44-45.

4450. ———. "The Whip Wins." COLLIER'S 81 (January 14, 1928):
       10-11, 30, 32.

       Examines KKK violence in Alabama during the 1920s.

4451. "Shots in the Shadows." NEWSWEEK 49 (February 4, 1957):
       26.

4452. Silverman, Joseph. "The Ku Klux Klan a Paradox." NORTH
      AMERICAN 223 (June-August 1926): 282-291.

4453. Simpkins, Francis B. "The Ku Klux Klan in South Caro-
      lina." JOURNAL OF NEGRO HISTORY 12 (October 1927):
      606-647.

4454. Skinner, R. Dana. "Is the Ku Klux Klan Katholik?" INDE-
      PENDENT 111 (November 24, 1923): 242-243.

4455. Sloan, Charles W., Jr. "Kansas Battles the Invisible
      Empire: The Legal Ouster of the KKK from Kansas, 1922-
      1927." KANSAS HISTORICAL QUARTERLY 57 (Autumn 1974):
      393-409.

4456. Sloan, John Z. "The Ku Klux Klan and the Alabama Election
      of 1872." ALABAMA REVIEW 17 (April 1965): 113-124.

4457. Smith, Norman W. "The Ku Klux Klan in Rhode Island."
      RHODE ISLAND HISTORY 37 (1978): 35-45.

4458. Smith, Robert B. "Klan Spooks in Congress." INDEPENDENT
      116 (June 19, 1926): 718-719.

4459. Snell, William R. "Fiery Crosses in the Roaring Twenties:
      Activities of the Revised Klan in Alabaman, 1915-1930."
      ALABAMA REVIEW 23 (October 1970): 256-276.

4460. "Solemn but Undignified Penguins." NATION 116 (January
      1923): 6-7.

4461. Sonnichsen, C.L., and M.G. McKinney. "El Paso - From
      War to Depression." SOUTHWESTERN HISTORICAL QUARTERLY
      74 (January 1971): 357-371.

      Includes discussion of the KKK in Texas.

4462. "South Carolina Race War." NEW REPUBLIC 123 (September
      11, 1950): 9.

4463. "The South: Its Dark Side." AMERICAN MISSIONARY MAGAZINE
      13 (October 1869): 230-231.

      Examines KKK violence in Tennessee during Reconstruc-
      tion.

4464. "Southern Reaction to the Arrest of Klansmen." NATION
      174 (March 8, 1952): 215.

4465. Stagg, J.C.A. "The Problem of Klan Violence: The South
      Carolina Up-Country, 1868-1871." JOURNAL OF AMERICAN
      STUDIES 8 (December 1974): 303-318.

4466. Stephens, Harold W. "Mask and Lash in Crenshaw." NORTH
      AMERICAN 225 (April 1928): 435-442.

      Reviews Klan violence in Alabama.

4467. Stockbridge, Frank Parker. "The Ku Klux Klan Revival."
      CURRENT HISTORY 14 (April 1921): 19-25.

4468. "The Strange Invasion; British Klans." NEWSWEEK 49 (May
      13, 1957): 58.

4469. "Subpoena the Klan." AMERICA 96 (February 9, 1957): 520.

4470. Sullivan, Mark. "Midsummer Politics and Primaries."
      WORLD'S WORK 44 (July 1922): 296-302.

      Examines KKK activity in Texas.

4471. Swallow, Craig A. "The Ku Klux Klan in Nevada During
      the 1920s." NEVADA HISTORICAL SOCIETY QUARTERLY 24
      (1981): 202-230.

4472. Sweeney, Charles. "The Great Bigotry Merger." NATION
      115 (July 5, 1922): 8-10.

4473. Swertfeger, Jack, Jr. "Anti-Mask and Anti-Klan Laws."
      JOURNAL OF PUBLIC LAW 1 (1952): 195-196.

4474. "Talent Rewarded: Mr. Justice Black." CATHOLIC WORLD
      146 (November 1937): 129-134.

4475. Tannebaum, Frank. "Books to Cure Clannishness." THE
      WORLD TOMORROW 7 (March 1924): 94.

4476. ———. "The Ku Klux Klan: Its Social Origin in the
      South." CENTURY 105 (April 1923): 873-882.

4477. Taylor, A.A. "The Negro in South Carolina: Opposition
      to the Reconstruction." JOURNAL OF NEGRO HISTORY 9
      (July 1924): 442-468.

4478. Taylor, Alva W. "Klan Seen Trying for a Comeback."
      CHRISTIAN CENTURY 67 (February 1, 1950): 148, 150.

4479. ————. "What the Klan Did in Indiana." NEW REPUBLIC
      52 (November 16, 1927): 330-332.

4480. Thornobrough, Emma L. "Segregation in Indiana During
      the Klan Era of the 1920s." MISSISSIPPI VALLEY HIS-
      TORICAL REVIEW 47 (March 1961): 594-618.

4481. Toll, William. "Progress and Piety: The Ku Klux Klan
      and Social Change in Tillamook, Oregon." PACIFIC
      NORTHWEST QUARTERLY 69 (April 1978): 75-85.

4482. Toy, Eckard V., Jr. "The Ku Klux Klan in Tillamook,
      Oregon." PACIFIC NORTHWEST QUARTERLY 53 (April 1962):
      60-64.

4483. Trent, William P. "A New South's View of Reconstruction."
      SEWANEE REVIEW 9 (January 1901): 13-29.

4484. "Trouble at Charlie's Place." NEWSWEEK 36 (September 11,
      1950): 36.

4485. Tyack, David B. "Perils of Pluralism: The Background of
      the Pierce Case." AMERICAN HISTORICAL REVIEW 74 (Octo-
      ber 1968): 74-98.

4486. "Uncle Henry on the Klan Komplex." COLLIER'S 72 (Janu-
      ary 27, 1923): 15-16.

4487. "United Against Ku Kluxism." THE MESSENGER 5 (August
      1923): 781-782.

4488. "United Front Against the Ku Klux Menace." THE MESSEN-
      GER 4 (September 1922): 478-479.

4489. "University of Oklahoma and the Ku Klux Klan." SCHOOL
      AND SOCIETY 16 (October 7, 1922): 412-413.

4490. Van Der Veer, Virginia. "Hugo Black and the K.K.K."
      AMERICAN HERITAGE 19 (April 1968): 60-64.

4491. Velie, Leslie. "The Klan Rides the South Again." COL-
      LIER'S 122 (October 1948): 13-15.

4492. Wald, Kenneth D. "The Visible Empire: The Ku Klux Klan
      as an Electoral Movement." JOURNAL OF INTERDISCIPLIN-
      ARY HISTORY 11 (Autumn 1980): 217-234.

4493. Wallace, Robert. "Freedom to Jim Crow: Part II: Back-
      ground to Segregation." LIFE 41 (September 10, 1956):
      99.

4494. ———. "New Forces in the Broken Land." LIFE 41 (Sep-
      tember 10, 1956): 99.

4495. Warwick, L. "Father's Private Miracle." CORONET 44
      (August 1958): 19-23.

4496. Weir, Sally B. "Reminiscences of the Ku Klux Klan."
      METROPOLITAN MAGAZINE 26 (April 1907): 97-106.

4497. Werly, John M. "Premillennialism and the Paranoid Style."
      AMERICAN STUDIES 18 (1977): 39-55.

4498. Wesberry, James P. "K.K.K. Holds Cross-Burning Near
      Atlanta." CHRISTIAN CENTURY 74 (January 9, 1957): 54.

4499. Wetta, Frank J. "Bulldozing the Scalawags." LOUISIANA
      HISTORY 21 (Winter 1980): 43-58.

4500. "What is Wrong with the Klan?" NATION 118 (June 18,
      1924): 698-699.

4501. "When Carolina Indians Went on the Warpath." U.S. NEWS
      & WORLD REPORT 44 (January 31, 1958): 14.

4502. White, Arthur Corning. "An American Fascismo." THE
      FORUM 72 (November 1924): 636-642.

4503. White, Walter F. "Election by Terror in Florida." NEW
      REPUBLIC 25 (January 12, 1921): 195-197.

4504. ———. "Reviving the Ku Klux Klan." FORUM 65 (April
      1921): 426-434.

4505. White, William Allen. "Annihilate the Klan!" NATION
      120 (January 7, 1925): 7.

4506. ———. "Patience and Publicity." THE WORLD TOMORROW
      7 (March 1924): 87.

4507. "W.H. Moses." THE MESSENGER 3 (October 1921): 264-266.

4508. "Why Kansas Bans the Klan." LITERARY DIGEST 75 (Novem-
      ber 11, 1922): 13-14.

4509. "Why They Join the Klan." NEW REPUBLIC 36 (November 21, 1923): 321-322.

4510. "William Allen White's War on the Klan." LITERARY DIGEST 83 (October 11, 1924): 16-17.

4511. Wilson, D.L. "The Beginning of the Ku Klux Klan." SOUTHERN BIVOUAC 4 (October 1885): 269-271.

4512. ———. "The Ku Klux Klan: Its Origin, Growth, and Disbandment." CENTURY 28 (July 1884): 398-410.

4513. Wilson, Walter. "The Meridian Massacre of 1871." THE CRISIS 81 (June 1980): 2.

4514. Wilson, William E. "Long Hot Summer in Indiana; 1924." AMERICAN HERITAGE 16 (August 1965): 56-64.

4515. "Wiping Out Oregon's School Law." LITERARY DIGEST 81 (April 26, 1924): 33-34.

4516. "With Malice Afore Thought." TIME 55 (March 13, 1950): 24.

    Reports a Klan murder in Alabama.

4517. Wood, W.D. "The Ku Klux Klan." QUARTERLY OF THE TEXAS STATE HISTORICAL ASSOCIATION 9 (April 1906): 262-268.

4518. Wrench, Evelyn. "English-Speaking World." SPECTATOR 130 (March 24, 1923): 506-507.

    Examines the 1920s Louisiana Klan.

4519. Zander, James W. Vander. "The Klan Revival." AMERICAN JOURNAL OF SOCIOLOGY 65 (March 1960): 456-462.

6. Lynching

a. Books

4520. Ames, Jessie D. THE CHANGING CHARACTER OF LYNCHING. REVIEW OF LYNCHING, 1939-1941, WITH A DISCUSSION OF RECENT DEVELOPMENTS IN THE FIELD. Atlanta, Ga.: Commission on Interracial Cooperation, 1942.

    Reveals that, while overall lynchings are on the decline nationwide, mob action is more often being used

to punish blacks for minor or nonexistent "offenses,"
such as petty theft and disrespect for whites.

4521. AN AMERICAN LYNCHING. BEING THE BURNING AT THE STAKE OF
HENRY LAWRY AT NODENA, ARKANSAS, JAN. 26, 1921, AS TOLD
IN AMERICAN NEWSPAPERS. New York: National Association
for the Advancement of Colored People, 1921.

4522. Cameron, James. A TIME OF TERROR. Milwaukee: T.D. Publications, 1980.

Reviews the case of a lynching at Marion, Ind.

4523. Cantril, Hadley. THE PSYCHOLOGY OF SOCIAL MOVEMENTS.
New York: John Wiley & Sons, 1941.

Attempts "to translate the objective descriptions of
lynching mobs into their probable subjective psychological counterparts."

4524. Chadbourn, James Harmon. LYNCHING AND THE LAW. Chapel
Hill, N.C.: University of North Carolina Press, 1933.

Includes proposals for federal laws designed to curb
mob violence.

4525. Collins, Winfield H. THE TRUTH ABOUT LYNCHING AND THE
NEGRO IN THE SOUTH, IN WHICH THE AUTHOR PLEADS THAT
THE SOUTH BE MADE SAFE AGAIN FOR THE WHITE RACE. New
York: The Neale Publishing Co., 1918.

Presents lynching as a "necessary evil" used by right-
thinking men to protect white society in the South. An
interesting look at the other side of the coin.

4526. Cutler, James Elbert. LYNCH LAWS: AN INVESTIGATION INTO
THE HISTORY OF LYNCHING IN THE UNITED STATES. New
York: Longmans, Green & Co., 1905.

4527. Fedo, Michael W. "THEY WAS JUST NIGGERS." Ontario,
Calif.: Brasch & Brasch, 1979.

Examines the lynching of multiple victims at Duluth,
Minnesota.

4528. Gambino, Richard. VENDETTA. New York: Doubleday, 1977.

Examines the New Orleans Mafia lynchings of 1891, their

background, and the international repercussions which
created a temporary rift between Italy and the United
States.

4529. Harris, Trudie. EXORCISING BLACKNESS: HISTORICAL AND
LITERARY LYNCHING AND BURNING RITUALS. Bloomington,
Ind.: Indiana University Press, 1984.

4530. Haywood, Harry, and Milton Howard. LYNCHING: A WEAPON
OF NATIONAL OPPRESSION. New York: 1952.

4531. Raper, Arthur F. THE TRAGEDY OF LYNCHING. Chapel Hill,
N.C.: University of North Carolina Press, 1938.

4532. Shay, Frank. JUDGE LYNCH. HIS FIRST HUNDRED YEARS. New
York: 1938.

4533. THIRTY YEARS OF LYNCHING IN THE UNITED STATES, 1889-1918.
New York: National Association for the Advancement of
Colored People, 1919.

4534. Wells-Barnett, Ida. ON LYNCHINGS; SOUTHERN HORRORS. New
York: Arno Press, 1892.

4535. White, Walter F. ROPE AND FAGGOT: A BIOGRAPHY OF JUDGE
LYNCH. New York: Alfred A. Knopf, 1929.

b. Articles

4536. "Act Against Lynching." MISSISSIPPI REVIEW 58 (June
1935): 306.

4537. Addams, J. "Respect for Law." INDEPENDENT 53 (January
1901): 18-20.

Reports events of 1900, in which 101 persons were
lynched in America.

4538. "Address by John Jay Chapman at a Prayermeeting Held in
Coatesville, Pennsylvania." HARPER'S WEEKLY 56 (September 21, 1912): 6.

4539. "Aftermath." NEWSWEEK 2 (December 16, 1932): 8-10.

Examines repercussions from the lynching, one month
earlier, of a Louisiana black man "charged" with insult-
ing two white women at Wisner, in Franklin Parish.

4540. "Against Lynching; Association of Southern Women for the
      Prevention of Lynching." COMMONWEAL 17 (April 19,
      1933): 675.

4541. "All Honor to the Women of Georgia!" CHRISTIAN CENTURY
      48 (January 28, 1931): 123.

4542. "Americanism in Action." WORLD TOMORROW 16 (October 26,
      1933): 581-582.

4543. "Anarchy in Delaware." OUTLOOK 74 (July 4, 1903): 543-
      546.

      Reports the lynching of George White, accused of mur-
      der and rape near Wilmington, on June 12.

4544. "Another Lynching; Alabama-Florida Outrage." COMMONWEAL
      21 (November 9, 1934): 49.

      Examines the case of Claude Neal, a black man accused
      of rape and murder, who was kidnapped from a jail in
      Brewton, Ala., and tortured to death by a mob at Marianna,
      Fla., on October 26.

4545. "Another Lynching on the Eastern Shore; What Will Gover-
      nor Ritchie Do About It?" CATHOLIC WORLD 138 (Decem-
      ber 1933): 261-262; 138 (February 1934): 521-523.

4546. "Anti-Lynch Fight; Filibuster Continues in Face of Closure
      Threats." NEWSWEEK 11 (January 31, 1938): 13-14.

4547. "Anti-Lynching Bill Approved by House." SCHOLASTIC 30
      (May 1, 1937): 33.

4548. "Anti-Lynching Bill Laid Aside in the Senate." CONGRES-
      SIONAL DIGEST 17 (April 1938): 98.

4549. "Anti-Lynching Campaign." CHAUTAQUA 38 (October 1903):
      11-12.

4550. "Anti-Lynching Legislation." NATION 164 (May 31, 1947):
      643.

4551. "Anti-Lynching Remedies." PUBLIC 22 (May 17, 1919): 511.

4552. Ashbridge, G. "Pennsylvania Lynching." NATION 93 (Oc-
      tober 26, 1911): 392-393.

TERRORISM IN THE UNITED STATES AND EUROPE

Covers the mob execution of Zacharia Walker, at Coatesville, on August 13.

4553. Babbitt, D.R. "Psychology of a Lynching Mob." ARENA 32
(December 1904): 586-589.

4554. "Back to Lynching." NEW REPUBLIC 107 (November 2, 1942):
560-561.

Reports the lynching of three Mississippi blacks within
a five-day period of October 1942.

4555. "Bad Men Hang." COMMONWEAL 18 (May 26, 1933): 89-90.

Examines the mob execution of Will Kinsey, a black man
accused of killing a white at Warrenton, Ga., on May 11.

4556. Baker, Ray S. "Thin Crust of Civilization." AMERICAN
MERCURY 71 (April 1911): 691-704.

4557. ————. "What is a Lynching." McCLURE'S 24 (January
1905): 299-314; 24 (February 1905): 422-430.

4558. Barrow, E.G. "On Lynching." NATION 103 (July 6, 1916):
11.

4559. "The Beast is Loose." SURVEY 69 (December 1933): 413.

Reviews October lynchings of blacks in Georgia, Louisiana, Maryland, and South Carolina.

4560. "Best People Won't Talk." TIME 48 (August 5, 1946): 25.

Examines the mob execution of four "uppity" blacks near
Monroe, Ga., on July 25.

4561. Bishop, J.B. "Lynching." INTERNATIONAL QUARTERLY 8
(September 1903): 199-208.

4562. Black, Paul W. "Lynchings in Iowa." IOWA JOURNAL 10
(April 1912): 151-254.

4563. "Black Shirts and Lynching." WORLD TOMORROW 13 (November 1930): 437-438.

4564. "Black's White; Anti-Lynching Bill." TIME 31 (January
24, 1938): 8-10.

4565. Bloom, L.B. (ed). "Lt. John Bourke's Description of a
       Lynching in 1873." NEW MEXICO HISTORICAL REVIEW 19
       (July 1944): 233-242.

4566. "Blot on Civilization: Coatesville Lynching." OUTLOOK
       98 (August 26, 1911): 899.

4567. Bond, H.M. "What Lies Behind Lynching." NATION 128
       (March 27, 1929): 370-371.

4568. Borah, William E. "Anti-Lynching Bill; Speech in the
       Senate, January 7, 1938." REFERENCE SHELF 11 (1938):
       17-38.

4569. Boynton, S.S. "Miners' Vengeance." OVERLAND MAGAZINE
       22 (September 1893): 303-307.

4570. Bradley, R. "Back of the Maryland Lynching." NATION
       137 (December 13, 1933): 672-673.

       Examines the October 18 lynching of George Armwood, a
       black man accused of attacking an elderly white woman in
       Somerset County. A mob of 5,000 persons participated in
       Armwood's lynching and public cremation.

4571. "Brisk Start of the 1923 Lynchings." LITERARY DIGEST 76
       (January 20, 1923): 11-12.

4572. Brooks, R.P. "Southern Professor on Lynching." NATION
       103 (October 5, 1916): 321-322.

4573. Bruce, W. "Lynch Law in the South." NORTH AMERICAN 155
       (September 1892): 379-381.

4574. Butler, H. "Lynch Law in Action." NEW REPUBLIC 67 (July
       23, 1931): 256-258.

4575. "By the Clock." TIME 49 (February 24, 1947): 29.

       Covers the lynching of black accused murderer Willie
       Earle, taken from jail by a mob at Pickens, N.C., on
       February 17.

4576. Cansler, F. "Lynching Statistics; Reply to 'When is a
       Lynching?'" CHRISTIAN CENTURY 55 (August 24, 1938):
       1016.

4577. Carter, C.F. "Lynching Infamy." CURRENT HISTORY MAGA-
      ZINE 15 (March 1923): 897-902.

4578. Cartwright, M. "Mob Still Rides." NEGRO HISTORY BULLE-
      TIN 19 (February 1956): 105-106.

4579. "Cause and Cure of Lynching." OUTLOOK 74 (August 15,
      1903): 927-929.

4580. Celler, Emmanuel. "Remarks on Proposed Anti-Lynching
      Law." CONGRESSIONAL DIGEST 29 (February 1950): 62+.

4581. Chamberlayne, L.P. "Lynching." NATION 103 (July 13,
      1916): 34-35.

4582. Chambers, W. "Lynch Law in America." CHAMBERS' JOURNAL
      23: 101.

4583. Chamlee, G.W., and J.P. Fort. "Is Lynching Ever Defen-
      sible?" FORM 76 (December 1926): 811-822; 77 (Febru-
      ary 1927): 308-309.

4584. Chapman, J.J. "Nation's Responsibility." EDUCATIONAL
      REVIEW 44 (December 1912): 460-465.

4585. ———. "Penitent at Coatesville." LITERARY DIGEST 45
      (October 5, 1912): 566-567.

      Provides further coverage of the Zacharia Walker lynch-
      ing in Pennsylvania.

4586. "Chicago Indicts the South." LITERARY DIGEST 51 (Octo-
      ber 2, 1915): 698-699.

4587. "Christian Responsibility for Lynchings." CURRENT LIT-
      ERATURE 51 (October 1911): 404-405.

4588. "Churches and Lynchings." CHRISTIAN CENTURY 48 (April
      1, 1931): 429.

4589. "Civilization and Evansville." INDEPENDENT 53 (July 16,
      1903): 1694-1695.

4590. Clark, W. "True Remedy for Lynching." AMERICAN LAW
      REVIEW 28: 801.

4591. "Coatesville Lynchers Free." LITERARY DIGEST 44 (May
      18, 1912): 1023-1024.

4592. "Collegiate Move on Lynching." LITERARY DIGEST 52
      (January 22, 1916): 178.

4593. "Columbia, Tenn." NEW REPUBLIC 77 (December 27, 1933):
      181.

      Examines the December 15 lynching of Cord Cheek, a black
      man accused of molesting a white girl in Maury County.

4594. "Combating Mobs: Campaign Against Lynching Dramatized by
      Banner on Fifth Avenue." LITERARY DIGEST 122 (August
      1, 1936): 32.

4595. "Commission to Investigate Lynchings." NATION 131 (Octo-
      ber 1, 1930): 337.

4596. "Congress Considers the Costigan-Wagner Anti-Lynching
      Bill." CONGRESSIONAL DIGEST 14 (June 1935): 165-192.

4597. Considine, J.L. "When Downieville Hanged a Woman." SUN-
      SET 50 (January 1923): 20.

4598. "Contagious Social Disease." INDEPENDENT 85 (February
      7, 1916): 178.

4599. Cooley, S. "Civic Backsliding." PUBLIC FORUM 18 (Aug-
      ust 6, 1915): 753-754.

4600. Cothran, B. "Ousting Judge Lynch." FORUM 98 (October
      1937): 158-163.

4601. Cox, Oliver C. "Lynching and the Status Quo." JOURNAL
      OF NEGRO EDUCATION 14 (Autumn 1945): 576-588.

4602. Cranfill, J.B. "Story of a Mob." INDEPENDENT 53 (Janu-
      ary 24, 1901): 213-214.

4603. "Crime: Lynchers' Due." NEWSWEEK 29 (March 3, 1947):
      26.

      Examines the legal repercussions of the Willie Earle
      lynching in Pickens, N.C.

4604. Curtis, G.T. "Law and the Lynchers." NORTH AMERICAN
      152 (June 1891): 691-695.

4605. "Curse of Lynching Agitates the Nation." LITERARY DI-
      GEST 116 (December 9, 1933): 5+.

396   TERRORISM IN THE UNITED STATES AND EUROPE

4606. Cutler, J.E. "Capital Punishment and Lynching." ANNALS
      OF THE AMERICAN ACADEMY 29 (May 1907): 622-625.

4607. ————. "Investigation Into the History of Lynching in
      the United States." AMERICAN HISTORY REVIEW 11 (Janu-
      ary 1906): 425-428.

4608. ————. "Lynch Law." NATION 81 (July 20, 1905): 57-58.

4609. ————. "Lynching and Colonel Lynch." NATION 76 (May
      21, 1903): 415.

4610. ————. "Proposed Remedies for Lynching." YALE REVIEW
      13 (August 1904): 194-212.

4611. ————. "Race Riots and Lynch Law: The Cause and the
      Cure; A Northern Professor's View." OUTLOOK 85 (Feb-
      ruary 2, 1907): 263-268.

4612. Dabney, V. "Dixie Rejects Lynching." NATION 145 (Novem-
      ber 27, 1937): 579-580.

4613. Daniels, J. "Native at Large." NATION 151 (September 14,
      1940): 219.

4614. Dashiell, A. "Moscow Comes to Maryland." NEW REPUBLIC
      70 (February 17, 1932): 20-21.

      Reviews the mob execution of Mack Williams, a black
      accused murderer lynched at Salisbury in December 1931.

4615. Davis, H.B. "Substitute for Lynching." NATION 130
      (January 1, 1930): 12-14.

4616. "Death of Picky Pie." TIME 53 (June 13, 1949): 23.

      Examines the lynching of a black victim at Irwinton,
      Ga.

4617. "Decline in Number of Lynchings." NEW REPUBLIC 73 (Jan-
      uary 11, 1933): 226.

4618. "Decrease in Lynching." OUTLOOK 134 (July 25, 1923): 449.

4619. "Deep Down Under Lynching." WORLD TOMORROW 16 (December
      21, 1933): 678.

4620. "Defeat of Judge Lynch." LITERARY DIGEST 105 (April 12, 1930): 24.

4621. "Democracy versus Demo-n-cracy." SURVEY 40 (August 3, 1918): 511-512.

4622. Dennis, A.P. "Political and Ethical Aspects of Lynching." INTERNATIONAL JOURNAL OF ETHICS 15: 149.

4623. "Diminishing Crime." SATURDAY EVENING POST 207 (June 22, 1935): 22.

4624. "Disgrace of Georgia and Alabama." CURRENT LITERATURE 37 (October 1904): 294-296.

Examines the September lynching of four victims in the states mentioned.

4625. "Dixie Blowtorch Sets Yankee Congressmen Afire." NEWS-WEEK 9 (April 24, 1937): 12.

Examines the case of two Mississippi blacks, accused of murdering a white man, who were taken from jail at Duck Hill and tortured to death with blowtorches on April 13.

4626. "Dixie Debunks Lynching; Findings of the Southern Commission on Lynching." LITERARY DIGEST 111 (November 21, 1931): 10.

4627. "Do We Need an Antilynch Law?" COLLIER'S 105 (February 10, 1940): 58.

4628. "Document the Nation Should Read: Plight of Tuscaloosa." CHRISTIAN CENTURY 51 (January 3, 1934): 10.

Examines recent lynchings of three black men at Tuscaloosa, Ala., in August and September 1933.

4629. Dorson, R.M. "Lynching of the McDonald Boys at Menominee." AMERICAN MERCURY 66 (June 1948): 698-703.

4630. "Double Lynching in Virginia." INDEPENDENT 52 (March 29, 1900): 783-784.

Reports the mob execution of Walter Colton and Brandt O'Grady, at Emporia, on March 24.

4631. Douglass, Frederick. "Lynch Law in the South." NORTH AMERICAN 155 (July 1892): 17.

4632. Dubay, Robert W. "Mississippi and the Proposed Federal Anti-Lynching Bills of 1937-1938." SOUTHERN QUARTERLY 7 (1968): 73-90.

4633. Durbin, W.T. "The Mob and the Law." INDEPENDENT 55 (July 30, 1903): 1790-1793.

4634. "Editorial Comment: Mobs, Governors, Citizens." CATHOLIC WORLD 138 (January 1934): 385-390.

4635. Ellet, E.L. "Fate of a Pennsylvania Coquette." MAGAZINE OF AMERICAN HISTORY 25 (April 1891): 372-333.

4636. Elliott, L. "Day Judge Lynch Cried Hang!" CORONET 40 (June 1956): 113-117.

4637. "Epidemic of Savagery." OUTLOOK 69 (September 7, 1901): 9-11.

     Examines the cases of 24 blacks lynched in Alabama and Georgia since the beginning of 1901.

4638. Ethridge, W.S. "Southern Women Attack Lynching." NATION 131 (December 10, 1930): 647.

4639. Ewing, Q. "How Can Lynching be Checked at the South?" OUTLOOK 69 (October 12, 1901): 359-361.

4640. "Excitement Over Picky Pie in Irwinton, Ga." NEWSWEEK 33 (June 13, 1949): 19-20.

4641. Featherstone, H.C. "Origin and History of Lynch Law." GREEN BAG 12: 150.

4642. "Federal Action Coming Against Lynching Following Recent Outrage in Florida." CHRISTIAN CENTURY 51 (November 14, 1934): 1444.

4643. "Federal Curb on Lynching." CHRISTIAN CENTURY 52 (May 8, 1935): 598-600.

4644. "Federal Power and Lynchings." CHAUTAQUA 35 (September 1902): 539.

4645. "Feeling in the South Against Proposed Anti-Lynching Law." NEW RPEUBLIC 82 (May 8, 1935): 352.

4646. "Fewer Lynchings." LITERARY DIGEST 68 (January 22, 1921): 15-16.

4647. "Fight in Texas Against Lynching." WORLD'S WORK 37 (April 1919): 111-113.

4648. "First 1934 Lynching." LITERARY DIGEST 117 (February 10, 1934): 16.

Florida leads the way, with the lynching of Robert Johnson, black accused chicken thief, murdered at Tampa on January 24.

4649. "First War-Lynching." LITERARY DIGEST 57 (April 20, 1918): 16-17.

Reviews the case of Claud Singleton, lynched by a white mob at Poplarville, Miss., on April 20.

4650. Fitelson, H.W. "Murders at Monroe, Ga." NEW REPUBLIC 115 (September 2, 1946): 258-260.

Examines the quadruple murder of blacks accused of "forgetting their place" in respect to local whites.

4651. "Floridians Stage a Lynching Up to Cannidy's." NEWSWEEK 4 (November 3, 1934): 38.

Reports the torture slaying of Claude Neal, black accused rape-slayer, who was lynched by whites at Marianna on October 26.

4652. Flower, B.O. "Burning of Negroes in the South: A Protest and a Warning." ARENA 7 (April 1893): 630-640.

4653. ————. "Rise of Anarchy in the U.S." ARENA 30 (September 1903): 305-311.

4654. "For Hanging Judge Lynch." LITERARY DIGEST 105 (May 17, 1930): 26.

4655. "Four Months Without Lynchings." LITERARY DIGEST 97 (June 2, 1928): 9.

4656. "Fund for the Suppression of Lynching." SURVEY 40 (August 24, 1918): 593.

4657. Gabrilowitsch, O. "Georgian Investigation." HARPER'S WEEKLY 61 (October 2, 1915): 335.

Authorities predictably fail to identify the lynchers of Leo Frank, a Northern Jew convicted of killing a girl in Atlanta. Sixty years later, Frank's innocence was proved and he was posthumously pardoned by the state.

4658. Galloway, C.B. "Some Thoughts on Lynching." SOUTH ATLANTIC QUARTERLY 5: 349.

4659. Gardner, K. "Anti-Lynching Bill." CHRISTIAN CENTURY 52 (January 30, 1935): 147.

4660. Gellhorn, M. "Justice at Night." LIVING AGE 351 (November 1936): 255-258.

Examines the case of Tom Finch, a black man taken from his home, in Atlanta, by lynchers impersonating police. The victim's "offense" is unclear, but the Atlanta police department actively participated in a cover-up, initially pretending Finch was killed by officers while "resisting arrest" for some unspecified crime.

4661. "Georgia's Body-Blow at Mob Murder." LITERARY DIGEST 91 (December 4, 1926): 10.

4662. "Georgia's Right to Lynch." LITERARY DIGEST 53 (September 9, 1916): 593.

4663. "Georgia's Shame." INDEPENDENT 83 (August 30, 1915): 280-281.

4664. Gerber, David A. "Lynching and Law and Order: Origin and Passage of the Ohio Anti-Lynching Law of 1896." OHIO HISTORY 83 (Winter 1974).

4665. Gibbons, J. "Lynch Law; Its Causes and Remedy." NORTH AMERICAN 181 (October 1905): 502.

4666. Gillard, J.T. "Can Law Stop Lynching." COMMONWEAL 19 (December 29, 1933): 235-237.

4667. ————. "Lynching and the Law." COMMONWEAL 19 (December 15, 1933): 175-177.

4668. Gilmour, A. "Mob Murder." READER'S DIGEST 28 (March 1936): 83-85.

4669. Glasson, W.H. "Statistics of Lynching." SOUTH ATLANTIC QUARTERLY 5: 342.

4670. Godkin, E.L. "The Educative Effect of Lynching." NATION 57: 222.

4671. ————. "Judge Lynch as an Educator." NATION 57 (September 28, 1893): 222-223.

4672. ————. "Lynching." NATION 69 (December 14, 1899): 440.

4673. ————. "Southern Lynching." NATION 57 (November 2, 1892): 322.

4674. "Good News on Lynching." COLLIER'S 121 (February 14, 1948): 82.

4675. Gould, B. "San Jose Ministers on Lynching." CHRISTIAN CENTURY 50 (December 20, 1933): 1611.

Presents local justifications for the lynching of two accused murderers. Both victims of the mob were white in this case, which led to the mob being publicly praised by California's governor.

4676. "Governor Lynch and His Mob." NATION 137 (December 13, 1933): 666-667.

Presents further coverage of San Jose's lynching.

4677. Gray, R.L. "Winning the War on Lynching." WORLD'S WORK 50 (September 1925): 507-511.

4678. "Great American Pastime." SURVEY 35 (January 15, 1916): 453.

4679. Gregg, R.B. "Following a Lynching." CHRISTIAN CENTURY 51 (November 7, 1934): 1426.

4680. Greuning, M. "Background of Scottsboro." NEW REPUBLIC 74 (May 3, 1933): 341.

Examines the atmosphere surrounding the case of blacks falsely accused of raping two white prostitutes in Alabama.

4681. ———. "Lynching of Norris Dendy." NEW REPUBLIC 79
      (June 6, 1934): 96-98.

      Reviews the year-old case of a black man lynched at
      Clinton, S.C., on July 4, 1933.

4682. ———. "Reflection on the South." NATION 140 (May 8,
      1935): 539-540.

4683. "Growing Social Effort in the South." SURVEY 36 (May 20,
      1916): 196.

4684. Haywood, A.G. "Black Shadow in the South." FORUM 16
      (October 1893): 167-175.

4685. "House for Fourth Time Since 1922 Considers a Federal
      Anti-Lynching Bill." TIME 35 (January 22, 1940): 18-19

4686. "House Passes Anti-Lynching Bill; Senate Will Block It."
      SCHOLASTIC MAGAZINE 35 (January 22, 1940): 7.

4687. Hovland, Carl I., and Robert R. Sears. "Minor Studies
      in Aggression: Correlation of Lynching with Economic
      Indices." JOURNAL OF PSYCHOLOGY 9 (1940): 301-310.

4688. "How Shall the Black Man's Burden Be Lifted?" CURRENT
      OPINION 67 (August 1919): 111-112.

4689. "How Tampa Treats Lynchers." LITERARY DIGEST 93 (June
      18, 1927): 12-13.

4690. "How to Put Down Lynching." NATION 77 (July 30, 1903):
      86.

4691. Huberman, L. "Lynching in America." SCHOLASTIC MAGAZINE
      25 (November 17, 1934): 21.

4692. "Incident at Pikesville." NEWSWEEK 24 (December 4,
      1944): 48-49.

4693. "Increase of Lynching During the Year 1914." SURVEY 33
      (March 27, 1915): 685.

4694. Innerst, J.S. "Capital Punishment and Lynching." CHRIS-
      TIAN CENTURY 48 (March 18, 1931): 381.

4695. "Insult to the Nation." OUTLOOK 82 (March 31, 1906): 721

4696. "Iowa Lynching." INDEPENDENT 62 (January 31, 1907):
      278-279.

      Examines the case of James Cullen, a white man accused
      of murder, killed by a mob at Charles City on January 9.

4697. "Is a Lynchless Year Coming?" LITERARY DIGEST 89 (April
      24, 1926): 14.

4698. "Is Burning at the Stake to Continue?" OUTLOOK 99 (No-
      vember 4, 1911): 551-552.

4699. "Is the Mob to Rule?" CHRISTIAN CENTURY 50 (December 13,
      1933): 1568-1570.

4700. Johnson, G.W. "Maryland: Storm Warning." NEW REPUBLIC
      77 (December 20, 1933): 159-161; 77 (December 27, 1933):
      199; 78 (March 21, 1934): 162.

      Discusses the case of George Armwood, lynched at Prin-
      cess Anne on October 18.

4701. Johnson, J.W. "Lynching, America's National Disgrace."
      CURRENT HISTORY 19 (January 1924): 596-607.

4702. ————. "Practice of Lynching." CENTURY 115 (November
      1927): 65-70.

4703. Jones, E.O. "Was an Innocent Man Lynched at San Jose?"
      NEW REPUBLIC 77 (February 7, 1934): 365-366.

      Reviews the case of the San Jose mob, casting doubt on
      its accuracy in the selection of victims.

4704. Jordan, J. "Lynchers Don't Like Lead." ATLANTIC MONTHLY
      177 (February 1946): 103-108.

4705. "Judge Lynch." CURRENT HISTORY 51 (February 1940): 6.

4706. "Judge Lynch and John Law." NEW REPUBLIC 77 (January 3,
      1934): 213.

4707. "Judge Lynch and the Pole Cat." NEWSWEEK 19 (February 9,
      1942): 59.

4708. "Judge Lynch Becomes Unpopular." LITERARY DIGEST 80
      (February 2, 1924): 31-32.

4709. "Judge Lynch in Decline." LITERARY DIGEST 86 (July 25, 1925): 32.

4710. "Judge Lynch Overruled." TIME 38 (July 7, 1941): 13.

4711. "Jury Makes Sheriff Pay for Negro's Lawless Death." NEWSWEEK 7 (May 30, 1936): 36.

Examines legal repercussions in the case of Willis Kees a black accused rapist lynched at Lepanto, Ark., in April

4712. Karlin, J.A. "New Orleans Lynchings of 1891 and the American Press." LOUISIANA HISTORICAL QUARTERLY 24 (January 1941): 187-204.

4713. Kennedy, N.J.D. "Englishman's View of the New Orleans Affair." REVIEW OF REVIEWS 5 (March 1892): 196.

4714. "Kentucky Cure for Lynching." LITERARY DIGEST 64 (February 28, 1920): 20-21.

4715. Kesler, J.L. "In Justice to Waco." NATION 103 (December 28, 1916): 609.

Reviews the May 15 lynching of Washington Jess, a black man accused of rape and murder.

4716. "King Mob Runs Amok in Texas." LITERARY DIGEST 105 (May 24, 1930): 11.

Describes events of May 9, at Sherman, Tex., where a mob burned the courthouse and blasted its vault to seize George Hughes, a black accused rapist.

4717. "Last Year's Lynching Record." OUTLOOK 115 (January 17, 1917): 97.

4718. "Last Year's Lynchings." LITERARY DIGEST 54 (January 27, 1917): 178.

4719. "Law and Lynching in Georgia." OUTLOOK 112 (March 1, 1916): 484.

4720. "Law Gaining on Lynching." LITERARY DIGEST 76 (January 13, 1923): 13-14.

4721. Law, R.A. "Punishment for Lynching." NATION 100 (March 25, 1915): 330-331.

4722. "Less Inclined to Lynch." OUTLOOK 142 (March 31, 1926):
      481-482.

4723. "Less Work for Judge Lynch." LITERARY DIGEST 46 (April
      26, 1913): 936.

4724. "Lessons of Coatesville." NATION 93 (August 31, 1911):
      183-184.

4725. Levell, W.H. "Lynching in the South." OUTLOOK 69 (No-
      vember 16, 1901): 678-679, 731-733.

4726. "Life and Liberty at Greenville, S.C." COMMONWEAL 46
      (June 6, 1947): 180.

      Reports the acquittal of 31 accused lynchers in the
      case of Willie Earle, murdered by a mob in February 1947.

4727. Lodge, Henry Cabot. "Lynching and Unrestricted Immigra-
      tion." NORTH AMERICAN 152 (May 1891): 602.

4728. "Look Before You Lynch." OUTLOOK 133 (February 7, 1923):
      253.

4729. "Louder Than Words: South Carolina." NEW REPUBLIC 116
      (March 24, 1947): 8.

      Praises the indictment of Willie Earle's lynchers,
      hopefully (and fruitlessly) anticipating convictions.

4730. "Louisiana Negro Lynched." NEWSWEEK 4 (July 21, 1934):
      8.

      Reports the lynching of Andrew McLeod, accused rapist,
      at Bastrop on July 9.

4731. "Lynch and Anti-Lynch." TIME 29 (April 26, 1937): 16-17.

4732. "Lynch-law and Treason; Lynching of Frank Little in
      Butte." LITERARY DIGEST 55 (August 18, 1917): 12-13.

4733. "Lynch Law: Congress Toys with Wagner-Van Nuys Anti-
      Lynching Bill." LITERARY DIGEST 123 (March 20, 1937):
      8-9.

4734. "Lynch Law in 1930." SURVEY 65 (October 15, 1930): 69.

4735. "Lynch Law in the South." INDEPENDENT 61 (October 11, 1906): 842-843.

4736. "Lynch Trial Makes Southern History." LIFE 22 (June 2, 1947): 27-31.

4737. "Lynch Week." TIME 40 (October 26, 1942): 23.

    Examines Mississippi's violent outburst, with three victims lynched in five days.

4738. "Lynchers Triumphant." NATION 93 (October 26, 1911): 386.

4739. "Lynching." NEW REPUBLIC 116 (March 3, 1947): 9.

4740. "Lynching a Family." LITERARY DIGEST 50 (January 30, 1915): 178-179.

    Reports a triple lynching at Monticello, Ga.

4741. "Lynching a National Evil." OUTLOOK 132 (December 6, 1922): 596-597.

4742. "Lynching Affair at New Orleans." SPECTATOR 66 (March 21, 1891): 400-402.

4743. "Lynching Again on the Increase." CHRISTIAN CENTURY 48 (January 7, 1931): 5.

4744. "Lynching: An American Kultur?" NEW REPUBLIC 14 (April 13, 1918): 311-312.

4745. "Lynching and the Axis." COMMONWEAL 37 (October 30, 1942): 27-28.

4746. "Lynching and the Criminal Law." REVIEW OF REVIEWS 34 (December 1906): 751-752.

4747. "Lynching and Criminal Procedure." OUTLOOK 83 (June 9, 1906): 301.

4748. "Lynching and Federal Law." CHAUTAQUA 40 (January 1905): 408-409.

4749. "Lynching and the Franchise Rights of the Negro." ANNALS OF THE AMERICAN ACADEMY OF POLITICAL SCIENCE 15 (May 1900): 493-497.

4750. "Lynching and Illiteracy." WORLD'S WORK 20 (October 1915): 637-638.

4751. "Lynching and New Negro Crime." HARPER'S WEEKLY 47 (August 29, 1903): 1395-1396.

4752. "Lynching and Public Sentiment in Florida." OUTLOOK 98 (June 10, 1911): 289-291.

Reports the mass-lynching of six blacks at Lake City on May 21. The victims, none of whom were identified, had been accused of killing a white man.

4753. "Lynching at All-Time Low." CHRISTIAN CENTURY 63 (January 16, 1946): 67.

4754. "Lynching Championship." LITERARY DIGEST 52 (February 5, 1916): 274-275.

Georgia wins hands-down, with the lynching of five blacks, including four members of the same family, at Sylvester on January 21.

4755. "Lynching Decreasing." LITERARY DIGEST 90 (July 24, 1926): 30.

4756. "Lynching et al." COMMONWEAL 18 (September 1, 1933): 417-418.

4757. "Lynching Evil." NEW REPUBLIC 19 (May 3, 1919): 7-8.

4758. "Lynching Evil from a Southern Standpoint." REVIEW OF REVIEWS 60 (November 1919): 531-532.

4759. "Lynching in America and English Interference." SPECTA-TOR 73 (August 11, 1894): 169.

4760. "Lynching in Cairo, Illinois." OUTLOOK 93 (November 27, 1906): 637-638.

4761. "Lynching in the Making." INDEPENDENT WOMAN 14 (January 1935): 7+.

4762. "Lynching in the Raw." CHRISTIAN CENTURY 52 (January 2, 1935): 10-11.

4763. "Lynching is a Community Crime." NATION 163 (August 3, 1946): 113.

4764. "Lynching Madness." NATION 77 (July 2, 1902): 4.

4765. "Lynching Mania at Large." REVIEW OF REVIEWS 23 (March 1901): 262.

4766. "Lynching Must Be Stopped!" CHRISTIAN CENTURY 54 (April 28, 1937): 544-546.

4767. "Lynching of Justice." COMMONWEAL 19 (December 8, 1933): 141-142.

4768. "Lynching on the Decrease." OUTLOOK 136 (January 9, 1924): 31.

4769. "Lynching on the Wane." LITERARY DIGEST 82 (August 23, 1924): 31.

4770. "Lynching Ratio Cut in Half." CHRISTIAN CENTURY 57 (January 3, 1940): 5.

4771. "Lynching Record." OUTLOOK 106 (February 28, 1914): 434.

4772. "Lynching Record for 1919." OUTLOOK 121 (January 22, 1919): 159.

4773. "Lynching Records Show Continued Gains." CHRISTIAN CENTURY 57 (May 29, 1940): 692.

4774. "Lynching Roll of Honor." LITERARY DIGEST 81 (April 5, 1924): 32-33.

4775. "Lynching the Innocent." NATION 133 (November 25, 1930): 561.

    Examines the case of Laci Mitchell, black star witness
    in the case of two white men charged with raping a black
    woman. Mitchell was lynched in Thomas County, Ga., on
    September 28, in an effort to scuttle the case.

4776. "Lynching Without 'Error of Law.'" PUBLIC FORUM 20 (October 5, 1917): 956.

4777. "Lynchings." OUTLOOK 156 (November 26, 1930): 489.

4778. "Lynchings in 1919." LITERARY DIGEST 64 (January 17, 1920): 20.

4779. "Lynchings Increase in 1940." CHRISTIAN CENTURY 58 (January 15, 1941): 76.

4780. "Lynchings North and South." GUNTON 25 (August 1903): 179-181.

4781. "Lynchings of 1934." LITERARY DIGEST 119 (January 12, 1935): 18.

4782. "Lynchings of Two Days." CHRISTIAN CENTURY 52 (November 27, 1935): 15-19.

   Examines mob violence which claimed the lives of two Louisiana victims and one from Tennessee in the first week of November 1935.

4783. "Lynching's Ominous Growth." LITERARY DIGEST 117 (January 13, 1934): 7.

4784. "Lynchings Stir Southern Debate." LITERARY DIGEST 120 (November 23, 1935): 6.

4785. "Lynchless South in 1933." COMMONWEAL 17 (November 30, 1932): 116.

4786. McClellan, John L. "Views on Proposed Anti-Lynching Laws." CONGRESSIONAL DIGEST 29 (February 1950): 63-64.

4787. McCrady, E. "Lynch Law and South Carolina." NATION 76 (January 15, 1903): 52.

4788. Mackreth, R.W. "Lynching Evil and Church Responsibility." LITERARY DIGEST 116 (December 23, 1933): 19-20; 117 (February 3, 1934): 47.

4789. "Major Legislation Moves Forward." CONGRESSIONAL DIGEST 16 (May 1937): 131.

4790. "Mark of the Beast." INDEPENDENT 117 (October 30, 1926): 489.

4791. "Maryland Has a Lynching." OUTLOOK 159 (December 23, 1931): 521.

   Recounts the lynching of Mack Williams, a black accused of killing his white employer at Salisbury.

4792. "Maryland Judge Censured for Tragedy." NEWSWEEK 2 (October 28, 1933): 8.

Examines repercussions of the George Armwood lynching, on October 18.

4793. "Maryland Lynching." NEW REPUBLIC 76 (November 8, 1933): 348.

4794. "Maryland's Eastern Shore." NATION 137 (November 1, 1933) 497.

Presents further coverage of the Armwood lynching.

4795. "Mass Murder in America." NEW REPUBLIC 77 (December 13, 1933): 116- 117.

4796. Matelis, V. "Merrily Lynching Along!" COMMONWEAL 16 (September 7, 1932): 443-445.

4797. Matthews, A. "History of the Term." NATION 75 (December 4, 1902): 719-721; 76 (January 29, 1903): 91.

4798. "Maysville Affair." NATION 69 (December 14, 1899): 440.

4799. Maxey, E. "Mob Rule." ARENA 30 (October 1903): 377-381.

4800. Means, D.M. "Lynch Law." NATION 65 (July 1, 1897): 6-7.

4801. Mecklin, J.M. "Confessio Nominis Non Examinato Criminis." NATION 104 (February 15, 1917): 186-187.

4802. "Men With Guns." NEWSWEEK 28 (August 5, 1946): 24.

Examines the murder of four blacks near Monroe, Ga., on July 25.

4803. Merrill, T. "Lynching the Anti-Lynching Bill." CHRISTIAN CENTURY 55 (February 23, 1938): 238-240.

4804. "Mexican Boycott." INDEPENDENT 69 (November 17, 1910): 1111-1112.

4805. Milston, G.F. "The Impeachment of Lynching." VIRGINIA QUARTERLY REVIEW (April 1932): 182-219.

4806. "Missouri Heads 1931 Lynching Parade." LITERARY DIGEST 108 (January 31, 1931): 17-18.

Reports the January 19 lynching of Raymond Gunn, at
Maryville. Charged with rape and murder of a local
teacher, Gunn was taken to the school where the crime
occurred, chained to a rooftree soaked with gasoline,
and cremated alive when the school was burned down
around him.

4807. "Missouri Mob Murder." OUTLOOK 157 (January 28, 1931):
      123.

4808. "Mr. Graves, Friend of the Mob." NATION 77 (August 30,
      1903): 146.

4809. "Mob at Springfield, Ohio." INDEPENDENT 60 (March 8,
      1906): 582-584.

      Examines the two-year-old case of Richard Dixon, lynched
      on March 7, 1904.

4810. "Mob Law." NEWSWEEK 2 (December 9, 1933): 6+.

4811. "Mob Law and the Negro." PUBLIC FORUM 20 (August 24,
      1917): 810-811.

4812. "Mob-Law and Prosperity." NATION 96 (March 16, 1911):
      259-260.

4813. "Mob-Law in Georgia." LITERARY DIGEST 51 (August 23,
      1915): 392.

4814. "Mob Spirit." CHAUTAQUA 38 (September 1903): 11-13.

4815. Morgan, C.T. "Lynched Death." CHRISTIAN CENTURY 56
      (February 8, 1939): 182-184.

      Examines the case of R.C. Williams, lynched on suspi-
      cion of rape and murder, in October 1938, at Ruston,
      Louisiana.

4816. "Morning in Bledsoe County." TIME 44 (December 4, 1944):
      22.

4817. Moton, R.R. "Lynchings Last Year." FORUM 79 (March
      1928): 475-476.

4818. "Moving Against Lynching." NATION 203 (August 3, 1916):
      101-102.

4819. "Murder." OUTLOOK 74 (August 8, 1903): 877-880.

4820. "Murder and the Law." NATION 96 (April 3, 1913): 326-327.

4821. Nack, A.J. "What We All Stand For: Coatesville Lynching."
      AMERICAN MERCURY 75 (February 1913): 53-57.

4822. Nash, R. "Lynching of Anthony Crawford." INDEPENDENT
      88 (December 11, 1916): 456+.

      Examines the case of a black farmer, lynched at Abbe-
      ville, S.C., after he cursed a white man in an argument
      over the price of cotton seed.

4823. "Nation Cheers as Tennessee Prevents a Lynching." LITER-
      ARY DIGEST 118 (December 29, 1934): 6.

4824. "New Phases of the Fight Against Lynching." CURRENT
      OPINION 67 (July 1919): 45.

4825. "New Twist." TIME 49 (March 3, 1947): 25.

4826. "Nine Negroes Have Been Lynched in Last Nine Months."
      NATION 163 (August 31, 1946): 225.

4827. "1933 Lynching Record." WORLD TOMORROW 17 (January 18,
      1934): 39.

4828. "1936 Score Jumps to Six." NEWSWEEK 7 (May 9, 1936): 11.

4829. "No Christian Condonation of Lynching." LITERARY DIGEST
      74 (September 9, 1922): 35.

4830. Nordyke, L.T. "Ladies and Lynchings." SURVEY GEOGRAPH-
      IC 28 (November 1939): 683-686.

4831. "North Carolina Slips." OUTLOOK 156 (September 3, 1930):
      14.

      Reports the lynching of Oliver Moore, a black man
      accused of rape at Tarboro, on August 19.

4832. "Northern Lynching." OUTLOOK 95 (July 23, 1910): 597-598.

      Examines the lynching of Carl Etherington at Newark,
      Ohio, on July 8.

4833. "Not by Violence." INDEPENDENT 53 (April 4, 1901): 796-
       797.

4834. "Note on Lynching." SCRIBNER'S COMMENTARY 9 (April 1941):
       68.

4835. Odum, H.W. "Lynchings, Fears, and Folkways." NATION 133
       (December 30, 1931): 719-720.

4836. "One Remedy for Mobs." WORLD'S WORK (September 1903):
       3829-3830.

4837. Oppenheim, J. "Lynching of Robert Johnson." INDEPENDENT
       73 (October 10, 1912): 823-827.

       Covers the case of a black man, charged with attempted
       rape (and later proved innocent), who was lynched at
       Bluefield, West Virginia, on September 4.

4838. "Organized Killings." NEW REPUBLIC 76 (October 4, 1933):
       197.

4839. Oswald, F.L. "Lynch Epidemics." NORTH AMERICAN 165
       (July 1897): 119.

4840. "Outlaw State: Lynching of Leo M. Frank." OUTLOOK 110
       (August 25, 1915): 945-947.

4841. Ovington, M.W. "Anti-Lynching Conference of the National
       Association for the Advancement of Colored People."
       SURVEY 42 (May 17, 1919): 292.

4842. Page, T.W. "Lynching of Negroes, Its Cause and Preven-
       tion." NORTH AMERICAN 178 (January 1904): 33-48.

4843. ———. "Lynching and Race Relations in the South."
       NORTH AMERICAN 206 (August 1917): 241-250.

4844. Page, W.H. "Last Hold of the Southern Bully." FORUM
       16: 303.

4845. Parrott, L. "Making History of Lynching." SURVEY 67
       (February 15, 1922): 532-533.

4846. "Pass Anti-Lynching Law Before Adjournment!" CHRISTIAN
       CENTURY 63 (August 7, 1946): 956.

4847. "Passing of Judge Lynch." LITERARY DIGEST 84 (January
      31, 1925): 30-31.

4848. Pell, E.L. "Prevention of Lynch Law." REVIEW OF REVIEWS
      17: 321.

4849. "Perhaps a Lex Talionis is Better Than No Lex." CHRISTIAN
      CENTURY 51 (March 21, 1934): 381.

4850. Petrie, J.C. "Lynching Shows Need for Federal Law."
      CHRISTIAN CENTURY 51 (January 24, 1934): 133.

4851. Pickens, W. "Aftermath of a Lynching." NATION 132 (Ap-
      ril 15, 1931): 406-407.

4852. ————. "American Congo; Burning of Henry Lowry." NATION
      112 (March 23, 1921): 426-428.

4853. Pierantoni, A. "Italian Feeling on American Lynching."
      INDEPENDENT 55 (August 27, 1903): 2040-2042.

4854. Poe, C.H. "Lynching, a Southern View." ATLANTIC MONTHLY
      93 (February 1904): 155-165.

4855. "Point No. 3: Anti-Lynching Proposals." CONGRESSIONAL
      DIGEST 29 (February 1950): 45.

4856. "Political Suicide." TIME 65 (January 24, 1955): 19.

4857. "Practical Way to Cut Down Lynchings." SURVEY 37 (Janu-
      ary 20, 1917): 461.

4858. "President on Lynching." NATION 77 (August 13, 1903):
      126.

4859. "Prevalence and Remedy." OUTLOOK 74 (August 13, 1903):
      126.

4860. "Prevention of Lynching." OUTLOOK 74 (August 22, 1903):
      959-961.

4861. Pruden, Durward. "A Sociological Study of a Texas
      Lynching." STUDIES IN SOCIOLOGY 1 (1936): 3-9.

4862. "Public Responsiblity for Mob Violence." OUTLOOK 82
      (April 28, 1906): 920-921.

4863. "Quiet Week." TIME 48 (August 26, 1946): 21.

    Congratulates Dixie on a "quiet week," following a
month in which five blacks were lynched and race riots
erupted in four states.

4864. "Quincy Ewing on Lynching." INDEPENDENT 53 (August 29,
    1901): 2059-2061.

4865. "Quintuple Lynching in Indiana." PUBLIC OPINION 23: 389.

4866. Randolph, T. "Governor and the Mob." INDEPENDENT 89
    (February 26, 1917): 347-348.

    Examines the case of five white burglars, lynched by
a Valparaiso, Ind., mob in 1897.

4867. Rascoe, B. "Caldwell Lynches Two Negroes." AMERICAN
    MERCURY 49 (April 1940): 493-498.

4868. "Reaping the Whirlwind." NATION 87 (November 5, 1908):
    428-429.

4869. Reed, John S. "An Evaluation of an Anti-Lynching Organ-
    ization." SOCIAL PROBLEMS 16 (1968): 172-182.

4870. Reilly, L.W. "Lynching: A National Crime." CATHOLIC
    WORLD 127 (July 1928): 396-403.

4871. "Report That Didn't Come." CHRISTIAN CENTURY 72 (Novem-
    ber 1954): 35.

4872. "Reversion to Savagery." OUTLOOK 110 (August 11, 1915):
    835-836.

4873. "Rewards to Catch Lynchers." NATION 107 (August 31,
    1918): 218-219.

4874. Richardson, W.H. "No More Lynchings! How North Carolina
    Has Solved the Problem." REVIEW OF REVIEWS 69 (April
    1924): 401-404.

4875. Robinson, N.T.N. "Anti-Lynching Bill; Progress to Date."
    CONGRESSIONAL DIGEST 14 (May 1935): 130-13i.

4876. Roosevelt, T. "Lynching and the Miscarriage of Justice."
    OUTLOOK 99 (November 25, 1911): 706-707.

4877. Ross, M. "Where Lynching is a Habit." SURVEY 49 (February 15, 1923): 626-627.

4878. Rousseau, B.G. "Juanita." OVERLAND MAGAZINE 52 (June 1924): 249-251.

4879. Sancton, T. "Greenville Acquittals." SURVEY GEOGRAPHIC 36 (June 1947): 349+.

       Examines the "not guilty" verdicts in the case of Willie Earle's lynchers, acquitted by an all-white jury.

4880. Seagle, W. "How to Put a Stop to Lynching." NATION 140 (May 29, 1935): 626.

4881. Seligman, H.J. "Protecting Southern Womanhood." NATION 10 (June 14, 1919): 938-939.

4882. "Sequel to Scottsboro." NEW REPUBLIC 76 (August 23, 1933): 34.

4883. "Shame of Pennsylvania." INDEPENDENT 71 (August 24, 1911): 427-429.

4884. "Shame to Mississippi." NATION 128 (January 16, 1929): 62.

4885. "Shelbyville Affair." COMMONWEAL 21 (January 4, 1935): 273.

4886. Sheldon, W.D. "Shall Lynching Be Suppressed, and How?" ARENA 36 (September 1906): 225.

4887. ———. "Shall Lynching Be Suppressed?" OUTLOOK 111 (September 15, 1915): 152.

4888. "Should America Have a Federal Anti-Lynching Law? Pro and Con." LITERARY DIGEST 124 (December 4, 1937): 12.

4889. "Silent Sentinel: South Carolina Lynching." NEW REPUBLIC 115 (May 26, 1947): 8-10.

4890. "Sledd, A. "Negro." ATLANTIC MONTHLY 90 (July 1902): 65-73.

4891. Smith, A.E. "Two Governors." NEW OUTLOOK 163 (January 1934): 11-12.

4892. Smith, B. "Memphis Lynching." NEW REPUBLIC 12 (August
      11, 1917): 51.

      Reviews the case of Ell Person, lynched on allegations
      of rape and murder, May 22, 1917.

4893. Somerville, H.M. "Some Causes of Negro Lynching." NORTH
      AMERICAN 177 (October 1903): 506-512.

4894. "Somewhere in America." COLLIER'S 109 (March 28, 1942):
      70.

4895. "South Carolina's Shame." NATION 123 (November 17, 1926):
      497.

4896. "Southern Church Speaks Out Against Lynching." CHRISTIAN
      CENTURY 47 (October 22, 1930): 1268.

4897. "Southern Commission Reports." CHRISTIAN CENTURY 48 (No-
      vember 25, 1931): 1477.

4898. "Southern Leaders Out to Track Down Judge Lynch." LIT-
      ERARY DIGEST 107 (October 18, 1930): 24-25.

4899. "Southern Protest Against Lynching." OUTLOOK 112 (Janu-
      ary 19, 1916): 124-125.

4900. "Southern Senators Filibuster." NEWSWEEK 5 (May 4, 1935):
      10.

      Dixie solons talk a federal anti-lynching bill to
      death, thus preserving "states' rights."

4901. "Southern Women Fight Lynching Evil." LITERARY DIGEST
      117 (January 27, 1934): 22.

4902. "South's Fight Against Mob Murders." LITERARY DIGEST
      84 (January 17, 1925): 30-31.

4903. "South's Latest Lynching." NEW REPUBLIC 80 (November
      7, 1934): 350.

4904. Spence, A.W. "Lynching and the Nation." COMMONWEAL 15
      (April 13, 1932): 658-659.

4905. "State Police a Cure for Lynching." WORLD'S WORK 35
      (April 1918): 585-586.

4906. "Statistics." INDEPENDENT 52 (January 11, 1900): 140.

4907. "Status of Anti-Lynching Bill." CONGRESSIONAL DIGEST 17
      (February 1938): 35.

4908. Stevens, W. Le C. "Lynching and the Law's Delays."
      NATIONS 61: 426.

4909. Stewart, H.L. "Casuistry of Lynch Law." NATION 103
      (August 24, 1916): 173-174.

4910. ———. "Southern View of Lynching." NATION 104 (Janu-
      ary 25, 1917): 102-103.

4911. "Story of a Lynching in Greenville, S.C." NEWSWEEK 29
      (May 26, 1947): 29-30.

4912. "Streicher Reminds American of Lynching Disgrace." CHRIS-
      TIAN CENTURY 52 (August 28, 1935): 1077.

4913. "Struggle Against Lynching Goes on in North Carolina."
      CHRISTIAN CENTURY 64 (August 20, 1947): 988.

4914. Summerbell, C. "Following a Lynching; Reply." CHRISTIAN
      CENTURY 51 (November 21, 1934): 1491.

4915. Taber, S.R. "Remedy for Lynching." NATION 75 (December
      18, 1902): 478.

4916. ———. "Remedy for Lynching." OUTLOOK 69 (November 16,
      1901): 678.

4917. "Talked Out." COLLIER'S 101 (March 5, 1938): 66.

4918. Taylor, A.W. "Lynchers Still Go Unpunished." CHRISTIAN
      CENTURY 51 (February 7, 1931): 200.

4919. ———. "Report on Responsibility for Lynchings, Tusca-
      loosa, Ala." CHRISTIAN CENTURY 50 (November 29, 1933):
      1509.

4920. "Tennessee Mobilizing for Law and Order." SURVEY 39
      (March 23, 1918): 690-691.

4921. Terrell, M.C. "Lynching from a Negro's Point of View."
      NORTH AMERICAN 178 (June 1904): 853-868.

4922. "Texas Anti-Lynch Law." NEW REPUBLIC 120 (March 7, 1949):
      7.

4923. "Texas Minds Its Own Business." TIME 53 (March 21,
      1949): 24.

4924. "Thirteen Lynchings." OUTLOOK 160 (January 6, 1932): 7.

      Reviews the body-count for 1931, with thirteen victims
      slain in eleven separate lynchings.

4925. "Thirty Years' Record in Lynching." WORLD'S WORK 39
      (March 1920): 433-444.

4926. Thompson, M. "Lynch Law." LIPPINCOTT'S MAGAZINE 64:
      254.

4927. Thornton, W. "Southern Comment on Lynching." NATION
      131 (October 22, 1930): 444.

4928. "To Lynch or Not to Lynch?" OUTLOOK 115 (January 24,
      1917): 137-138.

4929. Tobias, D.E. "Position of the Negro in America." 19th
      CENTURY AND AFTER 46 (December 1899): 966-968.

4930. "Torture and Lynching." OUTLOOK 71 (June 28, 1902):
      533-534.

4931. Townshend, R.B. "Trial by Lynch Law." 19th CENTURY AND
      AFTER 32; 243.

4932. "Trial by Jury in Greenville, S.C." TIME 49 (May 26,
      1947): 27.

      Reports the acquittal of lynchers in the Willie Earle
      case.

4933. "Trial by Jury in Lyons, Ga." NEWSWEEK 33 (January 24,
      1949): 20+.

      Accused lynchers are acquitted again, by an all-white
      jury.

4934. "Trial of Thirty-one White Men." NATION 164 (May 24,
      1947): 615.

4935. Tribble, E.   "Impeaching Judge Lynch."   NEW REPUBLIC 67
       (July 15, 1931): 226-227.

4936. "Troops Called Out in Shelbyville."   NEWSWEEK 4 (December 29, 1934): 5.

4937. "Tuscaloosa, Ala."   NEW REPUBLIC 76 (August 30, 1933): 58.

4938. "Twelve Good Men and True."   NEW REPUBLIC 116 (June 2,
       1947): 9.

       Provides further coverage of the Willie Earle lynching
       trial.

4939. "28 Lynchings in 1933): SURVEY 70 (February 1934): 49.

4940. "Two Lynchings Last Year."   CHRISTIAN CENTURY 66 (January 19, 1949): 67.

4941. "Undermining of Civilization."   CHRISTIAN CENTURY 50 (December 6, 1933): 1525.

4942. "Unusual and Different Punishment; Jury Made Legal Race
       History in Jackson, Miss."   TIME 41 (January 25, 1943):
       24.

4943. Upton, George P.   "Facts About Lynching."   INDEPENDENT
       57 (September 29, 1904): 719-721.

4944. "Uses and Abuses of Lynch Law."   AMERICAN WHIG REVIEW
       11: 459; 12: 494; 13: 213.

4945. Van Nuys, F.   "Report on the Anti-Lynching Bill, April 8,
       1940."   CONGRESSIONAL DIGEST 19 (August 1940): 208-210.

4946. Villard, O.G.   "Judge Lynch: His First Hundred Years."
       SATURDAY REVIEW OF LITERATURE 18 (July 30, 1938): 19-
       20.

4947.————.   "North Carolina Uprising."   NATION 83 (August 23,
       1906): 158-159.

       Records the lynching of three blacks at Salisbury, on
       August 6.

4948. "Virginia's Anti-Lynching Law."   LITERARY DIGEST 96
       (March 10, 1928): 14.

4949. "Wagner-Costigan Anti-Lynching Bill." NEW REPUBLIC 79
        (June 20, 1934): 139.

4950. Walter, David O. "Proposals for a Federal Anti-Lynching
        Law." AMERICAN POLITICAL SCIENCE REVIEW 28 (June
        1934): 436-442.

4951. "Wane of Lynching." OUTLOOK 137 (July 23, 1924): 459.

4952. Warren, N.J. "Inside Facts from Shelbyville." CHRISTIAN
        CENTURY 52 (January 30, 1935): 146.

4953. Washington, Booker T. "Lynchings and International Peace."
        OUTLOOK 100 (March 9, 1912): 554-555.

4954. Wells-Barnett, Ida B. "Lynch Law in America." ARENA 23
        (January 1900): 15-24.

4955. ————. "Lynching and the Excuse for It." INDEPENDENT
        53 (May 16, 1901): 1133-1136.

4956. ————. "The Negro's Case in Equity." INDEPENDENT 52
        (April 26, 1900): 1010-1011.

4957. ————. "Our Country's Lynching Record." SURVEY 29
        (February 1, 1913): 573-574.

4958. West, R. "Opera in Greenville." THE NEW YORKER 23
        (June 14, 1947): 33-36+.

4959. "What Alabama Thinks of Her Lynching." LITERARY DIGEST
        116 (September 2, 1933): 8.

4960. "When is a Lynching?" CHRISTIAN CENTURY 55 (August 10,
        1938): 957.

4961. Whipple, L. "Why We Lynch." SURVEY 63 (October 1,
        1929): 22.

4962. White, Walter. "I Investigate Lynchings." AMERICAN
        MERCURY 16 (January 1929): 77-84.

4963. Whittington, W.M. "Speech in the House, January 9, 1940,
        Opposing the Anti-Lynching Bill." CONGRESSIONAL DIGEST
        19 (August 1940): 217-218.

4964. "Who is to Blame for Mob Murders?" LITERARY DIGEST 106
        (July 19, 1930): 22.

4965. "Why Was Frank Lynched?" FORUM 56 (December 1916): 677-692.

4966. "Why Lynching Has Slumped." LITERARY DIGEST 78 (July 28, 1923): 16.

4967. "Will-to-Lynch." NEW REPUBLIC 8 (October 14, 1916): 261-262.

4968. Willis, G.S. "Lynch's Creek and the Name Lynch Law." NATION 76 (March 19, 1903): 225.

4969. Winston, J.T. "Lynching Defended." NATION 102 (June 22, 1916): 671.

4970. "Wiping Off a Smirch in Newark, Ohio." OUTLOOK 100 (January 6, 1912): 7-8.

4971. "With My Own Body! Gov. Stanley in Kentucky Prevents a Lynching." INDEPENDENT 89 (January 22, 1917): 135.

4972. "Women and Lynch Law." COMMONWEAL 13 (December 17, 1930): 171-172.

4973. Woofter, T.J. "Southern Backfires Against Lynch Law." SURVEY 51 (October 15, 1923): 99-100.

4974. Work, M.N. "Lynchings in the United States Since 1885." MISSISSIPPI REVIEW 54 (August 1931): 620.

4975. "Working for a Lynchless Year." LITERARY DIGEST 115 (January 7, 1933): 19.

4976. Yost, Genvieve. "History of Lynchings in Kansas." KANSAS HISTORICAL QUARTERLY 2 (May 1933): 182-219.

4977. Zangrando, Robert L. "The NAACP and a Federal Antilynching Bill, 1934-1940." JOURNAL OF NEGRO HISTORY 50 (1965): 106-117.

7. Political Violence

a. Books

4978. Abbott, Wilbur C. THE NEW BARBARIANS. Boston: Little, Brown, 1925.

Presents a critical view of 1920s radicals.

4979. Allen, James S. RECONSTRUCTION: THE BATTLE FOR DEMOCRACY
      (1865-76). New York: International Publishers, 1937.

      Examines post-Civil War reconstruction from the view-
      point of the American Communist Party.

4980. American Civil Liberties Union. WAR TIME PROSECUTION AND
      MOB VIOLENCE, 1917-1918. New York: A.C.L.U., 1918.

      Examines contemporaneous violence and "oppressive"
      prosecution aimed at "slackers," pacifists, and others
      who spoke out against American involvement in the First
      World War.

4981. Archer, Jules. THE PLOT TO SEIZE THE WHITE HOUSE. New
      York: Hawthorn Books, 1973.

      Documents an apparent effort by American military lead-
      ers and right-wing civilian elements to organize a coup
      against the New Deal regime of President Franklin Roose-
      velt.

4982. Bell, J. Bowyer. TRANSNATIONAL TERROR. Washington, D.C.:
      American Enterprise Institute for Public Policy Re-
      search, 1975.

4983. Bell, Leland V. HITLER'S SHADOW: THE ANATOMY OF AMERI-
      CAN NAZISM. Port Washington, N.Y.: Kennikat Press,
      1973.

4984. Billington, Ray A. THE PROTESTANT CRUSADE, 1800-1860: A
      STUDY OF THE ORIGINS OF AMERICAN NATIVISM. New York:
      Rinehart, 1938.

4985. Breihan, Carl W. QUANTRILL AND HIS CIVIL WAR GUERILLAS.
      Denver: A. Swallow, 1959.

      Follows the murderous career of Southern "guerilla
      fighters" who specialized in looting, rape, and the
      massacre of unarmed civilians in the Kansas-Missouri
      border country. Quantrill was run to earth and killed
      in May 1865, by Union troops. Surviving members of his
      troop, including the James and Younger brothers, went on
      to plague the nation with holdups and murders for another
      seventeen years before they were finally wiped out.

4986. Burligame, Roger. THE SIXTH COLUMN. Philadelphia: Lip-
      pincott, 1962.

      Includes coverage of violence by various right-wing
      groups, including the "respectable" American Legion, from
      the early 1920s onward.

4987. Burton, Anthony. REVOLUTIONARY VIOLENCE: THE THEORIES.
      New York: Crane, Russack, 1978.

4988. Carlson, John Roy (pseud.). THE PLOTTERS. New York:
      E.P. Dutton, 1944.

      Presents a sequel to item 4989 below, with further
      coverage of seditious activities by Axis sympathizers
      in America during World War II.

4989. ————. UNDER COVER. MY FOUR YEARS IN THE NAZI UNDER-
      WORLD OF AMERICA. New York: E.P. Dutton, 1943.

      An infiltrator of the racist right reports his various
      adventures with the KKK, German-American Bund, Silver
      Shirts, and other neo-fascist organizations in the 1940s.

4990. Clendenen, Clarence C. BLOOD ON THE BORDER: THE UNITED
      STATES ARMY AND THE MEXICAN IRREGULARS. New York: Mac-
      millan, 1969.

      Examines the era of tension between Mexico and America
      prior to World War I. Included is coverage of General
      Pershing's expedition to punish border outlaw Pancho
      Villa for his raids against New Mexico.

4991. Connelly, William. QUANTRILL AND THE BORDER WARS. Cedar
      Rapids, Iowa: The Torch Press, 1910.

4992. Cook, Adrian. THE ARMIES OF THE STREETS. THE NEW YORK
      CITY DRAFT RIOTS OF 1863. Lexington, Ky.: University
      Press of Kentucky, 1974.

      Examines the apocalyptic violence loosed upon New York
      when white civilians rose in arms against the prospect
      of military conscription. Most of the riot victims were
      blacks, as recent immigrants blamed slavery (and blacks
      in general) for the onset of the Civil War. Reliable
      body-counts are unavailable, but all sources agree that
      "hundreds" were killed in the riots.

4993. D'Arcy, William. THE FENIAN MOVEMENT IN THE UNITED
        STATES, 1858-1886. Washington, D.C.: Catholic Uni-
        versity of America, 1947.

        Examines Irish radicalism in America, with roots firmly
        planted in the auld sod. Active for nearly thirty years
        in America, the Fenians staged their most spectacular
        action in 1866, with an abortive invasion of Canada.

4994. Denison, Major George T. THE FENIAN RAID ON FORT ERIE
        WITH AN ACCOUNT OF THE BATTLE OF RIDGEWAY, JUNE, 1866.
        Toronto: G.N. Morang, 1866.

4995. Dennison, George M. THE DORR WAR. REPUBLICANISM ON TRIAL
        1831-1861. Lexington, Ky.: University Press of Kentucky,
        1975.

        Examines the struggle of Rhode Island citizens to force
        adoption of a new state constitution, superseding the
        ancient pre-Revolution documents then in force. Most of
        the actual fighting took place in 1841-42, prior to the
        arrest of leader Thomas Dorr.

4996. Desmond, Humphrey. THE A.P.A. MOVEMENT. New York: Arno
        Press, 1912.

        Examines the tawdry career of the American Protective
        Association, alias "Know Nothings," the leading 19th-
        century source of anti-Catholic agitation in America.

4997. Destler, Chester M. AMERICAN RADICALISM, 1865-1901.
        New York: Octagon Books, 1963.

4998. Feuerlicht, Roberta Strauss. AMERICA'S REIGN OF TERROR.
        WORLD WAR I, THE RED SCARE, AND THE PALMER RAIDS. New
        York: McGraw-Hill, 1962.

4999. Fast, Howard. PEEKSKILL: U.S.A. - A PERSONAL EXPERIENCE.
        New York: Civil Rights Congress, 1951.

        Presents a communist's view of the Peekskill, N.Y.,
        riots that erupted at a concert by black singer Paul
        Robeson in 1949. Accused of red sympathies, Robeson
        became a target for right-wing elements. There is per-
        suasive evidence that the riots were organized by local
        leaders of veterans groups like the VFW and American
        Legion.

5000. Forster, Arnold, and Benjamin Epstein. THE TROUBLE
MAKERS. Garden City, N.Y.: Doubleday, 1952.

Examines the recent growth of right-wing, racist, and
anti-semitic groups in the period following World War II.

5001. Fry, James B. NEW YORK AND THE CONSCRIPTION OF '63.
New York: D. Van Nostrand, 1885.

5002. Gettleman, Marvin. THE DORR REBELLION. A STUDY IN AMER-
ICAN RADICALISM, 1833-1849. New York: Random House,
1973.

5003. Gohmann, Mary de L. POLITICAL NATIVISM IN TENNESSEE TO
1860. Washington, D.C.: Catholic University of America, 1938.

5004. Goldberg, Harvey (ed.). AMERICAN RADICALS: SOME PROBLEMS
AND PERSONALITIES. New York: Monthly Review Press,
1957.

5005. Goldman, Emma. "The Psychology of Political Violence."
RED EMMA SPEAKS. Cited below as item 5038, p. 211+.

An excerpt from Goldman's autobiography presents her
views on the uses of violence as a means to political
change.

5006. Gregg, Robert D. THE INFLUENCE OF BORDER TROUBLES ON
RELATIONS BETWEEN THE UNITED STATES AND MEXICO, 1871-
1910. Baltimore: The Johns Hopkins Press, 1937.

5007. Headley, Joel T. THE GREAT RIOTS OF NEW YORK, 1712-1873.
New York: Dover Publications, 1873.

5008. Hernon, J.M. CELTS, CATHOLICS AND COPPERHEADS. Columbus, Ohio: State University Press, 1968.

5009. Hicks, Granville. JOHN REED: THE MAKING OF A REVOLUTION-
ARY. New York: Macmillan, 1936.

Examines the career of an early American communist,
who traveled to Russia for a first-hand look at the 1917
revolution.

5010. Higham, Charles. AMERICAN SWASTIKA. New York: Doubleday, 1985.

5011. Hoke, Henry Reed. BLACK MAIL. New York: Reader's Book
      Service, 1944.

5012. ———. IT'S A SECRET. New York: Reynal & Hitchcock,
      1946.

5013. Hoke, Travis Henderson. SHIRTS! A SURVEY OF THE NEW
      "SHIRTS" ORGANIZATIONS IN THE UNITED STATES SEEKING A
      FASCIST DICTATORSHIP. New York: American Civil Liber-
      ties Union, 1934.

5014. Jenkins, Brian. FENIANS AND ANGLO-AMERICAN RELATIONS
      DURING RECONSTRUCTION. Ithaca, N.Y.: Cornell Univer-
      sity Press, 1969.

5015. Keleher, William A. TURMOIL IN NEW MEXICO, 1846-1868.
      Santa Fe, N.M.: Rydal Press, 1951.

5016. ———. VIOLENCE IN LINCOLN COUNTY, 1869-1881. Albu-
      querque, N.M.: University of New Mexico Press, 1957.

      Updates item 5015 above, with further coverage of the
      lethal fight for political and economic control of New
      Mexico's Lincoln County. William "Billy the Kid" Bonney
      and Pat Garrett were two of the more renowned partici-
      pants in conflict spanning nearly two decades.

5017. Labor Research Association. THE PALMER RAIDS. New York:
      International Publishers, 1948.

      Presents a leftist view of the official reaction (and
      over-reaction) to radical activities in the years imme-
      diately after World War I.

5018. Lane, Roger. POLICING THE CITY: BOSTON, 1822-1885. Cam-
      bridge, Mass.: 1967.

      Includes police reactions to various outbreaks of
      political and religious violence in the capital of Mass-
      achusetts.

5019. Lasch, Christopher. THE NEW RADICALISM IN AMERICA, 1889-
      1963: THE INTELLECTUAL AS A SOCIAL TYPE. New York:
      W.W. Norton, 1965.

5020. Lee, Basil L. DISCONTENT IN NEW YORK CITY, 1861-1865.
      Washington, D.C.: 1943.

TERRORISM IN THE UNITED STATES AND EUROPE

5021. Leonard, Ira M., and Robert D. Parmet. AMERICAN NATIVISM,
1830-1860. New York: 1971.

5022. Leslie, Shane. THE IRISH ISSUE IN ITS AMERICAN ASPECT:
A CONTRIBUTION TO THE SETTLEMENT OF ANGLO-AMERICAN
RELATIONS DURING AND AFTER THE GREAT WAR. New York:
Charles Scribner's Sons, 1917.

5023. McCague, James. THE SECOND REBELLION: THE STORY OF THE
NEW YORK CITY DRAFT RIOTS OF 1863. New York: 1968.

5024. McGann, Agnes G. NATIVISM IN KENTUCKY TO 1860. Washington, D.C.: Catholic University of America, 1944.

5025. McMicken, Gilbert. THE ABORTIVE FENIAN RAID OF MANITOBA.
Winnepeg: The Author, 1888.

5026. Mowry, Arthur M. THE DORR WAR OR THE CONSTITUTIONAL
STRUGGLE IN RHODE ISLAND. Providence, R.I.: Preston
& Rounds, 1901.

5027. Murray, Robert K. RED SCARE: A STUDY IN NATIONAL HYSTER-
IA, 1919-1920. Minneapolis: University of Minnesota
Press, 1955.

5028. Neidhart, Wilfried. FENIANISM IN NORTH AMERICA. University Park, Pa.: Pennsylvania State University Press,
1975.

5029. Nichols, Alice. BLEEDING KANSAS. New York: Oxford University Press, 1954.

Examines the brutal border war between pro- and anti-
slavery forces, spanning half a dozen years before the
outbreak of the Civil War. John Brown, Quantrill's
raiders, and the anti-slavery "red-leg" terrorists all
contributed to the traumatic state of "Bleeding Kansas"
in the latter 1850s.

5030. Noonan, Carroll J. NATIVISM IN CONNECTICUT, 1828-1860.
Washington, D.C.: Catholic University of America, 1938.

5031. O'Neill, General John. OFFICIAL REPORT OF GENERAL JOHN
O'NEILL, PRESIDENT OF THE FENIAN BROTHERHOOD ON THE
ATTEMPT TO INVADE CANADA, MAY 25, 1870. New York:
The Author, 1870.

5032. Piller, Emanuel A. TIME BOMB. New York: Arco Pulishing
      Co., 1945.

      Examines the activities of alleged subversive elements
      during World War II.

5033. Preston, William, Jr. ALIENS AND DISSENTERS: FEDERAL
      SUPPRESSION OF RADICALS, 1903-1933. New York: Harper
      & Row, 1963.

5034. Rawley, James A. RACE AND POLITICS: "BLEEDING KANSAS"
      AND THE COMING OF THE CIVIL WAR. Philadelphia: 1969.

5035. Robinson, Charles. THE KANSAS CONFLICT. New York: Har-
      per & Brothers, 1892.

5036. Schmeckbier, Laurence F. HISTORY OF THE KNOW NOTHING
      PARTY IN MARYLAND. Baltimore: The Johns Hopkins Press,
      1899.

5037. Schonbach, Morris. NATIVE AMERICAN FASCISM DURING THE
      1930's AND 1940's: A STUDY OF ITS ROOTS, ITS GROWTH,
      AND ITS DECLINE. New York: Garland, 1985.

5038. Schulman, Alix K. RED EMMA SPEAKS. New York: Random
      House, 1972.

      Contains item 5005 above.

5039. Thomas, M. Evangeline. NATIVISM IN THE OLD NORTHWEST,
      1850-1860. Washington, D.C.: Catholic University of
      America, 1936.

5040. Werstein, Irving. JULY 1863: THE INCREDIBLE STORY OF
      THE BLOODY NEW YORK CITY DRAFT RIOTS. New York: 1957.

                          b. Articles

5041. Abbott, Wilbur C. "Political Warfare in Early Kansas."
      JOURNAL OF AMERICAN HISTORY 3 (1909): 627-632.

5042. "American Democracy vs. Fascism." LITERARY DIGEST 95
      (October 15, 1927): 16.

5043. "American Fascists; Institute for Propaganda Analysis
      Reports on Fascist Threat." NEW REPUBLIC 98 (March 8,
      1939): 117-118.

5044. Anderson, P.Y. "Fascism, American Style." NATION 146 (March 26, 1938): 347-348.

5045. "As Others See Us." LIVING AGE 346 (April 1934): 178-179.

Examines the rise of fascist groups in America during the Great Depression.

5046. "Assassination Attempt; with Message by Governor Munoz Marin." NEW REPUBLIC 123 (November 13, 1950): 6.

Covers the attempt by Puerto Rican nationalists to assassinate President Harry Truman.

5047. "Attack on the White House Shows Puerto Rican Discontent." CHRISTIAN CENTURY 67 (November 15, 1950): 1348.

5048. "Author, Author! Kamp and the Constitutional Educational League." NEW REPUBLIC 103 (October 7, 1940): 468.

5049. Basso, H. "Little Hitlers of Asheville." NEW REPUBLIC 88 (September 2, 1935): 100-101.

5050. Baum, Dale. "Know-Nothingism and the Republican Majority in Massachusetts: the Political Realignment of the 1850's." JOURNAL OF AMERICAN HISTORY 64 (1978): 959-986.

5051. Berkman, Alexander. "Legal Assassination." MOTHER EARTH 11 (October 1916): 635-639.

A noted anarchist spokesman castigates authorities for imposing the death sentence on radicals accused of murder.

5052. ———. "The Life and Death Struggle in San Francisco." MOTHER EARTH 11 (December 1916): 698-701.

5053. Billington, Monroe. "Red River Boundary Controversy." SOUTHWESTERN HISTORY QUARTERLY 62 (1958): 356-362.

Covers political "county seat wars" in the American Southwest.

5054. "Birth of a Riot? Peekskill Riots." NEWSWEEK 34 (December 12, 1949): 55.

5055. Blazer, Paul A. "The Fight at Blazer's Mill: A Chapter in the Lincoln County War." ARIZONA AND THE WEST 6 (1964): 203-210.

5056. Blum, John M. "Nativism, Anti-Radicalism, and the For-
      eign Scare, 1917-1290." MIDWEST JOURNAL 3 (1950): 46-
      53.

5057. "Bomb Plots Thicken." LITERARY DIGEST 52 (April 29,
      1916): 1205.

      German agents are suspected in a rash of domestic bomb-
      ings.

5058. Brazier, Richard. "The Mass I.W.W. Trial of 1918: a
      Retrospect." LABOR HISTORY 7 (1966): 178-192.

5059. "Bringing the War to America." LITERARY DIGEST 51 (No-
      vember 27, 1915): 1207-1209.

      Covers pre-war violence by reputed German agents in
      America.

5060. Britt, G. "Poison in the Melting Pot: Jew-Baiting in
      the United States." NATION 148 (April 1, 1939): 374-
      376.

5061. Calkin, Homer. "St. Albans in Reverse: The Fenian Raid
      of 1866." VERMONT HISTORY 35 (1967): 19-34.

5062. Calverton, V.F. "Our Future Dictator." SCRIBNER'S MAG-
      AZINE 97 (March 1935): 171-175.

      Examines Depression-era fascism in America.

5063. Carlson, John Roy (pseud.). "Inside the America First
      Movement." AMERICAN MERCURY 54 (January 1942): 7-25;
      54 (February-March 1942): 250, 378-379.

5064. ———. "Our Fascist Enemies Within." AMERICAN MERCURY
      54 (March 1942): 378-379.

5065. Carriere, Marcus. "Political Leadership in the Louisiana
      Know-Nothing Party." LOUISIANA HISTORY 21 (1980):
      183-195.

5066. Castel, Albert. "Kansas Jayhawking Raids into Western
      Missouri in 1861." MISSOURI HISTORICAL REVIEW 54
      (October 1959): 1-11.

5067. ———. "Quantrill's Missouri Bushwhackers in Kentucky."
      FILSON CLUB HISTORICAL QUARTERLY 38 (1964): 125-132.

5068. "Churches and American Fascism." CHRISTIAN CENTURY 52
      (March 13, 1935): 325-326.

5069. Clark, Charles B. "Baltimore and the Attack on the Sixth
      Massachusetts Regiment, April 19, 1861." MARYLAND HIS-
      TORY MAGAZINE 56 (1961): 39-71.

5070. ————. "Suppression and Control of Maryland, 1861-1865."
      MARYLAND HISTORY MAGAZINE 54 (1959): 241-271.

5071. Clement, Travers. "Mooney." AMERICAN MERCURY 17 (May
      1929): 26-33.

      Examines the case of Thomas Mooney, a "radical" framed
      by police in the 1916 Preparedness Day bombing in San
      Francisco.

5072. Coben, Stanley A. "A Study in Nativism: the American
      Red Scare of 1919-20." POLITICAL SCIENCE QUARTERLY
      79 (1964): 52-75.

5073. Coleman, Charles H., and Paul H. Spencer. "The Charles-
      ton Riot, March 26, 1864." JOURNAL OF THE ILLINOIS
      STATE HISTORICAL SOCIETY 33 (1940): 7-56.

5074. Colony, D.C. "Dictator Coughlin: Fascism Under the
      Cross." FORUM 52 (March 13, 1935): 196-201.

      Examines the leadership and program of the neo-fascist
      America First Committee.

5075. "Communiques Regarding Terrorist Uprising in Puerto Rico."
      U.S. STATE DEPARTMENT BULLETIN 23 (November 13, 1950):
      776-777.

5076. Congleton, Betty C. "George D. Prentice and Bloody Mon-
      day: a Reappraisal." KENTUCKY HISTORICAL SOCIETY REG-
      ISTER 63 (July 1965): 218-239.

5077. "Court and Fascism." NATION 144 (February 20, 1937): 200-
      201.

5078. Cowley, M. "Who's Fascist Now?" NEW REPUBLIC 110 (Feb-
      ruary 21, 1944): 246+.

5079. "Crime of Peekskill." LIFE 27 (September 26, 1949): 44.

      Examines the veteran's riot against Paul Robeson.

5080. Currey, Cecil. "Quakers in 'Bleeding Kansas'." QUAKER
      HISTORY 50 (1961): 96-101.

5081. "Dangerous Plot Discovered." OUTLOOK 111 (November 3,
      1915): 529.

      Examines evidence of pro-German terrorism in America
      prior to United States participation in World War I.

5082. Davis, F. "Father Coughlin." ATLANTIC MONTHLY 153 (De-
      cember 1935): 659-668.

5083. Davis, Harold A. "The Fenian Raid on New Brunswick."
      CANADIAN HISTORY REVIEW 36 (1955): 316-334.

5084. Dennis, L. "Fascism for America." ANNALS OF THE AMERI-
      CAN ACADEMY 180 (July 1935): 62-73.

5085. ———. "Portrait of American Fascism." AMERICAN MER-
      CURY 36 (December 1935): 404-413.

5086. DeRosier, Arthur H. "Importance of Failure: the Fenian
      Raids of 1866-1871." SOUTHERN QUARTERLY 3 (April
      1965): 181-197.

5087. Deusner, Charles E. "The Know Nothing Riots in Louis-
      ville, 1855." KENTUCKY HISTORICAL SOCIETY REGISTER
      61 (April 1963): 122-147.

5088. Dies, Martin. "Challenge to Democracy' Foreign Isms
      Threaten Us." VITAL SPEECHES 5 (October 1, 1939):
      762-765.

      The chairman of the House Committee on Un-American
      Activities expounds on the neo-fascist enemy within.

5089. "Does Mussolini Rule Millions Here?" LITERARY DIGEST
      103 (November 16, 1929): 14.

5090. "Does Wallace Know What Fascism Is?" SATURDAY EVENING
      POST 216 (March 11, 1944): 112.

5091. Duffield, M. "Mussolini's American Empire." HARPER'S
      159 (November 1929): 661-672.

5092. ———. "Mussolini's Red Herring." NATION 129 (Novem-
      ber 27, 1929): 644.

5093. Eastman, Crystal. "The Mooney Congress." LIBERATOR 1
      (March 1919): 19-24.

      Continues coverage of the Mooney-Billings bomb case.

5094. Egle, William H. "The Buckshot War." PENNSYLVANIA MAG-
      AZINE OF HISTORY AND BIOGRAPHY 23 (1899): 137-156.

      Examines political violence resulting from disputed
      Pennsylvania elections, circa 1838.

5095. Elliott, W.Y. "If America Goes Fascist." AMERICAN MER-
      CURY 44 (June 1938): 162-169.

5096. Emerson, E. "Hates Across the Sea." NEW OUTLOOK 165
      (January 1935): 2+.

5097. "Enlightened Rule." TIME 56 (July 1950): 36.

      Examines the background to modern Puerto Rican nation-
      alist violence.

5098. Ernst, Robert. "Economic Nativism in New York City
      During the 1890s." NEW YORK HISTORY 29 (April 1948):
      170-186.

5099. Etheridge, W.S. "Salesmen of Violence." OUTLOOK 156
      (November 19, 1930): 457-459.

5100. Eulau, H.H.F. "False Prophets in the Bible Belt." NEW
      REPUBLIC 110 (February 7, 1944): 169-171.

5101. Everett, Edward G. "The Baltimore Riots, April 1861."
      PENNSYLVANIA HISTORY 24 (1951): 331-342.

5102. Ewy, Marvi. "The United States Army in the Kansas Border
      Trouble, 1855-1856." KANSAS HISTORICAL QUARTERLY 32
      (1966): 385-400.

5103. "Fascism in America." LITERARY DIGEST 124 (August 14,
      1937): 16-17.

5104. "Fascism is Here!" CHRISTIAN CENTURY 53 (January 29,
      1936): 312-134.

5105. "Fascist Attitudes Found in America's Midwest." SCIENCE
      NEWS LETTER 31 (January 30, 1937): 70-71.

5106. "Fascisti in the United States." NATION 116 (April 15, 1923): 502-503.

5107. "Fascists in Our Armed Forces." NEW REPUBLIC 106 (May 4, 1942): 434.

5108. "Fight Against Fascism." WORLD TOMORROW 17 (March 29, 1934): 147-148.

5109. Fitch, John A. "The San Francisco Bomb Cases." SURVEY 38 (July 17, 1917): 305-312.

5110. ————. "The Strange Case of Tom Mooney." SURVEY GEOGRAPHIC 24 (December 1935): 586-590.

5111. "Fortune Survey; What is a Native Fascist?" FORTUNE 28 (November 1943): 10.

5112. Fowler, C. "Hates Across the Sea." NEW OUTLOOK 164 (November 1934): 39-43.

5113. Gay, Constance M. "The Campaign of 1855 in Virginia, and the Fall of the Know-Nothing Party." RICHMOND COLLECTION HISTORICAL PAPERS 1 (1916): 309-335.

5114. "German Bomb-Plot Convictions." LITERARY DIGEST 54 (January 27, 1917): 176-177.

5115. "German Bomb-Plots in the United States." LITERARY DIGEST 51 (November 6, 1915): 993-995.

5116. "German Campaign Against American Neutrality." OUTLOOK 110 (August 25, 1915): 934.

5117. "German Exposures." NATION 101 (August 19, 1915): 219.

5118. "German Plot Developments." INDEPENDENT 86 (May 1, 1916): 163-164.

5119. "German Plotters Arrested." INDEPENDENT 84 (December 27, 1915): 509.

5120. Goldman, Emma. "Stray Thoughts." MOTHER EARTH 11 (September 1916): 615-622.

    The veteran anarchist spokeswoman lays out her views on political violence as a necessity in America.

5121. Granber, J.C. "Civil Liberties in Texas." CHRISTIAN
      CENTURY 54 (October 27, 1937): 1526-1527.

5122. "Great Fascist Plot." NEW REPUBLIC 81 (December 5, 1934):
      37-39.

5123. Hammett, Theodore M. "Two Mobs of Jacksonian Boston:
      Ideology and Interest." JOURNAL OF AMERICAN HISTORY
      62 (1976): 845-868.

      Compares the August 1834 burning of an Ursuline convent
      with the October 1835 Anti-Slavery Society riot. Stress
      is placed on different motivations, leadership, and goals.

5124. Harding, Leonard. "The Cincinnati Riots of 1862." CIN-
      CINNATI HISTORICAL SOCIETY BULLETIN 25 (1967): 229-239.

5125. Hastings, W.F. "Our Puerto Rican Friends." CHRISTIAN
      CENTURY 67 (December 20, 1950): 1525.

5126. Haynes, G.H. "Local History of Know-Nothingism." NEW
      ENGLAND MAGAZINE 15: 82.

5127. Haynes, Robert V. "The Houston Mutiny and Riot of 1917."
      SOUTHWESTERN HISTORY QUARTERLY 76 (April 1973).

5128. Henry, M. St. "Nativism in Pennsylvania, with Particular
      Regard to Its Effect on Politics and Education, 1840-
      1860." RECORDS OF THE AMERICAN CATHOLIC HISTORICAL
      SOCIETY 47 (1936): 5-47.

5129. Herndon, B. "Pappy's Dixie Fascists; Christian Ameri-
      cans." NEW REPUBLIC 107 (July 20, 1942): 79-80.

5130. High, S. "Star-Spangled Fascists." SATURDAY EVENING
      POST 211 (May 27, 1939): 5-7+.

5131. Hindman, Jay A. "The Mooney Case." AMERICAN LAW REVIEW
      52 (September-October 1918): 743-746.

5132. "H.T.'s Attackers Not Ill." SCIENCE NEWS LETTER 58 (No-
      vember 11, 1950): 309.

      Disputes defense contentions that Puerto Rican gunmen
      who tried to kill President Truman should be acquitted
      on grounds of temporary insanity.

5133. Hugh-Jones, E.M. "Little Nest of Fascists." NEW REPUB-
      LIC 79 (May 30, 1934): 68-69.

5134. Hutcheon, Wallace S. "The Louisville Riots of August,
      1855." KENTUCKY HISTORICAL SOCIETY REGISTER 69 (1971):
      150-172.

5135. Hyman, Harold M. (ed). "New Yorkers and the Civil War
      Draft." NEW YORK HISTORY 36 (1955): 64-171.

5136. "Insurrection." TIME 56 (November 13, 1950): 38.

      Deals with anti-American violence in Puerto Rico.

5137. "Is Mooney Guilty?" COMMONWEAL 14 (March 1, 1938): 47-
      54.

5138. Isely, W.H. "The Sharps Rifle Episode in Kansas History."
      AMERICAN HISTORICAL REVIEW 12 (1906): 546-566.

5139. Jenkin, T.J. "Know-Nothingism in Kentucky." CATHOLIC
      WORLD 57: 511.

5140. Johnson, Benjamin S. "The Brooks-Boxer War." PUBLICA-
      TIONS OF THE ARKANSAS HISTORICAL ASSOCIATION 2 (1908):
      122-173.

5141. Kirchwey, F. "Curb the Fascist Press!" NATION 154 (March
      28, 1942): 357-358; 154 (April 11, 1942): 444, 499.

5142. ———. "Hart on Democracy." NATION 151 (September 14,
      1940): 3-4+.

      Reviews the activities of Depression-era fascists.

5143, Koesterm Leonard. "Louisville's 'Bloody Monday' - Aug-
      ust 6, 1855." HISTORICAL BULLETIN 26 (March 1958): 53.

5144. Kramer, D. "American Fascists Survey of the Principal
      Organizations and Groups in the United States Which
      Emulate Fascist or Nazi Methods." HARPER'S 181 (Sep-
      tember 1940): 380-393.

5145. Kraus, Carroll J. "A Study in Border Confrontation: the
      Iowa-Missouri Boundary Dispute." ANNALS OF IOWA 3
      (1969): 81-107.

5146. Lahey, E.A. "Fascism's Day in Court." NEW REPUBLIC 110 (June 5, 1944): 759-760.

5147. Lambert, G. "Dallas Tries Terror." NATION 145 (October 9, 1937): 376-378.

   Surveys recent violence against Texas radicals.

5148. Land, J. "Anatomy of Fascism." AMERICAN MERCURY 58 (April 1944): 497-502.

5149. Landon, M. "Is There a Fuhrer in the House? Fascists Make Bid for Seats in Congress." NEW REPUBLIC 103 (August 12, 1940): 212-213.

5150. ————. "Threat, Fear and Secrecy; What is Fascism?" VITAL SPEECHES 9 (September 1, 1943): 680-681.

5151. Larsen, Lawrence H. "Draft Riot in Wisconsin, 1862." CIVIL WAR HISTORY 7 (1961): 421-447.

5152. Lavine, H. "Fifth Column Literature." SATURDAY REVIEW OF LITERATURE 22 (September 14, 1940): 3-4+.

5153. Leder, Lawrence. "New York's Bloodiest Week." AMERICAN HERITAGE 10 (1959): 44-49.

   Presents a retrospective of the 1863 draft riots.

5154. Leonard, Ellen. "Three Days Reign of Terror." HARPER'S 34 (1867): 225-233.

5155. Lerner, M. "Epistle to the Right." AMERICAN MERCURY 46 (January 1939): 80-84; 46 (March 1939): 374-376.

   Examines the state of American fascism on the eve of World War II.

5156. Lindeman, E.C. "Fascist Sympathies in the United States." NATION 131 (September 10, 1930): 267-268.

5157. ————. "Trouble at the Grass Roots; Growing Confusions, Fears and Hates Found in a Swing Through Mid-America." SURVEY GEOGRAPHIC 33 (June 1944): 280-282.

5158. Loeb, H., and S. Rodman. "American Fascism in Embryo." NEW REPUBLIC 77 (December 27, 1933): 185-187.

5159. Lofton, Williston H. "Northern Labor and the Negro Dur-
      ing the Civil War." JOURNAL OF NEGRO HISTORY 34 (1949):
      251-273.

5160. "Lynch Jury in San Francisco Convicts Thomas Mooney."
      MOTHER EARTH 12 (March 1917): 11-14.

5161. McMaster, J.B. "The Riotous Career of Know-Nothingism."
      FORUM 17: 524.

5162. McWilliams, Carey. "Fascism in American Law." AMERICAN
      MERCURY 32 (June 1934): 192-183.

5163. ————. "Hollywood Plays with Fascism." NATION 140
      (May 29, 1935): 623-624.

5164. Malin, James C. "Judge Lecompte and the 'Sack of Lawr-
      ence,' May 21, 1856." KANSAS HISTORICAL QUARTERLY 20
      (1953): 465-493.

5165. Man, Albon P., Jr. "The Church and the New York Draft
      Tiots of '63." AMERICAN CATHOLIC HISTORICAL SOCIETY
      RECORDS 62 (March 1951): 33-50.

5166. ————. "Labor Competition and the New York Draft Riots
      of 1863." JOURNAL OF NEGRO HISTORY 36 (1951): 375-405.

5167. Martin, E.D., and Earl Browder. "Are We Going Communist?"
      FORUM 96 (November 1936): 202-208.

      These leaders of the American Communist Party hope so,
      but their evidence is specious, at best.

5168. Matthews, J.B., and R.E. Shallcross. "Must America Go
      Fascist?" HARPER'S 169 (June 1934): 1-15.

5169. Mayer, M.S. "Mrs. Dilling: Lady of the Red Network."
      AMERICAN MERCURY 47 (July 1939): 293-299.

      Examines the career of Elizabeth Dilling, an American
      fascist prosecuted for sedition during World War II.
      With other defendants, she was convicted and jailed.

5170. Milne, R. "Blood on the Hill." AMERICAN MERCURY 79
      (August 1954): 17-20.

      Examines a Puerto Rican nationalist attack on the House
      of Representatives, wounding several congressmen.

5171. Minor, Robert. "The San Francisco Bomb." MOTHER EARTH
      11 (September 1916): 608-612.

5172. Moley, R. "Primrose Path to Fascism." NEWSWEEK 23 (Feb-
      ruary 21, 1944): 104.

5173. Monti, Daniel J. "The Relation Between Terrorism and
      Domestic Civil Disorders." TERRORISM 4 (1980): 123-141.

      Examines 300 years of civil disturbances in New York
      City, pointing out the essentially conservative nature
      of collective violence and the conditions that might
      transform mob action into organized political terrorism.

5174. Mowry, Arthur M. "Tammany Hall and the Dorr Rebellion."
      AMERICAN HISTORY REVIEW 3 (1897): 292-301.

5175. Myers, Robert C. "Anti-Communist Mob Action: a Case
      Study." PUBLIC OPINION QUARTERLY 12 (1948): 57-67.

5176. "Nazis Are Here." NATION 148 (March 4, 1939): 253.

5177. "Need We Fear Fascism?" CHRISTIAN CENTURY 52 (July 24,
      1935): 357-359.

5178. Neighbours, Kenneth F. "The Taylor-Neighbors Struggle
      Over the Upper Rio Grande Region of Texas in 1850."
      SOUTHWESTERN HISTORY QUARTERLY 61 (1957): 431-463.

5179. "New York Meeting: Eye-witness Account of a Recent Chris-
      tian Front Meeting." COMMONWEAL 30 (September 1, 1939):
      428-429.

5180. Niebuhr, Reinhold. "Pawns of Fascism, Our Lower Middle
      Class." AMERICAN SCHOLAR 6 (1937): 145-152.

5181. "Nightmare in Peekskill." NATION 169 (September 10,
      1949): 43-44.

5182. "No Black Shirts or Red Shirts for Green." LITERARY DI-
      GEST 88 (January 9, 1926): 9.

5183. Nulle, S.H. "America and the Coming Order." AMERICAN
      REVIEW 7 (June 1936): 272-286.

      Examines the growth of domestic fascism during the
      Depression.

5184. Olson, C. "People v. the Fascist, U.S. 1944; Defamation of Groups." SURVEY GEOGRAPHIC 33 (August 1944): 356-357+.

5185. "Ominous Nomination." CHRISTIAN CENTURY 57 (July 31, 1940): 942-944.

Examines fascist agitation during the 1940 presidential campaign.

5186. "Our Black Shirts and the Reds." LITERARY DIGEST 77 (April 7, 1923): 16-18.

5187. Owen, William C. "The Los Angeles Explosion." MOTHER EARTH 5 (December 1910): 310-315.

5188. Palmer, P. "Why Hold an Election in 1940?" AMERICAN MERCURY 42 (October 1937): 147-150.

Critiques domestic fascist activities.

5189. Panunzio, C. "Italian Americans, Fascism, and the War." YALE REVIEW 31, (June 1942): 771-782.

5190. Parmet, Robert D. "Connecticut's Know-Nothings: A Profile." CONNECTICUT HISTORICAL SOCIETY BULLETIN 31 (July 1966): 84-90.

5191. "Peekskill Shadow; Part Played by Teen-Agers." CHRISTIAN CENTURY 66 (September 21, 1949): 1095-1097.

5192. Pemberton, P.L. "Christian Fascists." CHRISTIAN CENTURY 61 (May 10, 1944): 595.

5193. Phayre, I. "Dr. Wilson's Household Foes." LIVING AGE 289 (April 29, 1916): 308-312.

Examines the activities of pro-German activists prior to America's entry into World War I.

5194. Pitt, Leonard. "The Beginnings of Nativism in California." PACIFIC HISTORY REVIEW 30 (February 1961): 23-38.

5195. "Plots Against the U.S. by Terrorists." U.S. NEWS & WORLD REPORT 36 (March 12, 1954): 21-25.

5196. Prichett, John Perry. "The Origin of the So-Called Fenian Raid on Manitoba in 1871." CANADIAN HISTORICAL REVIEW Vol. IX.

5197. "Puerto Rican Hands Off." NEWSWEEK 33 (April 25, 1949): 47.

5198. "Puerto Rico." ATLANTIC MONTHLY 186 (July 1950): 14-17.

5199. "Puerto Rico is Not Free." TIME 63 (March 8, 1954): 19.

5200. "Puerto Rico Revolt Endangers Truman." LIFE 29 (November 13, 1950): 25-29.

5201. "Puerto Rico Storm Center." SCHOLASTIC 57 (November 15, 1950): 14.

5202. "Putting the Church in Her Place." COMMONWEAL 21 (April 5, 1935): 635-636.

     Refutes item 5074 above.

5203. "Rally to the Defense of Caplan and Schmidt." MOTHER EARTH 10 (July 1915): 168-172.

5204. Rasch, Philip J. "The Horrell War." NEW MEXICO HISTORY REVIEW 31 (1956): 223-231.

     Reviews 19th-century political violence in New Mexico.

5205. "Red-Baiting Fascists Nearly Caught in Trap They Set." NEWSWEEK 9 (March 27, 1937): 16-17.

5206. "Red-Sponsored Assassins." NEWSWEEK 36 (November 13, 1950): 23-26.

     Links international communism to the Puerto Rican nationalist attack on President Truman.

5207. Reed, John F. "Riot in Illinois, Charleston, 1864." MANUSCRIPTS 4 (1951): 23-27.

5208. Reekstin, William F. "The Draft Riots of July, 1863 on Staten Island." STATEN ISLAND HISTORY 19 (1958): 27-30.

5209. Rice, Philip M. "The Know-Nothing Party in Virginia, 1854-1856." VIRGINIA MAGAZINE OF HISTORY AND BIOGRAPHY 55 (April 1947): 61-75, 159-167.

5210. "Robeson Ruckus." NEWSWEEK 34 (September 12, 1949): 23.

Covers the veteran's riot at Peekskill, N.Y.

5211. Robey, R. "Who Are the Real Fascists in America?" NEWS-
WEEK 24 (October 30, 1944): 76.

5212. Robinson, D.B. "I Was in Journal Square." NEW REPUBLIC
95 (May 25, 1938): 66.

Presents a first-hand look at domestic fascists in action.

5213. Roche, John P. "Convicts, Bartenders, and New York Radicals: A Quaker View of Dorr's Rebellion." QUAKER
HISTORY 42 (1953): 41-44.

5214. "Roots of Tragedy; Assault on Truman's Life." NATION 171
(November 11, 1950): 423.

5215. Roseboom, Eugene H. "The Mobbing of the 'Crisis.'" OHIO
STATE ARCHIVES HISTORY QUARTERLY 59 (1950): 150-153.

Examines a violent anti-"copperhead" incident at Columbus, Ohio, in 1863. Objecting to editorials in a pro-
Southern paper, vigilantes trashed the presses and put
the opposition spokesmen out of business.

5216. "Same Old Coughlin." NEW REPUBLIC 106 (January 5, 1942):
7-8.

5217. Schall, Thomas D. "Why is Mooney in Prison?" PLAIN
TALK 4 (May 1929): 513-527.

5218. Schecter, A. "Fascism in Pennsylvania." NATION 140
(Jnue 19, 1935): 713-714.

5219. Schmidt, Matthew A. "Address Before His Executioner in
the Court of Los Angeles." MOTHER EARTH 10 (February
1916): 397-399.

5220. Schneider, John C. "Detroit and the Problem of Disorder:
The Riot of 1863." MICHIGAN HISTORY 58 (Spring 1974).

5221. ————. "Riot and Reaction in St. Louis 1854-1856."
MISSOURI HISTORICAL REVIEW 68 (January 1974).

5222. Schuchman, John S. "The Political Background of the Pol-
itical-Question Doctrine: the Judges and the Dorr War."
AMERICAN JOURNAL OF LEGAL HISTORY 16 (1972): 111-125.

5223. Schwartzkopf, Calvin F. "The Rush County-Seat War."
      KANSAS HISTORY QUARTERLY 36 (1970): 40-61.

5224. Seldes, G. "Father Coughlin" Anti-Semite." NEW REPUBLIC
      96 (November 2, 1938): 353-354.

5225. Seligman, H.J. "New Barbarian Invasion; Fascist Propa-
      ganda." NEW REPUBLIC 95 (June 22, 1938): 175-177.

5226. "Serpents and Vipers." TIME 42 (August 23, 1943): 97-98.

5227. Severance, Frank H. "The Fenian Raid of 1866." PUBLI-
      CATIONS OF THE BUFFALO HISTORICAL SOCIETY 25 (1921).

5228. Shankman, Arnold. "Vallandingham's Arrest and the 1863
      Dayton Riot: Two Letters." OHIO HISTORY 79 (1970):
      119-123.

5229. Shields, Art. "The Palmer-Hoover 'Red Raids.'" POLITI-
      CAL AFFAIRS 48 (1969): 20-30.

5230. Shockley, Ernest V. "County Seats and County Seat Wars
      in Indiana." INDIANA MAGAZINE OF HISTORY 10 (1914):
      1-46.

5231. Small, K.D., and V. Bradley, Jr. "Chicago, the Munich
      of America; Headquarters of the Incipient American
      Fascism." AMERICAN MERCURY 57 (November 1943): 543-551.

5232. Smith, A.J. "I Went to a Nazi Rally." CHRISTIAN CENTURY
      56 (March 8, 1939): 320-322.

5233. Socolofsky, Homer E. "The County-Seat Wars in Kansas."
      TRAIL GUIDE 9 (December 1964): 1-25.

5234. Sokolsky, George E. "America Drifts Toward Fascism."
      AMERICAN MERCURY 32 (July 1934): 257-264.

5235. Sowles, Edward A. "History of Fenianism and Fenian
      Raids in Vermont." VERMONT HISTORICAL PROCEEDINGS
      (1880).

5236. Spangler, Colin Irving. "Frame-Up or Square Deal?" SUN-
      SET 38 (May 1917): 28-29, 90-92.

5237. Starnes, J., and C. O'Day. "Should Congress Pass the
      Dies Bill to Deport Alien Fascists and Communists?"
      CONGRESSIONAL DIGEST 14 (November 1935): 283.

5238. Sterling, Robert E. "Civil War Draft Resistance in Illinois." JOURNAL OF ILLINOIS STATE HISTORICAL SOCIETY 64 (1971): 244-266.

5239. Sweeney, General Thomas W. "Official Report of General Thomas W. Sweeney, Secretary of War Fenian Brotherhood and Commander-in-Chief of the Irish Republican Army, Headquarters of F.B., September, 18-6." JOURNAL OF THE AMERICAN IRISH HISTORICAL SOCIETY 3 (1924).

5240. Swing, R.G. "Build-Up of Long and Coughlin." NATION 140 (March 20, 1935): 325-326.

5241. Symes, Lillian. "Fascism for America, Threat or Scarehead." HARPER'S 179 (June 1939): 35-43.

5242. ————. "Our American Dreyfuss Case: a Challenge to California Justice." HARPER'S 162 (May 1931): 641-652.

5243. Tate, A., and G. Lumpkin. "Fascism and the Southern Agrarians." NEW REPUBLIC 87 (May 27, 1936): 75-76.

5244. Taylor, R.L. "Reporter at Large; Kampf of Joe McWilliams." NEW YORKER 16 (August 24, 1940): 340.

   Covers fascist organizations in America.

5245. Theisen, Lee S. (ed). "The Fight in Lincoln, N.M., 1878: the Testimony of Two Negro Participants." ARIZONA AND THE WEST 12 (1970): 173-198.

5246. "They Want Wilkie; Fascist Organizations." NEW REPUBLIC 103 (September 9, 1940): 340.

5247. "They're At It Again; Outlook for Fascism in the United States." COMMONWEAL 19 (March 9, 1934): 509-510.

5248. Thompson, D. "Who Goes Nazi?" HARPER'S 183 (August 1941): 237-242.

5249. "Thorkelsonianism." NEW REPUBLIC 101 (November 8, 1939): 13.

   Examines yet another splinter of domestic fascism.

5250. Tigner, H.S. "Will America Go Fascist?" CHRISTIAN CENTURY 51 (May 2, 1934): 592-594.

5251. "Tinder for Fascist Fires." NATION 146 (June 4, 1938): 633.

5252. Tozier, R. "Moseley of the Fifth Column." NEW REPUBLIC 99 (June 7, 1939): 119-121.

5253. Tribble, E. "Black Shirts in Georgia." NEW REPUBLIC 64 (October 8, 1930): 204-206.

5254. Tucker, W.P. "Fascist Trend." WILSON BULLETIN 9 (March 1935): 377+.

5255. Tusca, Benjamin. "Know-Nothingism in Baltimore, 1854-1860." CATHOLIC HISTORY REVIEW (July 1925).

5256 Unionist (pseud.). "The Los Angeles Conspiracy Against Organized Labor." INTERNATIONAL SOCIALIST REVIEW 11 (1910): 262-266.

5257. "U.S. Indicts Fascists." LIFE 16 (January 17, 1944): 15-19.

5258. "Vanishing Un-American." NEW REPUBLIC 103 (August 26, 1940): 264.

5259. Varney, H.L. "Truth About American Fascism." AMERICAN MERCURY 41 (August 1937): 385-398.

5260. Villegas, Daniel Cosio. "Border Troubles in Mexican-United States Relations." SOUTHWESTERN HISTORY QUARTERLY 71 (1968): 34-39.

5261. "Wall Street's Fascist Wing." NATION 147 (December 24, 1938): 680.

5262. Wallace, H.A. "Fascism Comes to the Campus; the University of California as a Case in Point." NEW REPUBLIC 31 (January 9, 1935): 338-341.

5263. ———. "Wallace Defines American Fascism." NEW YORK TIMES MAGAZINE (April 9, 1944): 7+.

5264. Walsh, J.R. "Labor and Fascism." LITERARY DIGEST 124 (December 4, 1937): 24-25.

5265. Ward, H.F. "Christians and Communists." CHRISTIAN CENTURY 52 (December 25, 1935): 1651-1653.

5266. ――――. "Development of Fascism in the United States." ANNALS OF THE AMERICAN ACADEMY 180 (July 1935): 55-61.

5267. ――――. "Fascist Trends in American Churches." CHRISTIAN CENTURY 61 (April 19, 1944): 490-492.

5268. Warth, Robert D. "The Palmer Raids." SOUTH ATLANTIC QUARTERLY 48 (January 1949): 1-23.

5269. Wast, Klaus G. "German Immigrants and Nativism in Virginia, 1840-1860." SOCIAL HISTORY OF GERMANS IN MARYLAND 29 (1956).

5270. Watkins, Gordon S. "Revolutionary Communism in the United States." AMERICAN POLITICAL SCIENCE REVIEW 14 (1920): 14-33.

5271. "We Could Plan Ourselves Into Fascism." SATURDAY EVENING POST 217 (March 17, 1945): 108.

5272. Wechsler, J. "Coughlin Terror." NATION 149 (July 22, 1939): 87-88, 92-97; 149 (August 12, 1939): 164-165.

5273. Wegelin, Oscar. "Etienne Derbec and the Destruction of His Press at San Francisco, April, 1865." NEW YORK HISTORICAL SOCIETY QUARTERLY 27 (1943): 10-17.

      Covers mob action against a pro-Southern newspaper in the wake of President Lincoln's assassination.

5274. Weinbaum, Paul O. "Temperance, Politics, and the New York City Riots of 1857." NEW-YORK HISTORICAL SOCIETY QUARTERLY 59 (1975): 246-270.

5275. Whelpley, J.D. "German War in America." FORTUNE 104 (September 1915): 454-464.

5276. Whitmore, Allan R. "'A Guard of Faithful Sentinels': the Know-Nothing Appeal in Maine, 1854-1855." MAINE HISTORICAL SOCIETY QUARTERLY 20 (1981): 151-197.

5277. "Whose Shame?" NATION 169 (September 24, 1949): 291.

      Covers the veteran's riot at Peekskill, N.Y.

5278. "Why Puerto Rico Boils Over." U.S. NEWS & WORLD REPORT 29 (November 10, 1950): 22.

5279. Wiecek, William M. "Popular Sovereignty and the Dorr War - Conservative Counterblast." RHODE ISLAND HISTORY 32 (May 1973).

5280. Williams, Burton J. "Quantrill's Raid on Lawrence: a Question of Complicity." KANSAS HISTORICAL QUARTERLY 34 (1968): 143-149.

5281. Williams, James C. "The Long Tom Rebellion." OREGON HISTORICAL QUARTERLY 67 (1966): 54-60.

5282. Williamson, Chilston. "Rhode Island Suffrage Since the Dorr War." NEW ENGLAND QUARTERLY 28 (1955): 34-50.

5283. Wiltz, John E. "APA-ism in Kentucky and Elsewhere." KENTUCKY HISTORICAL SOCIETY REGISTER 56 (April 1958): 143-155.

5284. Winner, P. "Fascism at the Door." SCRIBNER'S MAGAZINE 99 (January 1936): 33-38.

5285. "Within the Gates." NATION 151 (July 27, 1940): 73-74; 151 (August 10, 1940): 112-113.

5286. Woodward, Earl F. "The Brooks and Baxter War in Arkansas, 1872-1874." ARKANSAS HISTORY QUARTERLY 30 (1971): 315-336.

8. Racial Violence

a. Books

5287. Aptheker, Herbert. AMERICAN SLAVE REVOLTS. New York: Columbia University Press, 1944.

An American communist presents his interpretation of 18th- and 19th-century slave rebellions.

5288. ———. NAT TURNER'S SLAVE REBELLION. TOGETHER WITH THE FULL TEXT OF THE SO-CALLED "CONFESSIONS" OF NAT TURNER MADE IN PRISON IN 1831. New York: Humanities Press, 1937.

5289. ———. NEGRO SLAVE REVOLTS IN THE UNITED STATES, 1526-1860. New York: International Publishers, 1939.

An earlier version of item 5287 above.

5290. Barber, John W. (ed). A HISTORY OF THE AMISTAD CAPTIVES:
      BEING A CIRCUMSTANTIAL ACCOUNT OF THE CAPTURE OF THE
      SPANISH SCHOONER AMISTAD. New Haven, Conn.: Arno Press,
      1840.

      Examines the revolt by captive passengers aboard a
      slave ship bound for the United States.

5291. Barnes, Gilbert H. THE ANTISLAVERY IMPULSE, 1830-1844.
      New York: Appleton-Century, 1933.

5292. Bates, Daisy. THE LONG SHADOW OF LITTLE ROCK. New York:
      David McKay, 1962.

      Examines riots sparked by efforts to desegregate a pub-
      lic school in Arkansas.

5293. Blasi, Anthony J. SEGREGATIONIST VIOLENCE AND CIVIL
      RIGHTS MOVEMENTS IN TUSCALOOSA. Washington, D.C.:
      University Press of America, 1980.

5294. Boskin, Joseph. URBAN RACIAL VIOLENCE IN THE TWENTIETH
      CENTURY. Beverly Hills, Calif.: Glencoe Press, 1976.

5295. Boyer, Richard O. THE LEGEND OF JOHN BROWN: A BIOGRAPHY
      AND A HISTORY. New York: Knopf, 1973.

      Reviews the career of an abolitionist whose "divinely-
      ordained" methods included murder and mutilation of
      slaveholders (and sometimes of innocent bystanders) in
      the name of freedom.

5296. Brearly, Henry Chase. "The Pattern of Violence." CUL-
      TURE IN THE SOUTH. Cited below as item 5311, pp.
      678-692.

5297. Bromley, Isaac H. THE CHINESE MASSACRE AT ROCK SPRINGS,
      WYOMING TERRITORY, SEPTEMBER 2, 1885. Boston: The
      Author, 1886.

5298. Brown, Earl. WHY RACE RIOTS? LESSONS FROM DETROIT.
      Washington, D.C.: New York Public Affairs Comm., 1944.

5299. Buck, Paul H. THE ROAD TO REUNION, 1865-1900. Boston:
      Little, Brown, 1937.

      Includes discussion of anti-black terrorism during
      Reconstruction.

450 TERRORISM IN THE UNITED STATES AND EUROPE

5300. Carroll, Stanley W. SLAVE INSURRECTIONS IN THE UNITED STATES, 1800-1865. New York: Negro Universities Press, 1938.

5301. Carter, Hodding. THE ANGRY SCAR: THE STORY OF RECONSTRUCTION. Garden City, N.Y.: Doubleday, 1959.

This, and all subsequent entries dealing with Reconstruction after the Civil War, includes discussion of white terrorism, the KKK, and other violent means employed to subjugate newly-freed blacks while following the letter of the 13th Amendment.

5302. ———. THE SOUTH STRIKES BACK. Garden City, N.Y.: Doubleday, 1959.

A Mississippi journalist examines angry, often violent reactions to the Supreme Court's order for public school desegregation after 1954. Particular attention is given to the White Citizens Councils which organized as an alternative to the "lower class" KKK.

5303. Cheek, William F. (ed). BLACK RESISTANCE BEFORE THE CIVIL WAR. Beverly Hills, Calif.: Glencoe Press, 1970.

5304. Chicago Commission on Race Relations. THE NEGRO IN CHICAGO: A STUDY OF RACE RELATIONS AND A RACE RIOT. Chicago: Chicago Commission on Race Relations, 1922.

5305. Clarke, John H. (ed). WILLIAM STYRON'S NAT TURNER: TEN BLACK WRITERS RESPOND. Boston: Beacon Press, 1968.

5306. Coffin, Joshua. AN ACCOUNT OF SOME OF THE PRINCIPAL SLAVE INSURRECTIONS. New York: Anti-Slavery Society, 1860.

5307. Conrad, Earl. JIM CROW AMERICA. New York: Duell, Sloan & Pearce, 1947.

Examines the history of racial segregation in America, including incidents of terrorism used by whites to enforce the "separate but equal doctrine."

5308. Conway, Alan. HISTORY OF THE NEGRO IN THE UNITED STATES OF AMERICA. London: London Historical Assn., 1968.

5309. ———. THE RECONSTRUCTION OF GEORGIA. Minneapolis: University of Minnesota Press, 1966.

5310. Corporation of Charleston. AN ACCOUNT OF THE LATE IN-
      TENDED INSURRECTION AMONG A PORTION OF THE BLACKS IN
      THIS CITY. Charleston, S.C.: Corp. of Charleston, 1822.

5311. Couch, William Terry (ed). CULTURE IN THE SOUTH. Chapel
      Hill, N.C.: University of North Carolina Press, 1935.

      Contains item 5296 above.

5312. Coulter, E. Merton. THE CIVIL WAR AND READJUSTMENT IN
      KENTUCKY. Chapel Hill, N.C.: University of North Car-
      olina Press, 1926.

5313. ———. THE SOUTH DURING RECONSTRUCTION, 1865-1877.
      Baton Rouge, La.: Louisiana State University Press,
      1947.

5314. Cronon, E.D. BLACK MOSES. Madison, Wis.: University of
      Wisconsin Press, 1955.

      Presents the biography of Marcus Garvey, black nation-
      alist and convicted swindler, whose "back to Africa"
      plan won the endorsement of the KKK.

5315. Crozier, E.W. THE WHITE CAPS: A HISTORY OF THE ORGANI-
      ZATION IN SEVIER COUNTY. Knoxville, Tenn.: The Author,
      1899.

5316. Curran, Thomas J. XENOPHOBIA AND IMMIGRATION, 1820-1930.
      Boston: Twayne Publishers, 1975.

5317. Daniels, Roger (ed). ANIT-CHINESE VIOLENCE IN NORTH
      AMERICA. New York: Arno Press, 1978.

5318. Davis, William W. THE CIVIL WAR AND RECONSTRUCTION IN
      FLORIDA. Gainesville, Fla.: University of Florida
      Press, 1964.

5319. Dees, Jesse W., Jr., and James S. Hadley. JIM CROW.
      Ann Arbor, Mich.: University of Michigan Press, 1951.

5320. de Ford, Miriam Allen. THEY WERE SAN FRANCISCANS.
      Caldwell, Idaho: Caxton Publishers, 1941, pp. 188-211.

      Pages cited cover violence against Chinese immigrants.

5321. Dillon, Merton L. ELIJAH P. LOVEJOY, ABOLITIONIST EDITOR.
      Urbana, Ill.: University of Illinois Press, 1961.

Examines the life of a leading abolitionist spokesman, murdered by pro-slavery vigilantes in 1837.

5322. Dillon, Richard H.   THE HATCHET MEN: THE STORY OF THE TONG WARS IN SAN FRANCISCO'S CHINA TOWN. New York: Coward, McCann, 1962, pp. 99-127.

Pages cited discuss white violence against Chinese.

5323. Drewry, William S. SLAVE INSURRECTIONS IN VIRGINIA, 1830-1865: THE SOUTHAMPTON INSURRECTION. Washington, D.C.: The Neale Co., 1900.

5324. Du Bois, William E.B. THE ATLANTA RIOT. New York: Holt, 1907.

5325. ————. BLACK RECONSTRUCTION IN AMERICA, 1860-1880. New York: Russell & Russell, 1935.

5326. ————. THE SOULS OF BLACK FOLK. Chicago: A.C. McClurg, 1903.

5327. Duff, John B., and Peter M. Mitchell (eds). THE NAT TURNER REBELLION. THE HISTORICAL EVENT AND THE MODERN CONTROVERSY. New York: Harper & Row, 1971.

5328. Dunning, William A. RECONSTRUCTION: POLITICAL AND ECONOMIC, 1865-1877. New York: Harper & Brothers, 1935.

5329. Edmonds, Helen G. THE NEGRO AND FUSION POLITICS IN NORTH CAROLINA, 1894-1901. Chapel Hill, N.C.: University of North Carolina Press, 1951.

5330. Eppse, Merl R. THE NEGRO, TOO, IN AMERICAN HISTORY. Nashville, Tenn.: National Educational Publishing Co., 1938.

5331. Evans, Maurice S. BLACK AND WHITE IN THE SOUTHERN UNITED STATES. New York: Longmans, Green and Co., 1915.

5332. Exell, John S. THE SOUTH SINCE 1865. New York: Macmillan, 1963.

5333. Feldstein, Stanely (ed). THE POISONED TONGUE: A DOCUMENTARY HISTORY OF AMERICAN RACISM AND PREJUDICE. New York: William Morrow, 1972.

5334. Fellman, Michael. "Rehearsal for the Civil War: Anti-slavery and Proslavery at the Fighting Point in Kansas, 1854-1856." ANTISLAVERY RECONSIDERED: NEW PERSPECTIVES ON THE ABOLITIONISTS. Edited by Lewis Perry and Michael Fellman. Baton Rouge: Louisiana State University Press, 1979, pp. 287-307.

5335. Filler, Louis. THE CRUSADE AGAINST SLAVERY, 1830-1860. New York: Harper, 1960.

5336. ———. THE MILITANT SOUTH, 1800-1861. Cambridge, Mass.: Harvard University Press, 1956.

5337. Fleming, Walter L. THE CIVIL WAR AND RECONSTRUCTION IN ALABAMA. Cleveland, Ohio: Arthur H. Clark Co., 1911.

5338. ——— (ed). DOCUMENTARY HISTORY OF RECONSTRUCTION. Cleveland, Ohio: Arthur H. Clark Co., 1907.

5339. Foner, Eric (ed). NAT TURNER. Englewood Cliffs, N.J.: Prentice-Hall, 1971.

5340. Franklin, John Hope. FROM SLAVERY TO FREEDOM: A HISTORY OF NEGRO AMERICANS. New York: Vintage Books, 1969.

5341. ———. THE MILITANT SOUTH, 1800-1861. Cambridge, Mass.: Harvard University Press, 1956.

5342. Frazier, E. Franklin. THE NEGRO IN THE UNITED STATES. New York: Macmillan, 1957.

5343. Friedman, Lawrence J. THE WHITE SAVAGE: RACIAL FANTASIES IN THE POST-BELLUM SOUTH. Englewood Cliffs, N.J.: Prentice-Hall, 1970.

5344. Frye, Charles A. (ed). VALUES IN CONFLICT: BLACKS AND THE AMERICAN AMBIVALENCE TOWARD VIOLENCE. Washington, D.C.: University Press of America, 1980.

5345. Fuller, Thomas O. PICTORIAL HISTORY OF THE AMERICAN NEGRO. Memphis, Tenn.: Pictorial History, Inc., 1933.

5346. Gill, John. TIDE WITHOUT TURNING: ELIJAH P. LOVEJOY AND THE FREEDOM OF THE PRESS. Boston: Starr King Press, 1958.

5347. Grimke, Archibald H. RIGHT ON THE SCAFFOLD; OR, THE MARTYRS OF 1822. Washington, D.C.: American Negro Academy, 1901.

Examines the abortive Denmark Vesey slave revolt in
South Carolina. Forty-seven black participants were
hanged as a result of their attempt to overthrow the
state's "peculiar institution" of slavery.

5348. Grimshaw, Allen Day. RACIAL VIOLENCE IN THE UNITED
STATES. Chicago: Aldine, 1970.

5349. ————. A STUDY IN SOCIAL VIOLENCE: URBAN RACE RIOTS
IN THE UNITED STATES. Philadelphia: University of
Pennsylvania Press, 1959.

5350. Hair, William I. CARNIVAL OF FURY: ROBERT CHARLES AND
THE NEW ORLEANS RACE RIOT OF 1900. Baton Rouge, La.:
Louisiana State University Press, 1976.

5351. Halasz, Nicholas. THE RATTLING CHAINS: SLAVE UNREST AND
REBELLION IN THE ANTEBELLUM SOUTH. New York: David
McKay, 1966.

5352. Harding, Vincent. "Religion and Resistance Among Ante-
Bellum Negroes, 1800-1860." THE MAKING OF BLACK AMER-
ICA. Edited by A. Meier and E. Rudwick. New York: 1969.

5353. Hayden, Harry. THE STORY OF THE WILMINGTON REBELLION.
Wilmington, N.C.: The Author, 1936.

Presents the white side of a brutal race riot against
blacks.

5354. Haynes, Robert V. NIGHT OF VIOLENCE. THE HOUSTON RIOT
OF 1917. Baton Rouge, La.: Louisiana State University
Press, 1976.

5355. Hensel, William U. THE CHRISTIANA RIOT AND THE TREASON
TRIALS OF 1851. New York: Press of the New Era Printing Co., 1911.

5356. Hinton, Richard J. JOHN BROWN AND HIS MEN. WITH SOME
ACCOUNT OF THE ROADS THEY TRAVELED TO REACH HARPER'S
FERRY. New York: Funk & Wagnalls, 1969.

5357. James, C.L.R. A HISTORY OF NEGRO REVOLT. London: Fact
Ltd., 1938.

5358. Janowitz, Morris. "Patterns of Collective Racial Vio-
lence." VIOLENCE IN AMERICA: HISTORICAL AND COMPARA-
TIVE PERSPECTIVES. Edited by Hugh Davis Graham and
Ted Robert Gurr. Cited above as item 3265, pp. 412-444.

5359. Johnson, F. Roy. THE NAT TURNER SLAVE INSURRECTION.
      Murfreesboro, N.C.: Johnson Publishing Co., 1966.

5360. Katz, Jonathan. RESISTANCE AT CHRISTIANA. THE FUGITIVE
      SLAVE REBELLION, CHRISTIANA, PA., SEPT. 11, 1851. A
      DOCUMENTARY ACCOUNT. New York: Crowell, 1974.

5361. Killens, John O. (ed). THE TRIAL RECORD OF DENMARK VESEY.
      Boston: Beacon Press, 1970.

5362. Kromer, Helen. THE AMISTAD, 1839: THE SLAVE UPRISING
      ABOARD THE SPANISH SCHOONER. New York: Watts, 1973.

5363. Landry, Stuart. SIDELIGHTS ON THE BATTLE OF NEW ORLEANS.
      New Orleans: Pelican Press, 1965.

      Examines the coup by white supremacists which toppled
      the "radical" city government during Reconstruction.

5364. Lane, A.J. THE BROWNSVILLE AFFAIR: NATIONAL CRISIS AND
      BLACK REACTION. London: Kennikat Press, 1971.

      Reviews the case of an alleged mutiny by black soldiers
      at Brownsville, Tex., during 1906. One white person was
      killed and two others wounded when members of the all-
      black 25th Regiment "shot up the town." As a result,
      President Theodore Roosevelt dismissed the entire regi-
      ment without honor, an action widely described at the
      time as an "executive lynching."

5365. Lane, Roger. ROOTS OF VIOLENCE IN BLACK PHILADELPHIA
      1860-1900. Cambridge, Mass.: Harvard University Press,
      1986.

5366. Lee, Alfred McClung, and Norman Daymond Humphrey. RACE
      RIOT: A FIRST HAND OBSERVATION OF THE 1943 DETROIT
      RIOTS. New York: The Dryden Press, 1943.

5367. Lincoln, Charles E. THE BLACK MUSLIMS IN AMERICA. Bos-
      ton: Beacon Press, 1961.

      Covers the growth of America's leading black separatist
      movement, including violent clashes with police.

5368. Litwack, Leon F. NORTH OF SLAVERY: THE NEGRO IN THE
      FREE STATES, 1790-1860. Chicago: University of Chicago
      Press, 1961.

5369. Lofton, John M. INSURRECTION IN SOUTH CAROLINA: THE
      TURBULENT WORLD OF DENMARK VESEY. Yellow Springs,
      Ohio: Antioch Press, 1964.

5370. Logan, Frenise A. THE NEGRO IN NORTH CAROLINA, 1876-
      1894. Chapel Hill, N.C.: University of North Carolina
      Press, 1964.

5371. Lovejoy, Joseph C., and Owen Lovejoy. MEMOIR OF THE REV.
      ELIJAH P. LOVEJOY, WHO WAS MURDERED IN DEFENSE OF THE
      LIBERTY OF THE PRESS AT ALTON, ILLINOIS, NOV. 7, 1837.
      New York: J.S. Taylor, 1838.

5372. Lyman, Theodore (ed). PAPERS RELATING TO THE GARRISON
      MOB. Cambridge, Mass.: The Author, 1870.

5373. McGowan, Joseph A. HISTORY OF THE SACRAMENTO VALLEY.
      Vol. 1. New York: Lewis Historical Publishing Co.,
      1961, pp. 321-333.

      Pages cited include discussion of violence against
      Chinese immigrants.

5374. McMillan, George. RACIAL VIOLENCE AND LAW ENFORCEMENT.
      Atlanta, Ga.: Southern Regional Council, 1966.

5375. McWilliams, Carey. NORTH FROM MEXICO. Philadelphia:
      J.B. Lippincott, 1949.

5376. ————. PREJUDICE - JAPANESE AMERICANS: SYMBOL OF RACIAL
      INTOLERANCE. Boston: Little, Brown, 1944.

5377. Mayor's Commission on Conditions in Harlem. THE COMPLETE
      REPORT OF MAYOR LA GUARDIA'S COMMISSION ON THE HARLEM
      RIOT OF MARCH 19, 1935. New York: Mayor's Commission
      on Conditions in Harlem, 1935.

5378. Meier, August. "Black Violence in the 20th Century: A
      Study on Rhetoric and Retaliation." VIOLENCE IN AMER-
      ICA. HISTORICAL AND COMPARATIVE PERSPECTIVES. Cited
      above as item 3265, pp. 399-412.

5379. Miller, Stuart C. THE UNWELCOME IMMIGRANT: THE AMERICAN
      IMAGE OF THE CHINESE, 1785-1882. Berkeley, Calif.:
      University of California Press, 1969.

5380. Mitchell, J. Paul (ed). RACE RIOTS IN BLACK AND WHITE.
      Englewood Cliffs, N.J.: Prentice-Hall, 1970.

5381. Moss, Frank. STORY OF THE RIOT. PERSECUTION OF NEGROES
      BY ROUGHS AND POLICEMEN IN THE CITY OF NEW YORK, AUG-
      UST 1900. New York: Citizens' Protective League, 1900.

5382. National Urban League. RACIAL CONFLICT, A HOME-FRONT
      DANGER: LESSONS OF THE DETROIT RIOT. New York: Nation-
      al Urban League, 1943.

5383. NEGRO YEAR BOOK: ANNUAL ENCYCLOPEDIA OF THE NEGRO. Tus-
      kegee, Ala.: Tuskegee Institute, 1912-1952 (yearly,
      except 1920-1921, 1923-1924, and 1927-1928).

5384. Newby, Idus A. JIM CROW'S DEFENSE: ANTI-NEGRO THOUGHT
      IN AMERICA, 1900-1930. Baton Rouge, La.: Louisiana
      State University Press, 1965.

5385. Oates, Stephen B. TO PURGE THIS LAND WITH BLOOD: A BIO-
      GRAPHY OF JOHN BROWN. New York: Harper & Row, 1970.

5386. Owens, William A. BLACK MUTINY: THE REVOLT ON THE SCHOO-
      NER AMISTAD. New York: Pilgrim Press, 1953.

5387. Panger, Daniel. OL' PROPHET NAT. Greenwich, Conn.:
      Yale University Press, 1968.

5388. Perlman, Selig. "The Anti-Chinese Agitation in Califor-
      nia." HISTORY OF LABOR IN THE UNITED STATES. Edited
      by John R. Commons. New York: Macmillan, 1918, pp.
      252-268.

5389. Quarles, Benjamin. ALLIES FOR FREEDOM: BLACKS AND JOHN
      BROWN. New York: Oxford University Press, 1974.

5390. ———— (ed). BLACKS ON JOHN BROWN. Urbana, Ill.: Uni-
      versity of Illinois Press, 1974.

      Contains essays by black authors on John Brown, his
      abolitionism, and his choice of violent means.

5391. Randall, James G. THE CIVIL WAR AND RECONSTRUCTION.
      New York: Heath, 1937.

5392. Ratner, Lorman A. POWDER KEG: NORTHERN OPPOSITION TO THE
      ANTI-SLAVERY MOVEMENT, 1831-1840. New York: Basic
      Books, 1968.

5393. Record, Wilson, and Jane Cassels Record (eds). LITTLE ROCK, U.S.A.: MATERIALS FOR ANALYSIS. San Francisco: Chandler Publishing Co., 1960.

5394. Rice, Lawrence D. THE NEGRO IN TEXAS, 1874-1900. Baton Rouge, La.: Louisiana State University Press, 1971.

5395. Richardson, Joe M. (ed). THE NEGRO IN THE RECONSTRUCTION OF FLORIDA, 1865-1877. Tallahassee: Florida State University Press, 1965.

5396. Richardson, Leonard L. GENTLEMEN OF PROPERTY AND STANDING. ANTI-ABOLITION MOBS IN JACKSONIAN AMERICA. New York: Oxford University Press, 1970.

5397. Rowan, Carl T. GO SOUTH TO SORROW. New York: Random House, 1957.

A black reporter visits Dixie in the wake of the Supreme Court's school desegregation ruling.

5398. ————. SOUTH OF FREEDOM. New York: Alfred A. Knopf, 1952.

5399. Ruchames, Louis (ed). A JOHN BROWN READER. New York: Abelard-Schuman, 1971.

5400. Rudwick, Elliott M. RACE RIOT AT EAST ST. LOUIS, JULY 2, 1917. Carbondale, Ill.: Southern Illinois University Press, 1964.

5401. Sandburg, Carl. THE CHICAGO RACE RIOT, JULY 1919. New York: Harcourt, Brace & World, 1919.

5402. Sandmeyer, Elmer Clarence. THE ANTI-CHINESE MOVEMENT IN CALIFORNIA. Urbana, Ill.: University of Illinois Press, 1939.

5403. Saxton, Alexander. THE INDISPENSABLE ENEMY: LABOR AND THE ANTI-CHINESE MOVEMENT IN CALIFORNIA. Berkeley, Calif.: University of California Press, 1971.

5404. Shofner, Jerrell H. NOR IS IT OVER YET: FLORIDA IN THE ERA OF RECONSTRUCTION, 1863-1877. Gainesville, Fla.: University Presses of Florida, 1974.

5405. Shogan, Robert, and Tom Craig. THE DETROIT RACE RIOT: A STUDY IN VIOLENCE. Philadelphia: Chilton Books, 1964.

5406. Simpkins, Francis B., and Robert H. Wood. SOUTH CAROLINA
       DURING RECONSTRUCTION. Chapel Hill, N.C.: University
       of North Carolina Press, 1932.

5407. Sprigle, Ray. IN THE LAND OF JIM CROW. New York: Simon
       & Schuster, 1949.

5408. Stampp, Kenneth. THE ERA OF RECONSTRUCTION, 1865-1877.
       New York: Alfred A. Knopf, 1965.

5409. Staples, Thomas S. RECONSTRUCTION IN ARKANSAS, 1862-1874.
       New York: Columbia University Press, 1923.

5410. Starobin, Robert S. (ed). DENMARK VESEY. THE SLAVE CON-
       SPIRACY OF 1822. Englewood Cliffs, N.J.: Prentice-Hall,
       1970.

5411. Styron, William. THE CONFESSIONS OF NAT TURNER. New
       York: Random House, 1967.

       Presents a fictionalized account of a famous slave re-
       volt. Considered controversial at the time, especially
       by blacks who felt that Turner's character had not rece-
       ived sufficient sympathy and understanding.

5412. Tanner, Henry. THE MARTYRDOM OF LOVEJOY. Chicago: The
       Author, 1881.

5413. Taylor, Alrutheus A. THE NEGRO IN THE RECONSTRUCTION OF
       VIRGINIA. Washington, D.C.: The Association for the
       Study of Negro Life and History, 1926.

5414. ————. THE NEGRO IN SOUTH CAROLINA DURING RECONSTRUC-
       TION. Washington, D.C.: The Association for the Study
       of Negro Life and History, 1924.

5415. ————. THE NEGRO IN TENNESSEE, 1865-1880. Washington,
       D.C.: Associated Publishers, 1941.

5416. Thompson, Clara Mildred. RECONSTRUCTION IN GEORGIA:
       ECONOMIC, SOCIAL, POLITICAL, 1865-1872. New York:
       Columbia University Press, 1915.

5417. Tindall, George B. SOUTH CAROLINA NEGROES, 1877-1900.
       Columbia, S.C. University of South Carolina Press,
       1952.

460 TERRORISM IN THE UNITED STATES AND EUROPE

5418. Tragle, Henry I. (ed). THE SOUTHAMPTON REVOLT OF 1831:
A COMPILATION OF SOURCE MATERIALS. Amherst, Mass.:
University of Massachusetts Press, 1971.

5419. Tuttle, William M, Jr. RACE RIOT IN CHICAGO IN THE RED
SUMMER OF 1919. New York: Atheneum, 1970.

5420. United States House of Representatives. EAST ST. LOUIS
RIOTS. REPORT OF THE SPECIAL COMMITTEE AUTHORIZED BY
CONGRESS TO INVESTIGATE THE EAST ST. LOUIS RIOTS. 65th
Congress, Second Session. Washington, D.C.: U.S. Gov-
ernment Printing Office, 1969.

5421. ———. MEMPHIS RIOTS AND MASSACRES. 39th Congress,
First Session. Washington, D.C.: U.S. Government Printing Office, 1969.

5422. ———. VICKSBURG TROUBLES. 43rd Congress, Second Session. Washington, D.C.: U.S. Government Printing Office, 1969.

5423. United States Senate. NEW ORLEANS RIOTS OF JULY 30,
1866. REPORT OF THE SELECT COMMITTEE OF THE SENATE.
39th Congress, Second Session. Washington, D.C.: U.S.
Government Printing Office, 1969.

5424. Van Dusen, John G. THE BLACK MAN IN WHITE AMERICA.
Washington, D.C.: Associated Publishers, 1969.

5425. Vessey, Denmark. THE TRIAL RECORD OF DENMARK VESSEY
1822. Boston: Beacon Press, 1970.

5426. Waskow, Arthur I. FROM RACE RIOT TO SIT-IN, 1919 AND
THE 1960s; A STUDY IN THE CONNECTIONS BETWEEN CONFLICT
AND VIOLENCE. Garden City, N.Y.: Doubleday, 1966.

5427. White, Walter, and Thurgood Marshall. WHAT CAUSED THE
DETROIT RIOT? New York: 1843.

The authors come down heavily on racist agitators and
incompetent police in this telling assessment of racial
upheaval during World War II. Marshall was moved to
call Detroit police "the Gestapo" for their kid-glove
handling of white rioters, counter-balanced by brutality
and use of deadly force against black prisoners.

5428. Williams, Lee D. ANATOMY OF FOUR RACE RIOTS; RACIAL CON-
FLICT IN KNOXVILLE, ELAINE, TULSA, AND CHICAGO, 1919-
1921. Hattiesburg, Miss.: University and College Pres
of Mississippi, 1972.

5429. Woodward, C. Vann. REUNION AND REACTION: THE COMPROMISE OF 1877 AND THE END OF RECONSTRUCTION. Boston: Little, Brown, 1951.

5430. ————. THE STRANGE CAREER OF JIM CROW. London: Oxford University Press, 1955.

5431. Wynes, Charles E. THE NEGRO IN THE SOUTH SINCE 1865. Tuscaloosa, Ala.: University of Alabama Press, 1965.

b. Articles

5432. Abernethy, Lloyd M. "The Washington Race War of July 1919." MARYLAND HISTORICAL MAGAZINE 58 (1963): 309-324.

5433. Abzug, Robert H. "The Influence of Garrisonian Abolitionists' Fears of Slave Violence on the Antislavery Argument, 1829-1840." JOURNAL OF NEGRO HISTORY 55 (1970): 15-28.

5434. Addington, Wendell G. "Slave Insurrections in Texas." JOURNAL OF NEGRO HISTORY 35 (1950): 408-434.

5435. Akers, Elmer R., and Vernon Fox. "The Detroit Rioters and Looters Committed to Prison." JOURNAL OF CRIMINAL LAW 35 (1944): 105-111.

5436. Alexander, H. "Race Riots and Lynch Law; the Cause and the Cure; a Southern Lawyer's View." OUTLOOK 85 (February 2, 1907): 259-263.

5437. "Anniversary of Hate." NEWSWEEK 33 (June 26, 1944): 49-50+.

Presents a one-year retrospective on the 1943 Detroit race riot.

5438. "Anti-Race Riot Insurance." COLLIER'S 112 (October 23, 1943): 86.

5439. "Appeal to America Not Yet Written by Woodrow Wilson." NATION 109 (August 9, 1919): 160.

In the closing days of a violent "red summer" marred by riots and lynchings, liberal editors chastise President Wilson for his failure to speak out forcefully against racial terrorism.

5440. Aptheker, Herbert. "Militant Abolitionism." JOURNAL OF
      NEGRO HISTORY 26 (1941): 438-484.

5441. ———. "Notes on Slave Insurrections in Confederate
      Mississippi." JOURNAL OF NEGRO HISTORY 29 (1944):
      75-79.

5442. ———. "Slavery, the Negro, and Militancy." POLITICAL
      AFFAIRS 46 (1967): 36-43.

5443. Arendt, Hannah. "Reflections on Little Rock." DISSENT
      6 (1959): 45-55.

      Reviews events in Arkansas, where opposition to public
      school integration turned violent in 1957.

5444. Ashe, Samuel A., and Lyon G. Tyler. "Secession, Insur-
      rection of Negroes, and Northern Incendiarism." TYLER'S
      QUARTERLY HISTORICAL AND GENEALOGICAL MAGAZINE (July
      1933).

5445. Asher, Robert (ed). "Documents of the Race Riot at East
      St. Louis." JOURNAL OF THE ILLINOIS STATE HISTORICAL
      SOCIETY 65 (1972): 327-336.

5446. "Atlanta Massacre." INDEPENDENT 61 (October 4, 1906):
      799-800.

5447. "Atlanta Outdone in Springfield." INDEPENDENT 65 (August
      20, 1908): 442-443.

5448. "Atlanta Riots: Symposium." OUTLOOK 84 (November 17,
      1906): 684-685.

5449. "Awaiting Action in Mississippi." TIME 48 (August 12,
      1946): 20.

      Follows developments in the case of Leon McTatie, a
      black man flogged to death by whites at Lexington, Miss.,
      after he was accused of stealing a saddle. Six whites
      were arrested in the case; all were ultimately freed.

5450. Baker, R.S. "Following the Color Line." AMERICAN MER-
      CURY 63 (April 1907): 563-579.

5451. Banay, Ralph S. "A Psychiatrist Looks at the Zoot Suit."
      PROBATION 22 (1944): 81-85.

Examines the attire of contemporary Latino street gangs in the wake of anti-Mexican violence by whites in Los Angeles. A classic case of blaming the victim.

5452. Barnard, H. "Emmett Lewis Till." NATION 181 (September 24, 1955): inside cover.

Reviews the case of a black teenager, murdered in Mississippi after he allegedly whistled at a white woman. Till's killers were acquitted by a jury, then confessed their crime (for money) in a national magazine.

5453. Beeler, Dorothy. "Race Riot in Columbia, Tennessee: February 25-27, 1946." TENNESSEE HISTORICAL QUARTERLY 39 (1980): 49-61.

5454. Bell, Leland. "Radicalism and Race: The IWW and the Black Worker." JOURNAL OF HUMAN RELATIONS 19 (1971): 48-56.

5455. Bernson, Sarah L., and Robert J. Eggers. "Black People in South Dakota History." SOUTH DAKOTA HISTORY 7 (1977): 241-270.

Includes coverage of the 1920s KKK in South Dakota.

5456. Blagden, W.S. "Arkansas Flogging." NEW REPUBLIC 87 (July 1, 1936): 236-237.

5457. "Blame for the Riot at Springfield." NATION 87 (September 24, 1908): 284.

5458. Blaser, Kent. "North Carolina and John Brown's Raid." CIVIL WAR HISTORY 24 (1978): 197-212.

Examines how the raid at Harper's Ferry shifted Southern white opinion from moderation toward militant extremism in the days preceding the Civil War.

5459. Bliven, B. "Judge Waring Moves North." NEW REPUBLIC 126 (May 5, 1952): 13-14.

A pro-integration judge is driven out of South Carolina by racist violence and harassment.

5460. "Blood and Oil." SURVEY 46 (June 11, 1921): 369-370.

Examines the recent race riot in Tulsa, Okla.

5461. "Blot on the Nation: Murder of H.T. Moore." SURVEY 88
      (February 1952): 86.

      Reviews the bombing death of Florida civil rights
      leader Harry Moore and his wife, assassinated in their
      home on Christmas Eve by members of the KKK.

5462. "Blunder of Race Riots." INDEPENDENT 99 (August 9, 1919):
      176-178.

5463. Bogen, David. "Concerning Zoot Suit Gangs." COMMUNITY
      COORDINATION 11 (1943): 1-3.

5464. "Bombs and Terror in Florida." NEWSWEEK 39 (January 7,
      1952): 15-16.

5465. Borome, Joseph A. "The Vigilant Committee of Philadel-
      phia." PENNSYLVANIA MAGAZINE OF HISTORY AND BIOGRAPHY
      92 (1968): 320-351.

      Examines a militant abolitionist society established
      after local race riots in 1842.

5466. Boyle, S.P. "Voice from the South." CHRISTIAN CENTURY
      69 (December 17, 1952): 1471-1473.

5467. Brown, E. "Truth About the Detroit Riot." HARPER'S
      187 (November 1943): 488-489.

5468. Brumbaugh, T.T. "Fault, Dear Brutus." CHRISTIAN CEN-
      TURY 61 (May 24, 1944): 643-644.

5469. ————. "Truce in Detroit." CHRISTIAN CENTURY 60 (Aug-
      ust 11, 1943): 913-914.

5470. Burms, J.H. "Tomorrow's Race Riots." CHRISTIAN CENTURY
      62 (March 21, 1945): 364-365.

5471. Butts, J.W., and Dorothy James. "The Underlying Causes
      of the Elaine Riot of 1919." ARKANSAS HISTORICAL QUAR-
      TERLY 20 (1961): 95-104.

5472. Cable, G.W. "Silent South." SURVEY GEOGRAPHIC 36 (Jan-
      uary 1947): 27-28.

      Examines the refusal of "decent" Southerners to speak
      out in the wake of recent racial violence.

5473. Caldwell, Erskine. "The Deep South's Other Venerable
      Tradition." NEW YORK TIMES MAGAZINE (July 11, 1965).

      Examines the extent to which violence and cruelty are
      "indigenous traits" in the South.

5474. Cantwell, D.M. "Postscript to the Cicero Riot." COMMON-
      WEAL 54 (September 14, 1951): 543-545.

5475. Carpenter, John A. "Atrocities in the Reconstruction
      Period." JOURNAL OF NEGRO HISTORY 47 (1962): 234-247.

5476. Carranco, Lynwood. "Chinese Expulsion from Humboldt
      County." PACIFIC HISTORY REVIEW 30 (1961): 329-340.

5477. Carter, Dan T. "The Anatomy of Fear: The Christmas Day
      Insurrection Scare of 1865." JOURNAL OF SOUTHERN HIS-
      TORY 42 (1976): 345-364.

      Examines a case in which mere rumors of an impending
      slave revolt panicked local whites and produced violent
      reactions against peaceful blacks.

5478. Carter, Hodding. "Racial Crisis in the Deep South."
      SATURDAY EVENING POST 228 (December 17, 1955): 26-27+.

5479. Carter, Hodding III. "A Wave of Terror Threatens the
      South." LOOK 19 (March 22, 1955): 32-36.

5480. Case, H.G. "A Claim for the Slaveship Amistad." LONG
      ISLAND FORUM 35 (1972): 238-241.

      Chronicles the trial which followed an 1839 shipboard
      slave revolt.

5481. Castel, Albert. "Bleeding Kansas." AMERICAN HISTORY
      ILLUSTRATED 10 (1975): 4-9, 42-49.

5482. "Causes of the Chicago Race Riot." WORLD'S WORK 45
      (December 1922): 131-134.

5483. Chick, C.A. "Which Way?" VITAL SPEECHES 18 (October
      1, 1952): 764-765.

5484. "Cicero Riots." COMMONWEAL 54 (July 27, 1951): 371-372.

5485. Clark, Kenneth B. "Group Violence: A Preliminary Study of the Attitudinal Pattern of Its Acceptance and Rejection: A Study of the 1943 Harlem Race Riot." JOURNAL OF ABNORMAL AND SOCIAL PSYCHOLOGY 19 (1944): 319-337.

5486. ————, and James Barker. "The Zoot Suit Effect in Personality: A Race Riot Participant." JOURNAL OF ABNORMAL AND SOCIAL PSYCHOLOGY 40 (1945): 143-148.

5487. "Climate of Fear." COMMONWEAL 63 (Ocotber 14, 1955): 28.

5488. Cohen, William. "Riots, Racism, and Hysteria: The Response of Federal Investigative Officials to the Race Riots of 1919." MASSACHUSETTS REVIEW 13 (1972): 373-400.

Federal investigators find "Negro subversion" at the root of several riots in which most of the victims were blacks, murdered by rampaging whites. A curious result, but typical of the times.

5489. Comstock, A. "Over There." SURVEY 46 (July 2, 1921): 460.

5490. "Convictions in Cicero." CHRISTIAN CENTURY 68 (July 16, 1952): 34.

White rioters go to jail for a change, following a violent outburst in Illinois.

5491. Cotter, Edwin N., Jr. "John Brown in the Adirondacks." ADIRONDACK LIFE 3 (1972): 8-12.

Brown takes a vacation from the war in Kansas, spending time on Gerritt Smith's 100,000-acre farm, where several of his Harper's Ferry raiders were recruited.

5492. "Courage in Action: Koinonia Farm, Georgia." NATION 183 (September 22, 1956): 229, 237-238.

Examines the tribulations of a racially integrated commune in Klan-ridden Georgia.

5493. Crane, Paul, and Alfred Larson. "The Chinese Massacre." ANNALS OF WYOMING 12 (1940): 47-55.

5494. Creed, David A. "Reconstruction in Madison Parish." NORTH LOUISIANA HISTORICAL ASSOCIATION JOURNAL 7 (1976): 39-47.

Violent episodes include clashes betweeh Jayhawker outlaws and Confederate guerillas in 1860 and a purge of black voters by white terrorists in the early 1870s.

5495. Cromwell, John W. "The Aftermath of Nat Turner's Insurrection." JOURNAL OF NEGRO HISTORY 5 (1920): 208-234.

5496. Crouthamel, James L. "The Springfield Race Riot of 1908." JOURNAL OF NEGRO HISTORY 45 (1960): 164-181.

5497. Crowe, Charles. "Racial Massacre in Atlanta, September 22, 1906." JOURNAL OF NEGRO HISTORY 54 (1969): 150-173.

5498. ————. "Racial Violence and Social Reform: Origins of the Atlanta Riot of 1906." JOURNAL OF NEGRO HISTORY 53 (1968): 234-256.

5499. Dabbs, J.M. "What is the White South Defending?" CHRISTIAN CENTURY 73 (February 8, 1956): 173-174.

5500. Dabney, Virginius. "Gabriel's Insurrection." AMERICAN HISTORY ILLUSTRATED 11 (1976): 24-32.

Covers a slave revolt in South Carolina during 1800.

5501. ————. "Is the South That Bad?" SATURDAY REVIEW OF LITERATURE 29 (April 13, 1946): 9-10.

5502. Dahlke, H. Otto. "Race and Minority Riots—a Study in the Typology of Violence." SOCIAL FORCES 30 (1952): 419-425.

5503. Daniell, Elizabeth Otto. "The Ashburn Murder Case in Georgia Reconstruction, 1868." GEORGIA HISTORICAL QUARTERLY 59 (1975): 296-312.

Examines the political career of George Ashburn and the military trial of his racist assassins in 1868.

5504. "Dark Anniversary." TIME 42 (August 23, 1943): 20-21.

5505. "Darkest Cloud." SURVEY 42 (August 2, 1919): 675-676.

5506. Davenport, W. "Race Riots Coming: America's Negro Problem." COLLIER'S 112 (September 18, 1943): 11+.

5507. Davids, R.C. "Sixteen Sticks in a Bundle." READER'S DIGEST 60 (April 1952): 51-53.

Examines recent bombings in the South, primarily aimed
at black families purchasing homes in formerly "white"
neighborhoods. Birmingham, Ala., so monopolized the
bombings for a time that it was known as "Bombingham"
among local blacks.

5508. Davison, Allison. "Caste, Economy and Violence." AMER-
ICAN JOURNAL OF SOCIOLOGY 51 (July 1945): 7-15.

Suggests that increasing violence indicates blacks are
starting to compete more effectively with whites, econom-
ically.

5509. "Deadlock in Yanceyville." NEWSWEEK 38 (November 26,
1951): 25-26.

Once again, white jurors fail to convict Caucasian
killers of a black man in the South.

5510. "Death in Mississippi." COMMONWEAL 62 (September 23,
1955): 603-604.

Reviews the case of Emmett Till.

5511. "Deep Trouble." TIME 41 (June 28, 1943): 19.

Reports the Detroit race riot of 1943.

5512. "Defeat at Detroit." NATION 157 (July 3, 1943): 4.

5513. "Defeat in Cicero." CHRISTIAN CENTURY 68 (July 25, 1951):
862-863.

White rioters prevent a black family from moving into
a Chicago suburb.

5514. Delatte, Carolyn E. "The St. Landry Riot: A Forgotten
Incident of Reconstruction Violence." LOUISIANA HIS-
TORY 17 (1976): 41-49.

Covers a major riot in Louisiana, during 1868, which
led to weeks of lethal violence against blacks. Delatte
notes the ominous circumstance in which "[t]he entire
population joined ranks to insure Negro subordination."

5515. Demos, John. "The Antislavery Movement and the Problem
of Violent 'Menas.'" NEW ENGLAND QUARTERLY 37 (1964)
501-526.

5516. "Deploring Florida Killings Is Not Enough." CHRISTIAN CENTURY 69 (January 16, 1952): 60-61; 69 (February 27, 1952): 251-252.

5517. "Detroit." COMMONWEAL 38 (July 2, 1943): 263.

5518. "Detroit, the Storm Bursts." CHRISTIAN CENTURY 60 (June 30, 1943): 759-761.

5519. Dew, Charles B. "Black Iron Workers and the Slave Insurrection Panic of 1856." JOURNAL OF SOUTHERN HISTORY 41 (August 1975).

5520. Dick, John. "Stances of 'The Standard': The 1919 Chicago Race Riot." FOUNDATIONS 16 (October-December 1973).

5521. Dorland, C.P. "The Chinese Massacre at Los Angeles in 1871." HISTORICAL SOCIETY OF SOUTHERN CALIFORNIA PUBLICATIONS 3 (1894): 22-26.

5522. ———. "A Prophecy Partly Fulfilled." OVERLAND MONTHLY 7 (1886): 230-234.

    Covers contemporaneous violence against the Chinese.

5523. Downing, F. "Murder on Christmas." COMMONWEAL 55 (January 11, 1952): 347-348; 55 (February 8, 1952): 447; 55 (March 14, 1952): 567-568.

    Covers the Harry Moore bombing case in Florida.

5524. ———. "Report from Detroit." COMMONWEAL 38 (July 30, 1943): 361-363.

5525. Drake, S.C. "Lawrenceburg Verdict; Reply." NEW REPUBLIC 115 (December 3, 1946): 727.

5526. Draughton, Ralph Brown, Jr. "The Mobile Register Interviews John Brown." ALABAMA REVIEW 27 (1974): 152-155.

    Brown denies insanity, but admits seeking martyrdom in this interview with a Southern journalist.

5527. Dubay, Robert W. "Mississippi and the Proposed Federal Anti-Lynching Bills of 1937-38." SOUTHERN QUARTERLY 7 (1968): 73-89.

5528. Du Bois, W.E.B., and Martha Gruening. "Massacre at East
      St. Louis." THE CRISIS 14 (1917): 219-238.

5529. Dudley, J. Wayne. "'Hate' Organizations of the 1940s:
      The Columbians, Inc." PHYLON 42 (1981): 262-274.

      Follows the career of a neo-fascist organization that
      briefly terrorized blacks and Jews in Atlanta, Ga. Sev-
      eral members of the group were sent to prison; survivors
      later joined the KKK or helped organize the violent
      National States Rights Party.

5530. "Dynamite and the Cop, Little Rock." TIME 74 (September
      21, 1959): 29.

5531. Eaton, Clement. "Mob Violence in the Old South." MISS-
      ISSIPPI VALLEY HISTORICAL REVIEW 29 (1942): 351-370.

5532. Edwards, G.C. "White Justice in Dallas; Akins Trials."
      NATION 161 (September 15, 1945): 253-255.

5533. Edwards, John Carver. "Radical Reconstruction and the
      New Orleans Riot of 1866." INTERNATIONAL REVIEW OF
      HISTORY AND POLITICAL SCIENCE 10 (August 1973): 48-64.

5534. Elliott, Robert N. "The Nat Turner Insurrection as Re-
      ported in the North Carolina Press." NORTH CAROLINA
      HISTORICAL REVIEW 38 (1961): 1-18.

5535. Ely, James W., Jr., and Daniel P. Jordan. "Harper's
      Ferry Revisited: Father Costello's 'Short Sketch' of
      Brown's Raid." RECORDS OF THE AMERICAN CATHOLIC HIS-
      TORICAL SOCIETY OF PHILADELPHIA 85 (1974): 59-67.

5536. "Facing the Negro Problem." MISSISSIPPI REVIEW 43 (No-
      vember 1919): 818-819.

5537. "Facts About Atlanta Murders." WORLD'S WORK 13 (November
      1906): 8147-8148.

5538. "Fair Brow." NEW REPUBLIC 116 (February 24, 1947): 6.

      Examines recent acts of racial violence in the South.

5539. Farley, Foster. "The Fear of Negro Slave Revolts in
      South Carolina, 1690-1865." AFRO-AMERICAN STUDIES 3
      (December 1972).

5540. Faulkner, William. "On Fear: The South in Labor." HAR-
      PER'S 212 (June 1956): 29-34; 213 (August 1956): 4.

5541. "FBI vs. Hate Bombs." SENIOR SCHOLASTIC 73 (October 31,
      1958): 34.

5542. "Festering Tension; Detroit's Race Riots Ebb, but U.S.
      Problems Remain." NEWSWEEK 22 (July 5, 1943): 35-36+.

5543. Fey, H.E. "Tornado Weather in Dixie." CHRISTIAN CENTURY
      73 (February 29, 1956): 263-265.

5544. "Find the Guilty." NEWSWEEK 46 (December 12, 1955): 37.

5545. Fingerhut, Eugene R. "Tom Watson, Blacks, and Southern
      Reform." GEORGIA HISTORICAL QUARTERLY 60 (1976): 324-
      343.

      Traces Watson's political career from idealistic Pop-
      ulism to the depths of gutter racism and anti-semitism
      after his initial campaigns fell flat at the polls.

5546. Fitelson, H.W. "Murders at Monroe, Ga." NEW REPUBLIC
      115 (September 2, 1946): 258-260.

5547. FitzSimons, Theodore B., Jr. "The Camilla Riot, 1868."
      GEORGIA HISTORICAL QUARTERLY 35 (1951): 116-125.

5548. Fleming, Thomas J. "The Right to Self-Defense." CRISIS
      76 (1969): 9-15.

      Examines the case of Dr. Ossian Sweet, a black physi-
      cian who defended his Detroit home against white attackers
      in September 1925 and was charged with murder as a re-
      sult. Attorney Clarence Darrow won the case for Sweet,
      but not before Detroit's simmering racial antagonisms
      were brought to light in a grim foretaste of things to
      come.

5549. ———. "The Trial of John Brown." AMERICAN HERITAGE
      18 (1967): 28-33, 92-100.

5550. Fogelson, Robert M. "Violence as Protest." PROCEEDINGS
      OF THE ACADEMY OF POLITICAL SCIENCE 29 (1968): 25-41.

      Compares the ghetto riots of 1964-67 with those of
      earlier periods, in which whites were the aggressors.

5551. Fornell, Earl W. "The Abduction of Free Negroes and
      Slaves in Texas." SOUTHWESTERN HISTORICAL QUARTERLY
      60 (1957): 369-380.

5552. Foster, V.C. "Racial Tensions Plague Alabama." CHRIS-
      TIAN CENTURY 73 (February 29, 1956): 280+.

5553. Fowler, C. "Racial Prejudice: A Racket." NEW OUTLOOK
      164 (October 1934): 10-14.

5554. Franklin, Vincent P. "The Philadelphia Race Riot of
      1918." PENNSYLVANIA MAGAZINE OF HISTORY AND BIOGRAPHY
      99 (1975): 336-350.

5555. Friedman, Lawrence J. "Antebellum American Abolitionsim
      and the Problem of Violent Means." PSYCHOHISTORY RE-
      VIEW 9 (1980): 23-58.

5556. "From a Faucet On Up: Explosion at Central High." REPOR-
      TER 19 (October 1958): 2.

      A year after riots failed to block integration at Cen-
      tral High School in Little Rock, bombers make a differ-
      ent attempt to gain the same objective.

5557. Galpin, W. Freeman. "The Jerry Rescue." NEW YORK HIS-
      TORY 26 (1945): 19-34.

      Runaway slaves are forcibly removed from the custody
      of trackers assigned to carry them south.

5558. "Gassed." TIME 48 (November 25, 1946): 27.

5559. Gatewood, Willard B. "Theodore Roosevelt and the Indian-
      ola Affair." JOURNAL OF NEGRO HISTORY 53 (1968): 48-69.

5560. "Gauntlet Flung in Florida." COMMONWEAL 55 (January 11,
      1952): 339-340.

      Examines the murder of Harry Moore and his wife.

5561. Gavit, J.P. "By Their Fruits Ye Shall Know Them." SUR-
      VEY GEOGRAPHIC 25 (July 1936): 434.

5562. George, Paul S. "Colored Town: Miami's Black Community,
      1896-1930." FLORIDA HISTORY QUARTERLY 56 (1978): 432-
      447.

5563. "Georgia Fascists." LIFE 21 (December 23, 1946): 28-29.

Examines the pathetic career of the Columbians, described by their prosecutor as "the juvenile delinquents
of the Klan."

5564. Gilbert, Arthur. "Violence and Intimidation in the
South." SOCIAL ORDER 10 (December 1960): 450-456.

Examines the relationship between racism and anti-
semitism in the segregationist movement of the 1950s.

5565. Goldstein, Leslie F. "Violence as an Instrument of Social Change; the Views of Frederick Douglas, 1817-1895."
JOURNAL OF NEGRO HISTORY 6 (1976): 61-72.

5566. "Governors Pass the Buck." NEW REPUBLIC 109 (July 12,
1943): 38.

5567. Granade, Ray. "Slave Unrest in Florida." FLORIDA HIS-
TORICAL QUARTERLY 55 (1976): 18-36.

5568. Grau, Richard. "The Christiana Riot of 1851: A Reapprais-
al." JOURNAL OF THE LANCASTER COUNTY HISTORICAL SOCIETY
68 (1964): 147-163.

5569. Graves, J.T. "South Won't Surrender." AMERICAN MERCURY
83 (July 1956): 39-46.

5570. ———, and W.E.B. Du Bois. "Tragedy at Atlanta."
WORLD TODAY 11 (November 1906): 1169-1175.

5571. Hachey, Thomas E. "The Wages of War: A British Commentary on Life in Detroit in July, 1943." MICHIGAN HIS-
TORY 59 (1975): 227-238.

5572. Hair, William Ivy. "'Inquisition for Blood': An Outlook
of Ritual Murder in Louisiana, Georgia and Texas,
1911-1912." LOUISIANA STUDIES 11 (1972): 274-281.

Examines the mass murders of mulattoes in three states,
possibly committed by an extreme religious organization
"cleansing" the race of "hybrid" individuals.

5573. Halberstam, David. "White Citizens Councils." COMMENTARY
22 (October 1956): 293-302.

5574. Halliburton, R., Jr. "The Tulsa Race War of 1921."
      JOURNAL OF BLACK STUDIES 2 (1972): 333-357.

5575. Hanson, H. "No Surrender in Farmville, Va." NEW REPUB-
      LIC 133 (October 10, 1955): 11-15.

5576. "Harlem Hoodlums." NEWSWEEK 22 (August 9, 1943): 48+.

5577. "Harlem's Wild Rampage Brings Death, Destruction, Looting
      and Shame." LIFE 15 (August 16, 1943): 32-33.

5578. Harrison, Theresa A. "George Thompson and the 1851 'Anti-
      Abolition' Riot." HISTORICAL JOURNAL OF WESTERN MASS-
      ACHUSETTS 7 (1976): 36-44.

5579. "Harry Moore, Negro." NEW REPUBLIC 126 (January 7, 1952):
      6.

5580. "Has the Negro Gone Bolshevik?" WORLD OUTLOOK 5 (October
      1919): 12-13.

5581. Haynes, G.E. "Race Riots in Relation to Democracy."
      SURVEY 42 (August 9, 1919): 697-699.

5582. ———. "What Negroes Think of Race Riots." PUBLIC
      FORUM 22 (August 9, 1919): 848-849.

5583. Haynes, Robert V. "The Houston Mutiny and Riot of 1917."
      SOUTHWESTERN HISTORY QUARTERLY 76 (1973): 418-439.

      Following the beating of a black soldier by local
      whites, a mixed group of soldiers attempted to shoot up
      the town, but were prevented by their officers from
      doing so. To prevent further incidents, the regiment
      was shipped overseas to combat duty in Europe.

5584. Headrick, W.C. "Race Riots, Segregated Slums." CURRENT
      HISTORY 5 (September 1943): 30-34.

5585. Heer, David M. "The Sentiment of White Supremacy: An
      Ecological Study." AMERICAN JOURNAL OF SOCIOLOGY 64
      (May 1959): 592-598.

5586. "Heil Columbians." NEW REPUBLIC 115 (December 23, 1946):
      26.

5587. Hennesey, Melinda Meek. "Race and Violence in Reconstruc-
      tion. New Orleans: the 1868 Riot." LOUISIANA HISTORY
      20 (1979): 77-92.

5588. Hermann, Janet S. "The McIntosh Affair." MISSOURI HIS-
      TORICAL SOCIETY BULLETIN 26 (1969): 123-143.

5589. Hewitt, John H. "The Sacking of St. Philip's Church,
      New York." HISTORICAL MAGAZINE OF THE PROTESTANT EPIS-
      COPAL CHURCH 49 (1980): 7-20.

      Examines the July 1834 attack on a black church by mem-
      bers of a racist, anti-abolitionist mob.

5590. Higginson, Thomas W. "Denmark Vesey." ATLANTIC MONTHLY
      7 (1861): 728-744.

5591. ———. "Gabriel's Defeat." ATLANTIC MONTHLY 10 (1862):
      337-345.

5592. ———. "Nat Turner's Insurrection." ATLANTIC MONTHLY
      8 (August 1861): 173-187.

5593. Hirsch, Leo H. "New York and the Negro, 1783-1865."
      JOURNAL OF NEGRO HISTORY 16 (1931): 382-473.

5594. Horrman, M.M. "Court-Martial Conversion; Fort Sam Hous-
      ton, 1917." CATHOLIC WORLD 172 (October 1950): 45-51.

5595. Holman, C.W. "Race Riots in Chicago." OUTLOOK 122
      (August 13, 1919): 566-567.

5596. Holmes, Jack D.L. "The Effects of the Memphis Race Riot
      of 1866." WEST TENNESSEE HISTORICAL SOCIETY PAPERS 12
      (1958): 195-221.

5597. ———. "The Underlying Causes of the Memphis Race Riot
      of 1866." TENNESSEE HISTORICAL QUARTERLY 17 (1958):
      195-221.

5598. Holmes, William F. "The Leflore County Massacre and the
      Demise of the Colored Farmers' Alliance." PHYLON 34
      (1973): 267-274.

5599. ———. "Whitecapping: Anti-Semitism in the Populist
      Era." AMERICAN JEWISH HISTORY QUARTERLY 63 (1974):
      244-261.

5600. Howard, Victor B. "John Brown's Raid at Harper's Ferry
      and the Sectional Crisis in North Carolina." NORTH
      CAROLINA HISTORY REVIEW 55 (1978): 396-420.

5601. Howington, Arthur F. "Violence in Alabama: A Study of
      the Late Ante-Bellum Montgomery." ALABAMA REVIEW 27
      (July 1974): 213-231.

5602. Hughey, Jeff. "Black Jack: 1856." CIVIL WAR TIMES IL-
      LUSTRATED 14 (1976): 38-42.

      Examines John Brown's role in the first battle for
      "Bleeding Kansas," conducted near the sight of present-
      day Lawrence.

5603. Huie, William Bradford. "Shocking Story of Approved
      Murder in Mississippi." LOOK 20 (January 24, 1956):
      46-48+; 20 (March 6, 1956): 12; 20 (March 20, 1956): 25.

      Chronicles the case of Emmett Till, including the pub-
      lic confession of his murderers.

5604. "Invisible Injustice." OUTLOOK 133 (January 3, 1923): 7.

5605. Jack, H.A. "Cicero Nightmare." NATION 173 (July 28,
      1951): 64-65.

5606. Johnson, David W. "Freesoilers for God: Kansas Newspaper
      Editors and the Antislavery Crusade." KANSAS HISTORY
      2 (1979): 74-85.

5607. Johnston, James H. "The Participation of White Men in
      Virginia Negro Insurrections." JOURNAL OF NEGRO HIS-
      TORY 53 (1931): 158-167.

5608. Jones, E.D. "Detroit Stunned by Race Rioting." CHRIST-
      IAN CENTURY 50 (July 7, 1943): 801.

5609. Jones, Howard. "The Peculiar Institution and National
      Honor: The Case of the 'Creole' Slave Revolt." CIVIL
      WAR HISTORY 21 (March 1975).

5610. "Justice; Batesburg, S.C." COMMONWEAL 45 (November 22,
      1946): 131.

5611. Karlin, Jules Alexander. "The Anti-Chinese Outbreak in
      Tacoma, 1895." PACIFIC HISTORICAL REVIEW 23 (August
      1954): 271-283.

5612. ————. "The Anti-Chinese Outbreaks in Seattle, 1885-
      1886." NORTHWEST QUARTERLY 37 (July 1952): 248-276.

UNITED STATES 477

5613. Kelley, Don Quinn. "What Price Freedom in America?" MONTHLY REVIEW 34 (1982): 24-39.

5614. Kelly, Donald B. "Harper's Ferry: Prelude to Crisis in Mississippi." JOURNAL OF MISSISSIPPI HISTORY 27 (1965): 351-372.

5615. Kendall, John S. "Shadow Over the City." LOUISIANA HISTORICAL QUARTERLY 22 (1939): 142-165.

5616. Kennedy, Stetson. "Bombs Bring Us Together." NATION 174 (February 2, 1952): 105-107.

5617. ————. "Murder by Bombing." NATION 174 (January 5, 1952): 4.

5618. Kerber, Linda K. "Abolitionists and Amalgamation: the New York City Race Riots of 1834." NEW YORK HISTORY 48 (1967): 28-39.

5619. Killian, Lewis M. "The Purge of an Agitator." SOCIAL PROBLEMS 7 (1959): 152-256.

5620. Kimball, William J. "The Gabriel Insurrection of 1800." NEGRO HISTORY BULLETIN 34 (1971): 153-156.

5621. Kleinman, Max L. "The Denmark Vesey Conspiracy: An Historigraphical Study." NEGRO HISTORY BULLETIN 37 (1974): 225-228.

5622. Knopf, Terry Ann. "Race, Riots, and Reporting." JOURNAL OF BLACK STUDIES 4 (March 1974).

5623. Lamon, Lester C. "Tennessee Race Relations and the Knoxville Riot or 1919." EAST TENNESSEE HISTORICAL SOCIETY PUBLICATIONS 41 (1969): 67-85.

5624. Lasker, B. "Unmaking of a Myth." SURVEY 49 (October 1, 1922): 46-49.

5625. "Last Word. Holmes County, Miss." TIME 66 (November 21, 1955): 75.

   Examines the murder of Emmett Till.

5626. "Law and Lawlessness: Violence in the South." AMERICA 101 (June 27, 1959): 463.

5627. "Leather Rule." LITERARY DIGEST 122 (July 22, 1936):
      1021.

5628. Le Berthton, T. "Lights Went Out." COMMONWEAL 44 (May
      17, 1946): 114-116.

5629. Leonard, Edward A. "Nonviolence and Violence in American
      Racial Protests, 1942-1967." ROCKY MOUNTAIN SOCIAL
      SCIENCE JOURNAL 6 (1969): 10-22.

5630. "Lesson from Tulsa." OUTLOOK 128 (June 15, 1921): 280-281.

5631. Levstik, Frank R. "The Toledo Riot of 1862: A Study of
      Midwest Negrophobia." NORTHWEST OHIO QUARTERLY 44
      (1972): 100-106.

      Examines the July 8 riot by white stevedores against
      blacks regarded as competitors for local jobs.

5632. Levy, Leonard W. "The 'Abolition Riot': Boston's First
      Slave Rescue." JOURNAL OF NEGRO HISTORY 42 (1952):
      85-92.

5633. "Light Turned on a Race Riot." LITERARY DIGEST 75 (Oc-
      tober 28, 1922): 11-12.

5634. Locke, Alain. "Harlem: Dark Weather-Vane." SURVEY GEO-
      GRAPHIC 25 (August 1936): 457-462, 493-495.

5635. Lofton, John M. "Denmark Vesey's Call to Arms." JOURNAL
      OF NEGRO HISTORY 33 (1948): 395-417.

5636. Lovett, Bobby L. "Memphis Riots: White Reaction to Blacks
      in Memphis, May 1865-July 1866." TENNESSEE HISTORICAL
      QUARTERLY 38 (1979): 9-33.

5637. Low, A.R. "Zigzagging Through Dixie." CHRISTIAN CENTURY
      63 (November 6, 1946): 1339-1440.

5638. Lubell, Samuel. "Racial War in the South." COMMENTARY
      24 (August 1957): 113-118.

5639. McCarthy, T.J. "Report from Los Angeles: Zoot Suit Inci-
      dent." COMMONWEAL 38 (June 25, 1943): 243-244.

5640. McCullough, J.E. "Another View of the Washington Riots."
      OUTLOOK 123 (September 3, 1919): 28-29.

5641. McDonald, John J. "Emerson and John Brown." NEW ENGLAND
      QUARTERLY 44 (1971): 377-396.

5642. McGill, Ralph. "Angry South." ATLANTIC MONTHLY 197
      (April 1956): 31-34.

5643. McIntyre, William R. "Spread of Terrorism and Hatemon-
      gering." EDITORIAL RESEARCH REPORTS (December 3, 1958):
      893-911.

5644. McKibben, Davidson B. "Negro Slave Insurrections in
      Mississippi, 1800-1865." JOURNAL OF NEGRO HISTORY 34
      (1949): 73-90.

5645. McKnight, C.A. "Troubled South: Search for a Middle
      Ground." COLLIER'S 137 (June 22, 1956): 25-31.

5646. McLean, P.J. "New Hate Group Appears in South." CHRIS-
      TIAN CENTURY 63 (November 20, 1946): 1412.

5647. McMillan, George. "Race Justice in Aiken." NATION 163
      (November 23, 1946): 579-580.

5648. McWilliams, Carey. "Zoot-Suit Riots." NEW REPUBLIC 108
      (June 21, 1943): 818-820.

5649. Maginnes, David R. "The Case of the Court House Rioters
      in the Rendition of the Fugitive Slave Anthony Burns,
      1854." JOURNAL OF NEGRO HISTORY 56 (1971): 31-42.

5650. Marshall, Thurgood. "The Gestapo in Detroit." THE CRI-
      SIS 50 (1943): 232-233, 246-247.

      A future Supreme Court justice reviews police perform-
      ance in the 1943 Detroit race riot.

5651. ———. "The Gestapo in New York." THE CRISIS 50 (1943):
      232-233.

      Another view of alleged police brutality against blacks,
      this time in Harlem.

5652. Marszalek, John F. "Battle for Freedom - Gabriel's In-
      surrection." NEGRO HISTORY BULLETIN 39 (1976): 540-543.

5653. Maund, A. "Grass-Roots Racism; White Council at Work."
      NATION 181 (July 23, 1955): 70-72.

5654. Mayer, Milton. "Deep in the Heart." PROGRESSIVE 21
(July 1957): 12-14.

5655. "Medicine for the Mob." OUTLOOK 85 (February 2, 1907):
249-250.

5656. Messner, William F. "Black Violence and White Response:
Louisiana, 1862." JOURNAL OF SOUTHERN HISTORY 41
(1975): 19-38.

5657. Mexerik, A.G. "Dixie in Black and White." NATION 164
(March 22, 1947): 324-327; 164 (March 29, 1947): 360-
363.

5658. Miles, Edwin A. "The Mississippi Slave Insurrection of
1835." JOURNAL OF NEGRO HISTORY 42 (1957): 48-60.

5659. Miller, M. Sammy. "Legend of a Kidnapper." CRISIS 82
(1975): 118-120.

Presents the story of Patty Cannon, Delaware kidnapper
of free blacks (whom she sold into slavery), murderess
of at least 11 persons, and accomplice to a dozen other
slayings.

5660. Milligan, John D. "Slave Rebelliousness and the Florida
Maroon." PROLOGUE 6 (Spring 1974).

5661. "Mink Slide: The Aftermath; Trial at Lawrenceburg, Tenn."
TIME 48 (October 14, 1946): 29.

Examines the dispensation of "justice" to black victims
of a white riot at Columbia, Tenn.

5662. "Miserable Columbians." NEW REPUBLIC 115 (December 23,
1946): 849.

5663. "Mob Fury and Race Hatred as a National Danger." LITER-
ARY DIGEST 69 (June 18, 1921): 7-9.

5664. "Mob Rule as a National Menace." LITERARY DIGEST 63
(October 18, 1919): 9-11.

5665. "Montgomery Pastor's Home is Bombed." CHRISTIAN CENTURY
73 (September 5, 1956): 1012.

Reports an act of violence linked to the continuing
boycott of segregated city buses.

5666. Morris, J.A. "Truth About the Florida Race Troubles."
      SATURDAY EVENING POST 224 (June 21, 1952): 24-25+.

5667. "Moving Toward Race War." NEW REPUBLIC 27 (June 22,
      1921): 96-97.

5668. Murrah, Bill. "The Knoxville Race Riot: 'To Make People
      Proud.'" SOUTHERN EXPOSURE 1 (1974): 105-111.

5669. Muse, Benjamin. "Moderates and Militants." NEW REPUBLIC
      (April 2, 1956): 8-10.

5670. ————. "Submerged Moderates." NEW REPUBLIC 134 (May
      28, 1956): 14-15.

5671. Nash, Roderick W. "The Christiana Riot: An Evaluation of
      Its National Significance." JOURNAL OF LANCASTER
      COUNTY HISTORICAL SOCIETY 65 (1961): 65-91.

5672. ————. "William Parker and the Christiana Riot." JOUR-
      NAL OF NEGRO HISTORY 46 (January 1961): 24-31.

5673. "Negroes at Columbia, Tenn., Acquitted." NATION 163
      (October 12, 1946): 393.

5674. "New Disgrace for Cicero." LIFE 31 (July 23, 1951): 22-
      23.

5675. Newman, Ewell L. "Death in the Heart of This People."
      CRISIS 80 (1973): 50-57.

5676. Nichols, E.G. "Abbeville Case; Rape of a Negro Woman by
      White Youths." CHRISTIAN CENTURY 62 (May 9, 1945):
      580-582.

5677. Nitoburg, E.L. "The Garvey Movement." VOPROSY ISTORII
      7 (1977): 137-151.

      Follows the fraudulent "Back to Africa" movement of
      the 1920s, which won support from many white racists.

5678. "No Day of Triumph; Murder of H.T. Moore." NATION 174
      (January 5, 1952): 3-4.

5679. "No Remedy in Law; Case of Emmett Till." NEW REPUBLIC
      133 (November 21, 1955): 5.

5680. Norton, W.J. "Detroit Riots and After." SURVEY GEOGRAPH-
IC 32 (August 1943): 317-318.

5681. Olson, James, and Sharon Phair. "The Anatomy of a Race
Riot: Beaumont, Texas, 1943." TEXANA 11 (1973): 64-72.

5682. "Omaha." NATION 109 (October 11, 1919): 491.

Examines a recent white pogrom against blacks in Nebraska's largest city.

5683. "Omaha; Riots in the Nebraska City." LITERARY DIGEST 63
(October 11, 1919): 16.

5684. "On the Firing-Line During the Chicago Race-Riots."
LITERARY DIGEST 62 (August 23, 1919): 44-46.

5685. "Our Own Race War." NORTH AMERICAN 210 (October 1919):
436-438.

5686. "Our Own Subject Race Rebels." LITERARY DIGEST 63 (August 2, 1919): 25.

5687. "Outbreaks of Violence." SURVEY 79 (July 1943): 202.

5688. Ovington, M.W. "Gunpowder of Race Antagonism." AMERICAN
CITY 21 (September 1919): 248-251.

5689. Owens, Harry B. "The Eufala Riot of 1874." ALABAMA RE-
VIEW 16 (1963): 224-237.

5690. "Pachuco Troubles; Zoot-Suit Riots in Los Angeles."
INTER-AMERICAN MAGAZINE 2 (August 1943): 5-6.

5691. Peek, Ralph L. "Curbing Voter Intimidation in Florida,
1871." FLORIDA HISTORICAL QUARTERLY 43 (1965): 333-348.

5692. Petersm W. "How to Fight Hate Merchants." CORONTE 45
(April 1959): 67-72.

5693. Petrie, J.C. "Flogging Arouses Varied Opinions." CHRIS-
TIAN CENTURY 53 (July 22, 1936): 1021.

5694. Phelps, Albert. "New Orleans and Reconstruction." AT-
LANTIC MONTHLY 88 (July 1901): 121-131.

5695. Phillips, C. "Integration Battle of Hoxie, Ark." NEW
      YORK TIMES MAGAZINE (September 25, 1955): 12.

      Members of the White Citizens Council and KKK did their
      best to foment mob violence in Hoxie prior to integration
      of the local schools. This article examines their tech-
      niques and degree of success.

5696. "Pogrom in Tennessee, and the Part Politics Plays."
      NEW REPUBLIC 114 (April 1, 1946): 429.

5697. "Portent of Storm; Los Angeles Zoot Suit Riots." CHRIS-
      TIAN CENTURY 60 (June 23, 1943): 735-736.

5698. "Prominent on the Credit Side of the Georgia Ledger."
      NATION 164 (March 1, 1947): 234.

      Examines the recent successful prosecution of a sheriff
      and his deputies who surrendered black prisoners to a
      white mob.

5699. Quailes, Benjamin (ed). "John Brown Writes to Blacks."
      KANSAS HISTORICAL QUARTERLY 41 (1975): 454-467.

      Reprints letters from John Brown, published by Freder-
      ick Douglass during 1851-56.

5700. "Race Riot Prescription." SCIENCE NEWS LETTER 44 (Decem-
      ber 11, 1943): 381.

5701. "Race Riots Hurt." BUSINESS WEEK (June 26, 1943): 102+.

5702. "Race Riots in Washington and Chicago." CURRENT HISTORY
      10 (September 1919): 453-454.

5703. "Race Riots on the Pacific Coast." OUTLOOK 87 (Septem-
      ber 21, 1907): 89.

5704. "Race Trouble to Grow in South." U.S. NEWS & WORLD RE-
      PORT 40 (February 24, 1956): 44-48+.

5705. "Race War in Detroit." LIFE 15 (July 5, 1943): 93-100.

5706. "Racial Self-Restraint." OUTLOOK 89 (November 3, 1906):
      551-553.

5707. "Racial Tension and Race Riots." OUTLOOK 122 (August 6,
      1919): 532-534.

484   TERRORISM IN THE UNITED STATES AND EUROPE

5708. "Racial: Trial and Error." NEWSWEEK 28 (November 4, 1946): 31.

5709. "Racists Resort to Terrorism." CHRISTIAN CENTURY 74 (January 23, 1957): 101.

5710. Ratliff, B.A. "In the Delta: the Story of a Man Hunt." ATLANTIC MONTHLY 125 (April 1920): 456-461.

5711. Rauschenbush, W. "How to Prevent Race Riots." AMERICAN MERCURY 57 (September 1943): 302-309; 58 (February 1944): 251.

5712. "Reading & 'Riting & Rubble." TIME 72 (November 24, 1958): 21.

Examines recent bombings aimed at integrated schools.

5713. "Reaping the Whirlwind." COMMONWEAL 69 (October 31, 1958): 117.

5714. Reddick, L.D. "Whose Ordeal?" NEW REPUBLIC 135 (September 24, 1956): 9-10.

5715. Reed, John S. "To Live—and Die—in Dixie: a Contribution to the Study of Southern Violence." POLITICAL SCIENCE QUARTERLY 86 (1971): 429-443.

5716. "Reign of Terror." TIME 74 (July 27, 1959): 22+.

5717. "Remedy for Race Riots." SCIENCE NEWS LETTER 45 (February 26, 1944): 132.

5718. "Resistance to Integration." COMMONWEAL 63 (Mqrch 20, 1956): 656.

5719. Reynolds, Donald E. "The New Orleans Riot of 1866 Reconsidered." LOUISIANA HISTORY 5 (1964): 5-27.

5720. Reynolds, Thomas J. "Pope County Militia War (1872-73)." PUBLICATIONS OF THE ARKANSAS HISTORICAL ASSOCIATION 2 (1908): 174-198.

5721. Richmond, Douglas W. "La Guerra de Texas se Renova: Mexican Insurrection and Carrancista Ambitions, 1900-1920." AZTLAN 11 (1980): 1-32.

Traces efforts of the Mexican government under President Carranza to foment rebellion among Mexicans in Texas.

5722. "Riot at Springfield." OUTLOOK 89 (August 22, 1908): 869-870.

5723. "Riotous Race Hate." NEWSWEEK 21 (June 28, 1943): 42+.

5724. "Riots in Harlem." NEW REPUBLIC 109 (August 9, 1943): 108.

5725. "Rise in School Bombings; What's Being Done About It." U.S. NEWS & WORLD REPORT 45 (November 21, 1958): 57.

5726. Robinson, Bernard F. "The Sociology of Race Riots." PHYLON 2 (1941): 162-171.

5727. ———. "War and Race Conflicts in the United States." PHYLON 4 (1943): 311-327.

5728. Robson, W.N. "Open Letter on Race Hatred." THEATER ARTS 28 (September 1944): 537-540+.

5729. Rogers, O.A., Jr. "The Elaine Race Riots of 1919." ARKANSAS HISTORICAL QUARTERLY 19 (1960): 142-150.

5730. Rose, Arnold M. "The Course of the South: Descent Into Barbarism." COMMENTARY 27 (June 1959): 495-499.

5731. Ruark, H.G. "South Carolinians Tighten the Screws." CHRISTIAN CENTURY 73 (May 30, 1956): 674-675.

5732. Rudwick, Elliott M. "Fifty Years of Race Relations in East St. Louis: the Breaking Down of White Supremacy." MIDCONTINENT AMERICAN STUDIES JOURNAL 6 (1965): 3-15.

5733. Runcie, John. "'Hunting the Nigs' in Philadelphia: the Race Riot of August, 1834." PENNSYLVANIA HISTORY 39 (1972): 187-218.

5734. "Rusty Weapons; Clumsy Tactics." NATION 184 (January 26, 1957): 69.

5735. Rutherford, Phillip R. "The 'Arabia' Incident." KANSAS HISTORY 1 (1978): 39-47.

Examines the foiled effort of the New England Emigrant

Aid Company to smuggle weapons to "free soilers" in Kansas. Seizure of the weapons led to a four-year legal battle for custody.

5736. Sancton, Thomas. "Race Clash." HARPER'S 180 (January 1944): 135-140.

5737. ———. "Race Riots." NEW REPUBLIC 109 (July 5, 1943): 9-13.

5738. Scarborough, W.S. "Race Riots and Their Remedy." INDEPENDENT 99 (August 16, 1919): 223.

5739. Scheer, J. "White Folks Fight Back." NEW REPUBLIC 133 (October 31, 1955): 9-12.

5740. Schneider, John C. "Detroit and the Problem of Disorder: the Riot of 1863." MICHIGAN HISTORY 58 (1974): 4-24.

5741. Schroeder, L. "Force and Violence in Illinois." NATION 174 (February 9, 1952): 124-126.

5742. Schuler, Edgar M. "The Houston Race Riot, 1917." JOURNAL OF NEGRO HISTORY 29 (1944): 30-38.

5743. Schuyler, G.S. "More Race Riots Are Coming." AMERICAN MERCURY 59 (December 1944): 686-691.

5744. Seligmann, H.J. "Race War in Washington." NEW REPUBLIC 20 (August 13, 1919): 48-50.

5745. ———. "What is Behind the Negro Uprisings?" CURRENT OPINION 67 (September 1919): 154-155.

The "uprisings" in question consisted of blacks using armed force to defend themselves from white rioters and lynch mobs in Chicago and other cities. At the time, self-defense was considered aberrant and radical behavior.

5746. Sevareid, Eric. "Hate Wave." REPORTER 19 (November 27, 1958): 4.

5747. "Shadows of Actions." FREEMAN 6 (January 3, 1923): 390-391.

5748. Shaffer, Helen B. "Violence and Non-Violence in American Race Relations." EDITORIAL RESEARCH REPORTS (March 25, 1960): 221-228.

5749. Sheean, V. "Lawrenceburg Verdict." NEW REPUBLIC 115
      (October 14, 1946): 472-473.

5750. Sheeler, J.R. "Methods for Control of the Negro Mind,
      Soul and Body." NEGRO HISTORY BULLETIN 21 (December
      1957): 67-69.

5751. Shepherd, W.G. "Poison Gas for Home Use." COLLIER'S
      76 (October 17, 1925): 11.

5752. "Sheriff Shoots in Florida's Lake County." TIME 58 (No-
      vember 19, 1951): 26-27.

      Examines the murder of a black prisoner by Sheriff
      Willis McCall. Years later, documented evidence linked
      McCall with a reign of terror in South Florida, includ-
      ing participation by McCall and his deputies in the
      bombing murder of Harry Moore.

5753. Shostack, David A. "Crosby Smith: Forgotten Witness to
      a Mississippi Nightmare." NEGRO HISTORY BULLETIN 38
      (1974): 320-325.

5754. Sinclair, Upton. "Mass Exodus from Mississippi." NEW
      REPUBLIC 134 (January 9, 1956): 23.

      Follows blacks who are being driven from their homes
      in the Magnolia State by a combination of economic pres-
      sure and old-fashioned violence.

5755. Singletary, Otis A. "Militia Disturbances in Arkansas
      During Reconstruction." ARKANSAS HISTORICAL QUARTERLY
      15 (1956): 140-150.

5756. Sitkoff, Harvard. "The Detroit Race Riot of 1943."
      MICHIGAN HISTORY 53 (1969): 183-206.

5757. Smith, H.A. "Not One Witness; Negro Murder, Broohaven,
      Miss." CHRISTIAN CENTURY 73 (June 6, 1956): 698-699.

      Examines the peculiar absence of witnesses in the broad-
      daylight murder of a local black man, shot to death by a
      state legislator on a public street. (In fact, a black
      eyewitness did exist, but he was murdered "by persons
      unknown" shortly after giving a statement to the FBI.)

5758. "The So-Called Race Riot of Springfield, Illinois." CHAR-
      ITIES AND THE COMMUNITY 19 (September 1908): 709-711.

5759. Stein, W. "White Citizens' Councils." NEGRO HISTORY BULLETIN 20 (October 1956): 2+.

5760. Story, Ronald. "Blacks, Brown, and Blood: the Hourglass Pattern." RESEARCH IN AMERICAN HISTORY 3 (1975): 213-218.

Examines the degree of black support for John Brown's guerilla campaigns.

5761. Street, A.L.H. "Municipal Liability for Mob Violence." AMERICAN CITY 32 (February 1925): 217-219.

5762. "Subversion in the South." NATION 183 (September 15, 1956): 209.

5763. "Summons Against Mob Violence." LITERARY DIGEST 96 (February 4, 1928): 31-32.

5764. Swan, L. Alex. "When Whites Riot: The E. St. Louis Massacre." INTERNATIONAL SOCIALIST REVIEW 34 (1973): 12-24.

5765. "Sweet Land of Liberty." NATION 117 (July 4, 1923): 11.

5766. "Target Terrorism; Racial Bombings." NEWSWEEK 51 (May 12, 1958): 27.

5767. "Taut String." TIME 42 (August 9, 1943): 19.

5768. Taylor, A.W. "One Justice for All." CHRISTIAN CENTURY 63 (December 11, 1946): 1501-1502.

5769. ———. "Race News: Some Good, Some Bad." CHRISTIAN CENTURY 63 (November 13, 1946): 1378+.

5770. ———. "Racial Tensions Rock the South." CHRISTIAN CENTURY 63 (September 18, 1946): 1124+.

5771. ———. "Sift Blame for Tennessee Riot; Federal Grand Jury Probes Charges." CHRISTIAN CENTURY 63 (April 24, 1946): 531-532.

5772. Taylor, G. "Chicago in the Nation's Race Strife." SURVEY 42 (August 9, 1919): 695-697.

5773. ———. "Race Riot in Lincoln's City." CHARITIES AND THE COMMUNITY 20 (August 29, 1908): 627-628.

5774. Taylor, R.H. "Slave Conspiracies in North Carolina."
      NORTH CAROLINA HISTORICAL REVIEW 5 (1928): 20-34.

5775. "Tennessee Race Riot a Danger Sign." CHRISTIAN CENTURY
      63 (March 13, 1946): 325.

5776. "Tension in the North: Race Riots Break Out Again." U.S.
      NEWS & WORLD REPORT 44 (June 13, 1958): 85-86.

5777. "Terror by Bombing: the Story Back of It." U.S. NEWS &
      WORLD REPORT 45 (October 24, 1958): 33-35.

      Attempts to blame "leftists" for recent racial bombings
      in the South, in a shabby effort to discredit the black
      civil rights movement.

5778. "Terror in Cicero." NEWSWEEK 38 (July 23, 1951): 17-18.

5779. "Terror in Mink Slide, Columbia, Tenn." NEWSWEEK 27
      (March 11, 1946): 28.

5780. "Terror, Inc." NEW REPUBLIC 115 (November 18, 1946): 657.

      Examines activities of the neo-fascist Columbians.

5781. Thornbrough, Emma L. "The Brownsville Episode and the
      Negro Vote." MISSISSIPPI VALLEY HISTORICAL REVIEW 44
      (1957): 469-493.

5782. "Thunderhead." TIME 48 (November 11, 1946): 25.

5783. "Tinder for Talmadge." NEWSWEEK 28 (July 1, 1946): 22.

      Racial violence in Georgia boosts the arch-segregation-
      ist campaign of Eugene Talmadge in his bid for the gov-
      ernor's mansion.

5784. Tinsley, James A. "Roosevelt, Foraker, and the Browns-
      ville Affray." JOURNAL OF NEGRO HISTORY 41 (January
      1956): 43-65.

5785. "Toy Hitlers." NEWSWEEK 28 (November 11, 1946): 31.

      Further examines the Columbians in Georgia.

5786. "Tragedy in Mink Slide, Columbia, Tenn." TIME 47 (March
      11, 1946): 23.

5787. Tragle, Henry L. "Southampton Slave Revolt." AMERICAN
      HISTORY ILLUSTRATED 6 (1971): 4-11, 44-47.

5788. Trapp, C.N. "Mob Victim." NEW REPUBLIC 56 (November 14,
      1928): 345-346.

5789. Tuck, R.D. "Behind the Zoot Suit Riots; Los Angeles and
      Its Mexican." SURVEY GEOGRAPHIC 32 (August 1943): 313-
      316+.

5790. Tucker, David M. "Miss Ida B. Wells and Memphis Lynch-
      ing." PHYLON 32 (1971): 112-122.

5791. "Tulsa." NATION 112 (June 15, 1921): 839.

5792. "Tulsa Race Riots." INDEPENDENT 105 (June 1921): 646-647.

5793. Turner, Ralph H., and Samuel J. Surace. "Zoot-Suiters
      and Mexicans: Symbols of Crowd Behavior." AMERICAN
      JOURNAL OF SOCIOLOGY 62 (1956): 14-20.

5794. Tuttle, William M. "Contested Neighborhoods and Racial
      Violence: Prelude to the Chicago Riot of 1919." JOUR-
      NAL OF NEGRO HISTORY 55 (1970): 266-288.

5795. ———. "Labor Conflict and Racial Violence: the Black
      Worker in Chicago, 1894-1919." LABOR HISTORY 10
      (1969): 408-432.

5796. ———. "'Red Summer': 1919." AMERICAN HISTORY ILLUS-
      TRATED 6 (1971): 32-41.

5797. ———. "Views of a Negro During the 'Red Summer' of
      1919 - A Document." JOURNAL OF NEGRO HISTORY 51 (1966):
      209-218.

5798. ———. "Violence in a 'Heather' Land: the Longview
      Race Riot of 1919." PHYLON 33 (1972): 324-333.

5799. "Two Stories; Negroes at Mount Pleasant, Tenn." TIME 48
      (October 28, 1946): 30.

5800. "Two-Way Squeeze; White Citizens Councils." NATION 181
      (December 24, 1955): 546.

5801. "Ugly Nights in Cicero." TIME 58 (July 23, 1951): 10-11.

5802. "Uninvited Guest: H.T. Moore." TIME 59 (January 7, 1952):
      14.

5803. "U.S. to Investigate Cicero Riots." CHRISTIAN CENTURY
      68 (October 10, 1951): 1149.

5804. Vance, W. Silas. "The Marion Riot." MISSISSIPPI QUAR-
      TERLY 27 (1974): 447-466.

      Examines the November 8, 1881 riot at Marion, Miss.,
      sparked by white resentment over black attempts to vote.

5805. Vander Zanden, James W. "Turbulence Accompanying School
      Desegregation." JOURNAL OF EDUCATIONAL SOCIOLOGY 29
      (Spring 1960): 204-206.

5806. "Violent Alien." NATION 117 (October 17, 1923): 427-428.

5807. Wade, Richard C. "The Vesey Plot: a Reconsideration."
      JOURNAL OF SOUTHERN HISTORY 30 (1964): 143-161.

5808. Wakefield, D. "Respectable Racism; Dixie's Citizens
      Councils." NATION 181 (October 22, 1955): 339-341.

5809. Wallace, R. "Voices of the White South." LIFE 41 (Sep-
      tember 17, 1956): 104-117; 41 (October 8, 1956): 22.

5810. Walling, William E. "The Race War in the North." INDE-
      PENDENT 65 (September 3, 1908): 529-534.

5811. Walsh, G.V. "Submerged Moderates; Reply." NEW REPUBLIC
      134 (June 4, 1956): 3+.

      Refutes item 5670 above.

5812. Walton, N.W. "Walking City, a History of the Montgomery
      Boycott." NEGRO HISTORY BULLETIN 20 (October 1956):
      16-20; 20 (November 1956): 27-33.

5813. Washington, Booker T. "Golden Rule in Atlanta." OUTLOOK
      84 (December 15, 1906): 913-916.

5814. "Washington Riots." INDEPENDENT 99 (August 2, 1919): 147.

5815. "Washington Riots." NATION 109 (August 9, 1919): 173.

5816. Weaver, Maurice, and Z. Alexander Looby. "What Happened
      at Columbia." THE CRISIS 53 (1946): 110-111.

5817. Weisberg, B. "Racial Violence and Civil Rights Enforce-
      ment." UNIVERSITY OF CHICAGO LAW REVIEW 18 (1951):
      769-783.

5818. Wells, Tom Henderson. "The Phoenix Election Riot."
      PHYLON 31 (1970): 58-69.

      Examines a riot in 1898, by whites, designed to stop
      blacks from voting in Phoenix, S.C.

5819. "What the South Thinks of Northern Race Riots." LITERARY
      DIGEST 62 (August 16, 1919): 17-18.

5820. "Where Terror Reigns." LIFE 46 (March 2, 1959): 38.

5821. White, Edward. "Eyewitness at Harper's Ferry." AMERICAN
      HERITAGE 26 (1975): 56-59, 94-97.

5822. White, Walter F. "Behind the Harlem Riots." NEW REPUB-
      LIC 109 (August 16, 1943): 220-222.

5823. ————. "Eruption at Tulsa." NATION 112 (June 29, 1921):
      909-910.

5824. ————. "Race Conflict in Arkansas." SURVEY 43 (Decem-
      ber 13, 1919): 233-234.

5825. White, William W. "The Texas Slave Insurrection of 1860."
      SOUTHWESTERN HISTORY QUARTERLY 52 (1949): 259-285.

5826. Whitman, Karen. "Re-evaluating John Brown's Raid at
      Harper's Ferry." WEST VIRGINIA HISTORY 34 (1972): 46-
      84.

      Contends that Brown was not a lunatic or religious fan-
      atic, but simply a man committed to social justice at
      any price.

5827. "Who Incites Southern Mobs, and Why?" CHRISTIAN CENTURY
      73 (February 22, 1956): 228.

5828. "Why the Negro Appeals to Violence." LITERARY DIGEST 62
      (August 9, 1919): 11.

5829. Wiggins, Sarah W. "The 'Pig Iron' Kelley Riot in Mobile,
      May 14, 1867." ALABAMA REVIEW 23 (1970): 45-55.

5830. Wilcox, B.P. "Anti-Chinese Riots in Washington." WASH-
      INGTON HISTORICAL QUARTERLY 20 (July 1929): 204-212.

5831. Wilson, Banjamin C. "Kentucky Kidnappers, Fugitives, and
      Abolitionists in Antebellum Cass County, Michigan."
      MICHIGAN HISTORY 60 (1976): 339-358.

      Examines the activities of Kentucky planters who led
      raids to recapture runaway slaves in 1847 and 1849.
      Their actions led to passage of a Fugitive Slave Act in
      1850, outraging abolitionists.

5832. "Wind and the Whirlwind." INDEPENDENT 61 (September 27,
      1906): 760-761.

5833. Wise, Leah. "The Elaine Massacre." SOUTHERN EXPOSURE 1
      (1974): 9-10.

5834. Wish, Harvey. "American Slave Insurrections Before 1861."
      JOURNAL OF NEGRO HISTORY 22 (1937): 299-320.

5935. ————. "The Slave Insurrection Panic of 1856." JOURNAL
      OF SOUTHERN HISTORY 5 (1939): 206-222.

5936. Woodbridge, W.A. "Why the Difference? Negro Crimes in
      Portsmouth, Va., and Springfield." INDEPENDENT 65
      (September 10, 1908): 605-606.

5937. Woodson, Carter G. "The Negroes of Cincinnati Prior to
      the Civil War." JOURNAL OF NEGRO HISTORY 1 (1916):
      1-22.

5938. Wortman, R.T. "Denver's Anti-Chinese Riot, 1880."
      COLORADO MAGAZINE 42 (1965): 275-291.

5939. Wright, Charles Allen. "School Integration: An Almost
      Lost Fight." PROGRESSIVE 22 (August 1958): 7-9.

5940. Wright, Charles H. "Paul Robeson at Peekskill." FREE-
      DOMWAYS 15 (1975): 101-111.

5941. Wyatt-Brown, Bertrun. "John Brown, Weathermen, and the
      Psychology of Antinomian Violence." SOUNDINGS 58
      (1975): 417-440.

      Compares militant abolitionists with anti-war radicals
      of the 1960s and 1970s, using the "psychocultural theory
      of antinomian deviancy" to find similarities. Wade through
      this at your own risk.

5842. Wynne, Lewis N. "Brownsville: the Reaction of the Negro Press." PHYLON 33 (1972): 153-160.

5843. "Yellow and White: the Coming War of Races." CONTEMPOR- ARY REVIEW 92 (October 1907): 577-579.

5844. Yeomans, G. Allan. "'Judicial Lynching at Brownsville': November 9, 1906." CRISIS 80 (1973): 15-17.

5845. Young, Erle Fiske. "The Relation of Lynching to the Size of Political Areas." SOCIOLOGY AND SOCIAL RE- SEARCH 12 (March-April 1928): 348-353.

5846. Zeitlin, J.I. "What Makes Race Riots Possible." NEW REPUBLIC 109 (October 18, 1943): 522.

5847. "Zoot-Suit Riots; 125 Hurt in Los Angeles Fights." LIFE 14 (June 21, 1943): 30-31.

5848. "Zoot-Suit War." TIME 41 (June 21, 1943): 18.

5849. "Zoot Suits and Service Stripes: Race Tension Behind the Riots." NEWSWEEK 21 (June 21, 1943): 35-36+.

9. Social Violence

5850. Brace, Charles L. THE DANGEROUS CLASSES OF NEW YORK AND TWENTY YEARS WORK AMONG THEM. New York: Wynkoop & Hallenbeck, 1865.

5851. Brown, Richard M. "The American Vigilante Tradition." VIOLENCE IN AMERICA: HISTORICAL AND COMPARATIVE PER- SPECTIVES. Cited above as item 3265, pp. 154-226.

5852. Dimsdale, Thomas J. THE VIGILANTES OF MONTANA. Virgin- ia City, Mont.: State Publishing Co., 1866.

5853. Moody, Richard. THE ASTOR PLACE RIOT. Bloomington, Ind.: Indiana University Press, 1958.

5854. Morris, Lucile. BALD KNOBBERS. Caldwell, Idaho: 1939.

5855. Stewart, George R. COMMITTEE OF VIGILANCE: REVOLUTION IN SAN FRANCISCO, 1851. Boston: Houghton Mifflin, 1964.

5856. Williams, Mary Floyd. HISTORY OF THE SAN FRANCISCO COM- MITTEE OF VIGILANCE OF 1851: A STUDY OF SOCIAL CONTROL ON THE CALIFORNIA FRONTIER IN THE DAYS OF THE GOLD RUSH. Berkeley, Calif.: University of California Press, 1969.

b. Articles

5857. Bitzes, John G. "The Anti-Greek Riot of 1909, South
      Omaha." NEBRASKA HISTORY 51 (1970): 199-204.

5858. Blew, Robert W. "Vigilantism in Los Angeles, 1835-1874."
      SOUTHERN CALIFORNIA QUARTERLY 54 (1972): 11-30.

5859. Bragg, James W. "Captain Slick, Arbiter of Early Alabama
      Morals." ALABAMA REVIEW 11 (1958): 125-134.

5860. Briggs, Harold E. "Lawlessness in Cairo, Illinois, 1848-
      1858." MID-AMERICA 33 (1951): 67-88.

5861. Briggs, John E. "Pioneer Gangsters." PALIMPSEST 21
      (1940): 73-90.

5862. Brown, Richard M. "Legal and Behavioral Perspectives on
      American Vigilantism." PERSPECTIVES 5 (1971): 95-146.

5863. Coxe, John E. "The New Orleans Mafia Incident." LOUISI-
      ANA HISTORICAL QUARTERLY 20 (1937): 1067-1110.

5864. Davis, David B. "Some Themes of Counter-Subversion: An
      Analysis of Anti-Masonic, Anti-Catholic, and Anti-
      Mormon Literature." MISSISSIPPI VALLEY HISTORICAL
      REVIEW 47 (September 1960): 205-224.

5865. Edwards, Linden F. "Body-Snatching in Ohio During the
      Nineteenth Century." OHIO STATE ARCHIVES HISTORICAL
      QUARTERLY 59 (1950): 329-351.

      Includes discussion of riots and vigilante attacks on
      suspected "resurrection men," accused of stealing corpses
      and selling them to medical schools for dissection.

5866. ————. "Resurrection Riots During the Heroic Age of
      Anatomy in America." MEDICAL HISTORY BULLETIN 25
      (1951): 178-184.

5867. Gower, Calvin W. "Vigilantes." COLORADO MAGAZINE 41
      (1964): 93-104.

      Examines vigilante activity in Colorado during the
      1860s.

5868. Graham, Orville F. "The Vigilance Committees." PALIMP-
      SEST 6 (1925): 359-370.

      Deals with Iowa's vigilantes during 1857-1859.

5869. Griffin, Harry L. "The Vigilance Committees of Attakapas
      County; or Early Louisiana Justice." MISSISSIPPI VALLEY
      HISTORICAL ASSOCIATION PROCEEDINGS 8 (1914): 146-159.

5870. Heard, William T. "Breaking Up a Party of Arkansas River
      Gamblers." PUBLICATION OF THE ARKANSAS HISTORICAL AS-
      SOCIATION 4 (1917): 312-325.

5871. Jones, Robert H. "Three Days of Violence. The Regulators
      of the Rock River Valley." JOURNAL OF THE ILLINOIS
      STATE HISTORICAL SOCIETY 59 (1966): 131-142.

5872. Karlin, J. Alexander. "The Italo-American Incident of
      1891 and the Road to Reunion." JOURNAL OF SOUTHERN
      HISTORY 8 (1942): 242-246.

5873. ————. "The New Orleans Lynchings of 1891 and the Am-
      erican Press." LOUISIANA HISTORICAL QUARTERLY 24 (1941):
      187-204.

5874. ————. "Some Repercussions of the New Orleans Mafia
      Incident of 1891." RESEARCH STUDIES OF THE STATE COL-
      LEGE OF WASHINGTON (December 1943).

5875. Kendall, John S. "Who Killa De Chief?" LOUISIANA HIS-
      TORICAL QUARTERLY 22 (1939): 492-530.

      Considers the assassination of a New Orleans police
      chief, which led directly to the 1891 lynching of alleged
      mafiosi.

5876. McKee, Irving. "The Shooting of Charles de Young."
      PACIFIC HISTORY REVIEW 16 (1947): 271-284.

      Examines the assassination of a San Francisco newspaper
      editor in 1880.

5877. Michelson, C. "Vigilantes of the West." MUNSEY MAGAZINE
      25 (May 1901): 200-212.

5878. Mueller, Oscar O. "The Central Montana Vigilante Raids
      of 1884." MONTANA MAGAZINE OF HISTORY 1 (January 1951):
      23-36.

5879. "New Orleans Levee Riot." HARPER'S WEEKLY 39 (March 30,
      1895): 295.

5880. Nicolosi, Anthony S. "The Rise and Fall of the New Jer-
      sey Vigilant Societies." NEW JERSEY HISTORY 86 (1968):
      29-53.

5881. Parish, John C. "White Beans for Hanging." PALIMPSEST
      1 (1920): 9-28.

      Examines Iowa vigilantes of the 1840s.

5882. Perrigo, Lynn I. "Law and Order in Early Colorado Mining
      Camps." MISSISSIPPI VALLEY HISTORICAL REVIEW 28 (1941):
      41-62.

5883. Potter, Chester D. "Reminiscences of the Socorro Vigi-
      lantes." NEW MEXICO HISTORICAL REVIEW 40 (1965): 23-54.

      Covers New Mexico vigilantes, circa 1880-1884.

5884. Price, Eliphalet. "The Trial and Execution of Patrick
      O'Connor at the Dubuque Mines, 1834." PALIMPSEST 1
      (1920): 86-97.

5885. Radabaugh, James H. "The Cincinnati Riot of 1884."
      MUSEUM ECHOES, OHIO HISTORICAL SOCIETY 32 (December
      1959): 91-94.

5886. Radlowski, Edmund E. "Law and Order at Cripple Creek,
      1890-1900." JOURNAL OF THE WEST 9 (1970): 346-355.

5887. Rister, Carl C. "Outlaws and Vigilantes of the Southern
      Plains, 1865-1885." MISSISSIPPI VALLEY HISTORICAL RE-
      VIEW 19 (1932): 537-554.

5888. "Tear Down the College." CONNECTICUT HISTORICAL SOCIETY
      BULLETIN 34 (1959): 50-53.

      Examines a riot against Yale medical school, suspected
      of employing body-snatchers in 1823.

5889. "The Vigilance Committee: Richmond During the War of
      1812." VIRGINIA MAGAZINE OF HISTORY AND BIOGRAPHY 7
      (1899): 225-241.

5890. Vincent, J.W. "The Slicker War and Its Consequences."
      MISSOURI HISTORICAL REVIEW 7 (1912): 138-145.

      Examines Missouri vigilantism during 1840.

5891. Webb, Stephen P. "A Sketch of the Causes, Operations,
      and Results of the San Francisco Vigilance Committee
      in 1856." ESSEX INSTITUTE HISTORICAL COLLECTION 84
      (1948): 97-130.

5892. Williams, Jack K. "Crime and Punishment in Alabama, 1819-
      1840." ALABAMA REVIEW 6 (1953): 14-30.

SUBJECT INDEX 501

4790, 4791, 4792, 4793,
4794, 4795, 4796, 4797,
4798, 4799, 4800, 4801,
4802, 4803, 4804, 4805,
4806, 4807, 4808, 4809,
4810, 4811, 4812, 4813,
4814, 4815, 4816, 4817,
4818, 4819, 4820, 4821,
4822, 4823, 4824, 4825,
4826, 4827, 4828, 4829,
4830, 4831, 4832, 4833,
4834, 4835, 4836, 4837,
4838, 4839, 4840, 4841,
4842, 4843, 4844, 4845,
4856, 4857, 4858, 4859,
4860, 4861, 4862, 4863,
4864, 4865, 4866, 4867,
4869, 4870, 4871, 4872,
4873, 4874, 4875, 4876,
4877, 4878, 4879, 4880,
4881, 4882, 4883, 4884,
4885, 4886, 4887, 4888,
4889, 4890, 4891, 4892,
4893, 4894, 4895, 4896,
4897, 4898, 4899, 4900,
4901, 4902, 4903, 4904,
4905, 4906, 4907, 4908,
4909, 4910, 4911, 4912,
4913, 4914, 4915, 4916,
4917, 4918, 4919, 4920,
4921, 4922, 4923, 4924,
4925, 4926, 4927, 4928,
4929, 4930, 4931, 4932,
4933, 4934, 4935, 4936,
4937, 4938, 4939, 4940,
4941, 4942, 4943, 4944,
4945, 4946, 4947, 4948,
4949, 4950, 9451, 4952,
4953, 4954, 4955, 4956,
4957, 4958, 4959, 4960,
4961, 4962, 4963, 4964,
4965, 4966, 4967, 4968,
4969, 4970, 4971, 4972,
4973, 4974, 4975, 4976,
4977, 4978, 4979, 4980,
4981, 4982, 4983, 4984,
4985, 4986, 4987, 4988,

4989, 4990, 4991, 4992,
4993, 4994, 4995, 4996,
4997, 4998, 5436, 5449,
5790, 5844, 5845, 5873
Molly Maguires 3507, 3508,
3512, 3523, 3561, 3576,
3735, 3799
Nazis in Austria 166, 168, 189,
191, 193, 197, 210, 228,
229, 233, 235, 236, 237,
238, 250, 251, 254, 255,
256, 258, 269, 270, 271,
277, 283, 285, 288, 297,
299; in Germany 15, 604,
605, 606, 607, 609, 610,
611, 613, 617, 618, 621,
622, 623, 625, 627, 630,
631, 632, 633, 635, 637,
638, 642, 648, 650, 651,
653, 654, 657, 658, 659,
661, 665, 668, 671, 684,
690, 693, 695, 696, 722,
725, 731, 732, 733, 734,
735, 736, 737, 738, 739,
740, 741, 754, 761, 773,
780, 781, 790, 793, 804,
806, 808, 818, 822, 824;
in Greece 920; in Ireland
1561; in Poland 2274; in
Spain 2773, 2893; in the
United States 4983, 4988,
4989, 5010, 5049, 5126,
5248
Range wars 3540, 3541, 3586,
3595, 3608, 3721, 3785,
3798
Revolution 1, 4, 6, 9, 14, 15,
17, 20, 26, 42, 47, 52, 55,
56, 57, 61, 65, 66, 67, 69,
71, 72, 75, 78, 81, 83, 85,
87, 95, 99, 100, 101, 102,
103, 104, 108, 109, 112,
114, 117, 119, 122, 127,
129, 130, 132, 133, 134,
135, 136, 137, 138, 139,
144, 146, 147, 151, 152,
156, 157; in Austria 161,